SAGE was founded in 1965 by Sara Miller McCune to support the dissemination of usable knowledge by publishing innovative and high-quality research and teaching content. Today, we publish over 900 journals, including those of more than 400 learned societies, more than 800 new books per year, and a growing range of library products including archives, data, case studies, reports, and video. SAGE remains majority-owned by our founder, and after Sara's lifetime will become owned by a charitable trust that secures our continued independence.

Los Angeles | London | New Delhi | Singapore | Washington DC | Melbourne

Media Metrics

Media Metrics

An Introduction to Quantitative Research in Mass Communication

Manoj Dayal

Professor, Former Dean & Chairperson,
Department of Communication Management & Technology,
Faculty of Media Studies, Guru Jambheshwar University of Science & Technology, Hisar, Haryana, India

SAGE | TEXTS

Los Angeles | London | New Delhi
Singapore | Washington DC | Melbourne

First published in 2017 by

SAGE | TEXTS

SAGE Publications India Pvt Ltd
B1/I-1 Mohan Cooperative Industrial Area
Mathura Road, New Delhi 110 044, India
www.sagepub.in

SAGE Publications Inc
2455 Teller Road
Thousand Oaks, California 91320, USA

SAGE Publications Ltd
1 Oliver's Yard, 55 City Road
London EC1Y 1SP, United Kingdom

SAGE Publications Asia-Pacific Pte Ltd
3 Church Street
#10-04 Samsung Hub
Singapore 049483

Published by Vivek Mehra for SAGE Publications India Pvt Ltd, typeset in 9.5/11.5 pt ITC Stone Serif Std by Zaza Eunice, Tamil Nadu, India.

Library of Congress Cataloging-in-Publication Data Available

ISBN: 978-93-860-6216-1 (PB)

SAGE Team: Amit Kumar, Indrani Dutta, Priya Arora, Megha Dabral and Ritu Chopra

In revered memory of my grandparents Late Justice Kameshwar Dayal and Late Bindeshwari Devi; parents Late Brijeshwar Dayal and Late Lalita Dayal; and sister Late Seema Dayal

BRIEF CONTENTS

Foreword by Prof. Sanjeev Bhanawat xiii
Foreword by Dr Tabitha Nyaboke Otieno xv
Preface xvii
About the Book xix
Acknowledgments xxi
About the Author xxv

1	Media Metrics: A Conceptual Framework	1
2	Mathematics in Media Research	24
3	Data Processing and Analysis in Mass Communication	51
4	Measures of Central Tendency in Media Research	72
5	Measures of Dispersion in Media Studies	99
6	Measures of Asymmetry in Mass Communication	134
7	Measures of Relationship and Other Measures in Media Research	175
8	Parametric Testing of Hypothesis in Media Studies	254
9	Nonparametric Testing of Hypothesis in Mass Communication	316
10	Chi-square Test in Media Research	339
11	Analysis of Variance in Media Studies	373
12	Multivariate Analysis Techniques in Mass Communication	403
13	Report Writing in Quantitative Media Research	425
14	Computer Applications in Quantitative Media Studies	440

Glossary G–1
Statistical Value Tables S–1
Index I–1
Answers to Questions and Problems A–1

DETAILED CONTENTS

Foreword by Prof. Sanjeev Bhanawat xiii
Foreword by Dr Tabitha Nyaboke Otieno xv
Preface xvii
About the Book xix
Acknowledgments xxi
About the Author xxv

CHAPTER 1 MEDIA METRICS: A CONCEPTUAL FRAMEWORK 1

1.1 Meaning and Concept of Media Metrics 1
1.2 Types of Media Metrics 2
1.3 Nature of Media Measurement 3
1.4 Application of Media Metrics in Mass Communication 7

CHAPTER 2 MATHEMATICS IN MEDIA RESEARCH 24

2.1 Meaning and Concept of Mathematics in Media Research 25
2.2 Use of Mathematics in Media and Communication Measurement 26
2.3 Procedures of Writing a Mathematical Notation 28
2.4 Types of Numbers 30
2.5 Set Descriptions 31
2.6 Classification of Sets 32
2.7 Set Operations 35
2.8 Partitions and Cross-partitions 39
2.9 Differentiation from First Principle 42
2.10 Matrix 47

CHAPTER 3 DATA PROCESSING AND ANALYSIS IN MASS COMMUNICATION 51

3.1 Meaning and Concept of Data Processing and Analysis in Mass Communication 52
3.2 Data 52
3.3 Data Processing 53
3.4 Data Analysis 67
3.5 Prominent Studies of Data Processing and Analysis in Media 68
3.6 Media Metrics in Scientific Data Processing and Analysis of Mass Communication 69

CHAPTER 4 MEASURES OF CENTRAL TENDENCY IN MEDIA RESEARCH 72

4.1 Meaning and Concept of Central Tendency in Media Research 73
4.2 Mean 73
4.3 Median 79
4.4 Mode 85

CHAPTER 5 MEASURES OF DISPERSION IN MEDIA STUDIES 99

5.1 Meaning and Concept of Measures of Dispersion in Media Studies 100
5.2 Methods of Dispersion 101
5.3 Mean Deviation (δ) 101
5.4 Meaning and Concept of Standard Deviation 104
5.5 Variance 117
5.6 Range 119

CHAPTER 6 MEASURES OF ASYMMETRY IN MASS COMMUNICATION 134

6.1 Meaning and Concept of Asymmetry in Mass Communication 135
6.2 Tests of Asymmetry 137
6.3 Measures of Asymmetry 137
6.4 Moments 146
6.5 Kurtosis 151
6.6 Normal Curve and Normal Distribution 153

CHAPTER 7 MEASURES OF RELATIONSHIP AND OTHER MEASURES IN MEDIA RESEARCH 175

7.1 Meaning and Concept of Measures of Relationship in Media Research 176
7.2 Meaning and Concept of Correlation 176
7.3 Significance of Study of Correlation 177
7.4 Types of Correlation 178
7.5 Correlation Coefficient 179
7.6 Properties of Correlation Coefficient 180
7.7 Methods of Correlation 181
7.8 Calculation of Correlation in a Time Series 203
7.9 Lag and Lead in Correlation 205
7.10 Meaning and Concept of Regression 207
7.11 Significance of Regression Analysis 208
7.12 Difference Between Correlation and Regression 208
7.13 Regression Equation 209
7.14 Method of Least Squares 209
7.15 Method of Deviations from Means 212
7.16 Properties of Regression Coefficients 213
7.17 Deviation from Assumed Mean 215
7.18 Standard Error of Estimate 224
7.19 Other Measures 226

CHAPTER 8 PARAMETRIC TESTING OF HYPOTHESIS IN MEDIA STUDIES 254

8.1 Meaning and Concept of Hypothesis Testing in Media Studies 255
8.2 Steps for Testing Hypothesis 255
8.3 Role of Standard Error and Sampling Distribution 260
8.4 Estimation 262

8.5 Test of Significance for Attributes 264
8.6 Test of Significance for Larger Samples 271
8.7 Test of Significance for Small Sample 293
8.8 Limitations of Tests of Significance 307

CHAPTER 9 NONPARAMETRIC TESTING OF HYPOTHESIS IN MASS COMMUNICATION 316

9.1 Meaning and Concept of Nonparametric Hypothesis Testing in Mass Communication 317
9.2 Types of Nonparametric Tests 317
9.3 Advantages of Nonparametric Tests 332
9.4 Limitations of Nonparametric Tests 333

CHAPTER 10 CHI-SQUARE TEST IN MEDIA RESEARCH 339

10.1 Meaning and Concept of Chi-square Test in Media Research 340
10.2 Applications of χ^2 Test 342
10.3 Additive Property of χ^2 343
10.4 Misuse of and Precautions in χ^2 Test 344
10.5 Illustration of Various Applications of the χ^2 Test 345

CHAPTER 11 ANALYSIS OF VARIANCE IN MEDIA STUDIES 373

11.1 Meaning and Concept of Analysis of Variance in Media Studies 374
11.2 Variance Test Ratio 374
11.3 Analysis of Variance in One-way Classification 377
11.4 Analysis of Variance in Two-way Classification 384
11.5 Precautions in Use of ANOVA 387
11.6 Illustrations Relating to Analysis of Variance in Media Studies 388

CHAPTER 12 MULTIVARIATE ANALYSIS TECHNIQUES IN MASS COMMUNICATION 403

12.1 Meaning and Concept of MVA Techniques in Mass Communication 404
12.2 Features and Uses of MVA 404
12.3 Types of Multivariate Techniques 405
12.4 Multiple Regression Analysis 405
12.5 Multiple Discriminant Analysis 409
12.6 Multiple Analysis of Variance 410
12.7 Canonical Correlation Analysis 410
12.8 Factor Analysis 411
12.9 Cluster Analysis 420
12.10 Multidimensional Scaling 421
12.11 Latent Structure Analysis 421

CHAPTER 13 REPORT WRITING IN QUANTITATIVE MEDIA RESEARCH 425

13.1 Meaning and Concept of Report Writing in Quantitative Media Research 426
13.2 Structure and Outline of Report Writing in Media Study 426
13.3 Importance of Report Writing of Quantitative Mass Communication Research 435
13.4 Precautions for Writing Research Report 436
13.5 Qualities of a Good Research Report 437

CHAPTER 14 COMPUTER APPLICATIONS IN QUANTITATIVE MEDIA STUDIES 440

14.1 Meaning and Concept of Computer Applications in Quantitative Media Research 441
14.2 Computer and Quantitative Media Research 441
14.3 Internet and Media Research of Quantitative Data 442
14.4 Electronic Data Collection Techniques in Quantitative Media Research 444
14.5 Internet and Referencing Techniques in Quantitative Media Studies 446
14.6 Applications of Software Packages in Quantitative Media Research 450

Glossary G–1
Statistical Value Tables S–1
Index I–1
Answers to Questions and Problems A–1

FOREWORD

This meticulous book is a pioneering creation in the field of quantitative research in communication and media studies by an eminent media teacher Professor Manoj Dayal.

The book comprehensively explains the foundation of media metrics and describes the proper applications of mathematics and statistics in media research. It cogently argues for the beginners to learn the mathematical and statistical tools manually as it will help them develop a strong base of the subject with precision and accuracy. Gradually, the students may develop their expertise in computer application for quick calculations of complex and multivariate data which has been largely and widely discussed in Chapter 14.

The 14-chapter book has provided various assignments for the students in each chapter in the form of questions and numerical problems with answers, in its purely mathematical and statistical chapters, and sufficient number of suggested websites and recommended books for further reading by the students. Wherever required, the book is full of solved numerical problems of a wide variety for the guidance, facility, and benefit of the students. Other than that, it also explains how to write an effective and systematic report of quantitative media data in Chapter 13.

I hope this innovative textbook from Professor Dayal turns out to be a milestone for the students, teachers, and professionals.

Professor Sanjeev Bhanawat
Head, Centre for Mass Communication,
Honorary Director, Centre for Jain Studies,
University of Rajasthan, Jaipur, India

FOREWORD

This book is a creative innovation in the area of quantitative media research by a senior media faculty-cum-researcher, Professor (Dr) Manoj Dayal, who has been teaching as a regular faculty and guiding media scholars for many years in different central and state universities of India.

The author broadly highlights media metrics and their interaction with quantitative mass communication research with his painstaking endeavor in the form of this book, which primarily employs mathematical and statistical tools in media research. The book comprehensively explains various scientific methods for measuring media variables to maintain accuracy, validity, reliability, and authenticity in media research. In his pioneering work on media metrics, the author describes the relationship between key media forces such as print media, electronic media, corporate communication and public relations, advertising, development communication, social marketing, web media, traditional media, and alternate media.

The author has made an exclusive endeavor in making this book important and relevant in the applications of descriptive media metrics and inferential media metrics and is worth reading to learn about internet referencing in media and communication research.

The author's effort in creatively producing this book and making it conducive to the applications of various software packages in quantitative media analysis will definitely add a new feather in this book's cap. Hence, this innovative art and craft will prove to be a wonderful instrument for students, researchers, faculties, and professionals of quantitative mass communication research.

Dr Tabitha Nyaboke Otieno
Professor,
Department of Social and Cultural Studies, Jackson State University,
Ridgeland, MS, USA

PREFACE

Research is basically a scientific study of finding new facts or testing the existing facts scientifically. However, one of the most important problems of communication and media research among students, researchers, faculties, and media professionals appears to be the lack of a scientific approach in research. They often lag far behind in the exact approach of scientific data collection and scientific data analysis. As a result, the findings are also unscientific.

This book on media metrics (use of mathematics and statistics in media research) is designed to help students in general and media researchers in particular in the scientific collection and analysis of communication and media data. Since media research often lacks appropriate measurement, precision, reliability, and validity, the book comprehensively explains the different mathematical and statistical tools to be used properly in such research. It largely and broadly discusses descriptive media metrics and inferential media metrics (from Chapter 2 to Chapter 12). In Chapter 2 (Section 2.2.1, with the help of a flow chart), the book clearly elaborates upon the different mathematical tools, beginning from the number system to matrix algebra. It explains natural numbers, irrational numbers, set description, set classification, set operation, differentiation from first principle, basics of integration, and matrix algebra. Moreover, in this chapter, there is a systematic discussion and elaboration on different statistical tools, from data processing and analysis to nonparametric statistics (chi-square test, *U*-test, *H*-test, and so on). The flow chart in Section 2.2.1 in this chapter systematically depicts the statistical tools of descriptive media metrics and inferential media metrics, such as data processing analysis, measures of central tendency (mean, median, and mode), measures of dispersion (mean deviation, standard deviation and variance, range, quartile deviation, and so on), measures of asymmetry (normal probability curve, skewness and kurtosis, and moments), measures of relationship (correlation and regression), and multivariate analysis techniques (multiple correlation, multiple regression, canonical correlation, factor analysis, cluster analysis, multidimensional scaling, and latent structure analysis). From Chapter 3 to Chapter 12, the book has systematically discussed one by one the above-mentioned mathematical and statistical tools, such as data processing and analysis in mass communication (Chapter 3), measures of central tendency in media research (Chapter 4), measures of dispersion in media studies (Chapter 5), measures of asymmetry in mass communication (Chapter 6), measures of relationship and other measures in media research (Chapter 7), parametric testing of hypothesis in media studies (Chapter 8), nonparametric testing of hypothesis in mass communication (Chapter 9), chi-square test in media research (Chapter 10), analysis of variance (ANOVA) in media studies (Chapter 11), and multivariate analysis techniques in mass communication (Chapter 12). The book strongly recommends students and researchers to learn statistics and mathematics manually in the beginning even if it is painstaking. This is mainly because it will help them understand variables and subvariables properly. After one has an accurate visualization of different types of variables, then only one can feed computer data systematically and scientifically to get appropriately scientific results. It must go step by step; for example, do it manually first, then use the calculator up to the desired extent, and in extreme cases, use the computer (whether offline or online) accordingly. On the same lines, it is recommended to perform a task manually, then use MS Excel, and at the end, use SPSS, which is the easiest and best tool for statistical and mathematical analysis. A process should not be done the other way round, that is, "Don't start the car in the top gear (SPSS version 23). Rather, begin with the first gear (manually), then second gear (calculator), third gear (computer offline), fourth gear (MS Excel), and finally the top gear (SPSS latest version)." Even top-notch industries of the world follow this step-by-step method systematically for achieving long-term outputs.

Once you learn properly about data and visualization of variables, you may drive the car most of the time in the fourth gear (MS Excel) and top gear (SPSS latest version) according to suitability and circumstances.

Write a project report manually in the first go and then switch to typing on a computer; thereafter, go on editing again and again till you are satisfied. Remember, it is not news writing where the deadline is transient. It is research writing where time lag is sufficient.

Therefore, on the noble advise of the publisher, I have added report writing in quantitative media research (Chapter 13) and computer applications in quantitative media studies (Chapter 14). Moreover, the book provides questions, problems (wherever required), and solutions to media and communication-related numerical issues. It also summarizes key points in each chapter. Further, it contains boxes of formulae for convenience and desirably enlists suggested reading and recommended website materials for the prospective target readers of the book.

ABOUT THE BOOK

The book comprehensively talks about media metrics that is basically the use of statistics and mathematics in media research. It is a method of measuring media variables in a scientific manner. It largely and broadly explains the technique of scientific data collection and scientific data analysis leading to appropriately scientific results, especially in the case of quantitative media data.

Media metrics in mass communication research is like "econometrics" in economic research, "psychometrics" in psychological research, "sociometrics" in sociological research, "edumetrics," or "educometrics" in educational research. However, unlike age-old sub-branches of social sciences—econometrics, psychometrics, sociometrics, and educometrics—media metrics is a new technical concept in communication and media research. This term is intensely getting importance and relevance all over the world as media research also demands accuracy, reliability, authenticity, and validity like other social and behavioral sciences. Since media research is still in its nascent stage and primitive phase, the term media metrics has been more than ignored in the glossary of mass communication.

Hence, this pioneering work on media metrics describes the relationship between key media forces such as print media, electronic media, corporate communication and public relations, advertising, development communication, social marketing, web media, traditional media, and alternate media.

This painstaking task on media metrics relates to the problems of media measurement, media quantification, media dimension, media datafication, media assessment, media agency and campaign review, and media audience analysis in a highly scientific manner. Therefore, the book comprehensively explains the various mathematical and statistical tools used in communication and media research with the following features:

1. Helpful in scientific analysis of communication and media variables
2. Useful in easily understanding the various mathematical and statistical tools used in media research
3. Instrumental in applications of descriptive media metrics and inferential media metrics
4. Worth learning about to understand internet referencing in quantitative media study
5. Conducive to applications of various software packages in quantitative media analysis
6. May be criticized by advocates of qualitative media research. However, on the lines of Bhutan, many countries are trying to develop a "gross happiness index" despite the fact that "happiness" is a qualitative term. A school of thought in mass communication is cogently arguing that even qualitative terms are quantifiable in this scientific era. On the same lines, we analyze the human development index in which India is lagging far behind.

Thus, the book has indicated and hinted at a possible way of converting the qualitative data into quantitative data, and describes various methods of measuring communication and media variables in a systematic and scientific manner. It is an approach to measure what is measureable and make measurable what is not.

ACKNOWLEDGMENTS

For their guidance time and again in this pioneering work, I am indebted to my media teachers of Indian Institute of Mass Communication, New Delhi:

Professor J.S. Yadava
Professor Devesh Kishore
Professor M.R. Dua
Professor Dasu Krishanamurthy
Professor B.B. Mohanthy
Professor Subhash Dhuliya
Professor N.N. Sarkar
Professor Rajeshwar Dayal
Professor Ramji Pd. Jangir

For their direct or indirect contributions to this painstaking task, I am extremely thankful to my colleagues:

Professor B.K. Kuthiala, Vice Chancellor, Makhanlal Chaturvedi National Journalism and Mass Communication University, Bhopal, and Honorary Professor, Faculty of Media Studies, Guru Jambheshwar University of Science & Technology (GJUST), Hisar

Professor Sushma Gandhi, Director, Amity School of Mass Communication, Maneshwar and former Dean, Faculty of Media Studies, GJUST, Hisar

Professor P.K. Jena, former Dean, Faculty of Media Studies, GJUST, Hisar

Professor Bandana Pandey, Director, Human Resources Development Centre, and Dean, Faculty of Media Studies, GJUST, Hisar

Professor Vikram Kausik, Chairperson, Department of Communication Management and Technology, GJUST, Hisar

Professor Umesh Arya, CMT, GJUST, Hisar

Dr Sushil K. Singh, CMT, GJUST, Hisar

Shri M.R. Patra, CMT, GJUST, Hisar

Professor Ved Pal, HSB, GJUST, Hisar

Professor Tika Ram, HSB, GJUST, Hisar

Dr Baljinder Kaur, CMT, GJUST, Hisar

Dr Pallavi, CMT, GJUST, Hisar

Ms Kusum, CMT, GJUST, Hisar

Ms Rashmi, CMT, GJUST, Hisar

Dr S.S. Joshi, Librarian, GJUST, Hisar

Dr Vinod Kr., Deputy Librarian, GJUST, Hisar

Padmashree Professor Anjan Kumar Banerji, former Dean, Faculty of Arts, Banaras Hindu University, Varanasi

Professor Santosh Kumar Tewari, Centre for Mass Communication, Central University of Jharkhand, Ranchi

Professor Sisir Basu, Department of Journalism and Mass Communication, Banaras Hindu University, Varanasi
Professor Biplab Loha Chawdhury, Centre for Mass Communication, Visva Bharati
Professor B. Balaswami, Department of Mass Communication, University of Hyderabad
Professor Ganesh Kawadia, Dean, Faculty of Social Sciences
Professor P.N. Mishra, Director, Institute of Management Studies, Devi Ahilya Vishwavidyalaya, Indore
Professor Sanjay Wadwalkar, School of Communication Studies, Punjab University, Chandigarh
Dr Sushma Kasbekar, Associate Professor in Mass Communication, Assumption University, Bangkok
Dr Sewa Singh Bajwa, Associate Professor in Mass Communication, CDLU, Sirsa
Mr Advitya Khurana, Assistant Professor in Mass Communication, Govt. College, Panchkula
Ms Kusum, Assistant Professor in Mass Communication, Govt. College, Narnaund
Mr A.J. Philip (veteran journalist)

Other colleagues of media education and media profession who directly or indirectly contributed their thoughts:

Professor K.V. Nagraj
Professor N.A.K. Durani
Professor Obaid Sidhqui
Professor Iftekar Ahmed
Professor Sanjeev Bhanawat
Professor Ram Mohan Pathak
Professor Shambhu Nath Singh
Professor O.P. Singh
Professor P. Bobby Vardhan
Professor Bala Subramaniam
Professor Ani Upadhyay
Professor Sunil K Behera
Professor H.P.S. Walia
Professor Navjot Singh Johal
Professor Hemant Joshi
Professor Jayant Petkar
Professor Archana R. Singh
Professor Mohanmeet Khosla
Professor Sarojini Nandal
Professor Rajbir Singh
Professor G.P. Pandey
Professor Tapati Basu
Professor Veerwala Aggrawal
Professor Jaishree Jethwani
Professor Shrikant Singh
Professor Ambrish Saxena
Professor Devashish Chakravorty
Professor Shafey Kidwai
Professor Biswajit Das

Professor Tripura Sundari
Professor Sonal Pandya
Professor Onkargounda Kakade
Professor Deepak Shinde
Professor Achyut Vaze
Professor Punita Harne
Dr Manoj Lodha
Dr Pradeep Nair
Dr Uma Shankar Pandey
Dr Surbhi Dahiya
Dr Pooja Rana
Dr Anubhuti Yadav
Dr Kiran Khanna
Dr Keerty Goyal
Dr Devi Lal Mishra
Shri Anuj Dayal, Executive Director, Delhi Metro Rail Corporation, and media researcher
Shri Sarvesh Tewari, Director and CEO, PR Professionals, Gurgaon

Thanks to my research scholars Dr Ashutosh Mishra, Dr Sahib Ram Godara, Dr Seth Singh Ranga, Dr Sunaina Narang, Dr Pragya Kausik, Dr Nisha Singh, Dr Sandeep Kumar Saini, Dr Dilawar Singh, Dr Krishan Kumar, Dr Prem Monga, Dr Pankaj Praveen Tripathi, Dr Kavita Dahiya, Dr Varinder Verma, Dr Ankita Bansal, and my current scholars Bhupinder Singh, Tanjum Khamboj, Bharti Batra, Mandev, Ritu Madad, Nidhi, Kulbir Chhikara, and Neeraj Kumar for their inquisitive questions that continuously kept me motivated for this uphill task.

For their regular encouragement in this tedious job, I am indebted to my mates from the Indian Institute of Mass Communication, New Delhi, Professor Ashok Ogra, Professor Geeta Bamzai, Professor Harish Kumar, Professor Devbrat Singh, Amit Sengupta, Chitra Subramaniam, David Devadas, Deepak Chaurasia, Sudhir Chaudary, Hasleen Kaur, Niret Alva, Ravish Kr., Rini Simon Khanna, Shriniwas Mishra, Sonal Kalra, Vartika Nanda, Vivek Agnihotri, Zeljka Malnar, Zafar Anjum, Debendra Prasad Majhi, Aditya Malviya, Jayant Singh Duia, Arindam Mukherji, Himanshu Joshi, Alok Shrivastav, Sanjay Sinha, Supriya Prasad, Darpan Singh, Arvind Das, Punit Kumar, Kunal Kanti, Rupam Ganguly, Meenakshi Sharma, Kavita Tandon, Ras Bihari, Sanjay Kumar, Jemini Shrivastav, Mini Ribeiro, Sushmita Chaterji, Deepshikha Seth, Mukta Rawat, Shilpa Sonal, Geetika Jain, Sonal Sharma, Swati, Reema Ganguly, Mary Ombara, Loretta Ann, and others.

I am equally obliged to my father-in-law Professor P.N.P. Sinha and my mother-in-law Professor Sudha Verma (both psychometricians), my brothers Shri Mukeshwar Dayal (legal luminary), brother-in-law Dr Sanjeev K. Sinha and Dr Rajiv Ranjan Sinha (both pure science researchers), Mr Sunil K. Sinha, Mr Neeraj K. Sinha (US-based industrial researcher), Mr Rajiv Ranjan Sinha (senior media person), Mr Praveen Kumar (crime researcher), Mr Rishi Kumar (industrial researcher), my sisters Ms Sushma Dayal, Ms Reshma Dayal, Ms Sama Dayal, my sister-in-laws Ms Manju Dayal, Dr Alka Sinha, Dr Rupshree Sinha, Ms Poonam Sinha (US-based industrial researcher), and Ms Mily Sinha. Last, but not the least, I am wholeheartedly grateful to my beloved wife Lily and my daughters Medha and Rachana for always inspiring me in this tough journey and sharing all my pains and losses.

ABOUT THE AUTHOR

The senior-most professor in mass communication at the Department of Communication Management & Technology, Faculty of Media Studies, Guru Jambheshwar University of Science & Technology, Hisar, Haryana, India, Manoj Dayal has been teaching media and communication research for more than 27 years (almost 13 years as a professor) and has the experience of working, pursuing, and guiding research for more than 30 years in different central and state universities of India. The founder head of the Department of Journalism and Mass Communication, University of Allahabad (1992–96), and the founder professor of Sirsa-based Chaudhary Devi Lal University (2004–05), Prof. Dayal has so far guided 17 PhD students, around two dozen MPhil students, and more than 200 postgraduate dissertations in journalism and mass communication. A member of editorial boards and referee boards of several national and international research journals, Prof. Dayal has 71 research publications (6 international and 65 national) in reputed national and international journals, has presented 77 research papers in international (21) and national (56) seminars, and has been nominated by the University Grants Commission (UGC), Delhi, for the postdoctoral commonwealth fellowship of United Kingdom in 2001. In addition, he has been the coordinator (2007–12) of a major departmental project (theme: research in internet journalism) of UGC under the Special Assistance Programme and is presently pursuing DLitt in mass communication from a central university of India. Further, Prof. Dayal has been honored by the ABP News channel with the National Education Award of Best Professor in the subject for the year 2014. Prof. Dayal's basic qualifications are a doctoral degree in the area of economic journalism, postgraduation in economics with econometrics as specialization, postgraduation in mass communication, and a postgraduate diploma in journalism (English) from the Indian Institute of Mass Communication, Jawaharlal Nehru University campus, New Delhi. Before joining the teaching profession, Prof. Dayal worked as a trainee journalist, *Financial Express* (Indian Express group), reporter-cum-subeditor in a Delhi-based feature agency (Newsmen Features), special correspondent in a Delhi- and Bhopal-based English fortnightly (*Mastak*), and subeditor in a national English daily (*Hindustan Times*, Delhi and Patna).

1

CHAPTER

Media Metrics: A Conceptual Framework

Measure what is measurable and make measurable what is not so.

—Galileo

Research is a scientific study. But media research often lacks exact scientific approach. This is because it broadly lacks measurement, precision, reliability, and validity. When we say the glass is half full or half empty, in both cases it is our qualitative judgment or attitude. In both these cases, we are biased. In the former situation, we are positively biased. And in the latter situation, we are negatively biased. But when we quantify it and say that there is 200 ml water in the glass, then it is measureable and hence it will have more precision, reliability, and validity.

Media metrics is a new technical concept in mass communication research. But the term is intensely getting importance all over the world as media research also demands accuracy, reliability, and validity like any other social and behavioral sciences. Since media research is still in its nascent stage, the term media metrics has been more than ignored in the glossary of mass communication.

This chapter focuses on the meaning and concept of media metrics, nature of measurement, variables, levels of measurement, application of media metrics in mass communication, media metrics in print media (precision journalism, database journalism, media metrics in electronic media, corporate communication and public relations, advertising, development communication, social marketing, web media, and social media and various other media).

In addition, the chapter will also cover the summary, related and suggested websites, references, related and recommended readings, and questions.

1.1 MEANING AND CONCEPT OF MEDIA METRICS

The linguistic meaning of any term helps in understanding the basic concept more clearly. Here are a few definitions of the term media metrics as defined in dictionaries. According to *Oxford Advanced Learner's Dictionary*, "*Metrics* is a method of measuring something or the results obtained from this." Hence, it denotes the science of measuring as applied to a specific field of study, for example, media metrics, econometrics, psychometrics, sociometrics, or edumetrics.

Business dictionaries define metrics as the standard of measurement by which efficiency, performance, progress, or quality of a plan, process, or product can be assessed. In the context of financial concerns, metrics may also be defined as parameters or measures of quantitative assessment used to measure, compare, or track performance, as defined by Investopedia.

Hence, media metrics may be defined as the use of statistics and mathematics in mass communication research to measure various aspects of the whole media phenomena such as communication variables and media issues. This term in media research has the same position and value as "econometrics" in economic research, "psychometrics" in psychological research, "sociometrics" in sociological research, "edumetrics" or "educometrics" in educational research, and so on.

Media metrics describes the numerical relationship within and between key media forces such as print media, electronic media, social media, corporate communication and public relations, advertising, development communication, social marketing, web media, traditional media, alternate media, and so on. Media metrics is related to the quantitative aspects of media measurement such as media evaluation, media quantification, media dimensions, media calculation, media datafication, media assessment, media agency and campaign reviews, media audience analysis, media trade marketing, and so on. Thus, media metrics is a broad term indicating a number of methods of gathering and analyzing data on the choice, communication, and interaction patterns of readers, listeners, viewers, users, and audience as a whole.

1.2 TYPES OF MEDIA METRICS

There are basically two types of media metrics: (a) theoretical media metrics and (b) applied media metrics.

In theoretical media metrics, theories, methods, and techniques of pure mathematics and pure statistics are studied, whereas in applied media metrics, these theories, methods, and techniques are used to solve various problems.

The applied media metrics may be further divided into two parts: (a) descriptive media metrics and (b) inferential media metrics.

Descriptive media metrics includes the following statistical techniques among others:

1. Data processing and analysis (including frequency distribution),
2. Measures of central tendency,
3. Measures of dispersion,
4. Measures of asymmetry,
5. Measures of relationship and other measures,
6. Multivariate analysis.

On the other hand, inferential media metrics is also called *inductive media metrics* and under this category the facts derived from descriptive media metrics are generalized. The inferential media metrics may be further divided into two categories: (a) parametric inferential media metrics and (b) nonparametric inferential media metrics.

Parametric inferential media metrics are those which have some parameters, that is, which have certain assumptions, whereas nonparametric inferential media metrics are those which do not have any parameters meaning that nonparametric inferential media metrics are assumption free.

Following are some of the prominent parametric inferential media metrics:

1. *F*-test,
2. *t*-test,
3. *Z*-test,
4. ANOVA.

Following are some of the prominent nonparametric inferential media metrics:

1. Chi-square test,
2. Sign test,
3. Signed test for paired observation,
4. Mann–Whitney *U* test
5. Kruskal–Wallis *H* test,
6. Alexander Mood's median test,
7. Wilcoxon signed-rank test,
8. McNemar test,
9. Fisher's exact probability test,
10. Wald–Wolfowitz runs test.

(Note: It is important to mention here that McNemar test, Fisher's probability test, and Wald–Wolfowitz test are generally not used in media metrics.)

1.3 NATURE OF MEDIA MEASUREMENT

By the help of media metrics, the data for mass communication are scientifically collected and interpreted. But to arrive at any scientific conclusion, the process of measurement is urgently required as research is a systematic and scientific inquiry of any phenomenon. The use and application of mathematics and statistics in mass communication research is of utmost importance. As aptly remarked by the measurement expert J.P. Guilford (cited in Wimmer and Dominick 2003, 48),

> The progress and maturity of a science are often judged by the extent to which it has succeeded in the use of mathematics.... Mathematics is a universal language that any science or technology may use with great power and convenience. Its vocabulary of terms is unlimited.... Its rules of operation ... are unexcelled for logical precision.

Hence, the nature of media measurement is very simple. For example, a researcher assigns numerals to objects, events, or properties according to certain rules. When it is given a quantitative meaning, it becomes a number and can be applied in mathematical and statistical computations. In order to measure media psychology such as "source credibility" or "attitude toward violence," meticulously explicated media measurement methods are required.

In mass communication, the researcher deals with human behavior which is not so easy to directly measure in quantitative terms, and just collection of qualitative responses is of no use unless they draw some generalization. For making such generalization, the responses of different individuals are clubbed together to retrieve public opinion. For such massive analysis, quantification of each response makes the task easy through application of media metrics in mass communication.

1.3.1 Variables

Variables are those measures of any phenomenon whose nature is dynamic. It varies and such variability may be dependent on or independent of other factors. The nature, traits, characteristics, features, or qualities of any individual or object, group, community, or society are called variables. For example, height, weight, intelligence level, or economic status of reporters of a newspaper is different. That is why height, weight, intelligence, or economic status here is called variables. Other examples of variables are gender, caste, religion, race, marital status, age, income, education, height, social class, organizational productivity, occupational mobility, level of aspiration, attitude, aptitude, anxiety, religious preference, political affiliation, ego, conformity, introversion, achievement, and so on. There are various types of variables (Figure 1.1):

1. Discrete variable and continuous variable,
2. Qualitative variable and quantitative variable,
3. Dependent variable and independent variable.

FIGURE 1.1
TYPES OF VARIABLES AS PER MEASURABILITY

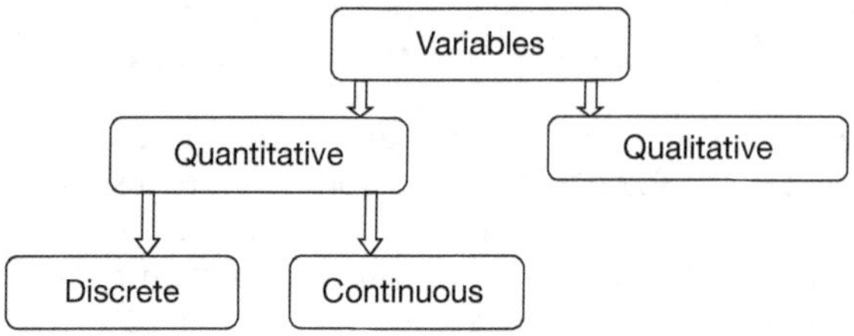

Source: Drawn by author.

1. A *discrete variable* is one whose basic unit of measurement cannot be subdivided. It is a whole number per case, for example, number of persons in a family, number of newspapers in a city, or number of reporters in a magazine. It can be 1, 2, 3, 4 and cannot be 2.43.

   On the other hand, a *continuous variable* can have any value (including fractions) and can be sub-divided into smaller subsections. A good example of such a variable is time spent in listening to radio. Person X spent 2.1315 hours listening to radio, while person Y spent 2.1314 hours. The average number of students in a media school is a continuous variable. Thus, in this reference, it is significant to say that there are 200.42 students. It is important to mention here that most of the measures in mass communication research tend to be discrete approximations of continuous variables.

FIGURE 1.2
TYPES OF VARIABLES AS PER CAUSE AND EFFECT

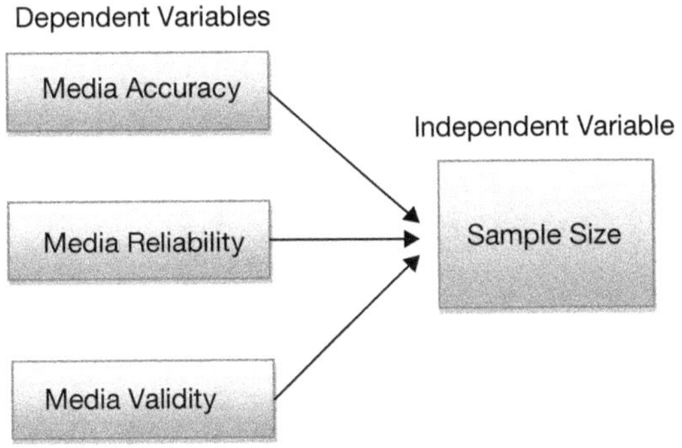

Source: Drawn by author.

2. A *qualitative variable* is the trait or quality of a person, object, or group, for example, aggression, attitude, aptitude, politeness, aspiration, ego, achievement, and so on. It can be measured in qualitative terms such as good and bad. However, their exact quantification is impossible but by assigning numerical codes to each trait they can be quantified to some extent and made easy for further analysis.
   On the other hand, a *quantitative variable* can be expressed numerically, for example, length, height, time, number of persons, and the likes.
3. A *dependent variable* is a consequence of some cause. For this reason, it is also called uncontrolled variable, result variable, outcome variable, effects variable, consequence variable, criterion variable, or attribute variable.

On the other hand an *independent variable* is the cause of some event. It is also called controlled variable, cause variable, active variable, predictor variable, or antecedent variable.

For example, media accuracy, media reliability, and media validity of a research depend on the sample size. Here, sample size is an independent variable, and media accuracy is a dependent variable. Similarly, the communication effectiveness is inversely proportional to the size of the audience. Here, the size of the audience is an independent variable and communication effectiveness is a dependent variable (Figure 1.2).

1.3.2 Levels of Measurement

A well-known psychometrician S.S. Stevens (1946) has divided measurement into four different levels of measurement, depending upon the rules that are used to assign numbers to objects or events. The four levels of measurement are as follows (Figure 1.3):

1. Nominal level of measurement,
2. Ordinal level of measurement,
3. Interval level of measurement,
4. Ratio level of measurement.

FIGURE 1.3
THE DIFFERENT LEVELS AND TYPES OF MEASUREMENT

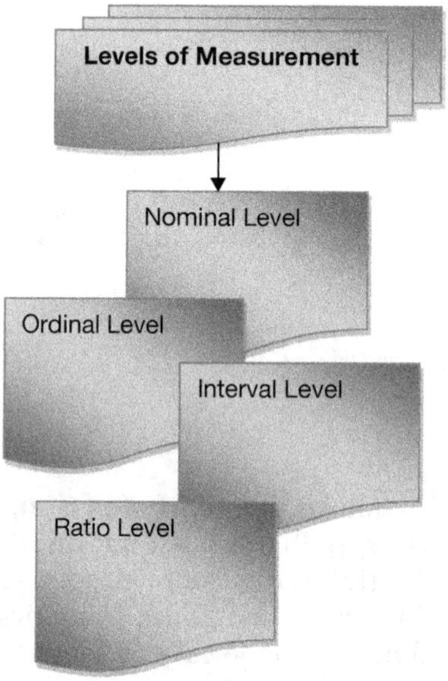

Source: Concept by S.S. Stevens, drawn by author's research scholar Bhupender Singh.

Nominal level of measurement is the most fundamental and the only universal measurement procedure to classify cases into the pre-established categories of a variable. Nominal relates to name, and both "nominal" and "name" have the same Latin root. Hence, it refers to categorically discrete data such as name of your university, name of media book, and gender (male or female). All measurements involve classification as a minimum. In nominal measurement, numerals or other symbols are used to classify persons, objects, or characteristics.

Nominal level of measurement possesses certain basic properties like equivalence and in this type of measurement, all categories are exhaustive and mutually exclusive.

Nominal level of measurement is often applied in mass communication research. In this, each category is coded and on these codes further quantitative analysis is applied like numerical codes: gender=Male/female, where code=1 is for male and code=2 for female. Hinkle and Elliot (cited in Wimmer and Dominick 2003, 50) categorized science coverage by supermarket tabloids and mainstream newspapers into medical coverage and hard technology stories and discovered that tabloids had much more medical stories. Weinberger and Spotts (cited in Wimmer and Dominick 2003, 50) categorized the application of humorous devices in British and American ads into six nominal categories—pun, understatement, joke, ludicrous, satire, and irony and their research revealed the facts that the use of humor was similar in both the countries.

Ordinal level of measurement is generally ranked on the basis of some order as the word "ordinal" and "order" has the same origin and hence order of a race or order of a rank in an examination I, II, III. Similar examples are high–low, minimum–maximum, more than/less than, short–average–tall, primary/secondary/higher education, lower–lower middle–middle–higher middle–higher–smallest to largest, and so on. For example, to measure the perception of audience on a specific matter, the questions are framed on a five-point Likert scale, that is, strongly agree to strongly disagree. As an ordinal scale, in numerical analysis they will be numbered as 1 for strongly disagree and 5 for strongly agree.

Ordinal level of measurement is applied in media research more often than not. Schweitzer (cited in Wimmer and Dominick 2003, 51) ranked 16 factors that were important to the success of media researchers. In yet another research work on electronic text news, Heeter, Brown, Soffin, Stanley, and Salwen (cited in Wimmer and Dominick 2003, 51) ranked audience evaluations of the importance of 25 various issues in the news items and finally observed little support of an effect on content, known as agenda setting.

The main disadvantage of ordinal level of measurement is that a particular score represents only position with respect to some other score. One can distinguish between high and low scores but the distance between the scores cannot be described in prescribed terms. Although we are aware that a score of 10 is more than a score of 5, yet we cannot say whether it is twice as much as 5. As the process of addition, subtraction, multiplication, and division assume equal intervals between scores, they are not permitted with variables measured at the ordinal level. For variables at this level, the most sophisticated mathematical and statistical operation granted is ranking categories and cases.

Interval data are the same as the ordinal data with equal split, such as time and temperature. Ratio data are the same as interval data with a natural or true zero, such as height and weight. Hence, the interval level of measurement and the ratio level of measurement are treated as the same at the primary stage of study as variables measured at the interval–ratio level not only permit classification and ranking but also permit the distance from score to score and category to category to be exactly defined. Interval–ratio variables are measured in units that have equal intervals and a true zero point. For example, interval–ratio variables are age, income, number of children, number of magazine subscriptions, number of newspaper readings at different places, and so on. All mathematical and statistical operations are granted for data measured at this level. Briefly, different types of media metrics call for various mathematical and statistical operations and, hence, the level of measurement considerations is the logical first guideline to use in selecting a statistic. Ratio scales are relatively less in media research, though some variables such as time spent listening to radio or number of words per story are ratio measurements. As, for instance, Gantz (cited in Wimmer and Dominick 2003, 52) measured news recall ability by asking subjects to report whether they had seen or heard 10 stories taken from the evening news. Giffard (cited in Wimmer and Dominick 2003, 52) counted the length of wire service reports relating to 101 developed and developing countries. Theoretically, scores could range from zero (no coverage) to hundreds of words.

1.4 APPLICATION OF MEDIA METRICS IN MASS COMMUNICATION

Media metrics may be applied in different branches of mass media such as print media, precision journalism, database journalism, electronic media, corporate communication and public relations, advertising, development communication, social marketing, web media, social media, and other media.

It means that media metrics can be used for the measurement of different variables of mass media to attain precision, reliability, and validity in mass media research. It can lead to quantification of any data relating to the variables of print media, precision journalism, database journalism, electronic media, corporate communication and public relations, advertising, development communication, social marketing, web media, social media, and other media. Since measurement in broader sense is the assignment of numerals to objects or events according to rules, measurement of print media variables includes no statement about the quality of the measurement procedure. It simply reflects that, somehow, numerals are assigned to objects or to events. Measurement is the game we play with objects and numerals. Games have rules. It is, of course, important for other reasons that the rules be "good" rules. But whether the rules are "good" or "bad," the procedure is still measurement. Measurement is important because it is often misunderstood. It is not hard to understand certain measurements used in the natural sciences—length, weight, and volume for example. But to understand that measurement of media involves basically and essentially the same thinking and general procedure is much harder.

Zandpour, and Tonny (2006) strongly opine and aptly remark in their paper entitled "Media Studies and Statistics: Real-world Demands, Classroom Quandaries, and On-line Solutions,"

> Communication professionals, faced with an explosive growth of numerical data, have to make sense of an increasingly complex world in an ever-changing media environment. For example, to ensure that their stories are accurate and credible, journalists have to examine a flood of information related to economic, political, and social phenomena, including scientific and academic research reports, public opinion data, academic, commercial and political polls, consumer surveys and countless other numerical data that are released on a daily basis. Advertising and public relations executives must be able to understand and utilize the latest available business information such as market trends, sales, competitive expenditures, audience ratings, click-thoughts and a host of other facts pertaining to consumers, products, companies and markets.

Since it is known that statistics is the basis of calculating any metrics, the importance of statistics in media metrics has been aptly highlighted by various scholars of the field as Fred and Tony (2006) argue,

> [T]he classroom training in statistical thinking that we offer our students is not up to responding to the challenges coming at us from the real-world media where we hope to place these students. We recognize that our students' interest in hands-on problem solving and their increasing sophistication with online technologies in building our argument in more disciplined-specific studies in statistics....

The study further argues, "Offer statistics education as part of the substantive areas of media and communication classes such as reporting, editing, media planning, campaign or communication management courses."

Given the enormous demand for up-to-date, accurate, and actionable information, it is reasonable to suggest that statistical thinking and reasoning (Butler 1990; Garfield et al. 2002; Snee 1990) should be considered a key learning goal for students of media and communication.

Frankenstein (cited in Healey 1999) in his pioneering work "Critical Mathematics Education: An Application of Paulo Freire's Epistemology" cogently opines,

> Knowledge of basic mathematics and statistics is important part of gaining real popular, democratic control over the economic, political and social structure of our society. Libratory social change requires an understanding of the technical knowledge that is too often used to obscure economic and social realities. When we develop specific strategies for an emancipator education, it is vital that we include such mathematical literacy.

In many disciplines, the aptitude to understand, interpret, and critically evaluate research data has become a crucial skill (Gal 2002; Gilsbrecht 1996). It is important to mention here that it is more demanding in a discipline like communication and mass media as this discipline now is an upcoming field in research, and the outcomes of these researches are directly linked, related, useful, and understandable even for the common man.

It appears that media and communication students are confronted with a dilemma. There is a growing need to include statistical understanding, reasoning, and thinking (Garfield et al. 2002) as learning goals in the curriculum while most communication students have a negative attitude toward statistics, perform poorly in statistics courses, and tend to avoid the subject of statistics altogether if they can.

Yilmaz (1996) remarked that advanced understanding of statistics in an introductory course may not be possible. However, introducing the statistical concepts within journalistic or marketing communication problems may strongly facilitate the development of opposite attitude toward statistics. This is to say that students are much more likely to be receptive to statistics training and they understand statistics when they see its utility in solving practical problems in the context of reporting case analysis or promotional projects.

1.4.1 Media Metrics in Print Media

We will discuss the use of media metrics in the measurement of different variables of print media to obtain accuracy, reliability, and validity in print media research. The supporters of qualitative research are of the opinion that quantitative research or measurement is not possible in media, especially print media. On the other hand, the supporters of media measurement schools strongly believe that if rules can be set up on some rational or empirical basis, measurement of anything in media is theoretically possible. This tremendously widens the horizons of media mathematicians. Such media mathematicians cannot reject the scope of measuring some property because the property is often complex and elusive. Here is an interesting story. A talented journalist of a grade 1 newspaper was not able to select a girl for his marriage, because the approach of his joint family was very complex. Some argued that "a male journalist should marry a female politician and a female journalist should marry a male bureaucrat." So, he should not be married to a female bureaucrat. Like this or that. Ultimately, the head, father of the family who was a scientist, fixed certain criteria and attributes of qualitative variables, quantitative variables, nominal level of measurement, ordinal level of measurement, interval level of measurement, and ratio level of measurement for giving marks to every proposal by every family member. These attributes and criteria were fixed to see only those girls for selection who scored more than 75 percent marks. Finally, in this process, the journalist got married to a simple and dedicated housewife.

Hence, the measurement game alters us to the essential neutral core of measurement procedures and the necessity for setting up good rules, that is, rules which have traits that can be empirically tested. Thus, no measurement procedure is any better than its rules.

Earlier, most of the researches in print media used to be qualitative in nature. The first issue of *Journalism Quarterly* published in 1928, succeeding *Journalism Bulletin* (started in 1924), contained qualitative research papers prominently on press law and ethics, comparison of international press, and press history. But second issue onwards, it widely covered quantitative research papers. In 1930s, countless numbers of research papers were published on print media advertising. As the methods and techniques of quantitative research became more widely accepted, adopted, and known, the research papers of newspapers and magazines became more empirical and applied. A well-known communication scientist Wilbur Schramm for the first time observed and recognized this trend of growth in 1957 in his pioneering research paper in a reputed journal called *Public Opinion Quarterly*. In this paper, Wilbur Schramm reviewed 20 years of research as reported in *Journalism Quarterly* and reached at a conclusion that only 10 percent of 101 research papers published between 1937 and 1941 were quantitative in nature. By 1952–56, 72 out of the 143 research papers published were quantitative. That means, in only 15 years, quantitative research increased by five times. According to Wilbur Schramm, the main reasons for this tremendous growth in quantitative research in mass media were the following:

1. Growing availability of basic data,
2. Development of more sophisticated research tools,
3. Increase in institutional support for research.

The trend of media changed by the end of 1960. As a result, the competition of newspapers and magazines with radio and television went on increasing. Due to this fact, newspapers and magazines managed to attract more readers and hence, advertisers increased their investment in the areas of print media. As a result, there was unexpected and unprecedented growth of quantitative media research in private sectors. Simultaneously, "News Research Centre" was established in the 1970s. It gave a new dimension and direction to quantitative research of news items. In 1976, the newspaper readership project was set up for the study of the problems of reducing circulation and deteriorating readership. This also raised several issues of quantitative print media research. In 1988, Jacobson found that quantitative research in magazine also played a vital role.

Print media research includes readership studies, circulation studies, management studies, typography and make-up studies, and readability studies. A common practice is to measure these variables with the help of a semantic differential rating scale. As for instance, Siskind (cited in Wimmer and Dominick 2003, 317) used a nine-point, 20-item differential scale with such adjective pair as "messy/neat," "informative/uninformative," "unpleasant/pleasant," "easy/difficult," "clear/unclear," "bold/timid," and "passive/active."

So many formulas have been developed to find out objectively the readability of text. One of the best known is the Flesch (cited in Wimmer and Dominick 2003, 319) Reading Ease Formula, which requires the researcher to choose systematically 100 words from the text, determine the total number of syllables in those words (wl), determine the average number of words per sentence (sl), and do the calculation as follows:

$$\text{Reading Ease} = 206.835 - 0.846\ \text{wl} - 1.01\ \text{sl}$$

There are many other measures of readability like fog index (Gunning cited in Wimmer and Dominick 2003, 319), SMOG grading (Mc laughling cited in Wimmer and Dominick 2003, 319), cloze procedure (Nestvold; Taylor cited in Wimmer and Dominick 2003, 320), and PMOSE/IKIRSCH (Mosenthal and Kirch cited in Wimmer and Dominick 2003, 320).

1.4.1.1 Precision Journalism

Precision journalism is also a very important approach of quantification of print media research. It is a technique of enquiry adopted by print media reporters who apply the research methodology of media research in their news reporting. This type of journalism

FIGURE 1.4
DATA-DRIVEN JOURNALISM = PROCESS

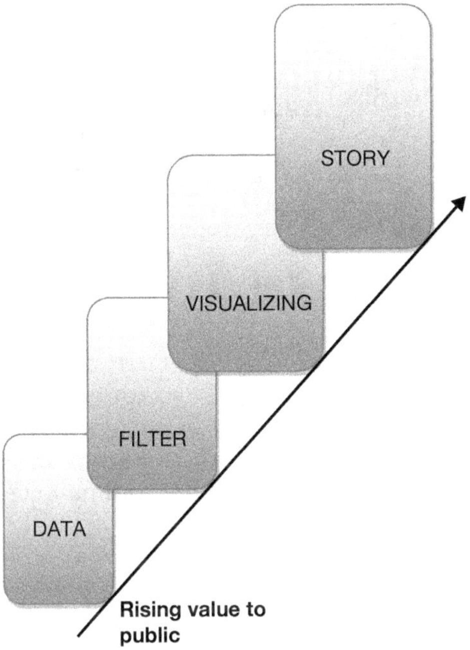

Source: Lorenz (2010).

was popularized by print media reporter and researcher Philip Meyer (cited in Wimmer and Dominick 2003, 322) in his pioneering book *Precision Journalism* (1973). That is why this type of journalism is called "Precision Journalism." This method relies primarily on the procedures of content analysis and survey research to generate quantitative data that are reported as news stories (Figure 1.4). For example, the *Detroit News* content analyzed almost 36,000 drunk-driving conviction records and arrived at a conclusion that big-city judges gave more lenient penalties than rural judges. In the same way, the *Charlotte Observer* analyzed campaign finance reports and noted a link between voting patterns and contributions.

1.4.1.2 Database Journalism

Yet another research-based quantitative journalism is database journalism (Figure 1.5) which was pioneered by news reporter Elliot Jaspin. This type of journalism depends on computer-based analysis of existing news file, an approach which has been accepted and adopted at several newspapers. Elliot Jaspin filed a story on school bus safety, by researching computerized records of traffic citations over a 3 years period and reached a conclusion that many bus drivers had frightful driving records.

Thus, the emergence of precision journalism and database journalism expects from our journalists to have a basic knowledge of media research methodology. Moreover, precision journalism requires the knowledge of mathematical and statistical measurement, research methodology, questionnaire design, sampling technique, and data presentation.

FIGURE 1.5
DATABASE JOURNALISM

Source: Drawn by author.

Hence, all such researches of print media such as readership research, circulation research, management research, typography and make-up research, readability research, precision journalism, and database journalism require the use and application of quantitative variables, qualitative variables, nominal level of measurement, ordinal level of measurement, interval level of measurement, and ratio level of measurement.

1.4.2 Media Metrics in Electronic Media

In this section, we will discuss the measurement and quantification of variables of electronic media in order to attain accuracy, authenticity, reliability, and validity in electronic media. It means evaluation and calculation of any data regarding the variables of radio, television, and film. Measurement is the assignment of numerals to objects or events according to rules. A numeral is a symbol of the form 1, 2, 3, and so on, or I, II, III, and so on. It has no quantitative meaning unless we give it such a meaning. It is simply a symbol of a special kind. It can be used to label objects, such as television viewers, radio listeners, or film viewers drawn in a sample from a universe. It is quite possible, even necessary, to assign symbols to objects according to rules. A numeral is used because measurement ordinarily uses numerals which after being assigned a quantitative meaning become numbers. A number then is a numeral that has been assigned a quantitative meaning. For example, we ask a male television channel owner to stand seven feet away from an attractive young girl who is to be selected for the channel. The TV owner is asked to look at the young girl and then estimate the degree to which she possesses five attributes: niceness, strength of character, personality, musical ability, and intelligence. The estimate is to be given numerically. In the number system, a scale of numbers from 1 through 5 is used; 1 indicating a very small amount of the characteristic in question and 5 indicating a great deal of it. This example may appear to be a little ridiculous. However, most of the people go through almost the same procedure all through their lives. We often judge how "nice," how "strong," how "intelligent" people are simply by looking at them and talking to them. It only seems silly when it is given a serious example of measurement. Whether silly or serious, it is an example of measurement, since it satisfies the definition. The television channel owner assigned numerals to objects according to rules. The objects, the numerals, and the rules for the assignment of the numerals to the objects were all specified. The numerals were 1, 2, 3, 4, and 5; the object was the young girl; the rules for the assignment of the numerals to the objects were contained in the instructions to the television channel owner. Then the end product of his work, the numerals, might be used to calculate measures of relation, ANOVA, and the like.

Electronic media research includes rating research, non-rating research, and miscellaneous research. Ratings research is the most visible form of electronic media research as well as the most influential in the decision-making process. However, non-rating approaches, such as auditorium testing, callout research, focus groups, music research, hook testing, image studies, and programmer testing, are frequently used in datafication. Other than rating methodology and non-rating methodology, there are several other researches of electronic media such as market studies, format studies, format search studies, program element importance, station image, personality studies, advertiser analysis, account executive research, sales research, diversification analysis, and TV program. Audience fragmentation has now emerged as an adopted and accepted phenomenon of the electronic media, and the competition for listeners and viewers has created a need for research data and their quantification. In datafication, instruments such as electronic meters, diaries, telephone interviews, and Nielson people meters are very useful. But at the same time, advanced statistical and mathematical tools are often used for electronic media assessment and mathesis.

1.4.3 Media Metrics in Corporate Communication and Public Relations

Media metrics is used for the calculation of several variables of corporate communication to get accuracy, reliability, and validity in corporate communication and public relations research. It relates to measurement of any data relating to the variables of environmental monitoring, public relations audits, communication audits, and social audits (Figure 1.6).

During the planning stage, quantitative and qualitative techniques are used to test several corporate communication and public relations strategies, and media audits are done to identify the most effective media for a campaign. Gate-keeping research and output analysis are performed during the program implementation phase. Eventually, evaluation research is applied both during and after a campaign to assess whether the stated goals were achieved. Benchmarking is the evolving methodology of evaluation research that is rapidly gaining popularity. But in any case, all such researches of corporate communication and public relations require the use of quantitative variables, qualitative variables, nominal level of measurement, ordinal level of measurement, and ratio level of measurement.

1.4.4 Media Metrics in Advertising

Media metrics in advertising relates to the datafication of numerous variables and factors of advertising to attain accuracy, reliability, and validity in advertising research. It can lead to the measurement and evaluation of any data relating to the variables of classified advertising, display advertising, and classified display advertising of newspapers, magazines or journals. It also evaluates the variables of radio jingles, television advertising, and film advertising. Here the variables are assigned quantitative meaning. The term assigned in the measurement definition is called mapping, which is basically the objects on one set onto the objects of another set. It is a rule that assigns to each member of one set some one member of another

FIGURE 1.6
THE VALID PUBLIC RELATIONS MATRIX FRAMEWORK

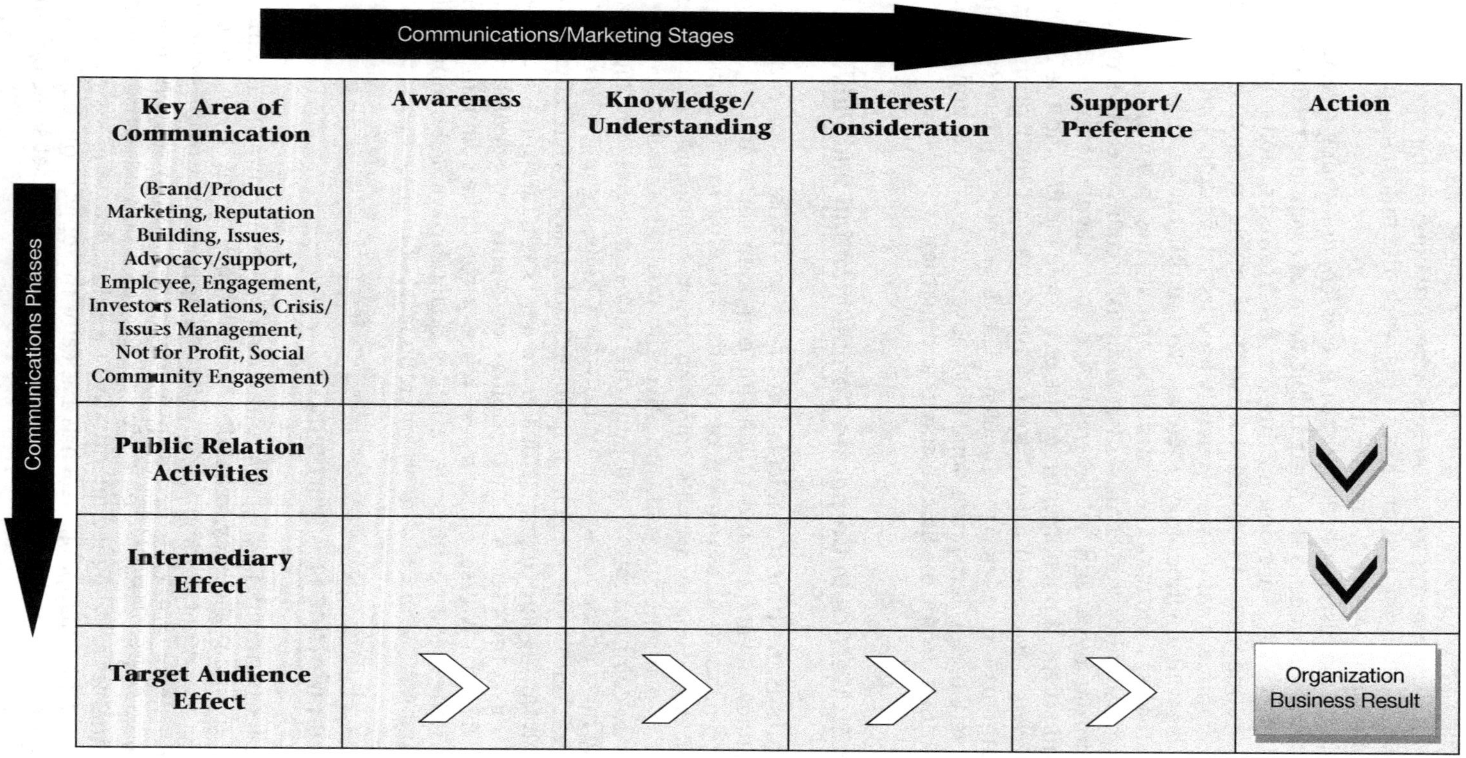

Source: Drawn by author.
Note: The figure shows the standard media metric table given under PRSI guidelines for the PR practitioners.

set. The members of the two sets can be any object. In mathematics, the members are generally numbers and algebraic symbols. In advertising research, the members of one set can be the audience, consumers, or symbols standing for audience or consumers, while members of the other set can be numerals or numbers. In most of the advertising measurement, numerals and numbers are mapped onto, or assigned to, consumers or target audience. Usually, in a mapping, the members of the domain are said to be mapped onto members of the range. In order to preserve consistency with the definition of measurement given above, and to always be able to conceive of measurement procedure as a function, the mapping has been turned around. The conception of mapping, furthermore, is consistent with the earlier definition of a function as a rule that assigns to each member of the domain of a set some one member of the range. The rule tells how the pairs are to be ordered (Figure 1.7).

Advertising research is considered to be the integral part of media research and marketing research. Under media research, the communicative and creative variables of advertising are studied, while under marketing research, the managerial, commercial, and planning variables of advertising are examined. That is why advertising research is not only audience-centered (readers, listeners, viewers, or users) but also consumer-centered (or buyer). Thus, whether it is media research or marketing research, advertising research is studied by bringing all such variables on an equilibrium point according to time or subject.

FIGURE 1.7

A SAMPLE OF MEDIA METRICS ELEMENTS CONSIDERED IN ADVERTISING

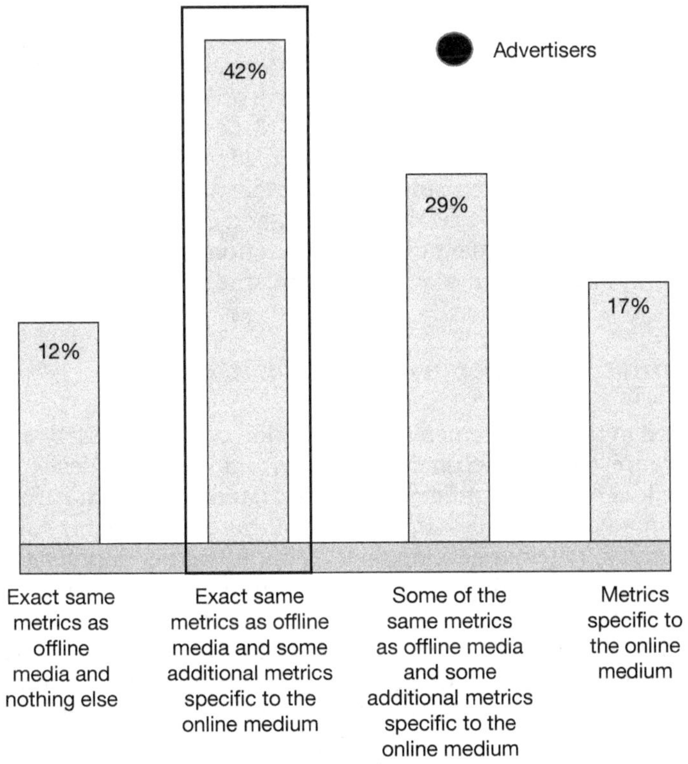

Source: Drawn by author.

Advertising is considered to be omnipotent and omnipresent. Vance Packard (1975) has described advertising as "hidden persuader." That is why advertising is also defined as "sellers of dreams" which compels a bald to buy a comb. It is also stated that "running business without advertising is like winking a girl in the dark."

Advertising research is also called evaluation research or effectiveness research. Advertising research can be mainly divided into three types, that is, copy research, media research, and campaign assessment research.

Since copy is an integral part of any advertisement, with the help of copy research, advertising can be made more and more effective. Under this study, it is also examined as to which advertisement is the most effective and which one is the most ineffective out of several advertisements. Copy research consists of studies that examine the advertisement or the commercial itself. Leckenby and Wedding (cited in Wimmer and Dominick 2003, 358) in 1982 divided advertising research into three categories, that is, cognitive (knowing), affective (feeling), and conative (doing). Under cognitive category, the most important dependent variables are attention, awareness, exposure, identification, understanding, and memory. These dependent variables are determined by consumer jury, eye-tracking study, tachistoscope (or T-scope), reader traffic score, memory test, rapid end measurement, day-after recall, magazine impact research service, and the likes, by using them under different circumstances.

Under affective category, projective test, theatre test, semantic differential scale, intensity measuring scale, peoples meter test, galvanic skin response, and the likes are used.

Under conative category, the actual consumer behavior is studied by Haskins buying intension scale, immediate testing, post-testing, and the likes. Also, media research helps determine which advertising vehicles are the most efficient and what type of media schedule will have the greatest impact. Campaign assessment research studies the overall response of consumers to a complete campaign. The two prominently known campaign assessment researches are the pre-test/post-test and the tracking study. So many private companies specialize in providing copy, media, and assessment data to advertisers. An emerging area in advertising research involves measuring the impact of "webertising" (web advertising).

Thus, all such researches of advertising, such as evaluation research, effectiveness research, copy research, cognitive research, affective research and conative research, require the application of quantitative variables, qualitative variables, nominal level of measurement, ordinal level of measurement, interval level of measurement, and ratio level of measurement.

1.4.5 Media Metrics in Development Communication

Media metrics is used in the measurement and evaluation of several variables and factor of development communication to attain accuracy, reliability, and validity in development communication research. It can lead to the quantification and calculation of any data relating to the variables of economic development, social development, political development, cultural development, intellectual development, religious development, and spiritual development (Figure 1.8).

The most interesting and difficult work of measurement is the rule. A rule is a guide, a method, a command that tells us what to do. A mathematical rule is f, a function; f is a rule for assigning the objects of one set to the objects of another set. In measurement, a rule might say: "Assign the numerals 1 through 5 to the development according to the positivity they have. If any development is very, very positive, let the number 5 be assigned to it. If the development is not all positive, let the number 1 be assigned." Thus, in the measurement of variables of development communication, the methods of econometrics, sociometrics,

FIGURE 1.8

QUANTITATIVE RESULTS OF A STUDY CONDUCTED BY AN INDUSTRIAL ORGANIZATION

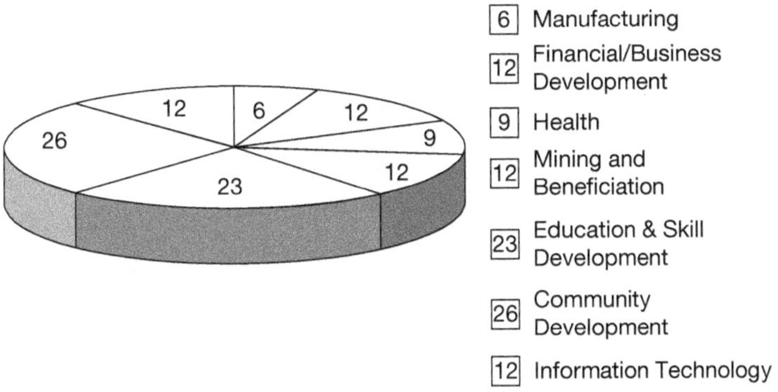

Source: Drawn by author.

psychometrics, or media metrics as a whole may be used for the application of advanced mathematical and statistical tools.

1.4.6 Media Metrics in Social Marketing

Media metrics is used in the measurement and calculation of several aspects and variables of social marketing to attain accuracy, reliability, and validity in social marketing research. It can lead to evaluation and quantification of any data relating to the variables of social research, marketing research, and advertising research (Figure 1.9). There is a method of bringing set, relation–function, and measurement ideas together. We must recall here that a relation is a set of ordered pairs. So is a function. Any measurement procedure then sets up a set of ordered pairs, the first member of each pair being the object measured and the second member, the numeral assigned to the object according to the measurement rule, whatever it is.

Thus, a general equation for any measurement procedure may be written as follows:

$$f=\{x, y\};\ x=\text{any object, and } y=\text{a numeral}$$

This is read: "The function, f, or the rule of correspondence is equal to the set of ordered pairs (x, y), such that x is an object and each corresponding y is a numeral." This is a very general rule and will fit in any case of measurement. Thus, in social marketing also other than media metrics, sociometrics, psychometrics, and econometrics may be used for the use of advanced mathematical and statistical tools.

1.4.7 Media Metrics in Web Media

Media metrics is used in the calculation and evaluation of many variables and factors of web media so as to attain accuracy, reliability, and validity in web media research. Web communication is the latest and the most modern form of media. So web media research is an integral and indispensable part of media research. Under web media research, internet journalism, new media, social media, webertising (web advertising), internet public relations, and the likes

FIGURE 1.9

GRAPHICAL REPRESENTATION OF METRICS OF MEDIA FORMS INCLUDED IN SOCIAL MARKETING

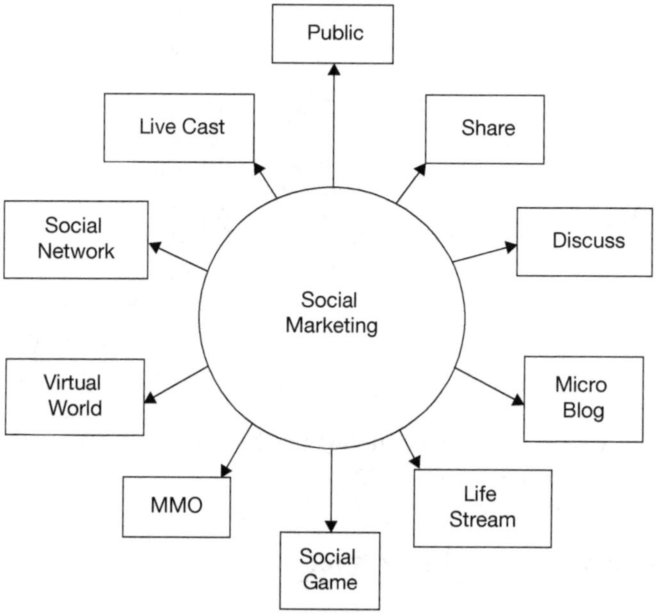

Source: http://www.advertisingmarketing.org.uk/niche-marketing/ (accessed February 1, 2017).

are studied and examined. In fact, a new word "compunication" has been created after marriage between computer and communication. Therefore, so many levels, categories, stages, phases, and dimensions of web media research have emerged very promptly. There are so many research problems relating to web media research, such as web communication: analysis and review, many facets of internet journalism and electronic journalism, webertizing and psychology of its users, relevance of e-PR, interface between multimedia and its users, internet journalism and rural development, internet journalism: origin and growth, internet through cable: A study, cyber journalism: past and present, cybernomic journalism and reactions of its users, interface between internet journalism and media metrics, application of media metrics in qualitative study of media, internet journalism and its management, internet journalism and its economy, sociology of web communication, interface between e-publication and e-administration, internet journalism and language, and so on.

As far as applying media metrics in the emerging areas of web media is concerned, it can lead to measurement and quantification of any data relating to the variables of web and different allied area of journalism and mass communication, such as print media, electronic media, advertising public relations and corporate communication, and social marketing.

1.4.8 Media Metrics in Social Media and Various Other Media

Media metrics is used in the measurement of numerous variables and factors of social media, new media, traditional media, alternate media, and the likes, to attain accuracy, reliability, and validity in such media (Figure 1.10).

FIGURE 1.10

ELEMENTS USED IN SOCIAL MEDIA METRICS AND THEIR QUANTITATIVE MEASUREMENT

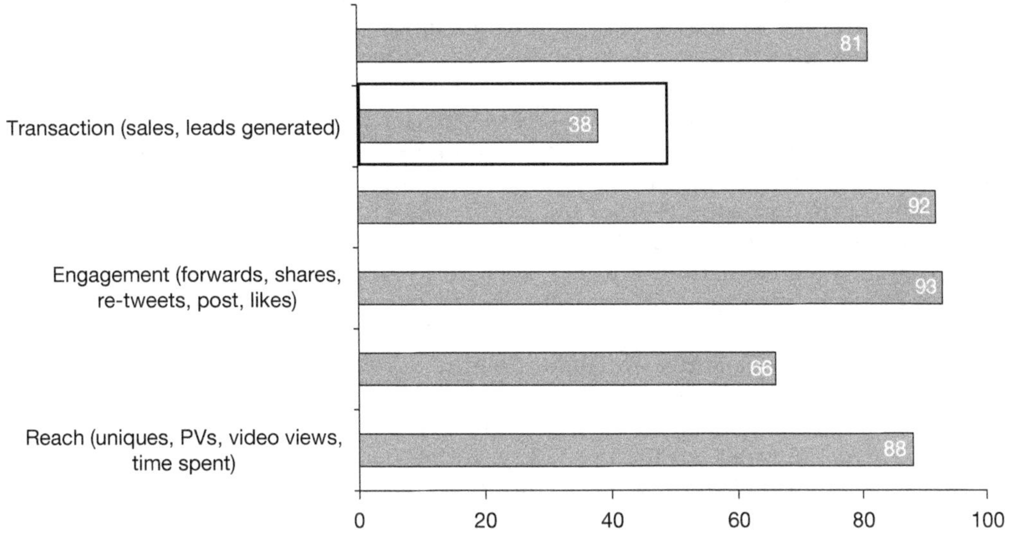

Source: Drawn by author.

It can lead to quantification and calculation of any data relating to puppetry, dance, drama, stage-show, documentary, docu-drama, stage-play, shadow-play, and alternate media like picnic, road-show, exhibition, and the likes. Thus, all such researches require the application of quantitative variables, qualitative variables along with nominal level of measurement, ordinal level of measurement, interval level of measurement, and ratio level of measurement.

Therefore, in the measurement of variables of such researches of interdisciplinarity, the methods of econometrics, sociometrics, and psychometrics and media metrics as a whole may be used for the application of advanced statistical and mathematical tools with a view of collecting the data scientifically and also interpreting them scientifically.

SUMMARY

Media metrics is a new buzz word in mass communication research. But the term is getting global importance as media research also demands accuracy, reliability, and validity like any other social and behavioral sciences. Media metrics means the use of statistics and mathematics in mass communication research for scientific collection and scientific interpretation of data. Media metrics relates to the problems of media measurement, media evaluation, media quantification, media dimension, media calculation, media datafication, media assessment, media agency and campaign reviews, media audience analysis, media trade marketing, and the likes.

Media metrics in print media means measurement of different variables of print media to attain accuracy, reliability, and validity in print media research. It can lead to the quantification of any data relating to the variables of newspapers, magazines, periodicals, journals, or news agencies. Print media research includes readership studies, typography, and make-up studies, and readability studies. In addition, precision journalism and database journalism are also very important issues of quantification of print media research.

Precision journalism is a technique of inquiry by print media reporters who apply the research methodology of media research in their news reporting. This type of journalism was popularized by print media reporter and researcher Philip Meyer in his pioneering book *Precision Journalism* (1973). That is why this type of journalism is called "precision journalism"; the method relies primarily on the procedures of content analysis and survey research to generate quantitative data that are reported as news stories.

Database journalism was pioneered by news reporter Elliot Jaspin. This type of journalism depends on computer-based analysis of existing news file, an approach which has been accepted and adopted at several newspapers. Hence, the emergence of precision journalism and database journalism expects from our journalists to have a basic knowledge of mathematical and statistical measurement, research methodology, questionnaire design, sampling technique, and data presentation. All such researches of print media like readership research, circulation research, management research, typography and make-up research, readability research, precision journalism, and database journalism require the use and application of quantitative variables, qualitative variables, nominal level of measurement, ordinal level of measurement, internal level of measurement, and ratio level of measurement.

Media metrics in electronic media relates to measurement and quantification of variables of electronic media in order to attain accuracy, authenticity, reliability, and validity in electronic media. It means evaluation and calculation of any data regarding the variables of radio, television, and films. Audience fragmentation has now emerged as an adopted and accepted phenomenon of the electronic media and the competition for listeners and viewers has created a need for research data and its quantification. In datafication, instruments such as electronic meters, diaries, telephone interviews, and Nielson People Meters are very useful. But at the same time, advanced statistical and mathematical tools are often used for electronic media assessment and mathesis.

Media metrics in corporate communication and public relations means calculation of several variables of corporate communication and public relations. It relates to measurement of any data relating to the variables of environmental monitoring, public relations audits, and social audits. Benchmarking is the evolving methodology of evaluation research. But in any case, all such researches of corporate communication and public relations require the use of quantitative variables, qualitative variables, nominal level of measurement, ordinal level of measurement, and ratio level of measurement.

Media metrics in advertising relates to the datafication of numerous variables and factors of advertising to attain accuracy, reliability, and validity in advertising research. It also evaluates the variables of radio jingles, television advertising, and film advertising. Hence, all researches of advertising such as evaluation research, effectiveness research, copy research, cognitive research, affective research, and conative research require the application of quantitative variables, qualitative variables, nominal level of measurement, ordinal level of measurement, interval level of measurement, and ratio level of measurement.

Media metrics in development communication means measurement and evaluation of several variables and factors of development communication to attain accuracy, reliability, and validity in development communication research. It can lead to the quantification and calculation of any data relating to the variables of economic development, social development, political development, cultural development, intellectual development, religious development, and spiritual development. Hence, in the measurement of variables of development communication, the methods of econometrics, sociometrics, psychometrics, or media metrics as a whole may be used for the application of advanced mathematical and statistical tools.

Media metrics in social marketing means measurement and calculation of several aspects and variables of social marketing to attain accuracy, reliability, and validity in social marketing research.

Media metrics in web media means calculation of many variables of web media so as to attain accuracy, reliability, and validity in media research. As far as applying media metrics in web media is concerned, it can lead to measurement and quantification of any data relating to the variables of web and different allied areas of journalism and mass communication, such as print media, electronic media, advertising, public relations, corporate communication, development communication, and social marketing.

Media metrics in social media and various other media means the measurement of numerous variables and factors of traditional media, alternative media, and so on, to attain accuracy, reliability, and validity in such media. It can lead to quantification of any data relating to puppetry, dance, drama, stage-show, documentary, docu-drama, stage-play, shadow-play, and alternative media such as picnic, road-show, and exhibition. Hence, all such researches require the application of quantitative variables, qualitative variables, nominal level of measurement, ordinal level of measurement, interval level of measurement, and ratio level of measurement. As a result in the measurement of variables of such researches of interdisciplinarity, the methods of econometrics, sociometrics, psychometrics, and media metrics as a whole may be used for the application of advanced statistical and mathematical tools with a view of collecting the data scientifically and also interpreting them scientifically.

With the growing importance, pertinence, and relevance of media metrics in different branches of mass communication research the world over, the basic knowledge of mathematics in mass communication research, use of mathematics in media and communication measurement, types of numbers, set descriptions, classification of sets, set operations, differentiation from first principle and rules for integration, related importance and use of mathematics with reference to media and communication measurement become extremely useful and highly desirable to discuss in the next chapter.

After a very comprehensive discussion on media metrics (a conceptual framework), it will be desirable to discuss data processing and analysis in mass communication for even better understanding of the descriptive statistics in media metrics (or descriptive media metrics) in the next chapter.

RELATED AND SUGGESTED WEBSITES

(As retrieved on December 1, 2015)

1. http://www.socialresearchmethods.net/kb/measlevl.php
2. http:/www.wimmerdominick.com.
3. http://www.ifabc.org/resources/metrics/print-metrics
4. http://learcenter.org/pdf/measuringmedia.pdf
5. http://mediaratingcouncil.org/Soc%20Guidelines%20v4.1%20Public%20Comment%20Version.pdf
6. http://www.web-strategist.com/blog/wp-content/uploads/2007/08/trackingtheinfluence.pdf
7. http://www.cdc.gov/metrics/

REFERENCES

Butler. 1990. Media Studies And Statistics: Real-world Demands, Classroom Quandaries, and On-line Solutions. Available at [iase_web.org/documents/papers/icots7/8A1_ZAND.pdf], accessed December 16, 2016.

Gal. 2002. Media Studies And Statistics: Real-world Demands, Classroom Quandaries, and On-line Solutions. Available at [iase_web.org/documents/papers/icots7/8A1_ZAND.pdf], accessed December 16, 2016.

Garfield et al. 2002. Media Studies And Statistics: Real-world Demands, Classroom Quandaries, and On-line Solutions. Available at [iase_web.org/documents/papers/icots7/8A1_ZAND.pdf], accessed December 16, 2016.

Gilsbrecht. 1996. Media Studies And Statistics: Real-world Demands, Classroom Quandaries, and On-line Solutions. Available at [iase_web.org/documents/papers/icots7/8A1_ZAND.pdf], accessed December 16, 2016.

Lorenz, Mirko. (2010). Information Architect. Available at http://www.mirkolorenz.com/?id=6, accessed on February 1, 2017.

Packard, Vance. 1957. *The Hidden Persuaders*. London, New York, Toronto: Longmans, Green & Co.

Snee. 1990. Media Studies And Statistics: Real-world Demands, Classroom Quandaries, and On-line Solutions. Available at [iase_web.org/documents/papers/icots7/8A1_ZAND.pdf], accessed December 16, 2016.

Steven, Stanley Smith. (1946). "On the Theory of Scales of Measurement" (PDF). *Science* 103 (2684): 677–680.

Wimmer, Roger D., and Joseph R. Dominick. 2003. *Mass Media Research: An Introduction*, 43–52, 317–32, 358. 7th ed. Belmont, CA: Wadsworth Publishing Company.

Yilmaz. 1996. Media Studies and Statistics: Real-world Demands, Classroom Quandaries, and On-line Solutions. Available at [iase_web.org/documents/papers/icots7/8A1_ZAND.pdf], accessed December 16, 2016.

Zandpour, Fred and Rimmer Tonny. 2006. Media Studies and Statistics: Real-world Demands, Classroom Quandaries, and On-line Solutions. Available at [iase_web.org/documents/papers/icots7/8A1_ZAND.pdf], accessed December 16, 2016.

RELATED AND RECOMMENDED READINGS

Flick, Uwe. 2010. *An Introduction to Qualitative Research*. 4th ed. London: SAGE Publications.

Healey, Joseph F. 1999. *Statistics: A Tool for Social Research*, 3–16. 5th ed. Belmont, CA: Wadsworth Publishing Company.

Kerlinger, Fred N. 1983. *Foundations of Behavioural Research*, 29–39, 426–30. 2nd ed. New Delhi: Surjeet Publication.

Sarangi, Prasant. 2010. *Research Methodology*. Delhi: Taxman Publication.

Zina, O Leary. 2010. *The Essential Guide to Doing Your Research Project*. 3rd ed. London: SAGE Publications.

QUESTIONS

1. What do you mean by media metrics? Discuss the types of media metrics.
2. Explain the nature of media measurement.
3. What is a variable? Discuss the various types of a variable.

4. Differentiate between nominal level of measurement, ordinal level of measurement, and interval–ratio level of measurement.
5. Describe the role of media metrics in print media.
6. Discuss the importance of media metrics in electronic media.
7. Explain the relevance of media metrics in public relations and corporate communication.
8. Describe the functions of media metrics in advertising.
9. Discuss the role of media metrics in development communication.
10. Explain the importance of media metrics in social marketing.
11. Throw light on media metrics in web media.
12. Describe the relevance of media metrics in social media and other media.

2

CHAPTER

Mathematics in Media Research

If people do not believe that mathematics is simple, it is only because they do not realise how complicated life is.

—John Neumann

Mathematics is a science of all sciences. That is why it is the soul of pure science. It has already become the heart of social science and marketing research. With the advancement of media research from its nascent stage to crescent stage, mathematics has fast entered into this domain and has become the mind and integral part of this micro-focused branch like media research the world over even for nonmathematical researchers.

Mathematics plays a vital role in the measurement of variables of media and communication science. Most of our development activities in the last few years have made it essential to apply mathematics to our real-life problems including media and communication fields. The use of mathematics in solving the media problems and real-world problems is fast becoming widespread at the global level. This is mainly because of the fast growing computational power of digital computers and computing methods. Both of these have facilitated the handling of lengthy, complex, and cumbersome problems. The process of translation of media and communication problems into a mathematical form can give a better representation and solution of certain problems in a more specific manner.

In ancient days, Babylonians, Chinese, Egyptians, Indians, and Greeks endeavored to understand and predict natural phenomena through their knowledge of mathematics, for example, a researcher wanting to measure height. From the knowledge of trigonometry, a researcher knows that if he has an angle of elevation and the distance from the foot of the plain-surfaced town, then he can calculate the height of the hilly town for the continuation of his further research.

Similarly, mathematics is used effectively to study the different situations of real life and communication activities. In cricket, a third umpire takes a decision of an LBW by looking at the trajectory of the ball, simulated, assuming that the batsman is not there. Mathematical equations are arrived at, based on the known paths of the ball before it hits the batsman's leg. This simulated model is used to take the decision of LBW. Similarly, if a university department or research center for Agriculture and Extension Education wants to estimate the yield of rice in India from the standing crops, mathematicians identify areas of rice cultivation and find the average yield per acre by cutting and weighing crops from some representative fields. Based on some mathematical techniques, decisions are made on the average yield of rice. Thus, mathematics is a representation that comprehends a situation more specifically and scientifically.

In the previous chapter, the conceptual framework of media metrics, that is, meaning and concept of media metrics, types of media metrics, nature of media measurement, variables, levels of measurement, media metrics in print media, media metrics in electronic media, media metrics in corporate communication and public relations, media metrics in advertising, media metrics in development communication, media metrics in social marketing, media metrics in web media, and media metrics in social media and various other media were discussed, and all these will be more relevant, valid, and complete if properly supplemented with some basic knowledge of mathematics in mass communication research—more so with the growing trend, significance, pertinence, and relevance of media metrics in different branches of mass communication research the world over. As a result, the use of mathematics in media and communication measurement, types of numbers, basic and relevant formulae, linear equation, quadratic equation, set descriptions, classification of sets, set operations, differentiation from first principle, rules for integration, matrix, and so on are indispensably required to be discussed in this chapter.

Hence, this chapter will focus the discussion on the following:

1. Meaning and concept of mathematics in media research
2. Use of mathematics in media and communication measurement (including tools of media metrics)
3. Procedures of writing mathematical notation
4. Types of numbers
5. Set descriptions
6. Classification of sets
7. Set operations
8. Partitions and cross-partitions
9. Differentiation from first principle and rules for integration
10. Matrix

In addition, the chapter will also cover the summary, related and suggested websites, references, related and recommended readings, and questions.

2.1 MEANING AND CONCEPT OF MATHEMATICS IN MEDIA RESEARCH

In our real-life communication problems and media issues, mathematical modeling is used more often which is an attempt to study some part (or form) of real-life problems in mathematical terms. Conversion of physical situation into mathematics with some suitable condition is known as mathematical modeling, which is nothing but a technique and the pedagogy taken from communication and fine arts and not from basic sciences. Mathematics basically is an attempt to study the essential characteristics of a real-life problem. On several occasions, model equations are obtained by assuming the situation in an idealized context. Mathematics will be useful only if it explains all the facts which we would like to explain scientifically. Otherwise, we will reject it, or else improve it, then verify it again. Thus, we measure the effectiveness of mathematics by comparing the results obtained from the mathematical model with the known facts about the real problem. This process is called validation of mathematics or mathematical model.

Hence, for quantitative research and quantity-based qualitative research (like Gross Happiness Index), mathematics is emerging as the primary need of every researcher in media and communication studies. The basics of set theory, set operations, set classifications, subset, superset, universal set, Venn diagram, basics of matrices (matrix algebra), basics of integral and differential calculus other than descriptive media metrics (measures of central tendencies, measures of dispersion, measures of skewness, measures of relationship, and other measures) and inferential media metrics (hypothesis testing, test of significance of nonparametric and parametric data such as ANOVA, *F*-test, *t*-test, and *Z*-test, multivariate analysis such as multiple correlation, canonical correlation, multiple regression, factor analysis, and cluster analysis) have become an integral part of media research the world over.

2.2 USE OF MATHEMATICS IN MEDIA AND COMMUNICATION MEASUREMENT

The use of mathematical techniques has been gaining popularity in media and communication science. As a matter of fact, the precision, accuracy, and exactness of mathematical methods and computational languages, and advancement of technology have made it possible to explore large areas of research in media and communication studies which remained hidden so far from the keen eyes of researchers. It can be said that today mathematics is the most reliable shoulder to lean on for not only pure sciences, but subjects like media, communication, psychology, sociology, anthropology, education commerce, economics, and management also. The valid reasons are that these days research has tended to be a more scientific than merely a descriptive branch of knowledge. Mathematics in its elementary form has not only made these areas more interesting but certainly also more comprehensive to the average human mind, thus opening more on evenness of investigation and throwing open greater challenges to communication scientists.

Mathematical expressions are facilitating the development of theory in media, communication, and social sciences, and making social dynamics increasingly intelligible to researchers. The induction and introduction of mathematics has made media research very exciting and revealing. The frontiers of media and communication research have considerably been extended and the scope for interdisciplinarity has also gone up tremendously. With the help of mathematics, in-depth studies have enriched the knowledge of communication scientists. To comprehend how and on what lines has media and communication research progressed in recent years, the knowledge of mathematics has become indispensable.

So many social and communication phenomena that give a vague idea of interrelationship among communication and media variables do not serve the purpose of the modern society. A good number of examples can be given wherein it is made amply evident that the use of elementary mathematical techniques not only simplifies the learning of media and communication science but also makes it more relevant to the modern society, wherein accuracy is putting vagueness out of circulation and ambiguity is giving way to better understanding of communication science.

Mathematics has become an intellectual short hand without pace with the fast-changing global scenario. Several media theories might have remained unnoticed without the use of mathematics. Beginners and learners are generally critical of use of mathematics in media and communication research. But the moment they become learned, they do not criticize it. Media researchers are generally unwilling to take mathematics, but when they plunge into it, they relish swimming across with excitement and generally with success.

Since mathematics is science of all sciences, it cannot leave out media and communication science from its purview. Preferably, simple and small doses of mathematics may be used in media and communication problems to improve their understanding and, hence, to find their solutions.

The knowledge of the types of numbers is the first step to study the numerical relationship between media and media-related social variables. So is the case with the study of set descriptions, classification of sets, Venn diagram, Cartesian product, De Morgan's law, set operations, differentiation from first principle, rules for integration, and matrix. All these mathematical tools and techniques are important for mass communication researchers to study the problems of media measurement, media evaluation, and media quantification.

2.2.1 Tools of Media Metrics

The different tools of media metrics can be very well understood by the following flowchart.

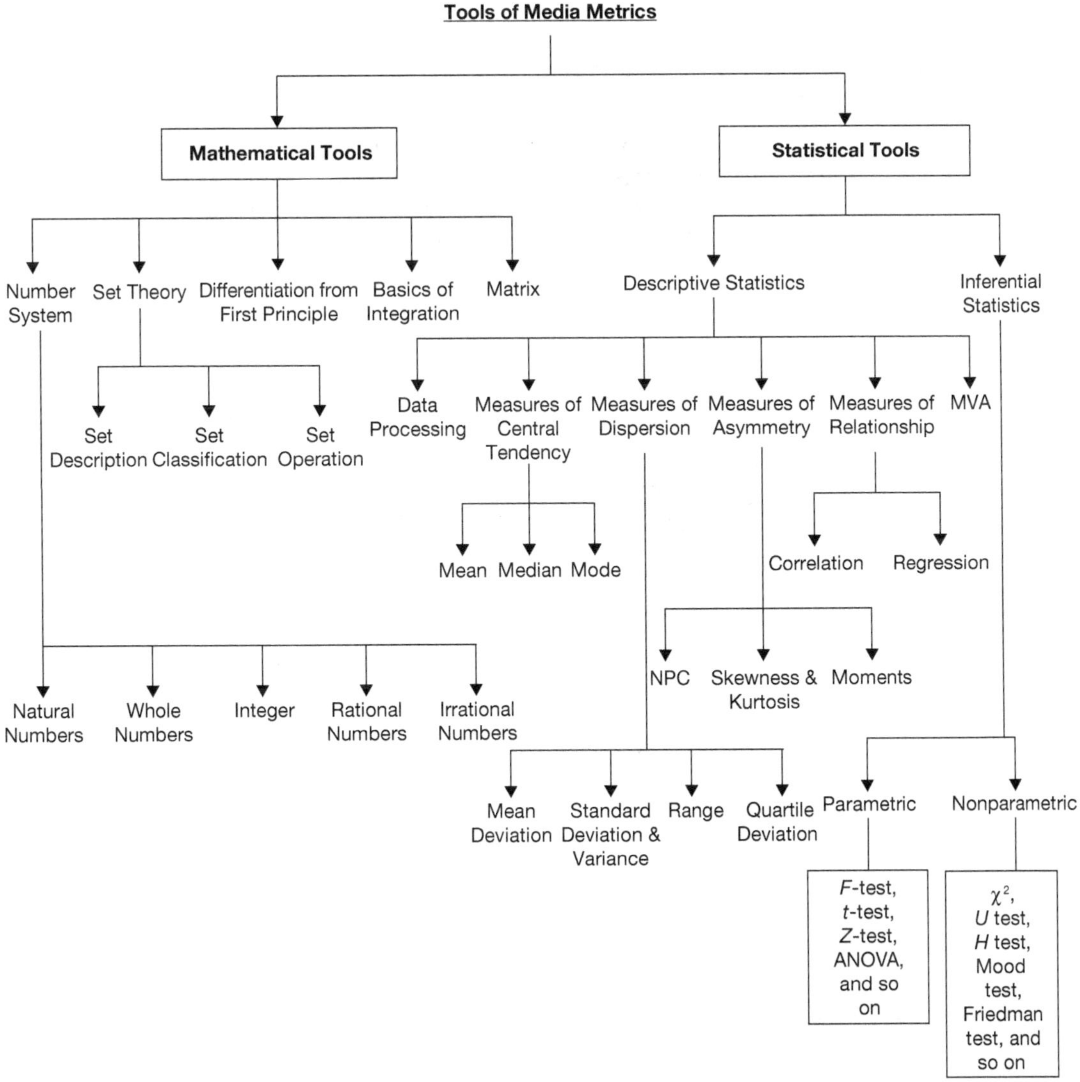

Source: Concept by author, drawn by author's research scholar Bhupender Singh.

As depicted in this flowchart, the tools of media metrics are number system, that is, different types of numbers such as natural numbers, whole numbers, integer (positive numbers and negative numbers), rational numbers, irrational numbers, real numbers, imaginary numbers, signed numbers, set theory (set classification, set description, and set operation), differentiation from first principle, basics of integration, and matrices. As far as statistical tools are concerned, these are mean, median, mode, average deviation, standard deviation (SD), variance, range, quartile deviation, normal probability curve (NPC), skewness, kurtosis, moments, *t*-test, *F*-test, *Z*-test, ANOVA, ANOCOVA, chi-square, *U* test, *H* test, correlation, regression, index numbers, and multivariate analysis tests such as multiple regression, multiple discriminant analysis, multivariate analysis of variance (MANOVA), canonical correlation analysis, factor analysis, cluster analysis, multidimensional scaling analysis, and latent structure analysis.

2.3 PROCEDURES OF WRITING A MATHEMATICAL NOTATION

It will be desirable for nonmathematics students of media and communication to get acquainted with some of the most relevant and widely used mathematical notations here. Again, it is indispensable for them to learn as to how these notations are written. These notations may be broadly divided into four categories as shown in Tables 2.1–2.4.

TABLE 2.1
NUMBERS

Mathematical Notation	Meaning	Example
$\mathbb{N}$	Natural numbers	1, 2, 3, ..., ∞
$\mathbb{W}$	Whole numbers	0, 1, 2, 3, ..., ∞
$\mathbb{Z}$	Integers	..., −1, −2, −3, 0, 1, 2, 3, ...
$\mathbb{R}$	Real numbers	$\frac{1}{3}, \sqrt{2}, \pi, \ldots.$
$\mathbb{Q}$	Rational numbers	$\frac{1}{2}, \frac{1}{4}, \frac{1}{2}, \frac{2}{7}, \frac{22}{7}$
$\mathbb{I}$	Irrational numbers	$\sqrt{2} = 1.41, \ldots \sqrt{3} = 1.732, \ldots, \sqrt{5} = 2.73, \ldots.$
$\dot{\mathbb{I}}$(iota)	Imaginary numbers	$\sqrt{-1}, \sqrt{-5}, \sqrt{-7}$
$\mathbb{C}$	Complex numbers	$5+\sqrt{-1} = 5+i, 4+\sqrt{-5} = 4+5i$ since $\sqrt{-1}$ is denoted by iota, i.e., i
Σ	Summation or sigma	$\sum X = x_1 + x_2 + x_3 + \cdots + x_n$ or $\sum_1^n X = x_1 + x_2 + x_3 + \cdots + x_n$

TABLE 2.2
SETS

Mathematical Notation	Meaning	Example
{............}	A set	{1,2,3,4,...}{a,e,i,o,u,...}
$\mathcal{X} \in A$	$\mathcal{X}$ is an element of set A	$u \in \{a,e,i,o,u\}$
{$\mathcal{X}$:.........} or |$\mathcal{X}$:.........}	the set of $\mathcal{X}$ such that	$\{\mathcal{X}: \mathcal{X}^2=4\}=\{-2,2\}$
|A|	cardinality in A (number of elements in A)	$\|\{1,2,3\}\|=3$
n(a)	Cardinal number	A={1,2,3,4,5}, then n(A)=5
$A \cup B$	A union B (set of elements in either A or B)	$\{1,2,3\} \cup \{2,4\}=\{1,2,3,4\}$
$A \cap B$	A intersection B (set of elements in both A and B)	$\{1,2,3\} \cap \{2,4\}=\{2\}$
$>$	Greater than	$4>2$
$\gg$	Much greater than	$1000 \gg 1$
$<$	Less than	$6<10$
$\ll$	Much less than	$1 \ll 1000$
$\geq$	Greater than or equal to	$\mathcal{X} \geq 8$, i.e., $\mathcal{X}=8$ or $\mathcal{X}>8$
$\leq$	Less than or equal to	$a \leq 10$, i.e., $a=8$ or $a \leq 8$
$A \subseteq B$	A is a subset of B or equal	$\{1,3\} \subseteq \{1,2,3\}$
$A'=A^c$	Compliment of A	Everything not in A
$\varnothing$	Null set or empty set or void set	$\{1,2\} \cap \{3,4\}=\varnothing$
$A \times B$	Cartesian product (set of all ordered pairs)	{1,2} × {1,3}={(1,1)},{(1,3),{92,1)},{(2,3)}

TABLE 2.3
DIFFERENTIATION AND INTEGRATION

Mathematical Notation	Meaning	Example
$\lim_{x \to 0} f(x)$	Limit value of a function	—
$\frac{dy}{dx}$	Derivative	$\frac{d(3x^3)}{dx}=9x^2$
$\frac{d^2y}{dx^2}$	Second derivative	$\frac{d^2(3x^3)}{dx^2}=18x$
$\frac{d^ny}{dx^n}$	N times derivative	$\frac{d^n(3x^3)}{dx^n}$
$\int$	Integration, i.e., opposite to differentiation	$\int x^2\, dx=\frac{x^3}{3}+C$, where C is a constant of integration

TABLE 2.4
GREEK ALPHABETS

Name	Capital	Lower Case
Alpha	A	α
Beta	B	β
Gamma	Γ	γ
Delta	Δ	δ
Theta	Θ	θ
Iota	I	ι
Lambda	Λ	λ
Mu	M	μ
Pi	Π	π
Rho	P	ρ
Sigma	Σ	σ
Chi	X	χ
Phi	Φ	ϕ

2.4 TYPES OF NUMBERS

Numbers are mathematical objects or statistical data used to count, measure, and label.

Before applying mathematics in media and communication measurement, it is very important, pertinent, and relevant here to know the types of numbers as these are the basic tools of mathematical description and mathematical operation of closure (i.e., addition, subtraction, multiplication, and division), commutativity (i.e., $a+b=b+a$, $a\times b=b\times a$) associativity (i.e., $[a+b]+c=a+[b+c]$), and distributivity (i.e., $a[b+c]=ab+ac$). These are also the base of understanding set descriptions, classification of sets, Venn diagram representation, Cartesian product, De Morgan's law, and the likes, which provide a systematic, yet practical approach for social science researchers, including media researchers, to combine all these set theories with standard statistical techniques and model testing (Smithson and Verkuilen 2006).

Different types of numbers are as follows:

1. Natural numbers: Numbers that start from 1 to infinity are called natural numbers. They are denoted by N and are also called counting numbers. Some of the main properties of natural numbers are closure, commutativity, associativity, and distributivity.
2. Whole numbers: Numbers that start from 0 to infinity are called whole numbers denoted by W. They do not have any decimal or fractional part. All whole numbers are not natural numbers, but all natural numbers are always whole numbers. Some of the main properties of whole numbers are closure, commutativity, associativity, and distributivity.
3. Integers: Whole numbers including negative numbers are called integers and are denoted by Z. The numbers 1, 2, 3, 4, 5, ..., which are generally used in counting, are known as positive integers. The corresponding numbers –1, –2, –3, –4, –5 are known as negative integers. All positive and negative integers and zero constitute the set of

integers. Some of the main properties of integers are closure, commutativity, associativity, and distributivity. Integers are of the following types: (a) even and odd numbers—A number is even if it is a multiple of two, and is odd otherwise, (b) prime numbers—Numbers that are only divisible by 1 or itself, for example, 2 and 3, (c) composite numbers—Numbers that have factors more than 2, for example, 8 and 16, (d) co-prime numbers—Pair of numbers that have only 1 factor, that is, a number having the highest common factor (HCF) 1.

4. Rational numbers: These are the numbers that can be written in the form of m/n, where m and n are integers and $n \neq 0$. Hence, a rational number may be terminating or non-terminating, but repeating (recurring). Rational numbers are denoted by Q. Some of the main properties of rational numbers are closure, commutativity, associativity, and distributivity.
5. Irrational numbers: These are the numbers that result in an infinite non-terminating and non-repeating (non-recurring) decimal fraction. Irrational numbers are denoted by I. For example, $\sqrt{2} = 1.414...$, $\sqrt{3} = 1.732...$ are irrational numbers.
6. Real numbers: Rational number and irrational number together constitute the set of real numbers. They are denoted by R.
7. Imaginary numbers: If m is a real number and greater than zero, then $\sqrt{-m}$ is known as an imaginary number. As such, all numbers such as $\sqrt{-4}, \sqrt{-25}$, and $\sqrt{-51}$ are imaginary. If we denote $\sqrt{-1}$ by "I" (iota), then $\sqrt{-4} = i2, \sqrt{-25} = i5$, and so on. Imaginary numbers are denoted by i.
8. Complex numbers: It includes real numbers and imaginary numbers—the square root of negative 1. The first part of a number is real and the second part is imaginary. They are denoted by C. Their most important characteristic is that if two complex numbers are equal, then the real number will be equal to the real number and the imaginary number will be equal to the imaginary number. For example, if ax+byi=cz+dwi, then ax=cz and byi=dwi.
9. Signed numbers: Such numbers are positive numbers, negative numbers, non-negative numbers, and non-positive numbers. Positive numbers are real numbers that are greater than zero. Negative numbers are real numbers that are less than zero. Non-negative numbers are real numbers that are greater than or equal to zero. Thus, a non-negative number is either zero or positive. Non-positive numbers, on the other hand, are real numbers that are less than or equal to zero. Thus, a non-positive number is either zero or negative.

2.5 SET DESCRIPTIONS

It is highly pertinent and relevant to study set descriptions in media and communication research as it provides a systematic, yet practical, approach for social science researchers, including media researchers, to combine set theory with standard statistical techniques and model testing (Smithson and Verkuilen 2006).

A set is defined as a well-defined collection of objects. For example, collection of qualitative attributes such as intelligent students, good players, positive-minded persons, honest persons do not form a set as these are not well-defined objects. These may vary from person to person. Similarly, the collection of interesting topics in mass communication is not a well-defined collection, as a particular topic of mass communication may be interesting for some students, but might not be interesting for others. However, the collection of all the topics of mass communication may be defined as well-defined objects.

A set may not consist of the same type of objects. It may consist of distinct objects. For example, the numbers 6, 8, and 10 are distinct objects when considered separately, but when they are considered collectively, they form a single set of size 3, written as {6, 8, 10}. Similarly, a bag, a pen, a box lying on a table may also form a set, their common property being that they form a collection of objects on the table. Another example of sets may be given like a set of natural numbers (N); if we describe a set of natural numbers by N, then we may describe set "N" as

$$N = \text{Set of natural numbers} = (1, 2, 3\ldots),$$

where the elements of a set are included within brackets. Similar examples of sets are: (a) the collection of all vowels in English alphabets, that is (a, i, e, o, u); (b) the collection of all editors of registered newspapers; (c) the collection of books on mass communication in our library, and (d) the collection of all positive integers, that is (1, 2, 3, 4...). The well-defined objects which belong to a set are called its members or elements.

A set is represented or expressed in two forms:

1. Tabular or roster form: In this form, all the members of a set are separated by commas, and are enclosed in curly or middle brackets. For example, the set N of natural numbers may be written as $N = \{1, 2, 3, 4\ldots\}$.
   Here, the dots denote that the set contains all the natural numbers.
2. Set builder form or rule method: Here, the set is written by some special properties satisfied by all its members like

$$N = \{x | x \text{ is a natural number}\}.$$

The symbol | stands for "such that" x is a natural number. Yet another example of all real numbers greater than 5 but less than 9 can be expressed symbolically as: $N = \{x | 5 < x < 9\}$.

In this case, the rule lays down that "N" is a set of all elements x such that x is an integer and $5 < x < 9$.

2.6 CLASSIFICATION OF SETS

It is extremely useful, important, pertinent, and relevant to focus on the classification of sets in mass communication research as it provides a systematic, yet practical approach for social science researchers, including media researchers, to combine set theory with standard statistical techniques and model testing (Smithson and Verkuilen 2006).

Sets may be classified as follows:

1. Finite set: When the element of a set are countable, the set is called a finite set. For example: (a) The set of all registered newspapers in a particular city or a set of all private TV channels in a particular city is a finite set; (b) The set of all countries on the earth is a finite set; (c) The set of all states in India is a finite set; (d) The set of months in a year is a finite set.
2. Infinite set: When the elements of a set are uncountable, the set is called an infinite set. For example, set of hair in our head or set of stars in the sky, or set of natural numbers, real numbers, whole numbers, complex numbers, rational numbers, and so on, are instances of infinite sets.

3. Singleton set: A set having only one element is known as singleton set. It is also called a unit set. For example, the set {a} is a singleton set in which the only element is "a."
4. Null set or empty set or void set: A set which does not have any member or element or component is called a null set or empty set or void set and is denoted by O| or by {}. For example, set of all those integers whose square is 7.
5. Universal set: It is a set of all components or elements that come in a particular situation and serve as a frame of reference. For example, in circumstances where reference is made to students of journalism and mass communication, all students of journalism and mass communication will constitute a universal set. It is generally denoted by U.
6. Subset: When each element of a set A is also the element of set B, then A is called the subset of B and B is called the superset of A. "A" is a subset of "B" is expressed as $A \subseteq B$. Accordingly, "B" is a subset of "A" is expressed as $B \subseteq A$. Number of subsets $= 2^n$ (where n is the number of elements).
7. Proper subset: B is said to be a proper subset of set A if every element of set B is an element of A, whereas every element of A is not an element of B. We write it as $B \subset A$ and read it as "B is a proper subset of A." Thus, B is a proper subset of A if every element of B is an element of A and there is at least one element in A which is not in B.

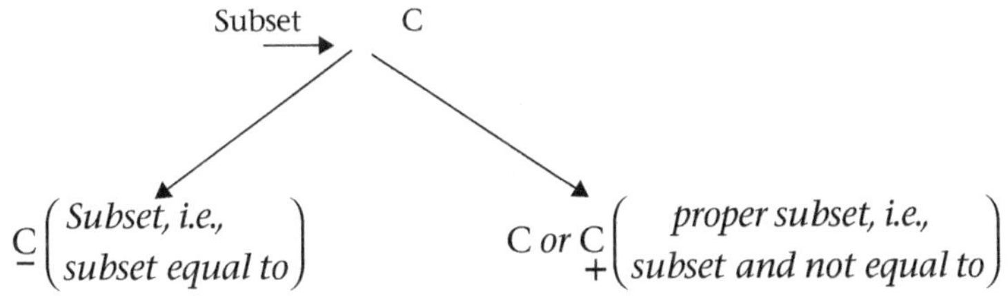

8. Power set: It is a collection of subsets.
9. Equal sets: Two sets A and B are said to be equal if every element of A is an element of B and every element of B is an element of A.
   For example:
   a. {5, 9, 11}={9, 11, 5} The order in which elements of a set are listed is immaterial.
   b. {3, 5, 9}={3, 5, 5, 9, 9, 3} The repetition of elements of a set is also immaterial.
10. Multiple sets: A multiple set is an unordered collection of elements in which an element may occur as a member more than once. The multiplicity of an element is the number of times the element occurs in the set.
    For example, the set A={b, c, c, d, d, e, e, e} is a multiple set.
    Multiplicity of element b in set A=1
    Multiplicity of element c in set A=2
    Multiplicity of element d in set A=2
    Multiplicity of element e in set A=3.
11. Equivalent sets: Two finite sets A and B are said to be equivalent sets if the number of elements in B are equal to the number of elements in A.
    that is, $n(A)=n(B)$.
    Equivalence of two sets is denoted by the symbol $\simeq$. Thus, if A and B are equivalent sets, we write $A \simeq B$ and it is read as "A is equivalent to B."
    For example, if A={1,2,3} and B={x,y,z}, then $n(A)=n(B)=3$ and, therefore, A and B are equivalent sets and we write A=B.
    (Note: Each pair of equal sets is an equivalent set, but equivalent sets need not be equal sets.)

12. Universal set: When all the sets under consideration are subjects of a larger set, then this larger set is called the universal set. For all these subsets, the universal set is denoted by U.
For example, let A={2, 4, 6}, B={1, 3, 5}, C={3, 5, 7, 11}, D={2, 4, 8, 16}, and U={1, 2, 3, 4, 5, 6, 7, 8, 10, 11, 16} be the given sets.
Here, sets A, B, C, and D are subsets of the set U. Hence, U is taken as the universal set.
Thus, it is a set of all components or elements that come up in a particular situation and serve as a frame of reference. Like, in a circumstance where reference is made to students of mass communication of India, all students of mass communication will constitute a universal set.
13. Comparable sets: Two sets A and B are said to be comparable if one of them is a subset of the other, that is, either $A \subseteq B$ or $B \subseteq A$.
For example, the sets {4, 5, 6, 7} and {4, 5, 6, 7, 8, 10} are comparable sets.
14. Disjoint sets: If A and B are two sets such that $A \cap B = \emptyset$, that is, there are no common elements in A and B, then these are called disjoint sets.
For example:

$$A=\{1, 2, 3, 4\}$$
$$B=\{8, 9, 10, 11\},$$

then A and B are disjoint sets because there are no common elements between the two sets.
The aggregate points on two parallel lines and the sets of odd natural numbers and even natural numbers can be described as disjoint sets.
15. Cartesian product: A set can be constructed by associating every element of one set with every element of another set. The Cartesian product of two sets A and B is denoted by $A \times B$.
For example:

a. $\{4, 5\} \times \{\text{Yellow}, \text{Green}\} = \begin{Bmatrix} (4, \text{Yellow}) \\ (4, \text{Green}) \\ (5, \text{Yellow}) \\ (5, \text{Green}) \end{Bmatrix}.$

b. $\{8, 20, \text{white}\} \times \{\text{Yellow, Green, White}\}$
$= \begin{Bmatrix} (8, \text{Yellow}), (8, \text{Green}), (8, \text{White}) \\ (20, \text{Yellow}), (20, \text{Green}), (20, \text{White}) \\ (\text{White}, \text{Green}), (\text{White, Yellow}), (\text{White, White}) \end{Bmatrix}.$

c. $\{4,5\} \times \{4,5\} = \{(4,4), (4,5), (5,4), (5,5)\}.$

Some other properties of Cartesian products are as follows:
a. $A \times \emptyset = \emptyset$,
b. $A \times (B \cup C) = (A \times B) \cup (B \times C)$,
c. $(A \cup B) \times C = (A \times C) \cup (B \times C)$.

2.7 SET OPERATIONS

The study of set operations is important and useful in media and communication research as it provides a systematic, yet practical, approach for social science researchers, including media researchers, to combine set theory with standard statistical techniques and model testing (Smithson and Verkuilen 2006).

Venn diagram may include universal set (represented by a rectangle) and there may be two, three or even more sets (represented by curves or circles). Some of the basic set operations include union, intersection, difference of sets, and their properties, and these can be depicted through Venn diagrams (Figure 2.1).

The relationship between two or more sets may be visualized by means of diagrams which are described as Venn diagrams. These diagrams are named after a British mathematician John Venn (1834–1883). In a Venn diagram, a universal set is generally expressed by the region enclosed by a rectangle and the properties of union, intersection and difference of sets by circles. There may be two, three or even more sets in a Venn diagram. This diagram represents sets logically, mathematically, and pictorially.

Properties of union of sets:

1. $A \cup B = B \cup A$ [commutative law]
2. $(A \cup B) \cup C = A \cup (B \cup C)$ [associative law]
3. $A \cup A = A$ [independent law]
4. $A \cup \varnothing = A$ [law of $\varnothing$]
5. $A \cup U = U$ [law of U]
6. If $A \subset B = A \cup B = B$
7. $A \subset A \cup B$

   $B \subset A \cup B$ $\left\{ \begin{array}{l} \text{i.e., both A and B are} \\ \text{subsets of } A \cup B. \end{array} \right\}$
8. $A \cup B = \varnothing \Rightarrow A = \varnothing, B = \varnothing$.

FIGURE 2.1

VENN DIAGRAM REPRESENTATION OF DISJOINT SETS

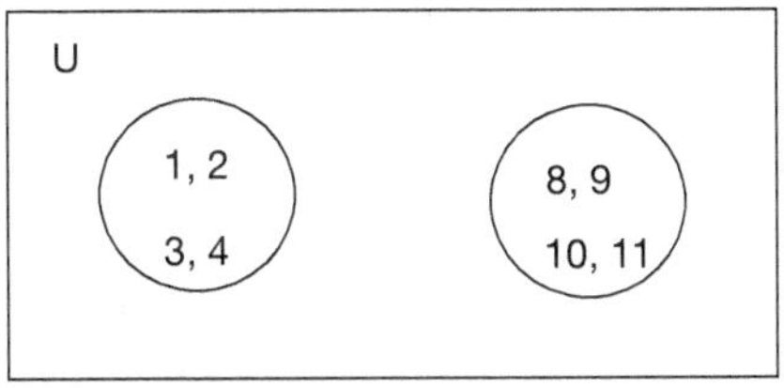

Source: Concept by British mathematician John Venn, drawn by author's research scholar Bhupender Singh.

Explanation of the properties of union of sets:

$A = \{1, 2, 3, 4\}$, $B = \{1, 2, 5, 7\}$

$C = \{1, 2, 8, 9, 13, 15\}$

$A \cup B = \{1, 2, 3, 5, 7\}$, $B \cup A = \{1, 2, 3, 5, 7\}$

$\therefore (A \cup B) \cup C = A \cup (B \cup C)$ Proved

and $A \cup (B \cup C) = 1, 2, 3, 5, 7, 8, 9, 13, 15$

$\therefore (A \cup B) \cup C = A \cup (B \cup C)$ Proved

$\therefore A \cup A = A$

$A \cup \emptyset = A$

$A \cup U = U \qquad U = \begin{Bmatrix} 1, 2, 3, 4, 5, 7, \\ 8, 9, 13, 15 \end{Bmatrix}.$

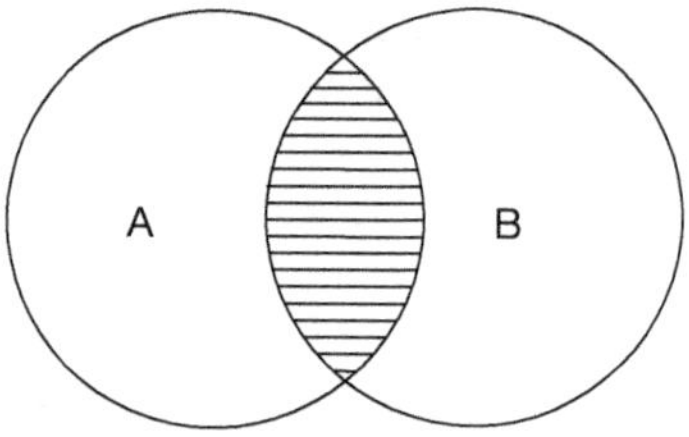

Properties of intersection of sets:

1. $A \cap B = B \cap A$ [commutative law]
2. $(A \cap B) \cap C = A \cap (B \cap C)$ [associative law]
3. $(A \cap A) = A$ [law of U]
4. $A \cap \emptyset = \emptyset$ [law of Ø]
5. $A \cap U = A$ [law of U]
6. If $A \subset B$, then $A \cap B = A$
7. $(A \cap B) \subset A$ {i.e., $(A \cap B)$ is a subset of both A and B}

$(A \cap B) \subset B$

Explanation of the above:

$A = \{1, 2, 3, 4\}$, $B = \{1, 2, 5, 7\}$, $C = \{1, 2, 8, 9, 13, 15\}$

$A \cap B = \{1, 2\}$, $B \cap A\{1, 2\}$, $(A \cap B) \cap C = \{1, 2\}$

$\therefore \{A \cap B\} \cap C = A \cap (B \cap C)$ Proved

$\therefore (A \cap A) = A$

$\therefore A \cap \emptyset = \emptyset$

$\therefore A \cap U = A.$

Combined properties of union and intersection:

1. $A \cap (B \cup C) = (A \cap B) \cup (A \cap B)$
2. $A \cup (B \cap C) = (A \cup B) \cap (A \cup C)$

Combined examples of union and intersection in media research: A union of male and female media persons can be represented as $M \cup F$; similarly, a union of print journalists and advertisers can be represented as $P \cup A$. Let A be all the desk persons of the editorial section of a newspaper organization and B be all the reporters/correspondents of the reporting section of the same organization. Then, $A \cup B$ is the set of all media persons of that newspaper organization and $A \cap B$ is the set of all common media persons who are looking after both the editorial and reporting sections.

Systematic difference of sets: The systematic difference of sets A and B is the union of sets (A–B) and (B–A). It is denoted as $A\Delta B$,

$$A\Delta B = (A - B) \cup (B - A)$$

For example:

$$\text{If} \quad A = \{4, 5, 6, 7\}, B = \{5, 7, 8, 9\},$$
$$\text{then} \quad (A - B) = \{4, 6\} \text{ and } (B - A) = \{8, 9\},$$
$$\therefore \quad A\Delta B = (A - B) \cup (B - A) = \{4, 6, 8, 9\}$$

Cardinal number of a finite set: The number of elements in a finite set A is known as the cardinal number and is denoted by $n(A)$.
For example, if $A=\{1, 2, 3, 4, 5\}$, then $n(A)=5$.
And if $B=\{a, b, e, f, g\}$, then $n(B)=5$.

Compliment of a set: The compliment of a given set is a set which contains all those members of the universal set that do not belong to the given set (Figure 2.2).
For example:

a. If the universal set is $U=\{4, 5, 6, 7, 8, 9, 10\}$ and $A=\{4, 5, 6, 7, 8\}$,

   then $$A'=A^C=\{9, 10\},$$

   where A' or A^C is compliment of a set.
b. If the universal set $U=\{p, q, r, s\}$ and $A=\{p, q, r\}$, then A' or $A^C=\{s\}$.

FIGURE 2.2
COMPLIMENT OF A SET

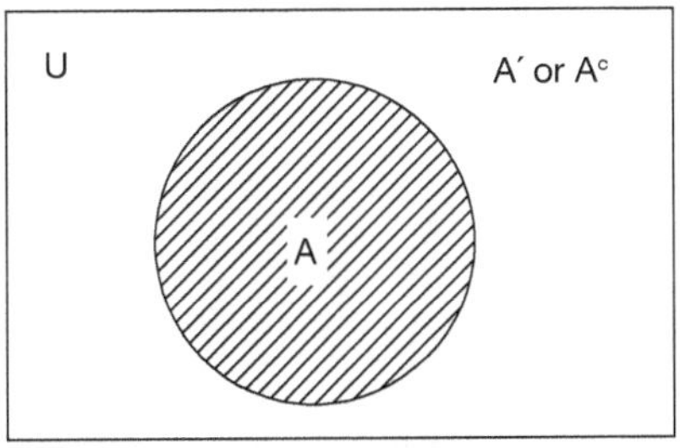

Source: Concept by British mathematician John Venn, drawn by author's research scholar Bhupender Singh.

Some properties of a compliment of a set are:

a. $A \cup A' = U$
b. $A \cap A' = \emptyset$
c. $(A')' = A$

De Morgan's law: Propounded by a British mathematician Augustus De Morgan in the 19th century, it is a law which states that the compliment of union of two sets is equal to the intersection of their complements and the complements and the intersection of two sets is equal to the union of their compliments, such as

$$(\mathbf{A} \cup \mathbf{B})^c = \mathbf{A}^c \cap \mathbf{B}^c.$$

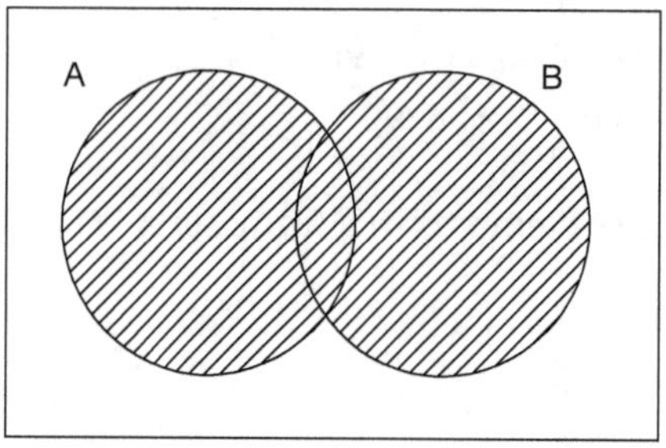

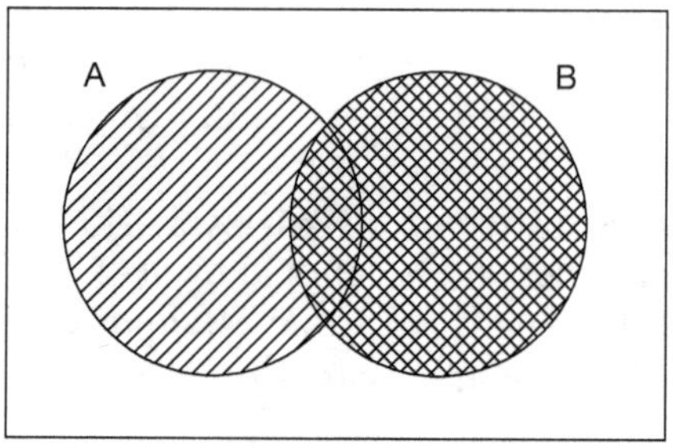

$(\mathbf{A} \cup \mathbf{B})^c$ is the plain white region in the figure.

Difference of sets: Two sets can be subtracted. If A and B are two sets, then the difference of sets A and B is the set of elements which are in A but not in B.

It is written as A–B and reads as "A difference B."

In general, $A-B \neq B-A$.

For example:

a. If $A=\{4, 5, 6, 7\}$ and $B=\{5, 7, 9, 10\}$,

then $A-B=\{4, 6\}$ and $B-A=\{9, 10\}$.

Hence, $A-B \neq B-A$.

b. If $A=\{10, 15, 17, 20, 21\}$
$B=\{10, 14, 16, 18, 21\}$
$C=\{15, 17, 18, 22\}$
then

$A - B = \{15, 17, 20\}$

$B - C = \{10, 14, 16, 21\}$

$C - A = \{18, 22\}$

$B - A = \{14, 16, 18\}$

$A - A = \emptyset.$

Thus, the set A–B, $A \cap B$, and B–A are mutually disjoint sets, that is, the intersection of any of these two sets is a null set.

2.8 PARTITIONS AND CROSS-PARTITIONS

We have already discussed earlier that set operations are not limited to two or more subsets of U which can also be broken down into subsets that do not exhaust all of U (unless we use set negation). On the other hand, U can also be broken down into subsets that do not intersect and exhaust all of U. When this is done, the process is called "partitioning" that breaks a universal set down into subsets that are disjoint and exhaustive of the universal set. In set language, let U be a universe, and A and B be the subsets of U that are partitions (Figure 2.3).

We label subsets of A and B as $A_1, A_2, \ldots, A_n$ and $B_1, B_2, \ldots, B_n$, respectively. Now, $[A_1, A_2]$ and $[B_1, B_2]$, for example, are partitions if

$$A_1 \cup A_2 = U \text{ and } A_1 \cap A_2 = E,$$
$$B_1 \cup B_2 = U \text{ and } B_1 \cap B_2 = E.$$

Diagrams make this clearer. The partitioning of U, represented by a rectangle, separately into subsets A_1 and A_2 and B_1 and B_2 is depicted in Figure 2.4(a). It is important to mention here that both the partitions have been created on the same U.

We generally come across many such examples: middle class–working class, high income–low income, introvert–extrovert, democrat–republican, field dependence–field independence, pass–fail, approve–disapprove, and so on. Some of these are true dichotomies; others are continuous variables.

It is quite possible to put two partitions together into a cross-partition. A cross-partition is a new partition of the same set U by forming all subsets of the form $A \cap B$. In other words, perform A partitioning and then B partitioning on the same U or the same square. This has been very well depicted in Figure 2.4(b). Each cell of the partition is an intersection of subsets of A and B. In due course of time, we will realize that such cross-partitioning is very important in research design and data analysis.

FIGURE 2.3
PARTITIONING AND CROSS-PARTITIONING
$A \cap B \cap C$

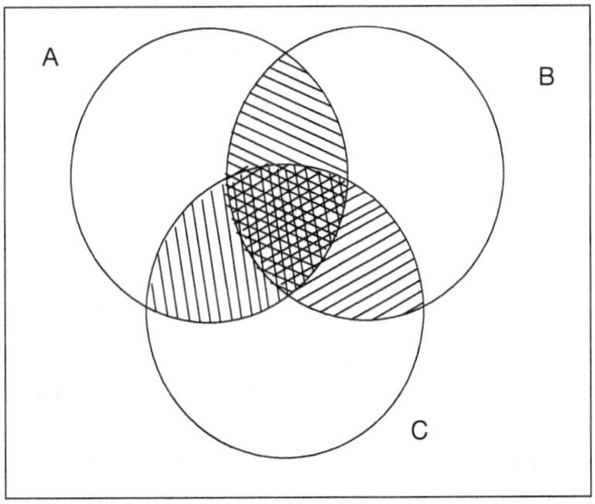

Source: Kerlinger (1983, 53).

FIGURE 2.4
MILLER AND SWANSON'S STUDY OF CHILD-REARING PRACTICES

(a)

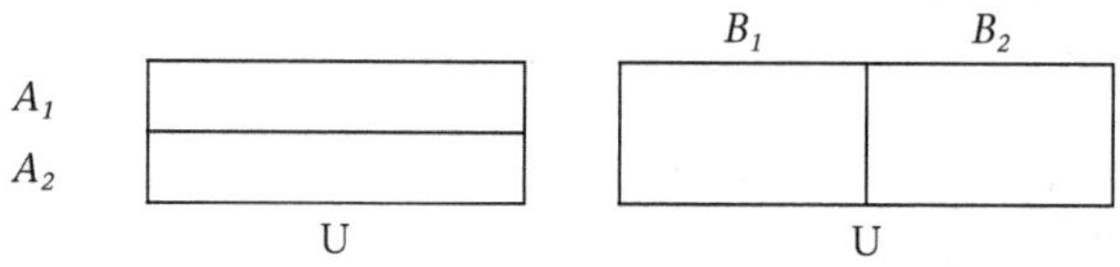

(b)

		B	
		B_1	B_2
	A_1	$A_1 \cap B_1$	$A_1 \cap B_2$
A	A_2	$A_2 \cap B_1$	$A_2 \cap B_2$

Source: Kerlinger (1983, 54–55).

FIGURE 2.5
RELATION BETWEEN SOCIAL CLASS AND WEANING (CROSSBREAK TABLE)

		Weaning	
		Early (B_1)	Late (B_2)
Social Class	Middle Class (A_1)	60% (33)	40% (22)
	Working Class (A_2)	35% (17)	65% (31)

Source: Miller and Swanson Study. (Kerlinger 1983, 54).

By predicting the future trends of media research, we give a research example for a cross-partition. Such examples are called crossbreaks. Crossbreaks provide the most elementary way to show a relation between two variables. The example here is taken from Miller and Swanson's study of child-rearing practices (Kerlinger 1983, 54). One of the tables in their report is a crossbreak in which the variables are social class (middle class and working class) and weaning (early and late). The data, converted to percentages by the author, are given in Figure 2.5. The frequencies reported by Miller and Swanson are given in the lower right corner of each cell. Evidently, there is a relation between social class and weaning. Middle-class mothers show a tendency to wean their children earlier than lower-class mothers do. The two conditions of disjointness and exhaustiveness are satisfied. The intersection of any two cells is empty, for example, $(A_1 \cap A_2) \cap (A_2 \cap B_2) = E$. Moreover, the cells exhaust all the cases: $(A_1 \cap B_1) \cup \cdots \cup (A_2 \cap B_2) = U$.

Partitioning extends beyond two partitions, of course. Instead of dichotomies, we can have polytomies: instead of success–failure, for instance, we can have success–partial success–failure. A variable can theoretically be partitioned into any number of subsets, though there are usually practical limitations. There is no theoretical limitation on the number of variables in a cross-partition, but practical considerations usually limit the number to three or four.

Here is an example of a larger and more complex cross-partition. We assign variable names to the set letters of a $2\times3\times2$ cross-partition. It has been laid out in the table below. Let U be all fourth grade children in the X school system. Let U be partitioned and cross-partitioned according to three variables A, B, and C, A being gender intelligence and C motivational communication. Let U be partitioned first into A_1 and A_2 or male and female. Let U be partitioned next into B_1, B_2, and B_3 or high, medium, and low intelligence. Finally, let U be partitioned into C_1 and C_2 or high and low motivational communication (to do school work).

Next, we cross-partition or crossbreak A_1 and A_2 and B_1, B_2, and B_3 by forming subsets from the intersections of A and B, such as $A_1 \cap B_1$, $A_1 \cap B_2, \ldots, A_2 \cap B_3$. We do the same, theoretically, for A and C and B and C. Actually, we do not have to do all this.

What we do after we have $A_1 \cap B_1, \ldots, A_2 \cap B_3$, is to cross-partition these intersection subsets with C_1 and C_2, arriving at the triple subsets: $A_1 \cap B_1 \cap C_1$, $A_1 \cap B_1 \cap C_2, \ldots, A_2 \cap B_3 \cap C_2$, (for simplicity, we write these subsets in the below table as $A_1\ B_1\ C_1$, $A_1\ B_1\ C_2$, and so forth.) This gives us $2\times3\times2=12$ cells, each of which represents the intersection of three sets.

	B_1		B_2		B_3	
	C_1	C_2	C_1	C_2	C_1	C_2
A_1	$A_1B_1C_1$	$A_1B_1C_2$	$A_1B_2C_1$	$A_1B_2C_2$	$A_1B_3C_1$	$A_1B_3C_2$
A_2	$A_2B_1C_1$	$A_2B_1C_2$	$A_2B_2C_1$	$A_2B_2C_2$	$A_2B_3C_1$	$A_2B_3C_2$

U

Source: Kerlinger (1983, 54–55).

To classify any single individual, we learn whether "the individual" is a male or a female whether he/she has high, medium, or low intelligence, and whether his/her motivational communication is high or low. We do this for each individual until all individuals or members of U are appropriately classified and assigned to their appropriate cells. Since our initial rules said that (a) the cells must be disjoint [$(A_1 \cap B_1 \cap C_2) \cap (A_2 \cap B_1 \cap C_3) = E$, for example] and (b) the union of all the cells must be the universe [$A_1 \cap B_1 \cap C_1) \cup (A_1 \cap B_1 \cap C_2) \cup \cdots \cup (A_2 \cap B_3 \cap C_2) = U$], no individual can be in more than one cell and every individual must be assigned to a cell. An example or two may clarify all this. If one of the children is female, has high intelligence, and low motivational communication, she is in cell $A_2\ B_1\ C_2$, whereas a boy of medium intelligence and high motivational communication is in cell $A_1\ B_2\ C_1$.

Moreover, set theory is a largely and widely applicable technique of interpersonal communication as well as analytical and conceptual thinking. Its most common applications pertinent to research methodology in this unexplored and emerging area of communication and media studies in the time to come will probably be the study of relations, logic, sampling, probability, measurement, and data analysis. For example, Piaget (1957) has applied set algebra in explaining the intrapersonal communication of children. On the other hand, Hunt (1962) has used set theories in his study of receiving the message and learning the process. Coombs (1960) explained his relevant theories of data largely in set terms. With their deep insight, Warr and Smith (1970) applied set theories to test different models of inference about personal traits, including communication skills. Further, for more clarity and scientific approach in basic principles of sampling, data analysis, and research design, set operations and set theories will hopefully be applied in the time to come in communication and media studies as well. Unfortunately, most of the communication scientists and media researchers seemingly are still not acquainted with generality, power, and flexibility of set operations and set theories. Hence, we may predict that researchers in communication and media studies will find set concepts, set operations, and set theories—as a whole—largely and widely applicable tools in conceptualization of theoretical and research problems.

2.9 DIFFERENTIATION FROM FIRST PRINCIPLE

Differentiation is an operation which allows media researchers to find out a function which gives the rate of change of one variable with respect to another variable. It is frequently used in engineering research, but moderately used in advanced media research to differentiate media variables and subvariables.

When we say that the effectiveness of communication is directly proportional to the presentation skill, in that case if the presentation skill is changed, then the effectiveness of communication will also change. Here, presentation skill is an independent variable and communication effectiveness is a dependent variable.

If we denote presentation skill by x and communication effectiveness by y, then let us consider the function

$$y=f(x).$$

If x changes by a small quantity (δx), then y also changes by (δy), corresponding to the change in x:

$$y+\delta y = f(x+\delta x)$$

or, $$\delta y = f(x+\delta x) - y$$

or, $$= f(x+\delta x) - f(x)$$

or, $$\frac{\delta y}{\delta x} = \frac{f(x+\delta x) - f(x)}{\delta x},$$

then $$\frac{\delta y}{\delta x} = \lim_{\delta x \to 0} \frac{\delta y}{\delta x} = \lim_{\delta x \to 0} \frac{f(x+\delta x) - f(x)}{\delta x}.$$

Example: Find $\frac{dx}{dy}$ of $y = 4x$ from the first principle.

Solution:

$$y = 4x$$

$$y + \delta y = 4(x+\delta x)$$

$$\delta y = 4x + 4\delta x - y = 4x + 4\delta - 4x$$

$$= 4\delta x$$

$$\therefore \frac{\delta y}{\delta x} = \frac{4\delta x}{\delta x} = 4.$$

Thus, whenever we want to know how quickly some quantity is changing, we are basically talking about a derivative.

2.9.1 Differentiation of a Power Function

Let us consider the following function:

$$y = f(x) = x^2.$$

Then
$$y + \delta y = (x + fx)^2$$
$$\delta y = (x + \delta x)^2 - y$$
$$= (x + \delta x)^2 - x^2$$
$$= x^2 + 2x\delta x + (\delta x)^2 - x$$
$$= 2x\delta x + (\delta x)^2$$

or
$$\frac{\delta y}{\delta x} = 2x + \delta x.$$

Hence,
$$\frac{\delta y}{\delta x} = \lim_{\delta x \to 0} \frac{\delta y}{\delta x} = \lim_{\delta x \to 0}(2x + \delta x)$$
$$= 2x.$$

We may now consider the function $y=x^n$ to build up a general case of differentiation of a power function:

$$y = x^n$$
$$y + \delta y = (x + \delta x)^n$$
$$\delta y = (x + \delta x)^n - y$$
$$= (x + \delta x)^n - x^n.$$

By using binomial expansion, we have,

$$\delta y = x^n + nc_1 x^{n-1}\delta x +^n c_2 x^{n-2}(\delta x)^2 + \cdots +^n c_n(\delta x)^n - x^n$$
$$= nc_1 \delta x +^n c_2 x^{n-2}(\delta x)^2 + \cdots +^n c_n(\delta x)^n$$

or,
$$\frac{\delta y}{\delta x} = nx^{n-1} + nc_2 x^{n-2}\delta x + \cdots + (\delta x)^{n-1}$$
$$\therefore \frac{\delta y}{\delta x} = \lim_{\delta x \to 0} \frac{\delta y}{\delta x} = \lim_{\delta x \to 0}\left[nx^{n-1} +^n c_2 x^{n-2}\delta x + \cdots (\delta x)^{n-1}\right].$$

Hence, the general formula for the derivative of a power function is:

$$\frac{d}{dx}(x^n) = nx^{n-1}.$$

Example: Find $\frac{dy}{dx}$ for $y = x^5$.

Solution:

$$y = x^5$$
$$\therefore \frac{dy}{dx} = \frac{d}{dx}x^5 = 5x^{5-1} = 5x^4 .$$

(Note: The derivative of a constant is always zero.)
The constant with a function remains unaffected in the process of differentiation.

Example:

1. Find $\frac{dy}{dx}$ for $y = 5$.
2. Find $\frac{dy}{dx}$ for $y = 4x^5$.

Solution:

1. $y = 5 \therefore \frac{dy}{dx} = 0.$
2. $y = 4x^5 \therefore \frac{dy}{dx} = 4\times\frac{d}{dx}x^5 = 4\times 5x^{5-1} = 4\times 5x^2 = 20x^4.$

2.9.2 Rules for Differentiation

Some important rules (such as sum rule, product rule, and quotient rule) of differentiation are as follows.

1. Sum rule: The derivative of a sum of a finite number of functions is the sum of their derivatives:

   Let $u+v+w...,$

   where y, u, v, w are all functions of x,
   then

$$\frac{\delta y}{\delta x} = \frac{du}{dx} + \frac{dv}{dx} + \frac{dw}{dx} + \cdots$$

   Example: Find $\frac{\delta y}{\delta x}$ of $y = 2x^2 + 3x^3 + 4x^5$.

   Solution: $\frac{\delta y}{\delta x} = 2\frac{d}{dx}(x)^2 + 3\frac{d}{dx}(x)^3 + 4\frac{d}{dx}(x)^5$

$$= 2\times 2x + 3\times 3x^2 + 4\times 5x^4$$
$$= 4x + 9x^2 + 20x^4.$$

2. Product rule: The derivative of the product of two functions is equal to the product of the first function and the derivative of the second function plus the product of the second and the derivative of the first function.
   If

$$y = uv, y, u, v \text{ are all the function of } x,$$

then

$$\frac{dy}{dx} = u\frac{dv}{dx} + v\frac{du}{dx}.$$

Extension of the product rule:
If

$$y = uvw,$$

then

$$\begin{aligned}\frac{dy}{dx} &= u\frac{d}{dx}(vw) + vw\frac{du}{dx}\\ &= u\left\{v\frac{dw}{dx} + w\frac{dv}{dx}\right\} + vw\frac{du}{dx}\\ &= uv\frac{dw}{dx} + uw\frac{dv}{dx} + vw\frac{du}{dx}.\end{aligned}$$

This rule can be further extended likewise.

Example: Find $\frac{dy}{dx}$ for $(x^2+2)(2x^4+5x^2)$.

Solution: By product rule, we have

$$\begin{aligned}\frac{dy}{dx} &= (x^2+2)\frac{d}{dx}(2x^4+5x^2) + (2x^4+5x^2)\frac{d}{dx}(x^2+2)\\ &= x^2 + 2(8x^3+10x) + 2x^4 + 5x^2 + 2x\\ &= x^2 + 2(8x^3+10x)(x^2+2) + 2x(2x^4+5x^2)\\ &= 2x(4x^2+5)(x^2+2) + 2x(2x^4+5x^2).\end{aligned}$$

3. Quotient rule: The derivative of the quotient of two functions is equal to the product of denominator and the derivative of the numerator minus the product of the numerator and the derivative of the denominator, whole divided by the square of the denominator.
   If

then

$$y = \frac{u}{v}, v \text{ and } y \text{ are functions of } x,$$

$$\frac{\left(\frac{dy}{dx} = v\frac{du}{dx} - u\frac{dv}{dx}\right)}{v^2}.$$

Example: Find $\frac{dy}{dx}$ or $y = \frac{X^3+3}{x^3+2}$

Solution: Using the quotient rule, we have,

$$\frac{dy}{dx} = \frac{\left((x^2+2)\frac{d}{dx}(x^3+3) - (x^3+3)\frac{d}{dx}(X^2+2)\right)}{x^2+2}$$

$$= \frac{[(X^2+2)\times 3x^2 - (x^3+3)\times 2x]}{(x^2+2)^2} = \frac{3x^4+6x^2-(2x^4+6x)}{(x^2+2)^2}$$

$$= \frac{3x^4+6x^2-2x^4-6x}{(x^2+2)^2}.$$

2.9.3 Rules for Integration

Integration is a process of finding a function when its derivatives are given. It is also called anti-differentiation. It is frequently applied in engineering research but is applied only rarely in advanced media research when variables and subvariables are integrated to find their function from the established derivatives. If F′(X)=f(X), then we say F(X) is an anti-derivative of f(X).

As far as rules of integration are concerned, these can be explained in the following ways:

1. $\int cf(x)dx = c\int f(x)dx.$
   This shows that the integral of the product of a constant and a function is equal to the product of the constant and the integral of the function.
2. $\int\{f_1(x)dx \pm f_2(x)dx \pm f_3(x)dx \pm \cdots \pm f_n(x)dx\}$
   $= \int f_1(x)dx \pm \int f_2(x)dx \pm \int f_3(x)dx \pm \cdots \pm \int f_n(x)dx.$

This shows the integral of the sum or the difference of their integrals.

Hence, the standard formula is:

$$\int x^n dx = \frac{x}{n+1} + c; n \neq -1.$$

Example: Evaluate $\int 5x^4 \times dx$.

Solution: $\int 5x^4 \times dx = 5\int x^4 \times dx = 5\frac{x^4+1}{4+1}$

$$= \frac{5x^5}{5} + c = x^5 + c.$$

Example 2: Evaluate $\int(6x^4+4x^3+5x^2+6x+2)dx.$

Solution: $= 6\int x^4dx + 4\int x^3dx + 5\int x^2dx + 6\int xdx + 2\int 1dx$

$$= 6\times\frac{x^{4+1}}{4+1} + 4\frac{x^{3+1}}{3+1} + 5\frac{x^{2+1}}{2+1} + 6\frac{x^{1+1}}{1+1} + 2x + c$$

$$= \frac{6}{5}x^5 + x^4 + \frac{5}{3}x^3 + 3x^2 + 2x + c.$$

The following examples of differentiation and integration make it clearer and more applicable in the area of communication studies.

Differentiation:

1. A person A chooses to specialize in art and craft by his introvert communication skills (he is basically differentiating himself from rest of the professionals) at time t. He chooses to work for a company C at time T (this is another point in time on his or her curve).
2. A person B specializes in selling goods and services by his extrovert communication skills at time t (he is also differentiating himself from rest of the professionals).

Integration: A few years later, they find themselves working together. That is only possible through integration of their differentiated skills. If we want, we can only focus on either one of those people discussed above and realize that their each step (points in time T, t) gives us a real snapshot of their journey. In retrospect, we are able to trace all those steps and by doing so we are already integrating seemingly disjoint twists, and it turns to give the wholeness of the subject in question.

Thus, the different types of variables of media and communication studies may be differentiated and integrated on the basis of the above-discussed basics of differentiation and integration and can be calculated in terms of numeric data.

2.10 MATRIX

Yet another dimension of mathematics used in media metrics is matrix, which is an integral part of mathematical algebra. Factor analysis, a type of multivariate analysis, is based on the study of matrix.

When data are explained in rows and columns, then it is called a matrix (plural is matrices). Matrix is a rectangular array of rows and columns in $m \times n$ form which will be discussed thoroughly in Chapter 12 of this book on multivariate analysis techniques.

SUMMARY

The use of mathematics in solving the problems of communication and media studies is fast becoming widespread at the international level. It is used effectively to study the different situations of communication and media. Mathematics is such a representation that comprehends communication more specifically and scientifically. The induction and introduction of mathematics has made media research very exciting and revealing. The frontiers of media and communication research have considerably been extended and scope for interdisciplinarity has also gone up tremendously. With the help of mathematics, the in-depth studies have enriched the knowledge of communication scientists. To understand how and on what lines media and communication research has progressed in recent years, the knowledge of mathematics has become indispensable. Several media theories might have remained unnoticed without the use of mathematics. Beginners and learners are generally critical of the use of mathematics in media research, but the moment they become learned, they don't criticize it. Mathematics is a science of all sciences. Hence, it cannot leave media and communication science from its purview. It has added a scientific approach to these exercises and made media research more relevant and useful for our modern society. Hence, there is a tremendous use of mathematics, specially use of numbers, set descriptions, classification of sets, set operations, Venn diagram, union of sets, intersection of disjoint sets, difference of sets, Cartesian product, some basic properties of Cartesian products, De Morgan's law, differentiation from first principles, rules for integration, and matrix.

With the growing applications of mathematics in media research, the knowledge of applied mathematics or statistics—such as data processing and analysis in mass communication, measures of central tendency in media research, measures of dispersion in media studies, measures of asymmetry in mass communication, measures of relationship and other measures in media research, parametric testing of hypothesis in media studies, nonparametric testing of hypothesis in mass communication, chi-square test in media research, ANOVA in media studies, and multivariate analysis techniques in mass communication—will be very important, pertinent, useful, relevant, and desirable to discuss in the following chapters one by one.

RELATED AND SUGGESTED WEBSITES

(As retrieved on December 1, 2015)

1. http://www.encyclopedia.com/doc/1G2-3407500183.html
2. http://www.laeuferpaar.de/Papers/SAGE-Math+Stat+SocScience.pdf
3. http://www.pearsonhighered.com/assets/hip/us/hip_us_pearsonhighered/samplechapter/0205638007.pdf
4. http://www.jstor.org/discover/10.2307/27951563?uid=2129&uid=2&uid=70&uid=4&sid=21104897400747
5. http://2000clicks.com/mathhelp/BasicSet.aspx

REFERENCES

Coombs, C. 1960. "A Theory of Data." *Psychological Review*, LXVII (3): 143–59.
Hunt, E. 1962. *Concept Learning*. New York: Wiley.
Kerlinger, F.N. 1983. *Foundations of Behavioural Research*, 49–59. New Delhi: Surjeet Publications.
Piaget, J. 1957. *Logic and Psychology*. New York: Basic Books.
Smithson, Michael, and Jay Verkuilen. 2006. *Fuzzy Set Theory Applications in Social Sciences*. Vol. 147. London: SAGE Publications.
Warr, P., and J. Smith. 1970. "Combining Information about People: Comparisons Between Six Models." *Journal of Personality and Social Psychology*, XVI: 55–65.

RELATED AND RECOMMENDED READINGS

Gupta, Santosh. 1999. *Research Methodology and Statistical Techniques*, 171–81. New Delhi: Deep and Deep Publication.
Inhelder, B., and J. Piaget. 1958. *The Growth of Logical Thinking from Children to Adolescence*. New York: Basic Books.
Kothari, C.R. 2000. *Research Methodologies: Methods and Techniques*, 97–115. New Delhi: Wishwa Prakashan.
NCERT. 2012. *Mathematics Textbook for Class XII* (I), 256–57. New Delhi: NCERT.

NCERT. 2012. *Mathematics Textbook for Class XII* (II), 287–391. New Delhi: NCERT.
Sarangi, Prasant. 2010. *Research Methodology*. Delhi: Taxman Publication.
Sharma, R.D. 2010. *Mathematics* (1), 1.1–1.51. New Delhi: Dhanpat Rai Publications.
Sharma, R.D. 2010. *Mathematics* (2). New Delhi: Dhanpat Rai Publications.
Wilkinson, T.S., and P.L. Bhandarkar. 1996. *Methodologies and Techniques of Social Research*, 192–293. Mumbai: Himalaya Publishing House.
Wimmer, Roger D., and Joseph R. Dominick. 2003. *Mass Media Research: An Introduction*. 7th ed. Belmont: Wadsworth Publishing Company.
Zina, O. Leary. 2010. *The Essential Guide to Doing Your Research Project*. 3rd ed. London: SAGE Publications.

QUESTIONS

1. Discuss the relevance and importance of mathematics in mass communication research.
2. Describe the use of mathematics in media and communication measurement.
3. Explain the types of numbers and their applications in communication and media research.
4. What is a set? Throw light on set operations with reference to mass communication research.
5. Discuss classification of sets with suitable examples in view of communication and media research.
6. Explain set operations with examples in light of mass communication research.
7. Make two overlapping circles, enclosed in a rectangle. Label the following parts: the universal set U, the subsets A and B, the intersection of A and B, and the union of A and B:
   a. If you were working on a communication research problem involving communication skills of fifth-grade children, what part of the diagram would indicate the children from whom you might draw samples?
   b. What meaning might the intersection of A and B have?
   c. How would you have to change the diagram to represent the empty set? Under what conditions would such diagram have research meaning?
8. Consider the following cross-partition:

	Print Journalist (B_1)	Advertiser (B_2)
Male Journalist (A_1)		
Female Journalist (A_2)		

   What is the meaning of the following sets—that is, what would we call any object in the sets?
   a. $(A_1 \cap B_1)$; $(A_2 \cap B_2)$
   b. A_1; B_1
   c. $(A_1 \cap B_1) \cup (A_2 \cap B_2) \cup (A_2 \cap B_1) \cup (A_2 \cap B_2)$
   d. $(A_1 \cap B_1) \cup (A_2 \cap B_1)$
9. Applying the following sets, make a cross-partition: communication level of third-grade children; socio-economic backgrounds of the children; the children's gender.

10. Under what conditions will the following set equations be true?

$$N(A \cup B) = n(A) + n(B),$$

where n(A) means the number of objects in the set A.
11. Suppose a researcher in communication studies of the influence of gender and communication level on occupational status. How can he/she conceptualize the problems in set terms?
12. How are sets related to variables? Can we talk about partitioning of variables? Is it meaningful to talk about subsets and variables?
13. Describe the basic rules for differentiation and its use in differentiating the media and communication variables.
14. Discuss the fundamental rules for integration and its application in integrating the different variables relating to mass communication research.

3

CHAPTER

Data Processing and Analysis in Mass Communication

It is a capital mistake to theorise before one has data. Insensibly one begins to twist facts to suit theories, instead of theories to suit facts.

—Arthur Conan Doyle

In mass communication research, the collection of relevant *data* in a scientific manner, its scientific processing, scientific analysis, scientific interpretation, and systematic report preparation are vital aspects to arrive at right conclusions. After the collection of relevant data, it has to be processed and analyzed in accordance with the outline laid down for the purpose at the time of research plan.

In the previous chapter, we have thoroughly discussed the conceptual framework of media metrics, including the meaning and concept of mathematics in media research, use of mathematics in media and communication measurement (including tools of media metrics), procedures of writing mathematical notations, types of numbers, linear equation, quadratic equation, set descriptions, classification of sets, set operations, differentiation from first principle, and rules for integration and matrix. Thus, in the previous section we have focused our attention on the mathematical tools, such as number system, set theory, differentiation from first principle, basics of integration, and matrix. Now, we will start our discussion on other aspects of tools of media metrics, that is, statistical tools such as descriptive statistics and inferential statistics, in the remaining chapters of this book. The first and foremost issue of descriptive statistics (as depicted in the flowchart in Section 2.2.1 of Chapter 2) is the processing and analysis of data. With the tremendous growth and development of applications of mathematics in media research the world over, the knowledge of applied mathematics, that is, statistics such as data processing and analysis, measures of central tendency, measures of dispersion, measures of asymmetry, measures of relationship and other measures, parametric testing of hypothesis, nonparametric testing of hypothesis, chi-square test, ANOVA, and multivariate analysis techniques will be very relevant, useful, applicable, important, pertinent, and desirable to discuss in the following chapters one by one.

Therefore, this chapter will focus the discussion on the following:

1. Meaning and concept of data processing and analysis in mass communication
2. Data
3. Data processing (editing, coding, classification, transcriptions of data, tabulation, graphs, charts)
4. Data analysis (types of data analysis, data interpretation)

5. Prominent studies of data processing and analysis in media
6. Media metrics in scientific data processing and analysis of mass communication

In addition, the chapter will also cover the summary, related and suggested websites, references, related and recommended readings, and questions of processing and analysis of data with general reference to statistics and special reference to media metrics.

3.1 MEANING AND CONCEPT OF DATA PROCESSING AND ANALYSIS IN MASS COMMUNICATION

In a micro-focused branch of social science like media and communication research, data processing and analysis are basically processes of understanding, diagnosing, inquiring, inspecting, investigating, cleaning, transforming, modeling, and mining the available data of the field of media such as print media, electronic media, web media, advertising, public relations, film studies, graphics, and animation. It is basically the data presentation method which is designed to discover relevant information and knowledge for coming out with useful conclusions and suggestions of such areas. The collected data from a variety of sources must be suitably processed, properly analyzed, and systematically organized for inferences. It may be required at some point of time to convert the data into tabular form, classified form, row–column form, or any other well-defined form for further analysis. Ultimately, it has to be processed and analyzed according to the suitability of outline with a goal to solve media research problems as framed in the research design.

3.2 DATA

Facts, statistics, or information in raw, unorganized, or unstructured form are called data. In any social science research including mass communication, the collected data are the subject matter on which various methods and tools are applied as per the research problems, research questions, and objectives. Thereafter, it is processed and analyzed as per the objectives, research questions, and hypothesis (if any) of the study. And at the end, the properly processed, managed, and presented data are interpreted as per the reflected findings to draw inferences of the study. In mass communication, the data are respondents' responses, contents, observations, and so on, as per the directed research aims and plans.

Data is generally collected from two types of sources: (a) primary sources and (b) secondary sources. *Primary sources* are the original sources from which the researcher collects the data directly. Primary data are the first-hand information collected through various methods, such as observation, interviewing, and mailing. *Secondary sources* are the sources containing data which have been collected and combined earlier or for another purpose. Such secondary sources consist of readily available compendia, already compiled statistical statements, census reports, annual reports and financial statements of companies, statistical reports of government departments, annual reports and publications of international organizations such as UNO, IMF, and WHO, trade and financial journals, newspapers, and the likes. These sources consist of not only published records but also unpublished records. The latter category includes different types of records and registers maintained by firms and organizations. The data collected in such a way is of no use at all until and unless presented in some easily understandable form. This involves data processing, analysis, and interpretation. Under these primary actions on collected data, the data is processed and arranged in a crystal clear, proper, and easily understandable format. The data processing steps are performed keeping an eye on the research questions or hypothesis of the study. The processing steps make and check the accuracy and verify with the aimed questions. Thus, the processed data is amenable to be analyzed with the help of statistical tools. The inferences drawn in such a way are interpreted to draw logical generalizations.

3.3 DATA PROCESSING

Processing of data implies editing, coding, classification, tabulation, and general explanation of the table. Analysis of data means to consider the data in light of hypothesis or research questions, research objectives, and the ever-evolving as well as prevailing theories, and drawing conclusions that are as amenable as theory formation.

Some researchers, like Johan Galtung (cited in Sharma 2007), differentiate between data processing and data analysis as discussed above, while some others, such as Seltiz et al. (cited in Kothari 2000, 151), do not effect such a precise difference. According to them, analysis of data seemingly involves processing, that is, operations designed to facilitate and increase amenability of data for analysis and also the operations designed to draw generalizations or to test hypothesis. They are of the opinion that analysis of data involves closely related operations which are performed with the purpose of summarizing the collected data and organizing them in such a systematic and scientific manner that they answer the research questions and hypothesis. To be more accurate and precise, it is desirable to observe the hairline difference between data processing and data analysis so that their implications become crystal clear.

Data processing is an important step between data collection and data interpretation. It is primarily the data presentation method which discovers the relevant information and knowledge for coming out with useful conclusions and suggestions. The data collected from wherever or whichever sources or methods are required to be made uniform for further analysis. The data collected is generally in different formats depending upon the data sources. No meaningful interpretations can be directly drawn from such collected data. To arrive at meaningful interpretations, the researcher is supposed to prepare the data as per the research objectives. This is carried out by identifying the structure, that is, the variables or group of variables, then coding, that is, assigning some uniform codes to different data to make them uniform, then classification as per categories, then editing, then transcription, that is, entering codes to data sheet to present collected data in one uniform form, then tabulation, and so on. This data preparation for analysis (as the tables are then used to apply statistical tools) is termed as data processing. Further, the selection of statistical tools depends on the results of this data processing.

The data gathered in the form of questionnaires/interview schedules/field notes/data sheets are mostly in the form of a large volume of research variables. The research variables are recognized as a result of the preliminary research plan, which also sets out the data processing methods beforehand. Processing of data requires advanced planning, and this planning may cover such aspects as identification of variables, hypothetical relationship among the variables, and the tentative research hypothesis.

3.3.1 Preparation of Analysis

The very first step of data preparation or data processing is to define the variables. In manual or mechanical data processing, the variables need to be clearly defined. It is done by preparing data structure. A data structure defines variables or group of variables that are interrelated to

FIGURE 3.1
DATA PROCESSING: IDENTIFYING STRUCTURES OF COLLECTED DATA

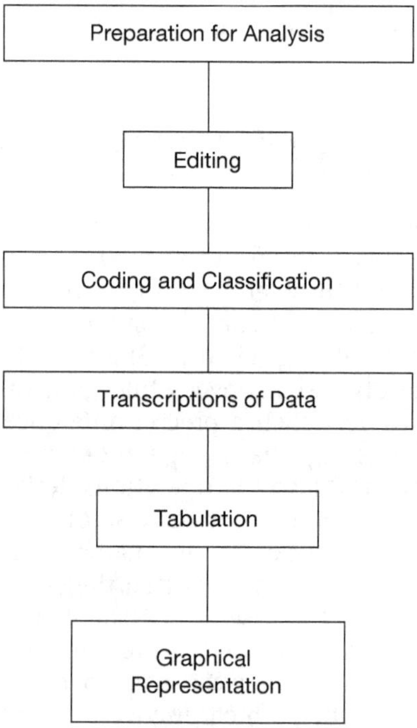

Source: Drawn by author.

reach at a conclusion. These are usually pre-planned by the researcher to derive the hypothesis or aimed research questions. Then the data is collected through various methods, which makes this process more complex. The interrelated variables are collected in a group to provide ease in understanding and analyzing.

As discussed earlier, data processing includes editing, coding, classification, and tabulation (Figure 3.1).

3.3.2 Editing

It is a process of converting the raw data into useful information by detecting errors and omissions. It includes perusal and careful examination of filled questionnaires and/or schedules. Editing is an art and craft which is executed to assure that the data are accurate and consistent with other facts gathered, uniformly entered as complete as possible, and have been systematically arranged to facilitate coding and tabulation. In the context of data processing, editing may be divided into (a) field editing and (b) central editing.

Field editing is essential because individual writing styles can often be difficult for others to decode. This type of editing should be done immediately after the interview is over.

Central editing is executed after the completion of all the schedules or forms. This type of editing should be done by a single expert editor in the case of a small research and by a team of expert editors in the case of a large study. Editors are supposed to correct the errors which are crystal clear, for example entry into a wrong column. In case the answer is incorrect or missing, then the editor may find out the correct answer just by observing the other information in the form/schedule. Sometimes, the respondents should also be contacted in the case of more ambiguity or complexity. All the obvious wrong answers should be finally dropped. Editors must take the following precautions:

1. Editors must be aware of the instructions given to them,
2. They should highlight entries in the form/schedule in some colors such as red or green,
3. They must put their signatures on the corrected or edited replies,
4. They must also sign and put a date of rectification on all completed forms or schedules.

3.3.3 Coding

Coding is proper placement of the unit of analysis into a particular category. It is a method of assigning numerals or symbols to replies from respondents so that the answers can be put into a limited number of categories or classes. It is essential for effective and efficient analysis which will reduce the data to a small number of classes. In the case of manual coding, the standard method is to code in the "margin" with a colored pencil. Whether the coding is executed electronically or manually, the researcher must see that coding errors are eliminated or minimized. It is better to keep a record sheet of codes, that is, a code sheet. Coding should be executed while preparing the data instrument. This helps in directly entering the code of each variable in the recording sheet. The codes can be numeric, alphabetic, or zero.

Numeric coding: It is like 1, 2, 3, and so on. The coding should be compulsorily numeric when the data is subjected to further parametric analysis.

Alphabetic coding: This type of coding is preferable when the data is just to be presented in tabulation and frequency count or geographical representation.

Zero coding: A "0" code refers to no response. If it is assigned to some response, then it will also be considered. And in the case of "Like," "Yes," or "No," both options are given a different code. For example,

Question Number	Observation/Variable	Response Categories	Code
1	Organization	Public	Pb
		Private	Pt
		Government	G
2	Owner of vehicle	Yes	2
		No	1

Each question is labeled by the variable included. And special care should be taken that a label should not be more than eight characters so as to make it easily feedable in statistical software packages for analysis. Sometimes it is not possible to directly enter the data; rather, it needs classification. That is to say that a set of responses from a specific class is required. Thereafter, the researcher needs to classify and code the responses. For this purpose, classification of the available data is required at the data entry stage.

3.3.4 Classification

The data collected generally becomes a large volume of raw data which must be reduced to homogeneous groups to make meaningful relationships. This is executed by creating classes through classification of data, through the process of arranging data in groups or classes on the basis of common characteristics. In accordance with the nature of phenomenon, classification may be done as follows:

1. Classification according to attributes: There are two types of variables—descriptive or numerical. The descriptive responses measure the presence or absence only. The descriptive characteristics refer to qualitative aspects which cannot be measured quantitatively, such as literacy and gender. Data collected in this way on the basis of some attributes is called classification attributes. In this, there is simple classification or manifold. In a simple type of classification, merely presence or absence is judged, while in manifold, two or more attributes are considered simultaneously and the data is divided into a number of classes (the attribute class of final order is given by $2n$ where n=number of attributes). It must be ensured while deciding attributes that there is no possibility of doubt/ambiguity regarding the said attributes.
2. Classification according to class intervals: The qualitative aspect has numerical characteristics which may be measured through statistical units. Data relating to income, production, age, weight, and so on, come under this type of category. These types of data are known as statistics of variables and are classified on the basis of class intervals. As for example, the age of respondents may be between class 5 and 10, 10 and 15, and so on. This is called class interval. Each class interval has a lower limit and an upper limit. The difference between them is called the length of the class. Here, the data or responses are grouped in their suitable class. In the process of classifying in this way, the following points should be considered.
   a. What should be the number of class interval: The most important and very first question in such classification arises as to what should be the number of classes and their magnitudes. First of all, there is no specific rule to the number of classes. Normally there may be 5–15 classes. The magnitude of each class could be equal and in some cases unequal. Therefore, the researcher's knowledge of the subject matter plays a very significant role in deciding class intervals. H.A. Sturges (cited in Kothari 2000, 154–155) has defined a formula to determine the size of a class interval.

$$I = R/(1 = 3.3 \log N)$$

   where I=size of a class interval

   R=range, that is, difference between the values of the largest item and the smallest item among the given items.

   N=number of items to be grouped.

   Generally, multiples of 2, 5, and 10 are preferred while determining class magnitudes. There are a few exceptions of this case which may be indifferent, like class interval under ₹500 or ₹1001 and over. All this is decided as per the nature of quantitative data. Secondly, how to choose class limit? Thirdly, how to determine the frequency of each class?
   b. How to choose a class limit: Class limit means grouping the range of qualitative data in which the data may be. In a class limit (also called class interval), there is a lower limit and an upper limit. The quantitative information as per statistics of variable is

put among the suitable class limit. To make it feasible and clear, it is preferred that the class limits are located at the multiples of 2, 5, 10, 20, 100, and such other figures.

Further there are two types of the class limit: (a) continuous and (b) overlapping.

In a continuous class limit, the data lying above the lower limit and below the upper limit are put such as:

10–20
20–30
30–40,

which means 10–20, that is, above 10 and below 20. This means that even the exact 20 value would be put in the next class interval, that is, 20–30. This is also called exclusive series or exclusive class limit.

In an overlapping class limit, the data of the upper limit's value is also considered in the same class interval. For example:

11–20
21–30
31–40.

The class limit 11–20 means the value above 11 to 20.9999..., and meaning 11–21.

c. How to determine the frequency of each class: The frequency of each class means the number of values put in a single class limit. It can be measured/counted by tally sheets or mechanical sheets. While executing it mechanically, the machine or software itself sorts the values under each class limit and counts the number of total values. While counting the frequency on tally sheets, the researcher has to calculate it manually as per the following steps:

Groups	Tally Marks	Total No. (Class Frequency)
Below 100	|||	3
100–200	𝍸	5
200–300	𝍸 𝍸 ||	12
300–400	𝍸	5
Total		25

i. On a paper sheet on the left-hand side, the class groups are written.
ii. In front of each class interval, for each value, a stroke is marked.
iii. On the count of 5, a slant stroke line is marked meaning a total of 5.
iv. The same process is further followed.
v. In the bottom and front of each column and row, the total is written. While determining classes, care should be taken to assure that the classes are exhaustive and mutually exhaustive. There should be option as others, which can be opted in case no mentioned class matches the very different few answers of the respondents.
vi. The number of categorization for a specific question/observation at the coding stage should be maximum permissible, since reducing the categorization at the analysis level would be easier than splitting an already classified group of responses. However, the number of categories is limited by the number of cases and the anticipated statistical analysis that are to be used on the observations.

3.3.5 Transcriptions of Data

It is the intermediary stage between data coding and data tabulation. The main aim of transcription is to minimize the shuffling process between several responses and observations. When the data collected by the instrument are not that much large, the simple inferences that can be drawn from the responses of observations can be transferred to data sheet, which is a summary of all responses on all observations from a research instrument. Suppose a research instrument contains 100 responses from 250 observations, to prepare a simple summary of one response from all 250 observations would require shuffling of 250 pages. The transcription, that is transferring data to data sheets, helps the researcher in presentation of all responses and observations on properly managed and clearly understood data sheets. The transcriptions can be prepared manually or electronically. The main requisite is the preparation of data sheets where observations are the rows of database and the responses/variables are the columns of data sheet. As explained earlier, each question is labeled by the variable name that too not exceeding the maximum length of eight characters. The label names are thus the links to specific questions in the research instrument. Once the labeling process has gone through for all the responses in the research instrument, the transcription of the responses is executed.

The worksheets can then be used for preparing tables for further analysis of data. The original research instruments can now be kept aside. The transcription process like editing, after once entering the data, is subject to a testing to ensure error-free transcription of data.

Transcription can be made as and when edited instruments are ready for processing. Once all the research instruments are transcribed, the frequency tables can be prepared straight from the worksheet. For computerized data transcription, care should be taken while assigning codes. In codes, logical coding and ordering of coding should be prepared, use of blank spaces should be avoided as different software packages have different principles, and the use of special characters or symbols in coding should also be avoided.

3.3.6 Tabulation

Tabulation is an orderly arrangement of data in columns and rows. After transcription, the summary is presented in the form of tables. Tables conserve space and time for understanding the presented variables. Tables represent the total of responses. They can be made manually by using the tally method or otherwise electronically by using some statistical analysis software. In the tally method, the number of each response in front of the column of its row (question/variable row) is represented with a stroke. And after every four strokes, the fifth one is drawn diagonally so as to make it easily understandable and countable. After the complete entry of responses, the total or the percentage of total is presented in the exact right column for rows and the last row for columns. In electronic data processing, it is much easier as one has to just enter the data and prepare data sheets, and the rest of the work is done with the help of simple commands for each operation. In the summary table, the frequencies are presented which are calculated through the tally method as explained earlier. While preparing tables in research, care should be taken in table presentation and its naming. When the tables are presented, each table is given a specific number, title, source, and so on. In each row, clearly defined stubs (row names/variable names) are recorded and columns, captions, and responses are mentioned. Some researchers give each column a specific number. This helps in clear and accurate interpretation and for the readers, it helps in easily correlating the interpretation of the table with the apt row/column. Abbreviations should be avoided in any table and the data entered should be as concise as possible. Each table should be numbered by appending the table number to the number of the chapter in which the tables are used (i.e., in Chapter 1, Table 1.1, 1.2, and so on). Or for grouped data, special consistent numberings should be used for all the incorporated tables.

Tables should be presented with appropriate interpretation to guide the readers as to how and what the table is telling about the represented data.

Tabulation is classified as simple and complex tabulation. Simple tabulation comprises one-way tables answering questions, such as the interrelationship of two variables. Complex tables can be used to present interrelationship of more than two to *N* number of variables. Complex tabulation is also called cross-tabulation. Tabulation can be very well understood by the following examples.

Simple table: Details of newspaper readers on the basis of age

Age (in yrs)	Readers
0–15	
15–30	
30–45	
45–60	
Above 60	
Total	

Complex table (bi-variate cross-tabulation): Details of newspapers' readers on the basis of age and gender.

	Readers		
Age (in yrs)	Male	Female	Total
0–15			
15–30			
30–45			
45–60			
Above 60			
Total			

Complex table (tri-variate cross-tabulation): Details of newspapers' readers on the basis of age, gender, and literacy.

	Male		Female		
Age (in yrs)	Literate	Illiterate	Literate	Illiterate	Total
0–15					
15–30					
30–45					
45–60					
Above 60					
Total					

Complex table (multivariate cross-tabulation): Details of newspaper readers from different states on the basis of age, gender, and literacy.

		Male		Female		
State	Age (in yrs)	Literate	Illiterate	Literate	Illiterate	Total
Delhi	0–15					
	15–30					
	30–45					
	45–60					
	Above 60					
	Total					
Haryana	0–15					
	15–30					
	30–45					
	45–60					
	Above 60					
	Total					
Punjab	0–15					
	15–30					
	30–45					
	45–60					
	Above 60					
	Total					
Uttar Pradesh	0–15					
	15–30					
	30–45					
	45–60					
	Above 60					
	Total					
Rajasthan	0–15					
	15–30					
	30–45					
	Above 60					

The other simple way to present data for further analysis other than tabulation is the graphical representation of the summary tables or data. These graphic forms such as graphics, chart, diagrams, and pictographs reduce large masses of statistical data to a form that can be quickly understood at a glance. Properly constructed graphs and charts relieve the mind of burdensome details by portraying the facts concisely, logically, and simply. The graphic devices of data presentation are useful to depict the data to general public. However, the graphic tools can never be treated as substitute for tables; they are just additional tools for the researcher to emphasize the research findings.

3.3.7 Graphical Representation of Data

A graph or chart is a diagrammatical representation of a set of data in which the data are represented by symbols. A diagrammatical representation is also called a graphical representation which is also described as a geometrical image of a set of data. It is basically a mathematical visualization. It helps us in visual thinking about a statistical problem. Hence, the graphical representation of data is a highly effective and more communicative method of processing, presenting, understanding, analyzing, and interpreting the collected data.

The benefits of graphical representation are many. In graphical representation, the data is eye-catching and eye-arresting because it is presented in a more attractive and crystal clear manner. It becomes easily understandable and makes it possible to have an immediate, instant, pertinent, and meaningful grasp of heavy data or even mines of data. Second, it helps a lot in comparative study of facts which becomes the base of further research. Third, measures of central tendencies such as mean, median, and mode and measures of dispersion such as average deviation, standard deviation, and quartile may be easily calculated, which further helps in deriving correlation and regression between two or more variables. Fourth, graphical representation helps in proper estimation, evaluation, and interpretation of the characteristics of different variables. Fifth, the real value of such representation lies in its economy, effectiveness, and communication power. Moreover, it helps a lot in forecasting and prognosticating as it indicates the trends, movements, and fluctuations of data in the past.

3.3.7.1 Graphical Representation of Ungrouped Data

The data in the form of raw scores is known as ungrouped data. The ungrouped data is not grouped or classified into a frequency distribution.

In ungrouped data, the following graphical representation is made.

1. Bar graph or bar chart: In a bar graph or chart, the data is represented by bars. Usually, these charts are drawn on a graph paper. Hence, these bar charts are also described as bar graphs. The bar graph or chart is of two types: (a) vertical bar graph and (b) horizontal bar graph.

   Example: 60 students of media and communication were asked to opt for different specializations. The details of these options are as follows:

Specialization	No. of Students	Percentage
Advertising	15	25%
Broadcasting	24	40%
Editing	06	10%
Photography	03	5%
Reporting	12	20%
Total	60	100%

Represent the above data through vertical and horizontal bar graphs.

Solution:

a. Vertical bar graph

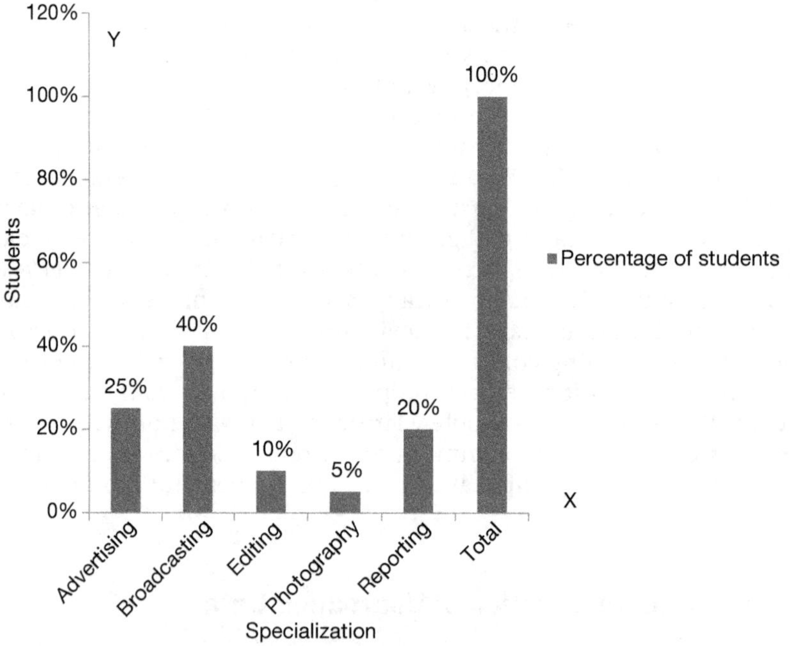

b. Horizontal bar graph

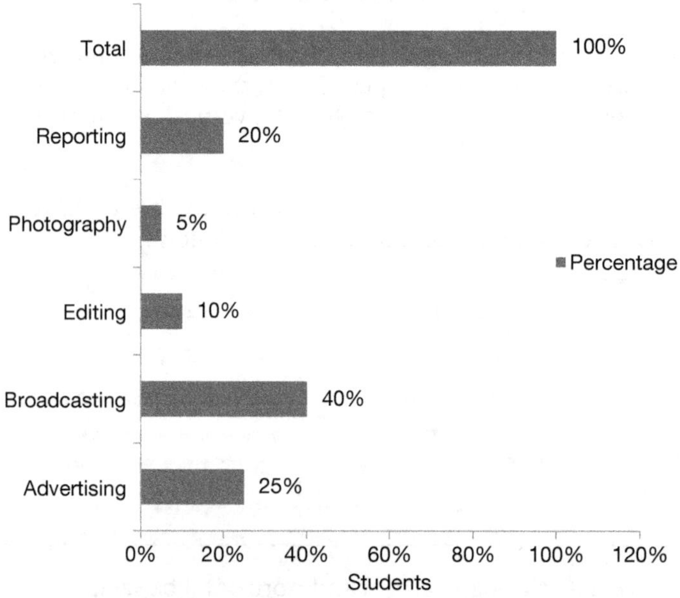

2. Circle graph, pie graph, or pie chart: In this type of graph, the data are represented through the sections or the portions of a circle. This graph is most popularly known as a pie chart.

   This can be very well understood with the help of the previous example. The numerical data from the example can easily be converted into angles of a circle:

Specialization	**No. of Students**	**Area of Circle**
Advertising	15	$\frac{15}{60} \times 360 = 90°$
Broadcasting	24	$\frac{24}{60} \times 360 = 144°$
Editing	06	$\frac{6}{60} \times 360 = 36°$
Photography	03	$\frac{3}{60} \times 360 = 18°$
Reporting	12	$\frac{12}{60} \times 360 = 72°$

The above numerical data can be easily represented through a pie chart as follows:

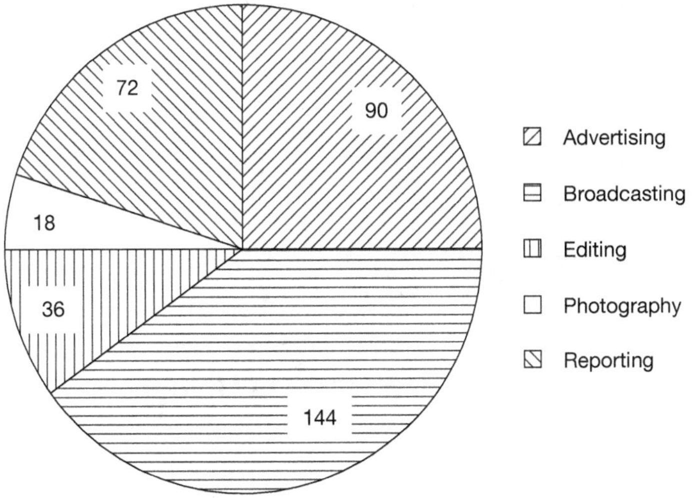

3. Line graph or line chart: This is a simple statistical line which is drawn on the graph paper by plotting the data, taking one variable on the horizontal *X*-axis and the other on the vertical *Y*-axis. This can be very well understood by the following diagram with the help of the previous example:

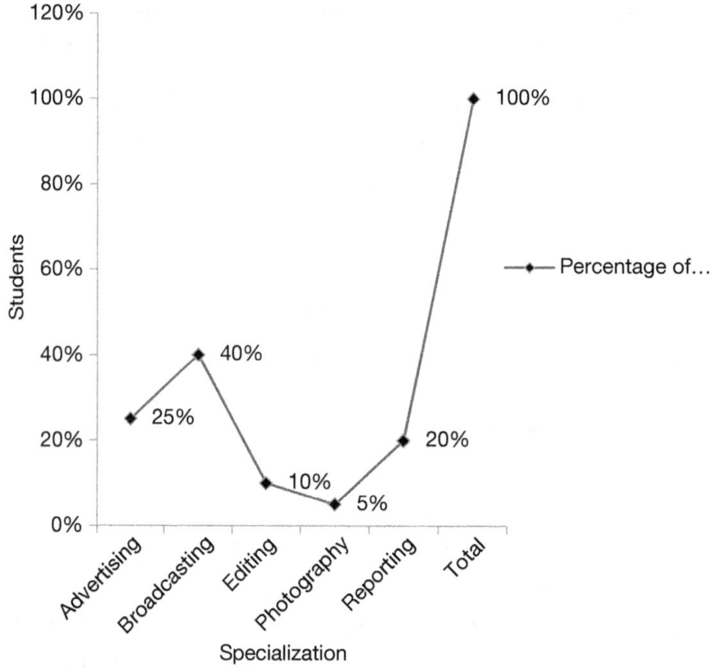

4. Pictogram: Statistical data may also be represented by pictures, which is described as a pictogram. This can be easily understood by the following diagram which shows the strength of broadcasters in Delhi for different years:

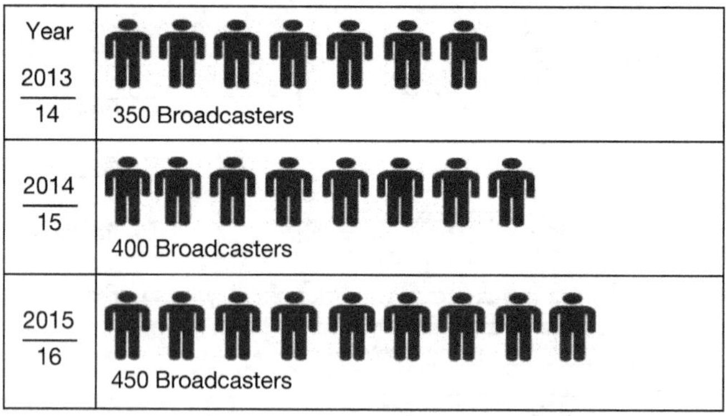

Note: Each picture represents the strength of 50 broadcasters.

3.3.7.2 Graphical Representation of Grouped Data

The data in the form of frequency distribution with class interval is described as grouped data. For grouped data, the following graphical representations are made:

1. Histogram: Also called a column chart or a column diagram, a histogram is essentially a bar graph of classified or grouped frequency distribution. This can be easily understood

TABLE 3.1
GROUPED FREQUENCY DISTRIBUTION BETWEEN AGE AND NUMBER OF NEWSPAPER READERS

Age (in yrs) Class	Mid-point	No. of Newspaper Readers (in Thousands); Frequency	Cumulative Frequency	Cumulative Percentage Frequency
0–10	5	2	2	2%
10–20	15	16	18	18%
20–30	25	15	33	33%
30–40	35	12	45	45%
40–50	45	10	55	55%
50–60	55	15	70	70%
60–70	65	12	82	82%
70–80	75	18	100	100%
Total		100		

by observing Table 3.1 of the grouped frequency distribution (of age and number of newspaper readers) followed by a bar graph.

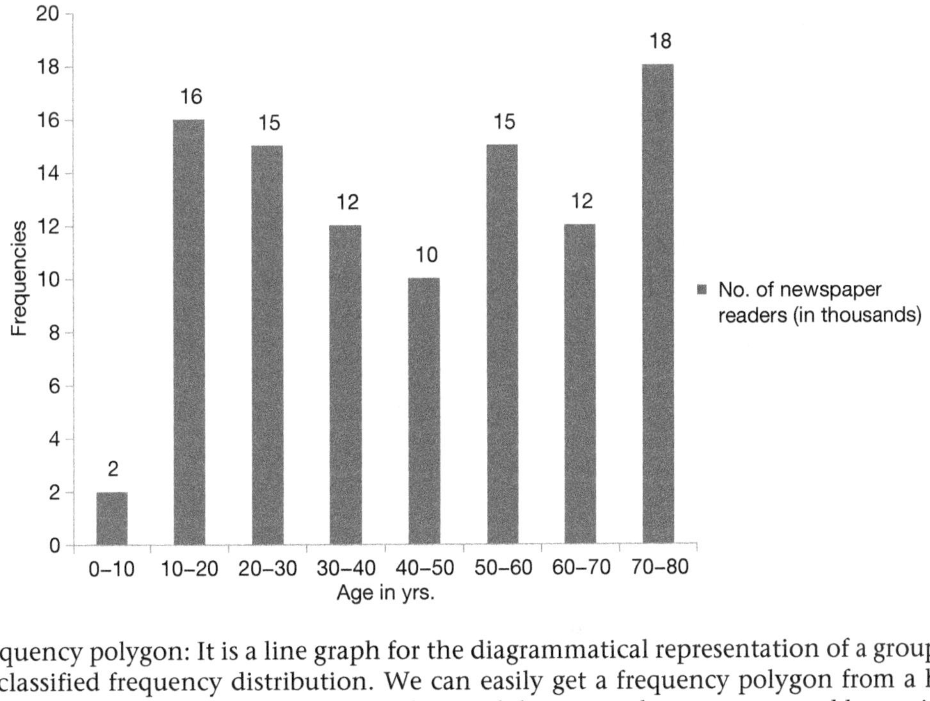

2. Frequency polygon: It is a line graph for the diagrammatical representation of a grouped or classified frequency distribution. We can easily get a frequency polygon from a histogram if the mid-points of the upper bases of the rectangles are connected by straight lines. But it is not mandatory to plot a histogram first to draw a frequency polygon. We may draw it directly from a given classified frequency distribution. It can be very well understood with the help of the following diagram drawn with the help of statistical data in Table 3.1.

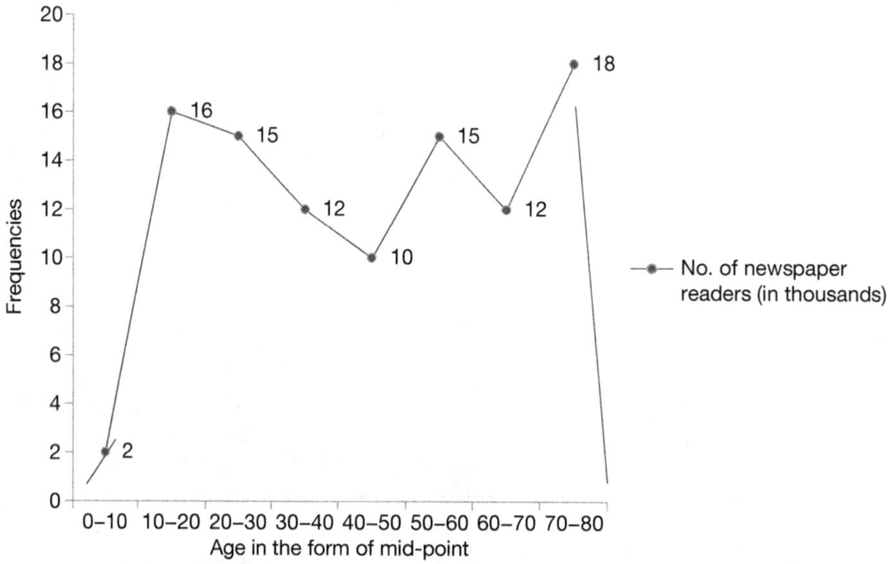

3. Cumulative frequency graph: The numerical data organized in the form of cumulative frequency distribution can be graphically represented through a cumulative frequency graph; it is a line graph for the graphical representation by plotting actual upper limits of the class intervals on the *X*-axis and the respective cumulative frequencies of these class intervals on the *Y*-axis. This can be easily understood with the help of the following diagram by using statistical data given in Table 3.1.

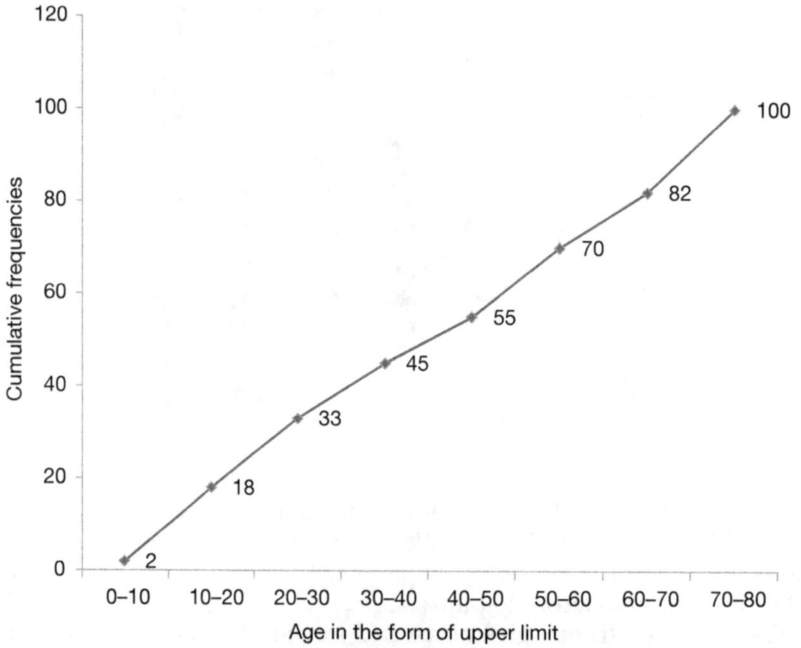

4. Ogive (cumulative frequency percentage graph): The cumulative frequency percentage graph or ogive is the diagrammatical representation of a cumulative percentage

frequency distribution as per the statistical data given in Table 3.1. It is, thus, a line graph drawn by plotting the actual upper limits of the classes on the *X*-axis and their respective cumulative percentage frequencies on the *Y*-axis. This can be easily understood by the following diagram with the help of the numerical data in Table 3.1.

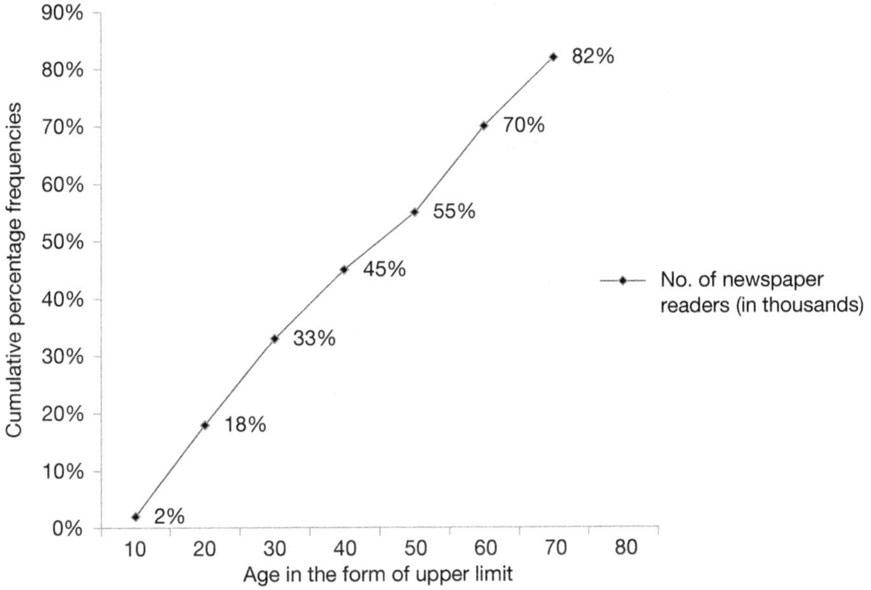

3.4 DATA ANALYSIS

As explained earlier, scholars of mass media, being a micro-branch of social sciences, consider hairline difference between data processing (or data presentation) and data analysis. Till now, we understood what is meant by or is included in the process of data. Extending this process to draw out inferences, now it is extremely desirable to discuss data analysis and interpretation.

The processed data is presentable and understandable, and drafts a clear picture of all the information gathered through different tools of data collection. The next step is to apply the appropriate measures on series of quantitative data presented in coding as per appropriate classifications. This is a process of applying statistical tools, presenting vast information in a very simple form, and enabling to test hypothesis or to know the data behavior.

Data analysis is the process of applying statistical measures on the data retrieved after the processing of data to know the relationship pattern among different data groups.

3.4.1 Types of Data Analysis

As data analysis means computation of certain statistical measures to draw inferences, and finding the relationship pattern between different data groups, it involves drawing parameters and testing hypotheses. In research, this analysis is of two types:

1. Descriptive analysis
2. Inferential analysis

3.4.2 Data Interpretation

This means drawing inference as per data behavior. This is a very significant step and the ending step in the process of research as it is the phase where the findings as per objectives and set hypotheses are highlighted. Through processing, the information gathered is given a valid form to be analyzed. Through applying statistical techniques, certain measures are computed which are selected as per data's nature and measures' applicability. After this, the outputs are interpreted and inferences are drawn. The relationship patterns of different data groups are explained. This is the most important step in any research. So care should be taken. Even language errors may change the actual expression of data. A few considerations to be kept in mind are:

1. The research should state what the data says.
2. The relationship patterns and inferences must be drawn as per data behavior.
3. The researcher should be very careful about the digits and percentages.
4. The researcher should never try to exaggerate the facts.
5. Biases should be carefully avoided and the researcher should just go with the data.
6. The researcher should always avoid his/her own personal opinion.

3.5 PROMINENT STUDIES OF DATA PROCESSING AND ANALYSIS IN MEDIA

Since data processing and analysis is the core of any social science research including mass communication, the discussion of some prominent studies of data processing and analysis becomes relevant to highlight here. According to a study by Riff, Lacy and Fico (2014), it was found that although the production of communications among humans is thousands of years old, the scholarly or scientific study of mass communication is fairly new. Riff and Freitag (cited in Wimmer and Dominick 2003) point out that during a 15-year period, one fourth of the articles of mass communication were published in Journalism and Mass Communication Quarterly as the content. Yet another journal entitled Communication Abstracts lists out that more than 90 content analytic studies for 1999 and 2000, shows the data trend that it is still one of the most important research techniques in media and communication research. The data analysis techniques we discuss in the following sections are those used most often in the articles. Unpublished examples of the data tables and analysis sections of 239 studies in *Journalism and Mass Communication Quarterly* from 1986 to 1995 indicate that content analysis relies on several basic techniques and a few more advanced ones. That is, a limited number of statistical tools turn out to be useful for a variety of tasks. As in many kinds of work, knowing what tool will serve adequately for what job is an essential knowledge.

Some of these analysis techniques are very simple indeed. Researchers who produced 28 percent of 239 content analysis studies have been able to achieve their objectives using only means, proportions, or simple frequency counts. When other techniques were used, they were often in combination with means and proportions. Techniques for analyzing the content data included chi-square and Cramer's V (used in 37% of studies), and Pearson's product-moment correlation (used in 15%) techniques to assess differences between means or proportions of two samples were used in 17 percent of studies. More advanced techniques included ANOVA (8% of studies). Only 7 percent of the studies employed statistical techniques more sophisticated than these.

3.6 MEDIA METRICS IN SCIENTIFIC DATA PROCESSING AND ANALYSIS OF MASS COMMUNICATION

Media metrics, as explained in earlier chapters and specially depicted in the flowchart in Section 2.2.1 of Chapter 2, is the use of statistics and mathematics in media research. And the role of statistics and mathematics in media research is to function as a foundational and basic tool in designing research, analyzing the collected data, and drawing inferences and conclusions therefrom. Hence, media metrics is considered to be a technical tool for scientific data processing and analysis. Media and communication research mostly studies the results in a large volume of raw data which must be suitably or logically reduced so that it can be easily understandable and can be used for further analysis. In this process, statistics and mathematics cannot be ignored by any researcher in case it is a scientific and systematic quantitative analysis. Then only we can adopt the process of generalization from all small groups (i.e., samples) of a population. As a matter of fact, there are two useful areas of statistics: (a) descriptive statistics and (b) inferential statistics.

Descriptive statistics relates to the development of certain indices from the raw data, while *inferential statistics* relates to the process of generalization. Inferential statistics is also called sampling statistics and is primarily related to two types of problems: (a) estimation of population parameters and (b) testing of statistical hypotheses.

In the present context, descriptive statistics may be defined as descriptive media metrics and inferential statistics may be defined as inferential media metrics. Hence, the most striking statistical measures in this context are: (a) data processing and analysis (already discussed), (b) measures of central tendency, (c) measures of dispersion, (d) measures of asymmetry, (e) measures of relationship and other measures, (f) parametric testing of hypotheses, (g) nonparametric testing of hypotheses, (h) chi-square test, (i) ANOVA, and (j) multivariate analysis techniques.

Further, the most important mathematical measures (already discussed) in this context are: (a) number system, (b) set theory, (c) differentiation from first principle, (d) basics of integration, and (e) matrix.

SUMMARY

In communication and media research, the data collected is processed and analyzed in accordance with the outline laid down for the purpose at the time of the research plan. Data are generally collected from two types of sources: (a) primary source and (b) secondary source. Primary source collects first-hand information, while secondary source collects second-hand information. Data processing implies editing, coding, classification, tabulation, and general explanation of the table. Data analysis means to consider the data in light of hypotheses or research questions, research objectives, and the ever-evolving theories, and drawing conclusions. Data processing includes editing, coding, classification, and tabulation. Editing is an art and craft which is carried out to ensure that the data are accurate, consistent with other facts gathered, uniformly entered as complete as possible, and have been systematically arranged to facilitate coding and tabulation. Coding is the proper placement of the unit of analysis into a particular category. It is essential for effective and efficient analysis which will reduce the data to a small number of classes. Classification of data is essential as the data collected generally becomes a large volume of raw data which must be reduced to homogeneous groups to make meaningful relationships. Tabulation of data is equally important as this is an orderly arrangement of data in columns and rows. Tables must be presented with appropriate interpretation in order to guide the readers as to how and what the table is telling about the represented data. This must be followed by graphical representation of data. Data analysis is the process of applying statistical measures on the data retrieved after the processing of the data. Data analysis is of two types: (a) descriptive analysis and (b) inferential analysis. On the other hand, data interpretation means drawing inference as per data behavior. The researcher must keep in mind that he/she should state what the data says. Second, the relationship pattern and inferences must be drawn as per data behavior. Third, the researcher should be very careful about the digits and percentages. Fourth, the researcher should never try to exaggerate the facts. Fifth, biases should be carefully avoided and the researcher should just go with the data. Sixth, the researcher should always avoid his/her own personal opinions.

There are different tools of media metrics in mass communication research. These tools are statistical and mathematical which help in designing research, analyzing the collected data, and deriving inferences and conclusions therefrom. Media and communication research mostly studies the results in a large volume of raw data which must be suitably and logically reduced so that it can be easily understood and can be used for further analysis. The most striking statistical and mathematical measures in this context are: (a) data processing and analysis, (b) measures of central tendency, (c) measures of dispersion, (d) measures of asymmetry, (e) measures of relationship and other measures, (f) parametric testing of hypotheses, (g) nonparametric testing of hypotheses, (h) chi-square test, (i) ANOVA, (j) multivariate analysis techniques (k) number system, (l) set theory, (m) differentiation from first principle, (n) basics of integration, and (o) matrix.

We have already discussed data processing and analysis in mass communication in this chapter. Hence, it will be very pertinent to discuss the measures of central tendency in media research in the next chapter.

RELATED AND SUGGESTED WEBSITES

(As retrieved on December 1, 2015)

1. http://www.socialresearchmethods.net/kb/measlevl.php
2. http:/www.wimmerdominick.com.
3. http://www.ifabc.org/resources/metrics/print-metrics
4. http://learcenter.org/pdf/measuringmedia.pdf
5. http://mediaratingcouncil.org/Soc%20Guidelines%20v4.1%20Public%20Comment %20Version.pdf
6. http://www.cdc.gov/metrics/
7. http://www.jstor.org/stable/3035554

REFERENCES

Kothari, C.R. 2000. *Research Methodologies: Methods and Techniques*, 122–31, 151, 154–55. New Delhi: Wishwa Prakashan.

Riff, D., S. Lacy and F. Fico. 2014. *Analysing Media Messages Using Quantitative Content Analysis in Research*, 5. 2nd ed. New York: Psychology Press.

Sharma, J.N. 2007. *Research Methodology: The Discipline and its Dimensions*, 255. New Delhi: Deep & Deep Publications.

Wimmer, Roger D., and Jospeh R. Dominick. 2003. *Mass Media Research: An Introduction*, 140. 7th ed. Belmont, CA: Wadsworth Publishing Company.

RELATED AND RECOMMENDED READINGS

Kerlinger, F.N. 1983. *Foundations of Behavioural Research*, 2nd ed., 134–54. New Delhi: Surjeet Publication.

Krishnaswami, O.R., and M. Ranganatham. 2005. *Methodology of Research*, 271–94. New Delhi: Himalaya Publications.

Negi, B.S. 2010. "Data Analysis and Interpretation." *Media Mimansa* 4 (1): 30–34.

Sarangi, Prasant. 2010. *Research Methodology*. Delhi: Taxman Publication.

Wilkinson, T.S., and P.L. Bhandarkar. 1996. *Methodologies and Techniques of Social Research*, 192–293. Mumbai: Himalaya Publishing House.

Zina, O. Leary. 2010. *The Essential Guide to Doing Your Research Project*. 3rd ed. London: SAGE Publications.

QUESTIONS

1. What is a data? Discuss the different sources of data.
2. Differentiate between data processing and data analysis.
3. Describe the role of editing, coding, classification, and tabulation in the processing of data.
4. Throw light on data analysis and interpretation.
5. Discuss the different tools of media metrics in mass communication research.
6. Describe the role of media metrics in scientific data processing and analysis of media research.

4

CHAPTER

Measures of Central Tendency in Media Research

Statistics may be rightly called the science of averages and their estimates.

—A.L. Bowley and A.L. Boddington

Measures of central tendency refer to the point about which items have a tendency to cluster. This is considered to be the most representative figure for the whole bunch of data. It gets a single value that describes the characteristics of the entire mass of scattered and wide data. Taking an example of media research, suppose there are 26 lakh media persons in India and each media person has some income. We say that the per capita income per media person per annum is ₹5 lakh. It reflects the entire picture of the income of media persons of the whole country with a single value. Hence, measures of central tendency in media research are generally the computation of mean, median, and mode in the field of print media, electronic media, advertising, corporate communication and public relations, web media, development communication and social marketing, social media, and various other media.

In the last chapter, we have thoroughly discussed the meaning and concept of processing and analysis of data in mass communication, data, data processing (editing, coding, classification, transcriptions of data, tabulation, graphical representation of data), data analysis (types of data analysis, data interpretation), prominent studies of data processing and analysis in media, and different tools of media metrics.

Therefore, the present chapter will focus the discussion on the following:

1. Meaning and concept of central tendency in media research,
2. Mean (including mean of simple distribution, mean of unclassified data with frequency distribution, mean of classified data with frequency distribution, mean by the shortcut method and mean by the step deviation method),
3. Median (including median of simple distribution, median of frequency distribution),
4. Mode (including mode of simple distribution, mode of frequency distribution, bi-modal values),
5. Important formulae.

In addition, the chapter will also cover the summary, related and suggested websites, references, related and recommended readings, questions and problems of measures of central tendency with general reference to statistics and special reference to media metrics relating to the problems of communication and media studies and their solutions.

4.1 MEANING AND CONCEPT OF CENTRAL TENDENCY IN MEDIA RESEARCH

Measures of central tendency are described as statistical averages which are fast becoming indispensable in the upcoming and emerging research areas of mass communication. As per the basic concept, the word "average" is commonly used in media research and in our day-to-day activities. But it has been differently defined in statistics.

According to Clark (cited in Gupta 2011, 178), "An average is an attempt to find one single figure to describe whole of figures."

Leabo (cited in Gupta 2011, 178) defines "average" as, "The average is sometimes described as a number which is typical of the whole group."

A.E. Waugh (cited in Gupta 2011, 178) defines it as, "An average is a single value selected from a group of values to represent them in some way—a value which is supposed to stand for whole group, of which it is a part, as typical of all the values in the group."

According to Ya-Lun-Chou (cited in Gupta 2011, 178), "An average is a typical value in the sense that it is sometimes employed to represent all the individual value in a series of a variable."

Croxton and Cowden (cited in Gupta 2011, 178) define average as, "An average value on a single value within the range of the data that is used to represent all of the values in the series. Since the average is somewhere within the range of the data, It is also called measures of central tendency."

Thus, the main objectives of average are to get a single value that describes the characteristics of the entire group and to facilitate comparison. Since the comparative and evaluative measurement concepts of unexplored variables of communication and media are more in demand these days due to the growing professionalism in this area, getting a single value of the mines of media data and then using such data in various comparisons is becoming the crying need of the hour.

There are three types of average (Figure 4.1): (a) mean, (b) median, and (c) mode.

4.2 MEAN

In media research, only arithmetic mean is applied, while geometric mean or harmonic mean are not required at any point of research. However, arithmetic mean is the most popular and widely used measure of representing the whole of media or communication data by one value. Its value is obtained by adding together all the items and by dividing this total by the number of items. In media research, arithmetic mean is so popular and relevant that when we talk of mean, we generally mean "arithmetic mean."

4.2.1 Mean of Simple Distribution (or Ungrouped or Unclassified Distribution)

Formula:

$$\bar{X} = \frac{\Sigma X}{N},$$

where (i) $\bar{X}$ (called X bar) is mean

(ii) X is score

FIGURE 4.1
TYPES OF MEASURES OF CENTRAL TENDENCY

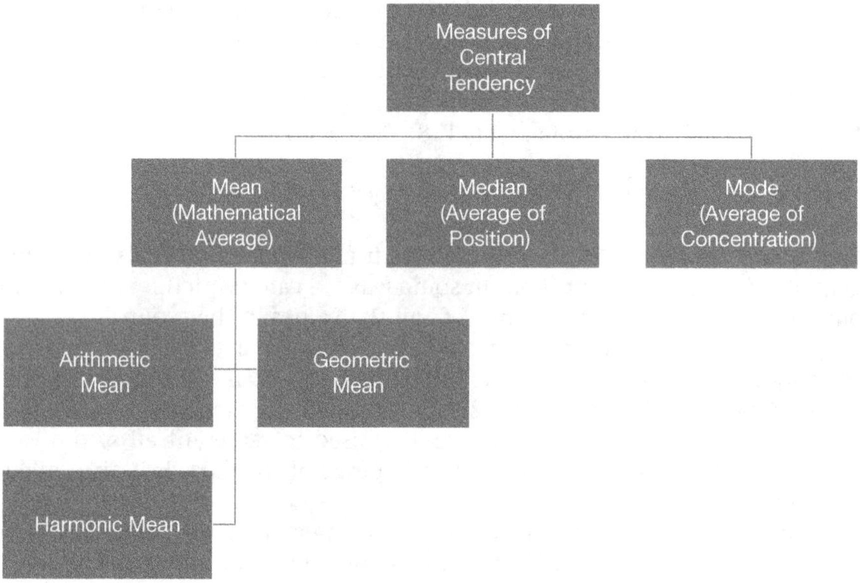

Source: Drawn by author.

(iii) N is number of scores
(iv) Σ is summation of....

Σ is a letter of Greek alphabets also called sigma.

Example: In a communication skill test, 10 students secured 10, 18, 16, 15, 19, 15, 14, 25, 16, and 18. Find the mean of the said data.

Solution:

No. of Students	Scores (X)
1	10
2	18
3	16
4	15
5	19
6	15
7	14
8	25
9	16
10	18
N=10	ΣX=166

$$\bar{X} = \frac{\Sigma X}{N} = \frac{166}{10} = 16.6.$$

Hence, the average score is 16.6 marks.

4.2.2 Mean of Unclassified Data with Frequency Distribution

Formula:

$$\bar{X} = \frac{\Sigma fX}{N},$$

where $\bar{X}$ is mean, X is score, N is the number of scores, and fX=frequency multiplied by X.

Example: Find the arithmetic mean of the unclassified data with the following frequency distribution of five media persons and their number of exclusive stories.

X (Media persons)	1	2	3	4	5
f (Exclusive stories)	2	9	9	7	3

Solution:

Variable (X)	Frequency (f)	fX
1	2	2
2	9	18
3	9	27
4	7	28
5	3	15
	$N = \Sigma f = 30$	$\Sigma fX = 90$

$$\therefore \bar{X} = \frac{\Sigma fX}{N} = \frac{90}{30} = 3.$$

Hence, the arithmetic mean of exclusive stories of five media persons is 3.

4.2.3 Mean of Classified Data with Frequency Distribution

Formula:

$$\therefore \bar{X} = \frac{\Sigma fX}{N}.$$

Example: Calculate the mean of the following frequency distribution of advertisers and their successful advertisement campaigning:

Class (advertisers)	0–8	8–16	16–24	24–32	32–40	40–48
Frequency (no. of successful ad campaigning)	10	20	14	16	18	22

Solution:

Class	Frequency (f)	Mid-value of Class (X)	fX
0–8	10	$\frac{0+8}{2}=4$	40
8–16	20	$\frac{8+16}{2}=12$	240
16–24	14	$\frac{16+24}{2}=20$	280
24–32	16	$\frac{24+32}{2}=28$	448
32–40	18	$\frac{32+40}{2}=36$	648
40–48	22	$\frac{40+48}{2}=44$	968
	$N=\Sigma f=100$		$\Sigma fX=2624$

$$\therefore \bar{X}=\frac{\Sigma fX}{N}=\frac{2624}{100}=26.24.$$

Hence, the mean of the advertisers and their successful ad campaigning is 26.

4.2.4 Mean by Shortcut Method

1. Simple distribution
2. Frequency distribution

Formula:

1. Simple distribution $\bar{X}=A+\frac{\Sigma d}{N}$,

   where A is assumed mean and d is deviation of scores from assumed mean.
   For assuming (A), any single value can be selected from X values.
2. Frequency distribution $\bar{X}=A+\frac{\Sigma fd}{N}$.

Example 1: In a communication skills test, 10 students secured 10, 18, 16, 15, 19, 15, 14, 24, 25, 16, and 18. Find the mean of this simple distribution by the shortcut method.

Solution: Let us take the assumed mean = 19.

X	$d=X-A$
10	10−19=−9
18	18−19=−1
16	16−19=−3
15	15−19=−4
19	19−19=0
15	15−19=−4
14	14−19=−5
25	25−19=6
16	16−19=−3
18	18−19=−1
N=10	$\Sigma d=-24$

$$\bar{X} = A + \frac{\Sigma d}{N} = 19 + \frac{-24}{10} = 19 - 2.4 = 16.6.$$

Hence, mean value is 16.

Example 2: Find the mean of the following frequency distribution (unclassified data) by the shortcut method of five public relations officers for the number of press conferences organized by them.

PR officer (X)	1	2	3	4	5
No. of Press conference (f)	2	9	9	7	3

Solution: Let the assumed mean be 3.

X	f	**Deviation of Score from Assumed Mean $d=(X-A)$**	fd
1	2	1−3=−2	−4
2	9	2−3=−1	−9
3	9	3−3=0	0
4	7	4−3=1	7
5	3	5−3=2	6
	$N=\Sigma f=30$		$\Sigma fd=0$

$$\therefore \bar{X} = A + \frac{\Sigma fd}{N} = 3 + \frac{0}{3} = 3 + 0 = 3.$$

Thus, the mean of five public relations officers for the number of press conferences organized by them is 3.

(Note: If we take the middle number from the series as the assumed mean, then the calculation becomes much easier).

Example 3: Calculate the mean of the following frequency distribution (classified data) by the shortcut method for the number of threats received by 100 press reporters per year.

Class (reporters)	0–8	8–16	16–24	24–32	32–40	40–48
Frequency (no. of threats)	10	20	14	16	18	22

Solution: Let us consider the mid-value of (16–24), that is 20, as the assumed mean.

Class	f	Mid-value	Deviation of X from Assumed Mean $d=(X-A)$	fd	fd_1 ($d_1=d/h$)
0–8	10	$\frac{0+8}{2}=4$	4−20=−16	−160	−20
8–16	20	$\frac{8+16}{2}=12$	12−20=−8	−160	−20
16–24	14	$\frac{16+24}{2}=20$	20−20=0	0	0
24–32	16	$\frac{24+32}{2}=28$	28−20=8	128	16
32–40	18	$\frac{32+40}{2}=36$	36−20=16	288	36
40–48	22	$\frac{40+48}{2}=44$	44−20=24	528	66
	$N=\Sigma f=100$			$\Sigma fd=624$	$\Sigma fd_1=78$

$$\therefore \bar{X}=A+\frac{\Sigma fd}{N}=20+\frac{624}{100}=20+6.24=26.24.$$

Thus, the number of threats received by 100 press reporters per year is 26.

4.2.5 Mean by the Step Deviation Method

Mean by the step deviation method can be derived only in the case of classified distribution.

Formula:

$$\bar{X}=A+\frac{h\Sigma fd_1}{N},$$

where $d_1=\frac{d}{h}$ and h is the height of class.

(Note: Instead of length of the class, height of the class is preferred because it is always the same whether the class is overlapping [continuous] or nonoverlapping [discrete]. In height, we have to just subtract the lower limit of any class from the lower limit of the nearest higher class. Or we have to just subtract the higher limit of any class from the higher limit of the nearest higher class. In case of use of height, there is no need to add +1 in nonoverlapping [discrete] class unlike length of the class.)

Example: Calculate the mean of the following frequency distribution (classified data) by the step deviation method for the number of threats received by 100 press reporters per year.

Class (reporters)	0–8	8–16	16–24	24–32	32–40	40–48
Frequency (no. of threats)	10	20	14	16	18	22

Solution: Let us consider the mid-value of (16–24), that is 20, as the assumed mean.

Class	f	Mid-value (X)	Deviation from Assumed Mean, i.e., $d=(X-20)$	$d_1=d/h$, where $h=8$	fd_1
0–8	10	$\frac{0+8}{2}=4$	$4-20=-16$	–2	–20
8–16	20	$\frac{8+16}{2}=12$	$12-20=-8$	–1	–20
16–24	14	$\frac{16+24}{2}=20$	$20-20=0$	0	0
24–32	16	$\frac{24+32}{2}=28$	$28-20=8$	1	16
32–40	18	$\frac{32+40}{2}=36$	$36-20=16$	2	36
40–48	22	$\frac{40+48}{2}=44$	$44-20=24$	3	66
	$N=100$				$\Sigma fd_1=78$

$$\bar{X} = A + \frac{h\Sigma fd_1}{N}$$

$$= 20 + \frac{8\times 78}{100} = 20 + \frac{624}{100}$$

$$= 20 + 6.24 = 26.24.$$

4.3 MEDIAN

Median refers to the middle value in the distribution. When all the observations are arranged in the order of their size, median is the value of the item that has equal number of observations on either side. In other words, median is the central value of the distribution or the value that divides the distribution into two equal parts. Hence, for the computation of median, it is the first condition that items be arranged in ascending or descending order. That is why it is also called the positional average or average of position, as it occupies a definite place in the given set of observations.

J. Wert, C. Neidt and J. Ahmmann (1954) have aptly defined median as "that point in the distribution above which and below which 50 percent of class lie."

4.3.1 Median of Simple Distribution (or Ungrouped or Unclassified Distribution)

Formula:

$$M = \left(\frac{N+1}{2}\right)\text{th term,}$$

where M is the median and N is the number of scores. When N is an odd number, deriving median is an extremely simple process.

Example: Find the median of 5, 8, 6, 11, and 9 of a public relations campaigning by different corporate organizations.

Solution: First, the scores are arranged in an ascending or descending order as follows: 5, 6, 8, 9, 11.

According to the formula,

$$\text{Median} = \left(\frac{N+1}{2}\right)\text{th term.}$$

Here,

$$N=5=5+1/2=6/2=3\text{rd term}$$

$$\therefore\ \text{Median}=8.$$

Thus, the median of public relations campaigning by different corporate organizations is 8.

When the median is an odd number, then also the same formula—$\left(\frac{N+1}{2}\right)$th term—may be applied, but there will be one more step in the calculation as it gives a 0.5 value, for example 2.5; in this step, we will find the mean of the second and third terms.

Example: Find the median of the following number of press conferences organized by different government bodies in a district: 5, 8, 9, 12, 11, 6.

Solution: First, the data is arranged in an ascending or descending order as follows: 5, 6, 8, 9, 11, 12.

According to the formula,

$$\text{Median} = \left(\frac{N+1}{2}\right)\text{th term.}$$

Here,

$$N = 5 = \frac{6+1}{2} = \frac{7}{2} = 3.5\text{th term.}$$

Here, the third term is 8 and the fourth term is 9, so the value of the 3.5th term will be the mean of 8 and 9, that is, $\frac{8+9}{2} = 8.5$

$$\therefore \text{Median} = 8.5.$$

Thus, the median of the press conferences organized by different government bodies in the district is 8.5.

4.3.2 Median of Frequency Distribution

1. Median of *unclassified* frequency distribution.

   First of all, the value of $\frac{N}{2}$ will be derived.

   Here, median will be the value of the variable having $cf \geq \frac{N}{2}$.

   (Note: When $N/2$ is not equal to any cumulative frequency, then cf, which is just greater than $N/2$, is taken.)

Example: Find the median of the following unclassified frequency distribution of marks secured by BA students of mass communication:

Marks (X)	11	12	13	14	15	16	17	18
No. of students	5	7	11	9	8	7	3	5

Solution:

X	f	cf
11	5	5
12	7	12
13	11	23
14 ←	9	32
15	8	40
16	7	47
17	3	50
18	5	55
	$N = 55$	

$$N/2 = 55/2 = 27.5$$

(cf is calculated by just adding previous frequency/frequencies. Like $5+7=12$, $12+11=\underline{23}$, $23+9=\underline{32}$, and so on.)

Here, cf just greater than 27.5 is 32, and the value of the variables corresponding to 32 is 14.

$$\therefore M=14.$$

Thus, the median of marks of BA students of mass communication is 14.

2. Median of the *classified* frequency distribution.
   Formula:

$$M = l + \left(\frac{\frac{N}{2} - cf_b}{f_m} \right) \times h,$$

where

l = lower limit of median class
(if total frequency is N, then class with $cf \geq N$ is called median class)
cf_b = cumulative frequency just below median class
f_m = frequency of median class
h = height of the class.

It is important to mention here that the lower limit of the median class is the same as that in the overlapping or continuous class, but 0.5 less in the nonoverlapping or discrete class.

(Note: Instead of length of the class, height of the class is preferred because it is always the same whether the class is overlapping [continuous] or nonoverlapping [discrete]. In height, we have to just subtract the lower limit of any class from the lower limit of the nearest higher class. Or we have to just subtract the higher limit of any class from the higher limit of the nearest higher class. In the case of use of height, unlike that of length, there is no need to add +1 in the nonoverlapping [discrete] class.)

Example 1: Find the median of the following class distribution of number of investigative stories covered by journalists of different age groups:

Age group of journalists	30–40	40–50	50–60	60–70	70–80
No. of investigative stories	50	54	85	45	30

Solution:

Class	Frequency	cf
30–40	50	50
40–50	54	104
50 – 60	85	189
60–70	45	234
70–80	30	264
	$N = 264$	

$$h = 50 - 40 = 10$$

$$\therefore \frac{N}{2} = \frac{264}{2} = 132.$$

Here, cf=189 is just greater than $N/2$, that is, 132. Hence, the corresponding class, that is, (50–60) is the median class and 104 is cf_b, that is, cumulative frequency just below the median class. Further, h is 70–60=10, 60–50=10, 50–40=10, or 40–30=10, that is, subtraction of the lower limit of any class from the lower limit of the nearest higher class as shown above in the class column.

As per the formula,

$$M = l + \left(\frac{\frac{N}{2} - cf_b}{f_m} \right) \times h$$

$$= 50 + \left(\frac{132 - 104}{85} \right) \times 10 = 50 + \left(\frac{280}{85} \right)$$

$$= 53.29.$$

Thus, the median of the number of investigative stories covered by journalists of the said age group is 53.

Example 2: Find the median of following classified distribution of scores obtained by the students of web media.

Scores	65–69	60–64	55–59	50–54	45–49	40–44	35–39	30–34	25–29	20–24
No. of web media students	1	3	6	8	10	7	7	5	2	1

Solution:

Scores	Frequency	cf
20–24	1	1
25–29	2	3
30–34	5	8
35–39	7	15
40–44	7	22
45 – 49	10 ←	32
50–54	8	40
55–59	6	46
60–64	3	49
65–69	1	50
	$\Sigma f = N = 50 \quad \therefore \frac{N}{2} = \frac{50}{2} = 25$	

Here, *cf*=32 is just greater than *N*/2, that is, 25. Hence, the corresponding class, that is, (45–49) is the median class and 22 is Cf_b, that is, cumulative frequency just below the median class. Further, *h* is 25−20=5, that is, subtraction of the lower limit of any class from the lower limit of the nearest higher class as shown above in the class column. Since class is nonoverlapping, the lower limit of the median class (45–49) is 44.5. It is important to mention here that the lower limit in a nonoverlapping class is always 0.5 less than the one given in the distribution.

$$\text{Now, } M = l + \left(\frac{\frac{N}{2} - cf_b}{f_m} \right) \times h$$

$$= 44.5 + \left(\frac{25 - 22}{10} \right) \times 5 = 44.5 + \frac{15}{10}$$

$$= 44.5 + 1.5 = 46.$$

Hence, the median of distribution of scores obtained by web media students is 46.

Example 3: Find the median of the following distribution.

Marks Obtained	No. of Students of BMC Distance Education
Less than 10	25
Less than 20	40
Less than 30	60
Less than 40	75
Less than 50	95
Less than 60	125
Less than 70	190
Less than 80	240

Solution: First of all, the frequency table will be prepared in the following manner.

Class	Cumulative Frequency	Frequency
0–10	25	25
10–20	40	40−25=15
20–30	60	60−40=20
30–40	75	75−60=15
40–50	95	95−75=20
50 − 60 ←	125	→ 125−95=30
60–70	190	190−125=65
70–80	240	240−190=50
		N=240

Here, *cf* 125 is just greater than $N/2$, that is, 120. Hence, the corresponding class, that is, cumulative frequency is just below the median class. Further, *h* is 10–0=10, that is, subtraction of the lower limit of any class from the lower limit of the nearest higher class as shown above in the class column.

$$\text{Now, } M = l + \left(\frac{\frac{N}{2} - cf_b}{f_m} \right) \times h$$

$$= 50 + \left(\frac{120 - 95}{30} \right) \times 10$$

$$= 50 + \frac{25}{3} = 50 + 8.33$$

$$= 58.33.$$

4.4 MODE

Mode is the score of the highest frequency. It refers to that point in the distribution which occurs most frequently. According to J.P. Guilford and B. Fructer (cited in Singh 1986), "The mode is defined as the point on the scale of measurement with maximum frequency in a distribution."

Croxton and Cowden (cited in Gupta 2011) define it as "The mode of a distribution is the value at the point around which the items tend to be most heavily concentrated. It may be regarded as the most typical of a series of values."

4.4.1 Mode of a Simple Distribution

It is the value in a series of observations which has the highest, greatest, or maximum frequency.

Example: Find the value of mode in the following data—3, 5, 6, 6, 7, 6, 8.

Solution: In this simple distribution of data, mode is "6" as it has the highest frequency "3".

4.4.2 Mode of Frequency Distribution

1. Mode of unclassified frequency distribution: Here, again it is the value of the highest frequency.

   Example: Find the mode of the following unclassified frequency distribution of scores secured by BA students of mass communication.

Scores (X)	11	12	13	14	15	16	17	18
No. of students	5	7	11	9	8	7	3	5

   Solution: Here mode is "13" as it has the highest frequency, that is, 11.

2. Mode of classified frequency distribution: Mode of a classified data is normally the mid-point of the class interval of the highest frequency. But for more accuracy and precision, the following formula is used:

$$M_0 = l + \left(\frac{f_a}{f_a + f_b}\right) \times h,$$

where M_0 is mode,

l is the lower limit of the modal class (class of highest frequency). It is the same in overlapping or continuous class and 0.5 less in nonoverlapping or discreet class,

f_a is the frequency of the pre-modal class,

f_b is the frequency of the post-modal class, and

h is the height of the class (height is the subtraction of the lower limit of any class from the lower limit of the nearest higher class).

Example 1: Find the mode of the scores obtained by the students of web media:

Scores (*X*)	65–69	60–64	55–59	50–54	45–49	40–44	35–39	30–34	25–29	20–24
No. of web media students (*f*)	1	3	6	8	10	7	7	5	2	1

Solution:

Class (*X*)	f
20–24	1
25–29	2
30–34	5
35–39	7
40–44	7
45 – 49	10
50–54	8
55–59	6
60–64	3
65–69	1

Modal class is the class of the highest frequency which is (45–49). So, mode should be the mid-point of (45–49), that is, $\frac{45+49}{2} = 47$.

Hence, the crude mode = 47.

But for more accuracy and precision,

$$M_0 = l + \left(\frac{f_a}{f_a + f_b}\right) \times h$$

$$= 44.5 + \left(\frac{7}{7+8}\right) \times 5 = 44.5 + \left(\frac{7}{15}\right) \times 5$$

$$= 44.5 + \frac{7}{3} = 44.5 + 2.33 = 46.83.$$

where

l = lower limit of modal class = 44.5
f_a = frequency pre-modal class = 7
f_b = frequency of post-modal class = 8
h = height of the class = 25 − 20 = 5

Example 2: Find the mode of the following distribution of journalists' success rate.

Class (no. of journalists)	6–10	11–15	16–20	21–25	26–30
Success rate (f)	20%	30%	50%	40%	10%

Solution: Since 50 is the highest frequency, the modal class is (16–20) and, hence,

$$\text{crude mode} = \frac{16+20}{2} = 18.$$

But for more accuracy and precision,
(the lower limit in an nonoverlapping class is always 0.5 less than the one given in the distribution)

$$M_0 = l + \left(\frac{f_a}{f_a + f_b}\right) \times h$$

$$= 15.5 + \left(\frac{30}{30+40}\right) \times 5$$

$$= 15.5 + \frac{30 \times 5}{70} = 15.5 + \frac{15}{7}$$

$$= 15.5 + 2.14 = 17.16.$$

Thus, the mode of journalists' success rate is 17.64 percent.

4.4.3 Bi-modal Values

When there are two values of mode, then it is called bi-modal values. There are two types of bi-modal situations:

1. Bi-modal value in unclassified frequency distribution
   Single value of mode is derived in bi-modal situations by the grouping method.

   Example: Find the single value of mode in the following distribution of number of awards won by the media persons.

No. of media persons (X)	5	6	7	8	9	10	11
No. of awards (f)	2	5	3	7	5	7	4

Solution: There are two modes, 8 and 10, as they have the highest frequency 7. If mode is determined by the method of grouping, the following table is prepared:

	Frequency of Groups					
	One-One	Two-Two		Three-Three		
Variable	I	II (1+2)	III (2+3)	IV (1+2+3)	V (2+3+4)	VI (3+4+5)
5	2	7		10		
6	5	(i.e., 2+5)	8		15	
7	3	10	(i.e., 5+3)	(i.e., 2+5+3)	(i.e., 5+3+7)	
8	7	(i.e., 3+7)	12			15
9	5	12	(i.e., 7+5)	19	16	(i.e., 3+7+5)
10	7	(i.e., 5+7)	11		(i.e., 5+7+4)	
11	4		(i.e., 7+4)	(i.e., 7+5+7)		

Working Rule:

In Group I, we write the frequencies of all the terms.
In Group II, we collect frequencies two by two from the beginning.
In Group III, we collect the succeeding frequencies two by two leaving the first frequency.
In Group IV, we collect the frequencies three by three taking the first frequency.
In Group V, we collect the frequencies three by three leaving the first frequency.
In Group VI, we collect the frequencies three by three leaving the first two frequencies.

Now, we take note of the maximum frequency in each column and its size. For example, in column II, the largest frequency is 12 and its size is 9 and 10. Similarly, the other columns are also observed. After that an *analysis table* is prepared. Since in column I the size of the largest frequency 7 is 8 and 10, we put a √ mark below 8 and 10 in line with I. Similarly, since in column II, the size of the largest frequency 12 is 9 and 10, we put a √ mark in the column for 9 and 10 in line with III and accordingly for the rest. After that, we count all these √ marks. The size whose column has the maximum number of marks is the mode.

ANALYSIS TABLE

	Variable Having Highest Frequency						
Group	5	6	7	8	9	10	11
I				✓		✓	
II					✓	✓	
III				✓	✓		
IV				✓	✓	✓	
V					✓	✓	✓
VI			✓	✓	✓		
			1	4	5	4	1

Accordingly, the size 9 has the maximum number of marks. So the term 9 has the highest frequency. Hence mode is 9. Thus, the mode of number of awards received by the media persons is 9.

2. Bi-modal in classified frequency distribution

Example: Find the mode of the following distribution of advertisers preparing ad campaign per year.

Class	0–10	10–20	20–30	30–40	40–50	50–60	60–70
Frequency	8	14	25	18	25	10	5

Solution: Here, there are two classes with the highest frequency 25. In this case too we find the modal class by the grouping method and then determine the mode by interpolation.

	Frequency of Groups					
	One-One	Two-Two		Three-Three		
Variable	**I**	**II(1+2)**	**III(2+3)**	**IV(1+2+3)**	**V(2+3+4)**	**VI(3+4+5)**
0–10	8	22				
10–20	14	(i.e., 8+14)	39	47	57	68
20–30	25	43	(i.e., 14+25)	(i.e., 8+14+25)	(i.e., 14+25+18)	(i.e., 25+18+25)
30–40	18	(i.e., 25+18)	43			
40–50	25	35	(i.e., 18+25)	53	40	
50–60	10	(i.e., 25+10)	15	(i.e., 18+25+10)	(i.e., 25+10+5)	
60–70	5		(i.e., 10+5)			

Now, according to the working rule, in Group I, we wrote the frequencies of all the terms. In Group II, we collected frequencies two by two from the beginning. In Group III, we collected the succeeding frequencies two by two. In Group IV, we collected the frequencies three by three taking the first frequency.

In Group V, we collected the frequencies three by three leaving the first two frequencies. In Group VI, we collected the frequencies three by three leaving the first two frequencies.

Thus, when the above table is prepared, we take note of the maximum frequency in each column and its class. For example, in column II, the highest frequency is 43 and its class is (20–30) and (30–40). Similar is the approach for other columns. Then we prepare for the table given ahead called the analysis table. Since in column I, the class of the highest frequency 25 is (20–30) and (40–50), we put a √ mark below (20–30) and (40–50) in line with I.

Again, since in column II, the class of the highest frequency 43 is (20–30) and (30–40), we put a √ mark below (20–30) and (30–40) in line with II, and similarly for the rest. Next, we count these marks. The class whose column has the highest number of marks is the modal class.

Group	Variable Having Highest Frequency						
	0–10	10–20	20–30	30–40	40–50	50–60	60–70
I			✓		✓		
II			✓	✓			
III				✓	✓	✓	
IV				✓	✓		
V		✓	✓	✓			
VI			✓	✓	✓		
		1	4	5	4	1	

Thus, the frequency of class (30–40) is the highest. Hence, (30–40) is the modal class.

$$
\begin{aligned}
M_0 &= l + \left(\frac{f_a}{f_a + f_b}\right) \times h \\
&= 30 + \left(\frac{25}{25 + 25}\right) \times 10 \\
&= 30 + \left(\frac{1}{2}\right) \times 10 \\
&= 30 + 5 = 35.
\end{aligned}
$$

Thus, the mode of the distribution of advertisers preparing an ad campaign per year is 35.

Hence, when choosing a measure of central tendency in media research out of the mean, media, and mode, mean is the most widely and largely used descriptive statistics in communication studies and media research or descriptive media metrics. This is mainly because so many statistical methods relating to media are based on means. So if we use something other than mean, we would need a lot of extra knowledge on the application of inferential statistics of mass communication or inferential media metrics.

SUMMARY

Measures of central tendency in media research, which are described as statistical averages, get a single value of largely and widely scattered data of mass media that describes the characteristics of the entire data. There are three types of averages—mean, median and mode. In media research when we talk of mean, we generally mean arithmetic mean. Median is the average of position, which refers to the middle value in the distribution. Hence, median is the central value in the distribution or the value that divides the distribution into two equal parts. Mode is the score of the highest frequency. When choosing a measure of central tendency in media research out of the mean, media, and mode, mean is the most widely and largely used descriptive statistics in media research or descriptive media metrics because so many statistical methods relating to media are based on means. So if we use something other than mean, we would need a lot of extra knowledge on the application of inferential statistics of mass communication or inferential media metrics.

After thorough discussion on measures of central tendency in media research, it will be desirable to discuss the measures of dispersion in media studies for even better understanding of the descriptive statistics in media metrics (or descriptive media metrics) in the next chapter.

IMPORTANT FORMULAE

1. Mean of Simple Distribution:

$$\bar{X} = \frac{\Sigma X}{N},$$

where $\bar{X}$ = mean,
X = scores,
N = no. of scores.
Hence, mean, that is X bar, is called sigma or summation X divided by N.

2. Mean of Frequency Distribution (Unclassified and Classified):

$$\bar{X} = \frac{\Sigma fX}{N},$$

where f is frequency
$N = \Sigma f$. Hence mean, that is, X bar is called summation $= \Sigma fX$ divided by N.

3. Shortcut Method:
   a. Simple distribution:

$$\bar{X} = A + \frac{\Sigma d}{N},$$

   where A = assumed mean,
   d = deviation from mean, that is, $(X - \bar{X})$

   b. Frequency distribution (unclassified and classified):

$$\bar{X} = A + \frac{\Sigma fd}{N}$$

4. Step-deviation Method (Classified Only):

$$\bar{X} = A + \frac{h\Sigma fd_1}{N},$$

where h = height of class

$$d_1 = \frac{d}{h}.$$

5. Median in Simple Distribution: $\left(\frac{N+1}{2}\right)$th term (easy when N is odd)
   $\left(\frac{N+1}{2}\right)$th term (more steps when N is even as it gives 0.5 value, like 2.5. Then, we will find the mean of the second and third terms)
6. Median in Unclassified Frequency Distribution:
   Here, median will be the value of variable having $cf \geq N/2$
7. Median in Classified Frequency Distribution:

$$M = l + \left(\frac{\frac{N}{2} - cf_b}{f_m}\right) \times h \quad \left(\begin{array}{c} \text{If total frequency be } N \text{, then the class whose} \\ cf \geq \frac{N}{2} \text{ is called the median class} \\ l = \text{lower limit of the median class} \\ \text{(Note: } l \text{ is 0.5 less in case of nonoverlapping)} \\ cf_b = \text{cumulative frequency below the median class} \\ f_m = \text{frequency of the median class} \\ h = \text{Height of the median class} \end{array}\right)$$

8. Mode in Simple Distribution or Unclassified Frequency Distribution:

$$M_0 = \text{variable having the highest frequency}$$

9. Mode in Classified Frequency Distribution:

$$M_o = l + \left(\frac{f_a}{f_a + f_b}\right) \times h \quad \left(\begin{array}{c} \text{The class of highest frequency is the modal class} \\ l = \text{lower limit of the modal class} \\ \text{(Note: } l \text{ is 0.5 less in case if the nonoverlapping class)} \\ f_a = \text{frequency of the pre-modal class} \\ f_b = \text{frequency of the post-modal class} \\ h = \text{height of the modal class} \end{array}\right)$$

10. Mode with the help of Median and Mean:

$$M_0 = 3\text{Median} - 2\text{Mean}$$

RELATED AND SUGGESTED WEBSITES

(As retrieved on December 1, 2015)

1. http://www.abs.gov.au/websitedbs/a3121120.nsf/home/statistical+language+-+measures+of+central+tendency
2. http://people.wku.edu/john.musalia/soc300/Chapter4.ppt

3. https://home.ubalt.edu/tmitch/631/PowerPoint_Lectures/chapter3/chapter3.ppt
4. http://www.authorstream.com/Presentation/aSGuest42880-372381-measures-central-tendency-education-ppt-powerpoint/
5. http://www4.uwsp.edu/psych/stat/5/ct-var.htm

REFERENCES

Gupta, S.P. 2011. *Statistical Methods*, 177–288. New Delhi: Sultan Chand & Sons.

Singh, Arun Kumar. 1986. *Basic Statistics in Psychology and Education*, 22–57. Patna: Novelty & Co.

Wert, J., C. Neidt and J. Ahmmann. 1954. *Statistical Methods in Educational and Psychological Research*, 55.

RELATED AND RECOMMENDED READINGS

Elhance, D.N., and Veena Elhance. 1990. *Fundamentals of Statistics*, 8.1–8.134. New Delhi: Kitab Mahal.

Gupta, Ashit Das, and S.N. Thakur. 1998. *Modern Approach to Intermediate Statistics and Probability*, 14–101. Patna: Bharti Bhawan.

Gupta, S.P, and Alka Gupta. 2008. *Statistical Method in Behavioral Sciences*, 62–86. Allahabad: Sharda Pustak Bhawan.

Husain, Shamshad. 1986. *Elementary Statistics in Psychology & Statistics*, 24–38. New Delhi: Motilal Banarasi Das.

Kerlinger, F.N. 1983. *Foundations of Behavioural Research*. New Delhi: Surjeet Publications.

Kothari, C.R. 2000. *Research Methodologies: Methods and Techniques*. New Delhi: Wishwa Prakashan.

Krishnaswami, O.R., and M. Ranganatham. 2005. *Methodology of Research*. New Delhi: Himalaya Publications.

Mangal, S.K. 1987. *Statistics in Psychology and Education*. New Delhi: McGraw Hill.

Sarangi, Prasant. 2010. *Research Methodology*. Delhi: Taxman Publication.

Wilkinson, T.S., and P.L. Bhandarkar. 1996. *Methodologies and Techniques of Social Research*. Mumbai: Himalaya Publishing House.

Wimmer, Roger D., and Joseph R. Dominick. 2003. *Mass Media Research: An Introduction*, 247–49. 7th ed. Belmont, CA: Thomson & Wadsworth.

QUESTIONS AND PROBLEMS

1. What do you mean by measures of central tendency? Throw light on it from the view-point of calculating them.
2. Write the formulae for calculating arithmetic mean.
3. Write the formulae for calculating median.
4. Write the formulae for calculating mode.
5. Find the arithmetic mean of the following scores secured by the students of bachelors of mass communication in reporting: 50, 40, 30, 45, 25, 42, 44, 38, 48, and 36.
6. Ten working journalists of a regional daily have the following monthly income in rupees: 14780, 15760, 26690, 27750, 24840, 24920, 16100, 17810, 27050, 26950. Find out the arithmetic mean of their income.

7. Fifty students of master of mass communication secured the following marks in the paper of editing. Find their mean, median, and mode:
32, 30, 45, 75, 35, 33, 51, 61, 44, 33, 45, 48, 56, 71, 70, 73, 80, 34, 46, 44, 48, 33, 31, 46, 61, 63, 64, 68, 69, 76, 77, 79, 71, 75, 55, 56, 34, 36, 38, 40, 32, 49, 51, 58, 55, 31, 62, 66, 45, 62.
8. Following are the monthly incomes in rupees of 12 journalist families. Calculate their arithmetic mean: 28000, 18000, 9600, 10400, 7500, 8000, 9400, 10000, 7500, 9800, 60000, 20000.
9. Calculate the arithmetic mean of the following frequency distribution by long method, shortcut method, and step-deviation method:

Class	65–69	60–64	55–59	50–54	45–49	40–44	35–39	30–34	25–29	20–24
Frequency	1	3	6	8	10	7	7	5	2	1

10. Calculate the arithmetic mean of the following frequency distribution by long method, shortcut method, and step-deviation method:

Class	11–13	13–15	15–17	17–19	19–21	21–23	23–25
Frequency	3	4	5	6	5	4	3

11. Calculate the arithmetic mean of the following frequency distribution by the long method, shortcut method, and step-deviation method:

Class	0–9	10–19	20–29	30–39	40–49	50–59	60–69	70–79
Frequency	15	20	25	24	12	31	71	52

12. In the following frequency distribution, find the unknown frequency if the arithmetic mean of the distribution is 67.45:

Class	60–62	63–65	66–68	69–71	72–74
Frequency	15	54	–	81	24

13. A student secures 36, 50, 82, 36, 62, and 65 marks in six papers of mass communication. Find the arithmetic mean of his marks by shortcut method.
14. Find the arithmetic mean of the following frequency distribution by long method, shortcut method, and step-deviation method:

Class	0–8	8–16	16–24	24–32	32–40	40–48
Frequency	10	20	14	16	18	22

15. Find the arithmetic mean of the following frequency distribution by long method, shortcut method, and step-deviation:

Class	18–22	23–27	28–32	33–37	38–42	43–47	48–52	53–57
Frequency	14	28	33	30	20	15	13	7

16. Find the arithmetic mean of the following frequency distribution of the marks obtained by the students of mass communication by long method, short method, and step-deviation method:

Marks obtained	Below 10	Below 20	Below 30	Below 40	Below 50	Below 60	Below 70	Below 80
No. of students	30	40	60	75	95	125	190	240

17. The marks obtained by 10 students of journalism are as follows. Find their arithmetic mean:

Roll no.	1	2	3	4	5	6	7	8	9	10
Marks	15	20	25	30	35	40	45	50	55	60

18. Find the arithmetic mean of the following frequency distribution by long method, shortcut method, and step-deviation method:

Class	140–150	150–160	160–170	170–180	180–190	190–200
Frequency	5	10	20	9	6	2

19. Find the arithmetic mean of the following data:

Variable	1	2	3	4	5
Frequency	2	9	9	7	3

20. Find the arithmetic mean of the following data:

Class	10–20	20–30	30–40	40–50	50–60	60–70
Frequency	5	18	24	32	38	40

21. Find the missing frequency in the following frequency table if the mean is 22.5:

Class	0–10	10–20	20–30	30–40	40–50
Frequency	2	4	3	–	2

if the mean is 22.5.

22. Find the unknown frequencies in the following table if the arithmetic mean is 10.8:

Class	0–4	4–8	8–12	12–16	16–20	Total
Frequency	3	–	–	8	2	20

23. Find the arithmetic mean of the following frequency distribution by step deviation method:

Class	0–2	3–5	6–8	9–11	12–14	15–17	18–20
Frequency	1	4	0	4	6	5	4

24. Find the mean, median, and mode of the following frequency distribution:

Class	57–59	54–56	51–53	48–50	45–47	42–44	39–41	36–38	33–35	30–32	27–29	24–26	21–23
Frequency	4	6	8	3	20	28	30	17	9	5	8	8	4

25. Find out the mean and median of the following data:
    (a) 30, 40, 10, 15, 16, 18, 30
    (b) 6, 5, 10, 8, 12, 14, 16, 20, 19
    (c) 40, 10, 8, 12, 14, 16, 20, 19
    (d) 30, 17, 15, 16, 18, 16, 19
    (e) 2.5, 3.8, 3.1, 6.2, 6.0, 0.6, 0.9
    (f) 3.7, 8.5, 1.1, 2.9, 6.9, 8.5, 8.6, 8.7
26. Why the mean cannot be calculated from the given data? Find the median and mode from the following distribution:

Class	100 and above	90–99	80–89	70–79	60–69	50–59	40–49	30–39	20–29	10–19
Frequency	9	1	6	3	6	10	16	2	3	4

27. Find mean, median, and mode from the following frequency distribution:
    (a)

Score	95	94	93	92	91	90	89	88
Frequency	2	0	1	3	10	2	1	1

(b)

Score	70	69	68	67	66	65	64	63	62	61	60	59	58
Frequency	1	0	1	3	6	8	8	2	3	0	1	0	2

28. Find mean, median, and mode from the following data:

Score	130–139	120–129	110–119	100–109	90–99	80–89	70–79	60–69	50–59	40–49	30–39
Frequency	2	0	3	0	4	7	20	18	2	3	1

29. Find the mean and median from the following ungrouped data:
    (a) 10, 6, 8, 20, 24, 27, 6
    (b) 1.2, 3.9, 0.9, 6.8, 5.2, 3.2, 4.1
    (c) 6.8, 4.3, 6.2, 4.3, 8.8, 9.1, 9.9
    (d) 6, 8, 12, 16, 12, 10, 20
    (e) 120, 130, 121, 140, 116, 110, 109, 109
    (f) 6, 8, 4, 3, 6, 8, 10, 20
30. Find mean, median, and mode from the following distribution:

Score	140–144	135–139	130–134	125–129	120–124	115–119	110–114	105–109	100–104	95–99	90–94
Frequency	2	0	4	0	8	40	6	7	0	2	1

31. Find the crude mode and true mode from the given frequency distribution:

Score	60 and above	50–59	50–54	45–49	40–44	35–39	30–34	25–29	20–24	15–19
Frequency	4	3	8	6	12	2	2	1	1	1

32. What type of mode calculation from the given data will be appropriate—crude or true? Find mean and median from following distribution.

Score	80–84	75–79	70–74	65–69	60–64	55–59	50–54	45–49	40–44	35–39	30–34
Frequency	1	2	6	3	5	12	10	12	3	4	6

33. Find the mean IQ for the eight media students whose individual IQ scores are as below: 80, 100, 105, 90, 112, 115, 110, 120.
34. Find the mean, median, and mode of the given distribution by long method:

Class	58–59	56–57	54–55	52–53	50–51	48–49	46–47	44–45	42–43	40–41
Frequency	3	3	2	4	7	9	5	4	3	2

35. Find the mean, median, and mode of the given data by step-deviation method:

Class	90–99	80–89	70–79	60–69	50–59	40–49	30–39	20–29	10–19	0–9
Frequency	4	8	12	12	15	40	22	13	10	6

36. Calculate the mean, median, and mode of the given data by step-deviation method:

Class	86–88	83–85	80–82	77–79	74–76	71–73	68–70	65–67	62–64	59–61	56–58	53–55	50–52
Frequency	3	4	4	5	5	5	20	15	10	8	6	3	2

37. Find the mean, median, and mode of the given distribution by long method:

Scores	85–89	80–84	75–79	70–74	65–69	60–64	55–59	50–54	45–49	40–44	35–39	30–34
Frequency	4	8	12	12	12	10	14	15	10	9	8	4

38. Find the mean, median, and mode of the following data by shortcut method:

Class	110–119	100–109	90–99	80–89	70–79	60–69	50–59	40–49	30–39	20–29	10–19
Frequency	2	4	3	2	6	16	10	5	5	4	3

39. Calculate the mean, median, and mode of the given data by step-deviation method:

Class	75–79	70–74	65–69	60–64	55–59	50–54	45–49	40–44	35–39	30–34	25–29	20–24
Frequency	4	3	2	5	8	11	16	10	8	5	4	4

40. Find the mean, median, and mode of the following distribution by long method:

Class	65–69	60–64	55–54	50–54	45–49	40–44	35–39	30–34	25–29	20–24	15–19	10–14	5–9
Frequency	4	8	10	15	12	12	30	24	14	12	8	6	5

41. In the situations described below, what measures of central tendency would you like to compute?
(a) The average achievement of a group,
(b) The most popular fashion of the day,
(c) Determining the mid-point of the scores of a group in an entrance examination.
42. Find the mode of the following data:

Class	0–10	10–20	20–30	30–40	40–50	50–60	60–70
Frequency	8	14	25	18	25	10	5

5

CHAPTER

Measures of Dispersion in Media Studies

When the head of a person is in freezer, foot in oven and stomach in cold water jacket, this will give an average temperature of that body. However there is dispersion in every sensing point in the body.

—Author

In mathematics, statistics, or media metrics, the word *dispersion* is often described as *variation*, *scatter*, or *spread*. It indicates the degree or extent of the available *stretched* or *squeezed* data. Measures of dispersion in media studies or media metrics are generally the mean deviation, coefficient of mean deviation, standard deviation, variance, range, semi-range, or interquartile range in the field of print media, electronic media, advertising, corporate communication and public relations, web media, development communication and social marketing, social media, and various other media. Thus, measures of dispersion in media metrics usually measure as to how spread out a set of media or communication data is.

In the previous chapter, we started discussing on statistical tools of media metrics called the measures of central tendency such as mean (including the means of simple distribution, frequency distribution, shortcut method, and step-deviation method), median (including the medians of simple distribution and frequency distribution), mode (including the mode of simple distribution, frequency distribution, and bi-modal values), and important formulae. It included a few general questions, illustrations, and solutions of basics of statistics in the beginning, but gradually focused more on media metrics. After the systematic discussion on the measures of central tendency, it is desirable to discuss the measures of dispersion for a better understanding of descriptive statistics in media metrics.

This chapter is focused on a statistical tool of media metrics called measures of dispersion (as shown in the flowchart in Section 2.2.1 of Chapter 2). In this chapter, we will discuss the following:

1. Meaning and concept of measures of dispersion in media studies
2. Methods of dispersion
3. Mean deviation
4. Meaning and concept of standard deviation
5. Variance
6. Range, interquartile range, and quartile deviation
7. Important formulae

This chapter will also cover the summary, related and suggested websites, references, related and recommended readings, questions and problems of measures of dispersion with general reference to statistics and special reference to media metrics relating to the problems of communication and media studies, and their solutions.

5.1 MEANING AND CONCEPT OF MEASURES OF DISPERSION IN MEDIA STUDIES

Measures of central tendency give a single value of lengthy and widely scattered data. But the average cannot adequately describe a set of observations unless all the observations are the same. In two or more distributions, the central value may be the same; yet, there may be huge disparities in the formation of the distribution. Measures of dispersion are instrumental in finding out this important characteristic of a distribution in media studies due to variability and fluctuation in various areas of mass communication. Different experts have defined measures of dispersion differently.

According to Simpson and Kafka (cited in Gupta 2011, 272), "The measurement of the scatteredness of the mass of figures in a series about an average is called measure of variation or dispersion."

A.L. Bowley (cited in D.N.S. Elhance and Veena Elhance 1990, 9.2) defines it as, "Dispersion is the measure of the variation of the items."

Spigel Opines (cited in D.N.S. Elhance and Veena Elhance 1990, 9.2), "The degree to which numerical data tend to spread about an average value is called the variation or the dispersion of the data."

Thus, it is crystal clear that dispersion (also described as scatter, spread, or variation) is the amount of variability in a set of scores, and it measures the extent to which the items vary from some central value. Since measures of dispersion give an average of the differences of various items from one average, they are also called averages of the second order.

For example, let there be two small groups of students of mass communication and advertising; their scores in a production portfolio test are as follows:

Scores of mass communication students	37, 41, 36, 17, 20, 19, 18, 3, 5, 4
Scores of advertising students	18, 21, 22, 18, 21, 23, 17, 20, 22, 18

Mean of mass communication students' scores=37+41+36+17+20+19+18+3+5+4=200/10=20.

Mean of advertising students' scores=18+21+22+18=21+23+17+20+22+18=200/10=20.

The value of mean in both the above situations is 20. Hence, as far as the mean is concerned, there is no difference in the performance of the two groups. Now, a valid question arises: Can we consider both sets of scores identical? No doubt, there are a lot of differences between the performances of the two groups. The scores of students of mass communication are found to range from 3 to 41, whereas the scores of students of advertising range from 18 to 23. The former group is composed of the students who have wide individual differences. It consists of either very intelligent students or very dull students. The latter group, on the other hand, is composed of average students. In this group, the students are less diverse than those in the former. Thus, if we want to describe or compare them, there is a great need of paying attention to the variability or dispersion of scores in the sets of scores or series. Thus, we may conclude that there is a tendency for data to be dispersed, scattered, or to show variability around the average; consequently, the variability or dispersion may also be defined as the tendency of the measures of the attributes of a group to deviate from the average or central value. Variability, thus, refers to the spread of scores from their central tendency.

5.2 METHODS OF DISPERSION

The degree of scattering or dispersion, that is, variability is measured by different methods. Of them, the following are popular:

1. Mean deviation
2. Standard deviation
3. Variance

Other than these, some are as follows:

4. Range
5. Interquartile range and quartile deviation

5.3 MEAN DEVIATION (δ)

Mean deviation of a distribution is the arithmetic mean of absolute deviations of the values of a variable from the measure of their either mean. Mean deviation is also known as average deviation and is generally denoted by AD or MD or δ (delta). It is the average difference between the items in a distribution and the median, mean, or mode of that series. It is the mean of deviations of all the separate scores in the series taken from their mean (occasionally from their median or mode) (Garnett cited in Mangal 1987, 63). It is the simplest measure of variability that takes into account the fluctuation or variation of all the items in a series. Theoretically, there is an advantage of taking deviations from a median merely because the sum of deviations of items from the median is minimum when signs are ignored. But in practice the mean is more frequently used in computing the value of average deviation. This is the reason why it is more commonly called mean deviation. This is also called the first moment dispersion. For mean deviation, we write δ; for mean deviation from a mean, we write $\delta_{\bar{x}}$; for mean deviation from a median, we write δ_M; and for mean deviation from a mode, we write δ_{M_0}.

5.3.1 Mean Deviation of a Simple Distribution or an Unclassified or Ungrouped Distribution

The simple formula for the mean deviation or average deviation is as follows:

$$\delta = \frac{\Sigma |d|}{N},$$

where δ is the mean or average deviation, d is the difference between the scores and their mean value $(|X - \bar{X}|), |d|$ is the mod of d, and N is the number of scores.

Example: Calculate the mean deviation of 12, 9, 8, 7, and 4.

X	$d = (X - \bar{X})$	$\|d\|$
12	12−8=4	4
9	9−8=1	1
8	8−8=0	0
7	7−8=−1	1
4	4−8=−4	4

$$\Sigma X = 40, N = 5,$$

$$\therefore \bar{X} = \frac{\Sigma X}{N} = \frac{40}{5} = 8, \text{ and } \Sigma |d| = 10.$$

$$\therefore \delta = \frac{\Sigma |d|}{N} = \frac{10}{5} = 2.$$

5.3.2 Mean Deviation of a Frequency Distribution

It is also called mean deviation of the grouped data. Such data or distributions are represented in a tabular or graphical form which indicates the frequency (number of times an observation occurs). There are two types of frequency distribution:

1. Unclassified frequency distribution
2. Classified frequency distribution

The mean deviation of a frequency distribution can be calculated as follows:

$$\delta = \frac{\Sigma |fd|}{N},$$

where f is the frequency of scores, $d = X - \bar{X}$, N is the total frequency, and $\bar{X} = \frac{\Sigma fX}{N}$.

Unclassified frequency distribution: Given below is a numerical problem of unclassified frequency distribution which makes the concept crystal clear.

Example: Find the mean deviation of the following data of newspapers' editors writing editorials per week.

No. of editors (X)	2	3	4	5	6	7
No. of editorials per week (f)	5	4	7	6	3	2

Solution:

X	f	fX	$d=(X-\bar{X})$	$\|d\|$	$\|fd\|$
2	5	10	2−4.15=−2.15	2.15	10.75
3	4	12	3−4.15=−1.15	1.15	4.60
4	7	28	4−4.15=−0.15	0.15	1.05
5	6	30	5−4.15=0.085	0.85	5.10
6	3	18	6−4.15=1.85	1.85	5.55
7	2	14	7−4.15=2.85	2.85	5.70
	$N=27$	$\Sigma fX=112$			$\Sigma\|fd\|=32.75$

$$\therefore \bar{X}=\frac{\Sigma fX}{N}=\frac{112}{27}=4.15 \quad \therefore \delta=\frac{\Sigma|fd|}{N}=\frac{32.75}{27}=1.21.$$

Thus, the mean deviation of newspapers' editors writing editorials per week is 1.21.

Classified frequency distribution: In the calculation of classified frequency distribution, a class interval is given and in that case the numerical value of X is the midpoint of the upper limit and the lower limit of the class interval. That is to say that the value of X is the average of the lower limit and the upper limit of the class interval.

5.3.3 Merits and Demerits of Mean Deviation

Merits

1. Simplicity in computation: The formula for computing mean deviation is simple. Hence, it is very useful for communication issues and media analysis.
2. Freedom of choice of mean: Mean deviation can be computed from any of the averages like mean, median, or mode. Thus, it is highly applicable in media research.
3. Importance of every term: The value of mean deviation is dependent on each and every term. Hence, it is very relevant in media metrics.
4. Distribution structure: The evaluation of mean deviation gives us an idea about how the terms are situated in the series of distribution. This type of distribution structure is very relevant in media analysis.

Demerits

1. Avoidance of negative sign: Since the formula of mean deviation carries only the absolute value, the negative sign is ignored. It tremendously affects a suitable media analysis.
2. Lack of certainty: Since it is calculated from any of the measures of central tendency, it lacks certainty. That is why it is sometimes avoided in the analysis of media issues. But mean deviation from a median is the least and considered to be the best in macro and micro media analysis.

Thus, mean deviation is highly practically relevant and useful in media research because of its simplicity in computation. It is particularly useful and effective for such group of communication studies which is not aware of statistical methods. Mean deviation is highly useful in media and communication studies for small samples with no elaborate analysis required. It is important to mention that the National Bureau of Economic Research has meticulously observed that the mean deviation is the most practical measure of dispersion, especially in social sciences, including communication studies.

5.3.4 Coefficient of Mean Deviation

It is the ratio of the mean deviation and the central value from which the deviation is measured.

Thus,

1. Coefficient of mean deviation from the mean $= \frac{\delta_{\bar{X}}}{\bar{X}}$
2. Coefficient of mean deviation from the median $= \frac{\delta_M}{M}$
3. Coefficient of mean deviation from the mode $= \frac{\delta_{M_0}}{M_0}$

5.4 MEANING AND CONCEPT OF STANDARD DEVIATION

The concept of standard deviation was first given by Karl Pearson in 1894. It is also called root mean square deviation or second moment dispersion (unlike mean deviation as the first moment dispersion). No doubt, it is the most relevant, important, and useful measure of study of dispersion. It is the most commonly used measure of dispersion in media research. It satisfies most of the properties laid down for an ideal measure of dispersion in communication and media studies. In social sciences, including communication studies, standard deviation is denoted by the small Greek letter σ(sigma). The greater the standard deviation, the greater will be the magnitude of the deviations of the values from their mean. Similarly, a small standard deviation means a high degree of uniformity of the observation as well as homogeneity of a series. Hence, if there are two or more comparable series, then the series with the smallest standard deviation has the most representative mean. Thus, it is largely and widely used in judging the representativeness of the mean.

Standard deviation is quite different from mean deviation. While computing mean deviation, negative signs are avoided. On the other hand, while calculating standard deviation no algebraic sign is ignored. Further, mean deviation can be calculated either from median, mean, or mode, whereas standard deviation is always calculated from the arithmetic mean as the sum of the squares of the deviation of items from the arithmetic mean is the least. Since it is root mean square deviation, it is the square root of the mean of the squared deviation from the arithmetic mean.

5.4.1 Standard Deviation of a Simple Distribution or an Unclassified or Ungrouped Distribution

The formula for standard deviation is as follows:

$$\sigma = \sqrt{\frac{\Sigma d^2}{N}},$$

where

σ = standard deviation

$d = X - \bar{X}$

X = Scores

$\bar{X}$ = mean of scores,

N = no. of scores

Example: Find the standard deviation of the following number of press conferences organized by the Press Information Bureau: 12, 9, 8, 7, and 4.

Solution:

X	$d = (X - \bar{X})$	d^2
12	12−8=4	16
9	9−8=1	1
8	8−8=0	0
7	7−8=−1	1
4	4−8=−4	16
$\Sigma X = 40$		$\Sigma d^2 = 34$

$$\therefore \bar{X} = \frac{\Sigma X}{N} = \frac{40}{5} = 8 \quad \therefore \sigma = \sqrt{\frac{\Sigma d^2}{N}} = \sqrt{\frac{34}{5}} = \sqrt{6.8} = 2.60.$$

Thus, the standard deviation of press conferences organized by the Press Information Bureau is 2.60.

5.4.2 Standard Deviation of a Frequency Distribution

Standard deviation of a frequency distribution is given by

$$\sigma = \sqrt{\frac{\Sigma fd^2}{N}}.$$

1. Unclassified or ungrouped frequency distribution.

   Example: Find the standard deviation of the following frequency distribution of newspaper correspondents filing news stories per month:

No. of correspondents (X)	0	1	2	3	4	5	6	7
No. of stories filed per month (f)	14	21	25	43	51	40	39	12

Solution:

X	f	Xf	$d = (X - \bar{X})$	d^2	fd^2
0	14	0	0−3.76=−3.76	14.14	197.96
1	21	21	1−3.76=−2.76	7.62	160.02
2	25	50	2−3.76=−1.76	3.10	77.50
3	43	129	3−3.76=−0.76	0.58	24.94
4	51	204	4−3.76=0.24	0.06	3.06
5	40	200	5−3.76=1.24	1.54	61.60
6	39	234	6−3.76=2.24	5.02	165.78
7	12	84	7−3.76=3.24	10.50	126.00
	N=245				$\Sigma fd^2 = 846.86$

$$\therefore X = \frac{\Sigma fX}{N} = \frac{922}{245} = 3.76 \quad \therefore \sigma = \sqrt{\frac{\Sigma fd^2}{N}} = \sqrt{\frac{846.86}{245}} = \sqrt{3.456} = 1.86.$$

Thus, standard deviation of the above-mentioned frequency distribution of newspaper correspondents filing news stories per month is 1.86.

2. Classified frequency distribution.

Example: Find the standard deviation of the following data of subeditors of different age groups making the page per day:

Age of subeditors (class)	45–49	40–44	35–39	30–34	25–29	20–24	15–19	10–14
No. of page make up per day (frequency)	1	2	2	6	5	2	1	1

Solution:

Class	f	Mid-value(X)	fX	$d = (X - \bar{X})$	d^2	fd^2
45–49	1	47	47	47−30.25=16.75	280.56	280.56
40–44	2	42	84	42−30.25=11.75	138.06	276.12
35–39	2	37	74	37−30.25=6.75	45.56	91.12
30–34	6	32	192	32−30.25=1.75	3.06	18.36
25–29	5	27	135	27−30.25=−3.25	10.56	52.80
20–24	2	22	44	22−30.25=−8.25	68.06	136.12
15–19	1	17	17	17−30.25=−13.25	175.56	175.56
10–14	1	12	12	12−30.25=−18.25	333.06	333.06
	N=20		$\sum fX = 605$			$\sum fd^2 = 1363.7$

$$\therefore \bar{X} = \frac{\Sigma fX}{N} = \frac{605}{20} = 30.25 \quad \therefore \sigma = \sqrt{\frac{\Sigma fd^2}{N}} = \sqrt{\frac{1363.7}{20}} = \sqrt{68.185}$$
$$= 8.25$$

Thus, the standard deviation of the above-mentioned data of subeditors of different age groups making the page per day is 8.25.

5.4.3 Standard Deviation by the Shortcut Method (or Assumed Mean Method)

1. In the case of the simple distribution,

$$\sigma = \sqrt{\frac{\Sigma d^2}{N} - \left(\frac{\Sigma d}{N}\right)^2}.$$

Example: Calculate the standard deviation of the following marks obtained by media students in a minor test: 10, 14, 7, 9, 5, 5, 4, 2

Solution:

X	$d=(X-A)$	d^2
10	10−7=3	9
14	14−7=7	49
7	7−7=0	0
9	9−7=2	4
5	5−7=−2	4
5	5−7=−2	4
4	4−7=−3	9
2	2−7=−5	25
N=8	$\Sigma d = 0$	$\Sigma d^2 = 104$

Let the assumed mean A be 7.

$$\therefore \sigma = \sqrt{\frac{\Sigma d^2}{N} - \left(\frac{\Sigma d}{N}\right)^2}$$
$$= \sqrt{\frac{104}{8} - \left(\frac{0}{8}\right)^2}$$
$$= \sqrt{\frac{104}{8}}$$
$$= \sqrt{13}$$
$$= 3.605.$$

2. In the case of the frequency distribution,

$$\therefore \sigma = \sqrt{\frac{\Sigma fd^2}{N} - \left(\frac{\Sigma fd}{N}\right)^2},$$

where

d = deviation from the assumed mean = $X - A$.

Example 1: Calculate the standard deviation of the following data of photo journalists of a news magazine clicking pictures per day.

No. of photo journalists (*X*)	2	4	6	7	8	9
No. of pictures clicked per day (*f*)	3	2	5	3	2	1

Solution:

X	f	$d=(X-A)$	d^2	fd	fd^2
2	3	2−7=−5	25	−15	75
4	2	4−7=−3	9	−6	18
6	5	6−7=−1	1	−5	5
7	3	7−7=0	0	0	0
8	2	8−7=1	1	2	2
9	1	9−7=2	4	2	4
	$N=16$			$\Sigma fd = -22$	$\Sigma fd^2 = 104$

Let the assumed mean A be 7.

$$\therefore \sigma = \sqrt{\frac{\Sigma fd^2}{N} - \left(\frac{\Sigma fd}{N}\right)^2}$$

$$= \sqrt{\frac{104}{16} - \left(\frac{-22}{16}\right)^2}$$

$$= \sqrt{6.5 - 1.89}$$

$$= \sqrt{4.61}$$

$$= 2.15$$

Thus, the standard deviation of the above-mentioned data of the photo journalists of a news magazine clicking pictures per day is 2.15.

Example 2: Calculate the standard deviation of the following distribution of the number of readers of a newspaper disliking the stories per day:

No. of readers (class)	0–4	5–9	10–14	15–19	20–24
Dislike of stories per day (frequency)	2	5	7	13	21

Solution:

Class	f	Mid-value (X)	$d=(X-A)$	d^2	fd	fd^2
0–4	2	2	2−12=−10	100	−20	200
5–9	5	7	7−12=−5	25	−25	125
10–14	7	12	12−12=0	0	0	0
15–19	13	17	17−12=5	25	65	325
20–24	21	22	22−12=10	100	210	2100
	$N=48$				$\Sigma fd = 230$	$\Sigma fd^2 = 2750$

Let the assumed mean A be 12.

$$\therefore \sigma = \sqrt{\frac{\Sigma fd^2}{N} - \left(\frac{\Sigma fd}{N}\right)^2}$$

$$= \sqrt{\frac{2750}{48} - \left(\frac{230}{48}\right)^2}$$

$$= \sqrt{57.29 + (4.8)^2}$$

$$= \sqrt{57.29 - 23.04} = \sqrt{34.25}$$

$$= 5.85.$$

5.4.4 Standard Deviation by the Step Deviation Method (Only in the Case of the Classified Distribution)

$$\sigma = h \times \sqrt{\frac{\Sigma fd_1^{\,2}}{N} - \left(\frac{\Sigma fd_1}{N}\right)^2},$$

where

h=the height of the class,

$d_1 = \frac{d}{h}$,

$d=X-A$.

Notes:

1. Standard deviation in the step deviation method takes place only in the case of the classified distribution.
2. Instead of the length of the class, the height of the class is preferred because it is always the same whether the class is overlapping (continuous) or nonoverlapping (discrete). From height, we have to just subtract the lower limit of any class from the lower limit of the nearest higher class, or we have to just subtract the higher limit of any class from the

higher limit of the nearest higher class. In the case of height, there is no need to add +1 in the nonoverlapping (discrete) class unlike when using the length of the class.

Example: Find the standard deviation of the following data of different ages of subeditors gate-keeping the stories per day by the step deviation method:

Age of subeditors (class)	10–20	20–30	30–40	40–50	50–60	60–70	70–80
No. of gate-keeping (f)	6	8	15	7	3	0	1

Solution:

Class	f	Mid-value (X)	$d=(X-A)$	$d_1=d/10$	d_1^2	fd_1	fd_1^2
10–20	6	15	$15-45=-30$	−3	9	−18	54
20–30	8	25	$25-45=-20$	−2	4	−16	32
30–40	15	35	$35-45=-10$	−1	1	−15	15
40–50	7	45	$45-45=0$	0	0	0	0
50–60	3	55	$55-45=10$	1	1	3	3
60–70	0	65	$65-45=20$	2	4	0	2
70–80	1	75	$75-45=30$	3	9	3	9
	$N=40$					$\Sigma fd_1=-43$	$\Sigma fd_1^2=113$

Let the assumed mean A be 45.

$$\therefore \sigma = h \times \sqrt{\frac{\Sigma fd_1^2}{N} - \left(\frac{\Sigma fd_1}{N}\right)^2}$$

$$= 10 \times \sqrt{\frac{113}{40} - \left(\frac{-43}{40}\right)^2} = 10 \times \sqrt{2.825 - 1.156}$$

$$= 10 \times \sqrt{1.1669} = 10 \times 1.292$$

$$= 12.92.$$

Thus, the standard deviation of the number of gate-keeping per day is 12.92.

5.4.5 Standard Deviation by the Nondeviation Method

This method is used when the deviation cannot be calculated or computed. That is why it is called the nondeviation method.

Using the nondeviation method, the standard deviation can be calculated as

$$\sigma = \sqrt{\frac{\Sigma X^2}{N} - \left(\frac{\Sigma X}{N}\right)^2},$$

where X denotes scores and N is the number of scores.

Example: Find the standard deviation of the following marks obtained by advertising students in a major test by the nondeviation method: 15, 14, 10, 16, 20, 30, 35, 18, 29, and 20.

Solution:

Scores (X)	X^2
15	225
14	196
10	100
16	256
20	400
30	900
35	1225
18	324
29	841
20	400
$\Sigma X = 207$	$\Sigma X^2 = 4867$
$N = 10$	

$$\therefore \sigma = \sqrt{\frac{\Sigma X^2}{N} - \left(\frac{\Sigma X}{N}\right)^2}$$

$$= \sqrt{\frac{4867}{10} - \left(\frac{207}{10}\right)^2}$$

$$= \sqrt{486.7 - (20.7)^2}$$

$$= \sqrt{486.7 - 428.5} = \sqrt{58.2}$$

$$= 7.628.$$

5.4.6 Merits and Demerits of Standard Deviation

Merits

1. Mathematically useful: In standard deviation since both positive and negative signs are taken into consideration, it is mathematically more correct, accurate, and useful. As a result, media researchers often rely on this method for measuring dispersion.
2. Dependence on every item: It is more reliable as it depends on all the terms. Hence, this method can be more dependable for the data analysis of media issues.
3. Effect of sampling is minimum: If the sample slightly changes, it will have the least effect on its computation. That is why its reliability is very high in communication and media studies.
4. Certainty: There is no ambiguity in its measurement. Due to its certainty attribute, it is emerging as one of the most dependable methods of measuring the dispersion of media variables.

5. Useful for more critical studies: As it is mathematically more convincing, it is more useful for critical analysis. That is why it is considered to be a standard device of dispersion in mass communication research.

Demerits:

1. Lengthy calculation: It is difficult to compute as compared to other measures. It is longer and lengthier. In media research, earlier it used to be avoided sometimes due to this demerit. But now with the rapid growth of information technology, lengthy computation is no more a problem. Since media researchers are generally more than average in the use of communication and information technology, this method is often adhered to.
2. Effect of the extreme value: It is normally more influenced and affected by extreme values, yet it is one of the most preferred devices in media and communication analysis as extreme values are automatically nullified in the process of squaring the data.

5.4.7 Differences Between the Mean Deviation and Standard Deviation

Both these measures are based on all the items of a variable, but they differ a lot in the following terms:

1. Mean deviation does not take into consideration the algebraic signs (plus or minus) in its calculation which is unreasonable and illogical. On the other hand, standard deviation consider the algebraic signs.
2. Mean deviation can be calculated from a median, mode, or mean, and its value differs in these cases (unless the distribution is normal). Standard deviation is always calculated from the arithmetic mean.
3. The mathematical properties possessed by standard deviation are much greater than those possessed by mean deviation.

5.4.8 Coefficient of Standard Deviation and Coefficient of Variation

It is important to mention here that standard deviation is an absolute measure of dispersion and is expressed in terms of units of variable. For the purpose of comparative studies, a relative measure of dispersion is computed. It is the coefficient of standard deviation which is equal to standard deviation divided by a mean.

Thus,

$$\text{The coefficient of SD} = \frac{\sigma}{\overline{X}}.$$

This value will often be in fraction and as such not ideal for any comparison and hence the coefficient of variation is calculated by multiplying the coefficient of standard deviation by 100.

Thus,

$$\text{The coefficient of variation or CV} = \frac{\sigma}{\overline{X}} \times 100.$$

This measure for the first time was evolved by Karl Pearson and is very useful for studying dispersion in more than one series.

A series in which the coefficient of variation is higher would have greater dispersion than the one in which it is lower. Similarly, when CV is high, the series is less consistent or less variable. This measure is largely, widely, and most commonly used for a comparative study of the variability or consistence of two or more series.

Example: Find the mean deviation, standard deviation, coefficient of standard deviation, and coefficient of variation of the following data: 5, 6, 9, 12, and 13.

Solution:

X	$d=(X-\bar{X})$	$\|d\|$	$\|d^2\|$
5	5−9=−4	4	16
6	6−9=−3	3	9
9	9−9=0	0	0
12	12−9=3	3	9
13	13−9=4	4	16
$\Sigma X = 45$		$\Sigma d = 14$	$\Sigma \|d^2\| = 50$
$N=5$			

$$\therefore \bar{X} = \frac{45}{5} = 9$$

$$\therefore \delta = \frac{|d|}{N} = \frac{14}{5} = 2.8$$

$$\sigma = \sqrt{\frac{\Sigma d^2}{N}}$$

$$= \sqrt{\frac{50}{5}} = \sqrt{10}$$

$$= 3.162$$

$$\text{The coefficient of SD} = \frac{\sigma}{\bar{X}} = \frac{3.162}{9} = 0.351$$

$$\text{The coefficient of variation or CV} = \frac{\sigma}{\bar{X}} \times 100$$

$$= \frac{3.162}{9} \times 100 = 35.13.$$

5.4.9 Combined Standard Deviation

An absolute measure of dispersion, called standard deviation, has some unique mathematical features which tremendously raise its importance in statistical analysis. It is very easy to calculate the combined mean of two or more groups. Similarly, the standard deviation of two or more groups can be found out from the standard deviation of its component parts and their means. The combined mean is denoted by $\bar{X}_{12}$ and the combined standard deviation is denoted by σ_{12}, and both of them are calculated, respectively, as follows:

$$\text{Combined mean} \quad (\bar{X}_{12}) = \frac{N_1\bar{X}_1 + N_2\bar{X}_2}{N_1 + N_2},$$

$$\text{Combined standard deviation} \quad (\sigma_{12}) = \sqrt{\frac{N_1\sigma_1{}^2 + N_2\sigma_2{}^2 + N_1 d_1{}^2 + N_2 d_2{}^2}{N_1 + N_2}},$$

where

$\bar{X}_{12}$ = Mean of a combined group
σ_{12} = Combined standard deviation
σ_1 = Standard deviation of the first group
σ_2 = Standard of the second group
$d_1 = \bar{X}_1 - \bar{X}_{12}$,
$\bar{X}_1$ = Mean of the first group
$d_2 = \bar{X}_2 - \bar{X}_{12}$
$\bar{X}_2$ = Mean of a second group
$\bar{X}_{12}$ = Mean of a combined group
N_1 = No. of scores for the first group
N_2 = No. of scores for the second group.

The above-mentioned formula can be further extended for more than two groups, that is, three or more groups. For example, the combined standard deviation (σ_{123}) for three groups can be written as

$$\sigma_{123} = \sqrt{\frac{N_1\sigma_1{}^2 + N_2\sigma_2{}^2 + N_3\sigma_3{}^2 + N_1 d_1{}^2 + N_2 d_2{}^2 + N_3 d_3{}^2}{N_1 + N_2 + N_3}}.$$

Here, $d_1 = \bar{X}_1 - \bar{X}_{123}$,
$d_2 = \bar{X}_2 - \bar{X}_{123}$
$d_3 = \bar{X}_3 - \bar{X}_{123}$

where $\bar{X}_{123}$ = Mean of a combined group
σ_3 = Standard deviation of the third group
N_3 = No. of scores for the third group.

Example 1: Find out the combined mean and combined standard deviation from the following data of news reports.

	Series A	Series B
No. of news items	100	500
Mean	50	60
Standard deviation	10	11

Solution:

$$\text{Combined mean, } \bar{X}_{12} = \frac{N_1\bar{X}_1 + N_2\bar{X}_2}{N_1 + N_2},$$

where $N_1 = 100, N_2 = 500, \bar{X}_1 = 50$, and $\bar{X}_2 = 60$

$$= \frac{100 \times 50 + 500 \times 60}{100 + 500} = \frac{5000 + 30000}{600} = \frac{35000}{600} = 58.3.$$

Now, the combined standard deviation,

$$\sigma_{12} = \sqrt{\frac{N_1\sigma_1{}^2 + N_2\sigma_2{}^2 + N_1 d_1{}^2 + N_2 d_2{}^2}{N_1 + N_2}},$$

where, $\sigma_1 = 10, \sigma_2 = 11, d_1 = |\bar{X}_1 - \bar{X}_{12}|, d_2 = |\bar{X}_2 - \bar{X}_{12}|$

$$d_1 = |\bar{X}_1 - \bar{X}_{12}| = |50 - 58.3| = 8.3$$

$$d_2 = |\bar{X}_2 - \bar{X}_{12}| = |60 - 58.3| = 1.7.$$

$$\therefore \quad \sigma_{12} = \sqrt{\frac{100 \times 10^2 + 500 \times 11^2 + 100 \times (8.3)^2 + 500 \times (1.7)^2}{100 + 500}}$$

$$= \sqrt{\frac{10000 + 60500 + 6889 + 1445}{600}} = \sqrt{\frac{78834}{600}} = \sqrt{131.39}$$

$$= 11.462.$$

Hence, the combined mean is 58.3 and combined standard deviation is 11.462.

Example 2: Following are the particulars of the number of stories and average words per intro of the stories in two newspapers.

	Newspaper 1	Newspaper 2
Number of stories	100	50
Average words per intro	60	45
Standard deviation	3	2

1. Find the standard deviation of the combined data.
2. Which of the two distributions is more variable?

Solution:

1. To find the combined SD (σ_{12}), we are supposed to compute the combined mean ($\bar{X}_{12}$) first.

$$\therefore \bar{X}_{12} = \frac{N_1\bar{X}_1 + N_2\bar{X}_2}{N_1 + N_2},$$

where $N_1 = 100, \bar{X}_1 = 60, N_2 = 50, \bar{X}_2 = 45$

$$= \frac{100 \times 60 + 50 \times 45}{100 + 50} = \frac{6000 + 2250}{150} = 55.$$

Now,

$$\sigma_{12} = \sqrt{\frac{N_1 \sigma_1{}^2 + N_2 \sigma_2{}^2 + N_1 d_1{}^2 + N_2 d_2{}^2}{N_1 + N_2}}$$

$$= \sqrt{\frac{100 \times 3^2 + 50 \times 2^2 + 100\,(\bar{X}_1 - \bar{X}_{12})^2 + 50\,(\bar{X}_1 - \bar{X}_{12})^2}{100 + 50}}$$

$$= \sqrt{\frac{900 + 200 + 100\,(60 - 55)^2 + 50\,(45 - 55)^2}{150}} = \sqrt{\frac{900 + 200 + 2500 + 5000}{150}}$$

$$= \sqrt{\frac{8600}{150}} = 7.57.$$

Hence, the combined average of words per intro of both the newspapers' stories is approximately 55 words and the combined standard deviation is 7.57.

2. To find out which distribution is more variable, we are supposed to compare the coefficient of variation of two distributions:

$$\text{Coefficient of variance (CV of Newspaper 1)} = \frac{\sigma_1}{\bar{X}_1} \times 100 = \frac{3}{60} \times 100 = 5$$

$$\text{Coefficient of variance (CV of Newspaper 2)} = \frac{\sigma_2}{\bar{X}_2} \times 100 = \frac{2}{45} \times 100 = 4.44$$

Since the coefficient of variation is more for the distribution of words in the intro of the stories of Newspaper 1, so the distribution of words in the same shows greater variability.

Example 3: The number of media persons employed, the mean wages (in ₹) per month, and the standard deviation (in ₹) in each section of a media organization are given below. Calculate the mean wages and standard deviation of all the media persons taken together.

Section	No. of Media Persons Employed	Mean Wages (in ₹)	Standard Deviation
X	50	11,130	60
Y	60	11,200	70
Z	90	11,150	80

Solution:

Now, the combined mean $(\bar{X}_{123}) = \frac{N_1\bar{X}_1 + N_2\bar{X}_2 + N_3\bar{X}_3}{N_1 + N_2 + N_3}$,

where $N_1 = 50, N_2 = 60, N_3 = 90, \quad \bar{X}_1 = 11{,}130, \bar{X}_2 = 11{,}200, \bar{X}_3 = 11{,}150$

$$= \frac{(50 \times 11130) + (60 \times 11200) + 90 \times 11150}{50 + 60 + 90}$$

$$= \frac{556500 + 672000 + 1003500}{200} = \frac{2232000}{200} = ₹\ 11160.$$

Again, combined standard deviation of three sections:

$$\sigma_{123} = \sqrt{\frac{N_1\sigma_1{}^2 + N_2\sigma_2{}^2 + N_3\sigma_3{}^2 + N_1 d_1{}^2 + N_2 d_2{}^2 + N_3 d_3{}^2}{N_1 + N_2 + N_3}}$$

$$d_1 = \left|\bar{X}_1 - \bar{X}_{123}\right| = |11130 - 11160| = 30$$

$$d_2 = \left|\bar{X}_2 - \bar{X}_{123}\right| = |11200 - 11160| = 40$$

$$d_3 = \left|\bar{X}_3 - \bar{X}_{123}\right| = |11250 - 11160| = 10$$

$$\sigma_{123} = \sqrt{\frac{500(60)^2 + 60(70)^2 + 90(80)^2 + 50(30)^2 + 60(40)^2 + 90(10)^2}{50 + 60 + 90}}$$

$$= \sqrt{\frac{180000 + 294000 + 576000 + 45000 + 96000 + 9000}{200}}$$

$$= \sqrt{\frac{1200000}{200}} = \sqrt{6000}$$

$$= 77.459$$

∴ Combined mean = ₹11,160

Combined standard deviation = 77.459.

5.5 VARIANCE

The term "variance" is used to describe the square of standard deviation. This term was first used by R.A. Fisher in 1913. The relevance and importance of the term "variance" lie in the fact that it is capable of a very exhaustive type of quantitative analysis. The concept of variance is very significant in advanced media research work where it is possible to split the total into several parts, each attributable to one of the factors causing variation in their original series. When we deal with a phenomenon affected by a number of variables in communication and media studies, the analysis of variance helps us in isolating the effects of various factors. Thus, variance is the sum of squared deviations of scores taken from mean and divided by their number (N).

Symbolically, variance $= \Sigma \frac{(X - \bar{X})^2}{N} = \sigma^2$.

Thus, $\sigma = \sqrt{\text{variance}}$.

In a frequency distribution where the assumed mean is taken and step deviations are calculated:

$$\text{Variance} = \left[\frac{\Sigma f d_1^2}{N} - \left(\frac{\Sigma f d_1}{N}\right)^2\right] \times h^2.$$

Here, $d = \frac{X - A}{H}$ and h = height of class.

Example 1: Five students of mass communication scored the following marks in their dissertation of print media: 20, 22, 25, 18, and 30. What is the variance and standard deviation?

Solution:

X	$d=(X-\overline{X})$	$\lvert d^2 \rvert$
20	20−23=−3	9
22	22−23=−1	1
25	22−23=2	4
18	18−23=−5	25
30	30−23=7	49
$\Sigma X = 115$		$\Sigma \lvert d^2 \rvert = 88$
$N=5$		

$$\therefore \overline{X} = \frac{\Sigma X}{N} = \frac{115}{5} = 23$$

$$\therefore \text{Variance} = \frac{\Sigma d^2}{N} = \frac{88}{5} = 17.6$$

$$\sigma = \sqrt{17.6} = 4.2.$$

Example 2: Compute the variance of the marks obtained by 80 students of bachelors of mass communication as shown in the following table.

Marks obtained	10–14	14–18	18–22	22–26	26–30	30–34	34–38	38–42	42–46	46–50	50–54	54–58
No. of students	2	4	4	8	12	16	10	8	4	6	2	4

Solution:

Marks	f	Mid-value (X)	$d=(X-A)/h$	$\lvert fd1 \rvert$	$\lvert fd1^2 \rvert$
10–14	2	12	−5	−10	50
14–18	4	16	−4	−16	64
18–22	4	20	−3	−12	36
22–26	8	24	−2	−16	32
26–30	12	28	−1	−12	12
30–34	16	32	0	0	0
34–38	10	36	1	10	10
38–42	8	40	2	16	32
42–46	4	44	3	12	36
46–50	6	48	4	24	96
50–54	2	52	5	10	50
54–58	4	56	6	24	144
	$N=80$			$\Sigma fd' = 30$	$\Sigma \lvert fd'^2 \rvert = 562$

$$\therefore \text{Variance} = \left[\frac{\Sigma fd'^2}{N} - \left(\frac{\Sigma fd'}{N}\right)^2\right] \times h^2$$

$$= \left[\frac{562}{80} - \left(\frac{30}{80}\right)^2\right] \times 4^2$$

$$= 6.884 \times 16$$

$$= 110.144.$$

5.6 RANGE

Range is the simplest possible measure of dispersion. It is calculated by subtracting the lowest score in the series from the highest. But it takes only extreme values into account and remains silent about the variation of different items.

Symbolically, range $(R) = L–S$,

where L is the largest value and S is the smallest value in a series.

If a range is divided by the sum of the extreme items, the resulting figure is called the "ratio of range" or "coefficient of range."

Symbolically, the coefficient of range or ratio of range $= \frac{L - S}{L + S}$.

Example 1: The range of the data 2,4,6,8,50.

Solution:

$$R = L - S,$$

where R is the range, L is the largest value (50) and S is the smallest value (2).

Hence, R = 50 − 2 = 48. Example 2: Find the range and coefficient of range of the following data.

Class	11–13	13–15	15–17	17–19
Frequency	3	4	5	26

Solution:

$$R = L - S$$

$$= 19 - 11 = 8.$$

$$\text{Coefficient of range} = \frac{L - S}{L + S}$$

$$= \frac{19 - 11}{19 + 11} = \frac{8}{30}$$

$$= 0.266.$$

(Note: In the calculation of range, only the values of the variables are taken into account and the frequencies are totally ignored.)

5.6.1 Merits and Demerits of a Range

A good measure of dispersion should be easily computed, rigidly defined, and readily understood. Moreover, it should be capable of further mathematical treatment and should not be much affected by fluctuations of the sampling.
Merits:

1. Range is easily calculated, readily understood, and hence, the simplest and the easiest method of studying dispersion. While carrying an economic journalism research, range is useful in the study of fluctuations in share prices, money, rates, exchange rates, gold prices, and the likes.
2. It takes the least time to compute the value of range. Thus, if we are interested to get a quick rather than a very accurate picture of variability, we may calculate range. Hence, in the applied research of communication and media analysis, range is often used as it is quickly computable.

Demerits:

1. It is not based on all the observations of the series. It has nothing to do with each and every item of the distribution as far as quality control is concerned. Since, it is subject to fluctuations of considerable magnitude from sample to sample, we may say that it is largely affected by fluctuations of sampling.
2. It is impossible to use it in the case of open-ended distributions. In such distributions, the lower limit of the lowest class and the upper limit of the highest class are quite unknown.

Despite several demerits of range of fluctuations of considerable magnitude from sample to sample, it is very useful in financial and commercial journalism research, especially in the study of fluctuations in share prices, money, rates, exchange rates, gold prices, and so on. It is very relevant in the overall mass communication research, in weather forecasts, and overall, in our everyday life. For example, if the salaries of the highest earning journalist and the lowest earning journalist remain unchanged and if the salaries of all other journalists are changed, the range will remain unaffected. The range of a symmetrical and an asymmetrical distribution can be identical. Two such distributions can never have the same dispersion. Thus, it is relevant and useful in media research.

5.6.2 Interquartile Range and Quartile Deviation

Interquartile range is also a measure of dispersion. It has an advantage over range because it is not affected by the values of the extreme items. For this purpose, a measure called interquartile range has been developed. This type of range includes the middle 50 percent of the distribution, that is, one quarter of the observations are at the lower end and another quarter of the distributions are excluded in calculating the interquartile range. Thus, interquartile range represents the difference between the third quartile and the first quartile.

Symbolically,

$$\text{interquartile range} = Q_3 - Q_1.$$

When the value of the interquartile range is divided by 2, it becomes a semi-interquartile range or a quartile deviation.

Thus,

$$\text{semi-interquartile range or quartile deviation} = \frac{Q_3 - Q_1}{2},$$

where Q_3 and Q_1 stand for the upper and lower quartiles, respectively.

In a symmetrical distribution, the median lies halfway on the scale from Q_1 to Q_1, that is, median $-Q_1 = Q_1 -$ median, and as such, the difference can be taken as a measure of dispersion. The median $\pm$ quartile deviation covers exactly 50 percent of the observations. However, in mass media such data are generally not available as there is a greater possibility of an asymmetrical distribution. In an asymmetrical distribution, Q_1 and Q_3 are not equidistant from the median. Thus, an asymmetrical distribution includes only approximately 50 percent of the observations.

If quartile deviation is very less, it indicates high uniformity or small variation of the central 50 percent items and a high quartile deviation means that the variation among the central item is large.

Thus, quartile deviation is described as an absolute measure of dispersion. When it is divided by the average value of the two quartiles, a relative measure of the dispersion is obtained. It is called "coefficient of quartile deviation."

Symbolically,

$$\text{Coefficient of a quartile deviation} = \frac{\frac{Q_3 - Q_1}{2}}{\frac{Q_3 + Q_1}{2}} = \frac{Q_3 - Q_1}{Q_3 + Q_1}.$$

(Note: It is important to mention here that coefficient of quartile deviation may be used to compare the degree of variations in different distributions.)

Example 1: Find the quartile deviation and its coefficient from the following data relating to the monthly income of seven freelance journalists.

Monthly Income (₹): 5000, 7000, 8000, 6000, 6500, 4000, 9000.

Solution: Here, the incomes are arranged in an ascending order, that is, 4000, 5000, 6000, 6500, 7000, 8000, and 9000.

$$Q_1 = \text{the value of} \left(\frac{N+1}{4}\right)\text{th or} \left(\frac{7+1}{4}\right)\text{th or 2nd item} = 5000,$$

$$Q_3 = \text{the value of } 3\left(\frac{N+1}{4}\right)\text{th or } 3\left(\frac{7+1}{4}\right)\text{th or 6th item} = 8000,$$

$$\therefore \quad \text{Quartile Deviation} = \frac{Q_3 - Q_1}{2} = \frac{8000 - 5000}{2} = \frac{3000}{2} = 1500.$$

$$\text{And, coefficient of quartile deviation} = \frac{Q_3 - Q_1}{Q_3 + Q_1} = \frac{8000 - 5000}{8000 + 5000} = \frac{3000}{13000} = 0.23.$$

Example 2: Calculate the value of quartile deviation and its coefficient from the data of seven students of broadcast journalism.

Roll No.	1	2	3	4	5	6	7
Marks	20	28	40	12	30	15	50

Solution: Marks arranged in an ascending order:
12, 15, 20, 28, 30, 40, 50

$$Q_1 = \left(\frac{N+1}{4}\right)\text{th term} = \frac{7+1}{4} = \text{2nd item} = 15$$

$$Q_3 = 3\left(\frac{N+1}{4}\right)\text{th term} = 3\left(\frac{7+1}{4}\right) = \text{6th item} = 40$$

$$\therefore \text{Quartile Deviation} = \frac{Q_3 - Q_1}{2} = \frac{40 - 15}{2} = \frac{25}{2} = 12.5.$$

$$\text{And, coefficient of quartile deviation} = \frac{Q_3 - Q_1}{Q_3 + Q_1} = \frac{40 - 15}{40 + 15} = \frac{25}{55} = 0.455.$$

5.6.3 Merits and Demerits of Quartile Deviation

Merits:

1. It is simply calculable and easily understandable.
2. As a measure of dispersion, it is superior to range in certain aspects.
3. It is relevant, significant, and useful in studying dispersion in open and series.
4. It is also relevant, significant, and useful in erratic or badly skewed distributions, where the other measures of dispersion would be warped by extreme values. Quartile deviation is not affected by the presence of extreme values.

Demerits:

1. Quartile deviation is not based on all the observations and it ignores 50 percent items, that is, the first 25 percent and the last 25 percent.
2. It is not capable of further algebraic manipulation and mathematical treatment.
3. It is, in a way, a positional average.
4. Its value is very much affected by sampling fluctuations. A change in the value of one item, may affect its value considerably.

Thus, due to considerable variation in the value of various items, it is not a suitable measure of dispersion. As its value does not depend upon every item of the series, it cannot be considered as a favorable method of measuring dispersion. Because of such limitations, it is not often useful for statistical inference. But communication and media researchers do use the term standard deviation and variance in measurements of differences between research units on what is being measured. And the knowledge of other measures is important for a proper understanding of standard deviation and variance.

SUMMARY

Dispersion, which is often described as scatter, spread, or variation, is the amount of variability in a set of scores and it measures the extent to which the item varies from some central value. There are five methods of dispersion: (a) mean deviation, (b) standard deviation, (c) variance, (d) range, (e) interquartile range and quartile deviation. Mean deviation is the average difference between the items in a distribution and the median or mean or mode of that series. Standard deviation is always calculated from the arithmetic mean, as the sum of squares of deviation of items from the arithmetic mean is the least. Variance is described as the square of standard deviation. Range is calculated by subtracting the lowest score in the series from the highest. Interquartile range represents the difference between the third and the first quartile. Most of such measures may not be practically so pertinent, but standard deviation and variance are highly relevant and pertinently applicable. Communication and media researchers do use the term standard deviation and variance in measurements of differences between research units on what is being measured. After the discussion of measures of dispersion in media studies, another important measure, that is, measures of asymmetry in mass communication will be discussed in the next chapter.

IMPORTANT FORMULAE

1. Mean Deviation of Simple Distribution or Unclassified or Ungrouped Distribution:

$$\delta\ (\text{MD or AD}) = \frac{\Sigma |d|}{N},$$

where δ (del) = mean deviation

$|d| = (X - \bar{X})$ positive value
N = no. of scores
X = scores
$\bar{X}$ = mean of scores
(When mean deviation is taken from mean, it is also written as $\delta_{\bar{X}}$).

2. Mean Deviation of Frequency Distribution:

$$\delta \quad \text{or} \quad \delta_{\bar{X}} = \frac{\Sigma |d|}{N},$$

where f = frequency of scores.

3. Coefficient of Mean Deviation from Mean $= \frac{\delta_{\bar{X}}}{\bar{X}}$,

   where $\delta_{\bar{X}}$ = mean deviation from the mean and $\bar{X}$ = mean

4. Coefficient of Mean Deviation from Median $= \frac{\delta_M}{M}$,

   where δ_M = mean deviation from median and M = median

5. Coefficient of Mean Deviation from Mode $= \frac{\delta_{M_0}}{M_0}$,

   where δ_{M_0} = mean deviation from mode and M_0 = mode

6. Standard Deviation of Simple Distribution or Unclassified or Ungrouped Distribution:

$$\sigma = \sqrt{\frac{\Sigma d^2}{N}},$$

   where σ (sigma) = standard deviation

$$d = X - \bar{X}, X = \text{scores}, \bar{X} = \text{mean of scores, and } N = \text{no. of scores}$$

7. Standard Deviation of Frequency Distribution:

$$\sigma = \sqrt{\frac{\Sigma fd^2}{N}},$$

   where f = frequency of scores.

8. Standard Deviation by Shortcut method (or Assumed Mean Method):
   a. In simple distribution:

$$\sigma = \sqrt{\frac{\Sigma d^2}{N} - \left(\frac{\Sigma d}{N}\right)^2},$$

   where $d = X - A$, X = scores and A = assumed mean

   b. In frequency distribution:

$$\sigma = \sqrt{\frac{\Sigma fd^2}{N} - \left(\frac{\Sigma fd}{N}\right)^2},$$

   where f = frequency and $d = X - A$.

9. Standard Deviation by Step Deviation Method (Only in the Case of Classified Distribution):

$$\sigma = h \times \sqrt{\frac{\Sigma f d_1^2}{N} - \left(\frac{\Sigma f d_1}{N}\right)^2},$$

where $d_1 = \frac{d}{h}$ and h=height of class.

10. Standard Deviation by Nondeviation Method:

$$\sigma = \sqrt{\frac{\Sigma X^2}{N} - \left(\frac{\Sigma X}{N}\right)^2},$$

where X=scores and N=no. of scores.

11. Coefficient of SD $= \frac{\sigma}{\overline{X}}$.
12. Coefficient of Variation or CV $= \frac{\sigma}{\overline{X}} \times 100$.
13. Combined Standard Deviation of Two Groups (σ_{12}):

$$\sigma_{12} = \sqrt{\frac{N_1\sigma_1^2 + N_2\sigma_2^2 + N_1 d_1^2 + N_2 d_2^2}{N_1 + N_2}},$$

where σ_{12}=combined standard deviation
σ_1=standard deviation of the first group
σ_2=standard deviation of the second group
$d_1 = \overline{X}_1 - \overline{X}_{12}$, $d_2 = \overline{X}_2 - \overline{X}_{12}$
N_1=no. of scores of the first group, N_2=no. of scores second group.

14. Combined Standard Deviation of Three Groups (σ_{123}):

$$\sigma_{123} = \sqrt{\frac{N_1\sigma_1^2 + N_2\sigma_2^2 + N_3\sigma_3^2 + N_1 d_1^2 + N_2 d_2^2 + N_3 d_3^2}{N_1 + N_2 + N_3}},$$

where $d_1 = \overline{X}_1 - \overline{X}_{123}$, $d_2 = \overline{X}_2 - \overline{X}_{123}$
$\overline{X}_{123}$ = mean of combined three group
σ_3=standard deviation of the third group
N_3=no. of scores of the third group.

15. Combined Mean of Two Groups ($\overline{X}_{12}$):

$$\overline{X}_{12} = \frac{N_1\overline{X}_1 + N_2\overline{X}_2}{N_1 + N_2},$$

where N_1 = no.of scores of group I
N_2 = no.of scores of group II
$\bar{X}_1$ = mean of group I
$\bar{X}_2$ = mean of group II.

16. Combined Mean of Three Groups ($\bar{X}_{123}$):

$$\bar{X}_{123} = \frac{N_1\bar{X}_1 + N_2\bar{X}_2 + N_3\bar{X}_3}{N_1 + N_2 + N_3},$$

where N_3 = no.of scores of group III
$\bar{X}_3$ = mean of group II.

17. Variance = σ^2.
18. Range: $R = L - S$,
where R = range, L = largest value in a score, and S = smallest value in a score.
19. Coefficient of Range or Ration of Range = $\frac{L - S}{L + S}$.
20. Interquartile Range = $Q_3 - Q_1$,
where $Q_3 = 3\left(\frac{N+1}{4}\right)$th term, $Q_1 = \left(\frac{N+1}{4}\right)$th term.
21. Semi-interquartile Range or Quartile Deviation = $\frac{Q_3 - Q_1}{2}$.
22. Coefficient of a Quartile Deviation = $\frac{Q_3 - Q_1}{Q_3 + Q_1}$.

RELATED AND SUGGESTED WEBSITES

(As retrieved on December 1, 2015)

1. http://teacher.buet.ac.bd/akmsaifulislam/dm/lec_dm_3.ppt
2. http://www.ncbi.nlm.nih.gov/pmc/articles/PMC3198538/
3. http://www.degreesofdemocracy.net/Soroka(JOP).pdf
4. http://www.itl.nist.gov/div898/handbook/eda/section3/eda35b.htm

REFERENCES

Elhance, D.N.S., and Veena Elhance. 1990. *Fundamentals of Statistics*, 9.1–9.54. New Delhi: Kitab Mahal.
Gupta, S.P. 2011. *Statistical Method*, 273–334. New Delhi: Sultan Chand & Sons.
Mangal, S.K. 1987. *Statistics in Psychology and Education*, 61–69. New Delhi: McGraw Hill.

RELATED AND RECOMMENDED READINGS

Gupta, Das, and S.N. Thakur. 1998. *Modern Approach to Intermediate Statistics and Probability*, 102–44. Patna: Bharti Bhawan.

Gupta, S.P and Gupta Alka. 2008. *Statistical Methods in Behavioural Sciences.* Allahabad: Sharda Pustak Bhawan.
Hussain, Shanshad. 1986. *Elementary Statistics in Psychology and Education,* 39–59. New Delhi: Motilal Banarasidas.
Kerlinger, F.N. 1983. *Foundations of Behavioural Research.* New Delhi: Surjeet Publications.
Kothari, C.R. 2000. *Research Methodologies: Methods and Techniques.* New Delhi: Wishwa Prakashan.
Krishnaswami, O.R., and M. Ranganatham. 2005. *Methodology of Research.* New Delhi: Himalaya Publications.
Sarangi, Prasant. 2010. *Research Methodology.* Delhi: Taxman Publication.
Singh, Arun Kumar. 1986. *Basic Statistics in Psychology and Education,* 86–111. Patna: Novelty & Co.
Wilkinston, T.S., and P.I. Bhandarkar. 1996. *Methodologies and Techniques of Social Research.* Mumbai: Himalaya Publishing House.
Wimmer, Roger D., and Joseph R. Dominick. 2003. *Mass Media Research: An Introduction,* 249–54. 7th ed. Belmont, CA: Thomson & Wadsworth.

QUESTIONS AND PROBLEMS

1. Describe the meaning and concept of measures of dispersion.
2. Explain the various methods of dispersion comprehensively.
3. What is mean deviation? Discuss the merits, demerits, and usefulness of mean deviation.
4. What is standard deviation? Discuss the merits, demerits, and usefulness of standard deviation.
5. Discuss the role of mean deviation in media and communication research.
6. Describe the significance of standard deviation in mass communication research.
7. Throw light on coefficient of mean deviation, coefficient of standard deviation, and coefficient of quartile deviation.
8. Differentiate between mean deviation and standard deviation.
9. What is variance? Discuss the significance of variance in media research.
10. Discuss the role of range, interquartile range, and semi-interquartile range in media and communication research.
11. Describe the merits and demerits of quartile deviation.
12. Throw light on combined standard deviation.
13. Discuss the significance of standard deviation in communication research.
14. Find the mean deviation of the following data:

Class	45–49	40–44	35–39	30–34	25–29	20–24	15–19	10–14
Frequency	1	2	2	5	4	2	1	1

15. Find the standard deviation by the nondeviation method of the following marks obtained by 10 students of advertising in a major test: 15, 14, 10, 16, 20, 30, 35, 18, 29, and 20.
16. Find the standard deviation of the following classified data:

Class	85–89	80–84	75–79	70–74	65–69	60–64	55–59	50–54	45–49	40–44
Frequency	1	1	2	3	9	8	2	1	1	2

17. Find the mean deviation, standard deviation, and variance of the following data: 10, 10, 9, 2, 6, 20, 28, and 25.
18. Find the mean deviation and standard deviation of the following data:

Class	80–89	70–79	60–69	50–59	40–49	30–39	20–29	10–19
Frequency	6	7	8	5	12	3	4	5

19. Find the standard deviation of the following data:

Class	50–54	45–49	40–44	35–39	30–34	25–19	20–24	15–19	10–14	5–9
Frequency	1	3	6	9	12	13	10	7	6	3

20. Find the standard deviation and the coefficient of Standard deviation of the following data by the step deviation method:

Class	10–20	20–30	30–40	40–50	50–60	60–70	70–80
Frequency	6	8	15	7	3	0	1

21. Find the standard deviation of the following data by the shortcut method and step-deviation method:

Class	50–54	45–49	40–44	35–39	30–34	25–19	20–24	15–19	10–14	5–9
Frequency	1	3	6	9	12	13	10	7	6	3

22. Find the mean deviation of the following distribution: 3, 9, 2, 8, 7, 1, 7, 7, 3.
23. Find the mean deviation of the following frequency distribution:

X	2	3	4	5	6
c.f.	3	7	9	16	19

24. Find the mean deviation from the median of the following frequency distribution:

Class	0–10	10–20	20–30	30–40	40–50
Frequency	5	7	4	3	2

25. The marks of nine students of MA (mass communication) in a minor test are as follows: 15, 10, 6, 15, 12, 9, 3, 5, 4, 2. Find their mean deviation from mean, mode, and median.
26. Calculate the mean deviation from the following data: 15, 10, 6, 8, 11.
27. Compute the mean deviation from mean, median, and mode of the following data: 2, 5, 4, 3, 5, 6, 5.
28. Calculate the mean deviation from the median of the 75 students of public relations from the following data:

Marks	10	11	12	13	14	15	16	17	18	19	20
No. of PR students	2	4	5	8	10	16	10	9	6	4	1

29. Compute the mean deviation from median of the following data:

Class	2–4	4–6	6–8	8–10
Frequency	3	4	2	1

30. Calculate the mean deviation from the median of the following data:

Class	0–10	10–20	20–30	30–40	40–50
Frequency	5	7	4	8	10

31. Calculate the mean deviation from the mean of the following data:

Class	30–39	40–49	50–59	60–69	70–79	80–89	90–99
No. of electronic media students	2	3	11	20	32	25	7

32. Compute the standard deviation of the following incomes (in ₹) of the stringers of an English daily: 3000, 4000, 4200, 4400, 4600, 4800, 5800.
33. Calculate the standard deviation of the following data:

Class	4–6	6–8	8–10	10–12	12–14	14–16
Frequency	13	10	9	5	8	5

34. Compute the standard deviation of the following distribution:

X	2	4	6	7	8	9
f	3	2	5	3	2	1

35. Calculate the standard deviation of the given data with the following frequency distribution:

Class	10	20	30	40
Frequency	2	3	5	2

36. Calculate the standard deviation of the following data: 2, 4, 5, 6, 9, 10.
37. Calculate the standard deviation of the marks secured by 48 students of editing in a minor test:

Marks Secured	0–4	5–9	10–14	15–19	20–24
No. of editing students	2	5	7	13	21

38. Find the standard deviation of the TV audience under different ages given as follows:

TV audience age under	10	20	30	40	50	60	70	80
No. of persons	15	30	53	75	100	110	115	125

39. Calculate the mean, standard deviation, and coefficient of standard deviation of the following distribution:

Class	10–20	20–30	30–40	40–50	50–60	60–70	70–80
Frequency	6	8	15	7	3	0	1

40. Stories filed per day by two reporters R_1 and R_2 of a daily newspaper are as follows. Calculate which reporter is more consistent in his/her performance:

	No. of Events Covered	
Stories Filed per Day	**Reporters (R_1)**	**Reporters (R_1)**
0	27	17
1	9	9
2	8	6
3	5	5
4	4	8

41. Compute the mean deviation from the mean and standard deviation of the following data:

Class	10–30	30–50	50–70	70–90	90–110	110–30
Frequency	4	7	15	12	7	5

42. The mean of 100 scores of students of reporting is 50 and their standard deviation is 4. Calculate the sum of all the scores and also the sum of the squares of the items.
43. Calculate the standard deviation and variance of the natural numbers 1, 2, 3,..., 10.
44. Compute the mean and the standard deviation of the following distribution:

Class	4–8	8–12	12–16	16–20	20–24	24–28	28–32	32–36	36–40
Frequency	6	10	18	30	15	12	10	6	2

45. The following data gives the distribution of ages of 500 media persons. Calculate their standard deviation:

Age in Year	20–25	25–30	30–35	35–40	40–45	45–50	50–55
No. of media persons	170	110	80	45	40	30	25

46. Compute the mean and standard deviation of the following distribution:

Class	5–15	15–25	25–35	35–45	45–55
c.f.	8	20	35	44	50

47. Calculate the standard deviation and coefficient of variation of the following distribution:

Class	0–9	10–19	20–29	30–39	40–49	50–59
Frequency	6	8	15	12	8	4

48. Compute the standard deviation of the following distribution:

Income in ₹	100–200	100–300	100–400	100–500	100–600
No. of stringers	15	33	63	83	100

49. Which of the following editors is more consistent in editing stories?

Editor X	5	7	16	27	39	53	56	61	80	101	105
Editor Y	0	4	16	21	41	43	57	78	83	90	95

50. Two TV newsreaders A and B read the following number of news items quarterly:

No. of News Items	0–25	25–50	50–75	75–100	100–125	125–150
A	17	8	4	3	1	2
B	22	5	6	3	3	1

Whose news reading was more consistent?

51. Find the mean deviation from the mean and the standard deviation of the following distribution:

Class	0–10	10–20	20–30	30–40	40–50	50–60
Frequency	5	15	25	20	10	5

52. Compute the mean deviation from the median and the standard deviation of the following data:

Class	0–20	20–40	40–60	60–80	80–100
Frequency	8	20	30	10	7

53. The first of two sub-groups of editors and reporters has 10 items with mean 15 and standard deviation 3. If the whole group of journalists has 250 items with mean 15.6 and standard deviation $\sqrt{13.44}$, find the standard deviation of the second sub-group of reporters.
54. The mean and standard deviation of normal distribution are 60 and 5, respectively. Calculate the interquartile range and the mean deviation of the distribution.
55. Trace the missing data from the following distribution:

	Group I	**Group II**	**Group III**	**Combined**
Number	50	?	90	200
Standard Deviation	6	7	?	7.746
Mean	113	?	115	116

56. An analysis of the daily income of the employees of two newspapers organizations A and B gave the following results:

	Newspaper Organizations	
	A	B
No. of employees	50	60
Average daily income	₹60	₹48
Variance	100	144

Find the average daily income and the standard deviation of all employees in the two newspaper organizations taken together. Which newspaper organization is more equitable in regard to payments?

57. A test in broadcast journalism was given to 400 students of bachelors of mass communication of a journalism university of whom 150 were boys and 250 girls. The results were,

$N_1 = 150$	$N_2 = 150$
$\bar{X}_1 = 72$	$\bar{X}_2 = 73$
$\sigma_1 = 7.0$	$\sigma_2 = 64$

Calculate the mean and standard deviation of the combined group.

58. Find out the coefficient of quartile deviation and the coefficient of variation from the following distribution of marks among the students of journalism.

Marks	No. of Journalism Students
Below 20	8
Below 40	20
Below 60	50
Below 80	70
Below 100	80

59. Compute the interquartile range and the coefficient of quartile deviation from the following distribution:

Marks in mass communication	Above 0	10	20	30	40	50	60	70	80
No. of students	150	140	100	80	80	70	30	14	0

60. From the given data, compute the standard deviation of X and Y variables:

$\Sigma X = 235$	$\Sigma Y = 250$
$\Sigma X^2 = 6750$	$\Sigma Y^2 = 6840$
$N = 10$	

61. The mean of 200 items is 48 and their standard deviation is 3. Compute the following:
    a. The sum of all the items,
    b. The sum of squares of all the items.
62. The mean and standard deviation of 20 items were found to be 10 and 2, respectively. Later it was found that the item 12 was misread as 8. Compute the correct mean and standard deviation.
63. The mean and standard deviation of a series of 20 items were calculated by a student as 20 cm and 5 cm, respectively. But while calculating them, an item 13 was misread as 30. Calculate the correct mean and standard deviation.

6

CHAPTER

Measures of Asymmetry in Mass Communication

Weighing scale is symmetrical while weighing is up to accuracy and is asymmetrical while it lacks accuracy of weight.

—Author

Symmetry means a balance between the two halves and asymmetry is just the reverse. The dictionary meaning of the word asymmetry is "lack of symmetry," "skewness," "uneven," "odd," "unequal," "not straight," "disharmony," or "uneven position on each side of a central point or line." In mathematics or statistics or media metrics, we may describe *asymmetry* as a synonym of skewness and may define it as a frequency distribution or its curve which lacks symmetry, evenness, balance, or harmony.

In the previous chapter, we extensively and intensively discussed the meaning and concept of measures of dispersion, methods of dispersion, meaning and concept of standard deviation, variance, range, interquartile range, quartile deviation, and important formulae. It included a few general questions, illustrations, and solutions of fundamentals of statistics in the beginning, but gradually focused more on media metrics. Thus, we have discussed statistical tool of media metrics like measures of dispersion in the previous chapter. Yet another statistical tool of media metrics in a proper sequence is measures of asymmetry (as shown in the flowchart in Section 2.2.1 of Chapter 2).

Hence, this chapter on measures of asymmetry will focus on the following:

1. Meaning and concept of asymmetry in mass communication
2. Tests of asymmetry
3. Measures of asymmetry
4. Moment
5. Kurtosis
6. Normal curve and normal distribution

In addition, the chapter will also cover the summary, important formulae, related and suggested websites, references, related and recommended readings, questions and problems of measures of dispersion with general reference to statistics and special reference to media metrics relating to the problems of communication and media studies and their solutions.

6.1 MEANING AND CONCEPT OF ASYMMETRY IN MASS COMMUNICATION

Asymmetry or skewness is opposite of symmetry and its presence tells us that a particular distribution is not symmetrical or in other words it is skew. When any data of media or communication is not increasing or decreasing in the same proportion, say for example, each time with the increase in presentation skill by 20 percent, the communication effectiveness is increasing by 8 percent, 2 percent, 3.5 percent, and so on, then it lacks symmetry and it will be described as uneven, odd, unequal, not straight, disharmonious, or skewed. Some relevant and significant definitions define asymmetry or skewness as follows:

According to Croxton and Cowden (cited in Gupta 2011, 338–87), "When a series is not symmetrical, it is said to be asymmetrical or skewed."

Garrett (cited in Gupta 2011, 338–87) defines it as: "A distribution is said to be 'skewed' when the *Mean* and the *Median* fall at different point in the distribution and the balance (or center of gravity) is shifted to one side or the other—to left side or right."

In the words of Marris Hamburg (cited in Gupta 2011, 338–87), "Skewness refers to the asymmetry or lack of symmetry in the shape of a frequency distribution."

Simpson and Kafta (cited in Gupta 2011, 338–87) aptly remark, "Measures of skewness tell us the direction and the extent of skewness. In the symmetrical distribution the *Mean, Median, and Mode* are identical. The more the Mean moves away from the Mode, the larger the asymmetry or skewness."

According to Riggleman and Frisbee (cited in D.N. Elhance and Veena Elhance 1990, 10.2), "Skewness (Asymmetry) is lack of symmetry. When a frequency distribution is piloted on a chart, skewness present in the items tends to be dispersed more on one side of the Mean than other."

Thus, asymmetry or skewness in mass communication research refers to lack of symmetry in the available data relating to media and communication. Any measure of asymmetry or skewness indicates the difference in the manner in which items are distributed in a particular distribution as compared with a symmetrical distribution. When a distribution is asymmetrical, there will be skewness in it, and the curve so drawn from the distribution is skewed; it will be slanted either to the left or the right side.

The meaning and the concept of asymmetry or skewness in mass communication research will be clearer from the following three figures, showing a symmetrical distribution, a positively skewed distribution, and a negatively skewed distribution, respectively, of data relating to media persons and their salaries.

1. Symmetrical distribution: It is crystal clear from the following figure that in a symmetrical distribution, the values of mean, median, and mode become equal and coincide at one point. Its shape is bell-shaped and the shapes of the frequencies are the same on both the sides of the central point of the curve. It is even and equally balanced at both the sides.

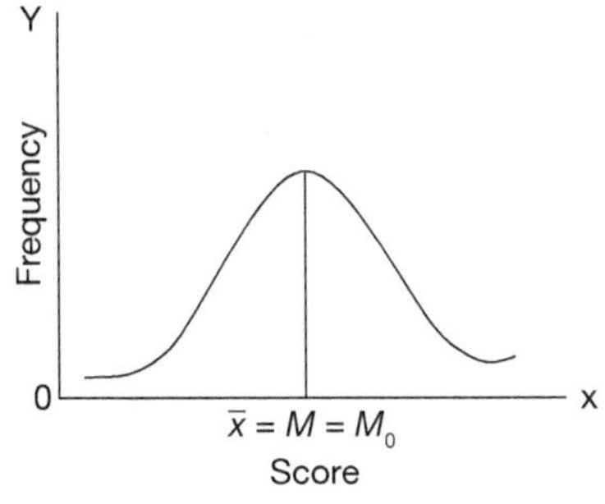

2. Asymmetrical distribution: A distribution which is not symmetrical is called asymmetrical distribution or skewed distribution, and this kind of distribution may be positively skewed or negatively skewed, which may be easily understood from the following discussion:
   a. Positively skewed distribution: In this type of distribution, the value of the mean ($\bar{X}$) is maximum and that of the mode (M_0) is minimum. Moreover, the median (M) lies in between as it is clear from the following figure:

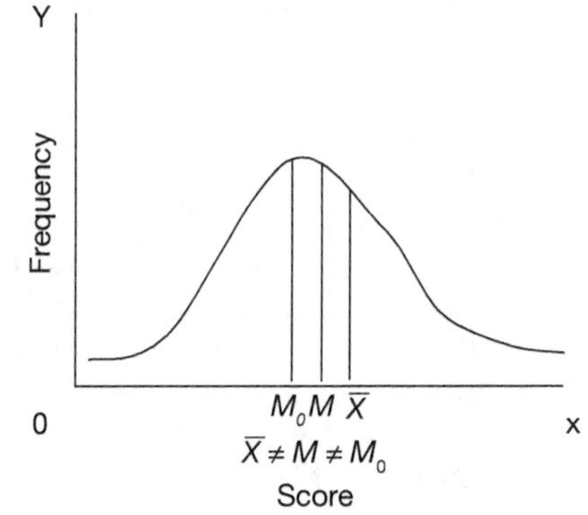

   b. Negatively skewed distribution: In this type of distribution, the value of the mean ($\bar{X}$) is minimum and that of the mode (M_0) is maximum. Further, the median (M) lies in between as it is clear from the following figure:

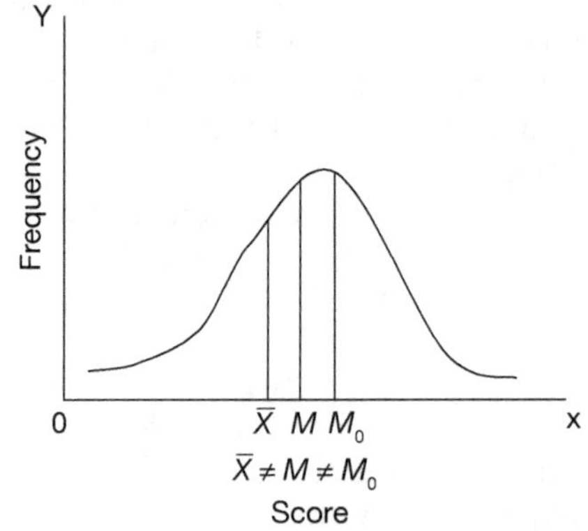

As far as positively skewed distribution is concerned, the frequencies are scattered over a greater range of values on the high-value end of the curve (the right-hand side) than they are on the low-value end. On the other hand, in a negatively skewed distribution, the position is just the reverse, that is, the excess tail is on the left-hand side.

Thus, it may be concluded here that

1. In a symmetrical distribution, $\bar{X} = M = M_0$
2. In a positively skewed distribution, $\bar{X} > M > M_0$
3. In a negatively skewed distribution, $\bar{X} < M < M_0$

6.2 TESTS OF ASYMMETRY

To explore whether a distribution is asymmetrical or skewed, the following tests are usually applied:

1. In an asymmetrical or skewed distribution, the values of mean, median, and mode will not coincide.
2. In an asymmetrical distribution, the two quartiles are not equidistant from the median, that is, $(Q_3-M)-(M-Q_1)$ will not be zero.
3. An asymmetrical distribution, when plotted on a graph paper, will not give a symmetrical bell-shaped curve.
4. The sum of positive deviations from the median is not equal to the sum of negative deviations.
5. Frequencies are not equally distributed at different points which are equidistant from the mode on either side.

Reversely, in the absence of asymmetry or skewness, that is, in the case of a symmetrical distribution, the following conditions are satisfied:

1. The values of mean, median, and mode converge on the same point.
2. When the data is plotted on a graph, it gives the normal bell-shaped form.
3. Sum of negative deviations from the median are equal to the sum of the positive deviations.
4. Quartiles are equidistant from the median.

6.3 MEASURES OF ASYMMETRY

Measures of asymmetry enlighten us in the direction and extent of asymmetry or skewness in a series and permit us to compare two or more series. There are two types of measures of asymmetry:

1. Absolute measures of asymmetry: Asymmetry may be measured in absolute terms by taking the difference between mean and mode.
   Absolute $S_k = \overline{X} - M_0$

   Example: Find out absolute skewness when $\overline{X} = 30$ and $M_0=20$.

   Solution: By formula, we know that absolute $S_k = \overline{X} - M_0$

   $$=30-20=10.$$

   Hence, absolute skewness=10.

   But if asymmetry is based on quartiles, absolute asymmetry may be given by the following formula:

   Absolute $S_{k=}Q_3+Q_{1-2}$ Median

   Example: Find absolute skewness when $Q_1=10$, $Q_3=30$, and $M=20$.

Solution: By formula, we know that absolute $S_k = Q_1 + Q_3 - 2M$

$$= 10 + 30 - 20 = 0.$$

Hence, absolute skewness is zero which means that the data is symmetrically distributed.

When the value of mean is greater than mode, asymmetry will be positive, and vice versa. But absolute measures of asymmetry are often avoided due to two reasons:

a. Distributions differ to a great extent and the difference between the mean and mode in absolute terms may be larger in one series and smaller in another, despite the fact that the frequency curves of two distributions were similarly skewed.
b. It is expressed in the unit of value of the distribution and could therefore not be compared with any other comparable series presented in various units.

Due to the above-mentioned reasons, absolute measures of asymmetry are often discarded and relative measures of asymmetry are preferred.

2. Relative measures of asymmetry: From the comparison point of view, it is important to accept the relative measures of asymmetry, which are obtained by dividing the absolute measures by any measure of dispersion. It is not advisable to divide the absolute measures of asymmetry by a measure of central tendency or any average. This is because here the issue is not to find out the extent of asymmetry in relation to the size of items, but it is to know the symmetry in relation to the dispersal of items around a central value. The main reason of knowing asymmetry is to find out how much more or less do the items on one side deviate from the items on the other side of a central value. Hence, absolute measures of asymmetry should always be divided by a measure of dispersion rather than a measure of central tendency. Relative measures of asymmetry are known as coefficients of skewness.

Thus, symbolically,
coefficient of skewness

$$S_k = \frac{\bar{X} - M_0}{\delta_{M_0}}, \qquad (i)$$

where $\bar{X}$ = mean, M_0 = mode, and δ_M = mean deviation from mode.

Example: Find the relative skewness of the data relating to commercialization of media when $\bar{X} = 60$, $M_0 = 40$, and $\delta_{M_0} = 15$.

Solution: By formula, we know that $S_k = \frac{\bar{X} - M_0}{\delta_{M_0}}$

$$= \frac{60 - 40}{15} = \frac{20}{15} = \frac{4}{3} = 1.33.$$

Hence, the relative skewness of the data relating to commercialization of media is 1.33.

When mode is ill defined, median can be used in lieu of mode:

$$S_k = \frac{\bar{X} - M}{\delta_M}, \qquad (ii)$$

where M = median and δ_M = mean deviation from median.

Example: find the relative skewness when $\bar{X}=50$, $M=45$, and $\delta_M=10$.

Solution: By formula, we know that $S_k = \dfrac{\bar{X} - M}{\delta_M}$

$$= \frac{50 - 45}{10} = \frac{5}{10} = 0.5.$$

Hence, relative skewness is 0.5.

Skewness can also be derived by finding out the difference of median and mode. Thus,

$$S_k = \frac{M - M_0}{\delta_{M_0}}. \qquad (iii)$$

Example: find the relative skewness when $M=60$, $M_0=10$, $\delta_{M_0}=5$.

Solution: By formula, we know that $S_k = \dfrac{M - M_0}{\delta_{M_0}}$

$$= \frac{60 - 10}{5} = \frac{50}{5} = 10.$$

Hence, relative skewness is 10.

But these measures of asymmetry (skewness) are not as useful and popular as those propounded by Karl Pearson, Arthur Lyon Bowley and Colleen Kelly, and the measures of skewness based on moments. However, the interpretation of measures of skewness is vague because skewness is categorized as "slight skewness," "marked skewness," or "moderate skewness."

a. Karl Pearson's coefficient of skewness: The well-known British biometrician and statistician Karl Pearson has propounded this method of measuring skewness. This is based on the difference between mean and mode divided by standard deviation to give a relative measure.
   Symbolically,

$$S_{k_p} = \frac{\bar{X} - M_0}{\sigma}, \qquad (iv)$$

   where S_{k_p} = Karl Pearson's coefficient of skewness.

   Example: Calculate Karl Pearson's skewness when $\bar{X}=20$, $M_0=10$, and $\sigma=8.5$.

   Solution: By formula, we know that $S_{k_p} = \dfrac{\bar{X} - M_0}{\sigma}$

$$= \frac{20 - 10}{8.5} = \frac{10}{8.5} = 1.176.$$

   Hence, Karl Pearson's skewness is 1.176.

But this formula has one major limitation that in practice the value given by this formula is rarely very high and it generally lies between + 1 and − 1.

In the case of symmetrical distribution, the value of coefficient of skewness will be zero because the values of mean, median, and mode become equal. If a distribution is positively skewed, the coefficient of skewness will have a plus sign, and reversely if the distribution is negatively skewed, the coefficient of skewness will have a minus sign. The extent of skewness will be derived by the numerical value, say 0.1, 0.7, or 0.9. Hence, this formula explains the direction and the degree of skewness. But the above-mentioned formula is not at all useful if mode is ill defined. Under the circumstance, Karl Pearson is of the view that its value should be computed on the basis of the empirical relationship which exists between the values of mean, median, and mode in a moderately asymmetrical distribution.

We are quite aware that in a moderately asymmetrically distribution,

$$\text{Mode} = 3\text{Median} - 2\text{Mean}$$

$$\therefore S_{k_p} = \frac{\bar{X} - (3\text{Median} - 2\text{Mean})}{\sigma} = \frac{\bar{X} - 3M + 2\bar{X}}{\sigma}$$

$$= \frac{3\bar{X} - 3M}{\sigma} \qquad (v)$$

$$= \frac{3(\bar{X} - M)}{\sigma}$$

Example: Compute the Pearson coefficient of skewness from the following distribution.

X	10	20	30	40	50	60	70
f	1	5	12	22	17	9	4

Solution:

X	*F*	Deviation from Assumed Mean $d = X - A$	$d_1 = \frac{d}{h}$ $h = 20 - 10 = 10$	d^2	fd_1	fd_1^2
10	1	10−40=−30	−30/10=−3	9	−3	9
20	5	20−40=−20	−20/10=−2	4	−10	20
30	12	30−40=−10	−10/10=−1	1	12	12
40	22	40−40=0	0/10=0	0	0	0
50	17	50−40=10	10/10=1	1	17	17
60	9	60−40=20	20/10=2	4	18	36
70	4	70−40=30	30/10=3	9	12	39
	$N=70$				$\Sigma fd_1=22$	$\Sigma fd_1^2 = 130$

Let the assumed mean (*A*) be 40.

By formula,

$$S_{k_p} = \frac{\bar{X} - M_0}{\sigma}$$

$$\bar{X} = A + \frac{\Sigma fd_1}{N} \times h = 40 + \left(\frac{22}{70} \times 10\right) = 43.1,$$

where $d_1 = d/h$, $h = 20 - 10 = 10$, $N =$ No. of scores.

Since the corresponding value of the highest frequency 22 is 40, $M_0 = 40$.

Now,

$$\sigma = \sqrt{\frac{\Sigma fd_1^2}{N} - \left(\frac{\Sigma fd_1}{N}\right)^2} \times h$$

$$= \sqrt{\frac{130}{70} - \left(\frac{22}{70}\right)^2} \times 10 = \sqrt{\frac{130}{70} - \frac{484}{4900}} = \sqrt{\frac{9100 - 484}{4900}} = \sqrt{\frac{8616}{4900}} \times 10$$

$$= \sqrt{1.759} \times 10 = 1.326 \times 10$$

$$= 13.26$$

$$\therefore S_{k_p} = \frac{43.1 - 40}{13.26} = +0.23.$$

Example: Find out the coefficient of skewness based on mean and median from the following distribution.

Class	0–10	10–20	20–30	30–40	40–50	50–60	60–70	70–80
Frequency	6	12	22	48	56	32	18	6

Solution:

Class	F	Mid-value (x)	$d = x - A$	$d_1 = \frac{d}{h}$ $h = 10 - a = 10$	d_1^2	fd_1	fd_1^2	c.f.
0–10	6	5	5−35=−30	−3	9	−18	54	6
10–20	12	15	15−35=−20	−2	4	−24	48	18
20–30	22	25	25−35=−10	−1	1	−22	22	40
30–40	48	35	35−35=0	0	0	0	0	88
40–50	56	45	45−35=10	1	1	56	56←	144
50–60	32	55	55−35=20	2	4	46	128	176
60–70	18	65	65−35=30	3	9	54	162	194
70–80	6	75	75−35=40	4	16	24	96	200
						$\Sigma fd_1 = 134$	$\Sigma fd_1^2 = 566$	

Let the assumed mean be 35.
By formula,

$$S_{k_p} = \frac{3(\bar{X} - M)}{\sigma} \quad \therefore \bar{X} = A + \left(\frac{\Sigma fd_1}{N} \times h\right)$$

$$= 35 + \frac{134}{200} \times 10 = 41.7.$$

Median is the $\frac{N}{2}$th value of the $\left(\frac{200}{2}\right)$th item which lies in the (45–50) class.

$$\therefore M = l + \left(\frac{\frac{N}{2} - cf_b}{f_m}\right) \times h$$

$$= 40 + \left(\frac{100 - 88}{56}\right) \times 10 = 42.14$$

$$\sigma = \sqrt{\frac{\Sigma fd_1^2}{N} - \left(\frac{\Sigma fd_1}{N}\right)^2} \times h = \sqrt{\frac{566}{200} - \left(\frac{134}{200}\right)^2} \times 10 = 15.43$$

$$\therefore S_{k_p} = \frac{3(\bar{X} - M)}{\sigma} = \frac{3(41.7 - 42.14)}{15.43} = -0.085.$$

b. Bowley's coefficient of skewness: This formula was propounded by the well-known Statistician Late Professor Bowley. His concept is based on quartiles. He does not take into account the values of mean and mode. It depends on the values of quartiles and median. This measure of skewness is also known as the second measure of skewness. In a symmetrical distribution, first and third quartiles are equidistant from the median as we can see from the following figure:

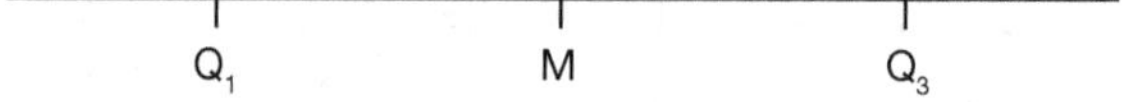

Hence, $Q_3 - M = M - Q_1$,
or $Q3 + Q_1 - 2M = 0$.

According to Bowley's coefficient of skewness,

$$S_{k_B} = Q_3 + Q_1 - 2M$$

or, the second measure of skewness $= Q_3 + Q_1 - 2M$.

But the above-mentioned formula is an absolute measure of skewness. The relative measure of skewness may be derived by dividing this absolute measure by the sum of (Q_3-M) and $(M-Q_1)$.

Thus, symbolically,

$$S_{k_B} = \frac{(Q_3 - M) - (M - Q_1)}{(Q_3 - M) + (M - Q_1)}$$

$$S_{k_B} = \frac{Q_3 + Q_1 - 2M}{Q_3 - Q_1} \qquad (vi)$$

It is important to mention here that the results derived by these two measures cannot be compared with one another, because Bowley's measure is limited to ±1, whereas Karl Pearson's measure has no such limits. However, if positional measures are required or if the extreme values are prominent or if a distribution is open-ended, Bowley's coefficient exhibits its superiority.

c. Kelly's coefficient of skewness: Another famous statistician Kelly has suggested that instead of quartiles, deciles and percentiles may be used in the computation of skewness. According to Kelly, the 10th and 90th percentiles or the first and the ninth deciles may be used for measuring the skewness.
Thus,

$$S_{k_k} = \frac{P_{90} + P_{10} - 2M}{P_{90} - P_{10}} \quad \text{or} \quad \frac{D_9 + D_1 - 2M}{D_9 - D_1},$$

where S_{k_k} = kelly's coefficient of skewness,
P_{90} = 90th Percentile, P_{10} = 10th Percentile,
D_9 = 9th decile, D_1 = 1st decile.
Thus, this method of measuring skewness is relevant, useful, and superior if skewness is dependent on percentiles or deciles. However, the above formula of Kelly is not very prominent in practice and usually Karl Pearson's formula is used to study skewness.

d. Measures of skewness based on moments: A measure of skewness can be computed by using the third moment about the mean.
The following examples will illustrate the application of the above-discussed methods. Pearson's formula has already been exampled earlier and the illustrations of Bowley's, Kelly's, and moments' methods follow.

Example 1: Compute Bowley's coefficient of skewness for the following data:

No. of magazines read	0	1	2	3	4	5	6
No. of media students	7	10	16	25	18	11	8

Solution: Computation of Bowley's coefficient of skewness.

No. of Magazines Read (X)	No. of Media Students (f)	cf
0	7	7
1	10	17
2	16	33
3	25	58
4	18	76
5	11	87
6	8	95
	N=95	

$$S_{k_B} = \frac{Q_3 + Q_1 - 2M}{Q_3 - Q_1}$$

$$Q_1 = \text{size of the } \frac{N+1}{4}\text{th term} = \frac{95+1}{4} = 24\text{th term} \therefore Q_1 = 2$$

$$Q_3 = \text{size of the } \frac{3(N+1)}{4}\text{th term} = \frac{3(95+1)}{4} = 72\text{th term} \therefore Q_3 = 4$$

$$M = \text{Size of the} \left(\frac{N+1}{2}\right)\text{th term} = \frac{96}{2} = 48\text{th term}$$

Size of the 48th term is 3; hence, $M = 3$

Now, $$S_{k_B} = \frac{4 + 2 - 2(3)}{4 - 2} = \frac{0}{2} = 0.$$

Hence, the distribution of the data is symmetrical.

Example 2: Compute Kelly's coefficient of skewness based on percentiles from the following data.

Marks	No. of Media Students
Less than 10	4
" 20	10
" 30	30
" 40	40
" 50	47
" 60	50

Solution: Computation of Kelly's coefficient of skewness.

Marks (X)	Frequency (f)	Cumulative Frequency (cf)
0–10	4	4
10–20	6	10
20–30	20	30
30–40	10	40
40–50	7	47
50–60	3	50
	$N=50$	

Median class is the value of $\frac{N}{2}=\frac{50}{2}$ or 25th item, which is in the 20–30 group.

P_{10} is the value of $\frac{10N}{100}=\frac{10(50)}{100}$ or 5th item which is in the 10–20 group.

P_{90} is the value of $\frac{90N}{100}=\frac{90(50)}{100}$ or 45th item which is in the 40–50 group.

$$M = l + \left(\frac{\frac{N}{2} - cf_b}{f_m}\right) \times h$$

$$M = 20 + \left(\frac{\frac{50}{2} - 10}{20}\right) \times 10$$

$$M = 20 + \frac{10}{20} \times (25 - 10) = 27.50$$

$$P_{90} = l + \left(\frac{\frac{90N}{100} - cf_b}{f_{P_{90}}}\right) \times h = 40 + \left(\frac{\frac{90 \times 50}{100} - 40}{7}\right) \times 10.$$

$$= 40 + \frac{(45 - 40) \times 10}{7} = 47.14$$

$$P_{10} = l + \left(\frac{\frac{10N}{100} - cf_b}{f_{P_{10}}}\right) \times h = 10 + \left(\frac{\frac{10 \times 50}{100} - 4}{6}\right) \times 10$$

$$= 10 + \frac{(5 - 4) \times 10}{6} = 11.67$$

$$\therefore S_{k_k} = \frac{P_{10} + P_{90} - 2M}{P_{90} - P_{10}} = \frac{11.67 + 47.14 - (2 \times 27.50)}{47.14 - 11.67}$$

$$= \frac{3.81}{34.47} = 0.11.$$

Example 3: Find out Pearson, Bowley, and Kelly's coefficients of skewness from the following data.

$$\bar{X} = 150, M = 142, Q_1 = 62, Q_3 = 195, D_1 = 30, D_9 = 230, \sigma = 30$$

Solution:
By formula,

$$S_{k_p} = \frac{3(\bar{X} - M)}{\sigma}$$

where S_{kp} = Karl Pearson's coefficient of skewness,

$$= \frac{3(150-142)}{30} = \frac{3 \times 8}{30} = 0.8.$$

Now,

$$S_{K_B} = \frac{Q_3 + Q_1 - 2M}{Q_3 - Q_1} = \frac{195 + 62 - 284}{195 - 62}$$
$$= -0.2$$

where S_{kB} = Bowley's coefficient of skewness.
Further,

$$S_{k_k} = \frac{D_1 + D_2 - 2M}{D_9 - D_1}$$

where S_{kk} Kelly's coefficient of skewness, D_1 and D_2 are the 1st and 9th deciles or 10th or 90th percentiles,

$$= \frac{30 + 230 - 284}{230 - 30} = \frac{-24}{200}$$
$$= -0.19.$$

6.4 MOMENTS

Unlike physics, the term moment in media metrics is used to explain the different features of a frequency distribution, such as central tendency variation and skewness, relating to media and communication issues. Here, it is crystal clear that the formula for calculating a moment $\frac{\Sigma fX}{N}$ is the same as we use in the computation of mean. In media metrics, the term moments is used with reference to frequencies and the respective values against them. In the computation of mean, we multiply the frequencies with respective values, add such products, and divide them with the total frequency, and the resulting value $\frac{\Sigma f\bar{X}}{N}$ is the mean.

For this reason, mean is also called the first moment about the origin. The concept moment may also be extended to higher powers.

Let us consider the symbol "d" as the deviation of any item in a distribution from the mean of that distribution. The mean of the various powers of these deviations in any distribution is called the moment of the distribution.

6.4.1 Moments about Arbitrary Origin

If the mean is in fraction, it is difficult to calculate moments. In such a situation, we calculate moments about an arbitrary origin "A" and then convert these moments about the mean. Moments about the arbitrary origin, also called "raw moments," are denoted by the symbol δ.

Hence δ_1 stands for the first moment about the arbitrary origin A, δ_2 for the second moment, and so on.

Symbolically,

$$\delta_1 = \frac{\Sigma(X-A)}{N}, \quad \delta_2 = \frac{\Sigma(X-A)^2}{N}, \quad \delta_3 = \frac{\Sigma(X-A)^3}{N}, \quad \delta_4 = \frac{\Sigma(X-A)^4}{N}.$$

For frequency distribution,

$$\delta_1 = \frac{\Sigma(X-A)}{N} \text{ or } \frac{\Sigma fd}{N} \text{ or } \frac{\Sigma fd_1}{N} \times h$$

$$\delta_2 = \frac{\Sigma(X-A)^2}{N} \text{ or } \frac{\Sigma fd^2}{N} \text{ or } \frac{\Sigma fd_1^2}{N} \times h^2$$

$$\delta_3 = \frac{\Sigma(X-A)^3}{N} \text{ or } \frac{\Sigma fd^3}{N} \text{ or } \frac{\Sigma fd_1^3}{N} \times h^3$$

$$\delta_4 = \frac{\Sigma(X-A)^4}{N} \text{ or } \frac{\Sigma fd^4}{N} \text{ or } \frac{\Sigma fd_1^4}{N} \times h^4.$$

6.4.2 Conversion of Moments about an Arbitrary Origin into Moments about Mean

The conversion of moments about an arbitrary origin (μ) into moments about mean (also called central moment) is as follows:

$$\mu_1 = \delta_1 - \delta_2 = 0,$$

$$\mu_2 = \delta_2 - \delta_1^2,$$

$$\mu_3 = \delta_3 - 3\delta_1\delta_2 + 2\delta_1^3$$

$$\mu_4 = \delta_4 - 4\delta_1\delta_3 + 6\delta_1^2\delta_2 - 3\delta_1^4.$$

6.4.3 Moments about Zero

Moments about zero are denoted by Z_1, Z_2, Z_3, Z_4, and so on.

Symbolically,

$$Z_1 = \frac{\Sigma fX}{N}, \quad Z_2 = \frac{\Sigma fX^2}{N}, \quad Z_3 = \frac{\Sigma fX^3}{N}, \quad Z^4 = \frac{\Sigma fX^4}{N}$$

Moreover,

$$\begin{aligned} Z_1 &= A + \delta_1 = \text{mean}, \\ Z_2 &= \mu_2 + Z_1^2, \\ Z_3 &= \mu_2 + 3\mu_2 Z_1 + Z_1^3, \\ Z_4 &= \mu_4 + 4\mu_3 Z_1 + 6\mu_2 Z_1^2 + Z_1^4. \end{aligned}$$

6.4.4 Measures of Moment

When we take the mean of the first power of the deviations, we will get the first moment about the mean. The mean of the squares of the deviations gives us the second moment about the mean. Similarly, the mean of the cubes of the deviations gives us the third moment about the mean, and so on and so forth. The moments about the mean called central moments are represented by the Greek letter μ (called mu). Hence, μ_1, μ_2, μ_3,... stands for the first moment about mean, second moment about mean, third moment about mean, and so on.

Thus, symbolically,

$$\mu = \frac{\Sigma X}{N} \text{ (first moment about origin)}$$

$$\mu_1 = \frac{\Sigma\, dx}{N}$$

where $dx = X - \bar{X}$

But Σdx is always zero, so the μ_1 (first moment from the mean) will always be zero.

$$\mu_2 = \frac{\Sigma\, dx^2}{N} = \text{variance} = \sigma^2$$

$$\mu_3 = \frac{\Sigma\, dx^3}{N}$$

$$\mu_4 = \frac{\Sigma\, dx^4}{N}.$$

Similarly, for frequency distribution,

$$\mu_1 = \frac{\Sigma fdx}{N} \quad \text{or} \quad \frac{\Sigma fdx_1}{N} \times h$$

$$\mu_2 = \frac{\Sigma fdx^2}{N} \quad \text{or} \quad \frac{\Sigma fdx_1^2}{N} \times h^2$$

$$\mu_3 = \frac{\Sigma fdx^3}{N} \quad \text{or} \quad \frac{\Sigma fdx_1^3}{N} \times h^3$$

$$\mu_4 = \frac{\Sigma fdx^4}{N} \quad \text{or} \quad \frac{\Sigma fdx_1^4}{N} \times h^4.$$

Usually, the first four moments are relevant and useful in media metrics. The study of moments can help us in measuring the central tendency of a set of observations, their variability, their asymmetry, and the height of the peak of the concerned curve.

The first four moments about the mean are very helpful in the analysis of simple distribution or frequency distribution which may be summarized as follows:

	Moment	Measures
1.	a. First moment about origin (μ)	Mean
	b. First moment about mean (μ_1)	Zero
2.	Second moment about mean (μ_2)	Variance
3.	Third moment about mean (μ_3)	Skewness
4.	Fourth moment about mean (μ_4)	Kurtosis.

Further, two important constants of a distribution are calculated from μ_2, μ_3, and μ_4 which tell us whether a distribution is symmetrical or not. But a symmetrical curve may or may not be a normal curve. They also tell us about the nature of symmetry—whether the symmetrical curve is (a) normal, (b) more flat then a normal curve, or (c) more peaked than a normal curve.

In fact, all normal curves are symmetrical, but all symmetrical curves may not be normal.

These constants are β_1 and β_2. β_1 is read as beta 1 and β_2 is read as beta 2. β_1 measures skewness which tells us whether a distribution is symmetrical or not. And β_2 measures kurtosis which tells us whether a curve is symmetrical or normal.

Here,

1. $\beta_1 = \frac{\mu_3^2}{\mu_2^2}$
2. $\beta_2 = \frac{\mu_4}{\mu_2^2}$.

It is important to mention here that in a symmetrical distribution, all odd moments, that is, μ_1, μ_3, and so on, would always be zero. When a curve is symmetrical, there will be a deviation below the mean which exactly equals each deviation above the mean and; hence, positive and negative deviations will neutralize and balance, and if added, will cancel out, that is, $\Sigma(X - \bar{X})$ will always be zero. Further, when the deviations are raised to even powers, their signs will always be positive. But the summation of the odd powers will all be equal to zero on account of the cancellations. Hence, odd moments always turn out to be zero in a symmetrical distribution. But this type of rule does not hold good in a skewed distribution.

Example: Compute the first four moments about the mean and analyze the following frequency distribution. Also measure the standard deviation, skewness, kurtosis, and the nature of the curve.

X	0	1	2	3	4	5	6	7	8
f	1	8	28	56	70	56	28	8	1

Solution:

X	f	f_X	$d = X - \bar{X} = X - 4$	fd	fd^2	fd^3	fd^4
0	1	0	–4	–4	16	–64	256
1	8	8	–3	–24	72	–216	648
2	28	56	–2	–56	112	–224	448
3	56	168	–1	–56	56	–56	56
4	70	280	0	0	0	0	0
5	56	280	1	56	56	56	56
6	28	168	2	56	112	224	448
7	8	56	3	24	72	216	648
8	1	8	4	4	16	64	256
	$N=256$	$\Sigma fX=1024$	$\Sigma d=0$	$\Sigma fd=0$	$\Sigma fd^2=512$	$\Sigma fd^3=0$	$\Sigma fd^4=2816$

$$\bar{X} = \frac{\Sigma fX}{N} = \frac{1024}{256} = 4$$

1. a. First moment of mean from the origin $= (\mu) = \dfrac{\Sigma fX}{N} = 4.$

   b. First moment about mean $(\mu) = \dfrac{\Sigma fd}{N} = \dfrac{0}{N} = 0.$

2. Second moment about mean $(\mu_2) = \dfrac{\Sigma fd^2}{N} = \dfrac{512}{256} = 2.$

3. Third moment about mean $(\mu_3) = \dfrac{\Sigma fd^3}{N} = \dfrac{o}{N} = 0.$

4. Forth moment about mean $(\mu_4) = \dfrac{\Sigma fd^4}{N} = \dfrac{2816}{256} = 11.$

It is important to mention here that the odd moments are zero which indicates that the distribution is symmetrical. Moreover, from these moments, we can calculate the standard deviation and skewness.

Standard deviation:

$$\sqrt{\mu_2} = \sqrt{2} = 1.414.$$

Skewness can be derived by the computation of β_1:

$$\beta_1 = \frac{\mu_3^2}{\mu_2^2} = \frac{0}{2^3} = 0.$$

In a symmetrical distribution, $\beta_1=0$. Hence, this distribution has no skewness.

We can also find out whether the distribution is normal or not with the help of moments. In the case of a normal distribution, the value of $\beta_2=3$

$$\beta_2 = \frac{\mu_4}{\mu_2^2} = \frac{11}{(2)^2} = \frac{11}{4} = 2.75.$$

Hence, the discussed distribution is symmetrical but not normal.

6.5 KURTOSIS

In media metrics, the term kurtosis refers to the degree of flatness or peakedness about the mode of a frequency curve pertaining to media problems and issues. It tells us the extent to which a distribution is more peaked or flat-topped than the normal curve. It enlightens us whether the distribution, if plotted on a graph, will give us a normal curve more flat than the normal curve or a curve more peaked than the normal curve.

Spiegel (cited in Gupta 2011, 338–87) in his pioneering book, *Theory and Problems of Statistics*, has defined it as, "[K]urtosis is the degree of peakedness of a distribution, usually taken relative to a normal distribution."

According to Simson and Kafa (cited in D.N. Elhance and Veena Elhance 1990, 10.31), "The degree of Kurtosis of a distribution is measured relative to the peakedness of a normal curve."

Croxton and Cowden define it as, "A measure of Kurtosis indicates the degree to which a curve of a frequency distribution is peaked or flat-topped." When a curve is more peaked than the normal curve, it is called "leptokurtic" and when it is more flat than the normal curve, it is called "platykurtic." The normal curve itself is known as "mesokurtic."

The following figure illustrates the three types of curves:

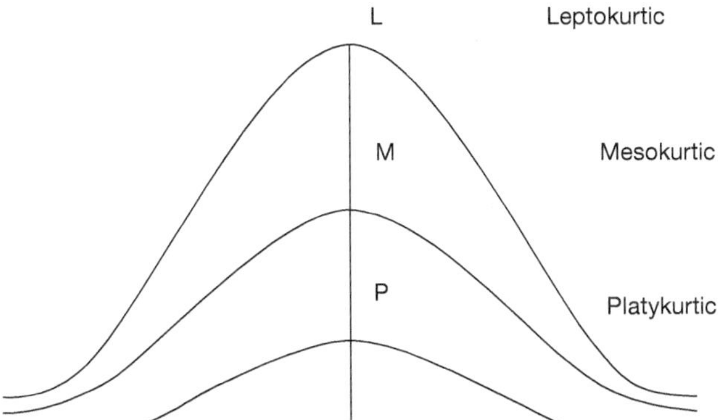

Here, curve M is normal or mesokurtic, curve L is more peaked than the normal curve and is leptokurtic, and curve P is more flat than the normal curve and is platykurtic.

6.5.1 Measures of Kurtosis

Kurtosis is usually measured by the value of coefficient β_2 or its derivation γ_2.

As we know, $\beta_2 = \frac{\mu_4}{\mu_2^2}$

where μ_4=fourth moment and μ_2=second moment.

The higher the value of β_2, more peaked is the distribution. For a normal curve, β_2=3. If the value of β_2 is more than 3, then the curve is more peaked than the normal curve, that is leptokurtic. If the value of β_2 is less than 3, then the curve is less peaked than the normal curve, that is, platykurtic. In a normal curve, the value of β_2=3 and is called mesokurtic.

Occasionally, the derivative of β_2, called γ_2, is used as a measure of kurtosis and is defined as

$$\gamma_2 = \beta_2 - 3.$$

In the case of a normal distribution, y_2=0. When γ_2 is positive, the curve is leptokurtic and when γ_2 is negative, the curve is platykurtic.

Example 1: The first four moments of a distribution are 0, 2.5, 0.7, and 18.75. Comment on the kurtosis of the distribution.

Solution: Here,

$$\beta_2 = \frac{\mu_4}{\mu_2^2} = \frac{18.75}{(2.5)^2}$$
$$= \frac{18.75}{6.25} = 3.$$

Since β_2 is 3, the data are normally distributed and the curve is also normal.

Example 2: From the following data, calculate whether the distribution is platykurtic:

$$N=100,\ \Sigma fd=50,\ \Sigma fd^2=1967.2,\ \Sigma fd^3=2958.8,\ \Sigma fd^4=86650.2.$$

Solution: To know the status of the curve, we are supposed to find out the value of β_2.

$$\beta_2 = \frac{\mu_4}{\mu_2^2}.$$

From the given data,

$$\delta_1 = \frac{\Sigma fd}{N} = \frac{50}{100} = 0.5$$
$$\delta_2 = \frac{\Sigma fd^2}{N} = \frac{1967.2}{100} = 19.672$$
$$\delta_3 = \frac{\Sigma fd^3}{N} = \frac{2925.8}{100} = 29.258$$
$$\delta_4 = \frac{\Sigma fd^4}{N} = \frac{86650.2}{100} = 866.502$$

$$\mu_1 = \delta_1 - \delta_1 = 0.5 - 0.5 = 0$$
$$\mu_2 = \delta_2 - \delta_1^2 = 19.672 - (0.5)^2 = 19.422$$
$$\mu_3 = \delta_3 - 3\delta_1\delta_2 + 2\delta_1^2 = 29.258 - (3 \times 0.5 \times 19.672) + 2(0.5)^2$$
$$= 29.258 - 29.5080 + 0.250 = 0$$
$$\mu_4 = \delta_4 - 4\delta_1\delta_2 + 6\delta_1^2\delta_1 - 3\delta_1^4$$
$$= 866.502 - (4 \times 0.5 \times 29.258) + [6 + (0.5)^2 \times 19.672] - 3 \times (0.5)^4$$
$$= 866.502 - 58.516 + 29.508 - 0.1875 = 837.3065$$
$$\beta_2 = \frac{\mu_4}{\mu_2^2} = \frac{837.3065}{(19.422)^2} = 2.22.$$

The value of β_2 is less than 3. Therefore, the distribution is platykurtic.

6.6 NORMAL CURVE AND NORMAL DISTRIBUTION

The dictionary meaning of the term "normal" is average. But in the field of measurement relating to the subject of communication, media, education, psychology, and sociology, those which are judged as average in terms of some qualities or characteristics are termed as normal and the others (below or above average) are considered away from the normal. Similar things happen with the data or distribution in terms of rating scores, readership scores, performance scores, and the likes, collected through tests, surveys, and experiments carried out in communication, media, education, psychology, and sociology on a randomly selected sample or population.

So far, we have discussed the measures of central tendency and variability. But these two do not reveal whether the dispersal of values on either side of an average is symmetrical or not. If observations are arranged in a symmetrical order around a measure of central tendency, we get what is called a symmetrical distribution. When plotted on a graph paper, such a distribution gives a normal or ideal curve. A normal curve has several mathematical characteristics.

As far as normal distribution is concerned, the values of mean, median, and mode coincide and quartiles are equidistant from the median. It is thus quite clear that in such cases, the sum of the deviation measured from the mean, median, or mode will be zero. It is important to mention here that the empirical relations between different averages and measures of dispersion hold good only in a normal distribution; a normal curve is a bell-shaped frequency curve in which the values on both the sides of a measure of central tendency are symmetrical. As a matter of fact, measures of central tendency and measures of dispersion should always be supplemented by what are called measures of asymmetry or skewness. Skewness is just opposite of symmetry and its presence tells us that a particular distribution is not normal. Hence, averages reveal the fact of the concentration of item around the central value, and measures of asymmetry tell us whether the dispersal of items from an average is normal.

Laplace and Gauss derived the normal curve by their independent efforts. Because of its discovery by Laplace and Gauss, the curve is also known as the Gaussian curve in the honor of Gauss. On the other hand, De Moivre used the normal curve mathematically in practice, so it is also called the De Moivre curve.

A normal curve, as follows, strongly considers the law, "[T]he greater a deviation from the *mean* or average value in a series, the less frequently it occurs."

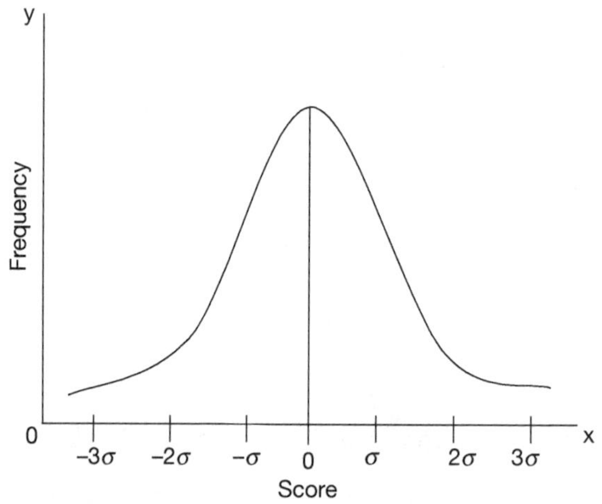

But it is not at all essential for a normal distribution to be described by an exactly perfect bell-shaped curve. Such a perfectly normal curve rarely exists in our practical day-to-day life. Absolute normalcy is a myth. In real-world situation, the slightly deviated or distorted bell-shaped curve is also accepted as a normal curve on the assumption of normal distribution of the characteristics measured in the universe. Hence, it should not be assumed that the distributions of the data in all cases will give normal curves or normal probability curves or approximately normal curves.

6.6.1 Characteristics and Properties of Normal Curve

Following are the striking characteristics and major properties of a normal curve:

1. Equality of central tendencies: For the curve to be normal, mean, median, and mode should be numerically equal and they should coincide at one point. Thus, $\bar{X} = M = M_0$.
2. Coefficient of skewness: A normal curve is perfectly symmetrical. That is, it is not skewed. The value of the measure of skewness calculated for this curve is zero. Thus, $S_k = 0$.
3. Coefficient of kurtosis: The normal curve serves as a model for explaining the peakedness or flatness of a curve through the measure of kurtosis. For the normal curve, the value of kurtosis is 3. When the value of kurtosis for a distribution is more than 3, the distribution is described as flatter at the top than the normal curve. But if the value of kurtosis is less than 0.263, the distribution is said to be more peaked than the normal curve. Thus, $K_u = 3$.
4. Shape: The shape of the normal curve is "bell-shaped," "completely symmetrical," "uni-modal," and "mesokurtic." In this curve, the frequencies at both extremes are low; it is higher toward the center and the highest at the peak point of the center.
5. Asymptotic: The normal curve tends to infinity in both the directions. It approaches but never touches the baseline. It extends from minus infinity to plus infinity. In other words, we may say that the curve touches the baseline at infinity. Thus, the curve is described as asymptotic.

6. Point of inflection: Point of inflection, as shown in the figure below, is that point where the curve changes its curvature. This point occurs at ± standard deviation unit ($\pm 1\sigma$) above and below the mean. Thus, the curve is concave to the baseline from $+1\sigma$ to -1σ, while it is convex to the tails above $\pm 1\sigma$ and below -1.

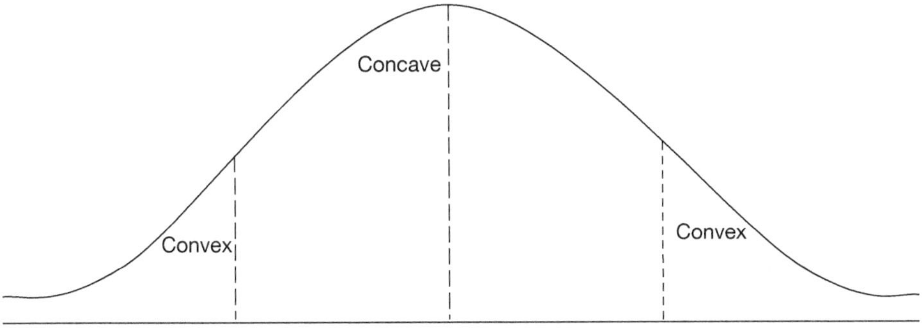

7. Equal distance of quartiles from median: In a normal curve, the distances of the third quartile and the first quartile from the median are the same. This difference is called quartile deviation, which is also described as probable error (PE). Thus, $Q_3 - M = M_1 - Q_1 = Q$ or PE.
8. Relationship between quartile deviation and standard deviation: In a normal curve, the value of quartile deviation is approximately 2/3rd of the standard deviation. $Q = 0.6745\sigma$ and $\sigma = 1.482Q$.
9. Highest ordinate: In a normal curve, the height of the mid-point of the baseline, that is, mean, is the highest and is equal to 0.3989 of the sum of frequencies (N), that is, $H = 0.3989N$.

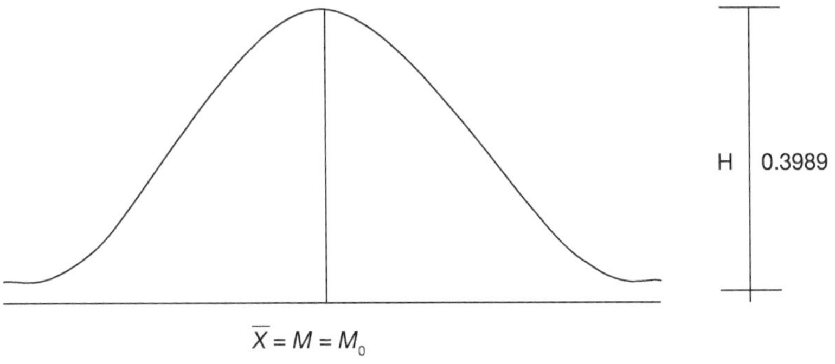

10. Area under a normal curve: The area between the normal curve and the baseline is called the area of the normal curve. We may find that 34.13 percent of the total area of the curve lies between the mean and $+1\sigma$ on the baseline of the normal curve. Similarly, another 34.13 percent cases lie between the mean and $-\sigma$ on the baseline. Consequently, 68.26 percent of the area of the curve falls within the limits ±1 standard deviation on $+1\sigma$ unit from the mean. Further, 95.44 percent cases lie from -2σ to $+2\sigma$ and 99.74 percent cases lie from -3σ to $+3\sigma$ So only 26 cases in 10,000 (10000−9974) should be expected to lie beyond the range $\pm 3\sigma$ in a large sample as shown in the following figure:

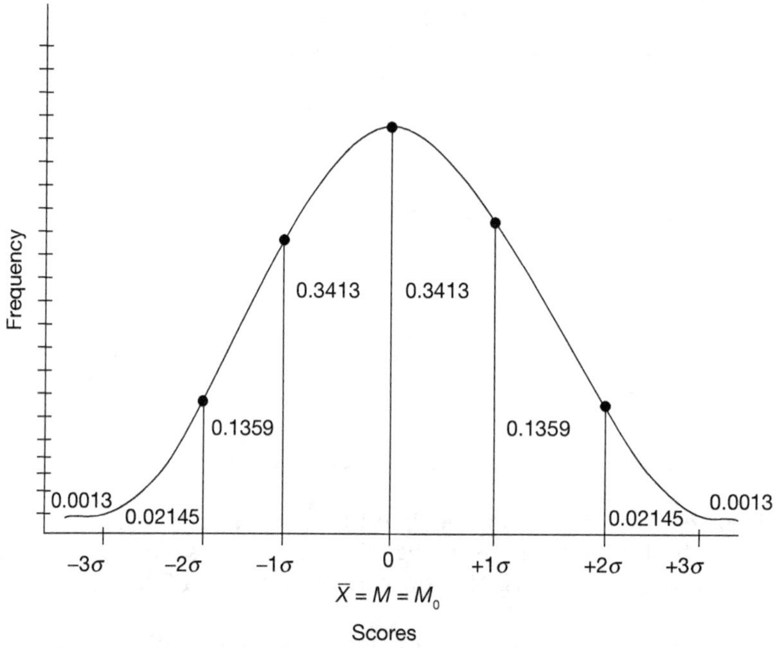

Details of the area under a normal curve can be seen as follows:

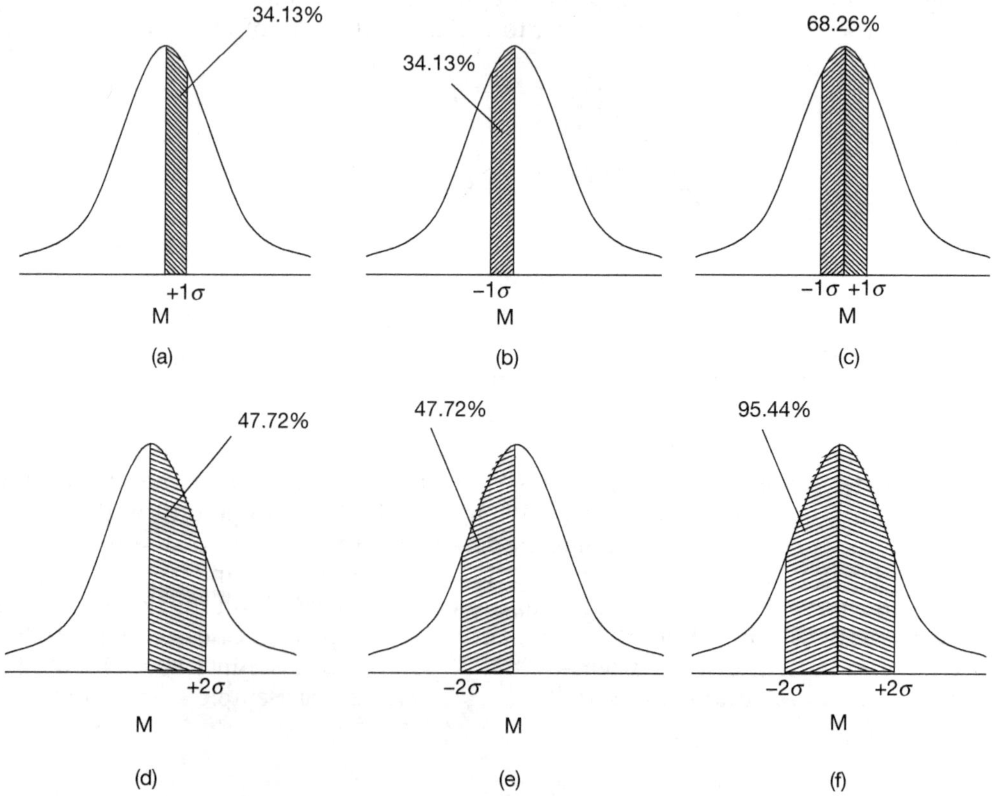

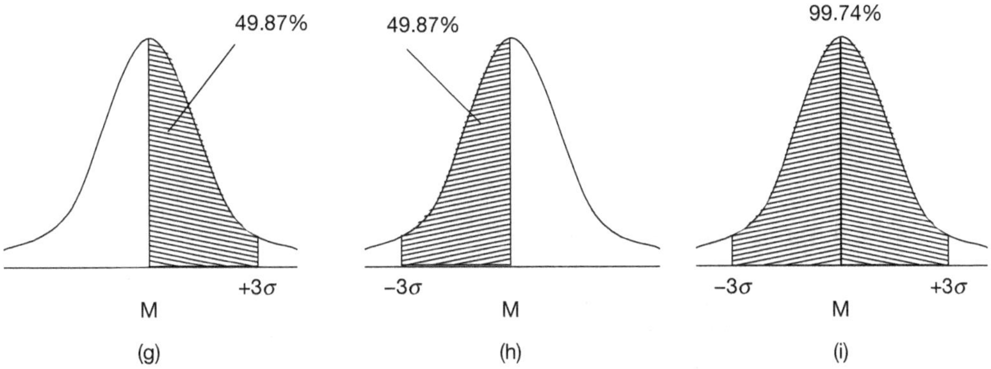

11. Mean as the starting point: As a normal curve does not touch the baseline, the mean $\overline{X}$ is used as the starting point.
12. Standard deviation as a unit of measurement: In order to go along some distance on the baseline of a normal curve above and below the point of departure (i.e., mean), standard deviation of the distribution (σ) is used as a unit of measurement.
13. Limit ($\pm 3\sigma$): For all the practical uses, the normal curve extends from -3σ distance on the left to $+3\sigma$ distance on the right.
14. Area beyond limit: In the normal curve, the limits of the distances $\pm 1.96\sigma$ include 95 percent and the limits of $\pm 2.58\sigma$ include 99 percent of the total area of the curve, 5 percent and 1 percent of the area, respectively, falling beyond these limits as depicted in the following figure.

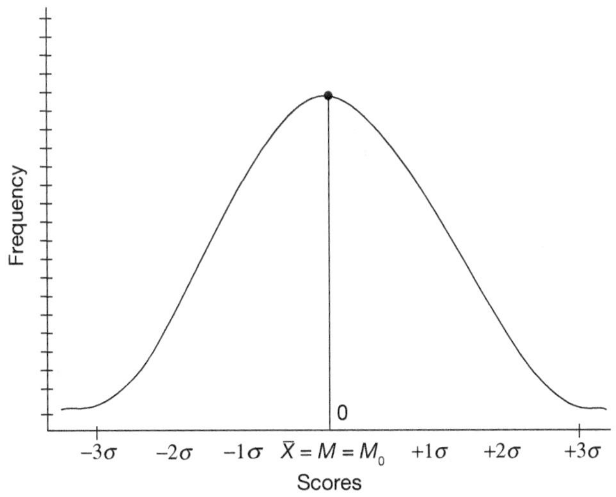

15. Mathematical equation: The mathematical equation of the normal curve is as follows.

$$Y = \frac{N}{\sigma\sqrt{2\pi}} e^{-d^2/2\sigma^2},$$

where Y = height of frequencies at the mid-point

$d = X - \bar{X}$, that is, distance and scores from mean
σ=standard deviation of scores
N=sum of frequencies
π=constant (value=3.1416)
e=constant (value=2.71828)

6.6.2 Applications of Normal Curve

A normal curve is highly relevant, significantly useful, and widely applicable in the field of measurement relating to communication and media studies. Some of its most important and relevant applications are discussed as follows.

1. As a research model: A normal curve can be widely applied as a model in media and communication research as it represents a model distribution. It is because of this reason that it may be first applied to compare various distributions with it, that is, to find whether the distributions are normal or not. If not, in what way they diverge from the normal curve. Second, it may be used to compare two or more distributions in terms of overlapping. Third, it may be applied to distribute marks and categorical ratings.
2. Percentile calculation: A normal curve may be easily used for calculating percentiles and percentile ranks in a normally distributed data of mass media and communication research.
3. Application of standard errors of measurement: A normal curve is well-known as the "curve of error" because of the strong reason that it is instrumental and helpful in comprehending the concept of standard errors and then applying the concept in measurement of the variables of media and communication.
4. Grouping into categories: A group of media persons or media industries may be easily grouped into certain categories as A, B, C, D, and E (outstanding, excellent, very good, good, and average) in terms of some traits (assumed to have normal distribution) with the help of a normal curve.
5. Transformation of qualitative data: It is under the assumption of a normally distributed variable that the sets of qualitative data—nature, personality, attitude, perception, judgment's ratings, grade divisions, and categorical ranks on a scale—may be easily transformed to quantitative data and combined to provide an average rating for each media person or each media industry.
6. Conversion of raw scores into normalized scores: A normal curve is helpful in converting the raw scores belonging to various scales of measurement into standard normalized scores such as sigma (or Z scores) and T scores. For converting an available raw score into a Z score, we subtract the mean from its raw score and divide it by the standard deviation of the distribution, that is, $Z = \frac{X - \bar{X}}{\sigma}$. Thus, a standard Z score finds out how many standard deviation units a raw score is above or below the mean and thus provides a standard scale for comparing the variables. Sometimes a Z score may have negative signs and decimals. Hence, for convenience in calculation, Z value is converted into T value by multiplying Z by the constant 10 and adding the constant 50. Thus, T=10Z+50.

7. Helpful in relative difficulty of test items: The normal curve avails the facility and turns out to be helpful in the simplest rational method of scaling test items for difficulty, and hence it may be easily applied for deciding the relative difficulty of test items, problems, questions, and so on.

6.6.3 Illustration of Applications of Normal Curve

Before illustrating the applications of a normal curve, we must be acquainted with converting raw scores into Z scores and vice versa.

Conversion of raw scores into Z scores:

As we know,

$$Z = \frac{X - \bar{X}}{\sigma},$$

where Z = standard normalized score,
X = raw scorcs
$\bar{X}$ = mean of raw scores
σ = standard deviation of raw scores (x).

Example 1: Calculate the Z score of the following data: Mean = 50, σ = 14, and Raw score = 80.

Solution: By formula,

$$Z = \frac{X - \bar{X}}{\sigma},$$

where X = 80, $\bar{X}$ = 50, and σ = 14.

$$\therefore Z = \frac{80 - 50}{14} = \frac{30}{14} = 2.14.$$

Example 2: Compute the raw score from the given distribution.
Mean = 50, σ = 10, and Z = 0.6

Solution: By formula,

$$Z = \frac{X - \bar{X}}{\sigma},$$

where Z = 0.6, X = ?, $\bar{X}$ = 50, and σ = 10

$$\therefore \quad 0.6 = \frac{X - 50}{10} \text{ or } X - 50 = 6$$

$$\therefore \quad X = 56.$$

Here are some examples of application of a normal curve.

Case 1: Comparing Scores on Two Different Tests

Example: A student obtains 80 marks in mass communication and 50 in advertising. If the mean and standard deviation for the scores in mass communication are 70 and 20 and for the scores in advertising are 30 and 10, find out in which subject (mass communication or advertising) he did better?

Solution: From the given data, direct comparison of the student's status in mass communication and advertising cannot be made because the marks secured do not belong to the same scale of measurement. For putting them into a common scale, let us convert these two scores into Z scores.

Here, raw scores in mass communication $(X_1)=80$, $\bar{X}_1=70$, and $\sigma_1=20$.

Raw scores in advertising $(X_2)=50$, $\bar{X}_2=30$, and $\sigma_2=10$.

$$\therefore Z \text{ score in mass communication} = \frac{X_1 - \bar{X}_1}{\sigma_1} = \frac{80-70}{20} = 0.5$$

$$Z \text{ score in advertising} = \frac{X_2 - \bar{X}_2}{\sigma_2} = \frac{50-30}{10} = 2.0.$$

Thus, the Z score of the student in advertising is 2.0 and that in mass communication is 0.5. That means the student performed better in advertising than in mass communication.

Case 2: Determining Percentage of the Individuals Whose Scores Lie Between Two Given Scores

Example: In a sample of 1,000 cases, the mean of test scores is 14.5 and standard deviation is 2.5. Assuming normal distribution, how many individuals scored between 12 and 16?

Solution: Both the raw scores 12 and 16 have to be converted into Z scores.

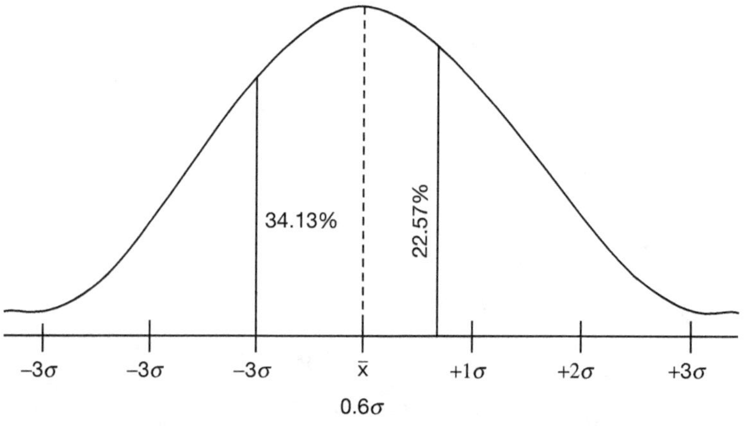

Z score equivalent to raw score 12

$$= \frac{X - \bar{X}}{\sigma}$$
$$= \frac{12 - 14.5}{2.5} = \frac{-2.5}{2.5}$$
$$= -1\sigma.$$

Z score equivalent to raw score $16 = \frac{16 - 14.5}{2.5}$

$$= \frac{1.5}{2.5} = 0.6\sigma.$$

From the normal curve figure, we see that 2,257 (out of 10,000), that is, 22.57 percent cases, lie between mean and 0.6σ. Similarly, 3,413, that is, 34.13 percent cases lie between -1σ and mean. Thus, it may be concluded that $22.57+34.13=56.7$ percent or 567 individuals out of 1,000 score between 12 and 16.

SUMMARY

In media metrics, we may describe asymmetry as a synonym of skewness and may define it as a frequency distribution or its curve which lacks symmetry, evenness, balance, or harmony. In a symmetrical distribution, $\bar{X} = M = M_0$, in a positively skewed distribution, $\bar{X} > M > M_0$, and in a negatively skewed distribution, $\bar{X} < M < M_0$. In an asymmetrical distribution, the two quartiles are not equidistant from the median, that is, $(Q_3-M)-(M-Q_1)$ will not be zero. Measures of asymmetry explore the direction and extent of asymmetry or skewness, which are of two types: Absolute measures of asymmetry (absolute $S_k = \bar{X} - M_0$ or $Q_3 + Q - 2\text{Median}$) and relative measures of asymmetry also known as coefficient of skewness $s_k = \left(\frac{\bar{X} - M_0}{\delta_{M_0}}, s_k = \frac{\bar{X} - M}{\delta_M}, s_k = \frac{M - M_0}{\delta_{M_0}}\right)$. But these measures of asymmetry (skewness) are not as popular as propounded by Karl Pearson, Bowley and Kelly, and measures of skewness based on moments.

s_{k_p} (Pearson's coefficient of skewness):

$$= \frac{\bar{X} - M}{\sigma} \text{ or } S_{k_p} = \frac{3(\bar{X} - M)}{\sigma}$$

S_{k_B} (Bowley's absolute coefficient of skewness also called the second moment of skewness)$=$ Q_3+Q_1-2M

and S_{k_B} (Bowley's relative coefficient of skewness) $= \frac{(Q_3 + Q_1 - 2M)}{(Q_3 - Q_1)}$

S_{k_K} (Kelly's coefficient of skewness)

$$= \frac{P_{90} + P_{10} - 2M}{P_{90} - P_{10}} \text{ or } \frac{D_9 + D_1 - 2M}{D_9 - D_1}.$$

In media metrics, the term moments is used with reference to frequencies and the respective values against them. In its computation, we multiply the frequencies with respective values, add such products, and divide them with the total of frequencies, and the resulting value $\frac{\Sigma fX}{N}$ is the mean. For this reason, mean is also called the first moment about the origin. The concept of moment may also be extended to higher powers.

Moment	Measures
1. a. First moment about origin $\left(\mu = \frac{\Sigma fx}{N}\right)$	Mean
b. First moment about mean $\left(\mu_1 = \frac{\Sigma fd}{N}\right)$	Zero
2. Second moment about mean $\left(\mu_2 = \frac{\Sigma fd^2}{N}\right)$	Variance
3. Third moment about mean $\left(\mu_3 = \frac{\Sigma fd^3}{N}\right)$	Skewness
4. Fourth moment about mean $\left(\mu_4 = \frac{\Sigma fd^4}{N}\right)$	Kurtosis.

All normal curves are symmetrical, but all symmetrical curves may not be normal. Constant β_1 measures skewness and β_2 measures kurtosis $\left(\beta_1 = \frac{\mu_3^2}{\mu_2^2} \text{ and } \beta_2 = \frac{\mu_4}{\mu_2^2}\right)$. Odd moments always turn out to be zero in symmetrical distribution, but this type of rule does not hold good in an asymmetrical (skewed) distribution. Kurtosis tells us the extent to which a distribution is more peaked or flat-topped than the normal curve. If a curve is more peaked than the normal curve, it is called "leptokurtic" and if more flat than the normal curve, it is called "platykurtic." The normal curve itself is known as "mesokurtic." Kurtosis is usually measured by $\beta_2 = \frac{\mu_4}{\mu_2^2}$ or $\gamma_2(\beta_3 - 3)$.

In a normal curve or normal distribution, $\beta_2 = 3$ or $\gamma_2 = \beta_2 - 3 = 0$. A normal curve (also called the Gaussian curve or De Moivre curve) has some basic properties like equality of central tendencies ($\bar{X} = M = M_0$); coefficient of skewness (S_k) is zero; coefficient of kurtosis is (Ku) 3; it is "bell-shaped," "completely mesokurtic," "unimodal," and "asymptotic" (never touches the baseline); it is concave to the baseline from $+1\sigma$ to -1σ, while convex to the tails above $+1\sigma$ and below -1σ; quartiles are equidistant from the median; $\phi = 0.6745\sigma$ and $\sigma = 1.482\phi$; height of the mid-point of the baseline is the highest, that is, $H = 0.3989N$; area covered by the normal curve is 99.74 percent (since $1\sigma = 34.13\%$, $2\sigma = 47.72\%$, $3\sigma = 49.87\%$, the total$=49.87+49.87=99.74$); mean ($\bar{X}$) is treated as the starting point; standard deviation (σ) is used as the unit of measurement; the curve extends from -3σ distance on the left to $+3\sigma$ distance on the right; the curve shows 5 percent and 1 percent cases lying beyond the limits of $\pm 1.96\sigma$ and $\pm 2.58\sigma$, respectively; and the mathematical equation of the height of frequencies on mid-point (Y) of the normal curve is given by the formula $\frac{N}{\sigma\sqrt{2\pi}}e^{-d^2/2\sigma^2}$. A normal curve is highly relevant, significantly useful, and widely applicable in the field of measurement relating to communication and media studies as a research model, helpful in percentile calculation. It can also be useful in applying the concept of standard error for measurement, grouping into categories, transformation of qualitative data into quantitative data, conversion of raw scores into standard normalized scores such as Z scores and T scores, by using the formula $Z = \frac{X - \bar{X}}{\sigma}$, $T = 10Z + 50$ (T value is used when Z has a negative sign and decimal).

After the thorough discussion on measures of asymmetry in mass communication, it will be extremely relevant, important, and pertinent to throw light on measures of relationship and other measures such as correlation, regression, and index number. Hence, these will be comprehensively discussed in the next chapter.

IMPORTANT FORMULAE

1. Absolute $S_K = \bar{X} - M_0$ or $(Q_3 + Q_1 - 2M)$,
   where S_k=skewness, $\bar{X}$=mean, M_0=mode, Q_3=third quartile, Q_1=first quartile).
2. Relative Skewness or Coefficient Skewness:
   a. $S_K = \frac{\bar{X} - M_0}{\delta_{M_0}}$,
      where δ_{M_0}=mean deviation from mode.
   b. $S_K = \frac{\bar{X} - M}{\delta_M}$,
      where δ_m=mean deviation from median.
   c. $S_K = \frac{M - M_0}{\delta_{M_0}}$,
      where δ_{M_0}=mean deviation from mode.
3. Karl Pearson's Coefficient of Skewness:
   a. $S_{k_P} = \frac{\bar{X} - M_0}{\sigma}$,
      where σ=standard deviation.
   b. $S_{k_P} = \frac{3(\bar{X} - M)}{\sigma}$,
      (where $M_0 = 3M - 2\bar{X}$).
4. Bowley's Coefficient of Skewness (Absolute):
   a. $S_{k_B} = Q_3 + Q_1 - 2M$

      or second measure of skewness $= Q_3 + Q_1 - 2M$

   b. $S_{k_B}\text{(Relative)} = \frac{(Q_3 + Q_1 - 2M)}{Q_3 - Q_1}$

5. Kelly's Coefficient of Skewness:

$$S_{k_K} = \frac{P_{90} + P_{10} - 2M}{P_{90} - P_{10}} \quad \text{or} \quad \frac{D_9 + D_1 - 2M}{D_9 - D_1},$$

where P_{90}=90th percentile, P_{10}=10th percentile, D_9=9th decile, D_1=1st decile.

6. a. μ (first moment about origin) $= \frac{\Sigma X}{N}$ = mean

   b. μ_1 (first moment from mean) $= \frac{\Sigma d}{N} = 0$ (where $d = X - \bar{X}$)

   c. μ_2 (second moment about mean) $= \frac{\Sigma d^2}{N}$ = variance = σ^2

   d. μ_3 (third moment about mean) $= \frac{\Sigma d^3}{N}$ = skewness

   e. μ_4 (fourth moment about mean) $= \frac{\Sigma d^4}{N}$ = kurtosis.

   Similarly, for frequency distribution:

$$\mu = \frac{\Sigma fX}{N},$$

$$\mu_1 = \frac{\Sigma fdx}{N} \quad \text{or} \quad \frac{\Sigma fd_{x1}}{N} \times h,$$

$$\mu_2 = \frac{\Sigma fdx^2}{N} \quad \text{or} \quad \frac{\Sigma fdx^2}{N} \times h^2,$$

$$\mu_3 = \frac{\Sigma fdx^3}{N} \quad \text{or} \quad \frac{\Sigma fdx^3}{N} \times h^3,$$

$$\mu_4 = \frac{\Sigma fdx^4}{N} \quad \text{or} \quad \frac{\Sigma fdx^4}{N} \times h^4$$

7. a. δ_1 (first moment about an arbitrary origin "A") $= \frac{\Sigma(X - A)}{N}$

   b. δ_2 (second moment about "A") $= \frac{\Sigma(X - A)^2}{N}$

   c. δ_3 (third moment about "A") $= \frac{\Sigma(X - A)^3}{N}$

   d. δ_4 (fourth moment about "A") $= \frac{\Sigma(X - A)^4}{N}$

   Similarly, for frequency distribution

$$\delta_1 = \frac{\Sigma fd}{N} \quad \text{or} \quad \frac{\Sigma fd_1}{N} \times h$$

$$\delta_2 = \frac{\Sigma fd^2}{N} \quad \text{or} \quad \frac{\Sigma fd_1^2}{N} \times h^2$$

$$\delta_3 = \frac{\Sigma fd^3}{N} \quad \text{or} \quad \frac{\Sigma fd_1^3}{N} \times h^3$$

$$\delta_4 = \frac{\Sigma fd^4}{N} \quad \text{or} \quad \frac{\Sigma fd_1^4}{N} \times h^4$$

8. a. $\mu_1 = \delta_1 - \delta_2 = 0$
   b. $\mu_2 = \delta_2 - \delta_1^2$
   c. $\mu_3 = \delta_3 - 3\delta_1\delta_2 + 2\delta^3$
   d. $\mu_4 = \delta_4 - 4\delta_1\delta_3 + 6\delta_1^2\delta_2 - 3\delta_1^4$
9. a. $Z_1 = \frac{\Sigma fX}{N}$ (where Z_1, Z_2, Z_3, Z_4, are moments about zero)
   b. $Z_2 = \frac{\Sigma fX^2}{N}$
   c. $Z_3 = \frac{\Sigma fX^3}{N}$
   d. $Z_4 = \frac{\Sigma fX^4}{N}$.

   Moreover, $Z_1 = A + \delta_1 = \text{mean}$

$$Z_2 = \mu_2 + Z_1^2$$
$$Z_3 = \mu_2 + 3\mu_2 Z_1 + Z_1^3$$
$$Z_4 = \mu_4 + 4\mu_3 Z_1 + 6\mu_2 Z_1^2 + Z_1^4$$

10. a. β_1 (skewness) $= \frac{\mu_3^2}{\mu_2^2}$, $\gamma_1 = \sqrt{\beta_1} = \frac{\mu_3}{\mu_2}$
    b. β_1 (kurtosis) $= \frac{\mu_4}{\mu_2^2}$ (if $\beta_2 = 3$, then the curve will be normal)
    c. $\gamma_2 = \beta_2 - 3$ (if $\gamma_2 = 0$, then the curve will be normal)

RELATED AND SUGGESTED WEBSITES

(As retrieved on December 1, 2015)

1. http://www.sciencedirect.com/science/article/pii/S0167715207000624
2. http://link.springer.com/article/10.1007%2Fs00362-011-0401-6#page-1
3. http://www.jstor.org/stable/3035554

REFERENCES

Elhance, D.N., and Veena Elhance. 1990. *Fundamentals of Statistics*, 10.1–10.48. New Delhi: Kitab Mahal.

Gupta, S.P. 2011. *Statistical Methods*, 338–87. New Delhi: Sultan Chand & Sons.

RELATED AND RECOMMENDED READINGS

Hussain, Shamshad. 1986. *Elementary Statistics in Psychology and Education*, 16–19. New Delhi: Motilal Banarsidass.
Kerlinger, F.N. 1983. *Foundations of Behavioural Research*. New Delhi: Surjeet Publications.
Kothari, C.R. 2000. *Research methodologies: Methods and Techniques*, 169–70. 2nd rev. ed. New Delhi: New Age International Publisher.
Krishnaswami, O.R., and Ranganatham, M. 2005. *Methodology of Research*. New Delhi: Himalaya Publications.
Mangal, S.K. 1987. *Statistics in Psychology and Education*, 105–27. New Delhi: McGraw Hill.
Wimmer, Roger D., and Joseph R. Dominick. 2003. *Mass Media Research: An Introduction*, 247–54. 7th ed. Belmont, CA: Wadsworth Publishing Company.
Zina, O Leary. 2010. *The Essential Guide to Doing Your Research Project*. 3rd ed. London: SAGE Publications.

QUESTIONS AND PROBLEMS

1. Explain the meaning and concept of asymmetry.
2. How will you explore whether a particular distribution is asymmetrical or not?
3. Differentiate between *absolute* measures of asymmetry and *relative* measures of asymmetry.
4. What is skewness? Throw light on Karl Pearson's coefficient of skewness and Kelly's coefficient of skewness.
5. Who has given the most useful and helpful coefficient of skewness from the point of view of media research? Explain why?
6. Explain the measures of skewness based on moments.
7. What is the meaning of moments in media metrics? Explain all the four types of moments.
8. What is kurtosis? How is it computed?
9. Explain the various properties and characteristics of a normal curve.
10. What do you mean by "point of inflection" in a normal curve? Explain.
11. Explain how the area under a normal curve can be measured?
12. Throw light on the applications of a normal curve.
13. Distinguish between skewness and kurtosis.
14. How does skewness differ from kurtosis?
15. Distinguish between dispersion, skewness, and kurtosis. Is the study of skewness useful in media research?
16. What are tests of skewness? Explain the role of skewness and kurtosis in analyzing a frequency distribution.
17. Suppose that a newspaper organization has selected a random sample of 100 from its journalists and has obtained data as follows:

Class	130–134	135–139	140–144	145–149	150–154	155–159	160–164
Frequency	3	12	21	28	19	12	5

Compute the following:
(a) mean, (b) standard deviation, and (c) Karl Pearson's coefficient of skewness.

18. Compute Karl Pearson's measure of skewness on the basis of mean, mode, and standard deviation:

X	14.5	15.5	16.5	17.5	18.5	19.5	20.5	21.5
F	35	40	48	100	125	87	43	22

19. Find out Karl Pearson's coefficient of skewness from the following data:

Marks	Above 0	Above 10	Above 20	Above 30	Above 40	Above 50	Above 60	Above 70	Above 80
No. of students	150	140	100	80	80	70	30	14	0

20. Compute the Pearson coefficient of skewness:

X	12.5	17.5	22.5	27.5	32.5	37.5	42.5	47.5
F	28	42	54	108	129	61	45	33

21. The following distribution of marks were obtained by advertising students and broadcast journalism students:

	Distribution of Advertising Students	Distribution of Broadcast Journalism Students
Mean	100	90
Median	90	80
Standard deviation	10	10

a. Distribution of advertising has the same degree of the variation as distribution of broadcast journalism.
b. Both the distributions have the same degree of skewness.
True/False? Give reasons.

22. Calculate Karl Pearson's coefficient of skewness from the following data:

Profit (₹ in lakhs)	70–80	80–90	90–100	100–110	110–120	120–130	130–140	140–150
No. of ad. agencies	12	18	35	42	50	45	30	8

23. Compute the coefficient of variation from the following data:
Pearson's measure of skewness = 0.42
Mean = 86
Median = 80.

24. Find out Karl Pearson's coefficient of skewness:

Class	70–80	60–70	50–60	40–50	30–40	20–30	10–20	0–10
Frequency	11	22	30	35	21	11	6	5

25. Compute the coefficient of variation from the following distribution:
    mean = 85, median = 80, and Karl Pearson's measure of skewness = 0.42.
26. Find out the coefficient of skewness based on quartiles and median from the following data:

x	70–80	60–70	50–60	40–50	30–40	20–30	10–20	0–10
f	4	7	15	22	38	26	16	12

27. Find the median and mode from the following data:
    Karl Pearson's coefficient of skewness = +0.40, mean = 30, and standard deviation = 8
28. Compute Bowley's coefficient of skewness for the following data:

Weights (in lbs)	200 and above	190–199	180–189	170–179	160–169	150–159	140–149	130–139	120–129	110–119	100–109	Below 99
No. of journalists	2	5	5	23	34	65	121	145	122	66	14	1

29. Find out Bowley's coefficient of skewness for the following continuous distribution:

Wages (₹)	90–100	80–90	70–80	60–70	50–60	40–50	30–40
No. of stringers	9	32	43	21	11	3	1

30. Analyze the following frequency distribution by the method of moments:

X	6	5	4	3	2
F	1	3	7	3	1

31. Compute the first four moments about the mean and analyze the distribution:

X	8	7	6	5	4	3	2	1	0
F	1	8	28	56	70	56	28	8	1

32. The first four moments of a distribution about the value 4 are –1.5, 17, –30, and 108. Calculate the moments about the mean and the origin.
33. Compute the first four moments about the mean and also the values of β_1 and β_2 from the following data:

Marks obtained	60–70	50–60	40–50	30–40	20–30	10–20	0–10
No. of editing students	5	10	15	30	20	12	8

34. The first four central moments of a distribution are 0, 2.5, 0.7, and 18.75. Analyze the kurtosis of the distribution.
35. For a group of ten items, $\Sigma X = 452$, $\Sigma X^2 = 24,270$, mode = 43.7. Calculate the Karl Pearson coefficient of skewness.
36. The first four moments of a distribution about $x = 2$ are 1, 2.5, 5.5, and 16. Find out the four moments about mean and about zero.

37. In a distribution of budding journalists, mean=65, median=70, and coefficient of skewness is –0.6. Calculate the mode and coefficient of variation.
38. Calculate the coefficient of skewness and kurtosis based on the following data of media persons:

X	94.5	84.5	74.5	64.5	54.5	44.5	34.5	24.5	14.5	4.5
F	8	1	3	8	9	17	22	12	4	1

39. The Pearson coefficient of skewness of a distribution of public relations officers is 0.32. Its standard deviation is 6.5 and mean is 29.6. Find the mode.
40. In a skewed distribution of advertisers, mean=160, mode=157, and standard deviation=50. Calculate the coefficient of variation, Karl Pearson's coefficient of skewness, and median.
41. Compute a measure of relative skewness and a measure of relative kurtosis, using moments, for the following distribution of broadcast journalists:

Class	150–170	130–150	110–130	90–110	70–90
Frequency	4	9	18	11	8

42. In a distribution of correspondents of a magazine, mean=50, CV=40 percent, and skewness=–0.4. Calculate the standard deviation, mode, and mean.
43. The income earned by 100 daily wagers in a large newspaper organization are as follows:

Daily wages (₹)	52.5–57.5	57.5–62.5	62.5–67.5	67.5–72.5	72.5–77.5	77.5–82.5	82.5–87.5	87.5–92.5	92.5–97.5
No. of workers	12	16	25	14	13	10	6	3	1

a. Compute the three quartiles.
b. Calculate the absolute measures of dispersion and skewness based on these quartiles.

44. The following details of wages of two advertising agencies from which it is concluded that the skewness and variability are the same for two ad. agencies:

	Ad. Agency A	**Ad. Agency B**
Mean	50	45
Mode	45	50
Variance	100	100

Calculate the coefficient of variations and skewness of both ad agencies.

45. In a skewed distribution of editors, the mean is 200, the coefficient of variation is 8, and Karl Pearson's coefficient of skewness is 0.3. Calculate the mode and the median.
46. Compute a measure of skewness of a group of working journalists based on mean, mode, and standard deviation from the following distribution.

x	80–70	70–60	60–50	50–40	40–30	30–20	20–10
f	50	23	136	180	34	77	185

47. In a group of 20 public relations practitioners, $\sum X = 1452$, $\sum X^2 = 144280$, and mode = 63.7. Calculate Karl Pearson's coefficient of skewness.
48. Compute Karl Pearson's coefficient of skewness for the following marks secured by advertising students:

Marks above	0	10	20	30	40	50	60	70	80
No. of ad. students	150	140	100	80	80	70	30	14	0

49. Calculate the coefficient of skewness from the given data of broadcast journalists: difference of two quartiles = 8, mode = 11, sum of two quartiles = 22, and mean = 8.
50. Find the measure of skewness based on mean, median, and standard deviation from the following data of freelance journalists:

X	600–500	500–400	400–300	300–200	200–100
F	79	206	146	88	45

51. Find out from the following data of income of editors of a daily newspaper, the coefficient of variation if the Pearson coefficient of variation = 0.42, mean = 86, and median = 80.
52. Compute the Pearson coefficient of skewness from the following data of radio broadcasters of All India Radio:

Class	40–50	50–60	60–70	70–80
Frequency	5	6	11	21

53. Find out the coefficient of skewness (Karl Pearson) from the given information of special correspondents of two daily newspapers:

Measure	**Newspaper A**	**Newspaper B**
Mean	150	140
Median	142	155
SD	30	55
Third quartile	195	200
First quartile	62	80

54. Compute Karl Pearson's measures of skewness on the basis of mean, mode, and standard deviation for the following data of media persons:

x	21.5	20.5	19.5	18.5	17.5	16.5	15.5	14.5
f	22	43	87	125	100	48	40	35

55. Find out the coefficient of skewness from the following data of advertisers:

Mid-point	15	20	25	30	35	40
Frequency	12	18	25	24	20	21

56. Calculate Bowley's coefficient of skewness for the following frequency distribution of journalists' families:

No. of children per family	0	1	2	3	4	5	6
No. of journalists per family	7	10	16	25	18	11	8

57. Find out Bowley's coefficient of skewness from the following data of sports reporters:

Mid-value	75	100	125	150	175	200	225	250
Frequency	35	40	48	100	125	80	50	22

58. Calculate the coefficient of skewness based on quartile from the following data:

Size	10–20	20–30	30–40	40–50	50–60	60–70	70–80
Frequency	358	2417	976	129	62	18	10

59. Compute Bowley's coefficient of skewness for the following income figures of stringers of a daily newspaper:

Income equal to or more than	100	200	300	400	500	600	700	800	900	1000
No. of stringers	1000	950	700	600	500	200	150	100	50	0

60. Find out Bowley's coefficient of skewness for the following distribution relating to the personal income tax paid by journalists:

Tax paid (in ₹)	0–100	100–150	150–200	200–250	250–300	300–500	500–800	800–1500	1500–2500	2500 and above
No. of journalists	8	11	14	20	27	8	6	2	2	2

61. Calculate the first four moments about mean and also the values of β_1 and β_2 from the following data of 50 contractual computer operators of a daily newspaper:

Daily wages (in ₹)	170–160	160–150	150–40	140–130	130–120	120–110	110–100
No. of computer operators	3	4	12	20	7	3	1

62. Find the standard deviation from the following distribution of an advertising agency: mean=45, median=48, and coefficient of skewness=–0.4

63. Compute the quartile coefficient of skewness for the following data of an English fortnightly:

Class	501–600	601–700	701–800	801–900	901–1000	1001–1100	1101–1200	1201–1300
Frequency	5	17	80	186	208	134	68	18

64. In a frequency distribution of media persons, the coefficient of skewness based on quartile is 0.6. If the sum of the upper and the lower quartiles is 100 and the median is 38, calculate the value of the upper quartile.
65. Compute Bowley's coefficient of skewness from the following data regarding the weight of working journalists:

Weight	190 and above	189–180	179–170	169–160	159–150	149–140	139–130	129–120	119–110	109–100	Below 100
No. of journalists	2	5	12	31	65	121	145	122	66	14	1

66. The first four moments of a distribution about $X=4$ are 1, 4, 10, and 45. Find out the skewness and kurtosis, and comment on the nature of the distribution.
67. The first two moments of distribution about the value 5 of the variable are 2 and 20. Find the mean and variance.
68. Calculate the coefficient of skewness from the following data: mode = 21 and mean = 18.
69. The first four moments of a distribution about $x=2$ are 1, 2.5, 5.5, and 16. Find out the four moments about the mean and about zero.
70. Compute the Pearson coefficient of skewness from the information of two TV channels:

Measure	**TV Channel A**	**TV Channel B**
Mean	256.5	240.8
Median	201.1	201.6
σ	215	181

71. The first three moments of distribution of a news agency about the value 7 calculated from a set of nine observations are 0.2, 19.4, and –41.0. Calculate the measure of central tendency and dispersion.
72. A frequency distribution of radio jockeys of an FM Radio station showed the following measures of location:
mean = 45, median = 48, and coefficient of skewness = –0.4. Calculate its standard deviation.
73. The first four moments of distribution of an advertising agency are 1, 4, 10, and 46, respectively. Calculate the first four central moments and the Beta constant. Comment on the nature of the distribution.
74. Compute the coefficient of skewness by the Pearson method and the values of β_1 and β_2 from the following data:

Profits (₹ lakhs)	60–50	50–40	40–30	30–20	20–10
No. of ad. agencies	10	22	20	30	18

75. For a distribution of working journalists of a news agency, the mean is 10, variance is 16, γ_2 is +1, and β_2 is 4. Obtain the first four moments about the origin, that is, zero.
76. From the following data of age of working journalists, compute the coefficient of skewness:

Age below (yrs)	55	50	45	40	35	30	25
No. of journalists	100	92	80	65	40	20	8

77. The first four moments of a distribution of a public relations society are 0, 2.5, 0.7, and 18.75. Test the skewness and kurtosis of the distribution.
78. From the following distribution of electronic media journalists, calculate the Pearson coefficient of skewness:

Class	32–28	27–23	22–18	17–13	12–8	7–3
Frequency	18	32	80	175	580	108

79. The first four moments of distribution of advertisers about the value 4 of the variable are –1.5, 17, –30, and 108. Calculate the value of the moments about the mean and zero.
80. The first four moments of distribution of special correspondents about the value 2 of the variable are –2, 12, –20, and 100. Compute the moment about mean. Also, compute and comment upon the distribution.
81. Karl Pearson's coefficient of skewness for a distribution is 0.4 and the coefficient of variation is 30 percent. Its mode is 88. Calculate the mean and the median.
82. A frequency distribution of intelligence of media persons of a TV channel gives the results of coefficient of variation=4, standard deviation=2, and Pearson coefficient of skewness=0.3. Calculate the mean and mode of the distribution.
83. When mean=49.5, σ=14.3 for a distribution of media persons, change the score 80 into Z score or sigma score.
84. If mean=48, σ=8 for a distribution of working journalists of a news agency, convert Z score (σ score) of the value of 0.625 into a raw score.
85. Find out which of the two distribution of subjects has more variability: editing or reporting, from the following data given:

	Editing	Reporting
M	60	30
σ	8	9
Achievement scores of a journalism student	70	67

86. In a normal distribution with a mean of 54 and σ of 5, compute the following:
    a. Q_1 and Q_3 (P_{25} and P_{75})
    b. Two scores between which lies the middle 50 percent cases.
    c. Number of journalists out of 600 who score below 57.
87. Given N=100, M=28.52, σ=4.66 percent, assuming the normality of the given distribution of advertisers, calculate the following:
    a. What percentage of cases lies between 23 and 25?
    b. What limits include the middle 60 percent?

88. Assuming a normal distribution of scores of students of mass communication, a test has a mean score of 100 and a standard deviation of 15. Find out the following:
    a. Score that cuts off the top 10 percent.
    b. Score that cuts off the lower 40 percent.
    c. Percentage of cases above 90.
    d. Score that occupies 68th percentile rank.
    e. Score limits of the middle 68 percent.
89. Of a large unrelated group, four problems are passed by 15 percent, 50 percent, 60 percent, and 75 percent, respectively. Assuming normality, calculate the relative difficulty value of each problem.

7

CHAPTER

Measures of Relationship and Other Measures in Media Research

All too often when liberals cite statistics, they forget the statisticians' warning that correlation is not causation.

—Thomas Sowell

Earlier, in our discussion regarding measures of central tendency, measures of dispersion, and measures of asymmetry, we have dealt with those statistical, mathematical, or media metrics related measures which are used in relation to univariate population, that is, the population consisting of measurement of only one variable. However, if the available data has two variables, then it is called bivariate population. Similarly, if the data happen to be on more than two variables, the population is known as multivariate population. For example, if we have a variable called advertisement, which affects the other variable called news, then the resulting pairs of values are described as bivariate population. Similarly, these variables may affect a third variable called feature or a fourth variable called editorial or a fifth variable called special article, and so on. Thus, the resulting pairs of all these variables—advertisement, news, feature, editorial, and special article—are described as multivariate population.

In the last chapter, we have comprehensively discussed the meaning and concept of asymmetry in mass communication, tests of asymmetry, measures of asymmetry, moment, kurtosis, normal curve, and normal distribution. It included a few general questions, illustrations, and solutions of basics of statistics in the beginning, but gradually focused more on media metrics. Thus, we have discussed statistical tools of media metrics like measures of asymmetry in the previous section. Yet another statistical tool of media metrics in a proper sequence is measures of relationship and other measures (as depicted in the flowchart in Section 2.2.1 of Chapter 2). Hence, this chapter on *measures of relationship and other measures* (in media research) will focus the discussion on the following:

1. Meaning and concept of measures of relationship in media research
2. Meaning and concept of correlation
3. Significance of study of correlation
4. Types of correlation
5. Correlation coefficient
6. Properties of correlation coefficient
7. Methods of correlation
8. Calculation of correlation in a time series
9. Lag and lead in a correlation

10. Concept and meaning of regression
11. Significance of regression analysis
12. Difference between correlation and regression
13. Regression equation
14. Method of least squares
15. Method of deviations from means
16. Properties of regression coefficients
17. Deviation from assumed mean
18. Standard error of estimate
19. Other measures (index numbers, time series, and so on)

In addition, the chapter will also cover the summary, important formulae, related and suggested websites, references, related and recommended readings, questions and problems of measures of dispersion with general reference to statistics and special reference to media metrics relating to the problems of communication and media studies, and their solutions.

7.1 MEANING AND CONCEPT OF MEASURES OF RELATIONSHIP IN MEDIA RESEARCH

When there is a directional or cause and effect relationship between two or more variables, then it can be measured numerically and is called a measure of relationship. In media and communication research, we often try to understand the relationship between two or more variables. For example, in a group communication when the number of audience increases, the effectiveness of communication decreases. So there is an adverse relationship between the number of members in an audience and effectiveness of communication.

Similarly, when the intelligence level of the audience increases or when the audience is changed from a lower intelligence level to a higher intelligence level, then the effectiveness of communication also increases. Hence, there is a direct relationship between intelligence level of the audience and effectiveness of communication. Thus, variables such as number, size, intelligence, gender, age, income, communication, and rigidity are related and connected. If one is affected, then other is also affected. Two valid and relevant questions arise here:

1. Is there any connection, relation, dependence, association, or correlation between two or more variables? If yes, then to what extent or what degree and which direction (positive, zero, negative)?
2. Does there exist any cause and effect relationship between two or more variables. If yes, then to what extent and in which direction?

The first question can be answered by *correlation analysis* and the second question can be answered by *regression analysis*.

7.2 MEANING AND CONCEPT OF CORRELATION

The dictionary meaning of the word correlation is mutual relationship. It is often used as a synonym of covariation, correlativity, mutuality, interrelation, association, relationship, and the likes. As per our discussion, the nearest synonym of correlation seems to be covariation, which indicates the relationship between two or more such variables in which with changes in the values of one variable, the values of the other variable(s) also change. The degree of relationship between the several variables under consideration is measured through the analysis of correlation. The measures of correlation called correlation coefficient or correlation index or the ratio between one variable and another summarize in one figure the direction and degree of correlation.

However, the term correlation has been technically defined by different well-known statisticians and prominent mathematicians differently. Some of the most significant and relevant definitions are as follows.

According to Croxton and Cowden (cited in D.N.S. Elhance and Veena Elhance 1990, 11.1–11.2), "When the relationship is of a qualitative nature, the appropriate statistical tool is for discovering and measuring the relationship and expressing it in a brief formula is known as *correlation*."

L.R. Connor (cited in D.N.S. Elhance and Veena Elhance 1990, 11.1–11.2) defines it as, "If two or more quantities vary in sympathy so that movements in one tend to be accompanied by corresponding movements in the other(s) then they are said to be correlated."

In the words of W.I. King (cited in D.N.S. Elhance and Veena Elhance 1990, 11.1–11.2), "*Correlation* means that between two series or groups of data there exists some causal connection."

According to Ya Lun Chou (cited in D.N.S. Elhance and Veena Elhance 1990, 11.1–11.2), "*Correlation analysis* attempts to determine the 'degree of relationship' between variables."

A.M. Tuttle (cited in Gupta 2011, 390) defines it as, "*Correlation* is an analysis of the covariation between two or more variables."

Thus, the above definitions make it crystal clear that the term correlation relates to the study of mutual relations or associations between two or more variables. Hence, in the field of media or communication, it is a type of statistical tool which helps us in analyzing the covariation of two or more variables of communication and media issues.

7.3 SIGNIFICANCE OF STUDY OF CORRELATION

The significance of the study of correlation is immense in our practical life, and in both physical as well as social sciences including communication and media studies. However, we will focus on the significance of correlation in social science in general and communication and media studies in particular.

1. Correlation helps us in reducing the range of uncertainty associated with decision-making. In communication and media analysis, forecasting is an important phenomenon and the study of correlation helps us immensely in making relatively more dependable forecasts.
2. With the analysis of correlation, we can measure, in one figure, the degree of relationship existing between the variables.
3. Correlation analysis is instrumental in understanding communication and behavior of the people. There is correlation between crime and poverty. There is correlation between communication behavior and frustration. So psychological cause like frustration and economic cause like poverty can reflect the communication behavior of an individual or a society.
4. The analysis of correlation helps us in finding out such variable on which other variables depend. It helps us to explore the probable variation in a variable with a particular amount of variation in a related variable. For example, with the increase in our age, the rigidity in our communication behavior also changes.

5. Mutually interconnected studies between variables are highly instrumental in the growth and development of research and opening of new frontiers and vistas.

Hence, correlation analysis is significantly relevant and widely useful in communication and media research. Thus, correlation is considered to be the basic conceptual as well as statistical tool for in-depth analysis and interpretation of data relating to two or more variables. But correlation analysis does not tell us anything about the cause and effect relationship. Even if there is a high degree of correlation between two variables, yet it does not necessarily indicate a cause and effect relationship between them. Thus, correlation is only a mathematical and statistical relationship and it does not necessarily signify a cause and effect relationship between the variables.

7.4 TYPES OF CORRELATION

Correlation may be broadly classified into the following three most important types.

7.4.1 Positive and Negative Correlation

When there is a direct relationship between two or more variables, then correlation is said to be positive. That is to say that when the values of two variables move in the same direction so that an increase in the value of one variable is related to an increase in the value of the other variable also and the decrease in the value of one variable is related to a decrease in the value of other variable also, then correlation is said to be positive. On the other hand, if variables are varying in opposite directions, that is, as one variable is increasing the other is decreasing or vice versa, then it is called an inverse relationship and the correlation is described as negative or inverse. For example, let us observe the change in the two variables "advertisement" and "news":

a. Positive correlation or direct correlation
    i. No. of news items=11, 15, 20, 22, 24, 26, 30
       No. of photographs=14, 20, 23, 24, 26, 32
    ii. No. of features=85, 70, 55, 35, 30
       No. of animated and graphic items=55, 45, 35, 20, 10
b. Negative correlation or inverse correlation
    i. No. of advertisements=25, 30, 40, 55, 75
       No. of news items=45, 40, 30, 15, 10
    ii. No. of advertisements=110, 95, 60, 40, 25
       No. of special articles=12, 15, 20, 30, 50

7.4.2 Simple, Partial, and Multiple Correlation

In simple correlation, there are only two variables. But in partial and multiple correlation, there are more than two variables. Now, the difference between partial correlation and multiple correlation is that in partial correlation there may be more than two variables, but only two variables are changing; others are considered to be constant. In multiple correlation, there are three or more variables and all are changing or variating simultaneously and the change is also studied simultaneously.

7.4.3 Linear and Nonlinear (Curvilinear) Correlation

In linear correlation, the change is in the same proportion. So it is a straight line. Linear correlation is based on the constancy of ratio of change between the variables. Further, if the amount of change in one variable tends to bear constant ratio to the amount of change in the other variable, then the correlation is described to be linear. For example, let us observe the change in the two variables "new media" and "political campaigning":

No. of posts on new media=15, 30, 45, 60, 75,90

No. of political campaigning=80, 160, 240, 320, 400, 480

Hence, the rate of change between the variables is equiproportionate or, in other words, the ratio of change between the two variables is the same. If it is systematically piloted on a graph, its resultant will be a straight line. Reversely, in a nonlinear correlation, the change is not in the same proportion and the curve is not straight, but it is skewed. Hence, it is also called curvilinear. Here, the *correlation* is not based on the constancy of the ratio of change between the variables; rather such ratio of change is always fluctuating. For example, let us observe the fluctuating change in the two variables "new channel" and "viewer":

Nonlinear correlation

No. of news channels: 400; 800; 1,600; 3,200; 6,400
No. of viewers: 6,00000; 8,00000; 15,00000; 20,00000; 30,00000

7.5 CORRELATION COEFFICIENT

It is also called the correlation index. It is the numerical value of correlation. It is calculated to study the extent or degree and direction of correlation between two or more variables.

J.P. Guilford in his pioneering book *Fundamental Statistics in Psychology and Education* has defined a correlation coefficient as follows: "A coefficient of correlation is a single number that tells us to what extent two things are related, to what extent variations in one go with variations in other." The value of a correlation coefficient ranges from –1 to 1, that is, ±1. The verbal description of correlation coefficient may be given by the following table.

Correlation Coefficient	Verbal Description
+1	Perfectly positive correlation
+0.90 to +1.00	Very highly positive correlation
+0.70 to +0.90	Highly positive correlation
+0.40 to + 0.70	Moderately positive correlation
+0.20 to +0.40	Low positive correlation
+0.00 to +0.20	Very low positive correlation
00	Zero correlation
–0.00 to –0.20	Very low negative correlation
–0.20 to –0.40	Low negative correlation
–0.40 to –0.70	Moderately negative correlation

Correlation Coefficient	Verbal Description
–0.70 to –0.90	Highly negative correlation
–0.10 to –0.20	Very highly negative correlation
–1	Perfectly negative correlation

7.6 PROPERTIES OF CORRELATION COEFFICIENT

Some of the properties of a correlation coefficient are as follows:

1. It ranges from –1 to +1.
2. It is a purely numerical value. It does not have any unit.
3. It is not affected or influenced by addition, subtraction, multiplication, or division of a constant.
4. It does not give the cause and effect relationship.

Perfectly positive correlation, positive correlation, perfectly negative correlation, and negative correlation can be represented by the following figures.

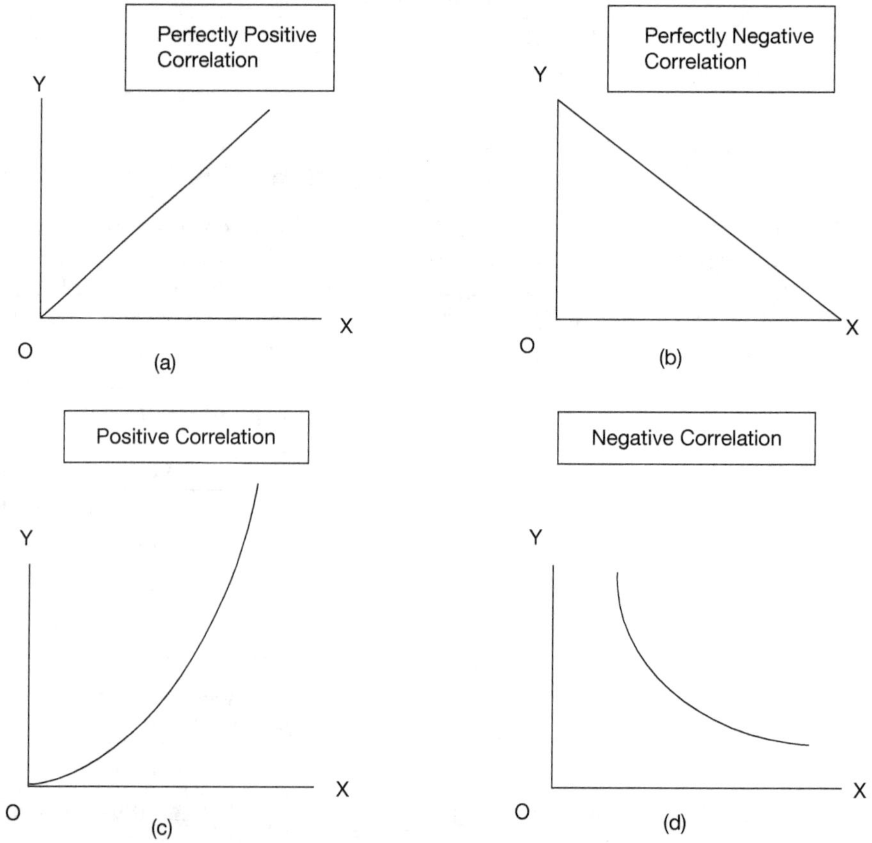

7.7 METHODS OF CORRELATION

There are methods for studying correlation, which are as follows:

1. Scatter diagram method
2. Graphic method
3. Karl Pearson's coefficient of correlation method
4. Spearman's coefficient of correlation method
5. Concurrent deviation method
6. Least squares method

Out of these six methods, the first two methods are based on the knowledge of diagrams and graphs, whereas the remaining four methods are mathematical and statistical methods.

7.7.1 Scatter Diagram Method

Let us suppose that in a distribution, each item has one value, each for two variables X and Y. For example, if the income and hours of work of 50 media persons are measured, then each media person assumes one value in each of the two variables—income and time. If the income of media persons is represented by X and time spent (in hours) by Y and further if X-variable is plotted on the horizontal scale and Y-variable on the vertical scale, only one point would be plotted for each set of the two values. On the horizontal scale, it would indicate the income and time spent by media persons. In this way, the whole data about 50 media persons can be plotted in the shape of 50 points. If these points show some trends either upward or downward, the two variables are said to be correlated. If the trend of the points is upward, rising from left bottom and going up toward the right top, correlation is positive. Similarly, if the tendency is reverse, showing downward trend of the graph from the left top to the right bottom, correlation is negative. The following scatter diagrams will explain the points clearly:

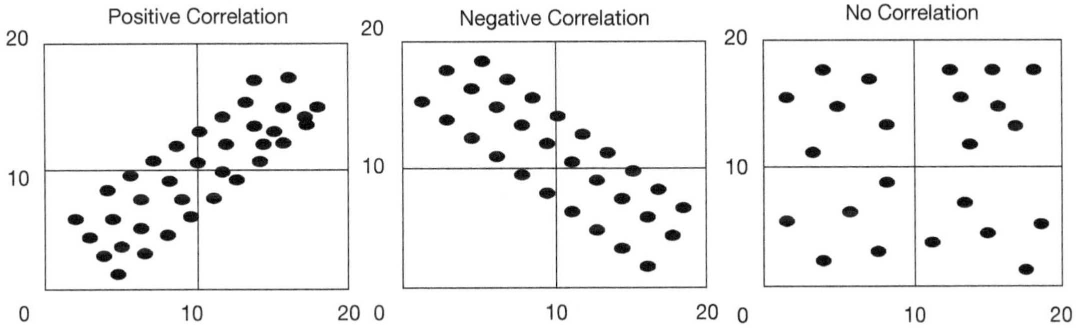

(a) (b) (c)

These diagrams reflect the scattering of different points. All these points do not have any mathematical relationship and they only reflect the trend of the data. Figure (a) reflects positive correlation as it indicates the values of the two variables in the upward direction. Figure (b) reflects negative correlation as the values of the two variables are moving in reverse directions. Figure (c) does not reflect any proper trend, and hence it indicates that there is no correlation between two variables.

7.7.1.1 Merits and Demerits of Scatter Diagram

Merits:

1. It is very easy to draw a scatter diagram. In a subject like mass communication, where media researchers are the least exposed to media metrics, or even those who do not have any mathematical or statistical background can easily understand the correlation between two variables.
2. It is easily understandable and interpretable without any special skills of media metrics.
3. Extreme item values do not affect the method. Such points are always separated in the scatter diagram.

Demerits:

1. The main demerit of this method is that it only gives a visual picture of the relationship of two variables. It only tells us whether there is correlation between the variables and their directions, that is, positive or negative.
2. It does not give the value of the correlation coefficient. So it fails to give an idea about the precise degree of relationship as it cannot explain it mathematically. So it does not help in accurate micro or macro media analysis.

7.7.2 Graphic Method

This method is very useful to find out correlation between two distributions and also the direction whether it is positively correlated or negatively correlated. When in a graph, the two curves representing the two variables show similar tendency, it is an indication of a positive correlation; on the other hand, when the two curves move in different directions, the correlation is negative.

The data mentioned in the following table are plotted in Figure 7.1.

	Price and Supply of Newsprint	
Year	Price per Quintal (₹)	Supply (in Quintals)
2003	3,200	22,000
2004	4,500	19,000
2005	3,200	22,000
2006	2,900	19,000
2007	4,400	27,000
2008	6,900	43,000
2009	4,000	24,000
2010	2,900	18,000
2011	3,100	20,000

Year	Price per Quintal (₹)	Supply (in Quintals)
2012	3,900	23,000
2013	5,300	32,000
2014	4,300	26,000
Average	4,000.5	25,400

For projecting the above data with the help of a graph, there will be two axis X and Y. The X-axis will represent the year and the Y-axis will represent the price of the newsprint per quintal (in ₹) and also the supply of the newsprint (in quintals).

Hence, there will be two line graphs from which the correlation will be observed. Figure 7.1 reflects that the two variables price and supply are positively correlated. Their curves always move in the same direction reflecting that the mutual relationship between them is very close.

7.7.2.1 Merits and Demerits of Graphic Method

This method is generally applied where the data are given over a period of time, that is, in the case of time series. However, just like the scatter diagram method, by this graphic method also we can only have an idea about the direction of the correlation, whether it is positive or negative. We cannot get a numerical value, its degree or magnitude, or the extent to which the variables are related. Thus, it does not help in scientific data analysis of micro or macro media issues.

7.7.3 Karl Pearson's Coefficient of Correlation

Karl Pearson, a well-known biometrician and mathematician, has propounded a formula for the measurement of coefficient of correlation for many mathematical methods of calculating

FIGURE 7.1

CORRELATION BETWEEN NEWSPRINT PRICE AND SUPPLY

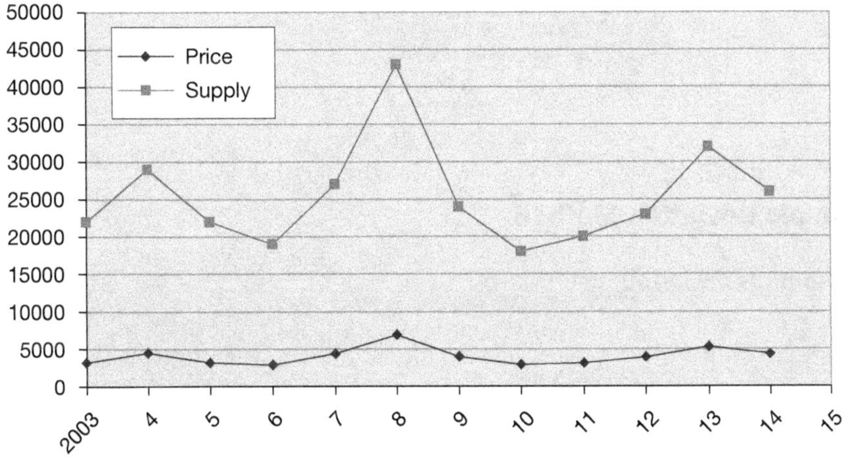

Source: Drawn by author.

correlation; this method is the most widely used in practice. Karl Pearson gave his formula for correlation (r) on the study of covariance between two series—$\left(\frac{\Sigma d_x d_y}{N}\right)$.

Here, d_x and d_y are deviations of two series from their respective means ($\bar{X}$ and $\bar{Y}$), that is, $d_x = X - \bar{X}$ and $d_y = Y - \bar{Y}$.

To find out correlation, the covariance between the two series is divided by the product of their standard deviations:

$$r = \frac{\text{covariance of two series}}{\text{SD of series } X \times \text{SD of series } Y}$$

$$= \frac{\frac{\Sigma d_x d_y}{N}}{\sigma_x \times \sigma_y}$$

where $d_x = X - \bar{X}$, $d_y = Y - \bar{Y}$,

σx = standard deviation of series X,

σ_y = standard deviation of series Y, N = no. of scores

$$= \frac{\Sigma d_x d_y}{N\sigma_x \times \sigma_y}.$$

This formula is known as the product moment formula of coefficient of correlation and this correlation coefficient is popularly known as the *product moment correlation coefficient.*

The above formula is called the *simple deviation method* and can also be extended as

$$= \frac{\Sigma d_x d_y}{N\sqrt{\frac{\Sigma d_x^2}{N}} \times \sqrt{\frac{\Sigma d_y^2}{N}}}$$

$$= \frac{\Sigma d_x d_y}{\frac{N\sqrt{\Sigma d_x^2 \times \Sigma d_y^2}}{N}}$$

$$= \frac{\Sigma d_x d_y}{\sqrt{\Sigma d_x^2 \times d_y^2}}.$$

7.7.3.1 Simple Deviation Method

Thus, by the simple deviation method:

$$r = \frac{\Sigma d_x d_y}{N\sigma_x \times \sigma_y} \quad \text{or} \quad \frac{\Sigma d_x d_y}{\sqrt{\Sigma d_x^2 \times d_y^2}}.$$

Example: Find the correlation coefficient using the product moment method of the fiction and non-fiction serials in five years:

Serial (in 5 yrs.)	1	2	3	4	5
Fiction (X)	15	25	20	30	35
Non-fiction (Y)	60	70	40	50	30

Solution:

Serial (in 5 yrs.)	Fiction (X)	Non-fiction (Y)	$d_x=X-\bar{X}$	$d_y=Y-\bar{Y}$	d_xd_y	d_x^2	d_y^2
1	15	60	−10	10	−100	100	100
2	25	70	0	20	0	0	400
3	20	40	−5	−10	50	25	100
4	30	50	5	0	0	25	0
5	35	30	10	−20	−200	100	400
$N=5$	$\Sigma X=125$	$\Sigma Y=250$			$\Sigma d_xd_y=-250$	$\Sigma d_x^2=250$	$\Sigma d_y^2=1000$

$$\bar{X}=\frac{\Sigma X}{N}=\frac{125}{5}=25,\quad \bar{Y}=\frac{\Sigma Y}{N}=\frac{250}{5}=50$$

$$\therefore r=\frac{\Sigma d_xd_y}{\sqrt{\Sigma d_x^2\times d_y^2}}=\frac{-250}{\sqrt{250\times 1000}}=-\frac{-250}{\sqrt{250\times 250\times 4}}=-\frac{250}{250\times 2}$$

$$=\frac{-1}{2}=-0.5$$

$\therefore$ product moment correlation coefficient=−0.5.

7.7.3.2 Direct/Nondeviation Method

This is a direct method. This is also a nondeviation method. So, we call it the direct/nondeviation method. This method is specially preferred when actual means or deviations are in fraction.

Thus,

$$r=\frac{N\Sigma XY-(\Sigma X)(\Sigma Y)}{\sqrt{N\Sigma X^2-(\Sigma X)^2}\sqrt{N\Sigma Y^2-(\Sigma Y)^2}},$$

where X and Y are scores of raw data and N is the number of series.

Example: Find the product moment correlation coefficient of the following data by the direct/nondeviation method.

Subject	Advertising	Broadcasting	Computer	Development Communication	Editing
Marks in Minor I	5	3	2	8	6
Marks in Minor II	12	15	11	10	18

Solution:

Subject	Minor I (*X*)	Minor II (*Y*)	*XY*	X^2	Y^2
Ad	5	12	60	25	144
Broadcast	3	15	45	9	225
Computer	2	11	22	4	121
DC	8	10	80	64	100
Editing	6	18	108	36	324
$N=5$	$\Sigma X = 24$	$\Sigma Y = 66$	$\Sigma XY = 315$	$\Sigma X^2 = 138$	$\Sigma Y^2 = 914$

$$r = \frac{N\Sigma XY - (\Sigma X)(\Sigma Y)}{\sqrt{N\Sigma X^2 - (\Sigma X)^2}\sqrt{N\Sigma Y^2 - (\Sigma Y)^2}}$$

$$= \frac{5 \times 315 - 24 \times 66}{\sqrt{5 \times 138 - (24)^2}\sqrt{5 \times 914 - (66)^2}}$$

$$= \frac{1575 - 1584}{\sqrt{690 - 576}\sqrt{4570 - 4356}}$$

$$= \frac{-9}{\sqrt{114 \times 214}} = \frac{-9}{\sqrt{24396}}$$

$$= \frac{-9}{156.2} = -0.0567.$$

7.7.3.3 Shortcut Method (or Assumed Mean Method)

$$r = \frac{N\Sigma d_x d_y - (\Sigma d_x)(\Sigma d_y)}{\sqrt{N\Sigma d_x^2 - (\Sigma d_x)^2}\sqrt{N\Sigma d_y^2 - (\Sigma d_y)^2}},$$

where r = coefficient of correlation
N = No. of scores
$d_x = X - A_x$ (X = Scores, A_x = Assumed Mean of x)
$d_y = Y - A_y$ (Y = Scores, A_y = Assumed Mean of y)

Example: Find the product moment correlation coefficient of the following data by the direct/nondeviation method and the shortcut or assumed mean method.

X	5	8	3	4	7	6	9	7	4	8
Y	3	7	4	5	6	8	8	6	2	7

Solution:

Direct/nondeviation method

X	Y	XY	X^2	Y^2
5	3	15	25	09
8	7	56	64	49
3	4	12	09	16
4	5	20	16	25
7	6	42	49	36
6	8	48	36	64
9	8	72	81	64
7	6	42	49	36
4	2	8	16	04
8	7	56	64	49
$\sum X = 61$	$\sum Y = 56$	$\sum XY = 371$	$\sum X^2 = 409$	$\sum Y^2 = 352$

By formula,

$$r = \frac{N\sum XY - (\sum X)(\sum Y)}{\sqrt{N\sum X^2 - (\sum X)^2}\sqrt{N\sum Y^2 - (\sum Y)^2}}$$

$$= \frac{10 \times 371 - 61 \times 56}{\sqrt{10 \times 409 - (61)^2}\sqrt{10 \times 352 - (56)^2}}$$

$$= \frac{3710 - 3416}{(4090 - 3721)(3520 - 3136)}$$

$$= \frac{294}{\sqrt{369 \times 384}} = \frac{294}{\sqrt{141696}} = \frac{294}{376.4} = 0.78$$

$\therefore$ product moment correlation coefficient=0.78

Shortcut method

X	$d_x = X - A_x$	Y	$d_y = Y - A_y$	$d_x d_y$	d_x^2	d_y^2
5	−2	3	−3	6	4	9
8	1	7	1	1	1	1
3	−4	4	−2	8	16	4
4	−3	5	−1	3	9	1
[7]	0	[6]	0	0	0	0
6	−1	8	2	−2	1	4
9	2	8	2	4	4	4
7	0	6	0	0	0	0
4	−3	2	−4	12	9	16
8	1	7	1	1	1	1
$N = 10$	$\sum d_x = -9$		$\sum d_y = -4$	$\sum d_x d_y = 33$	$\sum d_x^2 = 45$	$\sum d_y^2 = 40$

By formula,

$$r = \frac{N\Sigma d_x d_y - (\Sigma d_x)(\Sigma d_y)}{\sqrt{N\Sigma d_x{}^2 - (\Sigma d_x)^2}\sqrt{N\Sigma d_y{}^2 - (\Sigma d_y)^2}}$$

$$= \frac{10 \times 33 - (-9)(-4)}{\sqrt{10 \times 45 - (-9)^2}\sqrt{10 \times 40 - (-4)^2}}$$

$$= \frac{330 - 36}{\sqrt{450 - 81}\sqrt{400 - 16}}$$

$$= \frac{330 - 36}{\sqrt{450 - 81}\sqrt{400 - 16}}$$

$$= \frac{294}{\sqrt{369 \times 384}} = \frac{294}{\sqrt{141696}}$$

$$= \frac{294}{376.4} = 0.78$$

$$\therefore r = 0.78.$$

7.7.3.4 Classified Frequency Distribution Method

$$r = \frac{N\Sigma fd_x d_y - (\Sigma fd_x)(\Sigma fd_y)}{\sqrt{N\Sigma fd_x^2 - (\Sigma fd_x)^2}\sqrt{N\Sigma fd_y^2 - (\Sigma fd_y)^2}}.$$

Example: The following table gives the frequency according to groups of marks secured by the students of mass communication in an intelligence test.

	Age in Year				
Test Marks	**18**	**19**	**20**	**21**	**Total**
200–250	7	4	2	1	14
250–300	3	5	4	2	14
300–350	2	6	8	5	21
350–400	1	4	6	10	21
Total	13	19	20	18	70

Calculate the product moment correlation coefficient from the above-mentioned bivariate classified frequency distribution.

Solution:

x / y	d_y			Age in Year					
		18	19	20	21				
	d_x	−1	0	+1	+2	f	fd_y	fd_y^2	fd_xd_y
200–250	−1	7 7	4 0	2 −2	1 −2	14	−14	14	3
250–300	0	3 0	5 0	4 0	2 0	14	0	0	0
300–350	+1	2 −2	6 0	8 8	5 10	21	21	21	16
350–400	+2	1 −2	4 0	6 12	10 40	21	42	84	50
	Total	13	19	20	19	$N=70$	$\sum fd_y = 35$	$\sum fd_y^2 = 119$	$\sum fd_xd_y = 69$
fd_x		−13	0	20	36	$\sum fd_x = 43$			
fd_x^2		+13	0	20	72	$\sum fd_x^2 = 105$			
fd_xd_y		03	0	18	48	$\sum fd_xd_y = 69$			

Steps in calculation (check the table):

1. Take the step deviation of X and Y series from assumed means and denote them by d_x and d_y.
2. Multiply d_x and d_y and the frequency of the cell. This value, fd_xd_y, may be put at the top on the right- or left-hand side of the cell (which contains the frequency also).
3. Add all values of fd_xd_y (as in step 2) and, thus, obtain the value of Σfd_xd_y.
4. Multiply the frequency of x series with step deviation and total all such products to get Σfd_x. Similarly, get Σfd_y.
5. Then take the square of the step deviations of x series and multiply them with the frequency and total the products to get
6. fd_x^2. Similarly, we will get fd_y^2.
7. After that, substitute the values so obtained in the formula mentioned above and get the value of r.
8. The following examples of product movement correlation coefficient will clarify all the points.

$$r = \frac{N\Sigma fd_xd_y - (\Sigma fd_x)(\Sigma fd_y)}{\sqrt{N\Sigma fd_x^2 - (\Sigma fd_x)^2}\sqrt{N\Sigma fd_y^2 - (\Sigma fd_y)^2}}$$

$$= \frac{70 \times 69 - 43 \times 55}{\sqrt{70 \times 105 - (43)^2}\sqrt{70 \times 119 - (55)^2}} = \frac{4830 - 2365}{\sqrt{7350 - 1849}\sqrt{8330 - 3025}}$$

$$= \frac{2465}{\sqrt{5501}\sqrt{5305}} = \frac{2465}{\sqrt{5501 \times 5305}} = \frac{2465}{\sqrt{29182805}}$$

$$= \frac{2465}{5402.1} = 0.456.$$

7.7.3.5 Assumptions of Karl Pearson's Correlation Coefficient

1. It assumes linear relationship between variables. This means that covariance of X and Y should be equally distributed on both the sides of a straight line.
2. The two variables are affected by a large number of contributory causes so as to form a normal distribution.
3. Even if a cause and effect relationship cannot be studied by a correlation coefficient, yet there exists a cause and effect relationship between the pair of two series of observations.

7.7.3.6 Merits and Demerits of Karl Pearson's Coefficient of Correlation

The most important and striking merit of this correlation coefficient is that it not only gives an idea about the covariation of the two series, but also indicates the direction of relationship. Hence, this coefficient measures both the degree and direction of the correlation between two or more variables.

Out of the mathematical methods used for measuring the degree and direction of the mutual relationship between the variables, Karl Pearson's method is the most widely used method of measuring relationship between two or more variables. However, this method suffers from a few limitations worth mentioning here. These are:

1. It assumes that there is a linear relationship between the variables.
2. Highly correlated does not mean closely correlated. It is liable to be misinterpreted.
3. It is complex, tedious, and time-consuming to compute the value of a correlation coefficient.

7.7.3.7 Coefficient of Correlation and Probable Error

The probable error of Karl Pearson's correlation coefficient is calculated by the following formula:

$$\mathrm{PE}_r = 0.6745\frac{1-r^2}{\sqrt{N}}.$$

PE_r stands for the probable error of correlation coefficient, where r stands for the coefficient of correlation and N stands for the number of pair of two series.

When we omit 0.6745 from the formula, we get the standard error of the coefficient of correlation. Hence,

$$\mathrm{SE}_r = \frac{1-r^2}{\sqrt{N}},$$

where SE_r is the standard error of coefficient of correlation.

Example: Calculate the probable error and standard error of correlation coefficient when the correlation coefficient is=0.7 of 100 pairs of observations.

Solution: By formula,

$$
\begin{aligned}
PE_r &= 0.6745\frac{1-r^2}{\sqrt{N}} \\
&= 0.6745 \times \frac{1-(0.7)^2}{\sqrt{100}} \\
&= 0.6745 \times \frac{1-0.49}{10} \\
&= 0.6745 \times \frac{0.51}{10} \\
&= 6745 \times 0.051 = 0.34 \quad (\text{and } SE_r \text{ is} = 0.051)
\end{aligned}
$$

$$
\begin{aligned}
\therefore \quad \rho &= r \pm PE \\
&= 0.7 \pm 0.034 \\
&= 0.734 \quad \text{or} \quad 0.666.
\end{aligned}
$$

1. Thus, the limit of the coefficient of correlation in the above-mentioned case will range from 0.666 to 0.734.
2. If the value of r is less than the probable error, there is no evidence of correlation.
3. If the value of r is more than six times the probable error, it is significant correlation.
4. Probable error should be applied only when the number of pairs of observations is large. If N is small, probable error may give misleading outcomes.
5. Only in an unbiased and representative sample study, probable error is a measure for interpreting the coefficient of correlation.

7.7.3.8 Coefficient of Determination

Coefficient of determination is the square of coefficient of correlation, that is, r^2, and is defined as the ratio of explained variance to the total variance.

Hence,

$$\text{Coefficient of determination} = r^2 = \frac{\text{Explained variance}}{\text{Total variance}}.$$

The coefficient of nondetermination, on the other hand, is one minus the coefficient of determination and is denoted by K^2, whereas its square root is called the coefficient of alienation and is denoted by K.

Thus, symbolically,

$$K^2 = 1 - r^2 = 1 - \frac{\text{Explained variance}}{\text{Total variance}}$$

where K^2 is the coefficient of nondetermination

or
$$K = \sqrt{1 - r^2} = \sqrt{1 - \frac{\text{Explained variance}}{\text{Total variance}}},$$

where K is the coefficient of alienation.

7.7.4 Spearman's Correlation Coefficient Method

This method is also called the rank difference correlation coefficient and was propounded by the well-known British psychologist Charles Spearman in the year 1904. If we want to study association between two attributes such as intelligence and beauty, Karl Pearson's correlation cannot be calculated as these attributes cannot be assigned definite numerical values. Further, Karl Pearson's method is based on the assumption that the universe under study is normally distributed, is large, and the sample is unbiased and representative. Hence, there is a need for a measure of correlation when the shape of the distribution is not known. Under such circumstances, using ranks rather than actual observations gives the coefficient of rank correlation. This method is especially relevant, important, and useful when quantitative measures for certain factors (such as beauty, leadership, honesty, character, and morality) cannot be determined, but the individuals in the group can be assigned an order thereby obtaining for each individual a number indicating his or her rank in the entire group. Spearman's rank difference correlation coefficient is denoted by ρ (Rho) or R or r_s and calculated by the following formula:

$$\rho = \frac{1 - 6\sum D^2}{N(N^2 - 1)},$$

where ρ (Greek letter "Rho") is the correlation coefficient of rank, D is the difference in ranks, and N is the number of pair of cases.

Example: Find the correlation coefficient of the rank of the following articles and feature numbers published in magazines in one year.

Magazines	A	B	C	D	E	F	G	H	I	J	K
Articles (in 1 yr)	80	45	55	56	58	60	65	68	70	75	85
Features (in 1 yr)	82	86	50	48	60	62	64	65	70	74	90

Solution:

Magazines	Articles (in 1 yr)	Features (in 1 yr)	Rank (R_1)	Rank (R_2)	$D=R_1-R_2$	D^2
A	80	82	2	3	−1	1
B	45	86	11	2	9	81
C	55	50	10	10	0	0
D	56	48	9	11	−2	4
E	58	60	8	9	−1	1
F	60	62	7	8	−1	1
G	65	64	6	7	−1	1
H	68	65	5	6	−1	1
I	70	70	4	5	−1	1
J	75	74	3	4	−1	1
K	85	90	1	1	0	0
$N=11$					$\sum D=0$	$\sum D^2=92$

$$\therefore \rho = 1-\frac{6\sum D^2}{N(N^2-1)} = 1-\frac{6\times 92}{11(11^2-1)}$$
$$= 1-\frac{552}{11(121-1)} = 1-\frac{552}{11\times 120}$$
$$= 1-\frac{23}{55} = \frac{55-23}{55}$$
$$= 0.58.$$

Hence, the rank correlation between articles and features published in magazines is 0.58, that is, moderately positive correlation.

7.7.4.1 Characteristics of Spearman's Correlation Coefficient

1. The sum of the difference of ranks between two variables will always be zero, that is, $\sum D=0$.
2. This type of correlation coefficient is distribution-free or nonparametric. This is because there are no strict assumptions made about the form of the universe from which sample observations are drawn.
3. This method is nothing more, but Pearson's correlation coefficient between the ranks. Thus, it may be analyzed and interpreted in the same manner as Karl Pearson's correlation coefficient.
4. There are generally two types of problems while calculating this type of correlation coefficient:
   a. When actual ranks are given: In this case, the steps required to get the coefficient of correlation are as follows:
      i. We calculate the difference of the two ranks (R_1-R_2) and denote them by D.

ii. Then we compute D^2 and total them to get ΣD^2.

iii. There after, we apply the formula $\rho = 1 - \dfrac{6\Sigma D^2}{N(N^2-1)}$.

Example: The ranking of 10 newspapers are as follows:

English	6	5	3	10	2	4	9	7	8	1
Hindi	3	8	4	9	1	6	10	7	5	2

Compute the rank correlation coefficient.

Solution:

R_1	R_2	$D=(R_1-R_2)$	$(R_1-R_2)^2=D^2$
6	3	3	9
5	8	–3	9
3	4	–1	1
10	9	1	1
2	1	1	1
4	6	–2	4
9	10	–1	1
7	7	0	0
8	5	3	9
1	2	–1	1
$N=10$			$\Sigma D^2 = 36$

$$\rho = 1 - \frac{6\Sigma D^2}{N(N^2-1)} = 1 - \frac{6\times 36}{10(100-1)} = 1 - \frac{216}{990}$$
$$= 1 - 0.218 = 0.782.$$

Hence, the rank correlation between English and Hindi newspapers is 0.782, that is, highly positive correlation.

b. When actual ranks are not given: Rank formula can be applied even when we are dealing with variables which can be measured in quantitative terms. When we get the actual data and not the ranks, we have to convert the data into ranks. The highest or the smallest value is given rank 1 and the other variables are given ranks accordingly. It does not matter whether ranks are in ascending order or descending order, as long as the same approach is followed for both the variables.

Example: Compute the coefficient of rank correlation from the marks obtained by media students in editing and reporting:

X (editing)	60	34	40	50	45	41	22	43	42	66	64	46
Y (reporting)	75	32	34	40	45	33	12	30	36	72	41	57

Solution: Computing of the coefficient of rank correlation,

X	R_x	Y	R_y	$D=R_x-R_y$	D^2
60	3	75	1	2	4
34	11	32	10	1	1
40	10	34	8	2	4
50	4	40	6	–2	4
45	6	45	4	2	4
41	9	33	9	0	0
22	12	12	12	0	0
43	7	30	11	–4	16
42	8	36	7	1	1
66	1	72	2	–1	1
64	2	41	5	-3	9
46	5	57	3	2	4
					$\Sigma D^2 = 48$

$$\therefore \rho = 1 - \frac{6\Sigma D^2}{N(N^2-1)} = 1 - \frac{6 \times 48}{12(12^2-1)}$$

$$= 1 - \frac{288}{1716} = \frac{1428}{1716} = 0.82.$$

7.7.4.2 Equal Ranks

Whenever there is more than one item with the same value, a common rank is given to such items. In such a case, it is customary to give each item an average rank. Hence, if two items are ranked equal at the seventh place, they are each given the rank $\frac{7+8}{2}$, that is, 7.5, while if three are ranked equally at the seventh place, then they are given the rank $\frac{7+8+9}{3} = 8$. When this is done, the coefficient of rank correlation needs some correction, because the mentioned formula is based on the supposition that the ranks of various items are different and that no rank is given to more than one item. The adjustment consists of adding $\frac{1}{12}(m^3 - m)$ to the value of ΣD^2. m stands for the number of items whose ranks are common. When there are more than one such group of items with a common rank, this value is added as many times as the number of such groups. The formula can, thus, be modified as follows:

$$\rho = 1 - \frac{6\Sigma D^2 + \frac{1}{12}(m^3 - m) + \frac{1}{12}(m^3 - m) + \cdots}{N(N^2-1)}$$

(where m is the number of items whose terms are common).

The formula may be further modified as:

$$\rho = 1 - \frac{6\sum D^2 + \frac{1}{12}(m_1^3 - m_1) + \frac{1}{12}(m_2^3 - m_2) + \cdots}{N(N^2 - 1)}.$$

Example: Calculate the coefficient of rank correlation from the following data.

Newspapers	A	B	C	D	E	F	G	H	I	J
Sports news (*X*)	12	15	24	20	8	15	20	20	11	26
Political news (*Y*)	21	25	35	24	16	18	25	16	16	38

Solution:

Newspapers	X	R_x	Y	R_y	$R_x - R_y = D$	D^2
A	12	8	21	6	2	4
B	15	6.5	25	3.5	3	9
C	24	2	35	2	0	0
D	20	4	24	5	1	1
E	8	10	16	9	1	1
F	15	6.5	18	8	0.5	0.25
G	20	4	25	3.5	0.5	0.25
H	20	4	16	9	5	25
I	11	9	16	9	0	0
J	26	1	38	1	0	0
$N=10$					$\Sigma D=0$	$\Sigma D^2=40.5$

By formula,

$$\rho = 1 - \frac{6\sum D^2 + \frac{1}{12}(m_1^3 - m_1) + \frac{1}{12}(m_2^3 - m_2) + \frac{1}{12}(m_3^3 - m_3) + \frac{1}{12}(m_4^3 - m_4)}{N(N^2 - 1)}$$

$$\left[\begin{array}{c}\text{Since item 15 occurs 2 times and 20 occurs 3 times,} \\ m_1 = 2,\ m_2 = 3 \\ \text{Further , item 5 occurs twice and 16 occurs thrice} \\ \text{in } Y\text{-axis, so } m_3=2,\ m_4=3.\end{array}\right]$$

$$= 1 - \frac{6 \times 40.5 + \frac{1}{12}(2^3 - 2) + \frac{1}{12}(3^3 - 3) + \frac{1}{12}(2^3 - 2) + \frac{1}{12}(3^3 - 3)}{10(10^2 - 1)}$$

$$= 1 - \frac{6 \times 40.5 + \frac{1}{2} + 2 + \frac{1}{2} + 2}{10 \times 99}$$

$$= 1 - \frac{243 + 5}{990} = 1 - \frac{248}{990} = \frac{990 - 248}{990} = \frac{742}{990} = \frac{371}{495}$$

$$= 0.74.$$

7.7.4.3 Merits and Demerits of Rank Correlation

Merits:

1. This method is very easy to use and apply compared to the Pearson method. The answers obtained by this method and product moment method will be the same, provided no value is repeated, that is, no value reoccurs and all the items are different.
2. While the Pearson method is based on a set of full information, Spearman's coefficient is based only on the ranks.
3. Even if the data are of a qualitative nature, such as feeling, beauty, attitude, emotion, personality, and communication skill, this method is simpler to understand and easier to apply. For examples, the journalists of two newspaper industries can be ranked in order of efficiency and degree of correlation calculated by this method.
4. In the rank method, since the sum of differences between ranks, that is, ΣD, is always equal to zero, it always provides a check and makes the calculation much easier.
5. This method unlike the Pearson method does not assume normality in the distribution of the universe from which the sample has been drawn.
6. This is the one and only approach which can be applied where we are given the ranks and not the actual data.
7. Even if actual data are available, the rank method can be used for computing correlation.

Demerits:

1. The rank method cannot be applied in a bivariate classified frequency distribution, while the large volume of media data is often classified for suitable media analysis.
2. This method can be easily used if N is small, say 25 or 30, or else the calculation will become tedious.

7.7.5 Concurrent Deviation Method

This method is described as the simplest and quickest method of calculating the coefficient of correlation. This method mainly focuses on the direction of change of two variables (say X and Y) independently.

By formula,

$$r_c = \pm\sqrt{\pm\left(\frac{2c-n}{n}\right)},$$

where r_c is the correlation coefficient of concurrent deviation, c is the number of positive signs obtained after multiplying D_x and D_y, D_x is the direction of change (positive or negative) of X series, and similarly, D_y is the direction of change (positive or negative) of Y series, n is $(N-1)$, while N is the number of pairs of observations.

(Note: Here, n is always taken to be 1 less than the number of pairs of observations as there is no sign for the first value of X and Y. For example, if there are seven pairs of observations in the series, then n will be 6. Further, the meaning of ± signs both inside and outside the root is that only the positive value inside the root will be considered as the negative value inside the root will give only an imaginary number.)

7.7.5.1 Steps for Computation

1. First of all, we have to find out the direction of change (+, –, or zero) of X variable (D_x) and similarly of Y variable (D_y), independently. We will examine whether as compared to the first value of x, the second value of x is increasing, decreasing, or constant. If it is increasing, we will put a + sign, if decreasing, then a – sign, and if constant, then zero. Likewise, we will compare the second value of x with the third value, and so on. A similar treatment will be given to the Y variable.
2. Then, we will find D_xD_y by multiplying D_x with D_y
3. After that, we will find the value of c by summing the + sign of D_xD_y, that is, $c=\Sigma D_xD_y$ (in terms of the number of + signs only)

Lastly, we will apply the above-mentioned formula,

$$r_c = \pm\sqrt{\pm\left(\frac{2c-n}{n}\right)}.$$

Example 1: Find out the correlation coefficient of the time allotted in minutes to the news and non-fiction programs mentioned in the following X series and Y series by the concurrent deviation method.

TV Channel	A	B	C	D	E	F	G
(News time) X	110	120	130	130	115	100	120
(Non-fiction time) Y	50	40	60	80	80	55	60

Solution:

News Channel	X	D_x	Y	D_y	D_xD_y
A	110		50		
B	120	+	40	–	–
C	130	+	60	+	+
D	130	0	80	+	0
E	115	–	80	0	0
F	100	–	55	–	+
G	120	+	60	+	+
	$N=7$				$c=3$

$N=7 \therefore n=N-1=7-1=6$

$$\therefore r_c = \pm\sqrt{\pm\left(\frac{2c-n}{n}\right)} = \pm\sqrt{\pm\left(\frac{2\times 3-6}{6}\right)}$$

$$= \pm\sqrt{\pm\frac{0}{6}} = \pm\sqrt{0} = 0.$$

Hence, the correlation between the time allotted to news and non-fiction programs is 0, that is, no correlation.

Example 2: Calculate the correlation coefficient by the concurrent deviation method of the following data:

X	1	2	3	4	5	6
Y	30	15	9	5	1	0

Solution:

X	D_x	Y	D_y	D_xD_y
1		30		
2	+	15	−	−
3	+	9	−	−
4	+	5	−	−
5	+	1	−	−
6	+	0	−	−
$N=6$				$c=0$

$N=6, \therefore n=n-1=6-1=5$

$$\therefore r_c = \pm\sqrt{\pm\left(\frac{2c-n}{n}\right)} = \pm\sqrt{\pm\left(\frac{2\times 0-5}{5}\right)}$$

$$= \pm\sqrt{\pm\frac{0-5}{5}} = \pm\sqrt{\frac{-5}{5}}$$

$$= \pm\sqrt{-1} = -\sqrt{1} = -1.$$

Hence, the correlation between X and Y is –1, that is, perfectly negative correlation.

Example 3: Calculate the correlation coefficient of the following data by the concurrent deviation method.

X	250	300	350	400	450	500
Y	25	30	32	33	40	50

Solution:

X	D_x	Y	D_y	D_xD_y
250		25		
300	+	30	+	+
350	+	32	+	+
400	+	33	+	+
450	+	40	+	+
500	+	50	+	+
$N=6$				$c=5$

$N=6, \therefore n=N-1=6-1=5$

$$\therefore r_c = \pm\sqrt{\pm\left(\frac{2c-n}{n}\right)} = \pm\sqrt{\pm\left(\frac{2\times 5-5}{5}\right)}$$

$$= \pm\sqrt{\pm\frac{10-5}{5}} = \pm\sqrt{\pm\frac{5}{5}} = \pm\sqrt{\pm 1} = \sqrt{1} = 1.$$

Hence, the correlation between X and Y is +1, that is, perfectly positive correlation.

7.7.5.2 Merits and Demerits of Concurrent Deviation Method

Merits:

1. This method is the easiest, simplest, and quickest of all the methods. Hence, it is often applied when the media analysis is based on "very" short-term and short-term planning.
2. It is very convenient even when the number of pairs of observations is very large. Thus, it helps in data mining of media analysis or large volume of media data.

Demerits:

1. It is only a very rough indicator of correlation. Hence, it does not turn out to be very useful in scientific data analysis of media issues.
2. It does not differentiate between small and big changes of direction. For example, if the number of news items increases from 100 to 2000, the sign indicating change would be + and if the change is from 100 to 105, then also the sign of change would be +, without taking into consideration the magnitude of change. Again it is not suitable for accuracy in communication and media interpretation.

7.7.6 Method of Least Squares

It has been discussed earlier that the Pearson correlation coefficient is based on linear relationship between variables. This means that the covariance of x and y should be equally distributed on both sides of a straight line. One of the methods of finding out this linear relationship between x and y is by calculating the linear values of y corresponding to the values of x. This is carried out by the method of least squares:

$$r_1 = \frac{S_y}{\sigma_y}$$

where r_l=least squares correlation coefficient, σ_{yl}=*SD* of computed (linear) values of *Y*, σ_y=*SD* of original values of *Y*

Now, the computed (linear) value of *y* can be calculated by the equation of a straight line, that is,

$$Y=a+bx.$$

To calculate the values of *a* and *b*, the following two normal equations are applied:

$$\sum Y = Na + b\sum X \quad (i)$$

$$\sum XY = a\sum X + b\sum X^2 \quad (ii)$$

Thus, by putting the relevant values of *X* and *Y* in the above equations, we can compute the linear values of the equation $Y=a+bx$.

Example: Calculate the coefficient of correlation from the following data.

X	1	2	3	4	5
Y	166	184	142	180	338

Solution: Computing linear value of $Y=a+bx$

X	*Y*	*XY*	X^2
1	166	166	1
2	184	368	4
3	142	426	9
4	180	720	16
5	338	1690	25
$N=5$	$\Sigma Y=1010$	$\Sigma XY=3370$	$\Sigma X^2=55$

The two normal equations are:

$$\Sigma Y=Na+b\Sigma X$$

$$\Sigma XY=a\Sigma X+b\Sigma X^2$$

Substituting the values from the above table, we get,

$$1010 = 5a + 15b \quad (i)$$

$$3370 = 15a + 55b \quad (ii)$$

By multiplying Equation (*i*) by 3, we get,

$$3030 = 15a + 45b \quad (iii)$$

Now, by subtracting (*ii*) from (*iii*), we get

$$3030 = 15a + 45b$$
$$-3370 = -15a \pm 55b$$
$$-340 = -10b$$
$$b = 34$$

Putting the value of b in (*i*), we get,

$$1010 = 5a + 15 \times 34$$
$$\text{or,} \quad 5a = 1010 - 510$$
$$\text{or,} \quad 5a = 500$$
$$\therefore a = 100.$$

Thus, the equation of the straight line

$Y = a + bx$ becomes $Y = 100 + 34x$.

Now, we can calculate the computed (linear) values of Y for given values of X:

X	$Y = a + bx$
1	$100 + 34 \times 1 = 134$
2	$100 + 34 \times 2 = 168$
3	$100 + 34 \times 3 = 202$
4	$100 + 34 \times 4 = 236$
5	$100 + 34 \times 5 = 270$

Now, we are supposed to calculate the standard deviation of the original Y series and the computed (linear) Y series:

Original (Y)	$d_y = Y - \bar{Y}$ $Y - 202$	d_y^2	**Computed (linear) Y_c**	$d_{yc} = Y_c - \bar{Y}_c$ $Y_c - 202$	d_{yc}^2
166	-36	1296	134	-68	4624
184	-18	324	168	-34	1156
142	-60	3600	202	0	0
180	-22	484	236	34	1156
338	136	18496	270	68	4624
$\Sigma Y = 1010$	$\Sigma d_y = 0$	$\Sigma d_y^2 = 24200$	$\Sigma y_c = 1010$	$\Sigma d_{yc} = 0$	$\Sigma d_{yc}^2 = 11560$

$$N = 5, \therefore \bar{Y} = \frac{\Sigma Y}{N} = \frac{1010}{5} = 202 \quad \text{and} \quad \bar{Y}_c = \frac{\Sigma Y_c}{N} = \frac{1010}{5} = 202.$$

Now, standard deviation of the original Y series

or

$$\sigma_y = \sqrt{\frac{\Sigma d_y^2}{N}} = \sqrt{\frac{24200}{5}} = \sqrt{4800} = 69.57.$$

Standard deviation of the computed (linear) Y series
or

$$\sigma_{yc} = \sqrt{\frac{\Sigma d_{yc}^2}{N}} = \sqrt{\frac{11560}{5}} = \sqrt{2312} = 48.08$$

$$\therefore r_c = \frac{\sigma_{yc}}{\sigma_y} = \frac{48.08}{69.57} = 0.69.$$

7.8 CALCULATION OF CORRELATION IN A TIME SERIES

Times series is that series in which one variable is time. In this, we observe numerical data in relation to time. For example, when average prices of newsprint are given for the last 20 years, it will constitute a time series. Time series depict two types of changes: (a) long term and (b) short term. When we study correlation of two times series, it is necessary to study separately the correlation of long- and short-term changes. The reason is that it is not necessary that the relationship between the long-term changes in the two series and the relationship between their short-term fluctuations should be similar. It is quite likely that in two time series there may be positive correlation between long-term changes and negative correlation between short-term fluctuations. Under such circumstances, it is important to study correlation between long-term changes and short-term changes separately, or else misleading conclusions would be arrived at.

7.8.1 Correlation of Long-term Changes

For understanding and calculating the correlation of long-term changes, first of all the trend values of the two series must be obtained either by the moving average method or by the method of least squares. After this, the coefficient of correlation can be calculated between the trend values of two series by the methods discussed earlier and no separate or special method is necessary. Hence, in calculating correlation between long-term changes, the only special thing to remember is that instead of the original series, trend values are applied for the computation of the coefficient of correlation.

7.8.2 Correlation of Short-term Changes

This can be computed by the following steps:

1. Instead of original series, we will determine the trend values by the average method.
2. Then, we will deduct from the actual values the corresponding trend values by the moving average method. Thus, we will get the short-term fluctuations which will be denoted by d_x and d_y for short-term fluctuations of X series and Y series, respectively.
3. After that we will square the short-term fluctuations of the x series and get the total of Σd_x^2.
4. Similarly, we will square the short-term fluctuations of the Y series and get the total of Σd_y^2
5. Then, we will multiply d_x with d_y for each value and get the total $\Sigma d_x d_y$.

Thus,

$$r = \frac{\Sigma d_x d_y}{\sqrt{\Sigma d_x^2 \times \Sigma d_y^2}}.$$

As already mentioned in the above-mentioned steps, here d_x denotes deviation of the X series from the moving average and not from the actual mean. Similarly d_y denotes deviation of the Y series from the moving average and not from the actual mean. Thus, d_x and d_y in the above formula mentioned in this column is different from d_x and d_y of Karl Pearson's formula of correlation coefficient.

Example: Compute the Pearson coefficient of correlation of short-term changes for the following indices of supply and price of newsprint.

Year	2000	2001	2002	2003	2004	2005	2006	2007	2008	2009	2010	2011	2012	2013	2014
Supply index of newsprint	91	98	95	92	93	96	102	107	104	98	100	108	116	114	111
Price index of newsprint	117	97	102	108	105	96	77	68	77	93	89	83	78	84	93

Solution: By formula,

$$r = \frac{\Sigma d_x d_y}{\sqrt{\Sigma d_x^2 \times \Sigma d_y^2}}.$$

Now, we will calculate the coefficient of correlation of short-term changes for the indices of supply and price of newsprint.

Year	Supply Index (X)	5-yearly Moving Average ($\bar{X}$)	Derivation of Actual Value from Moving Average $d_x = (X - \bar{X})$	d_x^2	Price Index (Y)	5-yearly Moving Average ($\bar{Y}$)	Derivation of Actual Value from Moving Average $d_y = (Y - \bar{Y})$	d_y^2	$d_x.d_y$
2000	91	–	–	–	117	–	–	–	–
2001	98	–	–	–	97	–	–	–	–
2002	95	93.8	1.2	1.44	102	105.8	–3.8	14.44	–4.56
2003	92	94.8	–2.8	7.84	108	101.6	6.4	40.96	–17.92
2004	93	95.6	–2.6	6.76	105	97.6	7.4	54.76	–19.24
2005	96	98.0	–2.0	4.00	96	90.8	5.2	27.04	–10.40
2006	102	100.4	1.6	2.56	77	84.6	–7.6	57.76	–12.16
2007	107	101.4	5.6	31.36	68	82.2	–14.2	201.64	–79.52
2008	104	102.4	1.8	3.24	77	80.8	–3.8	14.44	–6.84
2009	98	103.4	–5.4	29.16	93	82.0	11.0	121.00	–59.40
2010	100	105.2	–5.2	27.04	89	84.0	5.0	25.00	–26.00
2011	108	107.2	0.8	0.64	83	85.4	–2.4	5.76	–1.92

Year	Supply Index (X)	5-yearly Moving Average ($\bar{X}$)	Derivation of Actual Value from Moving Average $d_{x=}(X-\bar{X})$	d_x^2	Price Index (Y)	5-yearly Moving Average ($\bar{Y}$)	Derivation of Actual Value from Moving Average $d_{y=}(Y-\bar{Y})$	d_y^2	$d_x.d_y$
2012	116	109.8	6.2	38.44	78	85.4	-7.4	54.76	-45.88
2013	114	–	–	–	84	–	–	–	–
2014	111	–	–	–	93	–	–	–	–
				$\Sigma d_x^2 = 152.48$				$\Sigma d_y^2 = 617.56$	$\Sigma d_x d_y = -283.84$

$$\Sigma d_x d_y = -283.84,\ \Sigma d_x^2 = 152.48,\ \Sigma d_y^2 = 617.56.$$

Putting all the values in the formula,

$$r = \frac{\Sigma d_x d_y}{\sqrt{\Sigma d_x^2 \times \Sigma d_y^2}} \qquad r = \frac{-283.84}{\sqrt{152.48 \times 617.56}}$$

$$\begin{aligned}
\log r &= \log 283.84 - \frac{1}{2}[\log 152.48 + \log 617.56] \\
&= 2.4531 - \frac{1}{2}[2.1831 + 2.7907] \\
&= 2.4531 - \frac{1}{2}[4.9738] \\
&= 2.4531 - 2.4869 = -0.0338 \\
&= \bar{1}.9662 \\
r &= A.L.\bar{1}.9662 = 0.925.
\end{aligned}$$

Hence, the correlation between the supply and price index is 0.925, that is, very highly positive correlation.

7.9 LAG AND LEAD IN CORRELATION

The understanding and knowledge of lag and lead is of valid relevance and special significance in studying communication skills, advertising, sales promotion, and many other types of business communication. In this type of study, one may find a time gap before a cause and consequence relationship is set up. For example, the supply of newsprint may increase today, but it may not have an instant impact on prices; it may take a few months or a few years for prices to adjust to the increased supply. This difference in the period before a cause and consequence relationship is set up is described as "lag." When we are calculating correlation, their time gap must be taken care of or else fallacious results may be drawn. Here, adjustment is made in pairing of items in accordance with the time lag.

Month	Supply of Newsprint	Price of Newsprint
January	501	72
February	505	69
March	509	80
April	412	72
May	518	75
June	520	70
July	525	74
August	504	76
September	522	78
October	516	80
November	522	78
December	527	75

Example: Of a firm of a media organization, the following were the monthly figures of advertising expenditure (in crore) and sales (in number). It is observed that advertising expenditure has its impact on sales generally after two years. Compute the coefficient of correlation, allowing for this time lag.

Year	2003	2004	2005	2006	2007	2008	2009	2010	2011	2012	2013	2014
Advertising Expenditure (in crores)	50	60	70	90	120	150	140	160	170	190	200	250
Sales (in no.)	1300	1400	1600	2000	2200	2500	2400	2600	2800	2900	3100	3900

Solution: Here, we allow for a time lag of 2 years, that is, link advertising expenditure of 2003 with sales of 2005, and so on.

Calculation of correlation coefficient:

Year	Ad Expenditure (X)	$d_x = \frac{x-\bar{x}}{10} = \frac{x-120}{10}$	d_x^2	Sales (Y)	$d_y = \frac{y-\bar{y}}{100} = \frac{y-2600}{100}$	d_y^2	$d_x d_y$
2003	50	–7	49	1600	–10	100	70
2004	60	–6	36	2000	–6	36	36
2005	70	–5	25	2200	–4	16	20
2006	90	–3	9	2500	–1	1	3
2007	120	0	0	2400	–2	4	0
2008	150	3	9	2600	0	0	0
2009	140	2	4	2800	2	4	4
2010	160	4	16	2900	3	9	12

Year	Ad Expenditure (X)	$d_x = \frac{x-\bar{x}}{10} = \frac{x-120}{10}$	d_x^2	Sales (Y)	$d_y = \frac{y-\bar{y}}{100} = \frac{y-2600}{100}$	d_y^2	$d_x d_y$
2011	170	5	25	3100	5	25	25
2012	190	7	49	3900	13	169	91
N=10	$\Sigma X=1200$	$\Sigma d_x=0$	$\Sigma d_x^2=222$	$\Sigma Y=26000$	$\Sigma d_y=0$	$\Sigma d_y^2=364$	$\Sigma d_x d_y=261$

$$\bar{X} = \frac{\Sigma X}{N} = \frac{1200}{10} = 120, \quad \therefore Y = \frac{26000}{10} = 2600$$

$$r = \frac{\Sigma d_x d_y}{\sqrt{\Sigma d_x^2 \times \Sigma d_y^2}}$$

$$= \frac{261}{\sqrt{222 \times 364}} = \frac{261}{284.267} = +0.918.$$

Hence, the correlation between advertising expenditure and sales is +0.918, that is, very highly positive correlation.

7.10 MEANING AND CONCEPT OF REGRESSION

After understanding the concept and meaning of correlation, another important measure of measuring relation between two or more variables is regression analysis. The correlation measures tell only the relation between variables, whereas regression also finds out the causation among variables. The dictionary meaning of the word "regression" is "stepping back," "act of returning," or "reversion."

The term "regression" was first used by Sir Francis Galton (1822–1911) in 1877, while studying the height of fathers and their sons. Galton introduced the word "regression" in his paper entitled "Regression towards Mediocrity in Hereditary Stature." He studied the relationship between the heights of fathers and their sons on more than 1,000 fathers and sons and arrived at a very interesting relationship, that is, tall fathers have tall sons and short fathers have short sons. But the average height of the sons of a group of tall fathers is less than that of the fathers and the average height of sons of a group of short fathers is greater than that of the fathers. The line explaining the tendency of stepping back, sliding back, or going back is called a "regression line" by Francis Galton. These days there is a tendency to use the word "estimating line" instead of "regression line."

Regression basically implies going back or returning toward the mean and it is the measure of the average relationship between two or more variables in terms of the original units of the data. And regression lines or estimating lines study the average relationship between two series and highlight their covariance. Suppose the coefficient of correlation between the heights of fathers and sons is +0.8, it means that if a group of fathers have heights which are more than the average by H inches, then their sons could have heights which will be more than average by 0.8 inches. What we mean to say is that the height of the sons regresses toward the mean.

The word regression has been aptly defined by different mathematicians and statisticians differently.

According to Morris Hamburg (cited in Gupta 2011), "The term 'Regression Analysis' refers to the method by which estimates are made of the values of the variable from a knowledge of the values of one or more other variables and to the measurement of the errors involved in the estimation process."

Ya Lun Chou defines it as "Regression analysis attempts to establish the 'nature of relationship' between variables—that is, to study the functional relationship between the variables and thereby provide a mechanism for production or forecasting."

7.11 SIGNIFICANCE OF REGRESSION ANALYSIS

The study of regression is highly meaningfully relevant and widely useful in almost all the branches of media and communication. It has the following significance, relevance, and utility, especially in the field of analyzing the media variables:

1. Regression analysis is carried out for estimating or predicting the unknown value of one variable from the unknown value of other variable.
2. This is a widely useful branch of statistical theory and a significantly relevant statistical tool which is often used in social sciences, especially media and communication studies.
3. In our day-to-day activities, we come across many such variables which are interconnected and interrelated. For example, the effect of expenditure on advertisement may lead to rise in the sales. Thus, in social sciences, especially communication and media studies, there is multiple causation, which means that a large number of factors affect many variables. The regression analysis that confines itself to a study of only two variables is called simple regression, whereas the analysis which finds out more than two variables at a time is called multiple regression.
4. In the study of simple regression, there are two variables one of which is known as an "independent variable" or a "regressor" or "predictor" or "explanator." It is exclusively on the basis of the values of this variable that the values of the other variable are predicted. This is called the "dependent" or "regressed" or "explained" variable.
5. The study of regression is so helpful and useful that we can also compute the value of the coefficient of correlation by applying regression. The square of correlation coefficient (r), called the coefficient of determination, measures the degree of association of correlation that exists between the two variables. It also measures the consequence of independent variable on the dependent variable and gives an indication about the predictive value of regression studies. Thus, greater the value of the coefficient of determination (r^2), the better is the fit and the more helpful the regression equations as a predictive tool.

7.12 DIFFERENCE BETWEEN CORRELATION AND REGRESSION

Both correlation and regression are highly significant statistical devices, which help us in studying the relationship between two variables, yet they are different in approach:

1. As far as correlation is concerned, it is meant for studying the covariation of two variables. It studies whether the variables are moving in the same direction or in reverse direction. The extent of covariation is also reflected in the correlation coefficient. But it does not study the nature of relationship. It does highlight the relative movement in the variables and we cannot predict the value of one variable by considering the value of the other variable. All these things are possible only in the study of regression.
2. Correlation does not talk about the cause and effect relationship. On the other hand, regression presumes one variable as a cause and the other as its effect. The range of a correlation coefficient lies between –1 and +1. The regression is also both negative and positive just like correlation. When the correlation coefficient is positive, the regression coefficient will also be positive and vice versa.
3. Correlation coefficient cannot exceed unity. On the other hand, one of the regression coefficients may be more than unity. But at the same time the product of regression coefficients can never be more than unity. This is because a correlation coefficient is the square root of the product of two regression coefficients.
4. In the study of correlation, r_{xy} is a measure of the extent and direction of linear relationship between two variables X and Y; r_{xy} and r_{yx} are symmetric ($r_{xy}=r_{yx}$). What we mean is that it is quite immaterial which of X and Y is a dependent variable and which is an independent variable. Just reversely, in regression analysis, b_{xy} and b_{yx} are neither equal nor symmetrical and, thus, it matters a lot here as to which variable is dependent and which is independent.

7.13 REGRESSION EQUATION

Regression equations are algebraic expressions of the regression lines. The regression equations are also known as estimating equations. Since we have two regression lines, we have two regression equations. Regression line of X and Y gives the best possible mean values of X for given values of Y. Similarly, the regression line of Y on X gives the best possible mean values of Y for given values of X. The regression equation of X and Y is used to describe the variation in the values of X for given changes in Y and the regression equation of Y on X is used to describe the variation in the values of Y for given changes in X.

7.14 METHOD OF LEAST SQUARES

The regression equation of Y on X is expressed as: $Y=a+bX$ and the regression equation of Y on X is expressed as $X=a+bY$. These are the equations of straight line. Here, in these two equations, the values of a and b are numerical constants because for any given straight line, their value does not change. The values of a and b in these equations are calculated by the method of least squares, that is, the values of a and b are computed with the help of the following normal equations:

1. $\sum Y = Na + b\sum X, \quad \sum XY = a\sum X + b\sum X^2,$
2. $\sum X = Na + b\sum Y, \quad \sum XY = a\sum Y + b\sum Y^2,$

Example: From the given data, obtain the two regression equations using the method of least squares:

X	2	4	6	8	10
Y	5	7	9	8	11

Solution: Computation of regression equations.

X	Y	X^2	Y^2	XY
6	9	36	81	54
2	11	4	121	22
10	5	100	25	50
4	8	16	64	32
8	7	64	49	56
$\Sigma X=30$	$\Sigma Y=40$	$\Sigma X^2=220$	$\Sigma Y^2=340$	$\Sigma XY=214$

Regression equation of Y on X:

$$Y=a+bX$$

To find out the values of a and b, the following two normal equations are used:

$$\sum Y = Na + b\sum X$$

$$40 = 5a + 30b \quad (i)$$

$$\sum XY = a\sum X + b\sum X^2$$

$$214 = 30a + 220b \quad (ii)$$

Multiplying Equation (*i*) by 6, we get Equation (*iii*) as follows:

$$30a + 180b = 240 \quad (iii)$$

Now, subtracting Equation (*ii*) from Equation (*iii*), we get,

$$\begin{aligned} 30a + 180b &= 240 \\ \underline{30a} \pm 220b &= \underline{214} \\ \hline -40b &= 26 \end{aligned}$$

$$\therefore b = \frac{26}{-40} = -0.65$$

Substituting the value of *b* in Equation (*i*), we get,

$$5a + 30\left(\frac{-65}{100}\right) = 40$$

$$\text{or,} \quad 5a = 40 + 19.50 = 59.50$$

$$\therefore a = \frac{59.50}{5} = 11.9.$$

Putting the values of *a* and *b* in the regression equation of *Y* on *X*,

$$Y = a + bX$$
$$= 11.9 + (-0.65) \times 11.9.$$

Again, to find out the values of *a* and *b*, two normal equations are used:

$$\Sigma X = Na + b\Sigma Y$$

$$30 = 5a + 40b \qquad (i)$$

$$\Sigma XY = a\Sigma Y + b\Sigma Y^2$$

$$214 = 40a + 340b \qquad (ii)$$

Multiplyiing Equation (*i*) by 8, we get

$$40a + 320b = 240 \qquad (iii)$$

Now, subtracting (*ii*) from (*iii*), we get,

$$40a + 320b = 240$$
$$40a \pm 340b = 214$$
$$-20b = 26$$

$$\therefore b = \frac{-26}{20} = -1.3$$

Substituting the value of *b* in Equation (*i*), we get,

$$5a + 40(-1.3) = 30$$
$$\text{or} \quad 5a - 52 = 30$$
$$\text{or} \quad 5a = 30 + 52$$
$$\text{or,} \quad 5a = 82 \therefore a = 16.4.$$

Now, putting the values of *a* and *b* in the regression equation of *X* on *Y*:

$$X = a + bY, \quad \text{or} \quad X = 16.4 + Y(-1.3)$$
$$= 16.4 - 1.3Y$$

$$\therefore Y = a + bX = 11.9 - 0.65X \text{ and } X = 16.4 - 1.3Y$$

Second method.

Regression of Y on X:

$$Y = a + bX$$

$$b = \frac{N\sum xy - (\sum x)(\sum y)}{N\sum x^2 - (\sum x)^2} = \frac{5 \times 214 - 30 \times 40}{5 \times 220 - (30)^2}$$

$$= \frac{1070 - 1200}{1100 - 900} = \frac{-130}{200} = -0.65$$

$$a = \frac{\sum Y - b\sum X}{N} = \frac{40 - (-0.65) \times 30}{5} = 11.9$$

$$\therefore Y = a + bX = 11.9 - 0.65X.$$

Now regression of X on Y:

$$X = a + bY$$

$$b = \frac{N\sum xy - (\sum x)(\sum y)}{N\sum y^2 - (\sum y)^2} = \frac{5 \times 214 - 30 \times 40}{5 \times 340 - (40)^2}$$

$$= \frac{1070 - 1200}{1700 - 1600} = \frac{-130}{100} = -1.3$$

and

$$a = \frac{\sum X - b\sum Y}{N} = \frac{30 - (-1.3) \times 40}{5} = 16.4$$

$$\therefore X = a + bY = 16.4 - 1.3Y.$$

7.15 METHOD OF DEVIATIONS FROM MEANS

The above-mentioned method of least squares for finding the regression equation is complex, cumbersome, and tedious. The entire calculation will become very easy if instead of dealing with the actual values of X and Y, we take the deviation of X and Y series from their respective means. Under this method, the two regression equations are expressed as follows:

1. Regression equation of X on Y:

$$X - \bar{X} = r\frac{\sigma_x}{\sigma_y}(Y - \bar{Y}),$$

where $\bar{X}$ is the mean of X series, $\bar{Y}$ is the mean of Y series, r denotes the coefficient of correlation between x and y series, and σ_x and σ_y are the standard deviations of X and Y series, respectively. $r\frac{\sigma_x}{\sigma_y}$ is known as the regression coefficient of X on Y and is denoted by b_{xy}.

Thus,

$$b_{xy} = r\frac{\sigma_x}{\sigma_y} = \frac{\Sigma d_x \cdot d_y}{N \cdot \sigma_x \sigma_y} \times \frac{\sigma_x}{\sigma_y} = \frac{\Sigma d_x \cdot d_y}{N.\sigma_y^{\ 2}} = \frac{\Sigma d_x d_y}{N \times \frac{\Sigma d_y^2}{N}} = \frac{\Sigma d_x d_y}{\Sigma d_y^2}$$

where d_x and d_y are deviations from means, i.e., $d_x = X - \bar{X}$ $d_y = Y - \bar{Y}$
Hence, instead of calculating the value of a correlation coefficient, σ_x, σ_y, and so on, we can directly find out the value of the regression coefficient by computing $\Sigma d_x d_y$ and $\Sigma d_y^{\ 2}$ and dividing the former by the latter.

2. Regression equation of Y on X:

$$Y - \bar{Y} = r\frac{\sigma_y}{\sigma_x}(X - \bar{X}),$$

where $r\frac{\sigma_y}{\sigma_x}$ is called the regression coefficient of Y on X and is denoted by:

$$b_{xy} = r\frac{\sigma_y}{\sigma_x} = \frac{\Sigma d_x \cdot d_y}{N \cdot \sigma_x \sigma_y} \times \frac{\sigma_y}{\sigma_x} = \frac{\Sigma d_x \cdot d_y}{N.\sigma_x^{\ 2}} = \frac{\Sigma d_x d_y}{N \times \frac{\Sigma d_x^2}{N}} = \frac{\Sigma d_x d_y}{\Sigma d_x^2}.$$

In case we are dealing with actual values of X and Y variables and not the deviations, then

$$b_{xy} = \frac{N\Sigma XY - (\Sigma X)(\Sigma Y)}{N\Sigma Y^2 - (\Sigma Y)^2}$$

$$b_{yx} = \frac{N\Sigma XY - (\Sigma X)(\Sigma Y)}{N\Sigma X^2 - (\Sigma X)^2}.$$

7.16 PROPERTIES OF REGRESSION COEFFICIENTS

The regression coefficient b_{xy} possesses some important properties. They are:

1. The product of b_{xy} and b_{yx} gives the value of the coefficient of correlation.
Hence,

$$r = \sqrt{b_{xy} \times b_{yx}}.$$

It can be easily proved here by the following steps:

$$b_{xy} = r\frac{\sigma_x}{\sigma_y}, \quad b_{yx} = r\frac{\sigma_y}{\sigma_x}$$

$$\therefore b_{xy} \times b_{yx} = r\frac{\sigma_x}{\sigma_y} \times r\frac{\sigma_y}{\sigma_x} = r^2$$

$$\therefore r = \sqrt{b_{xy} \times b_{yx}}.$$

2. The algebraic sign of b_{xy} would be determined by the signs of the correlation coefficient (r). If r is positive, both b_{xy} and b_{yx} would be positive. If r is negative, both b_{xy} and b_{yx} would be negative.
3. Since the value of coefficients of correlation (r) cannot be more than 1, one of the regression coefficients must be less than 1, or in other words both the regression coefficients cannot be greater than 1. The reason is that $r = \sqrt{b_{xy} \times b_{yx}}$ and if both b_{xy} and b_{yx} individually exceed unity, the coefficient of correlation or r would be more than 1, which is not feasible.

Example: From the following data, obtain the regression equations by deviation from actual means:

No. of news items (X)	6	2	10	4	8
No. of features (Y)	9	11	5	8	7

Solution:

X	Y	$d_x = X - \bar{X} = (X-6)$	d_x^2	$d_y = Y - \bar{Y} = (Y-8)$	d_y^2	$d_x d_y$
6	9	0	0	1	1	0
2	11	–4	16	3	9	–12
10	5	4	16	–3	9	–12
4	8	–2	4	0	0	0
8	7	2	4	–1	1	–2
$\Sigma X = 30$	$\Sigma Y = 40$	$\Sigma d_x = 0$	$\Sigma d_x^2 = 40$	$\Sigma d_y = 0$	$\Sigma d_y^2 = 20$	$\Sigma d_x d_y = -26$

$$\therefore \bar{X} = \frac{\Sigma X}{N} = \frac{30}{5} = 6, \ \bar{Y} = \frac{\Sigma Y}{N} = \frac{40}{8} = 8$$

$$\therefore X - \bar{X} = r\frac{\sigma_x}{\sigma_y}(Y - \bar{Y})$$

$$= \frac{\Sigma d_x.d_y}{\Sigma d_y^2}(Y - \bar{Y}) = \frac{-26}{20}(Y - 8)$$

$$= -1.3(Y - 8) = 10.4 - 1.3Y$$

$$\therefore X = 10.4 + 6 - 1.3Y$$
$$= 16.4 - 1.3Y$$

Similarly,

$$Y - \bar{Y} = r\frac{\sigma_y}{\sigma_x}(X - \bar{X})$$
$$= \frac{\Sigma d_x.d_y}{\Sigma d_x^2}(X - \bar{X}) = \frac{-26}{40}(X - 6)$$
$$= -0.65(X - 6)$$
$$= -0.65x + 3.9$$
$$\therefore Y = 3.9 + 8 - 0.65X$$
$$= 11.9 - 0.65X$$

$$\therefore \text{Regression of } X \text{ on } Y = 16.4 - 1.3Y$$
$$\text{Regression of } Y \text{ on } X = 11.9 - 0.65X.$$

Hence, the answer is the same by both the methods. However, the calculation is very much simplified in deviation from the mean method than in the least squares method.

7.17 DEVIATION FROM ASSUMED MEAN

If the actual means of the two series X and Y are in fractions, the method from actual means becomes very tedious and complex. In that case, the deviations are taken from assumed means. When deviations are taken from assumed means, the whole process of calculating regression equations remains the same—the only difference is that instead of taking deviations from actual means, we take the deviations from assumed means. Thus, the regression equation of X on Y:

$$X - \bar{X} = r\frac{\sigma_x}{\sigma_y}(Y - \bar{Y}).$$

The value of $r\frac{\sigma_x}{\sigma_y}$ will now be obtained as follows:

$$r\frac{\sigma_x}{\sigma_y} = \frac{N\Sigma d_x.d_y - (\Sigma d_x)(\Sigma d_y)}{N\Sigma dy^2 - (\Sigma d_y)^2},$$

where $d_x = X - Ax$ and $d_y = Y - Ay$

$$(Y - \bar{Y}) = r\frac{\sigma_x}{\sigma_y}(X - \bar{X}) = \frac{N\Sigma d_x.d_y - (\Sigma d_x)(\Sigma d_y)}{N\Sigma d_x^2 - (\Sigma d_x)^2}$$

Thus, in both the cases, the numerator is the same, but the denominator is different. If the regression coefficients are computed from the correlation table, their values are obtained as follows:

$$r\frac{\sigma_x}{\sigma_y} = \frac{N\Sigma fd_x.d_y - (\Sigma fd_x)(\Sigma fd_y)}{N\Sigma fd_y^2 - (\Sigma fd_y)^2} \times \frac{h_x}{h_y},$$

where h_x=height of class interval of X variable and h_y=height of class interval of Y variable.

Similarly,

$$r\frac{\sigma_y}{\sigma_x} = \frac{N\Sigma fd_x.fd_y - (\Sigma fd_x)(\Sigma fd_y)}{N\Sigma fd_x^2 - (\Sigma fd_x)^2}.$$

Example 1: From the following table, obtain the regression equations taking deviation by assuming 5 as the mean of X series of graphic inputs and 7 as the mean of Y series of page layouts.

X (Graphic inputs)	6	2	10	4	8
Y (Page layouts)	9	11	5	8	7

Solution:

X	$d_x=x-5$	Y	$d_y=y-7$	$d_x \cdot d_y$	d_x^2	d_y^2
6	1	9	2	2	1	4
2	-3	11	4	–12	9	16
10	5	5	-2	–10	25	4
4	-1	8	1	–1	1	1
8	3	7	0	0	9	0
$\Sigma x=30$ $N=5$	$\Sigma d_x=5$	$\Sigma Y=40$	$\Sigma d_y=5$	$\Sigma d_x \cdot d_y=-21$	$\Sigma d_x^2 = 45$	$\Sigma d_y^2 = 25$

$$b_{xy} = \frac{N\Sigma d_x.d_y - (\Sigma d_x)(\Sigma d_y)}{N\Sigma d_y^2 - (\Sigma d_y)^2}$$

$$= \frac{5\times(-21) - 5\times 5}{5\times 25 - (5)^2}$$

$$= \frac{-105-25}{125-25} = \frac{-130}{100} = -1.3$$

$$X - \bar{X} = b_{xy}(Y - \bar{Y})$$

$$X - 6 = -1.3(Y-8) = -1.3Y + 10.4$$

$$\therefore \quad X = 16.4 - 1.3y.$$

Similarly

$$b_{yx} = \frac{N\sum d_x.d_y - (\sum d_x)(\sum d_y)}{N\sum d_x^2 - (\sum d_x)^2} = \frac{5\times(-21) - 5\times 5}{5\times 45 - (5)^2}$$
$$= \frac{-105-25}{225-25} = \frac{-130}{200}$$
$$= \frac{-65}{100} = -0.65$$

$$Y - \bar{Y} = b_{yx}(X - \bar{X})$$
$$= -0.65(X-6)$$
$$= -0.65X + 6\times 0.65$$

$$\therefore Y = -0.65X + 3.9 + 8$$
$$= 11.9 - 0.65X$$

$$\therefore X = 16.4 - 1.3Y$$

$$Y = 11.9 - 0.65X.$$

Example 2: Find the regression equations directly from the following raw data of male–female ratio of users of smart language in the new media.

X (Male)	2	3	6	4	5	4
Y (Female)	1	3	4	2	5	3

Solution:

X	*Y*	X^2	Y^2	*XY*
2	1	4	1	2
3	3	9	9	9
6	4	36	16	24
4	2	16	4	8
5	5	25	25	25
4	3	16	9	12
$\Sigma X=24$, $N=6$	$\Sigma Y=18$	$\Sigma X^2=106$	$\Sigma Y^2=64$	$\Sigma XY=80$

$$\bar{X} = \frac{24}{6} = 4,\ \bar{Y} = \frac{18}{6} = 3$$

$$r\frac{\sigma_y}{\sigma_x} = \frac{N\sum XY - (\sum X)(\sum Y)}{N\sum X^2 - (\sum X)^2}$$

$$= \frac{480 - 432}{6 \times 106 - (24)^2} = \frac{48}{636 - 576} = \frac{48}{60} = \frac{4}{5} = 0.8$$

$$X - \bar{X} = r\frac{\sigma_x}{\sigma_y}(Y - \bar{Y})$$

$$r\frac{\sigma_x}{\sigma_y} = \frac{N\sum XY - (\sum X)(\sum Y)}{N\sum Y^2 - (\sum Y)^2}$$

$$= \frac{6 \times 80 - 24 \times 18}{6 \times 64 - (18)^2} = \frac{480 - 432}{384 - 324}$$

$$= \frac{48}{60} = \frac{4}{5} = 0.8$$

$$\therefore X - \bar{X} = r\frac{\sigma_x}{\sigma_y}(Y - \bar{Y})$$

$$X - Y = 0.8(Y - 3)$$

$$= 0.8Y - 2.4$$

$$\therefore X = 4 - 2.4 + 0.8Y$$

$$= 1.6 + 0.8Y$$

$$Y - \bar{Y} = r\frac{\sigma_y}{\sigma_x}(X - \bar{X})$$

$$Y - 3 = 0.8(X - 4)$$

$$= 0.8X - 3.2$$

$$\therefore Y = 0.8X - 3.2 + 3$$

$$= -0.2 + 0.8X.$$

Example 3: Following are the data relating to scores in tests of two subjects—reporting and editing.

Editing (X)	Reporting (Y)
Mean=25	Mean=30
σ_x=1.7	σ_y=1.6
r=0.95	

1. Determine the regression equation;
2. Predict scores of reporting of a student whose score in editing is 40;
3. Predict scores of editing of a student whose score in reporting is 50.

Solution: Given the data for two tests,

$$X - \bar{X} = r\frac{\sigma_x}{\sigma_y}(Y - \bar{Y})$$

$$X - 25 = \frac{0.95 \times 1.7}{1.6}(Y - 30) \qquad (i)$$
$$= 0.95 \times 1.06(Y - 30)$$
$$= 1.007(Y - 30) = 1.007Y - 30.21$$
$$\therefore X = 1.007Y - 5.21$$

Now,

$$(Y - \bar{Y}) = r\frac{\sigma_y}{\sigma_x}(X - \bar{X})$$
$$= \frac{0.95 \times 1.6}{1.7}(X - 25)$$
$$= \frac{1.6}{1.7}(X - 25)$$

$$Y = 0.94X - 23.5 + 30$$
$$= 0.94X + 6.5$$
$$\therefore X = 1.007Y - 5.21 \qquad (ii)$$
$$Y = 0.94X + 6.5.$$

Now, putting the value of editing $(X) = 40$ in Equation (*ii*),

$$Y = 0.94X + 6.5$$
$$= 0.94 \times 40 + 6.5$$
$$= 37.6 + 6.5$$
$$= 44.1.$$

Putting the value of reporting $(Y) = 50$ in Equation (*i*),

$$X = 1.007Y - 5.21$$
$$= 1.007 \times 50 - 5.21$$
$$= 50.35 - 5.21$$
$$= 45.14.$$

1. Regression scores are $X = 1.007\,Y - 5.21$

$$Y = 0.94X + 6.5.$$

2. Scores of a student in reporting subject whose score in editing subject is 40=44.1.
3. Scores of a student in editing subject whose score in reporting subject is 50=45.14.

Example 4: Calculate the value of the correlation coefficient through the method of regression analysis from the following data first by taking deviation from the actual mean of photo cropping and page design and secondly from assumed means 2 and 18 for series photo cropping and page design, respectively.

X (Photo cropping)	1	2	3	4	5
Y (Page design)	10	20	15	25	30

Solution:

1. Calculation of regression coefficient from the actual mean:

X	Y	$d_x = X - \bar{X} = X - 3$	$d_y = Y - \bar{Y} = y - 20$	d_x^2	d_y^2	$d_x \cdot d_y$
1	10	− 2	−10	4	100	20
2	20	− 1	0	1	0	0
3	15	0	−5	0	25	0
4	25	1	5	1	25	5
5	30	2	10	4	100	20
$\Sigma X = 15$	$\Sigma Y = 100$	$\Sigma d_x = 0$	$\Sigma d_y = 0$	$\Sigma d_x^2 = 10$	$\Sigma d_y^2 = 250$	$\Sigma d_x . d_y = 45$

$$\therefore r = \sqrt{b_{xy} \times b_{yx}}$$

Now, regression coefficient of X on Y,

$$b_{xy} = \frac{\Sigma d_x . d_y}{\Sigma d_y^2} = \frac{45}{250} = 0.18$$

Regression coefficient of Y on X,

$$b_{yx} = \frac{\Sigma d_x . d_y}{\Sigma d_x^2} = \frac{45}{10} = 4.5$$

$$\therefore r = \sqrt{b_{xy} \times b_{yx}} = \sqrt{0.18 \times 4.5} = \sqrt{0.81} = 0.9.$$

2. Calculation of regression coefficient from assumed means (given 2 and 8):

X	Y	$d_x = X - A_x = X - 2$	$d_y = Y - A_y = Y - 8$	d_x^2	d_y^2	$d_x d_y$
1	10	−1	−8	1	64	8
2	20	0	−2	0	4	0
3	15	1	−3	1	9	−3
4	25	2	7	4	49	14
5	30	3	12	9	144	36

Given the assumed mean of $X=2$ and $Y=18$, the regression coefficient of X on Y:

$$b_{xy} = \frac{N\sum d_x.d_y - (\sum d_x)(\sum d_y)}{N\sum d_y^2 - (\sum d_y)^2} = \frac{5\times 55 - 5\times 10}{5\times 270 - (10)^2}$$

$$= \frac{275-50}{1350-100} = \frac{225}{1250} = 0.18.$$

Regression coefficient of Y on X:

$$b_{yx} = \frac{N\sum d_x.d_y - (\sum d_x)(\sum d_y)}{N\sum d_x^2 - (\sum d_x)^2}$$

$$= \frac{5\times 55 - 5\times 10}{5\times 15 - (5)^2} = \frac{275-50}{75-25} = \frac{225}{50}$$

$$= 4.5$$

$$\therefore r = \sqrt{b_{xy}\times b_{yx}} = \sqrt{0.18\times 4.5} = \sqrt{0.81} = 0.9.$$

Hence, the correlation coefficient is 0.9 by both the above-mentioned methods.

Example 5: From the following data, obtain two regression equations.

Advertising	91	97	108	121	67	124	51	73	111	57
Sales	71	75	69	97	70	91	39	61	80	47

Solution:

Advertising (X)	Sales (Y)	$d_x = X - \bar{X}$ $= X - 90$	$d_y = Y - \bar{Y}$ $= Y - 70$	d_x^2	d_y^2	$d_x.d_y$
91	71	1	1	1	1	1
97	75	7	5	49	25	35
108	69	18	–1	324	1	–18
121	97	31	27	961	729	837
67	70	–23	0	529	0	0
124	91	34	21	1156	441	714
51	39	–39	–31	1521	961	1209
73	61	–17	–9	289	81	153
111	80	–21	10	441	100	210
57	47	–33	–23	1089	529	759
$\sum X=900$	$\sum Y=700$	$\sum d_x=0$	$\sum d_y=0$	$\sum d_x^2 = 6360$	$\sum d_y^2 = 2868$	$\sum d_x.d_y = 3900$

$$\bar{X} = \frac{\Sigma X}{N} = \frac{900}{10} = 90, \quad \bar{y} = \frac{700}{10} = 70$$

$$b_{xy} = \frac{\Sigma d_x.d_y}{\Sigma d_y^2} = \frac{3900}{2868} = 1.361$$

$$b_{yx} = \frac{\Sigma d_x.d_y}{\Sigma d_x^2} = \frac{3900}{6360} = 0.6132.$$

Regression equation of X on Y,

$$X - \bar{X} = b_{xy}(Y - \bar{Y})$$

$$X - 90 = 1.361(Y - 70) \qquad (i)$$

$$= 1.361Y - 95.27 + 90$$

$$\therefore X = 1.361Y - 5.27$$

Regression equation of Y on X,

$$Y - \bar{Y} = b_{yx}(X - \bar{X})$$

or $$Y - 70 = 0.6132(X - 90)$$

$$= 0.6132X - 55.188$$

$$\therefore Y = 0.6132X + 14.812.$$

Example 6: Two researchers A and B graded seven newspapers' editorials and independently awarded the following marks according to their research parameters.

Newspapers' editorials	1	2	3	4	5	6	7
Marks awarded by researcher A	40	34	28	30	44	38	31
Marks awarded by researcher B	32	39	26	30	38	34	28

And the eighth newspapers' editorial was awarded 36 marks by researcher A, while researcher B was not present. If researcher B were also present, how many marks would you expect him to award to the eighth newspapers' editorial assuming that the same degree of relationship exists in their judgment.

Solution:

Marks Awarded by Researcher A (X)	Marks Awarded by Researcher B (Y)	$d_x = X - A_x$ $= X - 35$	$d_y = Y - A_y$ $= Y - 32$	d_x^2	d_y^2	$d_x.d_y$
40	32	5	0	25	0	0
34	39	−1	7	1	49	−7
28	26	−7	6	49	36	42
30	30	−5	−2	25	4	10
44	38	9	6	81	36	54
38	34	3	2	9	4	6
31	28	−4	−4	16	16	16
$\Sigma X = 245$	$\Sigma Y = 227$	$\Sigma d_x = 0$	$\Sigma d_y = 3$	$\Sigma d_x^2 = 206$	$\Sigma d_y^2 = 145$	$\Sigma d_x.d_y = 121$

Since deviation from the actual means is in fraction, we have taken the assumed mean. Let the assumed mean of the X series be 35 and that of the Y series be 32.

$$b_{yx} = \frac{N\Sigma d_x.d_y - (\Sigma d_x)(\Sigma d_y)}{N\Sigma d_x^2 - (\Sigma d_x)^2} = \frac{7\times 121 - 0\times 3}{7\times 206 - (0)^2}$$

$$= \frac{847}{1442} = 0.587$$

$$\therefore Y - \bar{Y} = b_{xy}(X - \bar{X})$$

$$Y - 32.428 = 0.587(36 - 35)$$

$$\therefore Y = 0.587 + 32.428 = 33.01.$$

Thus, researcher B would have awarded 33 marks to the eighth newspapers' editorial.

Example 7: The following table gives ages (in years) of male journalists and female journalists.

	Age of Male Journalists (*X*)			
Age of Female Journalists (*Y*)	**20–25**	**25–30**	**30–35**	**Total**
16–20	9	14	–	23
20–24	6	11	3	20
24–28	–	–	7	7
Total	15	25	10	50

Calculate,

1. The regression line of male journalists on female journalists.
2. The age of a male journalist when a female journalist is 20 years old.

Solution: Let the age of male journalists be denoted by X and that of female journalists by Y.

Computation for regression equations:

X			Age in Years						
			20–25	25–30	30–35	f	fd_y	fd_y^2	fd_xd_y
Y	Mid point	d_y \ d_x	–1	0	+1				
16–20	18	–1	9⌊9	14⌊0	–	23	–23	23	9
20–24	22	0	6⌊0	11⌊0	3⌊0	20	0	0	0
24–28	26	+1	–	–	7⌊7	7	7	7	7
		Total f	15	25	10	$N=50$	$\Sigma fd_y = 16$	$\Sigma fd_y^2 = 30$	$\Sigma fd_xd_y = 16$
		fd_x	–15	0	10	$\Sigma fd_x = 5$			
		fd_x^2	15	0	10	$\Sigma fd_x^2 = 25$			
		fd_xd_y	9	0	7	$\Sigma fd_xd_y = 16$			

Regression line of X on Y:

$$X - \bar{X} = b_{xy}(Y - \bar{Y})$$

$$= \frac{N\Sigma fd_x.d_y - (\Sigma fd_x)(\Sigma fd_y)}{N\Sigma fd_y^2 - (\Sigma fd_y)^2} \times \frac{h_x}{h_y}$$

$$= \frac{50 \times 16 - (-5)(-16)}{50 \times 30 - (-16)^2} \times \frac{5}{4}$$

$$= \frac{800 - 80}{1500 - 244} \times \frac{5}{4} = \frac{72}{99.52} = 0.723$$

$$\bar{X} = A_x + \frac{\Sigma fd_x}{N} \times h_x$$

$$= 27.5 + \frac{(-5)}{50} \times 5$$

$$= 27.5 - 0.5 = 27$$

$$\bar{Y} = A_y + \frac{\Sigma fd_y}{N} \times h_y$$

$$= 22 + \frac{(-16)}{50} \times 4$$

$$= 22 - \frac{64}{50} = 22 - 1.28$$

$$= 20.72.$$

Substituting the value of $\bar{X}$ and $\bar{Y}$ in b_{xy} in the regression equation,

$$X - 27 = 0.723(Y - 20.72)$$

$$= 0.723y - 14.98$$

$$\therefore X = 0.723y + 12.02.$$

Putting $y = 20$ in the equation,

$$x = 0.723(20) + 12.02 = 14.46 + 12.02 = 26.48.$$

Thus, the likely age of a male journalist when the age of a female journalist is 20 years, is 26.48 years.

7.18 STANDARD ERROR OF ESTIMATE

The standard error of estimate is also called the standard error of regression. This standard error is similar to standard deviation, where we find out the deviation of the original values of Y from its estimated values (or computed linear values), square these deviations, total the square, divide the total by the number of observations in the series, and calculate the square root of that value. In this way, we will get the standard error of the estimate of Y:

$$S_y = \sqrt{\frac{\Sigma(Y - Y_c)^2}{N}},$$

where Y is the original value, Y_c is the computed (linear) value, also called the estimated value, and N is the number of observations in the series.

There are other formulae also which may be used from situation to situation for simplified calculations, that is,

$$S_y = \sigma_y\sqrt{1 - r^2} \quad \text{or} \quad \sqrt{\frac{\Sigma Y^2 - a\Sigma Y - b\Sigma XY}{N}}$$

(where σ_y is the standard deviation of the Y series, r is correlation coefficient, and a and b are numerical constants).

Similarly,

$$S_x = \sqrt{\frac{\Sigma(X - X_c)^2}{N}} = \sqrt{\frac{\Sigma X^2 - a\Sigma X - b\Sigma XY}{N}}$$
$$= \sigma_x\sqrt{1 - r^2}.$$

Thus, the smaller the value of the standard error of regression (or estimate), the better the estimates based on the equation for this line. If standard error is zero, then the correlation is perfect and the estimate is the best.

Example: From the following data, calculate the standard errors of regression of $Y(S_y)$ and $X(S_x)$

X	6	2	10	4	8
Y	9	11	5	8	7

Solution: In earlier examples with the same equation, we have found
$Y = 11.9 - 0.65X$ and $X = 16.4 - 1.3Y$

X	Y	$x_c = 16.4 - 1.3y$	$Y_c = 11.9 - 0.65x$	$(X - X_c)^2$	$(Y - Y_c)^2$
6	9	4.7	8.0	1.69	1.00
2	11	2.1	10.6	0.01	0.16
10	5	9.9	5.4	0.01	0.16
4	8	6.0	9.3	4.00	1.69
8	7	7.3	6.7	0.49	0.09
$\Sigma X = 30$	$\Sigma Y = 40$	$\Sigma x_c = 30$	$\Sigma Y_c = 40$	$\Sigma(X - X_c) = 6.20$	$\Sigma(Y - Y_c) = 3.1$

$$S_x = \sqrt{\frac{\Sigma(X - X)^2}{N}} = \sqrt{\frac{(6.2)^2}{5}} = \sqrt{1.24} = 1.114$$

$$S_y = \sqrt{\frac{\Sigma(Y - Y_c)^2}{N}} = \sqrt{\frac{(3.1)^2}{5}} = \sqrt{0.62} = 0.787.$$

Thus, the study of regression analysis is the most vital in future estimation and establishing a relationship between cause and effect. But at the same time, we must keep an eye on the fact that the relationship between two variables can be adversely affected by other variables that are "lurking" in the background. The "lurking" variables are often unrecognized, unidentified, and unmeasured, and it can tremendously change the results of a regression analysis.

7.19 OTHER MEASURES

In addition to the study of correlation analysis and regression analysis with reference to the measures of relationship, we have some other measures also such as index number and time series. As far as time series is concerned, we have comprehensively discussed this too, while discussing the calculation of correlation coefficients. We have thoroughly discussed calculation of correlation in time series, correlation of long-term changes, correlation of short-term changes, in addition to lag and lead in correlation in Sections 7.8, 7.8.1, 7.8.2, and 7.9, respectively. Thus, we will discuss index number at this point only to the extent which is useful and relevant in social sciences, in general, and communication and media studies, in particular.

7.19.1 Meaning and Concept of Index Numbers

The first index number was constructed in the year 1764 by an Italian statistician called "Carli." Index numbers have today become one of the most widely and largely used statistical tool and there is scarcely any phenomenon, field, or area which does not make use of the device of index numbers. Whenever and wherever a relative and comparative study has to be made, index numbers are very handy and useful. Index numbers are supposed to be barometers of communication and media events which measure the change in the level of a phenomenon. Newspapers and magazines headline the fact that crimes are rising and a variety of media and communication phenomena and tendencies are changing in a particular period compared to the previous period as disclosed by index numbers. Some of the striking definitions given by prominent statisticians, mathematicians, and communicologists are as follows.

According to Patterson (cited in Gupta 2011, 536),

> In its simplest form, an Index Number is the ratio of two index numbers expressed as a percent. An Index Number is a statistical measure—a measure designed to show changes in one variable or a group related variables over time, or with respect to geographic location, or in terms of some other characteristics.

In the words of John I. Riffin (cited in D.N.S. Elhance and Veena Elhance 1990, 13.1), "Index Numbers are used to measure changes over time in magnitudes, which are not capable of direct measurement."

A.M. Tuttle (cited in Gupta 2011) defines it as, "Index Number is a single ration (usually in percentages) which measures the combined (i.e., averaged) change of several variables between two different times, places or situations."

According to Croxton and Cowden (cited in D.N.S. Elhance and Veena Elhance 1990), "Index Numbers are devices for measuring differences in the magnitude of a group of related variables."

Spigel (cited in Gupta 2011, 536) aptly remarks in this context and emphasizes, "An Index Number is a statistical measure designed to show changes in a variable or a group of related variables with respect to time, geographic location and other characteristics such as income, profession, etc."

According to Berenson and Levine, (cited in Gupta 2011, 536) "Generally speaking, Index Number measures the size or magnitude of some object at a particular point in time as a percentage of some base or reference object in the past."

Morris Hamburg (cited in Gupta 2011, 536) aptly remarks, "In its simplest form, an Index Number is nothing more than a relative number or a 'relative' which expresses the relationship between two figures where one of the figures is used as base."

Thus, an index number is a specialized type of average which measures the central tendency of a time series or a spatial series. It is designed to measure the change in a group of related variables over a period of time. For example, if we say that the index number of wholesale prices of a standard field camera is 220 for January, 2015, compared to January, 2014, it means there is a net increase in the prices of wholesale commodities to the extent of 120 percent during the year. When the variation in the level of a single item is being studied, the index number will be called "univariate index." Further, when the changes in the average level of a number of items are being studied together, this index number will be called "composite index number."

7.19.2 Characteristics of Index Numbers

1. Index numbers are specialized averages. We already know that an average is a single value of the population which broadly represents the whole population. But to get an average, the items must be in the same unit. However, this is not the case with index numbers. They are used for the purposes of comparison in situations where two or more series are expressed in different units or where series are composed of different types of items. For example, while constructing a news price index under consumer price index, the various items are divided into broad heads, such as (a) newsprint, (b) ink, and (c) staff in news-making. These items are expressed in different units, such as newsprint in *rim*, ink in *kilograms*, and staff salary in *rupees*. An average of all these items expressed in different units is obtained by using the technique of index numbers.
2. Index numbers measure the net overall change in a group of related variables. They describe the increase or decrease in a single value about a group of related variables. Suppose the news price index has gone up to 220 in January, 2015, compared to January, 2014; it means that there is a net measure of 120 percent in the prices of commodities included in the index. It must be taken care and noted that even when an index is showing a net increase, it may include some items which have actually decreased in value and others which have remained constant.
3. Index numbers help us in policy formulation. They help us in studying trends of various phenomena and these trends and tendencies are the bases on which many policy

decisions are taken. Here, cost of living index numbers and consumer price index are often used by government in various capacities. Its use is equally relevant in the social sciences such as sociology, psychology, and communication. Sociologists and communicologists study demographic changes with the help of index numbers and accordingly suggest suitable future policies. Similarly, psychologists also study the intelligence level or educational attainments, and the likes of a population with the help of various indices framed for the purpose under the study.

4. Index numbers measure effect of changes over a period of time. They is most widely and largely used for measuring changes over a period of time. But it should be noted that index numbers not only measure changes over a period of time, but also compare, economic, social, psychological, and communication conditions of different location, industries, cities, or even countries.
5. Index numbers are also capable of exploring the effects of such factors which cannot be measured directly. According to Bowley (cited in D.N.S. Elhance and Veena Elhance 1990, 13.3), "Index Numbers are used to measure the changes in some quantity which we cannot observe directly." For example, charges in advertising and sales activity in a country cannot be measured directly. But it is quite possible to understand relative changes in advertising and sales activity by finding out the variation in the values of some such factors, which affect advertising and sales activity and which are capable of direct measurement.
6. The cost of living of certain group of persons may vary over two periods of time, or the cost of living may be different at two different places at the same time. The tools and techniques of index numbers are used to measure both these types of changes. It must be taken into account that index numbers measures only relative changes in the values of a phenomenon or an event.

7.19.3 Uses of Index Numbers

1. Index numbers are very helpful and useful in forecasting future trends. Moreover, a set of composite index numbers are very useful in decision-making, more so in economic and financial analysis of media industry.
2. Index numbers are excellent indicators of trends and tendencies. Since index numbers are largely and widely applied for measuring changes over a period of time, the time series so created help us to understand deeply the general trend of the phenomena or event relating to media economics.
3. Index numbers are extremely relevant and highly useful in forecasting future socio-economic, psychological, and communication-related activities. They are useful not only in understanding the past, but also prognosticating future socio-economic activities. Index numbers are frequently applied in time series analysis and historical study of sociology, communication, and the likes of long-term and seasonal variations so that we can have better information available for decision-making purposes.

7.19.4 Methods of Constructing Index Numbers

Broadly, the methods of constructing index numbers can be divided into two groups as shown in the following flowchart: (a) unweighted index numbers and (b) weighted index numbers.

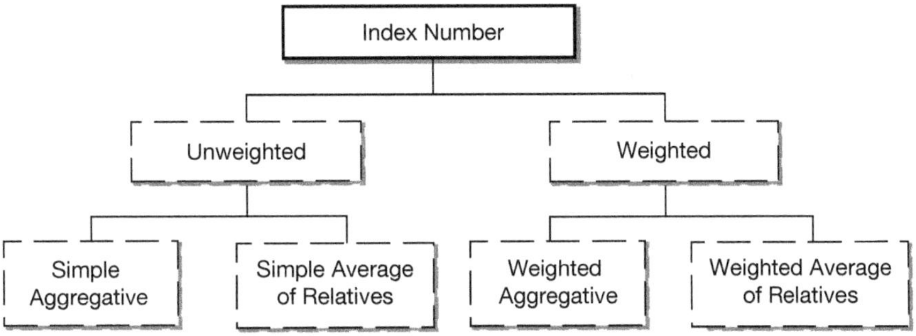

Source: Drawn by author.

Furthermore, unweighted index numbers are of two types: (a) simple aggregative method and (b) simple average of relatives method. And the weighted index numbers also may further be divided into two types: (a) weighted aggregative method and (b) Weighted average of relative method.

7.19.4.1 Unweighted Index Numbers

This type of index numbers is such that all the values considered in calculating the index numbers are of equal importance.

1. Simple aggregative method: This is the simplest, easiest, and quickest method of constructing index numbers. If this method is used to construct a price index, the total of the current year prices for the various items in question is divided by the total of the base year prices and the quotient is multiplied by 100.
   Symbolically,

$$P_{01} = \frac{\Sigma P_1}{\Sigma P_0} \times 100,$$

   where P_{01} is the index number of the current year, ΣP_1 is the total of the current year prices for various commodities, and ΣP_0 is the total of the base year prices for various items.
   The steps required in the calculation are as follows:
   a. We will add the current year prices of various items, that is, get ΣP_1;
   b. Then, we will add the base year prices for the same items, that is, get ΣP_0;
   c. After that, we will divide ΣP_1 by ΣP_0 and multiply the quotient by 100.

   Example: From the following data of monthly prices of different newspapers, construct an index number for 2015, taking 2014 as the base year.

Newspapers	A	B	C	D	E
Monthly price in 2013 (₹)	50	40	80	110	20
Monthly price in 2014 (₹)	70	60	90	120	20

Solution:

Newspapers	Monthly Price in 2014 (₹)	Monthly Price in 2015 (₹)
A	50	70
B	40	60
C	80	90
D	110	120
E	20	20
	$\Sigma P_0 = 300$	$\Sigma P_1 = 360$

$$\therefore P_{01} = \frac{\Sigma P_1}{\Sigma P_0} \times 100$$

$$= \frac{360}{300} \times 100 = 120.$$

This means that prices of newspapers in 2015 are 20 percent higher than the prices in 2014.

Limitation of unweighted index:

a. This is erroneous and defective as it is affected by the unit on which the price is quoted. The units applied in the price and quantity quotations can exert a big influence on the value of the index.
b. It is also influenced by the magnitude of the prices. That is to say that the higher the price of a product, the bigger is its influence. Hence, high-priced products get greater weightage as compared to low-priced products.
c. Since it is unweighted, the relative importance of different products is not considered in this index.

2. Simple average of relatives method: In this case, it is assumed that the prices of the commodities in the base year are 100 and the current year prices are presented as the percentage of the base year. This means that the current year's price is the price relative of the base year price. These price relatives are then converted into measures of central value to obtain the index numbers.
   In this context, generally the arithmetic mean is preferred for computation.
   Thus, symbolically,

$$P_{01} = \frac{\Sigma\left(\frac{P_1}{P_0}\right) \times 100}{N},$$

where N is the number of products or commodities or items from which the index number is to be constructed.

Example: From the given data of monthly prices of different newspapers, construct an index number for the year 2015, taking 2014 as the base year by simple average of relatives method:

Newspapers	A	B	C	D	E
Monthly price in 2014 (₹)	50	40	80	110	20
Monthly price in 2015 (₹)	70	60	90	120	20

Solution:

Newspapers	Monthly Price in 2014 (₹)	Monthly Price in 2015 (₹)	$\left(\frac{P_1}{P_0} \times 100\right)$
A	50	70	140
B	40	60	150
C	80	90	112.5
D	110	120	109.1
E	20	20	100
	$\Sigma P_0 = 300$	$\Sigma P_1 = 360$	$\Sigma\left(\frac{P_1}{P_0} \times 100\right) = 611.6$

$$P_{01} = \frac{\Sigma\left(\frac{P_1}{P_0}\right) \times 100}{N} = \frac{611.6}{5} = 122.32.$$

Merits of unweighted index numbers:

a. This index is not at all influenced by the units in which prices are quoted.
b. Here, in this method, the extreme items do not affect the index. All the items are treated equally.
c. This method gives such an index number which completely satisfies the unit test.

Demerits of unweighted index numbers:

a. The importance of all the items is assumed to be the same. This is because of the fact that it is unweighted average.
b. While constructing this index, in the measures of central tendency, the mode and median are avoided. The application of arithmetic mean is sometimes questionable as it has an upward bias.

7.19.4.2 Weighted Index Numbers

In this method of construction of index number, rational weights are assigned to different chains explicitly. Weighted index numbers are of two types:

1. Weighted aggregative method: Here, weights are assigned to different items and in lieu of computing the simple aggregate of prices, the weighted aggregate of prices is

obtained. As a result, many mathematicians and statisticians such as Laspeyres (1871), Paasche (German Statistician in 1874), Dorbish and Bowley, Fisher, and Marshall and Edgeworth further went on developing this method to make it more and more useful. But this method is more useful and applicable in subjects such as economics, commerce, and management. It has hardly any applicability in communication and media studies.

2. Weighted average of relatives method: In this method, the price relatives for the current year are computed on the basis of the base year price. This method too is more applicable, useful, and relevant in subjects such as economics, commerce, and management. It is of not much use in communication and media studies. So it is hardly relevant for media metrics.

Thus, in media metrics only simple aggregative method and simple average of relatives method are useful, relevant, and significant for the study of news price index as or like a part of consumer price index and several communication and media aspects as a part of living index number.

SUMMARY

In communication and media research, whether the variables are univariate, bivariate, or multivariate, we often try to understand the relationship between variables. For example, variables such as number, intelligence, gender, age, income, communication, and rigidity are related and connected. If one is affected, the other is affected. Two valid questions arise here: (a) Is there any connection, relation, dependence, association, or correlation between two or more variables? and (b) If yes, then to what extent or to what degree and which direction (positive, zero, negative)? Does there exist any cause and effect relationship between two or more variables? The first question can be answered by correlation analysis and the second question can be answered by regression analysis. The term correlation or covariation indicates the relationship between two or more such variables in which with changes in the values of one variable, the values of the other variable(s) also change. The measure of correlation called the correlation coefficient or correlation index or the ratio between one variable and another summarizes in one figure the direction and degree of correlation. Correlation analysis is widely and largely useful in communication and media research and is considered to be the basic conceptual as well as statistical tool for in-depth analysis and interpretation of data relating to two or more variables. Correlation is a mathematical and statistical relationship and it does not necessarily signify a cause and effect relationship between the variables. The most important types of correlation are positive and negative, simple, partial and multiple, and linear and nonlinear (or curvilinear). Correlation coefficient, which is also called the correlation index, is a numerical value of correlation. The value of correlation ranges from –1 to +1 which includes perfectly negative correlation (–1), very highly negative correlation (–0.10 to –0.20), highly negative correlation (–0.70 to –0.90), moderately negative correlation (–0.40 to –0.70), low negative correlation (–0.20 to –0.40), very low negative correlation (–0.00 to –0.20), zero correlation (00), very low positive correlation (+0.00 to +0.20), low positive correlation (+0.20 to +0.40), moderately positive correlation (+0.40 to +0.70), highly positive correlation (+0.70 to +0.90), very highly positive correlation (+0.90 to +1.00), and perfectly positive correlation (+1). There are mainly six methods for studying correlation: (a) scatter diagram method, (b) graphic method, (c) Karl Pearson's coefficient of correlation method, (d) Spearman's coefficient of correlation method, (e) concurrent deviation method, and (f) least squares method. For those who are not good at statistics and mathematics or those who wish to avoid statistics and mathematics may resort to the first two methods. Other four methods are mathematical and statistical methods. The probable error of Karl Pearson's correlation coefficient is calculated by the following formula:

$$\mathrm{PE}_r = 0.6745\frac{1-r^2}{\sqrt{N}},$$

where PE_r stands for probable error of correlation coefficient and N stands for the number of pairs of two series. When we take 0.6645 from the above formula, we get the standard error of coefficient of correlation. Hence,

$$\mathrm{SE}_r = \frac{1-r^2}{\sqrt{N}},$$

where SE_r stands for the standard error of coefficient of correlation.

Coefficient of determination$=r^2$, coefficient of nondetermination$=1-r^2$, and coefficient of alienation$=k=\sqrt{1-r^2}$. Time series is that series of correlation in which one variable is time. Time series depict two types of changes: (a) long-term changes and (b) short-term changes. In the study of lag and lead in correlation, one may find a time gap before a cause and effects relationship is established. The term "regression" was first used by Sir Francis Galton (1822–1911) in 1877. The line explaining the tendency of stepping back, sliding back, or going back is called by Francis Galton a regression line. Regression basically implies going back or returning toward the mean and it is the measure of the average relationship between two or more variables in terms of original units of the data. The study of regression is highly significant, meaningfully relevant, and widely useful in almost all branches of knowledge. Regression equations are algebraic expressions of the regression lines. Regression equations are also known as estimating equations. Since we have two regression lines, we have two regression equations. The regression equation of Y on X is expressed as $Y=a+bX$ and the regression equation of X on Y is expressed as $X=a+bY$. These are the equations of straight line. Here, in these two equations the values of a and b are numerical constants because for any given straight line, their values do not change. The values of a and b in these equations are calculated by the method of least squares, that is, the values of a and b are computed with the help of the following normal equations:

$$(i)\ \Sigma Y = Na + b\Sigma X,\ (ii)\ \Sigma X = Na + b\Sigma Y$$

$$\Sigma XY = a\Sigma X + b\Sigma X^2,\ \Sigma XY = a\Sigma Y + b\Sigma Y^2$$

By the method of deviation from means, the regression equation of X on Y is:

$$X - \bar{X} = r\frac{\sigma_x}{\sigma_y}(Y - \bar{Y}),$$

where $\bar{X}$ is the mean of X series, $\bar{Y}$ is the mean of Y series, r denotes the coefficient of correlation between X and Y series and σ_x and σ_y are standard deviations of X and Y series, respectively. $r\frac{\sigma_x}{\sigma_y}$ is known the regression coefficient of X on Y and is denoted by b_{xy} and equal to $\frac{\Sigma d_x d_y}{\Sigma d_y^{\ 2}}$, where d_x and d_y are deviations from means, that is, $d_x = X - \bar{X}$ and $d_y = Y - \bar{Y}$. Similarly, b_{yx} is equal to $\frac{\Sigma d_x d_y}{\Sigma d_x^2}$.

In case we deal with actual values of X and Y and not deviations, then

$$b_{xy} = \frac{N\Sigma XY - (\Sigma X)(\Sigma Y)}{N\Sigma Y^2 - (\Sigma Y)^2} \quad \text{and} \quad b_{yx} = \frac{N\Sigma XY - (\Sigma X)(\Sigma Y)}{N\Sigma X^2 - (\Sigma X)^2}.$$

The most important property of regression coefficient is that $r = \sqrt{b_{xy} \times b_{yx}}$. The standard error of estimate is also called the standard error of regression. This standard error is similar to standard deviation:

$$S_y = \sqrt{\frac{\Sigma(Y - Y_c)^2}{N}},$$

where S_y is the standard error of estimate of Y, Y is the original value, Y_c is the computed (linear) value, also called the estimate value, and N is the number of observations in the series. Also,

$$S_y = \sigma_y\sqrt{1 - r^2} \quad \text{or} \quad \sqrt{\frac{\Sigma Y^2 - a\Sigma Y - b\Sigma XY}{N}},$$

where σ_y is the standard deviation of the Y series, r is the correlation coefficient, and a and b are numerical constants. Similarly,

$$S_x = \sqrt{\frac{\Sigma(X - X_c)^2}{N}} = \sigma_x\sqrt{1 - r^2} \quad \text{or} \quad \sqrt{\frac{\Sigma X^2 - a\Sigma X - b\Sigma XY}{N}}.$$

Hence, the smaller the value of the standard error of regression (or estimate), the better the estimates based on the equation for this line. If the standard error is zero, then the correlation is perfect and the estimate is the best. Hence, the study of regression analysis is the most vital in future estimation and establishing a relationship between cause and effect. Index number, developed by the Italian Statistician Carli in 1764, is much superior to the central tendencies. It is a specialized type of central tendency and is designed to measure the change in a group of related variables over a period of time. For example, while constructing a news price index under consumer price index, the various items are divided into broad heads, such as (a) newsprint, (b) ink, and (c) staff in news making. These items or services are expressed in different units, like newsprint in rim, ink in kilograms, staff salary expenditure in terms of rupees, respectively. An average of all these items expressed in different units is obtained by using a special technique called index numbers. There are broadly two methods of constructing index numbers: (a) unweighted index numbers and (b) weighted index numbers. Unweighted index numbers are also of two types: (a) simple aggregative method and (b) simple average relatives method. Weighted index numbers are further divided into two types: (a) weighted aggregative method and (b) weighted average of relatives methods. The simple aggregative method can be expressed as follows:

Symbolically,

$$P_{01} = \frac{\Sigma P_1}{\Sigma P_0} \times 100,$$

where P_0 is the index number of the current year, ΣP_1 is the total of the current year prices for various commodities, and ΣP_0 is total of the base year prices for various commodities.

Simple average relatives method can be expressed as follows:

$$P_{01} = \frac{\Sigma P_1}{\Sigma P_0} \times 100,$$

where N is the number of products or commodities or items from which the index number is to be constructed. In media metrics, only simple aggregative and simple average of relatives methods are widely and largely used for the study of news price index like under consumer price index and several communication and media aspects as a part of living index number.

Since we have discussed almost all the aspects of descriptive statistics and media metrics, it will be extremely necessary now to focus our discussion on inferential statistics and media metrics which should be preferably started with hypothesis testing as will be discussed in the next chapter.

IMPORTANT FORMULAE

1. Correlation:
   a. Karl Pearson's correlation coefficient

$$r = \frac{\Sigma d_x d_y}{N\sigma_x \cdot \sigma_y},$$

where r=Karl Pearson's correlation coefficient or product moment correlation coefficient.

$$d_x = X - \bar{X},\ d_y = Y - \bar{Y}$$

σ_x=standard deviation of X series
σ_y=standard deviation of Y series
N=number of observations of pairs.

   b. Simple deviation method:

$$r = \frac{\Sigma d_x d_y}{\sqrt{\Sigma d_x^2 d_y^2}}$$

c. Direct nondeviation method:

$$r = \frac{N\sum XY - (\sum X)(\sum Y)}{\sqrt{N\sum X^2 - (\sum X)^2}\sqrt{N\sum Y^2 - (\sum Y)^2}},$$

where *X* and *Y* are score of raw data, *N* is the number of scores.

d. Shortcut method (or assumed mean method):

$$r = \frac{N\sum d_x d_y - (\sum d_x d_y)^2}{\sqrt{N\sum d_x^2 - (\sum d_x)^2}\sqrt{N\sum d_y^2 - (\sum d_y)^2}},$$

where r=coefficient correlation
N=number of scores

$$d_x = X - A_x \left[\begin{array}{c} X \text{ is score of } X \\ A_x \text{ is assumed mean} \\ \text{of } X \end{array}\right]$$

$$d_y = Y - A_y \left[\begin{array}{c} Y = \text{score of } Y \\ A_y = \text{Assumed mean} \\ \text{of } Y \end{array}\right]$$

e. Classified frequency distribution method:

$$r = \frac{N\sum fd_x d_y - (\sum fd_x)(\sum fd_y)}{\sqrt{N\sum fd_x^2 - (\sum fd_x)^2}\sqrt{N\sum fd_y^2 - (\sum fd_y)^2}}$$

f. Probable error of Karl Pearson's coefficient of correlation (PE_r):

$$PE_r = 0.6745\frac{1 - r^2}{\sqrt{N}}$$

g. Standard error of coefficient of correlation:

$$SE_r = \frac{1 - r^2}{\sqrt{N}},$$

where SE_r is the standard error of coefficient of correlation.

h. Limit $(\rho) = r \pm PE$,
where ρ(Rho) is the limit for coefficient of correlation.

i. Coefficient of determination $(r^2) = \frac{\text{Explained variance}}{\text{Total variance}}$

j. Coefficient of nondetermination $(K^2) = 1 - r^2 = 1 - \frac{\text{Explained variance}}{\text{Total variance}}$

k. Coefficient of alienation $(K) = \sqrt{1 - r^2}$

l. Spearman's rank correlation coefficient:

$$\rho = 1 - \frac{6\sum D^2}{N(N^2 - 1)},$$

where ρ(Rho) is the correlation coefficient of rank, D=differences in rank, and N=number of pair of cases.

m. In case of equal ranks:

$$\rho = 1 - \frac{6\sum D^2 + \frac{1}{12}(m^3 - m) + \frac{1}{12}(m^3 - m) + \cdots}{N(N^2 - 1)},$$

where m is the number of items whose terms are common.

This formula of equal ranks may be further modified as:

$$\rho = 1 - \frac{6\sum D^2 + \frac{1}{12}(m_1^3 - m_1) + \frac{1}{12}(m_2^3 - m_2) + \cdots}{N(N^2 - 1)}.$$

n. Concurrent deviation method:

$$r_c = \pm\sqrt{\pm\left(\frac{2c - n}{n}\right)},$$

where r_c is the correlation coefficient of concurrent deviation, c is the number of positive signs obtained after multiplying D_x and D_y, D_x is the direction of change (positive or negative) of the X series, and similarly D_y is the direction of the change (positive or negative) of the Y series, n is $(N-1)$, while N is the number of pairs of observations.

o. Least squares method:

$$Y = a + bX.$$

To calculate the values of constants a and b, the following two normal equations are applied:

$$\sum Y = Na + b\sum X \quad (i)$$

$$\sum XY = a\sum X + b\sum X^2 \quad (ii)$$

2. Regression:
   a. The regression equation of least squares is the same as least squares method of correlation.
   Hence, the regression equation of X on Y:

   $Y = a + bX$ and the regression equation of Y on X is expressed as

   $$X = a + bY.$$

   Here, the values of a and b are numerical constants of least squares, that is, computed with the help of the following normal equations:

   $$\text{(i) } \Sigma Y = Na + b\Sigma X \quad \text{(ii) } \Sigma X = Na + b\Sigma Y$$

   $$\Sigma XY = a\Sigma X + b\Sigma X^2 \quad \Sigma XY = a\Sigma Y + b\Sigma Y^2$$

   b. Second method,
   Regression equation of Y on X: $Y = a + bX$

   $$b = \frac{N\Sigma XY - (\Sigma X)(\Sigma Y)}{N\Sigma X^2 - (\Sigma X)^2}, \quad a = \frac{\Sigma X - b\Sigma Y}{N}$$

   c. Method of deviation from mean:
      i. Regression equation of X on Y:

      $$X - \bar{X} = r\frac{\sigma_x}{\sigma_y}(Y - \bar{Y}),$$

      where $\bar{X}$ is the mean of X series, $\bar{Y}$ is the mean of Y series, r denotes the coefficient of correlation between X and Y series, and σ_x and σ_y are the standard deviations of X and Y series. $r\frac{\sigma_x}{\sigma_y}$ is known as the regression coefficient of X on Y and is denoted by b_{xy}:

      $$b_{xy} = r\frac{\sigma_x}{\sigma_y} = \frac{\Sigma d_x \cdot d_y}{N \cdot \sigma_x \sigma_y} \times \frac{\sigma_x}{\sigma_y} = \frac{\Sigma d_x \cdot d_y}{N.\sigma_y{}^2} = \frac{\Sigma d_x d_y}{N \times \frac{\Sigma d_y^2}{N}} = \frac{\Sigma d_x d_y}{\Sigma d_y^2},$$

      where d_x and d_y are deviation from means i.e., $d_x = X - \bar{X}$, $d_y = Y - \bar{Y}$.
      ii. Regression equation of Y on X:

      $$X - \bar{X} = r\frac{\sigma_x}{\sigma_y}(Y - \bar{Y}),$$

      where $r\frac{\sigma_x}{\sigma_y}$ is called the regression equation of Y on X and is denoted by b_{yx}:

$$b_{yx} = r\frac{\sigma_y}{\sigma_x} = \frac{\Sigma d_x \cdot d_y}{N \cdot \sigma_x \sigma_y} \times \frac{\sigma_y}{\sigma_x} = \frac{\Sigma d_x \cdot d_y}{N.\sigma_x{}^2} = \frac{\Sigma d_x d_y}{N \times \frac{\Sigma d_x^2}{N}} = \frac{\Sigma d_x d_y}{\Sigma d_x^2}$$

In case we deal with actual values of X and Y and not the deviations, then:

$$b_{xy} = \frac{N\Sigma XY - (\Sigma X)(Y)}{N\Sigma Y^2 - (\Sigma Y)^2}$$

$$b_{yx} = \frac{N\Sigma d_x.d_y - (\Sigma d_x)(\Sigma d_y)}{N\Sigma d_x^2 - (\Sigma d_x)^2}$$

d. Deviation from assumed mean:

$$r\frac{\sigma_x}{\sigma_y} = \frac{N\Sigma d_x.d_y - (\Sigma d_x)(\Sigma d_y)}{N\Sigma d_y^2 - (\Sigma d_y)^2},$$

where $d_x = (X - A_x)$ and $d_y = (Y - A_y)$;
similarly,

$$r\frac{\sigma_y}{\sigma_x} = \frac{N\Sigma d_x.d_y - (\Sigma d_x)(\Sigma d_y)}{N\Sigma d_x^2 - (\Sigma d_x)^2}$$

e. Regression coefficient from correlation table:

$$r\frac{\sigma_x}{\sigma_y} = \frac{N\Sigma fd_x d_y - (\Sigma fd_x)(f\Sigma d_y)}{N\Sigma fd_y^2 - (\Sigma fd_y)^2} \times \frac{h_x}{h_y},$$

where h_x = height of class interval of X variable and h_y = height of class interval of Y variable.
Similarly,

$$r\frac{\sigma_y}{\sigma_x} = \frac{N\Sigma fd_x d_y - (\Sigma fd_x)(f\Sigma d_y)}{N\Sigma fd_x^2 - (\Sigma fd_x)^2} \times \frac{h_y}{h_x}.$$

f. Standard error of estimate (S_y):

$$S_y = \sqrt{\frac{\Sigma(Y - Y_c)^2}{N}},$$

where Y is the original value and Y_c is the computed (linear) value also called the estimated value and N is the number of observations in the series.

There are other formulae which may be used according to situation:

$$S_y = \sigma_y\sqrt{1-r^2} \quad \text{or} \quad \sqrt{\frac{\Sigma Y^2 - a\Sigma Y - b\Sigma XY}{N}},$$

where σ_y is the standard deviation of the Y series, r is the correlation coefficient, and a and b are numerical constants.

Similarly,

$$S_x = \sigma_x\sqrt{1-r^2} \quad \text{or} \quad \sqrt{\frac{\Sigma X^2 - a\Sigma X - b\Sigma XY}{N}}$$

$$= \sqrt{\frac{\Sigma(X - X_c)^2}{N}}$$

3. Index Numbers:
   a. Simple aggregative method:

$$P_{01} = \frac{\Sigma P_1}{\Sigma P_0} \times 100,$$

where P_{01} is the index number of the current year, ΣP_1 is the total of the current year prices for various commodities, ΣP_0 is the total of the base year prices for various commodities.

   b. Simple average of relatives method:

$$P_{01} = \frac{\Sigma\left(\frac{P_1}{P_0}\right) \times 100}{N},$$

where N is the number of products or commodities or items from which the index number is to be constructed.

RELATED AND SUGGESTED WEBSITES

(As retrieved on December 1, 2015)

1. http://faculty.uncfsu.edu/dwallace/lesson%2017.pdf
2. http://pages.stern.nyu.edu/~adamodar/New_Home_Page/littlebook/statisticsrelationships.htm
3. http://forrest.psych.unc.edu/research/vista-frames/help/lecturenotes/lecture11/overview.html
4. https://home.ubalt.edu/tmitch/631/PowerPoint_Lectures/chapter16/chapter16.ppt
5. http://www.utsc.utoronto.ca/~phanira/WebResearchMethods/validity.ppt

REFERENCES

Elhance, D.N.S., and Veena Elhance. 1990. *Fundamentals of Statistics,* 11.1–11.62, 12.1–12.41, 13.1–13.18. New Delhi: Kitab Mahal.

Gupta, S.P. 2011. *Statistical Method,* 390–557. New Delhi: Sultan Chand & Sons.

RELATED AND RECOMMENDED READINGS

Gupta, Das, and S.N. Thakur. 1998. *Modern Approach to Intermediate Statistics and Probability,* 102–44. Patna: Bharti Bhawan.

Hussain, Shanshad. 1986. *Elementary Statistics in Psychology and Education,* 60–92. New Delhi: Motilal Banarsidass.

Kerlinger, F.N. 1983. *Foundations of Behavioural Research.* New Delhi: Surjeet Publications.

Kothari, C.R. 2000. *Research Methodologies: Methods and Techniques,* 138–49. New Delhi: Wishwa Prakashan.

Krishnaswami, O.R., and M. Ranganatham. 2005. *Methodology of Research.* New Delhi: Himalaya Publications.

Mangal, S.K. 1987. *Statistics in Psychology and Education,* 71–104. New Delhi: McGraw Hill.

Sarangi, Prasant. 2010. *Research Methodology.* Delhi: Taxman Publication.

Singh, Arun Kumar. 1986. *Basic Statistics in Psychology and Education,* 112–22. Patna: Novelty & Co.

Wilkinson, T.S., and P.L. Bhandarkar. 1996. *Methodologies and Techniques of Social Research.* Mumbai: Himalaya Publishing House.

Wimmer, Roger D., and Joseph R. Dominick. 2003. *Mass Media Research: An Introduction,* 291–303. 7th ed. Belmont, CA: Thomson & Wadsworth.

QUESTIONS AND PROBLEMS

1. What do you mean by measures of relationship?
2. What is correlation? Describe the scatter diagram method of measuring correlation.
3. What is correlation? Point out the significance of its study to the students of communication and media studies.
4. Distinguish between positive, negative, and zero correlation.
5. Explain what is meant by the correlation between two variables. What are the methods of finding the existence of correlation? How can it be measured?
6. Define rank correlation. Write down Spearman's formula for rank correlation coefficient. What are the limits of correlation? Interpret the case when correlation assumes the minimum value.
7. Describe the merits and demerits of Spearman's rank correlation methods.
8. What kind of relationship between two variables does Karl Pearson's coefficient of correlation measure?
9. Why can correlation coefficient not exceed unity?
10. Explain the merits and demerits of the graphic method of correlation coefficient.
11. What is the significance of correlation? Does it always signify cause and effect relationship between two variables? How is the coefficient of correlation interpreted?
12. Explain simple, partial, and multiple correlations.
13. Throw light on the concurrent deviation method of correlation coefficient.

14. Describe the method of least squares of correlation coefficient.
15. How is correlation calculated in a time series?
16. Throw light on lag and lead in correlation.
17. What is regression analysis? Explain the significance of the study of regression.
18. Compare between correlation and regression.
19. Throw light on regression equations.
20. Describe the meaning and concept of index numbers.
21. Throw light on standard error of estimate.
22. Describe the meaning and concept of index numbers.
23. Explain the characteristics of index numbers.
24. Elaborate the uses of index numbers.
25. Throw light on methods of constructing index numbers.
26. Describe unweighted index numbers. What are the limitations of unweighted index numbers?
27. Explain the merits and demerits of unweighted index numbers.
28. Throw light on weighted index numbers.
29. Describe the relevance and significance of weighted index numbers in communication and media studies.
30. Analyze a scatter diagram from the following data of male and female correspondents:

Male correspondents	10	20	30	40	50	60	70	80
Female correspondents	32	20	24	36	40	28	48	44

31. Calculate the coefficient of correlation between the sales and expenses of the following 10 advertising agencies?

Ad agencies	1	2	3	4	5	6	7	8	9	10
Sales	50	50	55	60	65	65	65	60	60	50
Expenses	11	13	14	16	16	15	15	14	13	13

32. Compute the correction coefficient by the product moment method between the corresponding values of photo editing and visual impact of a magazine in the following table:

Photo editing	2	4	5	6	8	11
Visual impact	18	12	10	8	7	5

33. Compute the product moment correlation coefficient between the following scores of trainee journalists in current affairs and writing skills:

Current affairs	45	55	56	58	60	65	68	70	75	80	85
Writing skills	56	50	48	60	62	64	65	70	74	82	90

34. Calculate Karl Pearson's product moment correlation coefficient between ages of the trainee journalists and experienced journalists working in the same organizations from the following data:

Trainee journalists	15	16	17	18	19	20
Experienced journalists	80	75	60	40	30	30

35. Calculate Karl Pearson's correlation coefficient between the given ages of old and experienced media persons of India and China by the shortcut and nondeviation method?

Media persons of India	65	66	67	67	68	69	70	72
Media persons of China	67	68	65	68	72	72	69	71

36. Following are the results of entrance tests of the students of bachelors of mass communication:

Age of candidates	13–14	14–15	15–16	16–17	17–18	18–19	19–20	20–21	21–22	22–23
Candidates appeared	200	300	100	50	150	400	250	150	25	75
Successful candidates	124	180	65	34	99	252	145	81	12	33

Calculate the correlation coefficient between age and successful candidates.

37. Compute the product moment correlation coefficient from the advertisement cost and sales as per the following data:

Ad cost (in thousand ₹)	39	65	62	90	82	75	25	98	36	78
Sales (in lakhs ₹)	47	53	58	86	62	68	60	91	51	84

38. Calculate Karl Pearson's coefficient correlation between the following cases of modulation and the number of bulletins with improved voice effect:

Modulation	65	66	67	67	68	69	70	72
Effect	67	68	65	68	72	72	69	71

39. Compute Karl Pearson's coefficient correlation between the values of channel noise and declined performance of different television programs from the following data:

Channel noise	15	16	17	18	19	20
Declined TV performance	80	75	60	40	30	20

40. Product moment correlation coefficient between two variables, print media journalists and PR practitioners, is 0.28, their covariance is +7.6. If the variance of X is 9, calculate the standard deviation of the Y series.
41. Find out the product moment correlation coefficient between advertisement cost and sales as per the following data:

Ad cost (in thousand ₹)	39	65	62	90	82	75	25	98	36	78
Sales (in lakhs ₹)	47	53	58	86	62	68	60	91	51	84

42. Compute the product moment correlation coefficient from the following data, taking 100 and 50 as the assumed averages of male journalists and female journalists, respectively:

Male journalists (X)	104	111	104	118	117	105	108	106	100	104	105
Female journalists (Y)	57	55	47	45	50	64	63	66	62	69	61

43. Calculate Karl Pearson's correlation coefficient between years of experience of media persons and awards won by them from the following data:

Experience of media persons (in yrs)	1	2	3	4	5	6	7	8	9
No. of awards won	9	8	10	12	13	14	14	16	15

44. Find out the coefficient of correlation between the percentage of bonus given and the number of exclusive stories of different levels per annum from the following data by Karl Pearson's method:

Bonus (%)	2.52	2.49	2.49	2.45	2.43	2.42	2.41	2.40
Exclusive stories	730	710	770	890	970	1020	970	1040

45. Calculate the product moment correlation coefficient between the attacks on female journalists and those on male journalists in a district per year from the following data:

Female journalists (no. of attacks)	9	8	7	6	5	4	3	2	1
Male journalists (no. of attacks)	15	16	14	13	11	12	10	8	9

46. Find Karl Pearson's coefficient of correlation between the total number of absence from the duty of male reporters and female reporters of a newspaper organization during their service time from the given data and calculate the probable error:

Male reporters (No. of absence)	78	89	96	69	59	79	68	61
Female reporters (no. of absence)	125	137	156	112	107	136	123	108

Assume 69 and 112 as the mean values for X and Y, respectively.

47. Calculate Karl Pearson's coefficient of correlation from the following data:

Roll no.	1	2	3	4	5	6	7
Marks in editing	20	35	42	37	13	39	24
Marks in mass communication	32	37	50	30	25	24	40

48. Compute the coefficient of correlation by Karl Pearson's method between the number of printing machine break-ups of two newspaper organizations A and B from the following data:

Newspaper A	6	2	10	4	8
Newspaper B	9	11	?	8	7

Means of A and B are 6 and 8, respectively.

49. Calculate the product moment correlation from the following data taking deviation from 48 in the case of series of new media staff and 20 in the series of traditional media staff.

New media staff	40	42	46	48	50	56
Traditional media staff	10	12	15	23	27	30

50. Following are the results of media persons of experience of different years in terms of time in a promotional examination:

Yrs. of experience	**13–14**	**14–15**	**15–16**	**16–17**	**17–18**	**18–19**	**19–20**	**20–21**	**21–22**	**22–23**
Media persons appeared	200	300	100	50	150	400	250	150	25	75
Successful media persons	124	180	65	34	99	252	145	81	12	33

Calculate the coefficient of correlation between age and successful candidates in the examination.

51. Calculate the correlation coefficient between the marks obtained by 60 candidates in an examination in two subjects advertising and public relations from the following data:

	Marks in Ad			
Marks in PR	**5–15**	**15–25**	**25–35**	**35–45**
0–10	1	1	–	–
10–20	3	6	5	1
20–30	1	8	9	2
30–40	–	3	9	3
40–50	–	–	4	4

52. Find out Karl Pearson's coefficient of correlation from the given distribution:

	Age in Years				
Marks in Broadcasting	**18**	**19**	**20**	**21**	**22**
20–25	3	2	–	–	–
15–20	–	5	4	–	–
10–15	–	–	7	10	–
5–10	–	–	–	3	2
0–5	–	–	–	3	1

53. Calculate the coefficient of correlation from the following data:

	Marks in Reporting					
Marks in Editing	**0–10**	**10–20**	**20–30**	**30–40**	**40–50**	**Total**
0–10	4	6	–	–	–	10
10–20	–	5	9	1	–	15
20–30	–	–	4	3	3	10
30–40	–	–	–	6	3	9
40–50	–	–	–	4	2	6
Total	4	11	13	14	8	50

54. If covariance between journalists of a newspaper and those of a magazine is 10 and the variance of X and Y are, respectively, 16 and 9; find the coefficient of correlation?
55. Find the correlation coefficient of rank of the following marks obtained in reporting and editing:

Student	A	B	C	D	E	F	G	H
Scores of reporting	65	72	49	58	70	58	47	52
Scores of editing	60	65	40	52	67	60	45	44

56. From the following table, calculate the correlation coefficient between the ages of male journalists and female journalists:

No. of Female Journalists (Y Series)	Age of Male Journalists (X series)					
	20–30	30–40	40–50	50–60	60–70	Total
15–25	5	9	3	–	–	17
25–35	–	10	25	2	–	37
35–45	–	1	12	2	–	15
45–55	–	–	4	16	5	25
55–65	–	–	–	4	2	6
Total	5	20	44	24	7	100

57. From the following table, compute the correlation coefficient between ages of heroes and heroines of Bollywood:

	Age of Heroine (X)						
Age of Heroes (Y)	15–25	25–35	35–45	45–55	55–65	65–75	Total
15–25	1	1	–	–	–	–	2
25–35	2	12	1	1	–	–	15
35–45	–	4	10	6	–	–	15
45–55	–	–	3	2	1	–	10
55–65	–	–	–	–	4	2	8
65–75	–	–	–	–	1	2	3
Total	3	17	14	9	6	4	53

58. Find out the correlation coefficient between the number of successful male broadcasters and female broadcasters of the following data by the concurrent deviation method:

Male broadcasters	110	120	130	130	115	100	120
Female broadcasters	50	40	60	80	80	55	60

59. From the given data of the number of graphics and animation centers of two cities X and Y obtain the two regression equations using the methods of least squares:

Graphics and animation centers at city *X*	2	4	6	8	10
Graphics and animation centers at city *Y*	5	7	9	8	11

60. From the given data of male and female PR practitioners, obtain the regression equations by deviation from actual means:

Male PR practitioners	6	2	10	4	8
Female PR practitioners	9	11	5	8	7

61. From the data of the above question, calculate regression equations taking deviations by assuming 5 as the mean of the *X* series and 7 as the mean of the *Y* series.
62. Given the following data of two tests:

Marks in Advertising (*X*)	Marks in PR (*Y*)
$\bar{X} = 75.00$, SD for $X = 6.00$	$\bar{Y} = 70.00$, SD for $Y = 8.00$
$r = 0.72$	

Determine the regression equations and predict:
a. The marks in PR of students whose marks in advertising are 65, and
b. The marks in advertising of students whose marks in PR are 50.

63. Find the regression coefficient of the following data:

X	3	2	–1	6	4	–2	5
Y	5	13	12	–1	2	20	0

64. A panel of two advertising managers A_1 and A_2 grades the performance of creative artists by independently awarding the marks as follows:

Performance	1	2	3	4	5	6	7
Marks by A_1	46	42	44	40	43	41	45
Marks by A_2	40	38	36	35	39	37	41

The eighth performance which A_2 could not attend was awarded 37 by A_1. If A_2 has also been present, how many marks have been expected to be awarded by him to the eighth performance.

65. From the given data of monthly prices of different magazines, construct an index number for 2015 taking 2014 as the base year by the average of relatives method:

Magazines	Prices in 2014 (in ₹)	Prices in 2015 (in ₹)
A	40	48
B	50	60
C	60	80

66. The rank of 15 students in two subjects media writing and media law are as follows: (1, 10), (2, 7), (3, 2), (4, 6), (5, 4), (6, 8), (7, 3), (8, 1), (9, 11), (10, 15), (11, 9), (12, 5), (13, 14), (14, 12), (15, 13)
Use Spearman's formula to find the rank coefficient correlation.

67. Two news editors were asked to rank seven different types of news stories. The rank given by them are as follows:

News stories	NS_1	NS_2	NS_3	NS_4	NS_5	NS_6	NS_7
NE_1	2	1	4	3	5	7	6
NE_2	1	3	2	4	5	6	7

Calculate Spearman's rank correlation coefficient.

68. 10 TV News Readers' overall performances were ranked by three station directors in the following order:

SD_1	1	6	5	10	3	2	4	9	7	8
SD_2	3	5	8	4	7	10	2	1	6	9
SD_3	6	4	9	8	1	2	3	10	5	7

Use the rank correlation coefficient to determine which pair of station directors has the nearest approach to their overall performance.

69. Compute Spearman's coefficient of correlation between marks assigned to 10 media students in electronic media and mass communication examinations by two external experts *X* and *Y*, respectively with the following data:

S. No.	1	2	3	4	5	6	7	8	9	10
Marks by external (*X*)	52	53	42	60	45	41	37	38	25	27
Marks by external (*Y*)	65	68	43	38	77	48	35	30	25	50

70. Calculate Spearman's rank correlation for the following observation of eight students of public relations:

Students of PR	1	2	3	4	5	6	7	8
Examiner *X*	20	22	28	23	30	30	23	24
Examiner *Y*	28	24	24	25	26	27	32	30

71. Twelve customer executives are ranked in the order of merit efficiency by their advertising manager. They are also ranked in accordance with their length of service. What indication is there of a relation between length of service and efficiency?

CE	CE1	CE2	CE3	CE4	CE5	CE6	CE7	CE8	CE9	CE10	CE11	CE12
Service	5	2	10	8	6	4	12	2	7	5	9	3
Efficiency	7.5	11.5	2	4	6	9	1	11.5	5	7.5	3	10

72. Sixteen media industries have been ranked according to profit earned in 2013–14 and the working capital for that year. Compute the rank correlation coefficient:

Media industry (Profit)	1	2	3	4	5	6	7	8	9	10	11	12	13	14	15	16
Rank (working capital)	13	16	14	15	10	12	4	11	5	9	8	3	1	6	7	2

73. The ranking of 10 journalists at the start and finish of a journalism training course are as follows:

	A	B	C	D	E	F	G	H	I	J
Journalists rank (before)	1	6	3	9	5	2	7	10	8	4
Journalists rank (after)	6	8	3	7	2	1	5	9	4	10

Compute Spearman's coefficient of correlation.

74. Calculate the rank correlation between size of a family and readership of a newspaper from the following table:

	F1	F2	F3	F4	F5	F6	F7	F8	F9	F10
Size of family	17	13	15	16	06	11	14	9	7	12
Readership	36	46	35	24	12	18	27	22	2	8

75. Compute the coefficient of concurrent deviation from the following:

X	60	55	50	56	30	70	40	35	80	80	75
Y	65	40	35	75	63	80	35	20	80	60	50

76. The following table gives the frequency according to the group of marks secured by 67 media persons in an emotional quotient test. Calculate the degree of relationship between the age of media persons and emotional quotient test:

	Age of media persons in years				
Emotional Quotient Test Marks	**18**	**19**	**20**	**21**	**Total**
200–250	4	4	2	1	11
250–300	3	5	4	2	14
300–350	2	6	8	5	21
350–400	1	4	6	10	21
Total	10	19	20	18	67

77. Following are the marks secured by media students in creative writing and graphics in a minor test of 20 marks in each subject:

No. of students	1	2	3	4	5	6	7	8	9	10	11	12	13	14	15	16	17	18	19	20	21	22	23	24
Marks in creative writing	15	0	1	3	16	2	18	5	4	17	6	19	14	9	8	13	10	13	11	11	12	18	9	7
Marks in graphics	13	1	2	7	8	9	12	9	17	16	6	18	11	3	5	4	10	11	14	7	18	15	15	3

Prepare a correlation table taking the magnitude of each class interval as four marks and the first interval as equal to 0 and less than 4. Find out Karl Person's coefficient of correlation between marks in creative writing and marks in graphics.

78. The following data relate to the age of journalists and the number of days they were reported sick in a month:

	Journalists									
	1	2	3	4	5	6	7	8	9	10
Age (*X*)	30	32	35	40	48	50	52	55	57	61
Sick days (*Y*)	1	0	2	5	2	4	6	5	7	8

Find out Karl Pearson's coefficient of correlation.

79. If $r=0.6$ and $N=64$, calculate the probable error of the coefficient of correlation and determine the limits for population *r*.
80. Find out Karl Pearson's coefficient of correlation between age and job-seeking habits of media students from the following data. Also calculate the probable error:

Age	20	21	22	23	24	25
No. of students	500	400	300	240	200	160
Job seeker	400	300	180	36	60	24

81. Calculate the coefficient of correlation with the help of Karl Pearson's method:

	Marks in Media Research				
Mark in Media Law	19	20	30	40	50
5	2	4	1	4	1
10	8	2	5	1	–
15	–	3	2	1	–
20	–	1	3	2	4
25	–	–	4	2	–

82. If covariance between print journalists *X* and broadcast journalists *Y* is 10 and the variance for *X* and *Y* are, respectively, 16 and 9, find the coefficient of correlation.
83. The coefficient of correlation between two advertisers and PR practitioners is 0.64. Their covariance is 16. The variance of *X* is 19. Calculate the standard deviation of the *Y* series.
84. During an annual analysis of a media organization in a question of correlation, the value of *r* is 0.917 and its probable error is 0.034. What will be the value of the number of pairs of observations?
85. The value of *r* in an evaluation of an advertising agency was calculated as +0.72 for a question comprising five pairs of observations and it was concluded that there is high degree of correlation between variables. Do you justify this conclusion?
86. Find out the correlation coefficient between graphics and animation from the following data: $N=\Sigma 100$, $\Sigma x=140$, $\Sigma Y=150$, $\Sigma(X-10)^2=180$, $\Sigma(Y-15)^2=215$, $\Sigma(X-10)(Y-15)=60$. Also compute the coefficient of determination.
87. Find the number of pairs of observations between cub reporters and experienced journalists of a media agency from the following data: $r=0.5$, $\Sigma XY=120$, $\Sigma X^2=90$, $\sigma y=8$.

88. Compute the correlation coefficient of reporters and subeditors from the following data: $N=10$, $\Sigma x=140$, $\Sigma y=150$.
89. National daily newspapers in India are complaining that the rising level of unemployment is adversely affecting the level of crime in the country. To find out this claim, a research team studied a random sample of 12 states in India. For each state, they measured the level of unemployment rate and crime rate in the state. Then, the team did a ranking: X=level of unemployment, Y=crime rate. The result is shown in the following table. Higher X ranks mean more unemployment and higher Y ranks mean higher crime rate. Test the claim of the national daily newspaper.

States	1	2	3	4	5	6	7	8	9	10	11	12
Level of unemployment (X)	5	8	3	2	6	1	10	12	7	4	9	11
Crime rate (Y)	8	6	9	12	7	10	2	1	5	11	4	3

90. In a correlation analysis, the following values of male advertisers and female advertisers are obtained:

	Male Advertisers		**Female Journalists**
Mean	65		67
Standard Deviation	2.5		3.5
Coefficient Correlation		0.8	

Calculate the two regression equations.

91. For 50 students of a class, the regression equation of marks in editing (X) on the marks in reporting (Y) is $3y-5x+180=0$. The mean marks in reporting is 44 and the variance of marks in editing is 9/16th of the variance of the marks in reporting. Calculate the mean marks in editing and coefficient of correlation between marks in the two subjects.
92. Calculate the two regression equations and estimate the value of X when $Y=75$, from the following data:

	X	Y
Arithmetic Mean	36	85
Standard Deviation	11	8

Correlation coefficient between X and $Y=0.66$.

93. Following is the distribution of media persons in their height and weight:

	Weight in lbs			
Height in Inches	90–100	100–110	110–120	120–130
50–55	4	7	5	2
55–60	6	10	7	4
60–65	6	12	10	7
65–70	3	8	6	3

(a) Find out the coefficient of regression and (b) obtain the two regression equations.

94. An advertising agency summarized advertising expenditure and sales results as follows:

	Advertising Expenditure (₹ in Crore)	Sales (₹ in Crore)
Mean	20	200
SD	18	170
r	0.6	

Calculate the regression equations of advertising expenditure and sales results.

95. Find out the regression equation of advertisers (Y) on and creative writers (X) and estimate Y when $X=55$ from the following:

X	40	50	38	60	65	50	35
Y	38	60	55	70	60	48	30

96. If $b_{xy}=0.85$, $b_{yx}=0.89$, and $\sigma_x=6$, find the value of r and σ_y.
97. The following data about advertising and sales are given below:

	Advertising Expenditure (X) (₹ Crore)	Sales (Y) (₹ Crore)
Mean	20	100
SD	5	12
r	0.8	

a. Find out the two regression lines;
b. Calculate the likely sales when advertisement expenditure is ₹25 Crore;
c. What should be advertisement expenditure, if the company wants to attain a sales target of ₹130 Crore?

98. Calculate from the following information:
a. Two regression equations,
b. Coefficient of correlation between marks in advertising and public relations,
c. Most likely marks in PR when the marks in advertising is 30.

99. Calculate the regression coefficients of Y on X and X on Y from the following data: $\Sigma X=50$, $\overline{X}=5$, $\Sigma Y=60$, $\overline{Y}=6$, $\Sigma XY=350$, Variance of $X=4$, Variance of $Y=9$.
100. The correlation coefficient between two variables X and Y is $r=0.6$. If $S_x=1.50$, $S_y=2.00$, $\overline{X}=10$, $\overline{Y}=20$, find the regression lines of (a) Y on X, (b) X on Y.
101. The given data relate to advertisement expenditure (in lakhs of rupee) and their corresponding sales (in crore of rupees):

Advertisement Expenditure	10	12	15	23	20
Sales	14	17	23	25	21

Estimate:
a. Sales corresponding to advertisement expenditure of 30 lakhs,
b. The advertisement expenditure for a sales target of ₹35 crore.

102. Estimate from the following (a) the sale for advertising expenditure of ₹100 lakhs and (b) the advertisement expenditure for sales of ₹47 Crores:

Sales (₹Crore)	14	16	18	20	24	30	32
Adv. Exp. (₹lakhs)	52	62	65	70	76	80	78

103. The following data about advertisement expenditure and sales are as follows:

	Advt. Exp. (X)(₹ Crore)	Sales (Y) (₹ Crore)
Mean	20	120
SD	5	25
Correlation coefficient	0.8	

a. Find out two regression equations;
b. Calculate the likely sales when the advertisement expenditure is ₹25 Crore;
c. Compute the advertisement expenditure for the sales of ₹150 Crore?

104. The following table gives the aptitude test scores and productivity indices of 10 media persons selected at random:

Aptitude Scores (X)	60	62	65	70	72	48	53	73	65	82
Productivity Index (Y)	68	60	62	80	85	40	52	62	60	81

Calculate the two regression equations and estimate the productivity index of a media person whose test score is 92.

105. The following data relate to advertising expenditure and sales:

Adv. Exp. (₹ Lakhs)	60	62	65	70	73	75	71
Sales (₹ Crore)	10	11	13	15	16	19	14

Estimate (a) the sales for advertising expenditure of ₹90 lakhs and (b) the advertising expenditure for a sales target of ₹25 crore.

106. When the price of newsprint is given in lakh year-wise, compute the index number by taking:
a. 2006 as the base year,
b. 2013 as the base year,
c. 2006–08 as the base period.

Year	2006	2007	2008	2009	2010	2011	2012	2013	2014
Price	4	5	6	7	8	10	9	10	11

107. From the following data of printing commodities and prices construct the index number for the year 2015 taking 2014 as the base year by using arithmetic mean:

Printing commodities	A	B	C	D	E
Price in 2014 (₹)	6	2	4	10	8
Price in 2015 (₹)	10	2	6	12	12

8

CHAPTER

Parametric Testing of Hypothesis in Media Studies

There are two possible outcomes. If the result confirms the hypothesis, then you made a measurement. If the result is contrary to the hypothesis, then you made a discovery.

—Enrico Fermi

Parametric testing of hypothesis in media studies is often used to explore the basic qualities of sample parameters relating to the issues of mass communication or to examine whether estimates on a given parameter are equal for two samples of the media field. It proposes a null hypothesis against an alternative hypothesis. It tests whether or not the population mean is equal to a particular value. Then it applies suitable statistics to find out the probability of the null hypothesis being true. We may accept or reject the null hypothesis and the alternative hypothesis based on our statistical calculations.

In the previous chapter, we have comprehensively discussed the meaning and concept of measures of relationship in media research, meaning and concept of correlation, significance of study of correlation, types of correlation, correlation coefficient, properties of correlation coefficient, methods of correlation, calculation of correlation in a time series, lag and lead in a correlation, concept and meaning of regression, significance of regression analysis, difference between correlation and regression, regression equation, method of least squares, method of deviations from means, properties of regression coefficients, deviation from assumed mean, standard error of estimate, other measures, meaning and concept of index numbers, and important formulae.

Thus, we have discussed descriptive statistical tools of media metrics such as measures of relationship and other measures in the previous chapter. Since we have discussed almost all the aspects of descriptive statistics or descriptive media metrics, it will be extremely necessary now to focus our discussion on inferential statistics or inferential media metrics (we may say so in the present context). And that should be preferably started with hypothesis testing which will be discussed in this chapter.

Thus, we will start our discussion of inferential statistical tools of media metrics in this chapter and the following chapters. The first inferential statistics (as shown in the flowchart in Section 2.2.1 of Chapter 2) is parametric testing of hypothesis. Hence, this chapter on parametric testing of hypothesis will focus on the following:

1. Meaning and concept of hypothesis testing in media studies
2. Steps for testing hypothesis
3. Role of standard error and sampling distribution
4. Estimation

5. Test of significance for attributes
6. Test of significance for larger samples
7. Test of significance for small samples
8. Limitations of tests of significance

In addition, the chapter will also cover the summary, important formulae, related and suggested websites, references, related and recommended readings, questions and problems of measures of dispersion with general reference to statistics and special reference to media metrics relating to the problems of communication and media studies, and their solutions.

8.1 MEANING AND CONCEPT OF HYPOTHESIS TESTING IN MEDIA STUDIES

A hypothesis in media studies is a supposition or assumption of mass communication problems which becomes the base for reasoning. According to Palmer O. Johnson (cited in Gupta 2011, 882), "Hypothesis is like islands in the uncharted seas of thought to be used as bases for consolidation and recuperation as we advance into the unknown." Morris Hamburg (cited in Gupta 2011, 882) aptly remarks, "A hypothesis in statistics is simply a quantitative statement about a population." It is also a general observation about the population and its validity is tested statistically to know whether it is true or false. Hypothesis testing is testing the assumed supposition through appropriate statistical tests. In media studies, communication and media problems and issues are hypothesized and tested following the procedure of hypothesis testing.

8.2 STEPS FOR TESTING HYPOTHESIS

Formulating an appropriate hypothesis means completing half of the research work. In testing a hypothesis, the most important question is whether to accept the hypothesis or not. The procedure involved in hypothesis testing is explained below:

1. Establishing a hypothesis: The first and foremost issue in testing a hypothesis is to establish a hypothesis about a population parameter. For example, we may say that the average income of a journalist in Indian newspapers is ₹12,000. This is an assumption about the parameter mean. To test its validity, we are supposed to collect the data from the universe, which will give us simple statistics that will be used to determine how valid the hypothesis that we have made is. Hence, we will find out the difference between the hypothesized value and the actual value of the sample mean. Accordingly, with the help of the standard error, we will judge whether the difference is significant or it can be avoided as arising out of sampling fluctuations.

   Conventionally, a single hypothesis is not framed. If one of the hypotheses is accepted, the other is automatically rejected and vice versa.

   Such hypotheses are taken as:

   a. Null hypothesis or hypothesis of no difference
   b. Alternate hypothesis

   Null hypothesis is a highly important and relevant tool in testing the significance of difference. In its easiest and simplest form, the hypothesis asserts that there is no real difference in the sample and population in the particular matter under consideration and that the difference found is accidental and irrelevant arising out of fluctuations of sampling. A null hypothesis is based on the principles of law that a man is innocent until and unless he is proved guilty.

Unlike a null hypothesis, an alternate hypothesis assumes that the differences are not due to fluctuations of sampling; they are genuine and factual. Thus, if the null hypothesis is rejected, it means that the alternative hypothesis is accepted. Likewise, if the null hypothesis is accepted, it means that the alternate hypothesis is rejected.

A null hypothesis is denoted by H_0 and an alternative hypothesis by H_a. And μ (the lower case "m" in Greek and called mu) is the mean of the population.

As explained in the following example:

H_0: $\mu = 5$ kg (null hypothesis)
H_a: $\mu \neq 5$ kg, or
H_a: $\mu >$ or < 5 kg.

Similarly, if two samples have given us the mean income of media persons as ₹12,000 and ₹13,000 per month, then:

H_0: $\mu_1 = \mu_2$ or, $\mu_1 - \mu_2 = 0$ (null hypothesis)
H_a: $\mu_1 \neq \mu_2$ or, $\mu_1 - \mu_2 \neq 0$ (alternative hypothesis).

This means that null hypothesis and alternative hypothesis are mathematical opposites.

2. Determine a level of significance: After establishing the hypothesis, the next move is to determine a suitable level of significance at which the hypothesis will be tested. Here, we are supposed to test the validity of H_0 against that of H_a at a certain level of significance. Normally, the level of confidence for most hypothesis testing is 5 percent. This means that our decision to accept or reject a hypothesis will be 95 times out of 100 and the probability of our going wrong will be a 5 percent chance of our rejecting the null hypothesis which is true, or a 5 percent chance of our accepting the alternative hypothesis which is wrong. Suppose we want even greater precision, the hypothesis can be tested at 1 percent level of significance in which case, the probability of our going wrong is only 1 percent.
3. Deciding sampling distribution: The next step in hypothesis testing is to determine the suitable sampling distribution. Some of the common probability distributions which are applied more frequently in hypothesis testing are z, t, χ^2, F, and so on. The choice of test statistic will depend on the nature of the distribution and the size of the sample. If the sample is small, a normal distribution is not applicable and, hence, Z-test has to be replaced by a t-test.
4. Drawing conclusions: The last and final stage in hypothesis testing is to draw statistical conclusions and take decisions accordingly. A statistical conclusion is a decision either to accept or reject the null hypothesis. A null hypothesis will be rejected if the sample statistic falls in the rejection region. If we take at 5 percent level of significance, the mean of a sample would not represent the mean of the universe if its value is not within 95 percent value enclosed in a normal distribution. The rejection region will be 2.5 percent on either side of the normal curve. Under such circumstances, we reject the null hypothesis which leads us to the conclusion that the difference between the sample mean ($\bar{X}$) and the population mean (μ) could not be due to chance. The difference is significant and, hence, the null hypothesis stands rejected. Thus, the alternative hypothesis is accepted. Reversely, if the sample result is within 95 percent level of acceptance, we conclude that the difference between the sample mean and the population mean can be

used as a parameter value. The hypothesis of no difference, that is, the null hypothesis in this case is accepted, which means that the alternative hypothesis is rejected.

8.2.1 Errors in Hypothesis Testing

There are two types of errors in hypothesis testing: (a) type I error and (b) type II error. Type I error is that when the hypothesis is true, but our tests reject it. Type II error is that in which the hypothesis is false, but our tests accept it.

Type I error (rejecting a null hypothesis when it is true) is denoted by α.

Thus, α = Probability of type I error,

= Probability of rejecting H_0 when it is true.

Type II error (accepting a null hypothesis when it is not true) is denoted by β.

Thus, β = Probability of type II error,

= Probability of accepting H_0 when it is false.

When the difference between two population means is zero and when our tests indicate rejection of the null hypothesis, we commit type I error.

Similarly, if the difference between two means is not zero, but our tests signify acceptance of the null hypothesis, we commit type II error.

The following table explains the situations more explicitly:

	Accept H_0	**Reject H_0**
H_0 is true	No error	Type I error
H_0 is false	Type II error	No error

Decision based on sample	Truth about the population: H_0 true	Truth about the population: H_a true
Reject H_0	Type I Error	Correct Decision
Accept H_0	Correct Decision	Type II Error

Despite making every effort to reduce both type I and type II errors, it is not possible to reduce both at the same time. When we reduce the probability of type I error from 0.05 to 0.01, at the same time, we increase the probability of type II error. To get a low β, we will have to put a high α. However, it is erroneous to accept a false hypothesis (or commit type II error) than to reject a true hypothesis (or commit type I error). In most of the statistical tests, the level of significance is usually fixed at 5 percent. It clearly indicates that the probability of accepting a true hypothesis is 95 percent. In more simplified words, the critical region is 5 percent and the acceptance region is 95 percent.

8.2.2 Two-tailed and One-tailed Tests of Hypothesis

In the process of hypothesis testing, we often talk of two-tailed and one-tailed tests. A two-tailed test relates to both the sides of the normal curve, while a one-tailed test relates to only one side of this curve. The critical region (or the region of rejection) which is usually 5 percent is kept on both sides of the normal distribution in a two-tailed test. That is to say that 2.5 percent of the critical zone is on the extreme left and 2.5 percent on the extreme right of the normal curve. The middle 95 percent is the acceptance zone (Figure 8.1). In a one-tailed test (Figure 8.2), the 5 percent area would be either on the extreme left of the normal curve or on the extreme right. The remaining 95 percent will be the acceptance zone.

A two-tailed test is used if the mean income of journalists is ₹12,000 and the alternative hypothesis is that it is not ₹12,000. In such a situation the actual value of the population mean may be more than ₹12,000 or less than ₹12,000. In such situation, a two-tailed test is suitably preferred.

FIGURE 8.1
TWO-TAILED TEST FIGURES

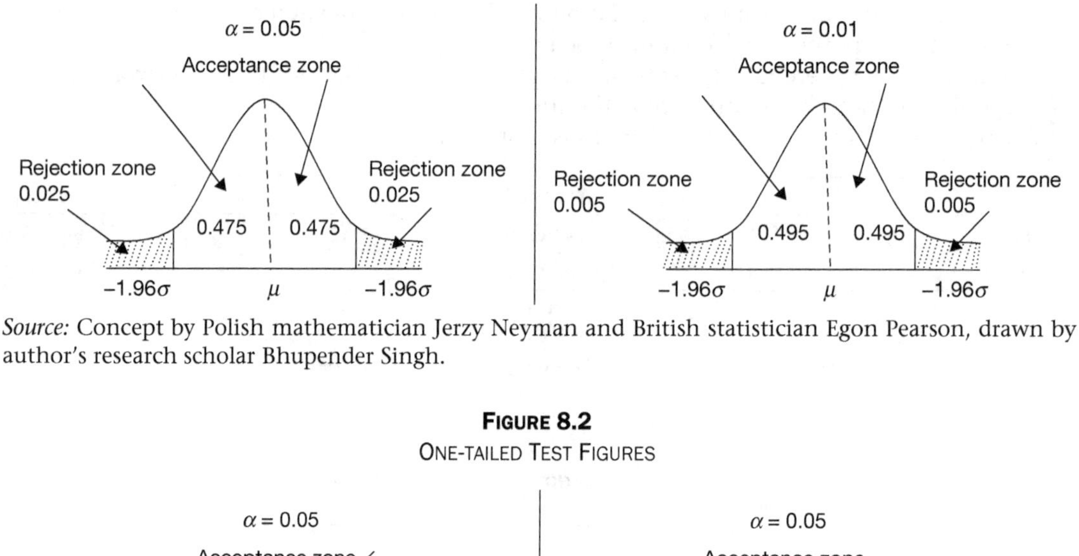

Source: Concept by Polish mathematician Jerzy Neyman and British statistician Egon Pearson, drawn by author's research scholar Bhupender Singh.

FIGURE 8.2
ONE-TAILED TEST FIGURES

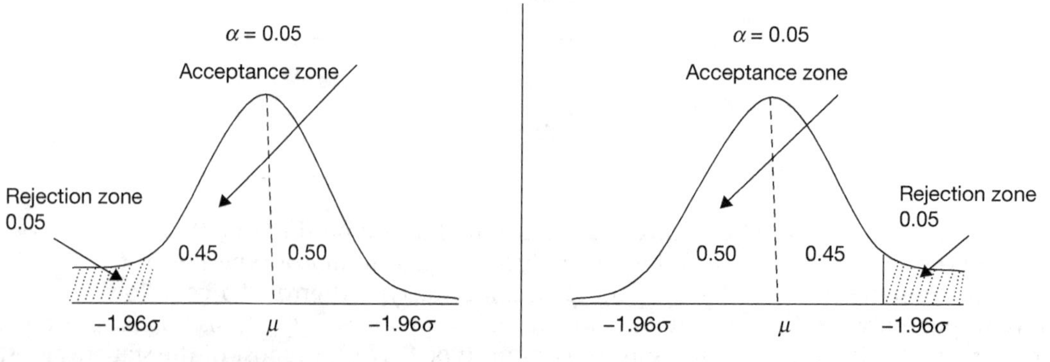

Source: Concept by Polish mathematician Jerzy Neyman and British statistician Egon Pearson, drawn by author's research scholar Bhupender Singh.

On the other hand when the null hypothesis is that the mean income of the journalists is ₹12,000 and the alternative hypothesis is that it can be more than ₹12,000, then a one-tailed test will be used and we will use the right tail for the purpose. Similarly, when the hypothesis is that the mean income of the journalists is ₹12,000 and the alternative hypothesis is that it is less than ₹12,000, then again we will apply the one-tailed test and apply the left tail of the normal curve.

Thus, when we want to test the hypothesis that the population has a specified mean, say μ_0, then the null hypothesis will be:

H_0: $\mu = \mu_0$.

And the alternative hypothesis could be:

1. H_a: $\mu \neq \mu_0$ (i.e., $\mu > \mu_0$ or $\mu < \mu_0$)
2. H_a: $\mu > \mu_0$
3. H_a: $\mu < \mu_0$

This can also be explicitly explained by the following table:

Sign of Alternative Hypothesis	Type of Test Used
=	Two-tailed test
>	Right-tailed test
<	Left-tailed test

This means that the alternative hypothesis in (1) is known as the two-tailed alternative and the hypotheses in (2) and (3) are known as the right-tailed and left-tailed alternatives, respectively. Hence, the corresponding tests of significance can be described as two-tailed, right-tailed, and left-tailed tests, respectively.

For convenience in analysis, the critical values of Z for both the two-tailed and one-tailed tests are presented in Table 8.1, which have been taken from the area table of the normal curve.

8.2.3 Judging the Power of Hypothesis Test

It is extremely important and relevant here to understand how properly, effectively, and powerfully a hypothesis test is working. The measure of how effectively the test is working is called the power of the test.

TABLE 8.1

CRITICAL VALUE OF Z

Level of Significance	1%	5%	10%
Z critical values for one-tailed test	+2.33 or −2.33	+1.645 or −1.645	+1.28 or −1.28
Z critical values for two-tailed test	+2.58 and −2.58	+1.96 and −1.96	+1.645 and −1.645

As discussed earlier, we may commit type I and Type II errors during hypothesis testing. In hypothesis testing, α (probability of type I error) and β (probability of type II error) should be negligible, small, and insignificant. It is quite well known to us that a hypothesis test cannot be foolproof. Sometimes the test does not reject H_0 when it is false and this way, type II error is committed. For hypothesis to be powerful, β (probability of accepting H_0 when H_0 is not true) should be as small as possible. Reversely, $1-\beta$ (probability of rejecting H_0 when H_0 is not true) should be as big as possible. If $(1-\beta)$ is near unity, we can say that the test is working effectively, leading us to the fact that the test is rejecting H_0 when H_0 is not true. Thus, $(1-\beta)$ value is the measure of how effectively the test is working or what is called the "power of a hypothesis test."

8.3 ROLE OF STANDARD ERROR AND SAMPLING DISTRIBUTION

Standard error and sampling distribution play a big role in hypothesis testing. So it is desirable here to understand the concept of standard error first, which is of fundamental importance in testing the hypothesis.

Standard deviation of a sampling distribution is described as the standard error. If the standard error is low, the sampling is more reliable and, hence, more representative to its universe. Standard error also measures the sampling variability due to chance or random forces. It is, thus, necessary to clarify a sampling distribution. When we select a number of independent random samples of a given size from a given universe and calculate some important statistical values such as mean and standard deviation from each sample, we will get a series of values of these statistics or functions. All these values obtained from different samples may be arranged in the form of a frequency table. The frequency distribution so formed of all possible values of a statistic is described as sampling distribution or the probability distribution of that statistic. Hence, when we draw 200 random samples from a given universe and calculate their mean, we will thus get a series of 200 means which will also form a frequency distribution. The distribution is called sampling distribution of the means.

It is important to mention here that the proper description of sampling distribution will be incomplete without explaining population distribution and sample distribution, and showing the relationship of these two with sampling distribution.

8.3.1 Population Distribution

When every unit of a universe or population is studied deeply, we obtain complete knowledge of its mean and standard deviation. The mean of the population, which is also described as the true mean, is symbolized by μ (the lower case m in Greek and called mu) and its standard deviation by σ (sigma). Measures characterizing a population such as μ and σ are described as parameters.

8.3.2 Sample Distribution

When we study a few units or a small part of a population instead of all the units, then we call it a sample distribution. The symbols $\bar{X}$ and S are used to designate the mean and the standard deviation of a sample distribution, respectively. It is important to mention here that several sample distributions are possible from an available population. A measure characterizing a sample, such as $\bar{X}$ or S, is described as a "statistic."

Following are some of the striking features of a statistic of a sampling distribution:

1. A sampling distribution is framed from a population distribution.
2. The same population may generate an infinite number of sampling distributions, each of special sample size, $N1$, $N2$, $N3$,..., $N\infty$.
3. A population may generate a sampling distribution for two or more varied statistics.

Sampling distributions are of utmost importance because they can lead to generalization about populations. Sampling distribution of a mean has the following striking features:

1. Mean, that is, the arithmetic mean of a sampling distribution is the same as the mean of the population from which the samples were generated. Due to this reason, the mean of a sampling distribution and the mean of the population may be denoted by the same symbol, that is, μ.
2. Sampling distribution of a mean is equal to the standard deviation (standard error of mean) divided by the square root of the size of the sample. Thus, symbolically, standard error of $\bar{X} = \sigma / \sqrt{N}$ (where σ is the standard deviation of the population and N is the size of the sample), which is equal to $S / \sqrt{N}$ (where S is the mean of the sample).
3. It is a known fact that the sampling distribution of means is normally distributed. As the sampling distribution of a mean has a normal distribution, we may develop a method in which we may use the mean of our sample to estimate the population mean. For example, when an interval of $\bar{X} \pm 1.96\, \sigma \sqrt{N}$ is computed, the interval will include 95 percent of all the sample means.

8.3.3 Importance of the Concept of Standard Error

The concept of standard error is of great relevance, significance, importance, and usefulness in media metrics. This is because of the following reasons:

1. Standard error is applied as a tool in testing the available hypothesis. The hypothesis is usually tested at 5 percent level of significance. When the difference between the observed and expected means is more than 1.90 standard error, we say that the result of the experiment does not support the hypothesis at 5 percent level. In other words, the difference is regarded as significant, that is, it could not have emerged owing to fluctuations of sampling. On the other hand, when the difference between the observed and expected results is less than 1.96 SE, it is not treated as significant. That is to say that it could have emerged owing to fluctuations of simple sampling, that is, we say that the result of experiment does not provide any evidence against the hypothesis. When the difference is more than 2.58 SE, it is treated as significant at 1 percent level. More often, a hypothesis is practically accepted when the difference is less than 3 SE This is because the probability of a difference being greater than 3 SE, coming out of chance, is only about 3 in thousand (2.7%) as 99.73 percent units are covered between mean$\pm 3\sigma$ on either side of the mean. Thus, it must be given due emphasis that the application of 3σ rule is justified only if N is large. Some students apply a criterion of 2 SE in order to determine whether or not the difference could have come up because of fluctuations of sampling. Hence, in lieu of 3 SE or 2 SE, it is suggested that we should

use either 5 percent level or 1 percent level of significance. But 5 percent level is more popular and generally applied.

2. Standard error tells us about the unreliability of a sample. The bigger the standard error, the bigger is the departure of the actual frequencies from the expected ones and, thus, the bigger the unreliability of the sample. The measure of reliability (or precision) of a sample is a reciprocal of standard error, that is, 1/SE Further, the precision or reliability of an observed proportion varies as the square root of the number of units in the given sample. Hence, when we want to double the reliability (which is the same thing as reducing the standard error to one-half), the number of observations should be increased to four times.
3. The limits within which the parameter values are expected to lie can be easily determined with the help of standard error. This is made possible because for large samples, sampling distributions tend to approximate a normal distribution. In a normally distributed sample, 68.27 percent of the samples will have their values (or any other constant) within a range of population mean$\pm$1 standard deviation or standard error. Likewise, a range of $\pm$2 SE will give 95.45 percent values and mean$\pm$3 SE will give 99.73 percent values. Hence, a range of $\pm$3 SE should be considered as the determining limit outside which the value of the parameter probability does not fall. The probability of a value lying between –3 and +3 SE limit is only 0.27 percent (i.e., nearly 3 in 1,000).

8.4 ESTIMATION

When sample studies are conducted, then broadly three problems arise: (a) How to estimate parameter values, or how to generalize the results of the sample to the population? (b) How to find out whether the generalizations made are valid or not? (c) What is the level of confidence with which a particular generalization can be made?

The answer to all these queries are given by the branch of statistical theory called "Statistical Inference" which can broadly be divided into two heads: (a) hypothesis testing and (b) estimation theory.

We have already thrown some light in this chapter on hypothesis testing. Now, we will focus our attention on estimation.

The theory of estimation was developed by the well-known statistician Professor R.A. Fisher in 1930. Estimation generally refers to the technique and methods by which population parameters are studied from sample studies. It may be pointed out that the real value of a parameter is quite unknown, hidden, and lurked which may be properly studied only by an extensive and intensive study of the population. But studying the entire population or universe will be highly time-consuming, money-consuming, energy-consuming, and resource-consuming. Thus, it becomes cost-ineffective from the economical and psychological point of view. In the case of a finite population, the cost of complete census may be prohibitive and in the case of an infinite population, complete calculations, computations, and enumerations are just impossible. A realistic approach may be to get an estimate or guess of the unknown real value or an interval of plausible values from the available sample. Hence, a proper procedure for estimation has been grouped by R.A. Fisher in two classes:

1. Point estimates
2. Interval estimates

8.4.1 Point Estimates

A point estimate is a particular single numeric value of the sample which is used to estimate the parameter value. It is also called "estimator of parameter." It is used as an estimate of the unknown population parameter. If we estimate the parameter value of a mean from a sample mean, we will say that the sample mean is an estimator of the parameter mean. Hence, a good estimator may be described as one which provides us a parameter value that is as close to the real value as possible. A good estimator is supposed to be unbiased, consistent, efficient, and sufficient.

A point estimate is applied as an estimate of an unknown population parameter. The main steps in point estimation is to first of all select a random sample of N observations, $x_1, x_2, x_{3,}\ldots,$ x_n from a population f(x,0) and then to apply some preconceived procedure to arrive from these observations at a number $\hat{\theta}$(called theta hat). $\hat{\theta}$ is dependent on the random variable which frames the sample and, thus, this is also a random variable with its own sampling distribution. Hence, this estimate is exactly a point which ultimately determines the parameter.

8.4.2 Interval Estimates

Unlike point estimate, an interval estimate is a statement of two values between which it is estimated that the parameter lies. Hence, it is a range instead of a particular point. Here, the question arises whether we can make some generalizations about the population values within a certain range. The answer is certainly "yes." The range within which a parameter value is estimated is called the "fiducial limits" or "confidence interval" or "confidence limits." This range will vary on the basis of the extent of precision which is the target to be attained. The bigger the extent of precision required, the larger will be the range between the lower limit and the upper limit of the range.

It is a known fact that in a normally distributed data, mean±1.96 SD includes 95 percent of the units of the distribution. When our limits are within mean±1.96 SD, the probability of any mistake is 0.05 or the probability of our being correct is 0.95.

Thus, we may say that the point estimated has the benefit of being accurate or precise or to the point. But it does specify how close the estimator is to the parameter being estimated. Further, it is not essential that in a scientific investigation, the precise value of a parameter will be determined. Hence, it is better to have some degree of the confidence that the value derived is within a well-defined certain range. The interval range is comfortably capable of providing such confidence leading to more applicability and practicality in the interval estimate.

8.4.3 Qualities of a Good Estimator

The qualities of a good estimator can be judged by its proximity to the parameter being estimated. An estimator can be evaluated on the basis of the following qualities:

1. A good estimator should be objective, neutral, and unbiased. An estimator will be described to be unbiased only when its expected value is similar to the population parameter being estimated. That is to say that if $\hat{\theta}$ is a neutral and unbiased estimate of θ, then we must have $E(\hat{\theta}) = \theta$. So many estimators are "asymptomatically unbiased" in the sense that the biases reduce to practically insignificant value zero when N becomes

very large. A good example here is estimator S^2. It is important to mention here that biases in estimation are not always bad or unwanted or unnecessary or undesirable. They may prove to be an asset in some situations. An estimator with a large bias but low variability is better than an estimator with low bias but high variability. If the variability in an estimator is large, the parameter value given by it will not be so reliable.

2. Another quality of a good estimator is that it should be consistent. An estimator is described to be consistent when with an increase in its size, its value (statistic) comes closer and closer to the parameter value. For example when an estimator $\hat{\theta}$ reaches the parameter θ closer and closer as the sample size N increases, $\hat{\theta}$ is said to be consistent estimator of θ. As N reaches near unity (1), then $\hat{\theta}$ is different from θ by no more than an arbitrary small constant. Further, when sample mean $\bar{X}$ comes closer to the parameter value of the population mean μ, it is inferred that the estimator is consistent. It means that consistency is a quality relating to the behavior of the estimator for a very large value of N. When the value of N is large and approaching infinity, then the value provided by the estimator would not vary from the real value of the parameter or the chance of it being very close to the real parameter value will be 1. Hence, the difference between the two values will be negligible, small, and insignificant.

   Thus, for larger and larger samples, consistency is a good, healthy, and desirable quality of an estimator. Reversely, in small samples, consistency is not so relevant, important, and useful.
3. A good estimator should be efficient and its efficiency depends on sampling variability. When two competing estimators are unbiased, the one with the smaller variance (for a given sample size) is said to be relatively more efficient. The lesser the variance of the estimator, the more concentrated will be the distribution of the estimator around and parameter being estimated and, hence, such estimator is considered to be much better and more efficient. In a normal distribution, both the mean and median are unbiased. But the variance of the sampling distribution of the mean would be less than the variance of the sampling distribution of the median. It is due to this reason only that the mean is considered to be a more efficient estimate than the median.
4. A good estimator is one which contains sufficiency of information in the sample about the parameter. When all the information that a sample can provide about the parameter has been used by an estimator, it will be described as a sufficient estimator.

In order to satisfy the above-mentioned qualities in an estimator, there are two very important methods which are the least square method and the maximum likelihood method.

After comprehensively discussing the concept of estimation, point estimates, interval estimates, and qualities of a good estimator, it is important to discuss the various situations in which we are supposed to apply various tests of significance. These tests are as follows:

1. Tests of significance for attributes
2. Tests of significance for variables (large samples)
3. Tests of significance for variables (small samples)

8.5 TEST OF SIGNIFICANCE FOR ATTRIBUTES

The word attribute means quality, property, characteristics, or traits. In this type of a test, we can only find out the presence or absence of a quality, property, characteristics, or traits.

Hence, the sampling of attributes may be described as drawing a sample from a universe "A" or lack of "A." For example, in the study of attribute, "journalists" may be taken as a sample and the universe may be classified as "journalists" and "non-journalists." The selection of an individual on sampling may be treated as an "event;" the presence of attribute A may be taken as "success" and its absence as "failure." Hence, if out of 500 people selected for the sample, 40 are found "journalists" and 460 "non-journalists," then it will be described as a sample consisting of 500 units out of which 40 are successes and 460 failures. The probability of success or $p=40/500$ or 0.08 and the probability of failure or $q=460/500$ or 0.92 so that $p+q=0.08+0.92=1$.

The different types of significance of attributes may be discussed under the following subheads:

1. Tests for number of successes
2. Tests for proportion of successes
3. Tests for difference between proportions

8.5.1 Test for Number of Successes

In this type of test for number of successes, the sampling distribution follows a binomial probability distribution. Thus, its standard error is symbolically given by the formula,

$$\text{SE of no. of successes} = \sqrt{Npq},$$

where N is size of sample, p is the probability of successes, and q is the probability of failure, that is, $q=(1-p)$.

Example 1: In a sample of 600 media persons, 320 are found to be journalists. Can we assume that both journalists and non-journalists equally exist in the sample?

Solution: Let us take the hypothesis that the journalists and non-journalists equally exist in the sample. The expected frequency for journalists and non-journalists will be 600/2=300 each,

$$\text{SE} = \sqrt{Npq} = \sqrt{600 \times \frac{1}{2} \times \frac{1}{2}} = \sqrt{150} = 12.247.$$

Difference between observed and expected number of journalists=320−300=20.

Now, $\dfrac{\text{Difference}}{\text{SE}} = \dfrac{20}{12.247} = 1.633.$

Since the difference is less than 1.96 SE (5% level), it can be concluded that journalists and non-journalists do not equally exist in the sample.

Example 2: In a sample of 500 journalists, 280 are found to be male journalists and the rest are female journalists. Can we assume that both male and female journalists equally exist in the sample?

Solution: Let us take the hypothesis that male and female journalists equally exist in the sample. Then, the expected frequency for male and female journalists will be 500/2=250.

$$\text{SE} = \sqrt{Npq} = \sqrt{500 \times \frac{1}{2} \times \frac{1}{2}} = 11.18.$$

Difference between the observed and expected number of male and female journalists= 280−250=30.

Now, $\frac{\text{Difference}}{\text{SE}} = \frac{30}{11.18} = 2.68.$

Since the difference is more than 2.58 SE (at 1% level), it could not have arisen due to fluctuations in the sample. Hence, we cannot assume that male and female journalists equally exist in the sample.

8.5.2 Test for Proportion of Successes

In this type of test for proportion of successes, instead of recording the number of successes in each sample, we may record the proportion of successes that is $1/N$ th of the number of successes in each sample. As this will lead to dividing all the figures by N, the mean proportion of successes and the standard deviation of the proportion of successes is $\sqrt{\frac{pq}{N}}$. Thus, we have the following formula:

$$\text{SE}p = \sqrt{\frac{pq}{N}}.$$

Example 1: 300 journalists are randomly selected by the government from a journalist association, out of which 30 are found to be having ill health. Estimate the proportion of sick journalists in the association and assign limits within which the proportion lies.

Solution: The proportion of sick journalists in the given sample $= \frac{30}{300} = 0.1.$

Hence, $p=0.1$ and $q=1-0.1=0.9$

$$\text{SE} = \sqrt{\frac{pq}{n}} = \sqrt{\frac{0.1 \times 0.9}{300}} = \sqrt{\frac{0.09}{300}} = 0.017.$$

The limit within which the percentage of sick journalists lies,

$$= \left[p \pm 3\sqrt{\frac{pq}{n}} \right] \times 100$$
$$= [0.1 \pm 3(0.017) \times 100$$
$$= [0.1 \pm 0.051] \times 100.$$

15.1 and 4.9

Thus, the percentage of sick journalists in the association almost certainly lies between 4.9 and 15.1.

Example 2: An advertising agency claims that only 4 percent employees are mentally defective. A random sample of 600 employees contained 36 mentally defective employees. Test the claim of the advertising agency.

Solution: The advertising agency claims that only 4 percent of the employees are mentally defective. Thus, the 95 percent confidence level is given by,

$$\overline{X} \pm 1.96 \text{ SE}$$

$$\text{SE}_p = \sqrt{\frac{pa}{n}} = \sqrt{0.96 \times \frac{0.4}{600}} = 0.008.$$

95 percent confidence limits $= \overline{X} \pm 1.96$ SE

$$= 0.96 \pm 1.96\ (0.008)$$
$$= 0.96 \pm 0.0157$$
$$= 0.9443 \text{ to } 0.9757.$$

Out of 600 employees, the good employees may vary between $0.9443 \times 600 = 566.58$ and $0.975 \times 600 = 585.42$, that is, 567 and 585.

Thus, the number of mentally defective employees is expected to lie between 15 and 33. Since the actual number is 36, the advertising agency's claim that only 4 percent of its employees are mentally defective cannot be accepted.

8.5.3 Test for Difference Between Proportions

In this type of test, the difference of proportions is studied. Suppose that we draw two samples from universe. We may be interested in calculating whether the difference between the proportion of successes is significant or not. Under such circumstances, we take the hypothesis that the difference between p_1, that is, the proportion of successes in one sample, and p_2, that is, the proportion of successes in another sample, is because of variation in random sampling. The standard error of the difference between proportions is computed by using the following formula:

$$\text{SE}(p_1 - p_2) = \sqrt{pq\left(\frac{1}{N_1} + \frac{1}{N_2}\right)},$$

where p is the pooled estimate of the actual proportion in the universe. The value of p is obtained by applying the following formula:

$$p = \frac{N_1 p_1 + N_2 p_2}{N_1 + N_2}, \quad \text{or} \quad p = \frac{X_1 + X_2}{N_1 + N_2}$$

where X_1 and X_2 stand for the number of occurrences in the two samples of sizes N_1 and N_2, respectively.

When $\frac{p_1 - p_2}{\text{SE}}$ is less than 1.96 SE (i.e., 5% level of significance), the difference is considered to be because of random sampling fluctuations, that is, not significant.

For further clarity, the following examples will be helpful to explain the method.

Example 1: In a random sample of 1,100 media persons from Patna and 800 media persons from Ranchi, 450 and 400, respectively, are found to be involved in drinking habit. Do these data reveal a significant difference between Patna and Ranchi so far as the proportion of drinking habit is concerned?

Solution: Let us take the hypothesis that the two capital cities Patna and Ranchi do not differ so far as the proportion of drinking habit of media persons is concerned,

That is, H_0: $p_1 = p_2$ against H_a: $p_1 \neq p_2$.

Now, calculating the standard error of the difference of proportions:

$$\text{SE}(p_1 - p_2) = \sqrt{pq\left(\frac{1}{N_1} + \frac{1}{N_2}\right)}$$

$$N_1 = 1100,\ p_1 = 450/1100 = 0.4,\ N_2 = 800,\ p_2 = 400/800 = 0.5,$$

$$P = \frac{(1100 \times 0.4) + (800 \times 0.5)}{1100 + 800} = \frac{440 + 400}{1100 + 800} = 840/1900 = 0.44$$

$$\therefore\ q = 1 - p = 1 - 0.44 = 0.56.$$

$$\text{Hence, SE}\ (p_1 - p_2) = \sqrt{0.44 \times 0.56\left(\frac{1}{1100} + \frac{1}{800}\right)}$$

$$= \sqrt{0.44 \times 0.56(0.009 + 0.0012)}$$

$$= \sqrt{0.44 \times 0.56 \times 0.0021}$$

$$= \sqrt{0.00051744}$$

$$= 0.022$$

$$p_1 - p_2 = 0.4 - 0.5 = -0.1.$$

Now, $Z = \frac{|\text{Difference}|}{\text{SE}} = \frac{0.1}{0.022} = 4.54.$

Since the difference is more than 2.58 SE (at 1% level of significance), it could have arisen due to fluctuations in the sampling. Thus, the data reveal a significant difference between two capital cities Patna and Ranchi so far as the proportion of drinking habit is concerned.

Example 2: In a simple random sample of 800 reporters of Chandigarh, 500 are found to be smokers. In another simple random sample of 900 reporters from Shimla, 450 are smoker. Do the data indicate that there is a significant difference in the habit of smoking in the two cities?

Solution: Let us take the hypothesis that there is no significant difference in the habit of smoking in the two capital cities.

$$\text{SE}(p_1 - p_2) = \sqrt{pq\left(\frac{1}{N_1} + \frac{1}{N_2}\right)}$$

Now, $$p_1 = \frac{500}{800} = 0.625,\ p_1 = \frac{450}{900} = 0.5$$

$$p = p = \frac{X_1 + X_2}{N_1 + N_2},\ q = 1 - p,\ N_1{=}800,\ N_2 = 900,\ X_1 = 500,\ X_2 = 450$$

$$p = \frac{500+450}{800+900} = 950 / 1700 = 0.55$$

$$q{=}1-0.55{=}0.45$$

$$\therefore \text{SE}\ (p_1 - p_2) = \sqrt{0.55{\times}0.45\left(\frac{1}{800} + \frac{1}{900}\right)}$$
$$= \sqrt{0.55 \times 0.45 \times (0.00125 + 0.00111)}$$
$$= \sqrt{0.55 \times 0.45 \times 0.00236}$$
$$= 0.21.$$

Now, $$Z = \frac{|\text{Difference}|}{\text{SE}} = \frac{0.625-0.5}{0.021} = \frac{0.125}{0.021} = 5.95.$$

Since the difference is more than 2.58 SE at 1 percent level of significance, the hypothesis is rejected. Thus, there is a significant difference in the smoking habits of reporters of Chandigarh and Shimla.

Example 3: 500 Subeditors out of a sample of 700 subeditors were found to be strong tea drinkers before an increase on excise duty on tea. After an increase on the duty, 400 subeditors were known to be strong tea drinkers in a sample of 600 subeditors. Do you think that there has been a significant decrease in the consumption of strong tea after the increase in the excise duty?

Solution: Let us take the hypothesis that there is no significant decrease in the consumption of strong tea after an increase in the excise duty.

Now, calculating the standard error in the difference of proportions:

$$\text{SE}_{p_1 - p_2} = \sqrt{pq\left(\frac{1}{N_1} + \frac{1}{N_2}\right)}$$

$$p_1 = \frac{500}{700} = 0.714,\ p_2 = \frac{400}{600} = 0.667.$$

$$p = \frac{X_1 + X_2}{N_1 + N_2} = \frac{500_1 + 400}{700 + 600} = \frac{900}{1300}$$
$$= \frac{9}{13}$$

$$q=1-p=1-9/13=4/13$$

$$\text{SE }(p_1-p_2)=\sqrt{\frac{9}{13}\times\frac{4}{13}\left(\frac{1}{700}+\frac{1}{600}\right)}$$

$$=\sqrt{\frac{9}{13}\times\frac{4}{13}\left(\frac{1}{700}+\frac{1}{600}\right)}=\sqrt{0.21(0.0014+0.0016)}$$

$$=\sqrt{0.21\times 0.003}=\sqrt{0.00063}$$

$$=0.025$$

$$Z=\frac{|\text{Difference}|}{\text{SE}}=\frac{0.714-0.667}{0.025}=\frac{0.047}{0.025}=1.88.$$

Since the difference is less than 2.58 SE (at 1% level) and also less than 1.96 SE (at 5% level), this might have arisen due to fluctuations of sampling. Hence, there is an insignificant decrease in the consumption of strong tea by subeditors even after the increase of excise duty.

Example 4: A printing machine produced 20 defective newspapers in a batch of 400. After overhauling, it produced 100 defective newspapers in a batch of 300. Has the printing machine improved?

Solution: Let us take the hypothesis that the printing machine has not improved after overhauling.

Hence, applying test of difference of proportions.

$$p_1=\frac{20}{400}=0.050,\ p_2=0.033.$$

Now, the pooled estimate of the actual proportion in the universe:

$$p=\frac{X_1+X_2}{N_1+N_2}=\frac{20+10}{400+300}=0.043$$

$$q=1-p=1-0.043=0.957$$

$$\text{SE}_{p_1-p_2}=\sqrt{pq\left(\frac{1}{N_1}+\frac{1}{N_2}\right)}$$

$$=\sqrt{0.43\times 0.957\left(\frac{1}{400}+\frac{1}{300}\right)}$$

$$=0.0155.$$

Now,

$$Z=\frac{|\text{Difference}|}{\text{SE}}=\frac{0.05-0.033}{0.0155}=1.1.$$

Since the difference is less than 1.96 (at 5% level), the hypothesis is accepted. Thus, the printing machine has not improved even after overhauling.

8.6 TEST OF SIGNIFICANCE FOR LARGER SAMPLES

After discussing the significance of attributes earlier, now we shall be discussing the sampling of variables. Sampling of variables is not only restricted to two variables such as success or failure, but there can also be more and more variables which may be restricted to some extent, practically or theoretically. Such values of variables given by different trials will be spread over a range, which will be unlimited.

There are three main objectives of studying the problems relating to the sampling of variables:

1. To compare actual or observed frequencies with those expected under certain assumptions and to see how much the deviation of one from another can be attributed to the sampling fluctuation;
2. To estimate from the samples, some basic characteristics of the universe, such as mean of a variable;
3. To assess the reliability of our estimates.

8.6.1 Difference Between Small and Large Samples

It is really very difficult to have a clear-cut line of demarcation between small samples and large samples. But it is normally a consensus among the statisticians that a sample is to be considered large if its size is more than 30. It is important to mention here that the tests of significance for large samples are different from the ones used for small samples for the simple reason that the assumptions of a large sample are quite different from that of a small sample.

The assumptions of a large sample are as follows:

1. There is a normal distribution of random sampling.
2. Sample values are very close to the population values and can be used for each other for calculating the standard error of estimate. To calculate the standard error, we can use standard deviation of the sample if the standard deviation of the universe is not available and vice versa. This is not possible in the case of a small sample.

During the study of significance of variable of large sampling, the concept of standard error as discussed earlier is frequently used here. A list of formulae for calculating the standard error of different statistics is given below:

1. SE of Mean $= \sigma_{\bar{X}} = \dfrac{\sigma}{\sqrt{N}} = \dfrac{S}{\sqrt{N}}$

where $\sigma_{\bar{X}}$ is SE of mean, σ (sigma) is standard deviation of population, S is standard deviation of sample, and N is the size of the sample.

2. SE of median $(\sigma_M) = \dfrac{1.253\sigma}{\sqrt{N}}$

3. SE of standard deviation $(\sigma_{SD}) = \frac{\sigma}{\sqrt{2N}} = \frac{0.71\sigma}{\sqrt{N}}$

4. SE of variance $= \sigma^2\sqrt{\frac{Z}{N}}$

5. SE correlation coefficient (Karl Pearson) $= \frac{1-r^2}{\sqrt{N}}$

6. SE of rank correlation coefficient $= \frac{1}{\sqrt{N-1}}$

7. SE of regression coefficient X on Y $(b_{xy}) = \frac{\sigma_x\sqrt{1-r^2}}{\sigma_y\sqrt{N}}$

8. SE of regression coefficient of Y on X $(b_{yx}) = \frac{\sigma_y\sqrt{1-r^2}}{\sigma_x\sqrt{N}}$

Example 1: Compute the standard error of mean from the following data showing the amount paid by 100 newspaper industries on the occasion of Durga Puja:

Mid value (₹)	39	49	59	69	79	89	99
No. of NP industries	2	3	11	20	32	25	7

Solution: $SE_{\bar{X}} = \frac{\sigma}{\sqrt{N}}$.

Calculation of standard deviation:

Mid-value (X)	F	$d_1 = X - A/h = X - 69/10$	fd_1	fd_1^2
39	2	–3	–6	18
49	3	–2	–6	12
59	11	–1	–11	11
69	20	0	0	0
79	32	+1	+32	32
89	25	+2	+50	100
99	07	+3	+21	63
	$N = 100$		$\Sigma fd_1 = 80$	$\Sigma fd_1^2 = 236$

$$\sigma = \sqrt{\frac{\Sigma fd_1^2}{N} - \left(\frac{\Sigma fd_1}{N}\right)^2} \times h$$

$$= \sqrt{\frac{236}{100} - \left(\frac{80}{100}\right)^2} \times 10$$

$$= \sqrt{2.36 - 0.64} \times 10$$

$$= 1.311 \times 10 = 13.11$$

$$\therefore \text{SE}_{\bar{X}} = \frac{\sigma}{\sqrt{N}} = \frac{13.11}{\sqrt{100}} = \frac{13.11}{10} = 1.311.$$

Example 2: Media persons were randomly selected to participate in a height competition. Their mean height is 65 inches. The standard deviation of the distribution of height of the population is known to be 3 inches. Test the statement that the mean height of the population is 67 inches at 5 percent level of significance. Also set up 99 percent limits of the mean height of the population.

Solution: Let us take the hypothesis that there is no significant difference between the sample mean and the population mean.

$$\text{SE} \quad \bar{X} = \frac{\sigma}{\sqrt{N}} = \frac{3}{\sqrt{100}} = \frac{3}{10} = 0.3$$

Now, $Z = \frac{|\text{Difference}|}{\text{SE}} = \frac{67-65}{0.3} = \frac{2}{0.3} = 6.6.$

Since the difference is more than 1.96 SE (5% level), the hypothesis is rejected. Thus, the mean height of the population of media persons cannot be 67.

99 percent probable limits of the mean height of the population $= \bar{X} \pm 2.58$ SE

$$= 65 \pm 2.58\ (0.3)$$
$$= 65 \pm 0.774$$
$$= 64.2 \text{ to } 65.7.$$

Example 3: For a given group, the coefficient of correlation between height and weight is 0.7, standard deviations of height and of weight are 2 inches and 10 lb, respectively, and the means of height and weight for the entire group are 70 inches and 130 lb, respectively. Calculate the best estimate of the weight that is 65 inches tall. Assign limits to these estimates in which in all probability of actual weight will be lying.

Solution: The regression of weight (Y) on height (X) is

$$Y - \bar{Y} = r\frac{\sigma_y}{\sigma_x}(X - \bar{X})$$

$$\bar{Y} = 130,\ \bar{X} = 70,\ \sigma_y = 10,\ \sigma_x = 2,\ r = 0.7$$

$$Y - 130 = 0.7 \times \frac{10}{2}(X - 70)$$

or $$Y - 130 = 3.5(X - 70)$$

or $$Y - 130 = 3.5X - 245$$

or $$Y = 3.5X - 115$$

when $X=65$, Y will be

$$Y=3.5(65)-115$$

or

$$Y=112.5 \text{ lb.}$$

The standard error of estimate of Y on X, SE_{yx}, is:

$$\begin{aligned} SE_{yx} &= \sigma_y\sqrt{1-r^2} \\ &= 10\sqrt{1-(0.7)^2} = 10\sqrt{0.51} = 10\times 0.714 = 7.14 \text{ lb.} \end{aligned}$$

Hence, the best estimate of the weight of a journalist who is 65 inches tall is 112.5 lb and the estimate cannot deviate from the actual weight by more than three times the standard error. Thus, in all probability, the actual weight would be lying between 112.5±3 (1.428) or 112.5±4.284, that is, 108.2 lbs and 116.8 lbs.

8.6.2 Two-tailed Test for Difference Between Means of Two Samples

1. When two independent random samples with sample sizes N_1 and N_2 (both sample sizes are greater than 30) are drawn from the same population of standard deviation σ, the standard error of the difference between the sample means is given by the following formula:

$$SE \text{ of difference between sample means } (SE_{\bar{X}_1-\bar{X}_2}) = \sigma_{\bar{X}_1-\bar{X}_2} = \sigma_D = \sqrt{\sigma^2\left(\frac{1}{N_1}+\frac{1}{N_2}\right)},$$

   where $\bar{X}_1 - \bar{X}_2 = D$.
   (Note: If σ is unknown, sample standard deviation for the combined samples must be substituted.)
2. When two random samples with X_1, σ_1, N_1, and $\dot{X}_2$, σ_2, N_2 are drawn from different populations, then the standard error of the difference between the means is given by the following formula:

$$SE_{\bar{X}_1-\bar{X}_2} = \sigma_D = \sqrt{\left(\frac{\sigma_1^2}{N_1}+\frac{\sigma_2^2}{N_2}\right)},$$

   where σ_1 and σ_2 are unknown.
   Now, the standard error of difference between sample means, that is,

$$SE_{\bar{X}_1-\bar{X}_2} = \sigma_D = \sqrt{\left(\frac{S_1^2}{N_1}+\frac{S_2^2}{N_2}\right)},$$

   where S_1 and S_2 represent standard deviations of the two samples. It is important to mention here that in a large sample, standard deviation of sample mean(s) becomes equal to standard deviation of population (σ), that is, $S=\sigma$.

The null hypothesis to be tested is that there is no significant difference in the means of the two samples, that is,

H_0: $\mu_1 = \mu_2$—Null hypothesis as there is no difference
H_a: $\mu_1 \neq \mu_2$—Alternative hypothesis as a difference exists

Example 1: In an achievement test of editing and communication skills, two groups of male journalists and female journalists were experimented and the following results obtained. Find out whether the difference of their means is significant:

	N	Mean	SD
Male journalists	50	22.25	8.15
Female journalists	40	25.30	10.50

Solution: Let us take the hypothesis that there is no difference in means of males and females. As per the formula,

$$\text{SE}_{\bar{X}_1-\bar{X}_2} = \sigma_D = \sqrt{\left(\frac{\sigma_1^2}{N_1} + \frac{\sigma_2^2}{N_2}\right)},$$

where $\sigma_1 = 8.15$, $N_1 = 50$, $\bar{X}_1 = 50$, $\sigma_2 = 10.50$, $N_2 = 40$, $X_2 = 25.30$

$$\text{SE}_{\bar{X}_1-\bar{X}_2} = \sigma_D = \sqrt{\left(\frac{(8.15)^2}{50} + \frac{(10.50)^2}{40}\right)}$$

$$= \sqrt{\frac{66.42}{50} + \frac{110.25}{40}}$$

$$= \sqrt{1.3284 + 2.7562}$$

$$= \sqrt{4.08} = 2.02$$

$$\therefore Z = \frac{\bar{X}_1 - \bar{X}_2}{\text{SE}_{\bar{X}_1-\bar{X}_2}}$$

$$= \frac{25.30 - 22.25}{2.02} = \frac{3.05}{2.02} = 1.51$$

$$d_f = (N_1 - 1) + (N_2 - 1) = (50 - 1) + (40 - 1)$$
$$= 49 + 39 = 88.$$

Since the critical value of Z for d_f=88 at 5 percent level=1.96 and at 1 percent level=2.64 and the calculated value of Z=1.51, which is lesser than the critical value at both the levels, the difference is insignificant. Thus, the null hypothesis is accepted and the assumed hypothesis is proved.

Example 2: A communication skill test was administered to a sample of 50 post graduated female students and 55 male students. The mean scores of females and males are given:

	N	Mean	SD
Female students	50	31.82	8.22
Male students	55	28.26	10.41

The problem is to test how significant is the difference between the two means?

Solution: Let us take the hypothesis that there is no significant difference between the two means.

By formula,

$$\mathrm{SE}_{\bar{X}_1-\bar{X}_2} = \sqrt{\left(\frac{\sigma_1^2}{N_1}+\frac{\sigma_2^2}{N_2}\right)}$$

$$= \sqrt{\frac{(8.22)^2}{50}+\frac{108.36}{55}}$$

$$= \sqrt{\frac{67.5}{50}+\frac{108.36}{55}}$$

$$= \sqrt{1.35+1.97} = \sqrt{3.3} = 1.82$$

$$\therefore Z = \frac{|D|}{\sigma_D} = \frac{|\bar{X}_1-\bar{X}_2|}{1.82} = \frac{31.82-28.26}{1.82} = \frac{3.56}{1.82} = 1.95$$

$$d_f = (N_1-1)+(N_2-1) = 50+55-2$$
$$= 103.$$

Critical value of 103 at 5 percent level = 1.96.

Since the calculated value is less than the critical value, the difference is insignificant. Hence, the null hypothesis is accepted and the hypothesis assumed is proved.

Example 3: A mass communication teacher wanted to know the relative effectiveness of the lecture cum demonstration method over the traditional lecture method. He divided his class into two equal random groups A and B and taught group A by the lecture cum demonstration method and group B by the conventional lecture method. After teaching for three months, he administered an achievement test to both groups. The data collected were as under:

	Group A	Group B
Mean	43	30
SD	8	7
No. of students	65	65

Form this data, what do you conclude about the effectiveness of one method of teaching over the other?

Solution: Let us take the hypothesis that there is no significant difference between the lecture cum demonstration method and conventional lecture method.

Hence,

$$\bar{X}_1 = 43,\ \bar{X}_2 = 30,\ \sigma_1 = 8,\ \sigma_2 = 7,\ N_1 = 65,\ N_2 = 65$$

$$\therefore \text{SE}_{\bar{X}_1-\bar{X}_2} = \sqrt{\left(\frac{\sigma_1^2}{N_1}+\frac{\sigma_2^2}{N_2}\right)} = \sqrt{\frac{8^2}{65}+\frac{7^2}{65}} = \sqrt{\frac{64+49}{65}} = \sqrt{\frac{113}{65}} = 1.32$$

$$\therefore Z = \frac{D}{\sigma_D} = \frac{\bar{X}_1-\bar{X}_2}{1.32} = \frac{43-40}{1.32} = \frac{3}{1.32} = 9.85$$

$$d_f = (N_1-1)+(N_2-2) = (65-1)+(65-2) = 64+63 = 127.$$

The critical value of Z at 5 percent level for $d_f = 127$ is 1.96, while the calculated value is 9.85. So the difference is very significant. Hence, the null hypothesis is rejected and the assumed hypothesis is disproved.

Thus, the lecture cum demonstration method is more effective than the conventional lecture method.

Example 4: On the social networking site Facebook, a political page was drafted to experiment voting decision impact on the audience through wall posts of a political leader. There were two pages; one was a general Facebook page of the leader and another, an experimental page specifically for political campaigning, hoping that such input will promote the voting numbers of the followers of that experimental page on Facebook.

The control group is not provided by such input. At the end of the experiment time period of 2 days before elections, following were the observations:

	Experimental Group	Control Group
Mean	35	30
SD	4	3
No. of followers	48	45

Is the gain significant enough to indicate that an extra input promotes vote count?

Solution: Let us take the hypothesis that an extra input has no significant gain in vote count.

Here,

$$X_1 = 35,\ \bar{X}_2 = 30,\ \sigma_1 = 4,\ \sigma_2 = 3,\ N_1 = 48,\ N_2 = 45$$

$$\text{SE}_{\bar{X}_1-\bar{X}_2} = \sigma_D = \sqrt{\left(\frac{\sigma_1^2}{N_1}+\frac{\sigma_2^2}{N_2}\right)}$$

$$= \sqrt{\frac{4^2}{48}+\frac{3^2}{45}} = \sqrt{\frac{16}{48}+\frac{9}{45}}$$

$$= \sqrt{\frac{1}{3}+\frac{1}{5}} = \sqrt{\frac{5+3}{15}} = \sqrt{\frac{8}{15}} = \sqrt{0.533} = 0.73$$

$$\therefore Z = \frac{D}{\sigma_D} = \frac{\bar{X}_1 - \bar{X}_2}{0.73} = \frac{35-30}{0.73} = \frac{5}{0.73} = 6.85$$

$$\begin{aligned} d_f &= (N_1 - 1) + (N_2 - 1) \\ &= (48-1) + (45-1) = 47 + 44 \\ &= 91. \end{aligned}$$

The critical value of Z at 5 percent level at d_f=91 is 1.96. Since the calculated value is greater than the critical value, the difference is significant. Hence, the null hypothesis is rejected and assumed hypothesis is disproved.

Thus, an extra input promotes vote count.

Example 5: Television sets manufactured by X and Y companies gave the following results:

	X Company	Y Company
No. of TV sets manufactured	100	100
Mean life in days	1300	1248
Standard deviation in days	82	93

Using standard error of the difference between means, state whether there is any significant difference between the mean lives of the two companies.

Solution: Let us take this hypothesis that there is no significant difference between the mean lives of the TV sets of the two companies.

Here,

$$\bar{X}_1 = 1300,\ \bar{X}_2 = 1248,\ S_1 = 82,\ S_2 = 93,\ N_1 = 100,\ N_2 = 100$$

$$\begin{aligned} SE_{\bar{X}_1 - \bar{X}_2} &= \sqrt{\left(\frac{\sigma_1^2}{N_1} + \frac{\sigma_2^2}{N_2}\right)} \\ &= \sqrt{\frac{S_1^2}{N_1} + \frac{S_2^2}{N_2}} \\ &= \sqrt{\frac{82^2}{100} + \frac{93^2}{100}} = \sqrt{\frac{6724}{100} + \frac{8649}{100}} = \sqrt{\frac{15373}{100}} \\ &= \sqrt{153.73} = 12.4 \end{aligned}$$

$$\therefore Z = \frac{D}{\sigma_D} = \frac{\bar{X}_1 - \bar{X}_2}{12.4} = \frac{1300-1248}{12.4} = \frac{52}{12.4} = 4.19.$$

$$\begin{aligned} d_f &= (N_1 + N_2 - 2) \\ &= (100 + 100 - 2) \\ &= 198. \end{aligned}$$

The critical value of Z at 5 percent level for d_f= 198 is 1.96. Since the calculated value is greater than the critical value, the difference is significant. Hence, the null hypothesis is rejected and the assumed hypothesis is disproved.

Thus, there is a significant difference between mean lives of company X and company Y.

Example 6: An examination was given to 50 students of a journalism university of Bhopal and 60 students of a journalism university of Rajasthan. At Bhopal, the mean grade was 75 with a standard deviation of 9. At Rajasthan, the mean grade was 79 with a standard deviation of 7. Is there a significant difference between the performances of the students at Bhopal and at Rajasthan, given that α=0.05 and α=0.01?

Solution: Let us take the hypothesis that there is no significant difference between the performances of the students of Bhopal and of Rajasthan.

Here,

$$\bar{X}_1 = 75,\ \bar{X}_2 = 79,\ S_1 = 9,\ S_2 = 7,\ N_1 = 50,\ N_2 = 60$$

$$SE_{\bar{X}_1-\bar{X}_2} = \sigma_D = \sqrt{\frac{S_1^2}{N_1} + \frac{S_2^2}{N_2}}$$

$$= \sqrt{\frac{9^2}{50} + \frac{4^2}{60}} = \sqrt{\frac{81}{50} + \frac{49}{60}}$$

$$= \sqrt{1.62 + 0.817} = \sqrt{2.437} = 1.56$$

$$\therefore Z = \frac{D}{\sigma_D} = \frac{\bar{X}_1 - \bar{X}_2}{1.56} = \frac{79-75}{1.56} = \frac{4}{1.56} = 2.56$$

$$d_f = (N_1 - 1) + (N_2 - 1)$$
$$= 50 + 60 - 2$$
$$= 108.$$

The critical values of Z at 5 percent level and at 1 percent level for d_f=108 are 1.96 and 2.57, respectively.

Since the calculated value at 5 percent level is greater than the critical value, the difference is significant at 5 percent and insignificant at 1 percent level. So the null hypothesis is rejected and the assumed hypothesis is also disproved at 5 percent level, but the null hypothesis is accepted and the assumed hypothesis is also proved at 1 percent level of significance.

Thus, there is no significant difference between the performances of students of Bhopal and Rajasthan.

Example 7: For the study of effectiveness of development communication, a random sample of 200 villages was taken from a district of China and the average population per village was found to be 485 with a standard deviation of 50. Another random sample of 200 villages from the same district gave an average population of 510 per village with a standard deviation of 40. Is the difference between the two samples statistically significant at 5 percent level of confidence?

Solution: Let us take the hypothesis that there is no significant difference between the two samples statistically at 5 percent level of confidence.

Hence,

$\bar{X}_1 = 485,$	$S_1 = 50$	$N_1 = 200$
$\bar{X}_2 = 510$	$S_2 = 40$	$N_2 = 200$

$$SE_{\bar{X}_1-\bar{X}_2} = \sigma_D = \sqrt{\frac{S_1^2}{N_1} + \frac{S_2^2}{N_2}}$$

$$= \sqrt{\frac{50^2}{200} + \frac{40^2}{200}} = \sqrt{\frac{2500}{200} + \frac{1600}{200}} = \sqrt{\frac{2500 + 1600}{200}}$$

$$= \sqrt{\frac{4100}{200}} = \sqrt{20.5} = 4.53$$

$$\therefore Z = \frac{D}{\sigma_D} = \frac{|\bar{X}_1 - \bar{X}_2|}{\sigma_D} = \frac{510 - 485}{4.53} = \frac{25}{4.53} = 5.5$$

$$d_f = (N_1 - 1) + (N_2 - 1)$$
$$= (200 + 200 - 2) = 398.$$

The critical value of Z at 5 percent level for $d_f = 398$ is 1.96. Since the calculated value is greater than the critical value, the difference is significant. Hence, the null hypothesis is rejected and the assumed hypothesis is also disproved.

Thus, there is a significant difference between the two samples statistically at 5 percent level of confidence.

Example 8: In newspaper A, 60 news have a mean space of 68.60 cm^2 and in newspaper B, 50 news have a mean space of 69.51 cm^2. Is the evidence conclusive that the mean space of newspaper B is greater than that of newspaper A if the standard deviation of the news space is 2.48 cm^2.

Solution: Let us take the hypothesis that the mean news space of newspaper B is greater and there is no significant difference in the given statement.

$N_1 = 60$ $\quad \bar{X}_1 = 68.60,$ $\quad \sigma = 2.48$

$N_2 = 50$ $\quad \bar{X}_2 = 69.51$

$$SE_{\bar{X}_1-\bar{X}_2} = \sigma_D = \sqrt{\sigma^2\left(\frac{1}{N_1} + \frac{1}{N_2}\right)}$$

$$= \sqrt{(2.48)^2\left(\frac{1}{60} + \frac{1}{50}\right)}$$

$$= (6.15)(0.167 + 0.02)$$

$$= \sqrt{6.15 \times 0.0367} = \sqrt{0.2257}$$

$$= 0.475$$

$$\therefore Z = \frac{D}{\sigma_D} = \frac{|\bar{X}_1 - \bar{X}_2|}{\sigma_D} = \frac{|68.60 - 69.51|}{0.475} = \frac{0.91}{0.475} = 1.92$$

$$d_f = (N_1 - 1) + (N_2 - 1)$$
$$= (60 + 50 - 2) = 108.$$

The critical value of Z at 5 percent level for $d_f = 108$ is 1.96 and at 1 percent is 2.58. Since the calculated value is smaller at both the levels, the difference is insignificant. Hence, the null hypothesis is accepted and the assumed hypothesis is also proved.

Thus, the mean news space of newspaper B is greater and there is no significant difference in the given statement of the problem.

Example 9: A sample of 83 male students and 95 female students was taken to test the communication skills of the students of Bangalore Medical College and Research Institute. The following results were found:

	N	Mean	SD
Female students	95	29.91	11.56
Male students	83	30.92	7.81

Is there a significant difference between the mean scores of male students and female students?

Solution: Let us take the hypothesis that there is no significant difference between the mean scores of male and female students.

Here, $N_1 = 95$ $\bar{X}_1 = 29.91,$ $S_1 = 11.56$
$N_2 = 83$ $\bar{X}_2 = 30.92$ $S_2 = 7.811$

$$SE_{\bar{X}_1 - \bar{X}_2} = \sigma_D = \sqrt{\frac{S_1^2}{N_1} + \frac{S_2^2}{N_2}}$$
$$= \sqrt{\frac{(11.56)^2}{95} + \frac{(7.81)^2}{83}}$$
$$= \sqrt{1.4067 + 0.7349} = \sqrt{2.1416} = 1.463$$

$$\therefore Z = \frac{D}{\sigma_D} = \frac{|\bar{X}_1 - \bar{X}_2|}{\sigma_D} = \frac{|29.91 - 30.92|}{1.463} = 1.169$$

$$d_f = (N_1 - 1) + (N_2 - 1)$$
$$= (95 + 83 - 2) = 176$$

The critical value of Z at 5 percent level for $d_f = 176$ is 1.96. Since the calculated value is smaller than the critical value, the difference is insignificant. Hence, the null hypothesis is accepted and the assumed hypothesis is also proved.

Thus, there is no significant difference between the mean scores of male and female students.

Example 10: Creativity test on two groups of boys and girls gave the following results:

	N	Mean	SD
Girls	150	75	15
Boys	250	70	20

Is there a significant difference between the mean scores of boys and girls regarding creativity?

Solution: Let us take the hypothesis that there is no significant difference between the mean scores of boys and girls regarding creativity.

Here,

$N_1=150 \quad \bar{X}_1=75, \quad \sigma_1=15$

$N_2=250 \quad \bar{X}_2=70 \quad \sigma_2=20$

$$SE_{\bar{X}_1-\bar{X}_2}=\sigma_D=\sqrt{\left(\frac{\sigma_1^2}{N_1}+\frac{\sigma_2^2}{N_2}\right)}$$

$$=\sqrt{\frac{(15)^2}{150}+\frac{(20)^2}{250}}=\sqrt{\frac{225}{150}+\frac{400}{250}}=\sqrt{1.5+1.6}=1.761$$

$$\therefore Z=\frac{D}{\sigma_D}=\frac{\bar{X}_1-\bar{X}_2}{1.761}=\frac{75-70}{1.761}=\frac{5}{1.761}=2.84$$

$$d_f=(N_1-1)+(N_2-1)$$
$$=(150+250-2)=398.$$

The critical value of Z at 5 percent level for $d_f=398$ is 1.96. Since the calculated value is more than the critical value, the difference is significant. Hence, the null hypothesis is rejected and the assumed hypothesis is also disproved.

Thus, there is a significance difference between the mean scores of boys and girls regarding creativity.

Example 11: A sample of height of 6,400 journalists has a mean of 67.85 inches and a standard deviation of 2.56 inches, while a sample of height of 1,600 advertisers has a mean of 68.55 inches and standard deviation of 2.52 inches. Do the data indicate that the journalists are, on the average, taller than the advertisers? Give reasons for your answers.

Solution: Let us take the hypothesis that there is no significant relation between the height of journalists and that of advertisers.

Here, $N_1=6400 \quad \bar{X}_1=67.85 \quad \sigma_1=2.56$

$N_2=1600 \quad \bar{X}_2=68.55 \quad \sigma_2=2.52$

$$SE_{\bar{X}_1-\bar{X}_2}=\sigma_D=\sqrt{\frac{\sigma_1^2}{N_1}+\frac{\sigma_2^2}{N^2}}$$

$$=\sqrt{\frac{(2.56)^2}{6400}+\frac{(2.52)^2}{1600}}=\sqrt{0.001+0.004}=0.0707$$

$$\therefore Z = \frac{D}{\sigma_D} = \frac{|\bar{X}_1 - \bar{X}_2|}{0.0707} = \frac{67.85 - 68.55}{0.0707} = 9.9$$

$$d_f = (N_1 - 1) + (N_2 - 1)$$
$$= (6400 + 1600 - 2) = 7898.$$

The critical value of Z at 5 percent level for $d_f = 7898$ is 1.96. Since the calculated value is greater than the critical value, the difference is significant. Hence, the null hypothesis is rejected and the assumed hypothesis is also disproved.

Thus, the data indicates that the journalists on the average are taller than the advertisers.

Example 12: Two samples of 100 radio sets each have means of 1,500 and 1,550 and standard deviations 50 and 60. Can it be concluded that two brands differ significantly at 1 percent level?

Solution: Let us take the hypothesis that two brands have no significant relation at 1 percent level.

Here, $N_1 = 100$, $\bar{X}_1 = 1500$, $\sigma_1 = 50$
$N_2 = 100$, $\bar{X}_2 = 1550$, $\sigma_2 = 60$

$$SE_{\bar{X}_1 - \bar{X}_2} = \sigma_D = \sqrt{\frac{\sigma_1^2}{N_1} + \frac{\sigma_2^2}{N^2}} = \sqrt{\frac{(50)^2}{100} + \frac{(60)^2}{100}}$$
$$= \sqrt{\frac{2500}{100} + \frac{3600}{100}} = \sqrt{\frac{2500 + 3600}{100}}$$
$$= \sqrt{\frac{4100}{100}} = 7.81$$

$$d_f = (N_1 - 1) + (N_2 - 1)$$
$$= (100 + 100 - 2) = 198.$$

The critical value of Z at 1 percent level for $d_f = 198$ is 2.58. Since the calculated value is greater than the critical value at 1 percent level, the difference is significant. Hence, the null hypothesis is rejected and the assumed hypothesis is also disproved.

Thus, it can be concluded that the two brands differ significantly at 1 percent level.

8.6.3 Standard Error of Difference Between Two Standard Deviations

When two large samples are drawn from normally distributed population, the standard error of difference between standard deviations is given by the formula:

$$SE_{\sigma_1 - \sigma_2} = \sqrt{\frac{\sigma_1^2}{2N_1} + \frac{\sigma_2^2}{2N_2}} \quad \text{or} \quad = SE_{S_1 - S_2} = \sqrt{\frac{S_1^2}{2N_1} + \frac{S_2^2}{2N_2}}.$$

Example 1: In a sample of 1000, the mean is 17.5 and the standard deviation is 2.5. In another sample of 800, the mean is 18 and the standard deviation is 2.7. Assuming that the samples are independent, discuss whether the two samples have the same standard deviation.

Here, $N_1 = 1000 \quad \bar{X}_1 = 17.5 \quad S_1 = 2.5$

$N_2 = 800 \quad \bar{X}_2 = 18 \quad S_2 = 2.7$

Solution: Let us take the hypothesis that two samples do not have the significant difference with the same population.

$$\begin{aligned}
SE_{S_1 - S_2} &= \sqrt{\frac{S_1^2}{2N_1} + \frac{S_2^2}{2N_2}} \\
&= \sqrt{\frac{(2.5)^2}{2 \times 1000} + \frac{(2.7)^2}{2 \times 800}} \\
&= \sqrt{\frac{6.25}{2000} + \frac{7.20}{1600}} \\
&= \sqrt{0.00312 + 0.00456} = 0.0876
\end{aligned}$$

$$\therefore Z = \frac{|D|}{SE_{\sigma_1 - \sigma_2}} = \frac{|\bar{X}_1 - \bar{X}_2|}{0.0876} = \frac{|17.5 - 18|}{0.0876} = \frac{0.5}{0.0876} = 2.283$$

$$\begin{aligned}
d_f &= (N_1 - 1) + (N_2 - 1) \\
&= (1000 + 800 - 2) = 1798.
\end{aligned}$$

The critical value at 5 percent level for $d_f = 1798$ is 1.96. Since the calculated value is greater than the critical value, the difference is significant. Hence, the null hypothesis is rejected and the assumed hypothesis is also disproved.

Thus, the two samples do not have the same standard deviations.

Example 2: Editing skills of two groups of boys and girls give the following results:

	N	Mean	SD
Girls	121	84	10
Boys	81	81	12

Solution: Let us take the hypothesis that there is no significant difference in the editing skills of boys and girls.

Here, $N_1 = 121 \quad \bar{X}_1 = 84, \quad \sigma_1 = 10$

$N_2 = 81 \quad \bar{X}_2 = 81 \quad \sigma_2 = 12$

$$\begin{aligned}
SE_{\sigma_1 - \sigma_2} &= \sqrt{\frac{\sigma_1^2}{2N_1} + \frac{\sigma_2^2}{2N_2}} \\
&= \sqrt{\frac{(10)^2}{2 \times 121} + \frac{(12)^2}{2 \times 81}} \\
&= \sqrt{\frac{100}{242} + \frac{144}{162}} = 1.14
\end{aligned}$$

$$\therefore Z = \frac{|D|}{SE_{\sigma_1 - \sigma_2}} = \frac{|\bar{X}_1 - \bar{X}_2|}{1.14} = \frac{|84-81|}{1.14} = \frac{3}{1.14} = 1.75$$

$$d_f = (N_1 - 1) + (N_2 - 1)$$
$$= (121 + 81 - 2) = 200.$$

The critical value of Z at 5 percent level for $d_f = 200$ is 1.96. Since the calculated value is less than the critical value, the difference is insignificant. Hence, the null hypothesis is accepted and the assumed hypothesis is also proved.

Thus, there is no difference in the editing skills of boys and girls.

8.6.4 Correlated Samples

When samples are correlated,

$$SE_{\bar{X}_1 - \bar{X}_2} = \sigma_D = \sqrt{(\sigma_{\bar{X}_1})^2 + (\sigma_{\bar{X}_2})^2 - 2r \cdot \sigma_{\bar{X}_1} \cdot \sigma_{\bar{X}_2}}$$

Example 1: A teacher of advertising gave a test in advertising appeal to 30 students of his class. Then he induced a test of anxiety among them and the achievement test was re-administered. The data obtained were as follows:

Initial Test Data		Final Test Data	
Mean	70	Mean	67
SD	6	SD	5.8
$R = 0.82$			

Find out the following on the basis of the above data:

1. Is there a significant difference between the two sets of scores?
2. Test the hypothesis that the population mean on the final test is significantly lower than the population mean on the initial test.
3. Did the introduction of the state of anxiety affect the ability of the students adversely?

Solution: Let us take the hypothesis that there is no significant difference between the two sets of scores, the population mean on the final test is lower than the population mean on the initial test, and there is no significant difference between the state of anxiety and the ability of the students.

Here, $N_1 = 30$ $\bar{X}_1 = 70$, $\sigma_1 = 6$
$N_2 = 30$ $\bar{X}_2 = 67$ $\sigma_2 = 5.8$ $r = 0.82$

Since the samples are correlated,

$$SE_{\bar{X}_1 - \bar{X}_2} = \sigma_D = \sqrt{(\sigma_{\bar{X}_1})^2 + (\sigma_{\bar{X}_2})^2 - 2r \cdot \sigma_{\bar{X}_1} \cdot \sigma_{\bar{X}_2}}.$$

$$\text{Now,}\quad \sigma_{\bar{X}_1} = \frac{\sigma_1}{\sqrt{N_1}} = \frac{6}{\sqrt{30}} = \frac{6}{5.477} = 1.09$$

$$\sigma_{\bar{X}_2} = \frac{\sigma_2}{\sqrt{N_2}} = \frac{5.8}{\sqrt{30}} = \frac{5.8}{5.477} = 1.06$$

$$\therefore \sigma_D = \sqrt{(1.09)^2 + (1.06)^2 - 2 \times 0.82 \times 1.09 \times 1.06}$$

$$= \sqrt{1.19 + 1.12 - 1.89} = \sqrt{0.42} = 0.648$$

$$\therefore Z = \frac{\bar{X}_1 - \bar{X}_2}{\sigma_D} = \frac{70 - 67}{0.648} = 4.628$$

$$d_f = (N_1 - 1) + (N_2 - 1)$$
$$= (30 + 30 - 2) = 58.$$

The critical value of Z at 5 percent level for $d_f = 58$ is 1.96 and at 1 percent, it is 2.58. Since the calculated value is more than the critical value, the difference is significant. Hence, the null hypotheses are rejected and all three assumed hypotheses are also disproved. Thus,

1. There is a significant difference between two sets of scores;
2. The population mean on the final test is lower than the population mean on the initial test; and
3. There is a significant difference between the state of anxiety and the ability of students.

Example 2: In a writing ability test administered to 60 journalists and 100 freelance writers, the following results were obtained:

Journalists mean score: 114, SD = 13

Freelance writers' mean score: 110, SD = 11 $r = 0.75$

Calculate the standard error of the difference of the two means and state whether the difference is significant?

Solution: Here, $N_1 = 60$ $\quad \bar{X}_1 = 114,$ $\quad \sigma_1 = 13$

$N_2 = 100$ $\quad \bar{X}_2 = 110$ $\quad \sigma_2 = 11$ $\quad r = 0.75$

Let us take the hypothesis that the difference is not significant.

$$\text{SE}_{\bar{X}_1 - \bar{X}_2} = \sigma_D = \sqrt{(\sigma_{\bar{X}_1})^2 + (\sigma_{\bar{X}_2})^2 - 2r \cdot \sigma_{\bar{X}_1} \cdot \sigma_{\bar{X}_2}}$$

$$\sigma_{\bar{X}_1} = \frac{\sigma_1}{\sqrt{N_1}} = \frac{13}{\sqrt{60}}$$

$$\sigma_{\bar{X}_2} = \frac{\sigma_2}{\sqrt{N_2}} = \frac{11}{\sqrt{100}} = \frac{11}{10}$$

$$\text{SE}_{\bar{X}_1-\bar{X}_2} = \sigma_D = \sqrt{\left(\frac{13}{\sqrt{60}}\right)^2 + \left(\frac{11}{10}\right)^2 - 2\times 0.75\times\frac{13}{\sqrt{60}}\times\frac{11}{10}}$$
$$= \sqrt{\frac{169}{60}+\frac{121}{100}-\frac{2\times 75\times 13\times 11}{100\times 10\times\sqrt{60}}}$$
$$= \sqrt{2.81+1.21-0.035} = \sqrt{4.02-0.35}$$
$$= \sqrt{3.97} = 1.99$$

$$\therefore Z = \frac{D}{\sigma_D} = \frac{114-110}{1.99} = \frac{4}{1.99} = 2.01$$

$$d_f = (N_1+N_2-2)$$
$$= (60+100-2) = 158.$$

The critical value of Z at 5 percent level for $d_f = 158$ is 1.96. Since the calculated value is greater than the critical value, the difference is significant. Hence, the null hypothesis is rejected and the assumed hypothesis is also disproved.

8.6.5 Comparing Mean of a Sample with Pooled Mean

Combined mean of two samples $(X_{12}) = \dfrac{N_1\bar{X}_1 + N_2\bar{X}_2}{N_1+N_2}$.

When the first sample is compared with the combined mean, then

$$\text{SE}_{\bar{X}_1-\bar{X}_{12}} = \sqrt{\frac{\sigma^2 N_2}{N_1(N_1+N_2)}}.$$

When the second sample is compared with the combined mean,

$$\text{SE}_{\bar{X}_2-\bar{X}_{12}} = \sqrt{\frac{\sigma^2 N_1}{N_2(N_1+N_2)}}.$$

Example 1: A random sample of 100 newspaper organizations in a state gives the mean population of 500 media persons per organization. Another sample of 150 newspaper organizations from the same state gives the mean at 504. If the standard deviation of the mean population of the newspaper organizations in that state is 20, find out if the mean of the first sample is significantly different from the combined means of the two samples taken together:

Solution: $N_1 = 100$ $\quad \bar{X}_1 = 500,$ $\quad \sigma = 20$
$N_2 = 150$ $\quad \bar{X}_2 = 504$

Let us take the hypothesis that there is no significant difference between the mean of the first sample and the combined mean of the two samples.

By formula,

$$\overline{X}_{12} = \frac{N_1\overline{X}_1 + N_2\overline{X}_2}{N_1 + N_2}$$
$$= \frac{100 \times 500 + 150 \times 504}{100 + 150}$$
$$= \frac{5000 + 75600}{250}$$
$$= \frac{125600}{250}$$
$$= 502.4.$$

Now, when the first sample is compared with combined mean, then by formula,

$$\text{SE}_{\overline{X}_1 - \overline{X}_{12}} = \sqrt{\frac{\sigma^2 N_2}{N_1(N_1 + N_2)}}$$
$$= \sqrt{\frac{(20)^2 \times 150}{150(100 + 150)}} = \sqrt{\frac{400 \times 150}{150 \times 250}}$$
$$= \sqrt{2.4} = 1.549$$

$$\therefore Z = \frac{|D|}{\sigma_D} = \frac{|\overline{X}_1 - \overline{X}_{12}|}{\sigma_D} = \frac{500 - 502.4}{1.549} = \frac{2.4}{1.549} = 1.549$$

$$d_f = (N_1 + N_2 - 2)$$
$$= (100 + 150 - 2) = 248.$$

The critical value of Z at 5 percent for $d_f = 248$ is 1.96. Since the calculated value is less than the critical value, the difference is insignificant. Hence, the null hypothesis is accepted and the assumed hypothesis is also proved.

Thus, the mean of the first sample is not significantly different from the combined mean of the two samples taken together.

Example 2: In an advertising agency, the median height of 400 advertising hoardings is found to be 160 inches with a standard deviation of 3 inches. Can it be said that the median height of the hoarding is 164 inches?

Solution: Let us take the hypothesis that the median height of the population is 164 inches.

Population median (M_1) = 164 inches
Sample median (M_2) = 160 inches
Sample standard deviation (S) = 3 inches
N = 400

$$\therefore \text{SE of median} = \frac{1.253S}{\sqrt{N}} = \frac{1.253 \times 3}{\sqrt{400}} = 0.188$$

$$\therefore Z = \frac{M_1 - M_2}{\text{SE of median}} = \frac{164 - 160}{0.188} = \frac{4}{0.188}$$

$$d_f = (N-1) = 400 - 1 = 399.$$

The critical value of Z at 5 percent for $d_f = 399$ is 1.96. Since the calculated value is much greater than the critical value, the difference is significant. Hence, the null hypothesis is rejected and the assumed hypothesis is also disproved. Thus, the median height of the advertising hoarding cannot be 164 inches.

Example 3: For the price distribution of 400 newspapers, the standard deviation was found to be ₹3. Can it be said that standard deviation in the price would be ₹2.5 at 5 percent level of significance?

Solution: Here $\sigma = ₹2.5$, $N = 400$, $S = ₹3$

$$\text{SE of SD} = \frac{S}{\sqrt{2N}} = \frac{3}{\sqrt{2 \times 400}} = \frac{3}{\sqrt{800}} = 0.106$$

$$\therefore Z = \frac{\text{Difference of SD}}{\text{SE of SD}} = \frac{3 - 2.5}{0.106} = \frac{0.5}{0.106} = 4.72$$

$$d_f = N - 1 = 400 - 1 = 399.$$

The critical value of Z at 5 percent for $d_f = 399$ is 1.96. Since the calculated value is greater than the critical value, the difference is significant. Hence, the null hypothesis is rejected and the assumed hypothesis is also disproved. Thus, the price cannot have a standard deviation of ₹2.5 at 5 percent level.

Example 4: A sample of 100 news items gives a variance of 25. Can it be said that the variance in the universe is 20 at 5 percent level of significance?

Solution: Let us take the hypothesis that the variance in the universe is 20 at 5 percent level of significance.

$$\text{SE of variance} = \sigma^2 \sqrt{\frac{2}{N}} = 25\sqrt{\frac{2}{100}} = 3.535$$

$$\therefore Z = \frac{\text{Difference of variance}}{\text{SE of variance}} = \frac{25 - 20}{3.535} = \frac{5}{3.535} = 1.414$$

$$d_f = N - 1 = 100 - 1 = 99.$$

The critical value of Z at 5 percent for $d_f = 99$ is 1.96. Since the calculated value is less than the critical value, the difference is insignificant. Hence, the null hypothesis is accepted and the assumed hypothesis is also proved. Thus, we can say that the variance in the universe is 20 at 5 percent level.

Example 5: The mean of a sample of 100 radio bulletins is 4.4 and the standard deviation is 0.79. Calculate the coefficient of variation. Also find out the limits within which the population coefficient of variation would vary.

Solution: Here, $N=100$, $\overline{X}=4.4$, $\sigma=0.79$

$$\text{CV}=\frac{\sigma}{\overline{X}}\times 100=\frac{0.79}{4.4}\times 100$$
$$=\frac{79}{4.4}=17.95.$$

$$\text{Now, SE of CV}=\frac{V}{\sqrt{2N}}\sqrt{1+\frac{2V^2}{104}}$$
$$=\frac{17.95}{\sqrt{200}}\sqrt{1+\frac{2(17.95)^2}{10^4}}$$
$$=1.27\times\sqrt{1+\frac{644.4}{10000}}=1.27\sqrt{1+0.064}$$
$$=1.27\times\sqrt{1.064}=1.27\times 1.03=1.31.$$

Range or limit of population coefficient of a variation:

$$\text{CV}\pm(3\times\text{SE}_{\text{cv}})=17.95\pm(3\times 1.31)$$
$$=17.95\pm 3.93$$
$$\text{or}\quad 14.02 \text{ and } 21.88.$$

Example 6: To study the correlation between advertising and sales, a sample of 900 is taken and a coefficient of correlation of 0.67 is observed. Can it be said that at 5 percent level of significance the correlation in the universe is +0.8?

Solution: Let us take the hypothesis that the population correlation is +0.8.
$N=900$ and $r=0.67$,

$$\text{SE}_r=\frac{1-r^2}{\sqrt{N}}=\frac{1-(0.67)^2}{\sqrt{900}}=\frac{1-0.4489}{30}=\frac{0.5511}{30}=0.018$$

$$\therefore Z=\frac{|D|}{\text{SE}_r}=\frac{0.8-0.67}{0.018}=7.2$$

$$d_f=N-1=900-1=899.$$

The critical value of Z at 5 percent for $d_f=899$ is 1.96. Since the calculated value is greater than the critical value, the difference is significant. Hence, the null hypothesis is rejected and the assumed hypothesis is also disproved. Thus, the correlation in the universe is not +0.8.

Now, the range of correlation $= r \pm 3$ SE

$$= 0.67 \pm 3 \times 0.08$$
$$= 0.67 \pm 0.054.$$

So it is between 0.616 and 0.724.

Example 7: The following data relate to the prices of a magazine in Mumbai and Kolkata:

	Mumbai	Kolkata
Mean Price of Magazine per Month	180	130
Standard Deviation	30	20

Coefficient of correlation between two prices from a sample of 900 quotations is +0.67. Find,

1. The regression coefficient and their standard error.
2. The price of magazine at Kolkata if the price in Mumbai is ₹150 per month and the standard error of the estimate.
3. The price of magazine at Mumbai if the price in Kolkata is ₹120 per month and the standard error of the estimate.

Solution: Let the prices in Mumbai be X and those in Kolkata be Y.
Here,

$$\bar{X} = 180 \quad \bar{Y} = 130, \quad \sigma_x = 30 \quad \sigma_y = 20$$
$$N = 900 \quad r = +0.67$$

1. Regression coefficient of the price in Mumbai over that in Kolkata or regression coefficient of X on Y

or

$$b_{xy} = r\frac{\sigma_x}{\sigma_y} = 0.67 \times \frac{30}{20} = 1.005$$

$$\text{SE}_{xy} = \frac{\sigma_x}{\sigma_y}\sqrt{\frac{1-r^2}{N}} = \frac{30}{20}\frac{\sqrt{1-(0.67)^2}}{900}$$
$$= \frac{30 \times \sqrt{0.5511}}{20 \times 30} = \frac{22.27}{600} = 0.037.$$

Now,

$$b_{yx} = r\frac{\sigma_y}{\sigma_x} = 0.67 \times \frac{20}{30} = 0.447$$

$$\text{SE}_{b_{yx}} = \frac{\sigma_y}{\sigma_x}\sqrt{\frac{1-r^2}{N}} = \frac{20}{30}\sqrt{\frac{1-(0.67)^2}{900}}$$
$$= \frac{20}{30} \times \frac{\sqrt{0.5511}}{30} = \frac{14.84}{900} = 0.016.$$

2. Now, we have to find out the value of Y when $X=150$. So, we use the regression equation of Y on X:

$$Y-\bar{Y}=b_{yx}(X-\bar{X})$$
$$Y-130=0.447(X-180)$$
$$Y=0.447-80.46+130$$
$$=0.447+49.54.$$

Since $X=150$ (given)

$$\therefore\ Y=0.447\times 150+49.54$$
$$=116.59$$

$$SE_{Y\text{ on }X}=\sigma_y\sqrt{1-r^2}=20\sqrt{1-(0.67)^2}$$
$$=20\times 0.742=14.84.$$

3. Now, we have to find out the value of X when $Y=120$.

$$X-\bar{X}=b_{xy}(Y-\bar{Y}),$$

or

$$X-180=1.005\ (120-130)$$
$$\therefore\ X=1.005\times 120+49.35$$
$$=169.95$$

$$SE_{X\text{ on }Y}=\sigma_x\sqrt{1-r^2}=30\sqrt{1-(0.67)^2}$$
$$=30\times 0.742=22.26.$$

Example 8: For a given group of media persons, the correlation coefficient between height and weight is 0.7, standard deviations of height and weight are 2 inches and 10 lb, respectively, and the means of height and weight for the entire group are 70 inches and 130 lb, respectively. Find out the best estimate of the weight of an individual who is 65 inches tall. Assign limits to this estimate in which in all probability his actual weight would be lying.

Solution: Here $r=0.7$, $\sigma_x=2$, $\sigma_y=10$, $\bar{X}=70$, $\bar{Y}=130$

$$b_{yx}=\frac{\sigma_y}{\sigma_x}\times r=\frac{10}{2}\times 0.7=5\times 0.7=3.5$$

$$\therefore\ Y-\bar{Y}=b_{yx}\ (X-\bar{X})$$
$$Y-130=3.5(65-70)$$
$$\therefore\ Y=3.5\times 65-70\times 3.5+130$$
$$=112.5\text{ lb}$$

$$SE_{Y\text{ on }X}=\sigma_y\sqrt{1-r^2}$$
$$=10\sqrt{1-(0.7)^2}=10\sqrt{0.51}$$
$$=10\times 0.714=7.14\text{ lb}$$

$$\therefore \text{Range} = Y \pm (3 \times 7.14) = 112.5 \pm 21.42$$
$$= 91.08 \text{ to } 133.92.$$

8.7 TEST OF SIGNIFICANCE FOR SMALL SAMPLE

In our discussion, we have comprehensively discussed problems concerning large samples. When a small sample (size$<$30) is considered, the tests that we have discussed so far become irrelevant and inapplicable. This is mainly because of the fact that the assumptions we made for large sample tests are not applicable for small samples. In the case of small samples, it is not possible to assume that (a) the random sampling distribution of a statistics is normal and (b) the sample values are sufficiently close to the population values to calculate the standard error of estimate. Hence, a totally new method and approach is required to deal with the problems of small samples. Thus, we must note that the methods, approaches, techniques, and theories of small samples are applicable to large samples, but not vice versa.

8.7.1 Student's *t*-distribution

This concept was introduced by W.S. Gosset (1876–1937) in 1905. He was working in an Ireland company of brewery called "Guinness and Sons" where employees were not permitted to publish their research work under their own name. Hence, he adopted a pen name "Student" for the publication of his research findings. Then onwards the distribution is known as Student's *t*-distribution. The *t*-distribution is used to test the hypothesis when the sample size is 30 or less and the population standard deviation or variance is unknown.

It is expressed by the following formula:

$$t = \frac{|\bar{X} - \mu|}{\sqrt{\frac{S^2}{N}}} = \frac{|\bar{X} - \mu|}{S} \times \sqrt{N},$$

where $\bar{X}$ is the sample mean, μ is the actual or hypothetical mean of the population, N is the sample size, and S is the standard deviation of the sample.

Here,

$$S = \sqrt{\frac{\Sigma d^2}{N-1}},$$

where $d = X - \bar{X}$.

It is important to mention here that "t" is distributed with $(N-1)$ degree of freedom (d_f or v).

8.7.2 Properties of *t*-distribution

1. The variable "*t*" distribution ranges from minus infinity (−∞) to plus infinity (+∞).
2. Like the standard normal distribution, it is also asymmetrical and has mean zero.
3. σ^2, that is, the variance of *t*-distribution is greater than 1. But it becomes 1 as *df* or *v* increases and, thus, the sample size becomes large. Hence, the variance of the *t*-distribution starts coming closer to the variance of the standard normal distribution as the sample size increases.
4. The *t*-distribution can be used even in the case of large samples. But the large samples theory cannot be applied to small samples.

The following diagram presents a comparative picture of a normal distribution curve and two *t*-distributions for two different samples.

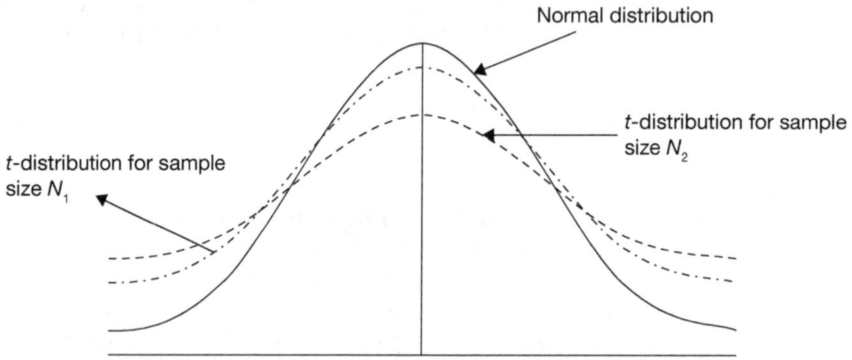

Source: Concept by British statistician William Sealy Gosset (1905), drawn by author's research scholar Bhupender Singh.

The diagram depicts two striking features of *t*-distribution:

1. A *t*-distribution is higher than the normal distribution on both the left and the right tails and it is lower in height at the point of the mean.
2. The *t*-distribution has a larger area in its tails than the normal distribution.

Thus, the interval widths of *t*-distributions are much wider than those of the normal curve.

8.7.3 Applications of *t*-distribution

t-distribution has several applications to test the significance of various results from small samples. Some of the most striking applications are mentioned as follows.

8.7.3.1 Testing the Significance of Single Mean

In order to find out whether the single mean of a random sample drawn from a normal population deviates significantly from a stated value (the actual or hypothetical value of the population mean) when the population variable is unknown, the following formula is used for the calculation:

$$t = \frac{|\bar{X} - \mu|}{S} \times \sqrt{N},$$

where $\bar{X}$ is the mean of the sample, μ is the actual or hypothetical mean of the population, N is the sample size, and S is the standard deviation of the sample.

$$S = \sqrt{\frac{\Sigma d^2}{N-1}},$$

where $d = X - \bar{X}$,

and

$$S = \sqrt{\frac{1}{N-1}\left(\Sigma d^2 - \frac{(\Sigma d)^2}{N}\right)},$$

where $d = X - A$, and A = assumed mean.

When the calculated value of $|t|$ exceeds the table value of $t_{0.05}$, then the difference between $\bar{X}$ and μ is said to be significant at 5 percent level and when the calculated value of t exceeds the table value of $t_{0.01}$, then the difference between $\bar{X}$ and μ is said to be significant at 1 percent level. Similarly, when $|t| < t_{0.05}$, then the difference between $\bar{X}$ and μ is not significant. This means that $\bar{X} = \mu$.

8.7.3.2 Confidence or Fiducial Limits of μ

If the sample is a random sample from a normal population of an unknown mean, the 95 percent confidence or fiducial limits of the population mean (μ) are:

$$\mu = \bar{X} \pm \frac{S}{\sqrt{N}} t_{0.01}.$$

Example 1: The manufacturer of a radio set claims that his radio sets have a mean life of 25 years with a standard deviation of 5 years. A random sample of six such radio sets gave the following value:

Life in years: 24, 26, 30, 20, 20, 18

Can you regard the producer's claim at 1 percent level of significance?

Solution: Let us take the hypothesis that there is no significant difference between the mean life of radio sets in the sample and that of a population:

That is, H_0: $\mu = \bar{X} = 25$ year. $t = \frac{|\bar{X} - \mu|}{S} \times \sqrt{N}$

Calculation of $\bar{X}$ and S

X	$d=X-23$	d^2
24	1	1
26	3	9
30	7	49
20	−3	9
20	−3	9
18	−5	25
$N=6$, $\Sigma X=138$		$\Sigma d^2=102$

$$\therefore \bar{X} = \frac{\Sigma X}{N} = \frac{138}{6} = 23$$

$$\therefore S = \sqrt{\frac{\Sigma d^2}{N-1}} = \sqrt{\frac{102}{6-1}} = \sqrt{\frac{102}{5}} = \sqrt{20.4} = 4.517$$

Here, $\bar{X} = 23,\ \mu = 25,\ S = 4.517$

Now,

$$t = \frac{|\bar{X} - \mu|}{S} \times \sqrt{N} = \frac{|23 - 25|}{4.517} \times \sqrt{6} = \frac{2 \times 2.449}{4.517}$$
$$= 1.084$$

$$d_f = N-1 = 5 \quad \text{for} \quad d_f = 5,\ t_{0.01} = 4.032.$$

Since the calculated value t is less than the critical value, the null hypothesis is accepted and the assumed hypothesis is also proved.

Hence, the producer's claim is not valid at 1 percent level of significance.

Example 2: The mean weekly sales of the chocolate bar in candy stores was 146.3 bars per store. After an advertising campaign, the mean weekly sales in 22 stores for a typical week increased to 153.7 and showed a standard deviation of 17.2. Was the advertising campaign successful?

Solution: Let us take the hypothesis that there is no significant difference between the sample mean and the hypothetical population mean.

That is, H_0: $\mu = 146.3 = \bar{X}$.

Here, $\mu = 146.3$, $N = 22$, $S = 17.2$, $\bar{X} = 153.7$.

Now,

$$t = \frac{|\bar{X} - \mu|}{S} \times \sqrt{N-1} = \frac{153.7 - 146.3}{17.2} \times \sqrt{22.1}$$
$$= \frac{7 \times \sqrt{21}}{17.2} = \frac{7.4 \times 4.5826}{17.2} = \frac{33.911}{17.2} = 1.97$$

$$d_f = N-1 = 22-1 = 21.$$

The critical value of t at 5 percent level of d_f=21 is 1.721. Since the calculated value is more than the critical value, the difference is significant. Hence, the null hypothesis is rejected and the assumed hypothesis is also disproved. Thus, the advertising campaigning has been successful in promoting sales.

Example 3: 10 Journalists are chosen at random from a population and their heights are found to be 63, 63, 66, 67, 68, 69, 70, 71, and 71. In light of the diet, discuss the suggestion that the mean height in the population is 66 inches.

Solution: Let us take the hypothesis that there is no significant difference between the mean height of the sample and the mean height of the population, that is, H_0: $\mu = \overline{X} = 66$.

Now,

$$t = \frac{|\bar{X} - \mu|}{S} \times \sqrt{N-1}.$$

Here, N=10, μ=66.

Calculation of mean and standard deviation:

X	$d = X - 67$	d^2
63	–4	16
63	–4	16
66	–1	1
67	0	0
68	1	1
69	2	4
70	3	9
70	3	9
71	4	16
71	4	16
$\Sigma X = 678$	$\Sigma d = 8$	$\Sigma d^2 = 88$

$$\therefore \bar{X} = a + \frac{\Sigma d}{N} = 67 + \frac{8}{10} = 67 + 0.8 = 67.8$$

$$\therefore S = \sqrt{\frac{\Sigma d^2}{N} - \left(\frac{\Sigma d}{N}\right)^2} = \sqrt{\frac{88}{10} - \left(\frac{8}{10}\right)^2}$$

$$= \sqrt{\frac{88}{10} - \frac{64}{100}}$$

$$= \sqrt{8.16} = 2.857$$

$$\therefore t = \frac{|\bar{X} - \mu|}{S} \times \sqrt{N-1}$$
$$= \frac{67.8 - 66}{2.857} \times \sqrt{10-1}$$
$$= \frac{1.8}{2.857} \times \sqrt{9} = \frac{1.8}{2.857} \times 3 = \frac{1.8}{0.952} = 1.89$$

$$d_f = N - 1 = 9.$$

The critical value of t at 5 percent level of d_f=9 is 2.262. Since the calculated value is less than the critical value, the difference is insignificant. Hence, the null hypothesis is accepted and the assumed hypothesis is also proved. Thus, the mean height of the population is 66 inches.

Example 4: A sample of 26 radio sets gives a mean life of 990 days with a standard deviation of 20 days. The manufacturer claims that the mean life of radio sets is 1,000 days. Is the sample not up to the standard?

Solution: Let us take the hypothesis that there is no significant difference between the sample mean and the hypothetical population mean.

That is, H_0: $\mu = \bar{X} = 1000$

$$N = 26,\ \bar{X} = 990,\ S = 20,\ \mu = 1000$$

$$t = \frac{|\bar{X} - \mu|}{S} \times \sqrt{N-1}$$
$$= \frac{|990 - 1000|}{20} \times \sqrt{26-1}$$
$$= \frac{10}{20} \times \sqrt{25}$$
$$= \frac{5}{2} = 2.5$$

$$d_f = N - 1 = 26 - 1 = 25.$$

The critical value of t at 5 percent level of d_f=25 is 1.708. Since the calculated value is greater than the critical value, the difference is significant. Hence, the null hypothesis is rejected and the assumed hypothesis is also disproved. Thus, the sample is not up to the standard.

8.7.3.3 Test for Difference of Means (of Two Independent Samples)

If two independent random samples of sizes N_1 and N_2 with means $\dot{X}_1$ and $\dot{X}_2$ have standard deviations S_1 and S_2, then the hypothesis of the samples coming from the same normal population can be tested by the following formula:

$$t = \frac{|\bar{X}_1 - \bar{X}_2|}{S} \times \sqrt{\frac{N_1 N_2}{N_1 + N_2}},$$

where $\bar{X}_1$ is the mean of the first sample, $\bar{X}_2$ is the mean of second sample, N_1 is the number of observations in the first sample, N_2 is the number of observations in the second sample, and S is the combined or pooled standard deviations of the two samples.

The value of S can be found out by the following formula:

$$S = \sqrt{\frac{\Sigma x_1^2 + \Sigma x_2^2}{N_1 + N_2 - 2}},$$

where $x_1 = X_1 - \bar{X}$, $x_2 = X_2 - \bar{X}_2$.

Further, the value of S when deviations have been taken from the assumed means A_1 and A_2 is,

$$S = \sqrt{\frac{\Sigma dx_1^2 + \Sigma dx_2^2 - N_1 \Sigma(\bar{X}_1 - A_1)^2 - N_2 \Sigma(\bar{X}_2 - A_2)^2}{N_1 + N_2 - 2}},$$

where $dx_1 = X_1 - A_1$, $dx_2 = X_2 - A_2$.

Moreover, when the standard deviations of the two samples are given (S_1 and S_2), the pooled or combined standard deviation is

$$S_{12} = \sqrt{\frac{(N_1 - 1)S_1^2 + (N_2 - 1)S_2^2}{N_1 + N_2 - 2}}.$$

Example 1: A group of five consumers treated after the advertising of medicine A weigh 42, 39, 48, 60, and 41 kgs. The second group of consumers treated after the advertising of medicine B weigh 38, 42, 56, 64, 68, 69, and 62 kgs. Do you agree with the claim that medicine B increases the weight significantly?

Solution:

X_1	$x_1 = X_1 - \bar{X}_1 = X_1 - 46$	x_1^2	X_2	$x_2 = X_2 - \bar{X}_2 = X_2 - 57$	x_2^2
42	−4	16	38	−19	361
39	−7	49	42	−15	225
48	2	4	56	−1	1
60	14	256	64	7	49
41	−15	225	68	11	121
$\Sigma X_1 = 230$		$\Sigma x_1^2 = 290$	69	12	144
			62	5	25
			$\Sigma X_2 = 399$		$\Sigma x_2^2 = 926$

$$\therefore \bar{X}_1 = \frac{230}{5} = 46, \therefore \bar{X}_2 = \frac{399}{7} = 57$$

$$\therefore S = \sqrt{\frac{\Sigma x_1^2 + \Sigma x_2^2}{N_1 + N_2 - 2}} = \sqrt{\frac{290 + 926}{5 + 7 - 2}} = \sqrt{\frac{1216}{10}} = \sqrt{121.6} = 11.027$$

$$\therefore t = \frac{|\bar{X}_1 - \bar{X}_2|}{S} \times \sqrt{\frac{N_1 N_2}{N_1 + N_2}}$$

$$= \frac{|46 - 57|}{11.027} \times \sqrt{\frac{35}{12}} = \frac{11 \times 1.708}{11.027} = \frac{18.786}{11.027} = 1.704$$

$$d_f = N_1 + N_2 - 2$$
$$= 5 + 7 - 2 = 10.$$

The critical value of t at 5 percent level of $d_f = 10$ is 1.81. Since the calculated value is less than the critical value, the difference is insignificant. Hence, the null hypothesis is accepted and the assumed hypothesis is also proved. Thus, medicine B is not more effective than medicine A.

Example 2: In three samples of 50 lines each from Khushwant Singh's column "With Malice towards One and All," the following number of weak endings were observed: 7, 9, and 10. In three similar samples, the weak endings were 15, 11, and 12. Discuss the suggestions that Khushwant Singh's column, as judged by the number of weak endings, increased with advancing years.

Solution: Calculation of mean and S for the two samples:

X_1	$dx_1 = X_1 - A_1$	dx_1^2	X_2	$dx_2 = X_2 - A_2$	dx_2^2
7	–2	4	15	4	16
9	0	0	11	0	0
10	1	1	12	1	1
$\Sigma X_1 = 26$	$\Sigma dx_1 = -1$	$\Sigma dx_1^2 = 5$	$\Sigma X_2 = 38$	$\Sigma dx_2 = 5$	$\Sigma dx_2^2 = 17$

$N_1 = 3$

$$\bar{X}_1 = \frac{26}{3} = 8.67, \quad \bar{X}_2 = \frac{38}{3} = 12.67$$

$$\therefore S = \sqrt{\frac{\Sigma dx_1^2 + \Sigma dx_2^2 - N_1 \Sigma(\bar{X}_1 - A_1)^2 - N_2 \Sigma(\bar{X}_2 - A_2)^2}{N_1 + N_2 - 2}}$$

$$= \sqrt{\frac{5 + 17 - 3\Sigma(8.67 - 9)^2 - 3\Sigma(12.67 - 11)^2}{3 + 3 - 2}}$$

$$= \sqrt{\frac{13.6333}{4}} = \sqrt{3.40} = 1.85$$

$$t = \frac{|\bar{X}_1 - \bar{X}_2|}{S} \times \sqrt{\frac{N_1N_2}{N_1 + N_2}}$$

$$= \frac{|8.67 - 12.67|}{1.85} \times \sqrt{\frac{3\times 3}{3+3}}$$

$$= \frac{4\times 3}{1.85\times\sqrt{6}} = 2.65$$

$$d_f = N_1 + N_2 - 2$$
$$= 3+3-2 = 4.$$

The critical value of t at 5 percent level of d_f=4 is 2.132. Since the calculated value is greater than the critical value, the difference is significant. Hence, hypothesis is rejected. Thus, Khushwant Singh's column has increased with advancing years.

Example 3: The mean life of a sample of 10 TV sets was found to be 1,456 days with a standard deviation of 423 days. A second sample of 17 TV sets chosen from a different batch showed the mean life of 1,280 days with a standard deviation of 398 days. Is there a significant difference between the means of the two batches?

Solution: Let us take the hypothesis that there is no significant difference between the means of two batches.

Here, $\bar{X}_1 = 1456$ $\bar{X}_1 = 1280,$ $S_1 = 423$ $S_2 = 398.$

Now,

$$S = \sqrt{\frac{(N_1 - 1)S_1^2 + (N_2 - 1)S_2^2}{N_1 + N_2 - 2}}$$

$$= \sqrt{\frac{(10-1)(423)^2 + (17-1)(378)^2}{10+17-2}}$$

$$= \sqrt{\frac{9\times(423)^2 + 16\times(398)^2}{25}} = \sqrt{\frac{1610361 + 2534464}{25}}$$

$$= 407.18$$

Now,

$$t = \frac{|\bar{X}_1 - \bar{X}_2|}{S} \times \sqrt{\frac{N_1N_2}{N_1 + N_2}}$$

$$= \frac{1456 - 1280}{407.18} \times \sqrt{\frac{10\times 17}{10+117}}$$

$$= \frac{176}{407.18} \times \sqrt{\frac{170}{27}} = \frac{176\times 2.51}{407.18}$$

$$= \frac{441.63}{407.18}$$

$$= 1.08.$$

The critical value of t at 5 percent level of d_f=25 for a two-tailed test is 2.06. Since the calculated value is less than the critical value, the difference is not significant. Hence, the null hypothesis is accepted and the assumed hypothesis is also proved. Thus, the two means do not significantly differ from each other.

8.7.3.4 Test for Difference Between Two Dependent Samples (or Paired Observations)

Earlier, we have discussed the *t*-test when two samples were independent. That is to say that the values of observations in one sample do not depend on the other. But there may be situations where the samples are not independent of each other and the values of the second sample depend on the values of the first sample. This is also called "matched paired observation" or simply "paired observations." Two samples are called dependent on each other when the units or components or items of one sample are related to those in the other, relevantly or meaningfully. If samples are dependent, they consist of the same number of elementary items. In this context, we may conduct some media research to examine the effect of media training on journalists, to study the efficacy of media workshop or conference or seminar and to find whether there is a significant difference. Generally, the application of dependent or paired samples will help us to carry out a more accurate study, because they will allow us to control the extraneous factors. Such researches or experiments are very useful in media especially in the field of advertising. For example, the effects of advertising on sales or the effect of increase of salary of media persons on the rise of their performance may be very relevant and meaningful in chalking out media policies.

In such media research, $N_1=N_2$ and every element has two values. Hence, the *t*-test of two dependent sample means or paired observations may be given by the following formula:

$$t = \frac{\bar{d} - 0}{S} \times \sqrt{N} \quad \text{or} \quad t = \frac{\bar{d}\sqrt{N}}{s},$$

where $\bar{d}$ is the mean of the differences of paired values and S is the standard deviation of the differences.

Here, the value of S is calculated by the following formula:

$$S = \sqrt{\frac{\Sigma(d - \bar{d})^2}{N - 1}} \quad \text{or} \quad \sqrt{\frac{\Sigma d^2 - N(\bar{d})^2}{N - 1}}.$$

It is important to mention here that t is based on $(N-1)$ degrees of freedom.

Example 1: To examine whether a media training in writing skills improves performance, a similar test was given to 12 participating journalists both before and after the training. The original marks recorded in alphabetical order of participating journalists were 44, 40, 61, 52, 32, 44, 70, 41, 67, 72, 53, and 72. After the media training, the marks were in the same order, 53, 38, 69, 57, 46, 39, 73, 48, 73, 74, 60, and 78. Was the media training useful?

Solution: Let us take the hypothesis that there is no significant difference in the marks obtained before and after the media training, that is, the training was not useful.

Now,
$$t = \frac{\bar{d}\sqrt{N}}{S}.$$

Participating Journalists	Before (1st Test)	After (2nd Test)	2nd – 1st Test (*d*)	d^2
1	44	53	9	81
2	40	38	–2	4
3	61	69	8	64
4	52	57	5	25
5	32	46	14	196
6	4	39	–5	25
7	70	73	3	9
8	41	48	7	49
9	67	73	6	36
10	72	74	2	4
11	53	60	7	49
12	72	78	6	36
			$\Sigma d=60$	$\Sigma d^2=578$

$$\bar{d} = \frac{\Sigma d}{N} = \frac{60}{12} = 5$$

$$S = \sqrt{\frac{\Sigma d^2 - N(\bar{d})^2}{N-1}} = \sqrt{\frac{578 - 12(5)^2}{12-1}}$$

$$= \sqrt{\frac{278}{11}} = 5.03$$

$$\therefore t = \frac{5 \times \sqrt{12}}{5.03} = \frac{5 \times 3.464}{5.03} = 3.443$$

$$d_f = N-1 = 12-1 = 11.$$

The critical value of t at 5 percent level of $d_f=11$ is 2.201. Since the calculated value of t is greater than the critical value, the difference is significant. Hence, the null hypothesis is rejected. Thus, the media training was useful.

Example 2: An interpersonal communication in the form of meditation and *pranayama* (breath exercise) was advised to 12 mentally disturbed media persons, resulting in the following change of their blood pressures: 5, 2, 6, –1, 3, 0, –2, 1, 5, 0, 4, 6.

Can it be concluded that the stimulus in the form of interpersonal communication will be accompanied by an increase in their blood pressures?

Solution: Let us take the hypothesis that the interpersonal communication in the form of meditation has no effect on the change of blood pressure.

D	d^2
5	25
2	4
8	64
−1	1
3	9
0	0
−2	4
1	1
5	25
0	0
4	4
6	36
$\Sigma d=31$	$\Sigma d^2=185$

$$\therefore \bar{d} = \frac{\Sigma d}{N} = \frac{31}{12} = 2.583$$

$$\text{Now, } S = \sqrt{\frac{\Sigma d^2 - N(\bar{d})^2}{N-1}} = \sqrt{\frac{185 - 12(2.583)^2}{12-1}}$$

$$= \sqrt{\frac{185 - 80.06}{11}} = 3.09$$

$$t = \frac{\bar{d}\sqrt{N}}{S} = \frac{2.583 \times \sqrt{12}}{3.09}$$

$$= \frac{2.583 \times 3.464}{3.09} = \frac{8.948}{3.09} = 2.296$$

$$d_f = N-1 = 12-1 = 11.$$

The critical value of t at 5 percent level of $d_f = 11$ is 1.796. Since the calculated value of t is more than the critical value, the null hypothesis is rejected and the assumed hypothesis is also disproved. Thus, the interpersonal communication in the form of meditation results in increase in the blood pressure.

8.7.3.5 Significance Test of an Observed Correction Coefficient

If a random sample from a bivariate normal population is available for study and we have to test the hypothesis that the correlation coefficient of the population is zero, that is, the variables in the population are uncorrelated, then the t can be derived by the following formula:

$$t = \frac{r}{\sqrt{1-r^2}} \times \sqrt{N-2}.$$

It is important to mention here that t is dependent on $(N-2)$ degree of freedom.

Example 1: A random sample of 18 from a normal distribution of advertisers gives a correlation coefficient of +0.5. Is this significant at 5 percent level of confidence?

Solution: Let us take the hypothesis that there is no significant difference in the sample correlation and correlation in the population.

Here, $r=0.5$, $N=18$.

Now,

$$t = \frac{r}{\sqrt{1-r^2}} \times \sqrt{N-2}$$
$$= \frac{0.5}{\sqrt{1-(0.25)^2}} \times \sqrt{18-2}$$
$$= \frac{0.5}{\sqrt{1-0.25}} \times \sqrt{16}$$
$$= \frac{0.5 \times 4}{0.867}$$
$$= 2.3068$$

$$d_f = N-2 = 18-2 = 16.$$

The critical value of t at $d_f = 16$ at 5 percent level is 2.12. Since the calculated value of t is more than the critical value, the difference is significant. Hence, the null hypothesis is rejected and the assumed hypothesis is also disproved.

Example 2: How many pairs of observations of a media event must be included in a sample in order that an observed correlation coefficient of value 0.42 shall have a calculated value of t greater than 2.72?

Solution:

$$t = \frac{r}{\sqrt{1-r^2}} \times \sqrt{N-2}$$

Here, $r=0.42$

$$\therefore t = \frac{0.42}{\sqrt{1-(0.42)^2}} \times \sqrt{N-2}$$
$$= 0.42 \times \sqrt{N-2} > 2.72 \times 0.908$$
$$= \sqrt{N-2} > \frac{2.72 \times 0.908}{0.42}$$
$$= 5.88$$

or, $$N-2 > (5.88)^2 = 34.57$$

$$\therefore N = 34.57 + 2 = 36.57 \quad \text{or} \quad 37.$$

Thus, we must include 37 observations.

Example 3: A random sample of 27 pairs of observations of press conferences from a normal population gives a correlation coefficient of 0.42. Is it likely that the variables in the population are uncorrelated?

Solution: Let us take the hypothesis that there is no significant difference in the sample correlation and population correlation.

Here, $r=0.42$, $N=27$.

Now,

$$
\begin{aligned}
t &= \frac{r}{\sqrt{1-r^2}} \times \sqrt{N-2} \\
&= \frac{0.42}{1-(0.42)^2} \times \sqrt{27-2} \\
&= \frac{0.42}{0.908} \times 5 \\
&= 2.31
\end{aligned}
$$

$$d_f = N-2 = 27-2 = 25.$$

The critical value of t at $d_f=25$ at 5 percent level is 1.708. Since the calculated value of t is more than the critical value, the hypothesis is rejected. Thus, the variables in the population are correlated.

Example 4: The following table gives the ages of 10 media persons and their wives at marriage. Find out the correlation coefficient and test for its significance.

Media person's age	23	27	28	29	30	31	33	35	36	39
Their wives age	18	22	23	24	25	26	28	29	30	32

Solution: Let us take the hypothesis that the given correlation coefficient is not significant.

Here, $r=0.5$, $N=11$.

Now,

$$
\begin{aligned}
t &= \frac{r}{\sqrt{1-r^2}} \times \sqrt{N-2} \\
&= \frac{0.5}{\sqrt{1-(0.5)^2}} \times \sqrt{11-2} = \frac{0.5}{\sqrt{1-0.25}} \times \sqrt{9} \\
&= \frac{0.5}{0.866} \times 3 \\
&= 1.732
\end{aligned}
$$

$$d_f = N-2 = 11-2 = 9.$$

The critical value of t at $d_f=9$ at 5 percent level is 2.26. Since the calculated value of t is less than the critical value, the given correlation coefficient is not significant.

8.8 LIMITATIONS OF TESTS OF SIGNIFICANCE

Statistical significance test has a great role to play in scientifically testing the hypothesis leading to complete research based on scientific analysis of data. But this too suffers from some demerits which may be perceived only by the experts with their experience, knowledge, and expertise of the subject.

These limitations are as follows:

1. First of all, statistical tests should not be used mechanically. They should be used technically and scientifically, understanding each and every variable suitably and properly. There may be situations where real differences exist but they fail to produce evidences which are statistically significant or the other way round. Therefore, great care, expertise, and experience of the researcher or his supervisor are required in each case. It does require the population to be normal, the sample to be random, and the variance to be homogenous unlike in a nonparametric test. In mass communication, sometimes it becomes the compulsion to apply the non-probability sampling test, such as purposive sampling, judgment sampling, cluster sampling, and snowball sampling. Then parametric tests become more difficult and cumbersome to apply, specially in macro media analysis.
2. Second limitation of a statistical significance test is that conclusions are based on probabilities and not on certainties. Hidden or lurking factors also affect the situation sometimes which can be better judged by the experiences of the supervisor or the project leader. A little ignorance or deviation destroys the whole media data in proper media analysis.
3. Third, these types of tests sometimes fail to reason out why the significant or insignificant differences exist. However, they do give us the clue or the basis for further investigation till a satisfaction point is arrived at. This does help in media analysis, but when there is large volume of media data, then it becomes time-consuming and trouble-causing.
4. Fourth, we often violate the basic assumptions of hypothesis testing while applying such a testing. Therefore, extra care should be taken in understanding the assumptions before applying the test or else our labor of love will be lost without any suitable outcome. Due to the fact that media researchers are the least exposed to media metrics or media-related statistics, it becomes more cumbersome in this field.
5. Last but not the least, hypothesis testing should be carried out with confidence and support beyond the statistical basis. It is often ignored by researchers in significance tests. Hence, the hypothesis must be designed with extreme reasonability in the sense of concordance with a prior expectation. Moreover, the hypothesis must fit logically and suitably. This definitely requires proper exposure of media metrics to communication and media researchers.

As a result, we must take extra care while applying the statistical procedures in hypothesis testing, more so in a microscopic branch of social sciences such as communication and media studies. Our wisdom, common sense, experience, judgment, and expertise must also be coupled with such applications of statistical tests in micro and macro media analysis in order to avoid some hidden, clandestine, and lurking elements inside.

SUMMARY

A hypothesis is an assumption on which the research is based for further reasoning. It can also be a quantitative statement about the population. It is also a general observation about the population which is tested statistically to know whether it is true or false. Conventionally, a single hypothesis is not framed. If one of the hypotheses is accepted, the other is automatically rejected and vice versa. Such hypotheses are taken as null hypothesis (or hypothesis of no difference) and alternate hypothesis. In its easiest and simplest form, the hypothesis asserts that there is no real difference in the sample and the population and difference found are irrelevant and accidental arising out of fluctuations of sampling. The null hypothesis is based on the principles of law that a man is innocent until and unless he is proved guilty. On the other hand, alternate hypothesis assumes that the differences are not due to fluctuations of sampling; they are genuine and factual. A null hypothesis is denoted by H_0 and an alternate hypothesis is denoted by H_a. There are two types of errors in hypothesis testing: (a) type I error and (b) type II error. Type I error is that in which the hypothesis is true, but our tests reject it. Type II error is that in which the hypothesis is false, but our tests accept it. We have two-tailed and one-tailed tests of hypothesis. Two-tailed test relates to both the sides of the normal curve, while one-tailed test relates to only one side: left or right. Understanding standard error and sampling distribution is extremely important in the process of the study of hypothesis testing. The standard deviation of the sampling distribution is called the standard error. When we study a few units of a population instead of all the units, then it is called sampling distribution. During sampling, some basic problems arise as to how to generalize the results of the sample, how to find out whether the generalizations made are valid or not and what is the level of confidence with which a particular generalization can be made. All these queries are answered by estimation theory and hypothesis testing. The theory of estimation was developed by the well-known Statistician Professor R.A. Fisher in 1930. After understanding the theory of estimation, it is important to discuss the situations in which we are supposed to apply tests of significance. These tests are: (a) test of significance for attributes, (b) test of significance for variables (large samples), and (c) test of significance for variables (small samples).

The word "attribute" means quality, property, trait, and so on. In this type of a test, we find the presence or absence of a trait. We have three types of significance of attributes (a) tests for number of successes, (b) test for proportion of successes, and (c) test for difference between proportions.

The sampling of variables are not only restricted to two variables such as success or failure, there can also be more and more variables which may be restricted to some extent, practically or theoretically. There are three main objectives of sampling of variables: (a) to compare actual or observed frequencies, (b) to estimate from the samples, some basic characteristics from the universe, and (c) to assess the reliability of our estimates.

Again it is really very difficult to have a clear-cut line of demarcation between small and large samples. A small sample has a sample size of 30 or less than 30, while a large sample has a sample size of more than 30. There is a difference between a large sample test and small sample test because their assumptions are quite different. In a large sample, (a) there is a normal distribution of random sampling and (b) sample values are sufficiently close to the population values and are used for each other. Whether it is significance of attributes or significance of variables (large or small), tests of significance have some limitations. So they should not be used mechanically. They should be used technically and scientifically. These types of test are not based on certainty, but based on probability. So they should be suitably judged by the expertise or experience. These types of tests also fail to study the significance in true sense.

But they give us the base for further study to reach a satisfactory conclusion. Moreover, we do violate the hypothesis testing assumptions while applying them. So care should be taken before their application, more so in a microscopic branch of social sciences like communication and media studies. Our wisdom, common sense, experience, judgment, and expertise must also be coupled with such applications of statistical tests in micro and macro media analysis in order to avoid some hidden, clandestine, and lurking elements inside.

IMPORTANT FORMULAE

1. Tests of Significance of Attributes
   a. Standard error of:
      i. No. of successes (SE) $= \sqrt{Npq}$

      ii. Proportion of successes (SE_p) $= \sqrt{\dfrac{pq}{N}}$

      iii. Difference of Proportions ($SE_{p_1-p_2}$) $= \sqrt{pq\left(\dfrac{1}{N_1}+\dfrac{1}{N_2}\right)}$,

   where $p = \dfrac{X_1+X_2}{N_1+N_2}$, N=size of sample, p=probability of success, q=probability of failure, $q=1-p$, X_1 and X_2 stand for the number of occurrences in two sample sizes N_1 and N_2, respectively.

   Or $SE_{p_1-p_2} = \sqrt{pq\left(\dfrac{1}{N_1}+\dfrac{1}{N_2}\right)}$,

   where p is the pooled estimate of the actual proportion in the universe, $z = \dfrac{|\text{Difference}|}{\text{SE}}$ or $\dfrac{|D|}{\sigma_D}$.
2. Tests of Significance of Large Samples
   a. $SE_{\bar{X}} = \sigma_{\bar{X}} = \dfrac{\sigma}{\sqrt{N}} = \dfrac{S}{\sqrt{N}}$

   b. $SE_{\bar{X}_1-\bar{X}_2} = \sigma_D = \sqrt{\dfrac{\sigma_1^2}{N_1}+\dfrac{\sigma_2^2}{N_2}}$

   c. $SE_{\sigma_1-\sigma_2} = \sqrt{\dfrac{\sigma_1^2}{2N_1}+\dfrac{\sigma_2^2}{2N_2}}$

   d. $SE_r = \dfrac{1-r^2}{\sqrt{N}}$,

   where σ (sigma) is standard deviation of population, $\sigma_{\bar{X}}$ is the standard error of the mean ($SE_{\bar{X}}$), S is standard deviation of sample, N is the size of the sample, N_1 is the size of sample$_1$, N_2 is the size of sample$_2$, $SE_{\bar{X}_1-\bar{X}_2}$ is the standard error of the difference between two means $\bar{X}_1$ and $\bar{X}_2$, $SE_{\sigma_1-\sigma_2}$ is the standard error of difference between two standard deviations of population, SE_r is standard error of correlation, r is the correlation coefficient.

3. Test of Significance of Small Samples
   a. To test the significance of the mean of a random sample: $t = \frac{\bar{X} - \mu}{S} \times \sqrt{N}$,

      where t is the t-value, $\bar{X}$ is the mean of the sample, μ is the mean of the population, S is the standard deviation of the sample, and N is the size of the sample. $S = \sqrt{\frac{\Sigma d^2}{N-1}}$, $d_f = v = N - 1$, where $d = (X - \bar{X})$.
   b. To test difference of means of two samples which are not independent: $t = \frac{|\bar{X}_1 - \bar{X}_2|}{S} \times \sqrt{\frac{N_1 N_2}{N_1 + N_2}}$

      where $d_f = v = (N_1 + N_2 - 2)$,

      where $S = \sqrt{\frac{(N_1 - 1)S_1^2 + (N_2 - 1)S_2^2}{N_1 + N_2 - 2}}$.
   c. To test the difference of means of two samples which are not independent $t = \frac{\bar{d}\sqrt{N}}{S}$,

      where $d_f = v = N_1 - 1$, $\bar{d}$ is the mean of differences. $S = \sqrt{\frac{\Sigma(d - \bar{d})^2}{N-1}}$ or $\sqrt{\frac{\Sigma d^2 - N(\bar{d})^2}{N-1}}$.
   d. To test the significance of an observed correlation coefficient: $t = \frac{r}{\sqrt{1 - r^2}} \times \sqrt{N-2}$, where $d_f = v = N - 2$.
   e. To test the significance of correlated samples:

      $SE_{\bar{X}_1 - \bar{X}_2} = \sigma_D = \sqrt{(\sigma_{\bar{X}_1})^2 + (\sigma_{\bar{X}_2})^2 - 2r \cdot \sigma_{\bar{X}_1} \cdot \sigma_{\bar{X}_2}}$.

RELATED AND SUGGESTED WEBSITES

(As retrieved on December 1, 2015)

1. http://sphweb.bumc.bu.edu/otlt/MPH-Modules/BS/BS704_Nonparametric/BS704_Nonparametric_print.html
2. http://www.gs.washington.edu/academics/courses/akey/56008/lecture/lecture7.pdf
3. http://www.uio.no/studier/emner/medisin/helseadm/HMM4101/h05/undervisningsmateriale/Lecture10.ppt
4. http://people.bath.ac.uk/jb335/Supporting%20Files/Lecture%206%20(Handout).ppt

REFERENCE

Gupta, S.P. 2011. *Statistical Methods*, 882–951. New Delhi: Sultan Chand & Sons.

RELATED AND RECOMMENDED READINGS

Elhance, D.N., and Veena Elhance. 1990. *Fundamentals of Statistics*, 21.1–21.26, 22.1–22.34 and 23.1–23.38. New Delhi: Kitab Mahal.

Gupta, S.P and Gupta Alka. 2008. *Statistical Methods in Behavioural Sciences.* Allahabad: Sharda Pustak Bhawan.

Hussain, Shamshad. 1971. *Elementary Statistics in Psychology and Education*, 96–119. 9th ed. New Delhi: Motilal Banarsidass.

Kanji, Gopal K. 2011. *100 Statistical Tests*, 1–13. 3rd ed. London: SAGE Publication, New Delhi: Vistaar Publication.

Kerlinger, F.N. 1983. *Foundations of Behavioural Research*, 198–213. 2nd ed. New Delhi: Surjeet Publications.

Kothari, C.R. 2000. *Research Methodology: Methods and Techniques*, 223–76. New Delhi: Wishwa Prakashan.

Mangal, S.K. 1987. *Statistics in Psychology and Education*, 128–68. New Delhi: McGraw Hill.

Shrivastav, G.P. 1995. *Statistics in Psychology and Education*, 60–74. Patna: Bharti Bhawan.

Wimmer, Roger D., and Joseph R. Dominick. 2003. *Mass Media Research: An Introduction*, 266–304. 7th ed. Belmont, CA: Thomson & Wadsworth.

QUESTIONS AND PROBLEMS

1. Explain the concept of sampling distribution and standard error. Discuss the role of standard error in large sample theory.
2. Throw light on the meaning and concept of hypothesis testing.
3. What is a hypothesis? Explain the steps for testing one.
4. Describe two-tailed and one-tailed tests of hypothesis.
5. How will you measure the power of hypothesis testing?
6. Differentiate between population distribution and sampling distribution.
7. What is estimation theory? Discuss the properties of a good estimator.
8. Throw light on point estimates and interval estimates.
9. What is the test of significance of attributes? Describe with examples,
   1. Test for number of successes,
   2. Test for proportion of successes,
   3. Test for difference between proportions.
10. Write a note on sampling distribution of statistic and random sampling.
11. Differentiate between null hypothesis and alternate hypothesis.
12. What do you mean by confidence level? How will you determine the confidence interval for normal population mean?
13. Explain the notion of sampling distribution of an estimator. Why is the knowledge of sampling distribution important in statistical theory?
14. Explain the concept of statistical significance. What is meant by the statement "the sample mean is significant at 5 percent level of significance?"
15. Explain briefly the procedure followed in testing a hypothesis.
16. Distinguish clearly between large sample and small sample test of significance. Explain the assumptions in large sampling theory.
17. Explain how *t*-test is applied to test the quality of two population means.
18. Explain how the student's *t*-distribution may be used to:
    1. Test the significance of the sample correlations coefficient in a sample drawn from a bivariate normal population.
    2. Test the significance of the difference between the mean yield of two varieties in an experiment.

19. Explain the concept of standard error. How is it useful in testing of hypothesis?
20. What is t-distribution? Explain some of its applications.
21. Explain the uses of t-distribution in testing the hypothesis.
22. Differentiate between the concepts in the following pairs (a) statistics and parameter, and (b) null and alternative hypothesis.
23. What is a point estimator? How will you proceed to construct an interval estimate of the mean of normal population with known variance?
24. Explain the role of standard error in large sample test.
25. What is sampling distribution of the mean? State its important properties.
26. Differentiate between standard deviation and standard error of estimate.
27. State the limitations of tests of significance.
28. What is t-distribution? How will you test the significance of mean of a random sample?
29. How will you test the difference between means of independent samples?
30. How will you test the difference between two dependent samples?
31. How will you test the significance of an observed correlation coefficient?
32. What is standard error? Discuss its role in large sample theory.
33. 500 news items were taken at random by a news editor from a large number of news items from the folder selected by trainee subeditors, and 50 news items were found to be senseless by the news editor. Estimate the proportions of the senseless news items in the folder and assign limits within which percentage most probably lie.
34. In an achievement test of communication skills of media students, two groups of boys and girls were experimented and the following results were obtained:

	N	Mean	SD
Girls	50	78	10
Boys	100	73	15

Find out whether the difference of their means is significant.

35. In an examination of mass communication, 12 students in one class had a mean grade of 78 with a standard deviation of 6, while 15 students in another class had a mean grade of 74 with a standard deviation of 8. Is there a significant difference between the means of the two groups?
36. In a random sample of 600 male journalists from London, 400 were found to be smokers, while in another random sample of 900 female journalists in Washington, 450 were found to be smokers. Discuss the question whether the data reveal a significant difference in London and Washington so far as the proportion of smokers is concerned.
37. Random samples of 200 newspapers produced by a printing machine A and 100 newspapers produced by a printing machine B showed 13 and 5 defective newspapers, respectively. Is there a significant difference between the performances of the two machines?
38. A communication skill test of advertising students was administered to a sample of 145 female students and 82 male students. The mean score of female and male students and standard deviation are given as follows:

	N	Mean	SD
Female students	145	32	6.2
Male students	82	36	7.4

Is there a significant difference between the two means?

39. A mass communication teacher wanted to know the relative effectiveness of the lecture cum demonstration method over the traditional lecture method. He divided his class into two equal random groups A and B and taught group A by the lecture cum demonstration method and group B by the lecture method. After teaching for three months, he administered an achievement test to both the groups. The data collected were as follows:

	Group A	Group B
Mean	22.25	25.30
SD	8.15	10.50
No. of students	50	40

From the data what do you conclude about the effectiveness of one method of teaching over the other?

40. A journalism teacher divides his class into two random groups. He provides an extra input in writing skills for an hour daily to an experimental group hoping that such input will promote the writing skills of the students of this group. The control group is not provided any such input. At the end of the session, he administered an achievement test and collected data as follows:

	Experimental Group	Control Group
Mean	140	120
SD	15.5	1.22
No. of students	12	16

Is the gain significant enough to indicate that an extra input promotes writing skills?

41. A group of 20 media students were given an achievement test of creative writing under two conditions (a) when tense and (b) when relaxed. Test the significance of the difference of means at 0.05 level and 0.01 level on the basis of the following data:

Roll no.	1	2	3	4	5	6	7	8	9	10	11	12	13	14	15	16	17	18	19	20
Score (when tense)	18	16	18	12	20	17	18	20	22	20	10	8	20	12	16	16	18	20	18	21
Score (when relaxed)	20	22	24	10	25	19	20	21	23	20	10	12	22	14	12	20	22	24	23	17

42. Two groups of media students, each consisting of 20 students of a class were matched in pairs on the basis of IQs. The use of film strip was the method used to teach the experimental group. The control was exposed to a conventional "read and discuss" method. The researcher wanted to test the null hypothesis that there was difference between the mean achievements of the two groups at 0.05 level. The data obtained are as follows:

	Experimental Group	Control Group
Mean	53.20	49.80
SD	7.4	6.5
No. of students	20	20
R=0.60		

43. An examination was given to 125 students of mass communication of a university of Bhopal and students of mass communication of a university of Raipur. At Bhopal, the mean grade was 51.42 with a standard deviation of 6.245. At Raipur, the mean grade was 51.38 with a standard deviation of 7.14. Is there a significant difference between the performance of the students of Bhopal and those at Raipur, given that (a) α=0.05? (b) α=0.01?
44. For the study of effectiveness of development communication, a random sample of 200 villages was taken from a district of Japan and the average population per village was found to be 250 with a standard deviation of 50. Another random sample of 200 villages from the same district gave an average population of 580 per village with standard deviation of 60. Is the difference between the averages of the two samples statistically significant?
45. A sample of 60 male students and 80 female students of a journalism college was taken to test the creativity skills. The following results were found:

	N	Mean	SD
Female students	80	107.76	7.92
Male students	60	109.28	4.36

Is there a significant difference between the mean scores of male students and female students?

46. Copy writing skills on two groups of boys and girls gave the following results:

	Mean	SD	N
Girls	100	8	64
Boys	80	10	61

Is the difference between boys and girls regarding copy writing skills significant?

47. Two samples of 100 TV sets each have means of 1500 and 1550, and standard deviations 50 and 60. Can it be concluded that the two brands differ significantly at 1 percent level?
48. Radio sets manufactured by Australian and British companies gave the following results:

	Australian Company	British Company
No. of radio sets manufactured	100	100
Mean life in days	1300	1248
Standard deviation in days	82	93

Using standard error of the difference between means, state whether there is any significant difference between the mean life of the Australian and British companies?

49. Communication skills test of two groups of boys and girls of a media school gives the following results:

	N	Mean	SD
Girls	12	84	10
Boys	8	81	12

Examine if the difference of means is significant?

50. A data entry operator working in a daily newspaper claims that she can take dictation at the rate of 120 words per minute. Can we reject her claim on the basis of 100 trials in which she demonstrates a mean of 116 words with a standard deviation of 15 words? Use 5 percent level of confidence.
51. An advertising teacher gave a test in an advertising appeal to 25 students of his class. Then he induced a test of anxiety among them and the achievement test was re-administered. The data obtained were as follows:

	Initial Test Data	**Final Test Data**
Mean	80	84
SD	8	10

r between the initial and final test was 0.40. Find out the following:

1. Is there a significant difference between two sets of scores at 5 percent level and 1 percent level?
2. Test the hypothesis that the population mean on the final test is significantly lower than the population mean on the initial test?
3. Did the introduction of the state of anxiety affect the ability of the students adversely?

52. Two types of TV sets T1 and T2 are tested for their length of life and the following results are obtained:

TV Sets	**Sample Size**	**Mean (days)**	**Variance (days)**
T1	10	1000	100
T2	12	1020	121

Can you conclude that the two types of TV sets have the same mean life?

53. A random sample from 200 villages was taken from a district of France and the average population per village was found to be 420 with a standard deviation of 50. Another random sample of 200 villages from the same district gave an average population of 480 per village with a standard deviation of 60. Is the difference between the averages of the two samples statistically significant?
54. In a sample of 1,000 media persons, 520 are found to be journalists. Can we assume that both journalists and non-journalists exist in equal numbers in the sample?
55. A group of media students consisting of boys and girls were given a test in graphics and animation. The details of the data are as follows:

	N	**Mean**	**SD**
Girls	61	118.2	10.2
Boys	84	121.3	12.1

Is the difference between mean scores of the boys and girls significant?

9

CHAPTER

Nonparametric Testing of Hypothesis in Mass Communication

It is hypothesis that the sun will rise tomorrow: and this means that we do not know whether it will rise.

—Ludwig Wittgenstein

Nonparametric statistics is quite different from parametric statistics. But it is very relevant and useful in a micro-focused branch of social sciences like mass communication. This is because in communication and media studies, it often becomes a complex and cumbersome problem to decide the parameters of the variables of media and communication issues. As a result, media researchers frequently opt for a wrong statistical tool for hypothesis testing of media issues because of underexposure of this technique and complexities of the problems.

In the last chapter, we have comprehensively discussed the parametric statistics where the central limit theorem allows the normality assumption to be bypassed for samples which are sufficiently large. Further, we have already discussed the meaning and concept of hypothesis testing in media studies, steps for testing hypothesis, role of standard error and sampling distribution, estimation, test of significance for attributes, test of significance for larger samples, test of significance for small samples, limitations of tests of significance, summary, and important formulae. Thus, we have discussed the first inferential statistical tool of media metrics like parametric testing of hypothesis in the previous section. Yet another inferential statistics (as shown in the flowchart in Section 2.2.1 of Chapter 2) is nonparametric testing of hypothesis. Hence, this chapter on *nonparametric testing of hypothesis* will focus on the following:

1. Meaning and concept of nonparametric hypothesis testing in mass communication
2. Types of nonparametric tests
3. Advantages of nonparametric tests
4. Limitations of nonparametric tests

In addition, the chapter will also cover the summary, important formulae, related and suggested websites, related and recommended readings, questions and problems relating to nonparametric testing of hypothesis in research in general, and media metrics, communication and media measurement in particular.

9.1 MEANING AND CONCEPT OF NONPARAMETRIC HYPOTHESIS TESTING IN MASS COMMUNICATION

A nonparametric statistics is also known as *distribution-free* statistics or *assumption-free* statistics or *order statistics*. Data relating to media and communication problems and issues which are nominal (such as "increase," "decrease" or "no-change") or ordinal (rank) do not give powerful, efficient, or meaningful results. This makes nonparametric statistics very relevant and useful in handling the distribution-free media variables and subvariables.

Mathematics and statistics have developed an alternate method which may be used to test hypotheses about data which are non-normal. Since such tests do not depend on population parameters such as the mean and the standard deviation, they are also called "nonparametric" tests.

Nonparametric hypothesis testing does not depend on random sampling or normal distribution. It can be applicable on any data. This type of hypothesis testing does not require any assumption and, hence, it is simple to understand and easy to apply. Such nonparametric hypothesis testing does not require lengthy and laborious computations. Hence, it is less time-consuming, less money-consuming, less energy-consuming, and less resource-consuming. Moreover, this type of test is applicable to all sorts of data whether qualitative, nominal, ordinal, interval, or ratio-scaled. Such studies make it possible to work with small samples like pilot study, especially in the field of media studies relating to health communication on patients who have rare diseases and who are not easily available and communicative. Other than health communication, it is very much in demand in mass communication in the cases of assumption-free situations. Though all parametric tests are a crying need in the field media in general, yet chi-square is specially, largely, and widely used as a tool of media research.

9.2 TYPES OF NONPARAMETRIC TESTS

There are many nonparametric tests available in the statistical world. But here we will focus on the widely used and largely applicable tests which are as follows:

1. Sign test
2. Rank test (*U* test)
3. One-sample runs test
4. One-sample Wilcoxon rank test
5. *H* Test
6. Rank correlation test
7. Mood's median test
8. Friedman's test
9. Chi-square test

9.2.1 Sign Test

The sign test is one of the simplest and the easiest nonparametric tests. It is called sign test because it is based on the (+) or (–) sign of observations. It is not based on any numeric value. The sign test may be categorized as follows.

9.2.1.1 One-sample Sign Test

It is a very simple nonparametric test. Under this test, we test the null hypothesis $\mu = \mu_0$ against an appropriate alternative on the basis of a random sample of size N.

We replace the value of each and every item of the sample with a plus (+) sign if it is greater than μ_0 and with a minus sign (–) if it is less than μ_0. But if the value happens to be equal to μ_0, then it is simply discarded. Thereafter, we test the null hypothesis that these plus and minus signs are values of a random variable having a binomial distribution with $p = \frac{1}{2}$. Here, the critical value (K) for a two-tailed alternative at 0.05 level can be derived by the following formula:

$$K = \frac{(N-1)}{2} - (0.98)\sqrt{N}$$

H_0 is rejected if $S \leq K$ for the sign test. (Here, S is the number of minus signs.)

9.2.1.2 Two-sample Sign Test

This type of a sample test has a very relevant use in problems relating to double data or paired data. Here, each pair of sample values can be replaced with a plus sign if the first value is more than the second, with a minus sign if the first value is less than the second, or be discarded if the two values are equal.

Example 1: In a media school, a typing trainer claims that in a six-week intensive course, she can train students to type, on the average, at least 60 words per minute. A random sample of 15 graduates is given a typing test and the median number of words per minute typed by each of these students is given in the table below. Test the hypothesis that the median typing speed of graduates is at least 60 words per minute.

Students	Words per Minute	Direction of Change
1	78	+18
2	75	+15
3	53	–7
4	71	+11
5	66	+6
6	59	–1
7	88	+28
8	73	+13
9	80	+20
10	66	+6
11	58	–2
12	70	+10
12	60	0
14	56	–4
15	55	–5
		$S=5$

Solution: By adopting the method step-wise, we have:

1. H_0: $M_d = 60$

   H_a: $M_d > 60$

2. Level of significance = 5 percent
3. Criteria: Since the alternate hypothesis is one-sided, we get the probability of our result from the following table and compare with 0.05. If the probability is less than 0.05, we reject H_0.
4. Result:
   No. of "+" signs = 9
   No. of "–" signs = 5
   No. of 0ˢ = 1
   Total = 15
   $\therefore N = 14$ (discarding "0")
   $S = 5$ (Here, S is the no. of minus signs)
   Now by formula:

$$K = \frac{(N-1)}{2} - (0.98)\sqrt{N}$$
$$= \frac{14-1}{2} - 0.98\sqrt{14}$$
$$= 6.5 - 3.67$$
$$= 2.83.$$

Since $S > K$, the null hypothesis is accepted.

Example 2: Before and after the publication of editorial matters in newspapers and magazines about a new collection policy regarding receivable account, calculate the difference between the number of days until the collection of the account by using the sign test at 0.05 level.

Before:	25	27	34	35	40	42	33	38	34	45	28	27	25	41	36
After:	30	28	33	32	37	43	40	41	37	44	27	33	30	38	36

Solution: Calculating the number of plus and minus signs,

Before (1st)	After (2nd)	(1st–2nd)
25	30	–
27	28	–
34	33	+
35	32	+
40	37	+
42	43	–
33	40	–
38	41	–
34	37	–

Before (1st)	After (2nd)	(1st–2nd)
45	44	+
28	27	+
27	33	–
25	30	–
41	38	+
36	36	0
		$S=8$

Now, applying the formula,

$$K = \frac{(N-1)}{2} - (0.98)\sqrt{N}$$
$$= \frac{14-1}{2} - 0.98\sqrt{14}$$
$$= 6.5 - 3.67$$
$$= 2.83.$$

Since $S>K$, the null hypothesis is accepted. There is no significant difference before and after the new collection policy in accounts receivable even after its publication in the newspapers.

9.2.2 Rank Sum Test

This type of test is a whole family of tests. But here we will discuss only one most relevant and important types. And that is the Mann–Whitney test, which is popularly known as the *U* test. With the help of this, we may determine whether two independent samples have been drawn from the same population. In fact, it is the best nonparametric substitute of the *t*-test or *Z*-test. This test was sporadically presented by Frank Wilcoxon. But it was properly picked up and suitably developed by H.B. Mann and D.R. Whitney. So it is popularly known as the Mann–Whitney test. But a few statisticians are of the view that it should be called the Wilcoxon–Mann–Whitney test. So it is occasionally referred to as the Wilcoxon–Mann–Whitney test.

The rank sum test can also test the null hypothesis $\mu_1=\mu_2$ without assuming whether the populations sampled roughly have the normal distribution.

Again, if it is true that the two samples have come from the same population, it is reasonable to assume that the means of the ranks assigned to the values of the two samples are more or less the same. Here, the alternate hypothesis is that the means of the population are not equal and if this is the case, most of the smaller ranks will go to the values of one sample, whereas most of the higher ranks will go to those of the other sample.

Thus, to execute this test, first of all the data are ranked jointly, taking them as belonging to a single sample in either an increasing or decreasing order of magnitude. Generally, a low to high ranking process is adhered to. That means, we assign rank 1 to an item with the lowest value, rank 2 to the next higher item, and so on and so forth. In the case of ties, we will assign each of the tied observation the mean of the ranks which they jointly had. For example, if the second, third, and fourth values are identical, then each of them will be assigned the rank (2+3+4)/3=3. Thereafter, we will note down the sum of the ranks assigned to the values of the first sample (may be called R_1) and also the sum of the ranks assigned to the values of the second sample (may be called R_2). Then we will calculate the value of *U* which is a measurement of the difference between the ranked observations of the two samples. If the sample sizes are N_1 and N_2, the sum of R_1 and R_2 is simply the sum of the first N_1+N_2, which is known to be:

$$\frac{(N_1+N_2)(N_1+N_2+1)}{2}.$$

This formula will be very helpful to find out the value of R_1 if R_2 is known and vice versa.

Now, how to measure the value of *U*?

$$U_1 = N_1N_2 + \frac{N_1(N_1+1)}{2} - \Sigma R_1$$
$$U_2 = N_1N_2 + \frac{N_2(N_2+1)}{2} - \Sigma R_2,$$

where N_1 and N_2 are the sample sizes and R_1 and R_2 are the rank sums of the corresponding samples. For small samples, if both N_1 and N_2 are less than 10 (a few statistical experts say 8), a special table must be used. If *U* is smaller than the critical value, H_0 can be associated with the standard normal curve. Under such circumstances, *Z*-transformation might be used if there is no way out. Here, it is a non-issue.

By formula,

$$Z = \frac{U - \frac{N_1N_2}{2}}{\sqrt{\frac{N_1N_2(N_1+N_2)}{12}}}.$$

Again, it is important to note here that *U* test is applied when values of N_1 and N_2 are less than 20. If any of the two is more than 20, then the *U* value will be transformed into a *Z* value, which is called *Z*-transformation.

Example 1: For the post of producers in a television, 24 applicants were interviewed by three media experts and rated on the scale of 5 as per the suitability of the position. Each applicant is given a "suitability" score which is the sum of the three numbers. Although media education is not a requirement for the position, the personnel media director felt that it might have some bearing on the suitability of the position. Experts made their ratings on the basis of individual interviews and were not told the educational background of applicants. Twelve of the applicants had completed at least two years of media education. Apply the *U* test to determine whether there was a difference in the scores of the two groups. Use a 0.05 level. Group A of media persons had an educational background of less than 2 years of media education, while group B of media persons had completed at least two years of media education.

Solution: Let us take the hypothesis that there is no difference between the scores of two groups.

Now calculating U_1 and U_2 by formula:

Group A	Group B
9	10
4	11
7	14
11	13
6	9
8	8
12	12
11	14
9	13
10	9
11	10
11	8
$N_1=12$	$N_2=12$

Group A	Rank of Combined Group (R_1)	Group B	Rank of Combined Group (R_2)
9	8.5	10	12
4	1	11	16
7	3	14	23.5
11	16	13	21.5
6	2	9	8.5
8	5	8	5
12	19.5	12	19.5
11	16	14	23.5
9	8.5	13	21.5
10	12	9	8.5
11	16	10	12
11	16	8	5
$N_1=12$	$\Sigma R_1=123.5$	$N_2=12$	$\Sigma R_2=176.5$

$$U_1 = N_1N_2 + \frac{N_1(N_1+1)}{2} - \Sigma R_1$$

$$= 12 \times 12 + \frac{12(12+1)}{2} - 123.5$$

$$= 144 + \frac{12 \times 13}{2} - 123.5 = 144 + 78 - 123.5$$

$$= 222 - 123.5$$

$$= 98.5.$$

If a table with the critical values of U for $N_1 = 12$ and $N_2 = 12$ is available, we may use it. If not, then Z-transformation will be done:

$$Z = \frac{U - \frac{N_1 \times N_2}{2}}{\sqrt{\frac{N_1 N_2 (N_1 + N_2)}{12}}} = \frac{98.5 - \frac{12 \times 12}{2}}{\sqrt{\frac{12 \times 12 (12 + 12)}{12}}}$$

$$= \frac{98.5 - 72}{\sqrt{\frac{12 \times 12 \times 24}{12}}} = \frac{26.5}{12\sqrt{2}}$$

$$= \frac{26.5}{12 \times 1.414} = \frac{26.5}{16.97} = 1.56.$$

Since the calculated value is less than 1.96 (at 5% level), the null hypothesis is accepted. Hence, there is no difference between the scores of the two groups.

Example 2: Two groups of media students of print media and advertising secured the following marks out of 20 in a minor test of their dissertations:

Print: 10, 12, 8, 15, 14, 16

Ad: 18, 10, 12, 11, 9

Is the difference of marks between print media and advertising significant?

Solution: Since the two sample sizes are so small, the U test will be most suitable. First, we will treat the two groups as one combined group and rank them from a lower score to higher score.

Scores of Print	Rank of Combined Group (R_1)	Score Ad	Score Combined Group (R_2)
10	3.5	18	11
12	6.5	10	3.5
8	1	11	5
15	9	12	2
14	8	9	
16	10		
$N_1 = 6$	$\Sigma R_1 = 38$	$N_2 = 5$	$\Sigma R_2 = 28$

Now calculating U_1 and U_2: As we know the formula,

$$U_1 = N_1 N_2 + \frac{N_1(N_1 + 1)}{2} - \Sigma R_1$$

$$= 6 \times 5 + \frac{6 \times 7}{2} - 38 = 30 + 21 - 38 = 13$$

$$U_2 = N_1 N_2 + \frac{N_2(N_2 + 1)}{2} - \Sigma R_2$$

$$= 6 \times 5 + \frac{5 \times 6}{2} - 28 = 30 + 15 - 28 = 17.$$

Hence, $U = 13$.

Since N_1 and N_2 both are less than 20, we will have to see their table values (critical values) at $N_1=6$ and $N_2=5$ at levels 0.05 and 0.01. It was found from the table that U at 0.05 is 4 and at 0.01 level is 1. Since the calculated value of $U=13$ is more than the critical value at both the levels, the difference of marks between print media and advertising is not significant.

(Note: In case of the U test, if the calculated value is more than the critical value, then the null hypothesis is accepted and the difference is considered to be insignificant. This is a special and exceptional situation applicable to the U test only.)

Example 3: The marks obtained in electronic media by boys and girls are as follows:

Boys	5	8	12	10	3	6	10	13	5	9	19	7	22	11	7	15	16	11	12	17	11	18
Girls	20	24	15	8	15	20	10	18	16	18	23	26	27	25	26							

Compare the difference of significance of boys and girls by U test.

Solution:

Boys (Scores)	Rank of Combined Group (R_1)	Girls (Scores)	Rank of Combined Group (R_2)
5	2.5	20	29.5
8	7.5	24	33
12	16.5	15	20
10	11	8	7.5
3	1	15	20
6	4	20	29.5
10	11	10	11
13	18	18	26
5	2.5	16	22.5
9	9	18	26
19	28	23	32
7	5.5	26	35.5
22	31	27	37
11	14	25	34
7	5.5	26	35.5
15	20		
16	22.5		
11	14		
12	16.5		
17	24		
11	14		
18	26		
$N_1=22$	$\Sigma R_1=304$	$N_2=15$	$\Sigma R_2=399$

Now, calculating U_1 and U_2:

By formula,

$$U_1 = N_1N_2 + \frac{N_1(N_1+1)}{2} - \Sigma R_1$$
$$= 22 \times 15 + \frac{22 \times 23}{2} - 304$$
$$= 330 + 253 - 304 = 279$$

$$U_2 = N_1N_2 + \frac{N_2(N_2+1)}{2} - \Sigma R_2$$
$$= 22 \times 15 + \frac{15 \times 16}{2} - 399 = 330 + 120 - 399 = 51$$
$$U = 51.$$

$N_1=22$ and $N_2=15$, which means that one of the groups is bigger than 20. So U will be transformed into Z (though it always carries a negative value, but its numeric value is treated as positive) for the test of significance.

$$Z = \frac{U - \frac{N_1 \times N_2}{2}}{\sqrt{\frac{N_1N_2(N_1+N_2)}{12}}} = \frac{51 - \frac{22 \times 15}{2}}{\sqrt{\frac{22 \times 15(22+15+1)}{12}}}$$
$$= \frac{51 - 165}{\sqrt{1045}} = \frac{-114}{32.33}$$
$$= -3.53.$$

3.53 is bigger than 2.58 which is the table value of Z at 0.01 level. So the difference at 0.01 level is significant.

9.2.3 One-sample Runs Test

This test is primarily based on the *Theory of Runs*. A run is a succession of identical letters or words or symbols. For example, let us see the following arrangement of letters:

XXX YYYY ZZZZ WWWWWW AA BBB

Here, the first set is a run of three Xs, then a run of four Ys, then a run of four Zs, then a run of six Ws, then a run of two As, and lastly a run of three Bs. Thus, there are six runs of different sizes. Here, too many or too few runs in a sample indicate something other than chance when the items were selected.

The number of runs is indicated by the symbol "r." To derive the mean of r (μ, or μ_r), the following formula is applied:

$$\mu \text{ or } \mu_r = \frac{2N_1N_2}{N_1+N_2} + 1.$$

The standard error of r (σ_1 or σ_r) is derived by the following formula:

$$\sigma_1 \quad \text{or} \quad \sigma_r = \frac{\sqrt{2N_1N_2(2N_1N_2 - N_1 - N_2)}}{(N_1 + N_2)^2(N_1 + N_2 - 1)}.$$

It is important to mention here that the sampling distribution of r can be closely approximated by the normal distribution if either N_1 or N_2 is greater than 20.

$$Z = \frac{r - \mu_r}{\sigma_r}.$$

Example 1: Following is an arrangement of 25 journalists (J) and 15 advertisers (A) lined up to apply for accreditation.

J AA JJJ A JJ A J A J AAA JJJ A JJ AAA JJJJJ AAA JJJJJ

Are they randomly arranged?

Solution: Let us take the hypothesis that both journalists and advertiser are randomly arranged.

Here, $N_1 = 25$ and $N_2 = 15$, $r = 17$

$$\therefore \mu_1 \text{ (or } \mu_r) = \frac{2N_1N_2}{N_1 + N_2} + 1$$

$$= \frac{2 \times 25 \times 15}{25 + 15} + 1 = \frac{750}{40} + 1$$

$$= \frac{750 + 40}{40} = \frac{790}{40} = \frac{79}{4}$$

$$= 19.75.$$

$$\text{Now, } \sigma_1 (\text{or } \sigma_r) = \frac{\sqrt{2N_1N_2(2N_1N_2 - N_1 - N_2)}}{(N_1 + N_2)^2(N_1 + N_2 - 1)}$$

$$= \frac{\sqrt{2 \times 25 \times 15(2 \times 25 \times 15 - 25 - 15)}}{(25 + 15)^2(25 + 15 - 1)}$$

$$= \frac{\sqrt{750 \times 710}}{1600 \times 39} = 2.92$$

$$\text{Now, } Z = \frac{r - \mu_r}{\sigma_r}$$

$$= \frac{17 - 19.75}{2.92} = -0.94.$$

Since the value of $Z = -0.94$ is less than 1.96 (5% level), the null hypothesis is accepted. Thus, we can say that both journalists and advertisers are randomly arranged.

Example 2: In a focus group discussion about news coverage of elections, there are 9 boys and 7 girls. Are they randomly sitting in the group if their sitting arrangement is as follows?

BBB GG B G BB G B GG BB G

Solution: Let us take the hypothesis that boys and girls are sitting randomly.

Here, $r=10$, $N_1=9$, and $N_2=7$.

Since r at 0.05 level is between 4 and 14, the calculated value of r is less than the table value. Hence, the null hypothesis is accepted. Thus, the boys and girls are sitting randomly.

9.2.4 One-sample Wilcoxon Rank Test

It assumes the data to be a symmetric distribution, such as the uniform or Cauchy distribution. If the researcher cannot verify this assumption of symmetry, he/she should use the nonparametric one-sample sign test. That is why this is not very popular as it is neither properly parametric nor nonparametric. Hence, a better option is always preferred.

9.2.5 Kruskal–Wallis Test (or *H* Test)

It is an extension of the Mann–Whitney test and the best nonparametric substitute of the ANOVA test if there is no assumption, as we know that the ANOVA procedure is adopted if there are more than two means or medians or correlations or any statistics. In other words, if there are more than two independent samples involved, then Kruskal–Wallis one-way ANOVA or *H* test is the best if no assumptions are available. This means that in the absence of the parametric ANOVA test, this is the best and the most effective nonparametric test. That is why it is also called "ANOVA by ranks." This test helps in understanding the null hypothesis that *K* number of independent random samples come from identical populations against the alternative hypothesis that the means of these samples are not all equal.

Here, all the data are ranked as if they were in one sample. It is carried out just on the lines of the Mann–Whitney *U* test where data are ranked from the lowest to the highest and samples are considered as a combined group. Here, the rank sums of each sample (*H*) are calculated by following formula:

$$H = \frac{12}{N(N+1)}\left(\frac{R_1^2}{N_1} + \frac{R_2^2}{N_2} + \cdots + \frac{R_K^2}{N_K}\right) - 3(N+1),$$

where $N=N_1+N_2+N_3+\cdots+N_k$.

$N_1, N_2, N_3, \ldots,$ or N_k are the numbers in each of the *K* samples and $R_1, R_2, \ldots, R_k$ are the rank sums of each sample. In the case of ties, again the usual procedure of the *U* test is followed.

But if there are so many ties, then the correlation method may also be adopted as H is very sensitive to ties. Again, H is nearly distributed as chi-square with $(k-1)$ degrees of freedom and the prescribed table may be used in that condition if the size of the sample is 5 or more than 5. Here, the null hypothesis generally assumes that all the samples are equal and, reversely, the alternative hypothesis assumes that the samples are not equal.

Example 1: Classes of first year, second year of MA (mass communication), and pre-PhD (mass communication) have obtained the following marks out of 25 in a seminar presentation independently.

Classes (Mass Communication)	Marks Obtained out of 25
MA (first year)	17, 16, 12
MA (second year)	13, 16, 18, 20
Pre-PhD	19, 21, 15, 22

Find whether the difference between three samples is significant?

Solution: Since the size of the sample is very small, it will be suitable and advisable to apply the Kruskal–Wallis *H* test.

Now, let us take the null hypothesis that all the three samples are equal, that is, there is no difference between them.

Hence, ranking the data from the lowest to the highest and considering the samples as a combined group, the following table is prepared:

MA (Mass Comm., First Year)		MA (Mass Comm., Second Year)		Pre-PhD (Mass Comm.)	
Score	Rank of Combined Group (R_1)	Score	Rank of Combined Group (R_2)	Score	Rank of Combined Group (R_3)
17	6	13	2	19	8
16	4.5	16	4.5	21	10
12	1	18	7	15	3
		20	9	22	11
$N_1=3$	$\Sigma R_1=11.5$	$N_2=4$	$\Sigma R_1=22.5$	$N_3=4$	$\Sigma R_1=32$

$$N = N_1 + N_2 + N_3 = 3 + 4 + 4 = 11$$

$$H = \frac{12}{N(N+1)}\left(\frac{R_1^{\ 2}}{N_1} + \frac{R_2^{\ 2}}{N_2} + \cdots + \frac{R_K^{\ 2}}{N_K}\right) - 3(N+1)$$

$$H = \frac{12}{11(11+1)}\left(\frac{11.5^2}{3} + \frac{22.5^2}{4} + \cdots + \frac{32^2}{4}\right) - 3(11+1)$$

$$= \frac{12}{11 \times 12} \times 426.65 - 36 = 38.79 - 36$$

$$= 2.79.$$

Since the calculated value of H is less than the table value, the difference is significant. Hence, the null hypothesis is rejected and, thus, the three samples are not equal.

Example 2: Three groups of students of BA (mass communication) of first year, second year, and third year independently get the following marks in a surprise tutorial test out of 40.

BA (mass comm.) first year: 21, 30, 20, 22, 25

BA (mass comm.) second year: 35, 22, 28, 25, 26, 29, 32, 30

BA (mass comm.) third year: 15, 26, 27, 28, 25, 23

Compare the three samples and find whether the difference between these samples is significant.

Solution:

BA (Mass Comm., First Year)		BA (Mass Comm., Second Year)		BA (mass comm., Third Year)	
Score	Rank of Combined Group (R_1)	Score	Rank of Combined Group (R_2)	Score	Rank of Combined Group (R_3)
21	3	35	19	15	1
30	16.5	22	4.5	26	10.5
20	2	28	13.5	27	12
22	4.5	25	8	28	13.5
25	8	26	10.5	25	8
		29	15	23	6
		32	18		
		30	16.5		
$N_1=5$	$\Sigma R_1=34$	$N_2=8$	$\Sigma R_2=105$	$N_3=6$	$\Sigma R_3=51$

$$N = N_1 + N_2 + N_3 = 5 + 8 + 6 = 19.$$

$$\text{By formula}: H = \frac{12}{N(N+1)}\left(\frac{R_1^2}{N_1} + \frac{R_2^2}{N_2} + \cdots + \frac{R_K^2}{N_K}\right) - 3(N+1)$$

$$H = \frac{12}{19(19+1)}\left(\frac{34^2}{5} + \frac{105^2}{8} + \frac{51^2}{6}\right) - 3(19+1)$$

$$= \frac{12}{19 \times 20} \times 2042.825 - 3 \times 20$$

$$= 64.51 - 60 = 4.51.$$

Since one of the sizes of the samples is greater than 5, the test of significance of the H test at $d_f = K - 1$ will be done in accordance with the chi-square table. At $d_f = 3 - 1 = 2$, the table value of chi-square at 0.05 level is 5.991 and at 0.01 level is 9.210. Since the calculated value of H is less than the table value of chi-square at both levels, the difference between samples is not significant and the assumed null hypothesis is also rejected. Thus, all the three samples are equal.

Example 3: A newspaper's trainee subeditors were randomly assigned to groups which were given some training tips on headline-cum-intro writing by three different methods. At end of the training period, they were tested for headline-cum-intro writing.

Following were their scores:

Method T_1: 68, 83, 79, 85, 90, 80
Method T_2: 91, 84, 60, 72, 86, 67, 82
Method T_3: 88, 65, 77, 78, 93

To know, whether the three method of training were equally effective, use the *H* test at 0.05 level.

Solution: Since the size of the sample is very small, it will be proper and advisable (as desired) to apply the Kruskal–Wallis *H* test.

Now, let us take the null hypothesis that all three samples are equally effective, that is, there is no difference between them.

Hence, ranking the data from the lowest to the highest and considering the samples as a combined group, the following table is prepared:

Method T_1		Method T_2		Method T_3	
Score	Rank of Combined Group (R_1)	Score	Rank of Combined Group (R_2)	Score	Rank of Combined Group (R_3)
68	4	91	17	88	15
83	11	84	12	65	2
79	8	60	1	77	6
85	13	72	5	78	7
90	16	86	14	93	18
80	9	67	3		
		82	10		
$N_1=6$	$\Sigma R_1=61$	$N_2=7$	$\Sigma R_2=62$	$N_3=5$	$\Sigma R_3=48$

$$N = N_1 + N_2 + N_3 = 6 + 7 + 5 = 18$$

By formula:

$$H = \frac{12}{N(N+1)}\left(\frac{R_1^{\,2}}{N_1} + \frac{R_2^{\,2}}{N_2} + \cdots + \frac{R_K^{\,2}}{N_K}\right) - 3(N+1)$$

$$H = \frac{12}{18(18+1)}\left(\frac{61^2}{6} + \frac{62^2}{7} + \frac{48^2}{5}\right) - 3(18+1)$$

$$= \frac{12}{18 \times 19}(620.17 + 549.14 + 460.8) - 3 \times 19$$

$$= 57.197 - 57 = 0.197$$

$d_f = 3-1 = 2$, at d_{f2}, $\chi^2 = 5.991$ at 5 percent level.

Hence, the calculated value of H is less than the critical value of χ^2 at 0.05 level, so the difference is insignificant and the assumed null hypothesis is also accepted.

Thus, all three samples are equally effective.

9.2.6 Rank Correlation Test

As discussed earlier also, the rank correlation coefficient test was developed by Spearman, which is described as a measure of association based on the ordinal feature of data. This test is one of the simplest statistical methods to use and the easiest to apply. It is even superior to Karl Pearson's product moment correlation coefficient in the sense that unlike the Pearson approach, it does not require normal distribution of data and random sampling. It can be easily applied on ordinal data through the ranking method.

Spearman's correlation coefficient ρ (Rho) is given by the following formula:

$$\rho = 1 - \frac{6\Sigma D^2}{N(N^2-1)}.$$

It varies from –1 to +1 including zero. The closer to unity (either positive or negative), the higher the value of the correlation coefficient. Reversely, the closer to zero, the lower the value of the correlation coefficient. Moreover, the standard error of the rank correlation coefficient is given by the formula $Z = r\sqrt{N-1}$. We need not repeat again the entire aspect of rank correlation as we have comprehensively discussed it earlier in Chapter 7.

Example: Find the correlation coefficient of the rank of the following news and feature numbers published in magazines in one year.

Magazines	A	B	C	D	E	F	G	H	I	J	K
News (in 1 yr)	80	45	55	56	58	60	65	68	70	75	85
Features (in 1 yr)	82	86	50	48	60	62	64	65	70	74	90

Solution:

Magazines	News (in 1 yr)	Features (in 1 yr)	Rank (R_1)	Rank (R_2)	$D=R_1-R_2$	D^2
A	80	82	2	3	–1	1
B	45	86	11	2	9	81
C	55	50	10	10	0	0
D	56	48	9	11	–2–1	4
E	58	60	8	9	–1	1
F	60	62	7	8	–1	1
G	65	64	6	7	–1	1
H	68	65	5	6	–1	1
I	70	70	4	5	–1	1
J	75	74	3	4	0	1
K	85	90	1	1		0
$N=11$					$\Sigma D=0$	$\Sigma D^2=92$

$$\therefore \rho = 1 - \frac{6\Sigma D^2}{N(N^2-1)} = 1 - \frac{6\times 92}{11(11^2-1)}$$

$$= 1 - \frac{552}{11(121-1)} = 1 - \frac{552}{11\times 120}$$

$$= 1 - \frac{23}{55} = \frac{55-23}{55}$$

$$= 0.58.$$

Hence, the rank correlation between news and features published in magazines is 0.58, that is, a moderately positive correlation.

9.2.7 Mood's Median Test

Alexander M. Mood propounded this nonparametric median test which is used to test the equality of medians from two or more populations. Hence, it gives a nonparametric alternative to the one-way ANOVA and sometimes also to Pearson's chi-square test. This test works when Y variable is continuous, discrete-ordinal, or discrete-nominal and X variable is discrete with two or more attributes.

9.2.8 Friedman's Test

It is a nonparametric test and an alternative to one-way ANOVA with repeated measures. It is applied to test for differences between groups when the dependent variable is ordinal.

9.2.9 Chi-square Test

This is such a widely and largely used method in media and communication that it will be separately discussed in Chapter 10.

9.3 ADVANTAGES OF NONPARAMETRIC TESTS

1. Nonparametric tests are assumption- and distribution-free. In a subject like mass communication, sometimes it becomes extremely difficult and complex to determine the parameters of the variables. Then the application of this test automatically becomes more relevant and useful in this subject.
2. They do not require the population to be normal, the sample to be random, and the variance to be homogenous unlike a parametric test. In mass communication, sometimes it becomes a compulsion to apply the non-probability sampling tests such as purposive sampling, judgment sampling, cluster sampling, and snowball sampling. Then, nonparametric tests become more suitable and pertinent to apply, especially in macro media analysis.
3. Since these tests are based on no assumption, they are extremely easy to understand, exorbitantly comfortable to use, and absolutely simple to apply in media research.
4. They are time-saving, money-saving, energy-saving, and resource-saving, as most of the nonparametric tests do not require lengthy, tough, tedious, laborious, and cumbersome computations. When they start giving relevant, significant, and satisfactory results, then there is no need for further use of any statistics. Hence, researchers of mass communication prefer to use these tests, sometimes due to least exposure to statistics and least time, and sometimes due to their nonparametric tendencies of no assumption and no distribution.

5. These type of tests are easily applicable to all types of communication and media data—ordinal or rank, qualitative or nominal, and even interval or ratio.
6. Such tests make it possible to work with very small samples. It is really an extremely useful to the researcher collecting pilot data. It is especially useful for researchers belonging to the media studies, particularly when they are dealing with health communication relating to rare patients having rare diseases.
7. As compared to classical procedures or parametric tests, these types of tests hardly require any assumption or pre-supposition. So they are not dependent on any conditionality; rather they are quite free from distribution and assumption. They have less assumption, so less restrictions or less limitations. Leading to more application in applied subjects such as communication and media studies.

9.4 LIMITATIONS OF NONPARAMETRIC TESTS

1. These types of tests are, however, considered to be less efficient, less accurate, less effective, and less powerful as compared to the classical procedures of parametric tests. When a media researcher wants scientific analysis of data having normally distributed media data with randomization and homogeneity of variance, then these tests totally fail.
2. Nonparametric tests have less assumption. That means they lead to less inferences. A media analysis with probability sampling is unable to apply these tests.
3. In communication and media analysis, it is highly disadvantageous to use nonparametric tests if all the assumptions of the classical procedures and parametric tests are available and the media data are measurable either on interval or ratio scale.
4. With the increase in the size of the data getting larger and larger in media studies, data management and its proper manipulations required for nonparametric methods are sometimes more tedious, cumbersome, lengthy, and laborious until and unless appropriate and advanced computer software or tools are available for quick computations.
5. Moreover, a collection of tabulated critical values for several nonparametric tests under situations dealing with small and large "N" is not easily available. This creates a lot of problems and complexities in communication and media analysis.

Thus, it depends on situations and circumstances of the available media data to apply parametric tests or nonparametric tests. If assumptions are met such as population is normal, samples are independent, and standard deviations are known, then researcher can think of applying parametric tests for hypothesis testing. But if assumptions cannot be met, then we can easily depend on nonparametric tests for hypothesis testing.

It is doubtless to say that nonparametric tests are crystal clear to understand, easy to explain, and simple to apply. Due to these features, nonparametric tests are gaining popularity day in and day out. It is true that the less one assumes, the less one can infer. But these tests are based on the principle, "the more one assumes, the more one limits the applicability of one's methods." Thus, we can say that both the methods are equally important and relevant depending upon the circumstances, situations, assumptions distributions, availability of conditions of data other than time, money, facilities, and resources.

SUMMARY

A nonparametric statistics is also known as distribution-free statistics or assumption-free statistics or order statistics. Since such tests do not depend on population parameters such as the mean and standard deviation, they are also called nonparametric tests. Such tests do not depend on random sampling or normal distribution; rather they can be applicable to any data, that is, qualitative, nominal, ordinal, interval, or ratio. Nonparametric tests can be broadly categorized as (a) sign test, (b) rank test, (c) one-sample test, (d) *H* test, and (e) rank correlation test. The sign test can further be categorized as (a) one-sample sign test and (b) two-sample sign test. The rank sum test is popularly known as the *U* test and is considered to be the best nonparametric substitute of the *t*-test or *Z*-test. This test was sporadically presented by Frank Wilcoxon, but was properly picked up and suitably developed by H.B. Mann and D.R. Whitney. So it is popularly known as the Mann–Whitney *U* test, though a few statisticians still call it "the Wilcoxon–Mann–Whitney *U* test." The *U* test is applied when the values of N_1 and N_2 (i.e., size of the sample) are less than 20. If any of the two is more than 20, then the *U* value will be transformed into a *Z* value, which is called *Z*-transformation. Unlike other tests, the *U* test is the only test which has a special and exceptional situation in which when the calculated value is more than the critical value, then the null hypothesis is accepted and the difference is considered to be insignificant. One-sample run test is primarily based on the "Theory of Runs." The Kruskal–Wallis *H* test is an extension of the Mann–Whitney *U* test and is considered to be the best nonparametric substitute of the ANOVA test without any assumption or assumption-free ANOVA or ANOVA by rank where data are ranked from the lowest to the highest and samples are considered as a combined group. Developed by Spearman, rank correlation is a measure of association based on the ordinal feature of data. Unlike the Pearson approach or any other parametric tests, it does not require normal distribution of data and random sampling. It can be easily applied on qualitative and ordinal data through the ranking method. Nonparametric test is based on the principle "No assumption, no restriction, no limitation." It is clear to understand, easy to use, simple to apply, and does not require the population to be normal, the sample to be random, and the variance to be homogenous. It is time-saving, money-saving, energy-saving, resource-saving, and makes it possible to work with very small samples. But it is considered to be less efficient, less accurate, less effective, and less powerful. It has "less assumption, less inference." In a subject like mass communication, sometimes it becomes extremely difficult and complex to determine the parameters of variables. Then, the application of this test automatically becomes more relevant and useful in this subject.

It is disadvantageous to use nonparametric tests if all the assumptions of the classical procedure and parametric tests are measurable either on an interval or a ratio scale. When a media researcher wants scientific analysis of data having normally distributed media data with randomization and homogeneity of variance, then this tests totally fails.

Hence, it depends on situations to apply nonparametric tests or parametric tests. After discussion of nonparametric tests, it is important to discuss yet another exclusive type of nonparametric test called the chi-square test which is widely used in media research. Hence, the next chapter is dedicated to the chi-square test in mass communication research.

IMPORTANT FORMULAE

1. One-sample Sign Test

$$k = \frac{(N-1)}{2} - (0.98)\sqrt{N},$$

where K=critical value for two-tailed alternative and N=size of the sample. If $S>k$, the null hypothesis is accepted and the difference is insignificant (S=no. of minus signs).

2. Mann–Whitney Rank Sum Test (U test):

   a. $U_1 = N_1N_2 + \frac{N_1(N_1+1)}{2} - \Sigma R_1$

   b. $U_2 = N_1N_2 + \frac{N_2(N_2+1)}{2} - \Sigma R_2,$

   where N_1 and N_2 are the sample sizes, R_1 and R_2 are the rank sums of the corresponding samples.

   c. $Z = \dfrac{U - \frac{N_1N_2}{2}}{\sqrt{N_1N_2\frac{(N_1+N_2)}{12}}},$

   where Z is the value of Z-transformation.

   The numeric value of Z will be counted only in plus or positive for any further analysis.

3. One-sample Runs Test:

   a. $\mu_1 \text{ or } \mu_r = \frac{2N_1N_2}{N_1+N_2} + 1,$

   where μ_1 or μ_r is the mean of r and r is the number of runs.

   b. $\sigma_1(\text{or } \sigma_r) = \dfrac{\sqrt{2N_1N_2(2N_1N_2 - N_1 - N_2)}}{(N_1+N_2)^2(N_1+N_2-1)},$

   where σ_1 (or σ_r) is the standard error of r.

   c. $z = \dfrac{r - \mu_r}{\sigma_r}$

4. Kruskal–Wallis Test (or H test):

$$H = \frac{12}{N(N+1)}\left(\frac{R_1{}^2}{N_1} + \frac{R_2{}^2}{N_2} + \cdots + \frac{R_K{}^2}{N_K}\right) - 3(N+1),$$

where $N=N_1+N_2+N_3 + \cdots + N_k$, that is, N is the total number of samples, N_1, N_2, N_3, and N_k are the number in each of the k samples and R_1, R_2, R_3, $+ \cdots +R_k$ are the rank sums of each sample.

5. Spearman's Rank Correlation Test:

$$\rho = 1 - \frac{6\sum D^2}{N(N^2-1)},$$

where ρ (Rho) is the rank correlation coefficient, D is the difference in rank, and N is the number of cases.

RELATED AND SUGGESTED WEBSITES

(As retrieved on December 1, 2015)

1. http://www.gs.washington.edu/academics/courses/akey/56008/lecture/lecture7.pdf
2. http://www.uio.no/studier/emner/medisin/helseadm/HMM4101/h05/undervisnings-materiale/Lecture10.ppt
3. http://people.bath.ac.uk/jb335/Supporting%20Files/Lecture%206%20(Handout).ppt

RELATED AND RECOMMENDED READINGS

Elhance, D.N.S., and Veena Elhance. 1990. *Fundamentals of Statistics*, 22.1–22.22, 23.1–23.27. New Delhi: Kitab Mahal.

Gupta, S.P. 2011. *Statistical Methods*, 1150–71. New Delhi: Sultan Chand & Sons.

Gupta, S.P., and Alka Gupta. 2008. *Statistical Methods in Behavioural Sciences*, 437–70. Allahabad: Sharda Pustak Bhawan.

Kerlinger, F.N. 1983. *Fundamental of Behavioural Research*, 285–96. 2nd ed. New Delhi: Surjeet Publications.

Kothari, C.R. 2000. *Research Methodology: Methods & Techniques*, 331–65. New Delhi: Wishwa Parkash.

Krishnaswami, O.R., and M. Ranganatham. 2005. *Methodology of Research*. New Delhi: Himalaya Publications.

Sarangi, Prasant. 2010. *Research Methodology*. Delhi: Taxman Publication.

Wilkinson, T.S., and P.L. Bhandarkar. 1996. *Methodologies and Techniques of Social Research*. Mumbai: Himalaya Publishing House.

Wimmer, Roger D., and Joseph R. Dominick. 2003. *Mass Media Research: An Introduction*, 266–304. 7th ed. Belmont, CA: Thomson and Wadsworth.

QUESTIONS AND PROBLEMS

1. What do you mean by nonparametric test of hypothesis? How is it different from a parametric test.
2. Discuss the meaning and concept of nonparametric testing of hypothesis with reference to media and communication research.

3. Explain briefly the advantages and limitations of nonparametric tests.
4. Describe the various types of nonparametric tests and the specific situations in which they are applicable in communication and media research.
5. Give your understanding of nonparametric or assumption-free or distribution-free methods, explaining their important characteristics.
6. What is the sign test? Explain with suitable examples.
7. Describe the concept of the sign test. When is it used and what are its limitations?
8. Throw light on the Mann–Whitney *U* test with suitable examples.
9. Describe the working of the one-sample run test with the help of an example.
10. Throw light on the Kruskal–Wallis *H* test with suitable examples.
11. Explain Spearman's rank correlation test. How is it superior to Pearson correlation coefficient?
12. Discuss the various nonparametric tests explaining the significance of each such test.
13. Write formulae for nonparametric hypothesis testing.
14. How is the *U* test a substitute for the *t*-test or *Z*-test? Explain.
15. Why is the Mann–Whitney *U* test also called the Wilcoxon–Mann–Whitney *U* test? How is it useful?
16. Under what conditions is the *U* test applicable? Explain with suitable examples.
17. What is *Z*-transformation? How is it different from the *Z*-test?
18. How is the null hypothesis tested in the *U* test?
19. Why is the Kruskal–Wallis *H* test called an ANOVA by ranks? Describe.
20. Under what conditions the Kruskal–Wallis *H* test is suitable and advisable? Explain.
21. Is nonparametric test based on the principle, "No assumption, No restriction?" Discuss.
22. Why is a nonparametric statistics also called distribution-free statistics or assumption-free statistics or order statistics? Explain.
23. For the post of subeditors, the applications of male and female applicants are arranged as given below. Can we accept the arrangement of applications as random?

FMMFMMFFFMFFFMMMMFFFMMMFFFMFMM

24. After a gap of one year with two training programs, the work efficiencies of 100 journalists were rated as given below. Is the difference in the work efficiency of journalists significant?

	Work Efficiency after One Year	
Initial Work Efficiency	**Excellent**	**Not Excellent**
Excellent	30	18
Not Excellent	12	40

25. Before and after treatment of an experiment, the scores of reporters of a daily newspaper were changed as follows:

Before treatment	21	19	14	15	14	16	12	19	16	17
After treatment	25	12	17	14	23	12	15	27	15	14

(a) Find the significance of treatment by the sign test.
(b) Find the significance of treatment by the Wilcoxon method pairs signed rank test.

26. In an experiment, the scores of a control group and two experimental groups are as follows:

Control Group	Experimental Group A	Experimental Group B
27	35	29
24	29	35
22	30	22
17	31	39
19	27	27
23	41	
29		

Compare the groups by using the *H* test.

10

CHAPTER

Chi-square Test in Media Research

> *A game of observed and expected frequencies which can be described as a table to show whether or not a six sided dice will land on the three side once out of every six times it is rolled.*
>
> —yourdictionary.com

Chi-square test, one of the easiest, simplest, and most popular nonparametric tests in media research, has a vital role in statistical analysis and statistical inference. But nonparametric tests in communication and media studies are still not as reliable as parametric tests. If both parametric and nonparametric tests can be applied under any situation, then parametric tests are considered to be more suitable, powerful, and effective.

In the previous chapter, we have already discussed the meaning and concept of non parametric hypothesis testing in mass communication, types of nonparametric tests, advantages of nonparametric tests, limitations of nonparametric tests, summary, and important formulae. Thus, we have discussed the inferential statistical tool of media metrics like nonparametric testing of hypothesis in the previous section. After a thorough discussion of nonparametric tests, it is important to discuss this exclusive type of nonparametric test called the chi-square test.

Thus, yet another inferential statistics (as shown in the flowchart in Section 2.2.1 of Chapter 2) is the chi-square test which is widely used in media research. Hence, this chapter on the chi-square test will focus on the following:

1. Meaning and concept of chi-square test in media research
2. Applications of chi-square test
3. Additive property of chi-square
4. Misuse and precaution of chi-square test
5. Illustration of various applications of the chi-square test

In addition, the chapter will also cover the summary, important formulae, related and suggested websites, references, related and recommended readings, and questions and problems relating to the chi-square test in general and media metrics, communication, and media measurement in particular.

10.1 MEANING AND CONCEPT OF CHI-SQUARE TEST IN MEDIA RESEARCH

Chi-square, which is widely and largely used in media research, is denoted by the Greek letter χ^2, which was first applied by British statistician Karl Pearson in the year 1900. It is given by the following formula:

$$\chi^2 = \Sigma \frac{(f_0 - f_e)^2}{f_e},$$

where f_0 is observed frequencies and f_e is expected frequencies.

This formula is applied by the following steps:

1. First of all, expected frequency is generally calculated by simply averaging all the observed frequencies. In a situation of multiple expected frequencies, the expected frequency is calculated by the following formula:

$$f_e = \frac{\text{RT} \times \text{CT}}{N},$$

   where RT is row total, CT is column total, and N is the total number of observations.
2. Then we will take the difference between observed frequencies (f_0) and expected frequencies (f_e), that is, ($f_0 - f_e$).
3. After that, we will find out $(f_0 - f_e)^2$ and divide each value of $(f_0 - f_e)^2$ by f_e, that is, find out the sum of all the values of $\frac{(f_0 - f_e)^2}{f_e}$.
4. After totaling all the values of $\frac{(f_0 - f_e)^2}{f_e}$, we will get the value of χ^2. In other words, $\chi^2 = \Sigma \frac{(f_0 - f_e)^2}{f_e}$.
5. Then we will compare the calculated value of χ^2 with the table value (or critical value) for the given degrees of freedom and at the desired level of significance.
6. If the calculated value of χ^2 is more than the table value, then the difference between observed frequencies and expected frequencies is significant. Similarly, if the calculated value of χ^2 is less than the table value, then the difference between the observed frequencies and expected frequencies is not significant and it may have arisen due to sampling fluctuations.

10.1.1 Degrees of Freedom

During the comparison between the calculated value and the table value of χ^2, we are supposed to find out the degrees of freedom. Here the degrees of freedom (d_f or v) is calculated by the following formula:

$$d_f = (c-1)\,(r-1),$$

where c is the number of columns and r is the number of rows.

In addition, if we fit a binomial distribution, the number of degrees of freedom is one less than the number of classes. If we fit a Poisson distribution, the degrees of freedom is 2 less than the number of classes, and if we fit a normal curve, the number of degrees of freedom is small by 3 than the number of classes.

The critical or table values of χ^2 are available only up to 30 degrees of freedom. Beyond that, the distribution of $\sqrt{2\chi^2}$ approximates the normal distribution. For d_f beyond 30, the approximation is acceptably close. The mean of the distribution $\sqrt{2\chi^2}$ is $\sqrt{2d_{f-1}}$ and $\sigma=1$. Thus, the application of the test is simple. Deviation $\sqrt{2\chi^2}$ from $\sqrt{2d_{f-1}}$ may be interpreted as a normal deviate with unit standard deviation. Thus, $z=\sqrt{2\chi^2}=\sqrt{2d_{f-1}}$. Here, z is like "t" value for a larger sample.

10.1.2 Constant of χ^2 Distribution

The constants of χ^2 distribution with d_f degrees of freedom are:

1. Mean $=2d_f$, mode $=d_f-2$, variance $=2d_f$.
2. Moments $=\mu_0=0,\ \mu_2=2d_f,\ \mu_3=8d_f$, and $\mu_4=48d_f+12d_f^{\ 2}$.
3. $\beta_1=\dfrac{\mu_3^2}{\mu_2^2}=\dfrac{64df^2}{8df^2}=\dfrac{8}{df}\quad \therefore \gamma_1=\sqrt{8/df}$.
4. $\beta_2=\dfrac{\mu_4}{\mu_2^2}=\dfrac{48df+12df^2}{4df^2}=3+\dfrac{12}{df}$

$$\therefore \gamma_2=\beta_2-3=\frac{12}{df}.$$

10.1.3 Alternative Method of χ^2

When the data are arranged into a 2×2 consistency table as shown below:

A	B	A+B
C	D	C+D
(A+C)	(B+D)	N

then

$$\text{then } \chi^2=\frac{N(AD-BC)^2}{(A+B)(C+D)(A+C)(B+D)}.$$

When in four cells of a 2×2 consistency table, any one of the frequencies is less than 5, then Yate's correction is applied and the value of χ^2 is determined by the following formula:

$$\chi^2=\frac{N(|AD-BC|-N/2)^2}{(A+B)(C+D)(A+C)(B+D)}.$$

χ^2 can also be calculated by the following formula:

$$\chi^2 = \Sigma \frac{f_0^2}{f_e} - N.$$

This formula is helpful if there are fractions in the deviations and the use of earlier direct formula becomes tedious.

10.2 APPLICATIONS OF χ^2 TEST

This test is widely used and is a very popular and prevalent method in mass communication today as it is applicable under a variety of conditions and situations. Since it is an assumption-free nonparametric test, it can be easily applied to several problems of communication and media studies. Most important applications of χ^2 are as follows:

1. Test of independence
2. Test of goodness of fit
3. Test of homogeneity
4. Test of population variance

10.2.1 As a Test of Independence

With the application of χ^2, we can easily test whether two or more attributes, such as the benefits of new media in education and readers' opinions about the same, are independent of each other or they are associated or related. We normally take the null hypothesis that "there is no association (or relation) in attributes" or in other words, "the two attributes are independent." If the calculated value of χ^2 is more than the table value at a particular level of significance, then we say that the difference is significant at that level and the null hypothesis is rejected. That is to say that there is some association (or relation) between the attributes or, in other words, the two attributes are not independent. Similarly, if the calculated value of χ^2 is less than the table value at a particular level of significance, then we say that the difference is not significant at that level and the null hypothesis is accepted. That is to say that there is no association (or relation) between the attributes or in other words the two attributes are independent.

10.2.2 As a Test of Goodness of Fit

It is also known as a test of concordance which enables us to understand how well the assured theoretical distribution fits to the observed data. If some probability distribution (theoretical distribution) is fitted to the given data, we can understand how well this distribution fits with the observed data. When the calculated value of χ^2 is less than the critical value (or tabulated value) at a particular level of significance, the null hypothesis is accepted and the fit is considered to be a good one, which means the difference between the observed and expected frequencies (or hypothesized value) is due to sampling fluctuations. But if the calculated value of χ^2 is greater than its critical value, the fit is not considered to be a good one. Thus, this test also helps in judging whether the distribution is continuous or discrete.

10.2.3 As a Test of Homogeneity

It is basically an extension of the test of independence. Test of homogeneity tries to understand whether two or more independent random samples are drawn from the same universe or from different universes. It is important to mention here that in both tests of independence and tests of homogeneity, we are related to cross-classified data. Hence, both tests are performed similarly. Test of independence is related to the problem of whether one attribute is independent of the other or not. But the test of homogeneity is related to the problem whether different samples come from the same universe. Moreover, the test of independence involves a single sample taken from one universe. But the test of homogeneity involves two or more independent samples, one from each of the probable universe under the study.

10.2.4 As a Test of Population Variance

This type of test is applied to find out whether the variance in the population could be a specified numeric value. This has a vital role in the scientific accuracy of media analysis. Hence, the value of χ^2 can be derived by the following formula:

$$\chi^2 = \frac{NS^2}{\sigma^2} = \frac{\Sigma(X - \overline{X})^2}{\sigma^2},$$

where N is the size of the sample,
S is the standard deviation of the sample, and
σ is the standard deviation of the universe.

Hence, the degree of freedom is taken as $(N-1)$. Thus, by comparing the calculated value and the critical value at about d_f and at a particular level of significance, the null hypothesis may be accepted or rejected.

It is important to mention here that this test is applicable only when the universe is normal.

10.3 ADDITIVE PROPERTY OF χ^2

χ^2 has a unique characteristic of addition which is very useful in the field of communication and media. When a number of sample studies are conducted in the same field of communication and media, then the results can be combined together for achieving an accurate idea about the actual position. It must be noted that during addition of the values of χ^2, two important aspects must be taken care of:

1. The pooled result in a single inclusive test is proper if the samples are independent.
2. If the values of χ^2 are to be combined together, Yate's corrections should be avoided because the addition theorem is applicable only for uncorrelated constituent elements.

10.4 MISUSE OF AND PRECAUTIONS IN χ^2 TEST

This test is the most widely, largely, and frequently used technique. But at the same time, this test is also described as the most widely, largely, and frequently misused procedure in the field of communication and media studies because of underexposure of this statistical device. It is very easy to learn its formula and computation, but very difficult to apply this test in a scientific, reasonable, and judicious manner.

Its most common misuse in mass communication is the violation of independence between measures. This assumption of independence should not be confused and misunderstood as a test of independence. The misuse of the χ^2 test in the field of behavioral communication and media studies has been suitably manifested in the *Journal of Experimental Psychology* as follows:

1. It is often applied even when the frequencies are very small. This is nothing but misuse of this test. Normally, no frequency should be less than 10. If the frequency is less than 5, then either it should be with the adjacent frequency or Yate's corrections should be used.
2. Frequency of nonoccurrence is often neglected. But it should never be omitted.
3. χ^2 is often used even if the original data is not available. This can be described as a misuse. For example, when we have only proportions, percentages, or rates, this test of χ^2 should not be applied.
4. Often the repeated measurements are made on the same units. This should be strictly avoided. For example, if the frequencies are given in percentage, then it does not reflect the size of *N*. If it is mentioned that out of 20 journalists, 8 are taken or out of 100 advertisers, 40 are taken, then the percentage is 40 percent. But this cannot be treated as the size of *N*. Such percentages must be multiplied by $N/100$ for computations.
5. Another misuse of this test is that there are often failures to equalize the sum of observed frequencies and the sum of expected frequencies. This should be taken care of and precautions should be taken to equalize the same.
6. Many a time, the expected values are not calculated on a rational basis.
7. Often the hypothesis is not properly set up. It can destroy the entire calculation and even the final results. So precautions are needed here too.
8. Similarly, the calculations of the degree of freedom are often mistaken. This is a very important and conclusive aspect. So it should not be avoided.
9. Often there are confusions between critical value and calculated value. This is again a serious matter. The calculated value is derived and the table value is available. The table value is also called the tabulated value or the critical value. The table must be seen at a particular level which is generally at 0.05 level or at 0.01 level of significance.
10. Further, the misuse of indeterminate theoretical frequencies, incorrect or questionable categorizing, incorrect calculations, and use of non-frequency data should be avoided.

It is highly surprising that the rate of growth of misuse of the χ^2 test is increasing faster than the rate of growth of its use. Joseph Stegar (cited in Gupta 2011, 1002) in his pioneering work *"Readings in Statistics for the Behavioral Scientist"* and further Lewis and Burke (cited in Gupta 2011, 1002) in their joint research paper have mentioned a strict precaution, "One cannot simply use a statistic because one knows how to calculate it. One must understand the rationale behind its development and its limitations on its applications imposed by its assumptions underlying it." Hence, precautions must be taken carefully and meticulously to avoid the various misuses of χ^2 as discussed above.

10.5 ILLUSTRATION OF VARIOUS APPLICATIONS OF THE χ^2 TEST

In media metrics, all the uses, misuses, precautions, and suitability of the various applications will be further exemplified and simplified by the following problem-solving illustrations.

Example 1: In a classroom of 60 students of mass communication, 40 said "yes" to a proposal, 10 said "no", and 10 remained neutral about the same. Find whether the opinion of the students is significant?

Solution: Let us take the hypothesis that the opinion of the students is not significant. Now, let us put the question into the following table:

	Yes	No	Neutral	Total
f_0	40	10	10	$N=60$
f_e	20	20	10	
f_0-f_e	20	−10	−10	
$(f_0-f_e)^2$	400	100	100	
$(f_0-f_e)^2/f_e$	20	5	5	

$$\therefore \chi^2 = \Sigma\frac{(f_0 - f_e)^2}{f_e} = 20 + 5 + 5 = 30.$$

$$d_f=(r-1)\ (c-1)=(2-1)\ (3-1)=2.$$

The table value of χ^2 with $d_f=2$ at 0.01 level is 9.21 and at 0.05 level is 5.99. Since the calculated value with $d_f=2$ at both the levels is much more than the table value, the difference is very significant. Hence, the null hypothesis is rejected. Thus, the opinion of the students is significant.

Example 2: In a journalism institute, 45 students were asked to express their attitude, in which 25, 12, and 8 students expressed their attitudes as liked, disliked, and neutral, respectively. Is this difference of attitude significant?

Solution: Let us take the hypothesis that the difference of attitude of students is not significant. Now, putting the questions in the following table:

	Liked	Disliked	Neutral	Total
f_0	25	12	8	$N=45$
f_e	15	15	15	
f_0-f_e	10	-3	-7	
$(f_0-f_e)^2$	100	9	49	
$(f_0-f_e)^2/f_e$	6.67	0.60	3.26	

$$\therefore \chi^2 = \Sigma\frac{(f_0 - f_e)^2}{f_e} = 6.67 + 0.60 + 3.26 = 10.52.$$

$$d_f=(r-1)\ (c-1)=(2-1)\ (3-1)=2.$$

The table value of χ^2 with d_f=2 at 0.01 level is 9.21 and at 0.05 level is 5.99. Since the calculated value with d_f=2 at both the levels is much more than the table value, the difference is significant. Hence, the null hypothesis is rejected. Thus, the difference of attitudes of students is significant.

Example 3: In a media school, 90 students were asked to give their preference for specialization, in which electronic media, print media, and advertising preferences were given by 28, 35, and 27 students, respectively. Is this difference of preference significant?

Solution: Let us take the hypothesis that there is no significant difference of preference of specialization among the students. Now, let us put the question into the following table:

	Electronic Media	Print Media	Advertising	Total
f_0	28	35	27	N=90
f_e	30	30	30	
f_0-f_e	−2	5	-3	
$(f_0-f_e)^2$	4	25	9	
$(f_0-f_e)^2/f_e$	0.133	0.833	0.30	

$$\therefore \chi^2 = \Sigma \frac{(f_0 - f_e)^2}{f_e} = 0.133 + 0.833 + 0.30 = 1.266$$

$$d_f = (r-1)\ (c-1) = (2-1)\ (3-1) = 2.$$

The table value of χ^2 with d_f=2 at 0.01 level and 0.05 level is 9.21 and 5.99, respectively. Since the calculated value is less than the table value with d_f=2 at both the levels, the difference is not significant. Hence the null hypothesis is accepted. Thus, the difference of preference of specialization among students is not significant.

Example 4: In a media center, 180 media persons were asked to express their attitude toward national service scheme, in which 54 media persons liked it, 70 disliked it, while 56 remained neutral. Is this difference of attitude significant?

Solution: Let us take the hypothesis that the difference of attitude of media persons is not significant. Now putting the problem in a tabular form:

	Liked	Disliked	Neutral	Total
f_0	54	70	56	N=180
f_e	60	60	30	
f_0-f_e	−6	10	−4	
$(f_0-f_e)^2$	36	100	16	
$(f_0-f_e)^2/f_e$	0.6	1.66	0.27	

$$\therefore \chi^2 = \Sigma \frac{(f_0 - f_e)^2}{f_e} = 0.6 + 1.66 + 0.27 = 2.53$$

$$d_f = (r-1)\ (c-1) = (2-1)\ (3-1) = 2.$$

The table value of χ^2 with d_f=2 at 0.01 level is 9.21 and at 0.05 level is 5.99. Since the calculated value at both the levels is less than the table value, the difference is not significant. Hence, the null hypothesis is accepted. Thus, the difference of attitude is not significant.

Example 5: On 50 viewers of television advertisement, the color preference was experimented in which 14 viewers preferred red, 8 preferred blue, 12 preferred yellow, 9 preferred green, and 7 preferred orange. Find whether this difference of color preference is significant?

Solution: Let us take the hypothesis that there is no difference of color preference among viewers. Now, putting the problem in a tabular form:

	Red	Blue	Yellow	Green	Orange	Total
f_0	14	8	12	9	7	N=50
f_e	10	10	10	10	10	
f_0-f_e	4	-2	2	-1	-3	
$(f_0-f_e)^2$	16	4	4	1	9	
$(f_0-f_e)^2/f_e$	1.6	0.4	0.4	0.1	0.9	

$$\therefore \chi^2 = \Sigma \frac{(f_0 - f_e)^2}{f_e} = 1.6 + 0.4 + 0.4 + 0.1 + 0.9 = 3.4$$

$$d_f = (r-1)\ (c-1) = (2-1)\ (5-1) = 4.$$

At d_f=4, the table value of χ^2 at 0.05 level is 9.48 and at 0.01 level is 13.27. Since the calculated value of χ^2 is less than the table value at both the levels, the difference is not significant. Hence, the null hypothesis is accepted. Thus, there is no difference of color preference among viewers of television advertisements.

Example 6: Whether new media is helpful in education or not? 100 users of new media were asked to give their views in which 24 strongly agreed, 17 agreed, 18 remained neutral, 23 disagreed, and 18 strongly disagreed. Is this difference of views significant?

Solution: Let us take the hypothesis that there is no significant difference of views of users of new media. Now, converting the problem into a table:

	Strongly Agreed	Agreed	Neutral	Disagreed	Strongly Disagreed	Total
f_0	24	17	18	23	18	N=100
f_e	20	20	20	20	20	
f_0-f_e	4	-3	-2	3	-2	
$(f_0-f_e)^2$	16	9	4	9	4	
$(f_0-f_e)^2/f_e$	0.8	0.45	0.2	0.45	0.2	

$$\therefore \chi^2 = \Sigma \frac{(f_0 - f_e)^2}{f_e} = 0.8 + 0.45 + 0.2 + 0.45 + 0.2 = 2.10$$

$$d_f = (r-1)\ (c-1) = (2-1)\ (5-1) = 4.$$

At $d_f = 4$, the table value of χ^2 at 0.05 level is 9.48 and at 0.01 is 13.27. Since the calculated value of χ^2 at both the levels is less than the table value, the difference is not significant. Hence, the null hypothesis is accepted. Thus, there is no significant difference among users of new media as far as education is concerned.

Example 7: When the opinions of 100 students of mass communication about a political party were collected, 30 students strongly supported, 25 supported, 10 remained neutral, 17 opposed, and 18 strongly opposed. Find whether the difference of opinion is significant?

Solution: Let us take the hypothesis that the difference of opinion of students is not significant. Now putting the question in a tabular form:

	Strongly Supported	Supported	Neutral	Opposed	Strongly Opposed	Total
f_0	30	25	10	17	18	$N=100$
f_e	20	20	20	20	20	
f_0-f_e	10	5	−10	−3	−2	
$(f_0-f_e)^2$	100	25	100	9	4	
$(f_0-f_e)^2/f_e$	5	1.25	5	0.45	0.2	

$$\therefore \chi^2 = \Sigma \frac{(f_0 - f_e)^2}{f_e} 5 + 1.25 + 5 + 0.45 + 0.2 = 11.90$$

$$d_f = (r-1)\ (c-1) = (2-1)\ (5-1) = 4.$$

At $d_f = 4$, the table value of χ^2 at 0.05 level and 0.01 level is 9.48 and 13.27, respectively. The calculated value of χ^2 at 0.05 level is more than the table value and at 0.01 level is less than the table value, so the difference is significant at 0.05 level and not significant at 0.01 level. Hence, the null hypothesis is rejected at 0.05 level and is accepted at 0.01 level. Thus, the difference of opinion of students at 0.05 level is significant and at 0.01 level is not significant.

Example 8: The number of attacks on journalists per month in a certain town was as follows: 12, 8, 20, 2, 14, 10, 15, 6, 9, 4. Use the chi-square test to determine if these frequencies are in agreement with the belief that attacks on journalist in that town were the same during the 10-month period.

Solution: Let us take the hypothesis that attacks on journalists were the same during the period we should expect:

$$= \frac{12 + 8 + 20 + 2 + 14 + 10 + 15 + 6 + 9 + 4}{10}$$

=10 attacks per month.

Applying the χ^2 test

f_0	12	8	20	2	14	10	15	6	9	4
f_e	10	10	10	10	10	10	10	10	10	10
f_0-f_e	2	-2	10	-8	4	0	5	-4	-1	-6
$(f_0-f_e)^2$	4	4	100	64	16	0	25	16	1	36
$(f_0-f_e)^2/f_e$	0.40	0.40	10	6.4	1.6	0	2.5	1.6	0.1	3.6

$$\chi^2 = \Sigma\frac{(f_0 - f_e)^2}{f_e} = 26.60$$

$$d_f = (n-1) = (10-1) = 9$$

$$\text{At } d_f = 9 \ \chi^2_{0.05} = 16.92.$$

Since the calculated value of χ^2 is more than the table value, the difference is significant. Hence, the null hypothesis is rejected. Thus, the frequencies are not in agreement with the belief that the number of attacks was the same as during the last 10-months period.

Example 9: From a sample of 50 female journalists, 60 percent females were highly educated, whereas 40 percent were moderately educated. Compare the distribution of females from the point of view of equal distribution.

Solution: Let us take the hypothesis that there is no significant difference between observed frequencies and expected frequencies of highly educated and moderately educated female journalists in the sample. Now, let us convert the question into a table:

	Highly Educated	Moderately Educated
f_0	60%	40%
f_e	50%	50%
f_0-f_e	10%	10%
$(f_0-f_e)^2$	100	100
$(f_0-f_e)^2/f_e$	2	2

$$\chi^2 = \Sigma\frac{(f_0 - f_e)^2}{f_e} = 2 + 2 = 4$$

Now, we are supposed to multiply the percentage value of χ^2 by $N/100$ to convert it into numeric value.

Hence,

$$\chi^2 = 4 \times \frac{N}{100} = 4 \times \frac{50}{100} = 2$$

$$d_f = (r-1)\ (c-1) = (2-1)\ (2-1) = 1.$$

At $d_f = 1$, the table value of χ^2 at 0.05 level is 3.84 and at 0.01 level is 6.63. Since the calculated value of χ^2 is less than the table value at both the levels, the difference is insignificant. Hence, the null hypothesis is accepted. Thus, there is no significant difference between the observed frequencies of highly educated and moderately educated female journalists in the sample. That means there is an equal distribution of highly educated and moderately educated female journalists in the sample.

Example 10: In an issue, out of 50 Hindus, 10 said "yes," 25 said "no," and 15 remained "undecided," while out of 45 Muslims, 20 said "yes," 20 said "no," and 5 remained "undecided" and out of 55 Christians, 30 said "yes," 15 said "no," and 10 remained "undecided." Find out whether the difference of opinion among Hindus, Muslims, and Christians is significant?

Solution: Let us take the hypothesis that there is no significant difference of opinion among the Hindus, Muslims, and Christians regarding the issue. Now, converting the problem into a tabular form:

Religion	Yes	No	Undecided	Total
Hindu	$f_{o_1} = 10$	$f_{o_2} = 25$	$f_{o_3} = 15$	$N_1 = 50$
	$f_{e_1} = 20$	$f_{e_2} = 20$	$f_{e_3} = 10$	
Muslim	$f_{o_4} = 20$	$f_{o_5} = 20$	$f_{o_6} = 5$	$N_2 = 45$
	$f_{e_4} = 18$	$f_{e_5} = 18$	$f_{e_6} = 9$	
Christian	$f_{o_7} = 30$	$f_{o_8} = 15$	$f_{o_9} = 10$	$N_3 = 55$
	$f_{e_7} = 22$	$f_{e_8} = 22$	$f_{e_9} = 11$	
Total	60	60	30	$N = N_1 + N_2 + N_3 = 50 + 45 + 55 = 150$

Calculation of $fe = \dfrac{RT \times CL}{N}$

$$\therefore \quad fe_1 = \frac{60 \times 50}{150} = 20$$

$$fe_2 = \frac{60 \times 50}{150} = 20$$

$$fe_3 = \frac{30 \times 50}{150} = 10$$

$$fe_4 = \frac{60 \times 45}{150} = 18$$

$$fe_5 = \frac{60 \times 45}{150} = 18$$

$$fe_6 = \frac{30 \times 45}{150} = 9$$

$$fe_7 = \frac{60 \times 55}{150} = 22$$

$$fe_8 = \frac{60 \times 55}{150} = 22$$

$$fe_9 = \frac{30 \times 55}{150} = 11.$$

Now calculation of χ^2:

f_0	10	25	15	20	20	5	30	15	10
f_e	20	20	10	18	18	9	22	22	11
f_0-f_e	−10	5	5	2	2	−4	8	7	-1
$(f_0-f_e)^2$	100	25	25	4	4	16	64	49	1
$(f_0-f_e)^2/f_e$	5	1.25	2.5	0.22	0.22	1.77	2.91	2.33	0.03

$$\chi^2 = \Sigma\frac{(f_0 - f_e)^2}{f_e} = 5 + 1.25 + 2.5 + 0.22 + 0.22 + 1.77 + 2.91 + 2.33 = 16.23$$

$$d_f = (r-1)\ (c-1) = (3-1)\ (3-1) = 4.$$

At $d_f=4$, the table value of χ^2 at 0.05 level and 0.01 level is 9.48 and 13.27, respectively. The calculated value of χ^2 at both the levels is more than the table value. So the difference is significant at both the levels. Hence, the null hypothesis is rejected. Thus, there is a significant difference of opinion among Hindus, Muslims, and Christians regarding the issue.

Example 11: An innovative training was imparted to 250 working journalists suffering from the habit of yellow journalism. From the data given below, state whether innovative training is superior to conventional training?

	Number of Working Journalists		
Training	**Favorable**	**Not Favorable**	**Total**
Innovative	140	30	170
Conventional	60	20	80
Total	200	50	250

Solution: Let us take the hypothesis that there is no significant difference between innovative training and conventional training. Applying the formula for calculating f_e:

$$fe = \frac{RT \times CT}{N}$$

$$\therefore \quad fe_1 = \frac{200 \times 170}{250} = 136$$

$$fe_2 = \frac{50 \times 170}{250} = 34$$

$$fe_3 = \frac{200 \times 80}{250} = 64$$

$$fe_4 = \frac{50 \times 80}{250} = 16.$$

Now, calculation of χ^2:

f_0	140	30	60	20
f_e	136	34	34	16
$f_0 - f_e$	4	4	4	4
$(f_0 - f_e)^2$	16	16	16	16
$(f_0 - f_e)^2/f_e$	0.118	0.250	0.471	1

$$\chi^2 = \Sigma \frac{(f_0 - f_e)^2}{f_e} = 0.118 + 0.250 + 0.47 + 1 = 1.839$$

$$d_f = (r-1)\ (c-1) = (2-1)\ (2-1) = 1 \times 1 = 1.$$

At $d_f = 1$, the table value of χ^2 at 0.05 level is 3.84. Since the calculated value is less than the table value, the difference is insignificant. Hence, the null hypothesis is accepted. Thus, there is no significant difference between innovative training and conventional training.

Example 12: A certain spiritual feature writing is claimed to be effective in eliminating the negative attitude. In an experiment on 500 readers with negative attitude, half of them were asked to read the spiritual feature and half of them were asked to read the spiritual news. The readers' reactions after such treatment are recorded in the following table:

	Helped	**Harmed**	**No Effect**	**Total**
Spiritual feature	150	30	70	250
Spiritual news	130	40	80	250
Total	280	70	150	500

On the basis of the data, can it be concluded that there is a significant difference in the effect of the spiritual feature and spiritual news?

Solution: Let us take the null hypothesis that there is no significant difference in the effect of spiritual feature and spiritual news. Applying the formula for calculating f_e:

$$fe = \frac{RT \times CT}{N}$$

$$\therefore \quad fe_1 = \frac{280 \times 250}{500} = 140$$

$$fe_2 = \frac{70 \times 250}{500} = 35$$

$$fe_3 = \frac{150 \times 250}{500} = 75$$

$$fe_4 = \frac{280 \times 250}{500} = 140$$

$$fe_5 = \frac{70 \times 250}{500} = 35$$

$$fe_6 = \frac{150 \times 250}{500} = 75.$$

Now calculating χ^2,

f_0	150	30	70	130	40	80
f_e	140	35	75	140	35	75
f_0-f_e	10	5	5	10	5	5
$(f_0-f_e)^2$	100	25	25	100	25	25
$(f_0-f_e)^2/f_e$	0.714	0.714	0.333	0.714	0.714	0.333

$$\chi^2 = \Sigma \frac{(f_0 - f_e)^2}{f_e} = 0.714 + 0.714 + 0.333 + 0.714 + 0.714 + 0.333 = 3.522$$

$$d_f = (r-1)\ (c-1) = (2-1)\ (3-1) = 2.$$

At d_f=2, the table value of χ^2 at 0.05 level is 5.99. Since the calculated value is less than the table value, the difference is not significant. Hence, the null hypothesis is accepted. Thus, there is no significant difference between the effects of spiritual feature and spiritual news.

Example 13: A film producer is bringing out a new film. In order to map out his advertising campaign, he wants to determine whether the film will appeal most to particular age group or whether it will appeal equally to all the of groups. The producer takes a random sample from persons attending preview of the new film and gets the following data:

	Age Groups				
	Under 20	**20–39**	**40–59**	**60 and Above**	**Total**
Liked	146	78	48	28	300
Disliked	54	22	42	22	140
Neutral	20	10	10	20	60
Total	220	110	100	70	500

What inference will you draw from this results?

Solution: Let us take the hypothesis that the film equally appeals to all age groups. Applying the formula for calculating f_e:

$$fe = \frac{RT \times CT}{N}$$

$$\therefore \quad fe_1 = \frac{220 \times 300}{500} = 132$$

$$fe_2 = \frac{110 \times 300}{500} = 66$$

$$fe_3 = \frac{100 \times 300}{500} = 60$$

$$fe_4 = \frac{70 \times 300}{500} = 42$$

$$fe_5 = \frac{220 \times 140}{500} = 61.6$$

$$fe_6 = \frac{110 \times 140}{500} = 30.8$$

$$fe_7 = \frac{100 \times 140}{500} = 28$$

$$fe_8 = \frac{70 \times 140}{500} = 19.6$$

$$fe_9 = \frac{220 \times 60}{500} = 26.4$$

$$fe_{10} = \frac{110 \times 60}{500} = 13.2$$

$$fe_{11} = \frac{100 \times 60}{500} = 12$$

$$fe_{12} = \frac{70 \times 60}{500} = 8.4.$$

Now, calculating the value of χ^2:

f_0	146	78	48	28	54	22	42	22	20	10	10	20
f_e	132	66	60	42	61.6	30.8	28	19.6	26.4	13.2	12	8.4
f_0-f_e	14	12	−12	−14	−7.6	−8.8	14	2.4	−6.4	−3.2	−2	11.6
$(f_0-f_e)^2$	196	144	144	196	57.76	77.44	196	5.76	40.96	10.24	4	134.56
$(f_0-f_e)^2/f_e$	1.485	2.182	2.4	4.6	0.93	2.51	7	0.29	1.55	0.77	2	16.01

$$\chi^2 = \Sigma \frac{(f_0 - f_e)^2}{f_e} = 1.485 + 2.182 + 2.4 + 4.6 + 0.93 + 2.51 + 7 + 0.29 + 1.55 + 0.77 + 2 + 16.01 = 40.16$$

$$d_f = (r-1)(c-1) = (3-1)(4-1) = 6.$$

For $d_f = 6$, $\chi^2_{0.05} = 12.59$.

Since the calculated value is more than the table value at 0.05 level, the difference is significant. Hence, the null hypothesis is rejected. Thus, the film does not equally appeal to all age groups.

Example 14: An ad agency gives us the following information about age groups and the liking for a particular model of a car, which it plans to advertise:

	Age Groups				
	Below 20	**20–39**	**40–59**	**60 and Above**	**Total**
Liked	140	80	40	20	280
Disliked	60	50	30	80	220
Total	200	130	70	100	500

On the basis of this data, can it be concluded that the model appeal is independent of the age group?

Solution: Let us take the hypothesis that the model appeal is independent of the age group. Applying the formula for calculating f_e:

$$fe = \frac{RT \times CT}{N}$$

$$fe_1 = \frac{200 \times 280}{500} = 112$$

$$fe_2 = \frac{130 \times 280}{500} = 72.8$$

$$fe_3 = \frac{70 \times 280}{500} = 39.2$$

$$fe_4 = \frac{100 \times 280}{500} = 56$$

$$fe_5 = \frac{200 \times 220}{500} = 88$$

$$fe_6 = \frac{130 \times 220}{500} = 57.2$$

$$fe_7 = \frac{70 \times 220}{500} = 30.8$$

$$fe_8 = \frac{100 \times 220}{500} = 44$$

Now, calculating the value of χ^2:

f_0	140	80	40	20	60	50	30	80
f_e	112	72.8	39.2	56	88	57.2	30.8	44
$f_0 - f_e$	28	7.2	0.8	–36	–28	-7.2	–0.8	36
$(f_0 - f_e)^2$	784	51.84	0.64	1296	784	51.84	0.64	1296
$(f_0 - f_e)^2/f_e$	7	0.712	0.016	23.143	8.910	0.906	0.021	29.454

$$\chi^2 = \Sigma\frac{(f_0 - f_e)^2}{f_e} = 7 + 0.712 + 0.016 + 23.143 + 8.910 + 0.906 + 0.021 + 29.454 = 70162$$

$$d_f = (r-1)\ (c-1) = (2-1)(4-1) = 3.$$

For $d_f = 3$, $\chi^2_{0.05} = 7.815$.

Since the calculated value is much more than the table value, the difference is significant. Hence, the null hypothesis is rejected. Thus, the model appeal is not independent of the age group.

Example 15: The following results were obtained when two sets of media persons were subjected to two different trainings X and Y, to enhance their writing skills. Training X was imparted to 400 media persons and 80 were found to have improved their writing skills. Training Y was imparted to 400 media persons and 20 were found to have improved their writing skills. Is the training Y superior to training X?

Solution: Let us take the null hypothesis that there is no significant difference in the two types of trainings X and Y. The given results can be put into a table in the following manner:

Training	Improved	Not Improved	Total
X	80	320	400
Y	20	380	400
Total	100	700	800

Calculating the value of f_e:

$$fe = \frac{RT \times CT}{N}$$

$$\therefore \quad fe_1 = \frac{400 \times 100}{800} = 50$$

$$fe_2 = 400 - 50 = 350$$

$$fe_2 = 400 - 50 = 350$$

$$fe_4 = 700 - 350 = 350.$$

Now, calculating the value of χ^2:

f_0	80	320	20	380
f_e	50	350	50	350
$f_0 - f_e$	30	30	30	30
$(f_0 - f_e)^2$	900	900	900	900
$(f_0 - f_e)^2/f_e$	18	2.571	18	2.571

$$\chi^2 = \Sigma \frac{(f_0 - f_e)^2}{f_e} = 18 + 2.571 + 18 + 2.571 = 41.142$$

$$d_f = (r-1)\ (c-1) = (2-1)(2-1) = 1.$$

At $d_f = 1 \therefore \chi^2_{0.05} = 3.84$.

Since the calculated value of χ^2 is much higher than the table value, the difference is significant. Hence, the null hypothesis is rejected. Thus, there is significant difference between the two types of trainings X and Y.

Example 16: Three samples were taken consisting of 120 reporters, 150 subeditors and 130 advertisers. Each person chosen is asked to select one of the three categories that best represents his feeling toward a certain national policy. The three categories are in favor of policy (A), against it (B), and indifferent toward it (C). The results of the interview are given below:

Occupation	A	B	C	Total
Reporters	80	30	10	120
Subeditors	70	40	40	150
Advertisers	50	50	30	130
Total	200	120	80	400

On the basis of this data, can it be concluded that the views of reporters, subeditors, and advertisers are homogenous as far as the national policy under discussion is concerned?

Solution: Let us take the hypothesis that the three classifications are homogenous as far as the opinions of three different groups of people about the national policy under consideration are concerned.

Calculating the value of f_e:

$$fe = \frac{RT \times CT}{N}$$

$$\therefore \quad fe_1 = \frac{200 \times 120}{400} = 60$$

$$fe_2 = \frac{120 \times 120}{400} = 36$$

$$fe_3 = 120 - (60 + 36) = 24$$

$$fe_4 = \frac{200 \times 150}{400} = 75$$

$$fe_5 = \frac{120 \times 150}{400} = 45$$

$$fe_6 = 150 - (75 + 45) = 30$$

$$fe_7 = 200 - (60 + 75) = 65$$

$$fe_8 = 120 - (36 + 45) = 39$$

$$fe_9 = 80 - (24 + 30) = 26$$

f_0	80	30	10	70	40	40	50	50	30
f_e	60	36	24	75	45	30	65	39	26
f_0-f_e	20	−6	−14	−5	−5	10	−15	11	4
$(f_0-f_e)^2$	400	36	196	25	25	100	225	121	16
$(f_0-f_e)^2/f_e$	6.667	1	8.167	0.3333	0.556	0.333	3.462	3.103	0.615

$$\chi^2 = \Sigma \frac{(f_0 - f_e)^2}{f_e} = 6.667 + 1 + 8.167 + 0.333 + 0.556 + 0.333 + 3.462 + 3.103 + 0.615 = 27.236$$

$$d_f = (r-1)\,(c-1) = (3-1)(3-1) = 2 \times 2 = 4.$$

For $d_f = 4$, $\chi^2_{0.05} = 9.488$.

Since the calculated value is much more than the table value, the difference is significant. Hence, the null hypothesis is rejected. Thus, the three classifications are not homogenous as far as the opinions of three different groups of people (reporters, subeditors and advertisers) about the national policy under consideration are concerned.

Example 17: From the following data of advertisers, find out whether there is any relationship between gender and preference of color:

Color	Males	Females	Total
Red	10	40	50
White	70	30	100
Green	30	20	50
Total	110	90	200

Solution: Let us take the hypothesis that there is no relationship between gender and preference of color. Now, calculating the value of f_e:

$$fe = \frac{RT \times CT}{N}$$

$$\therefore \quad fe_1 = \frac{110 \times 50}{200} = 27.5$$

$$fe_2 = 50 - 27.5 = 22.5$$

$$fe_3 = \frac{110 \times 100}{200} = 55$$

$$\therefore \quad fe_4 = 100 - 55 = 45$$

$$fe_5 = 110 - (fe_1 + fe_3)$$

$$= 110 - (27.5 + 55)$$

$$= 27.5$$

$$fe_6 = 50 - 27.5 = 22.5.$$

f_0	10	40	70	30	30	20
f_e	27.5	22.5	55	45	27.5	22.5
$f_0 - f_e$	–17.5	17.5	15	–15	2.5	–2.5
$(f_0 - f_e)^2$	306.25	306.25	225	225	6.25	6.25
$(f_0 - f_e)^2/f_e$	11.14	13.61	4.09	5	0.23	0.28

$$\chi^2 = \Sigma \frac{(f_0 - f_e)^2}{f_e} = 11.14 + 13.61 + 4.09 + 5 + 0.23 + 0.28 = 34.35$$

$$d_f = (r-1)\ (c-1) = (3-1)(2-1) = 2.$$

At $d_f = 2$, $\chi^2_{0.05} = 5.99$.

Since the calculated value is much more than the table value, the difference is significant. Hence, the hypothesis is rejected. Thus, there is relationship between gender and preference of color.

Example 18: A manufacturer of TV sets was trying to find out what variable influenced the purchase of a TV set. Level of income was suggested as a possible variable influencing the purchases of TV sets. A sample of 500 households was selected and the information obtained was classified as shown below:

	Have TV Set	Don't Have TV Set
Low income group	0	250
Middle income group	50	100
High income group	130	370

Is there evidence from the above data of a relation between ownership of TV sets and level of income?

Solution: Let us take the hypothesis that ownership of TV sets is independent of the level of income. Now, calculating the f_e:

$$fe = \frac{RT \times CT}{N}$$

$$\therefore \quad fe_1 = \frac{130 \times 250}{500} = 65$$

$$fe_2 = 250 - 65 = 185$$

$$fe_3 = \frac{130 \times 150}{500} = 39$$

$$fe_4 = 150 - 39 = 111$$

$$\therefore \quad fe_5 = 130 - (65 + 39) = 26$$

$$fe_6 = 370 - (111 + 185) = 74$$

f_0	0	250	50	100	80	20
f_e	65	185	39	111	26	74
$(f_0 - f_e)$	-65	65	11	-11	54	-54
$(f_0 - f_e)^2$	4225	4225	121	121	2916	2916
$(f_0 - f_e)^2/f_e$	65	22.838	3.103	1.090	112.154	39.405

$$\chi^2 = \Sigma\frac{(f_0 - f_e)^2}{f_e} = 65 + 22.838 + 3.103 + 1.090 + 112.154 + 39.405 = 243.59$$

$$d_f = (r-1)\ (c-1) = (2-1)(3-1) = 2.$$

At $d_f = 2$, $\chi^2_{0.05} = 7.82$.

Since the calculated value of χ^2 is much more than the table value, the difference is significant. Hence, the hypothesis is rejected. Thus, ownership of TV sets is not independent of income.

Example 19: A survey among women journalists was conducted to study the family life. The data is given below:

Family Life	Happy	Not Happy	Total
Highly educated	70	30	100
Moderately educated	60	40	100
Total	130	70	200

Test whether there is any association between family life and level of education.

Solution: Let us take the hypothesis that there is no association between family life and level of education. Now, calculating f_e:

$$fe = \frac{RT \times CT}{N}$$

$$\therefore\ \ fe_1 = \frac{130 \times 100}{200} = 65$$

$$\therefore\ \ fe_2 = 100 - 65 = 35$$

$$fe_3 = \frac{130 \times 100}{200} = 65$$

$$fe_4 = 100 - 65 = 35.$$

f_0	70	30	60	40
f_e	65	35	65	35
(f_0-f_e)	5	−5	−5	5
$(f_0-f_e)^2$	25	25	25	25
$(f_0-f_e)^2/f_e$	0.385	0.714	0.385	0.714

$$\chi^2 = \Sigma\frac{(f_0 - f_e)^2}{f_e} = 0.385 + 0.714 + 0.385 + 0.714 = 2.198$$

$$d_f = (r-1)\ (c-1) = (2-1)(2-1) = 1.$$

At $d_f = 1$, $\chi^2_{0.05} = 3.84$.

Since the calculated value of χ^2 is less than the table value, the difference is not significant. Hence, the null hypothesis is accepted. Thus, there is no association between family life and level of education.

Example 20: A controlled experiment to test the effectiveness of a communication model was conducted. Under this experiment, 300 media students were treated with this new communication model and 200 were not treated with this model. The results of the experiment are given below:

Details	Favorably Effected	Unfavorably Effected	No Effect	Total
Treated with new communication model	200	40	60	300
Not treated with the new communication model	120	30	50	200
Total	320	70	110	500

Use χ^2 and comment on the effectiveness of the new communication model.

Solution: Let us assume that there is no effectiveness of the new communication model on media students. Now, calculating the value of f_e:

$$fe = \frac{RT \times CT}{N}$$

$$\therefore \quad fe_1 = \frac{320 \times 300}{500} = 192$$

$$fe_2 = \frac{70 \times 300}{500} = 42$$

$$\therefore \quad fe_3 = 300 - (192 + 42) = 66$$

$$fe_4 = 320 - 192 = 128$$

$$fe_5 = 70 - 42 = 28$$

$$fe_6 = 110 - 66 = 44.$$

Now,

f_0	200	40	60	120	30	50
f_e	192	42	66	128	28	44
f_0-f_e	8	-2	-6	-8	2	6
$(f_0-f_e)^2$	64	4	36	64	4	36
$(f_0-f_e)^2/f_e$	0.333	0.095	0.545	0.5	0.143	0.818

$$\chi^2 = \Sigma \frac{(f_0 - f_e)^2}{f_e} = 0.333 + 0.095 + 0.545 + 0.5 + 0.143 + 0.818 = 2.434$$

$$d_f = (n-1)\ (c-1) = (2-1)\ (3-1) = 2.$$

For $d_f = 2$, $\chi^2_{0.05} = 5.49$.

Since the calculated value of χ^2 is less than the table value, the difference is not significant. Hence, the null hypothesis is accepted. Thus, there is no significant difference between the media students treated with the new communication model and those not treated with the same.

Example 21: Out of 150 students, 56 out of 80 girls described a decision as right and 24 as wrong, while 34 out of 70 boys described it as right and 36 as wrong. Find out whether there is a significant difference between the decisions of right and wrong.

Solution: Let us take the hypothesis that there is no significant difference between the decisions of right and wrong. Now let us put the problem into a tabular form:

	Right	**Wrong**	
Girls	(A)	(B)	$A+B$
	56	24	80
Boys	(C)	(D)	$C+D$
	34	36	70
	$A+C=90$	$B+D=60$	$N=150$

Since the data are in a 2×2 consistency table,

$$\chi^2 = \frac{N(AD - BC)^2}{(A+B)(C+D)(A+C)(B+D)}$$

$$= \frac{150(56\times 36 - 24\times 34)^2}{80\times 70\times 90\times 60}$$

$$= \frac{150(2016 - 816)^2}{30240000}$$

$$= \frac{150(1200)^2}{30240000}$$

$$= \frac{150\times 1440000}{30240000}$$

$$= \frac{150\times 144}{3024} = 7.14$$

$$\therefore \quad \chi^2 = 7.14$$

$$d_f = (r-1)\ (c-1) = (2-1)\ (2-1) = 1.$$

The table value of χ^2 with $d_f = 1$ at 0.05 level is 3.84 and at 0.01 level is 6.63. Since the calculated value of χ^2 is more than the table value at both the levels, the difference is significant. Hence, the null hypothesis is rejected. Thus, there is a significant difference between the decisions of right and wrong.

Example 22: 30 students (18 from public schools and 12 from government schools) participated in a debate on the topic, "Media is creating more tension than awareness." Some of them spoke in favor while some spoke against the motion. The data are as follows:

	Favor	Against	Total
Public Schools	12	6	18
Govt. Schools	2	10	12

Find whether the difference between favor and against is significant?

Solution: Let us take the hypothesis that there is no significant difference between favor and against.

In a 2×2 contingency table, if any one of the frequencies is less than 5, then Yate's correction is applied and the value of χ^2 is determined by the following formula:

$$\chi^2 = \frac{N\left(|AD - BC| - \frac{N}{2}\right)^2}{(A+B)(C+D)(A+C)(B+D)}.$$

Now, converting the question into a tabular form:

	Favor	Against	
Public Schools	12 (*A*)	6 (*B*)	$A+B=18$
Govt. Schools	2 (*C*)	10 (*D*)	$C+D=12$
	$A+C=14$	$B+D=16$	$N=30$

$$= \frac{N\left(|AD - BC| - \frac{N}{2}\right)^2}{(A+B)(C+D)(A+C)(B+D)}$$

$$= \frac{30\left(|12\times 10 - 6\times 2| - \frac{30}{2}\right)^2}{18\times 12\times 14\times 16} = \frac{30\times 93\times 93}{18\times 12\times 14\times 16}$$

$$= 5.36$$

$$d_f = (r-1)\ (c-1) = (2-1)\ (2-1) = 1\times 1 = 1.$$

At $d_f = 1$, the table value of χ^2 at 0.05 level is 3.84 and at 0.01 level is 6.63. Since the calculated value of χ^2 is more than the table value at 0.05 level and is less than the table value at 0.01 level, the difference at 0.05 level is significant and the same at 0.01 level is not significant. Hence, the null hypothesis is rejected at 0.05 level and is accepted at 0.01 level. Thus, there is a significant difference between favor and against at 0.05 level, while there is no significant difference between the two at 0.01 level.

Example 23: The number of mistakes per newspaper in a sample of 330 newspapers was found as follows:

No. of Mistakes	0	1	2	3	4
No. of Newspapers	214	92	20	3	1

Fit a Poisson distribution to the data and test for goodness of fit.

Solution: Let us take the hypothesis that there is no significant difference between observed frequencies and expected frequencies by fitting Poisson distribution.

The expected frequencies can be calculated by the following formula of theoretical distribution as $f_{e1}=212.75$, $f_{e2}=93.4$, $f_{e3}=20.5$, $f_{e4}=3$, $f_{e5}=0.35$.

Now, calculating χ^2,

f_0	214	92	20	3	1
f_e	212.75	93.4	20.5	3	0.35
f_0-f_e	1.25	–1.4	–0.5	0	–0.65
$(f_0-f_e)^2$	1.56	1.96	0.0625	0	0.4225
$(f_0-f_e)^2/f_e$	0.0073	0.0210	0.0031	0	1.20

$$\chi^2 = \Sigma\frac{(f_0 - f_e)^2}{f_e} = 1.2314$$

$$d_f = 3 - 2 = 1 \quad \therefore \chi^2_{0.05} = 3.84.$$

Since the calculated value of χ^2 is less than the table value, the difference is significant. Hence, the null hypothesis in accepted. Thus, the fit is good.

SUMMARY

Though parametric tests are more reliable, suitable, powerful, and effective than the non-parametric tests, yet the chi-square test is considered to be the most popular and widely used nonparametric tests for statistical analysis and statistical inference. Applied by the British Statistician Karl Pearson in 1990 and denoted by the Greek letter χ^2, chi-square is given by the following formula:

$$\chi^2 = \Sigma\frac{(f_0 - f_e)^2}{f_e}.$$

In a situation of multiple expected frequencies, the expected frequency is calculated by the following formula: $fe = \frac{RT \times CT}{N}$.

The degree of freedom is denoted by d_f or v and is given by the formula: d_f(or v) = $(n-1)$ $(r-1)$. When data are arranged into a 2×2 consistency table, then $\chi^2 = \frac{N(AD - BC)^2}{(A+B)(C+D)(A+C)(B+D)}$.

When in four cells of a 2×2 consistency table, any one of the frequencies is less than 5, then Yate's correction is applied and the value of χ^2 is determined by the following formula:

$$\chi^2 = \frac{N(|AD - BC| - N/2)^2}{(A+B)(C+D)(A+C)(B+D)}.$$

Most important applications of χ^2 are: (a) test of independence, (b) test of goodness of fit, (c) test of homogeneity, and (d) test of population variance. As a test of independence, one can test whether two or more attributes are independent of each other or they are associated or related. As a test of goodness of fit, one can test how well the assumed theoretical distribution is fitted to the given data. Test of homogeneity, an extension of the test of independence, involves two or more independent samples, one from each of the probable universe under study. Test of population variance is applied to test whether the variance in the population could be a specified numeric value. The rate of growth of misuse of χ^2 is increasing faster than the rate of growth of its use.

IMPORTANT FORMULAE

1. a. $\chi^2 = \Sigma \dfrac{(f_0 - f_e)^2}{f_e}$,

   where χ^2 is chi-square, f_0 is observed frequency, and f_e is expected frequency.

   b. $\chi^2 = \Sigma \dfrac{f_0^2}{f_e} - N.$

   (This formula is used only when there are fractions in deviations and the use of this direct formula becomes tedious.)

2. $fe = \dfrac{\text{RT} \times \text{CT}}{N}$,

   where RT is the row total, CT is the column total, and N is the total number of observations.

3. a. d_f or $v = (c-1)\ (r-1)$,

   where d_f or v is the degree of freedom, c is the number of columns, and r is the number of rows.

   b. $d_f = (N-1)$,

   in the case of population variance, where $\chi^2 = \dfrac{NS^2}{\sigma^2}$, S=SD of sample, σ=SD of population, and N=size of sample.

4. $Z = \sqrt{2\chi^2} = \sqrt{2d_f - 1}$,

   where z is the t value for a larger sample (this formula is applied only when the d_f is more than 30).

5. a. Mean=2 d_f, mode=$d_f - 2$, variance=$2d_f$

   b. Moments=$\mu_0 = 0$, $\mu_2 = 2d_f$, $\mu_3 = 8d_f$, $\mu_4 = 48d_f + 12d_f^2$

   c. $\beta_1 = \dfrac{\mu_3^2}{\mu_2^2} = \dfrac{64d_f^2}{8d_f^2} = \dfrac{8}{d_f} \qquad \therefore \gamma_1 = \sqrt{8/d_f}$

   d. $\beta_2 = \dfrac{\mu_4}{\mu_2^2} = \dfrac{48d_f + 12d_f^2}{4d_f^2} = 3 + \dfrac{12}{d_f}$

   e. $\gamma_2 = \beta_2 - 3 = \dfrac{12}{d_f}$

6. When the data are arranged into a 2×2 consistency table like the following:

A	B	$(A+B)$
C	D	$(C+D)$
$(A+C)(B+D)$	N	

then

a. $$\chi^2 = \frac{N(AD - BC)^2}{(A+B)(B+D)(A+C)(B+D)}$$

b. $$\chi^2 = \frac{N(|AD - BC| - N/2)^2}{(A+B)(B+D)(A+C)(B+D)}$$

(applicable if any one of the frequencies is less than 5 in the above 2×2 consistency table)

7. $$\chi^2 = \frac{NS^2}{\sigma^2} = \frac{\Sigma d^2}{\sigma^2} = \frac{\Sigma(X - \overline{X})^2}{\sigma^2} \qquad \left(\because S = \frac{\Sigma d^2}{N}\right),$$

where N is the size of the sample, S is the standard deviation of the sample, σ is the standard deviation of the population, and d is the deviation of the sample mean $(\overline{X})$ from the sample score (X), that is, $d = (X - \overline{X})$.

In light of the above-mentioned most widely and largely used nonparametric hypothesis testing like chi-square and parametric hypothesis testing like ANOVA in media studies will be very relevant, pertinent, and important to discuss in the next chapter.

RELATED AND SUGGESTED WEBSITES

(As retrieved on December 1, 2015)

1. http://www2.lv.psu.edu/jxm57/irp/chisquar.html
2. http://math.hws.edu/javamath/ryan/ChiSquare.html
3. http://www.stat.purdue.edu/research/technical_reports/pdfs/1-527/tr-469.pdf
4. https://repositori.upf.edu/bitstream/handle/10230/890/412.pdf?sequence=1
5. http://academic.csuohio.edu/zhao_w/teaching/Old/EEC685-F05/lecture18-web-2up.pdf
6. http://www.stats.org.uk/statistical-inference/Berkson1938.pdf

REFERENCE

Gupta, S.P. 2011. *Statistical Methods*, 954–1003. New Delhi: Sultan Chand & Sons.

RELATED AND RECOMMENDED READINGS

Elhance, D.N.S., and Veena Elhance. 1990. *Fundamentals of Statistics*, 24.1–24.54. New Delhi: Kitab Mahal.

Gupta, S.P., and Alka Gupta. 2008. *Statistical Methods in Behavioural Sciences*, 412–36. Allahabad: Sharda Pustak Bhawan.

Hussain, Shamshad. 1986. *Elementary Statistics in Psychology and Education*, 120–36. New Delhi: Motilal Banarsidass, Delhi.

Kerlinger, F.N. 1983. *Fundamental of Behavioural Research*, 162–72. 2nd ed. Holt, Rinehart and Winston.

Kothari, C.R. 2000. *Research Methodology: Methods and Techniques*, 277–99. New Delhi: Wishwa Parkash.

Krishnaswami, O.R., and M. Ranganatham. 2005. *Methodology of Research*. New Delhi: Himalaya Publications.

Mangal, S.K. 1987. *Statistics in Psychology and* Education, 169–91. Delhi: McGraw Hill.

Sarangi, Prasant. 2010. *Research Methodology*. Delhi: Taxman Publication.

Wilkinson, T.S., and P.L. Bhandarkar. 1996. *Methodologies and Techniques of Social Research*. Mumbai: Himalaya Publishing House.

Wimmer, Roger D., and Joseph R. Dominick. 2003. *Mass Media Research: An Introduction*, 280–84. 7th ed. Thomson & Wadsworth.

QUESTIONS AND PROBLEMS

1. What is the χ^2 test? Under what conditions is it applicable? Why is χ^2 test called the test of the goodness of fit?
2. Describe the χ^2 test of significance and state the several uses to which it can be put.
3. What is the χ^2 test of goodness of fit? What precautions are necessary?
4. What are the basic conditions for the application of the χ^2 test?
5. The χ^2 test is a test of independence, homogeneity, and goodness of fit. Discuss briefly.
6. Why is the χ^2 test so popular despite being a nonparametric test?
7. Describe the meaning and concept of χ^2. Explain the conditions for using the χ^2 test.
8. Explain the applications of the χ^2 test: (a) as a test of independence, (b) as a test of goodness of fit, (c) as a test of homogeneity, (d) as a test of population variance.
9. Explain the alternative method and additive property of the χ^2 test.
10. It is said that the χ^2 test is more of a widely misused test, even though it the most popular parametric test; comment.
11. How is the χ^2 test used if the degree of freedom is more than 30?
12. Explain the constants of chi-square distribution.
13. Enumerate the various formulae for measuring the value of χ^2.
14. Which formula will you use for measuring the value of χ^2 if there are more fractions in the deviations and the use of earlier direct formula becomes tedious?
15. The following grades were given to a class of 100 media students:

Grade	*A*	*B*	*C*	*D*	*E*
Frequency	18	14	16	32	20

Test the hypothesis at 0.05 level that the distribution of grade is uniform.

16. 60 media students (40 from print media and 20 from electronic media) participated in a debate on the topic, "New media is flattening the world." 25 students spoke against the motion. The detailed data are as follows:

	Favor	Against	Total
Print media	12	28	40
Electronic media	13	7	20

Find whether the difference between favor and against is significant.

($\chi^2 = 3.84$ at $d_f = 1$ at 5% level of significance)

17. From a sample of 75 female advertisers, 60 percent were highly educated. Compare the distribution of female advertisers from the point of view of equal distribution.
(Given $\chi^2 = 3.84$ at $d_f = 1$ at 5% level of significance)
18. An innovative training was imparted to 200 working journalists suffering from the habit of yellow journalism. From the data given below, state whether innovative training is superior to conventional training?

	No. of Working Journalists		
Training	**Favorable**	**Not Favorable**	**Total**
Innovative	60	20	80
Conventional	70	50	120
Total	130	70	200

19. A certain spiritual feature writing is claimed to be effective in eliminating a negative attitude. In an experiment on 500 readers with negative attitudes, 300 of them were asked to read the spiritual feature and 200 of them were asked to read spiritual news.
The readers' reactions after such treatment are recorded in the following table:

	Helped	Harmed	No Effect	Total
Spiritual feature	200	40	60	300
Spiritual news	120	30	50	200
Total	320	70	110	500

On the basis of the data, can it be concluded that there is a significant difference in the effect of the spiritual feature and spiritual news?

Given degree of freedom	1	2	3
$\chi^2_{0.05}$	3.84	5.99	7.81

20. A movie producer is bringing out a new movie. In order to map out his advertising campaign, he wants to determine whether the movie will appeal most to a particular age group or whether it will appeal equally to all the age groups. The producer takes a random sample from persons attending the preview of the new movie and gets the following data:

	Age Groups				
	Below 20	20–39	40–59	60 and Above	Total
Liked	140	80	40	20	280
Disliked	60	50	30	80	220
Total	200	130	70	100	500

What inference will you draw from these results? ($\chi^2_{0.05}$ at d_f 3 = 7.815)

21. An advertising agency gives us the following information about the age group of the sample informants and their liking for a particular model of scooter which the agency plans to advertise:

	Age Group of Informants			
	Below 20	20–39	40–59	Total
Liked	125	420	60	605
Disliked	75	220	100	395
Total	200	640	160	1000

On the basis of the above data, can it be concluded that the model appeal is independent of the age group of the informants?
(At d_f= 2, $\chi^2_{0.01}$ = 9.21, $\chi^2_{0.05}$ = 5.99)

22. From the following data of advertisers, find out whether there is any relationship between gender and preference of color:

Color	Males	Females	Total
Red	40	60	100
White	35	25	60
Green	25	15	40
Total	100	100	200

(At d_f= 2, $\chi^2_{0.01}$ = 9.21, $\chi^2_{0.05}$ = 5.99)

23. A newspaper production supervisor is interested in knowing if the number of breakdowns of four printing machines is independent of the shift using the machines. Test this hypothesis based on the following sample information:

	Machine			
Shift	A	B	C	D
Morning	10	15	18	15
Evening	08	12	15	10

24. 1,000 media students at university level are graded according to their IQ and their economic conditions. Use the chi-square test to find out whether there is any association between economic conditions and the level of IQ:

Economic Conditions	IQ High	Medium	Low	Total
Rich	160	300	140	600
Poor	140	100	160	400
Total	300	400	300	1000

25. 200 words are chosen at random from a set of stories. The frequencies of the words are as follows:

Words	0	1	2	3	4	5	6	7	8	9
Frequency	18	19	23	21	16	25	22	20	21	15

Use the χ^2 test to assess the correctness of the hypothesis that the words were distributed in equal numbers in the table from which they were chosen.

26. The figures given below are (a) the theoretical frequencies of a distribution, and (b) the frequencies of the normal distribution have the same mean, standard deviation, and the total frequency as:

(a)	1	5	20	28	42	22	15	5	2
(b)	1	6	18	25	40	25	18	6	1

Apply χ^2 for goodness of fit.

27. Two research scholars adopted different sampling techniques while investigating the same group of students to find the number of students falling in different intelligent levels.

The results for the number of students in each level are as follows:

Researcher	Below Average	Average	Above Average	Genius	Total
X	86	60	44	10	200
Y	40	33	25	2	100
Total	126	93	69	12	300

Would you say that the sampling techniques adopted by the two researchers are not significantly different?
(For d_f=3, $\chi^2_{0.05} = 7.82$).

28. 1,000 families of media persons were selected at random in a city to test the belief that high-income families usually send their children to public schools and low-income families often send their children to government schools. The following results were obtained:

Income	Schools Public	Govt.	Total
Low	370	430	800
High	130	70	200
Total	500	500	1000

Test whether income and type of schooling are independent?

29. In a survey of 200 journalists, of which 75 were intelligent, 40 had educated fathers, while 85 of unintelligent journalists had uneducated fathers. Do these figures support the hypothesis that educated fathers have intelligent journalist sons? Use χ^2 test. (Value of $\chi^2_{0.05} = 3.84$ at $d_f = 1$).

30. From the following data of advertisers, find out whether there is any relationship between gender and color preference.

Color	Males	Females	Total
Green	40	60	100
White	35	25	60
Yellow	25	15	40
Total	100	100	200

31. In a sample of 200 respondents on a statement that "TV programs are increasing the aggressiveness of children," 47, 35, 36, 45, and 37 respondents reacted as "completely agreed," "agreed," "neutral," "disagreed," and "completely disagreed," respectively. Is the difference in reactions significant?
32. In a survey of 500 students of a university, it was asked whether there should be election of student union. 290 students said "Yes," while 210 said "No." Is the difference of opinion significant?
33. In a sample of 400 media persons, the following results regarding their intelligence were recorded. Is this distribution of media persons normal? (At $d_f = 4$, $\chi^2_{0.01} = 13.27$, $\chi^2_{0.05} = 9.48$)
34. Out of 200 respondents, three different opinions about "newspapers creating awareness" were obtained. Is their difference of opinion significant? (At $d_f = 4$, $\chi^2_{0.01} = 13.27$, $\chi^2 = 9.48$)

	Agreed	Can't Say	Disagree	Total
Teenagers	15	15	40	70
Adult	25	40	25	90
Old persons	10	15	15	40
Total	50	70	80	200

35. In a sample of 200 media students, there are 120 boys and 80 girls. Among boys, 80 opted for Hindi medium and 40 opted for English medium, while among girls, 30 opted for Hindi medium and 50 opted for English Medium. Is there any relationship between gender and choice of medium?
36. In a sample of 10 students of electronic media, 7 students answered wrongly on a factual question. Is the difference significant?
37. A group of 30 college students were asked to respond on a five-point scale to the statement "Seeing Hindi films are a waste of time." The distribution of responses is shown below:

Strongly Agree	Moderately Agree	Neutral	Moderately Disagree	Strongly Disagree
5	8	8	6	3

In there a significant difference in their responses?

38. In a survey, a few media students belonging to two different socio-economic groups were asked to express their opinion in three categories: "yes," "no," "cannot say" on the subject "do you prefer radio news to reading a newspaper?" Obtained responses were as follows:

	Yes	No	Can't Say	Total
Middle class	25	12	5	42
Lower class	20	10	8	38
Total	45	22	13	80

Are socio-economic classes and the opinion expressed independent of each other at 1 percent level of significance?

11

CHAPTER

Analysis of Variance in Media Studies

The analysis of variance is not a mathematical theorem but rather a convenient method of arranging the mathematics.

—Ronald Fisher

In quantitative research of communication and media studies, we often come across situations where we are required to test the significance of the difference between several means of several samples instead of only two sample means capable of testing with the help of *Z*- or *t*-tests. *Analysis of Variance (ANOVA)* is a parametric test of inferential media metrics. It really seems odd and ambiguous sometimes that this technique is described as analysis of "variance" rather than analysis of "means." But as a matter of fact, the nomenclature is reasonably suitable because inferences about means are finally derived by analyzing variances. This technique is frequently applied in communication media studies to examine general rather than specific differences among means.

In the previous chapter we have already discussed the meaning and concept of the chi-square test in media research, its application, its misuse and precautions, illustration of various applications of the test, summary, important formulae, and so on. Thus, we have discussed the inferential statistical tool of media metrics like the chi-square test in the previous chapter. Yet another inferential statistics (as shown in the flowchart in Section 2.2.1 of Chapter 2) is ANOVA. Hence, this chapter on ANOVA will focus on the following:

1. Meaning and concept of ANOVA in media studies
2. Variance tests ratio
3. ANOVA in one-way classification
4. ANOVA in two-way classification
5. Precautions in use of ANOVA
6. Illustrations relating to ANOVA in media studies

In addition, the chapter will also cover the summary, important formulae, related and suggested websites, related and recommended readings, and questions and problems relating to ANOVA in research in general and media metrics and mass communication research in particular.

11.1 MEANING AND CONCEPT OF ANALYSIS OF VARIANCE IN MEDIA STUDIES

The concept of ANOVA which has started cropping up in media studies bit by bit, was first coined by R.A. Fisher in the 1920s. It provides a statistical analysis of simultaneously testing the difference between many sample means. Thus, it helps us to tell whether any of the differences between means of the given samples are significant. Variance analysis was found to be extremely useful in communication and media research, where the effects of one or two variables on a problem under study had to be determined on the basis of a number of experiments conducted simultaneously. Variance analysis in mass communication studies the significance of the difference of means by analyzing variance relating to the issues and problems of mass communication.

11.2 VARIANCE TEST RATIO

It is the ratio between greater variance and smaller variance, that is,

$$F = \frac{\text{Greater Variance}}{\text{Smaller Variance}}$$

$$= \frac{S_1^2}{S_2^2},$$

where $S_1^2 = \frac{\Sigma(X_1 - \overline{X}_1)^2}{n_1 - 1}$ and $S_2 = \frac{\Sigma(X_2 - \overline{X}_2)^2}{n_2 - 1}$.

(Here, F is the ratio of the variance of the smaller sample to the variance of the larger sample, S_1 is the variance of the smaller sample, and S_2 is the variance of the larger sample.)

It is important to mention here that $S_1{}^2$ should always be the variance of the larger sample, that is, $S_1{}^2 > S_2{}^2$.

Here, $d_{f1} = n_1 - 1$, $d_{f2} = n_2 - 1$;

d_{f1} = degree of freedom of sample having larger variance
d_{f2} = degree of freedom of sample having smaller variance.

If the calculated value of F is more than the table value at d_{f1} and d_{f2} at 1 percent level and 5 percent level of significance, respectively, the difference is significant. Hence, the null hypothesis is rejected. Similarly, if the calculated value of F is less than the table value, then the difference is not significant. Hence, the null hypothesis is accepted and it is concluded that both the samples have come from the population having the same variance.

F-test is also called the variance ratio test as it is based on the ratio of two variances.

11.2.1 Assumptions in *F*-test

Following are the assumptions of the *F*-test:

1. The universe should be normally distributed.

2. Samples drawn from the universe should be representative and should be independent of each other.
3. There should not be a significant difference between the variances of the samples. Thus, we start the solution with the null hypothesis $H_0 : \sigma_1^2 = \sigma_2^2 = \sigma_3^2 \ldots \sigma_n^2$.

11.2.2 Applications of *F*-test

The following illustrations will clearly depict the several applications of the *F*-test.

Example 1: Two representative samples from a normally distributed universe of advertisements and news were drawn and their values are as follows:

Advertisements:	75	67	66	76	82	84	88	90	92		
News:	74	66	64	78	82	85	87	92	93	95	97

Test whether the two populations have the same variance at 5 percent level of significance (F=3.36 at 5% level for d_{f1}=10 and d_{f2}=8).

Solution: Let us take the hypothesis that there is no significant difference between the variance of two normally distributed universes.

Applying the *F*-test,

$$F = \frac{S_1^2}{S_2^2},$$

where $S_1^2 > S_2^2$.

Advertisements	News	$(X_1 - \overline{X}_1)$	$(X_2 - \overline{X}_2)$	d_1^2	d_2^2
(X_1)	(X_2)	$(d_1 = X_1 - 80)$	$(d_2 = X_2 - 83)$		
75	74	−5	−9	25	81
67	66	−13	−13	169	289
66	64	−14	−12	196	361
76	78	−4	−5	16	25
82	82	2	−1	4	1
84	85	5	2	16	4
88	87	8	4	64	16
90	92	10	9	100	81
92	93	12	10	144	100
	95		12		144
	97		14		196
$\Sigma X_1 = 720$	$\Sigma X_2 = 913$			734	1298

$$\therefore \overline{X}_1 = \frac{\Sigma X_1}{N_1} = \frac{720}{9} = 80, \quad \overline{X}_2 = \frac{\Sigma X_2}{N_2} = \frac{913}{11} = 83$$

$$\therefore \quad S_1^2 = \frac{\Sigma d_1^2}{N_1 - 1} = \frac{734}{9-1} = \frac{734}{8} = 91.75$$

$$S_2^2 = \frac{\Sigma d_2^2}{N_2 - 1} = \frac{1298}{11-1} = \frac{1298}{10} = 129.8.$$

Since $S_2^2 > S_1^2$

$$\therefore F = \frac{\text{Greater variance}}{\text{Smaller variance}} = \frac{S_2^2}{S_1^2} = \frac{129.8}{91.75} = 1.41.$$

Now for $df_1 = 10$ and $df_2 = 8$, $F_{0.05} = 3.36$.
Since the calculated value of F is less than the table value, the difference is not significant. Hence, the null hypothesis is accepted. Thus, the variances of the two universes are the same.

Example 2: In a sample of eight students of electronic media specialization, the sum of the squared deviations from the mean was 84.4. In yet another samples of 10 students of print media, the value was found to be 102.6. Test whether the difference is significant at 5 percent level. (At 5% level and at $d_f = 7$ and $d_f = 9$, the table value of $F = 3.29$ and at $d_f = 8$ and $d_f = 10$, its value is 3.07.)

Solution: Let us take the hypothesis that the difference between samples of variance is not significant.
Now, $N_1 = 8$, $\Sigma(X_1 - \overline{X}_1)^2 = 84.4$, $N_2 = 10$, $\Sigma(X_2 - \overline{X}_2)^2 = 102.6$

$$\therefore S_1^2 = \frac{\Sigma d_1^2}{N_1 - 1} = \frac{(84.4)}{8-1}$$

$$= \frac{84.4}{7} = 12.06$$

$$S_2^2 = \frac{\Sigma d_2^2}{N_2 - 1} = \frac{(102.6)}{10-1}$$

$$= \frac{102.6}{9} = 11.4.$$

Since $S_1^2 > S_2^2$,

$$\therefore F = \frac{\text{Greater Variance}}{\text{Smaller Variance}} = \frac{S_1^2}{S_2^2}$$

$$= \frac{12.06}{11.4}$$

$$= 1.06.$$

11.3 ANALYSIS OF VARIANCE IN ONE-WAY CLASSIFICATION

In one-way classification, we take into account only one variable, that is, the data are classified according to only one criteria. More frequently, such an analysis has cropped up in media studies in recent days, especially after the realization of application of statistical testing of hypothesis for more scientific studies.

We start with the null hypothesis, which is not different in the universe, that is,

$$H_0 : \mu_1 = \mu_2 = \mu_3 \ldots = \mu_k$$

Here, the alternate hypothesis will be:

$$H_1 : \mu_1 \neq \mu_2 \neq \mu_3 \ldots \neq \mu_k$$

That is to say that the means of the universe from which the k samples were randomly drawn are equal to one another.

With the above hypothesis, we will calculate the analysis one by one:

1. The variance between the samples,
2. Variances within the samples,
3. Total sum of squares,
4. F-ratio,
5. Compare the calculated value of F with the table value of F for the degrees of freedom at a certain level.

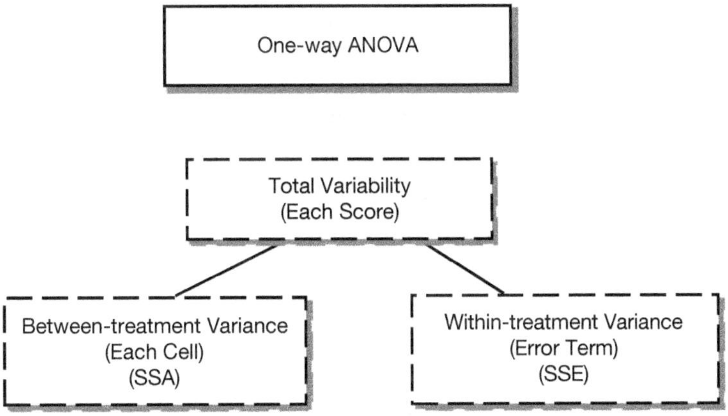

1. Variance between the samples: To measure the variance between the samples, we follow the following steps.

   a. The mean of each sample is calculated.
   b. Grand average (pronounced as "X double bar") should be calculated by the following formula:

$$\overline{\overline{X}} = \frac{\overline{X}_1 + \overline{X}_2 + \overline{X}_3 + \cdots + \overline{X}_k}{N_1 + N_2 + N_3 + \cdots + N_k}.$$

c. Then we will find out the difference between means of the various samples and the grand average.
d. After that, we will square these deviations and obtain the total, which will give the sum of the squares between the samples.
e. Thereafter, we will divide the total obtained in step (d) by the degrees of freedom. Here, the degree of freedom will be one less than the number of samples. For example, if there are 5 samples, then the degrees of freedom will be $5-1=4$ or $d_f=k-1$, where k is the number of samples.

2. Variance within the samples: It is denoted by SSE, which means the sum of squares within the samples (rows). The variance within the samples measures variability around the mean of each group. In order to find out the variance within the samples, we take the total of sums of squares of the deviation of several items from the mean values of the respective sample and then it is divided by the degrees of freedom. Following steps will be taken to suitably measure the variance within the samples.

$$\text{Sample} = \overline{X}_1, \overline{X}_2, \overline{X}_3, \ldots, \overline{X}_4$$

a. We will find out the mean value of each sample.
b. Then the deviations from the several items in a sample from the mean values of the respective samples will be taken.
c. After that, we will square these deviations and get the total which gives the sum of the squares within the sample.
d. Then the total obtained in step (c) will be divided by the degrees of freedom. Here, the d_f or $v=N-K$, where K refers to the total number of all the observations.

3. Total sum of squares: This is denoted by SST and can be obtained by adding the variance between samples and variance within samples.
4. *F*-ratio: It can be derived by the following formula:

$$F = \frac{\text{Between} - \text{column variance}}{\text{Within} - \text{column variance}}$$

$$= \frac{\text{variance between samples}}{\text{variance within samples}}$$

$$= \frac{\text{MSC}}{\text{MSE}}$$

MSN = Mean Sum of squares between samples
MSE = Mean Sum of square within samples

It is important to mention here that if the variance within the samples is more than the variance between the samples, then the numerator and the denominator should be interchanged and the degrees of freedom adjusted accordingly.

One-way ANOVA may be illustrated as follows:

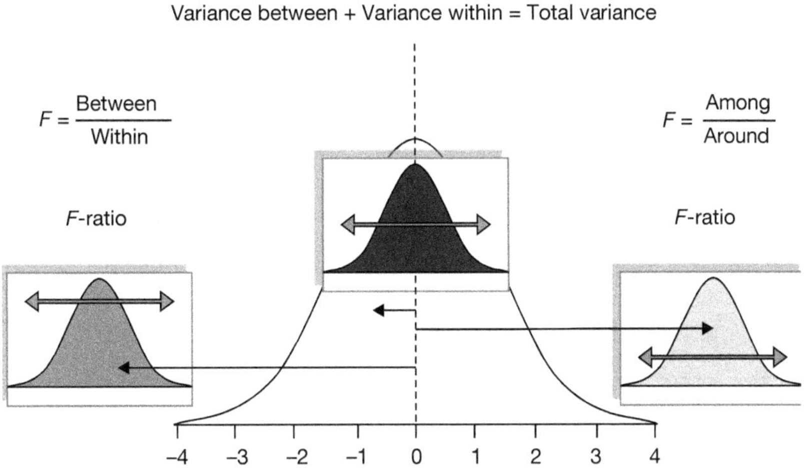

Source: Concept by British statistician Ronald Aylmer Fisher, drawn by author's research scholar Bhupender Singh.

5. Comparison of the calculated and table values of F: If the calculated value of F is more than the table value, then the difference between means is significant and the null hypothesis is rejected. If the calculated value of F is less than the table value, then the difference is not significant and has arisen due to sampling fluctuations.

All the above-mentioned points regarding one-way classification can be summarized in the following table, which is popularly known as the ANOVA table.

Source of Variation	Sum of Squares	Degree of Freedom	Mean Square	F-ratio
Between sample	SSC	$d_{fb}=C-1$	$MSC = \frac{SSC}{C-1}$	$\frac{MSC}{MSE}$
Within samples	SSE	$d_{fu}=N-C$	$MSE = \frac{SSE}{N-C}$	
Total	SST	$d_{fT}=N-1$		

Here, SSC = Sum of squares between samples,
SSE = Sum of squares within samples,
SST = Total sum of squares,
MSC = Mean square between samples,
MSE = Mean square within samples.

Example 1: Find out the significance of the possible variation in the performance of advertisement of a particular ad campaign in four different media. The monthly results are given as follows. Make an ANOVA table of data:

Media			
A	*B*	*C*	*D*
8	12	18	13
10	11	12	9
12	9	16	12
8	14	6	16
7	4	8	15

Solution:

Sample I	Sample II	Sample III	Sample IV
X_1	X_2	X_3	X_4
8	12	18	13
10	11	12	9
12	9	16	12
8	14	6	16
7	4	8	15
Total 45	50	60	65
$\bar{X}$ 9	10	12	13

$$\text{Grand Mean or } \bar{\bar{X}} = \frac{\bar{X}_1 + \bar{X}_2 + \bar{X}_3 + \bar{X}_4}{N},$$

where $\bar{X}_1$, $\bar{X}_2$, and so on represent the mean of each sample and N is the number of sample.

$$\bar{\bar{X}} = \frac{9 + 10 + 12 + 13}{4}$$

$$= \frac{44}{4} = 11.$$

$$\text{Grand mean of all samples or } \bar{\bar{X}} = \frac{45 + 50 + 60 + 65}{20}$$

$$= 11.$$

Variance between samples: In order to get the variance between samples, we will find out the square of the deviation of the various samples from the grand average. The mean of sample I is 9, but the grand mean is 11. So we will take the difference between 9 and 11 and square it. Similarly, for sample II the mean is 10, but the grand average is 11 and so we will take the difference between 10 and 11 and square it. Hence, we make the following table:

Sample I	**Sample II**	**Sample III**	**Sample IV**
$(X_1 - \bar{X}_1)^2$	$(X_2 - \bar{X}_2)^2$	$(X_3 - \bar{X}_3)^2$	$(X_4 - \bar{X}_4)^2$
4	1	1	4
4	1	1	4
4	1	1	4
4	1	1	4
4	1	1	4
20	5	5	20

Sum of the squares between the samples = 20 + 5 + 5 + 20 = 50.

Mean sum of squares between the samples is $\frac{50}{4-1} = 16.7$.

(Because there are four samples and degrees of freedom are 4 – 1 = 3.)

Variance within the samples: It is quite clear that the sum of the squares is the deviations of various items in a sample from the mean values of the respective samples. Hence, for the first sample, the mean is 9 and, thus, we will take deviations from 10 and so on. The squared deviations are given in the following table:

Sample I		**Sample II**		**Sample III**		**Sample IV**	
X_1	$(X_1 - \bar{X}_1)^2$	X_2	$(X_2 - \bar{X}_2)^2$	X_3	$(X_3 - \bar{X}_3)^2$	X_4	$(X_4 - \bar{X}_4)^2$
8	1	12	4	18	36	13	0
10	1	11	1	12	0	9	16
12	9	9	1	16	16	12	1
8	1	14	16	6	36	16	9
7	4	4	36	8	16	15	4
	$\Sigma(X_1 - \bar{X}_1)^2 = 16$		$(X_2 - \bar{X}_2)^2 = 58$		$\Sigma(X_3 - \bar{X}_3)^2 = 104$		$\Sigma(X_4 - \bar{X}_4)^2 = 30$

According to the above table, the total sum of squares within the samples = 16 + 58 + 104 + 30 = 208.

$$\text{Mean sum of squares within the samples} = \frac{208}{20-4} = \frac{208}{16} = 13.$$

For the verification of the above calculation, it is desirable to calculate the total variation. Total variation can be found out by taking the squares of the deviation of each item from the grand average.

Sample I		Sample II		Sample III		Sample IV	
X_1	$(X_1 - \bar{X}_1)^2$	X_2	$(X_2 - \bar{X}_2)^2$	X_3	$(X_3 - \bar{X}_3)^2$	X_4	$(X_4 - \bar{X}_4)^2$
8	9	12	1	18	49	13	4
10	1	11	0	12	1	9	4
12	1	9	4	16	25	12	1
8	9	14	9	6	25	16	25
7	16	4	49	8	9	15	16
	$\Sigma(X_1 - \bar{X}_1)^2 = 36$		$\Sigma(X_2 - \bar{X}_2)^2 = 63$		$\Sigma(X_3 - \bar{X}_3)^2 = 109$		$\Sigma(X_4 - \bar{X}_4)^2 = 50$

Hence, the total sum of squares $= 36 + 63 + 109 + 50 = 258$.

Degrees of freedom $= 20 - 1 = 19$.

If we add the sum of squares between samples and sum of squares within samples, we get the same total, that is, $50 + 208 = 258$. Thus, the calculation is correct.

All the above results can be tabulated as follows:

Source of Variation	Sum of Squares	Degrees of Freedom	Mean Square
Between samples	50	3	16.7
Within samples	208	16	13.0
Total	258	19	

$$F = \frac{\text{Variance between samples}}{\text{Variance within samples}} = \frac{16.7}{13} = 1.285.$$

The table value of F for $d_{f1} = 3$ and $d_{f2} = 16$ at 5 percent level is 3.24. Since the calculated value of F is less than the table value, the difference in the mean values of the sample is not significant, that is, the samples could have come from the same universe.

Shortcut Method.

Since the above method of calculating the F-ratio is very tedious, cumbersome, and time-taking, it is advisable to apply a shortcut method. The various steps in the calculations of variance ratio by the shortcut methods are as follows:

Sample I		Sample II		Sample III		Sample IV	
X_1	X_1^2	X_2	X_2^2	X_3	X_3^2	X_4	X_4^2
8	64	12	144	18	324	13	169
10	100	11	121	12	144	9	81
12	144	9	81	16	256	12	144
8	64	14	196	6	36	16	256
7	49	4	16	8	64	15	255
$\Sigma X_1 = 45$	$\Sigma X_1^2 = 421$	$\Sigma X_2 = 50$	$\Sigma X_2^2 = 558$	$\Sigma X_3 = 60$	$\Sigma X_3^2 = 824$	$\Sigma X_4 = 65$	$\Sigma X_4^2 = 825$

The sum of all the items of various samples:

$$=\Sigma X_1+\Sigma X_2+\Sigma X_3+\Sigma X_4=45+50+60+65=220.$$

$$\text{Correction factor}=\frac{T^2}{N}=\frac{(220)^2}{20}=\frac{18400}{20}=2420.$$

$$\text{Total sum of squares}=\Sigma X_1^2+\Sigma X_2^2+\Sigma X_3^2+\Sigma X_4^2-\frac{T^2}{N}$$

$$=421+558+824+875-2420=2678-2420=258 \text{ (as before).}$$

Sum of squares between sample

$$=\frac{\Sigma(X_1)^2}{N}+\frac{\Sigma(X_2)^2}{N}+\frac{\Sigma(X_3)^2}{N}+\frac{\Sigma(X_4)^2}{N}-\frac{T^2}{N}$$

$$=\frac{45^2}{5}+\frac{50^2}{5}+\frac{60^2}{5}+\frac{65^2}{5}-2420$$

$$=\frac{2025}{5}+\frac{2500}{5}+\frac{3600}{5}+\frac{4225}{5}-2420$$

$$=405+500+720+845-2420$$

$$=2470-2420=50 \text{ (as before).}$$

Sum of squares within samples =

Total sum of squares – Sum of squares between samples

$=258-50=208$ (as before).

Coding Method.

This method refers to the addition, multiplication, subtraction, or division of data by a constant. Since in the *F*-test the final quality is a ratio, the original measurement can be coded to simplify the calculations.

In the above-mentioned question, let us subtract 10 from each measurement. Now, the coded data will be as follows:

A	B	C	D
X_1	X_2	X_3	X_4
−2	+2	+8	+3
0	+1	+2	−1
+2	−1	+6	+2
−2	+4	−4	+6
−3	−6	−2	+5
$\Sigma X_1=-5$	$\Sigma X_2=0$	$\Sigma X_3=10$	$\Sigma X_4=15$
$\bar{X}_1=-1$	$\bar{X}_2=0$	$\bar{X}_3=2$	$\bar{X}_4=3$

$$\text{Grand mean or } \bar{\bar{X}}=\frac{\bar{X}_1+\bar{X}_2+\bar{X}_3+\bar{X}_4}{4}$$

$$= \frac{-1+0+2+3}{4} = 1.$$

Sum of squares between samples:

$(\bar{X}_1 - \bar{\bar{X}})^2$	$(\bar{X}_2 - \bar{\bar{X}})^2$	$(\bar{X}_3 - \bar{\bar{X}})^2$	$(\bar{X}_4 - \bar{\bar{X}})^2$
4	1	1	4
4	1	1	4
4	1	1	4
4	1	1	4
4	1	1	4
$\Sigma(\bar{X}_1 - \bar{\bar{X}})^2 = 20$	$\Sigma(\bar{X}_2 - \bar{\bar{X}})^2 = 5$	$\Sigma(\bar{X}_3 - \bar{\bar{X}})^2 = 5$	$\Sigma(\bar{X}_4 - \bar{\bar{X}})^2 = 20$

Sum of the squares between samples = 20 + 5 + 5 + 20 = 50.

Mean squares between samples $= \frac{50}{4-1} = 16.7$ (as before).

Sum of squares within samples:

X_1	$(X_1 - \bar{X}_1)^2$	X_2	$(X_2 - \bar{X}_2)^2$	X_3	$(X_3 - \bar{X}_3)^2$	X_4	$(X_4 - \bar{X}_4)^2$
−2	1	2	4	8	36	3	0
0	1	1	1	2	0	−1	16
2	9	−1	1	6	16	2	1
−2	1	4	16	−4	36	6	9
−3	4	−6	36	−2	16	5	4
	$\Sigma(X_1 - \bar{X}_1)^2 = 16$		$\Sigma(X_2 - \bar{X}_2)^2 = 58$		$\Sigma(X_3 - \bar{X}_3)^2 = 104$		$\Sigma(X_4 - \bar{X}_4)^2 = 30$

Total sum of squares within samples = 16 + 58 + 104 + 30 = 208.

Mean square within samples

$$= \frac{208}{20-4} = \frac{208}{16} = 13 \text{ (as before).}$$

11.4 ANALYSIS OF VARIANCE IN TWO-WAY CLASSIFICATION

With the realization of scientific analysis of data in the field of communication and media studies, two-way classification of ANOVA has also become equally relevant in this micro-focused branch of social sciences. The procedure for analysis in a two-way classification table takes the following form:

Source of Variation	**Sum of Squares**	**Degrees of Freedom**	**Mean Sum of Squares**	**Variance Ratio**
Total	SST			
Between columns	SSC	$d_{fc}=(c-1)$	MSC=SSC/$(c-1)$	MSC/MSE
Between rows	SSR	$d_{fr}=(r-1)$	MSR=SSR/$(r-1)$	MSR/MSE
Residual or error	SSE	$d_{fe}=(c-1)(r-1)$	MSE=SSE/$(c-1)(r-1)$	

Here, SSC=Sum of squares between columns,
SSR=Sum of squares between rows,
SSE=Sum of squares between errors,
SST=Total sum of squares.

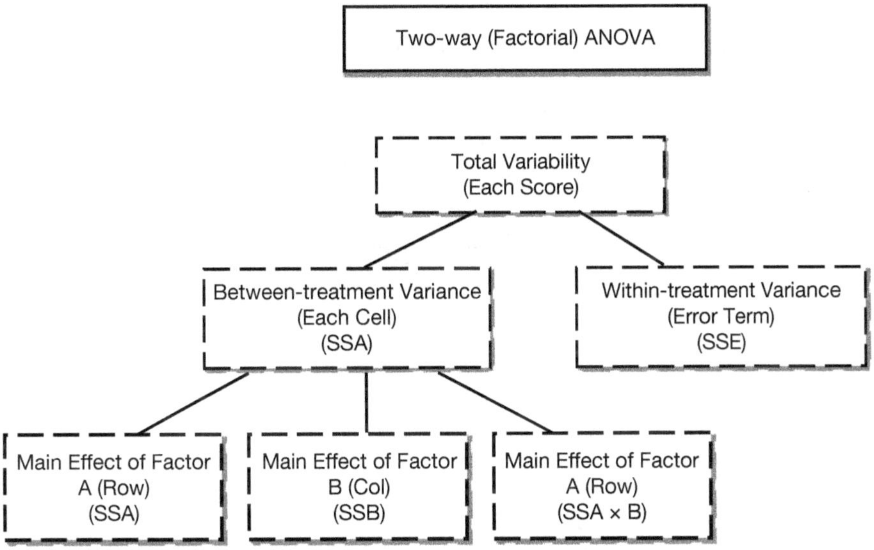

Source: Drawn by author.

The SSE or residual sum of squares is calculated by subtracting the total of SSC and SSR from the total sum of squares.

In two-way classification, the degree of freedom is calculated differently. For column figures, it is $(c-1)$, for row total it is $(r-1)$, and for the residual it is $(c-1)$ $(r-1)$. The total sum of squares for between columns and sum of squares for between rows are calculated in the same way as done before in one-way analysis.

Here,

$$F_{(d_{fc},d_{fe})} = \frac{\text{MSC}}{\text{MSE}},$$

where $d_{fc}=(c-1)$, $d_{fe}=(c-1)(r-1)$.

Thus, in two-way analysis, "residual" is the measuring rod for testing the significance. It represents the magnitude of variation due to forces called "chance."

Example: A newspaper-circulating agency appoints four agents A_1, A_2, A_3, and A_4 and observes their circulations in three different periods—election period, festival period, and normal period. The figures (in lakhs) are given in the following table.

	Agents				
Period	**A1**	**A2**	**A3**	**A4**	**Total**
Election	35	36	21	36	128
Festival	32	29	31	28	120
Normal	29	28	29	26	112
Agents' total	96	93	81	90	360

1. Do the agents significantly differ in performance?
2. Is there significant difference between the three above-mentioned periods?

Solution: The given data are classified according to two criteria: (a) agents and (b) periods.
By using the coding method to simplify the calculations, we code the data by subtracting 30 from each figure. Hence, the coded table will be as follows:

	Agents				
Periods	**A1**	**A2**	**A3**	**A4**	**Total**
Election	5	6	–9	6	
Festival	2	–1	1	–2	
Normal	1	–2	–1	–4	
	6	3	–9	0	Grand total (T)=0

$$\text{Correlation factor} = \frac{T^2}{N} = \frac{0}{12} = 0.$$

Sum of squares between agents: This will be calculated by squaring up the agents' total, dividing each total by the number of items included in it, adding these figures, and then subtracting the correction factor from them. Hence, the sum of squares between agents is,

$$= \frac{(6)^2}{3} + \frac{(3)^2}{3} + \frac{(-9)^2}{3} + \frac{(0)^2}{3} - \frac{T^2}{N}$$
$$= 12 + 3 + 27 + 0 = 42.$$

Sum of squares between periods: This will be found out by dividing the squares of the period totals by the number of items that make up each total, adding all such figures, and subtracting therefrom the correction factor.
Hence, the sum of squares between periods is:

$$= \frac{(-8)^2}{4} + \frac{(0)^2}{4} + \frac{(8)^2}{4} - \frac{T^2}{N}$$
$$= 16 + 0 + 16 - 0 = 32$$
$$d_f = (3 - 2) = 2.$$

Total sum of squares: This will be calculated by adding the squares of all the items in the table and subtracting the correction factor therefrom. Hence,

$$\text{total sum of squares} = (5)^2 + (2)^2 + (-1)^2 + (6)^2 + (-1)^2 + (-2)^2 + (-9)^2$$
$$+(1)^2 + (-1)^2 + (6)^2 + (-2)^2 + (-4)^2 - \frac{T^2}{N}$$
$$= 210 - 0 = 210$$
$$d_f = (12 - 1) = 11.$$

The above-calculated facts will be put in the following ANOVA table:

Source of Variation	Sum of Squares	d_f	Mean Squares
Between columns (agents)	42	3	14
Between rows (periods)	32	2	16
Residual	136	6	22.67
Total	210	11	

Now, let us take the hypothesis that there is no difference between the circulation of agents and the periods. This means that the three independent estimates of variance are the estimates of variance of a common population.

Comparing the agents' variance estimate with the residual variance estimate:

$$F = \frac{22.67}{14} = 1.619.$$

The table value of F for d_f=6, d_f=3 at 5 percent level of the significance is 8.94. Since the calculated value is less than the table value, the circulation of newspapers of different agents does not differ significantly.

Now, comparing the period variance estimate with the residual variance estimate,

$$F = \frac{22.67}{16} = 1.417.$$

The table value of F for d_{f1}=6 and d_{f2}=2 at 5 percent level of significance is 19.33. Since the calculated value of F is less than the table value, there is no significant difference in the periods as far as the circulations of the newspapers are concerned.

Hence, the test proves that the agents and periods are similar as far as the circulation of the newspapers is concerned.

11.5 PRECAUTIONS IN USE OF ANOVA

No doubt, the use and application of ANOVA is very relevant and significant in the statistical inference. But at the same time, the use of wrong and erroneous kind of ANOVA has often been practiced by media researchers due to the least exposure of this statistical tool. It can be extremely harmful. For example, applying one-way ANOVA where two-way analysis is more suitable can destroy the whole procedure and result in a very ineffective consequence. Further, if ANOVA is applied without following the requisite assumptions, then the results can be misleading and disoriented. Hence, utmost care should be taken in the interpretation of this procedure, failing which its effects will be detrimental and the entire labor of love will be lost.

11.6 ILLUSTRATIONS RELATING TO ANALYSIS OF VARIANCE IN MEDIA STUDIES

1. Perform a two-way ANOVA on the data given below:

Performance of Newspaper Production	Treatment			
	T_1	T_2	T_3	T_4
NP1	38	40	41	39
NP2	45	42	49	36
NP3	40	38	42	42

Solution: Subtracting 40 from all the given measurements to use the coding method and also assuming the hypothesis that there is no significant difference in the treatment and performance of newspaper production.

Now, applying the ANOVA procedure on subtracting 40 from each value, the table becomes as follows:

Performance of Newspaper production	Treatment				
	T_1	T_2	T_3	T_4	Total
NP1	–2	0	1	–1	–2
NP2	5	2	9	–4	12
NP3	0	–2	2	2	2
Total	3	0	12	–3	12

Correction factor:

$$\frac{T^2}{N} = \frac{(12)^2}{12} = 12.$$

Sum of squares between treatments:

$$= \frac{(3)^2}{3} + \frac{(0)^2}{3} + \frac{(12)^2}{3} + \frac{(-3)^2}{3} - \frac{T^2}{N}$$
$$= 3 + 0 + 48 + 3 + 12 = 42$$
$$d_f = 4 - 1 = 3.$$

Sum of squares between performances of newspaper production:

$$= \frac{(-2)^2}{4} + \frac{(12)^2}{4} + \frac{(2)^2}{4} - \frac{T^2}{N}$$
$$= 1 + 36 + 1 - 12 = 26$$
$$d_f = 3 - 1 = 2.$$

Total sum of squares:

$$= (-2)^2 + (5)^2 + (0)^2 + (0)^2 + (2)^2 + (-2)^2 + (1)^2 + (9)^2 + (2)^2 + (-1)^2 + (-4)^2 + (-2)^2 - \frac{T^2}{N}$$
$$= 4 + 25 + 0 + 0 + 4 + 4 + 1 + 81 + 4 + 1 + 16 + 4 - 12 = 132.$$

ANOVA table:

Source and Variation	Sum of Squares	d_f	Mean Squares	F
Between columns	42	3	14	$\frac{14}{10.67} = 1.312$
Between rows	26	2	13	$\frac{13}{10.67} = 1.218$
Between residuals	64	6	10.67	
Total	132	11		

For d_{f3} and d_{f6}, $F_{0.05} = 4.76$, and for d_{f2} and d_{f6}, $F_{0.05} = 5.14$. Since the calculated values of F is less than the table value at 5 percent level of significance, the difference is not significant. Hence, the null hypothesis is accepted. Thus, there is no significant difference between treatments and performances of newspaper production.

2. The following table gives the number of units of production per day turned out by four different types of printing methods of a newspaper:

	Type of Printing Methods			
Employee	P_1	P_2	P_3	P_4
E_1	40	36	45	30
E_2	38	42	50	41
E_3	36	30	48	35
E_4	46	47	52	44

By applying ANOVA,

a. test the hypothesis that the mean production is the same for the four printing methods, and
b. test the hypothesis that the employees do not differ with respect to mean productivity.

Solution: Let us take the hypothesis that (a) the mean production does not differ for the four printing methods and (b) the employees do not differ with respect to mean productivity.

Subtracting 40 from all the given values to use the coding method and simplifying the calculations, we get:

Employee	Printing Methods				Total
	P_1	P_2	P_3	P_4	
E_1	0	−4	5	−10	−9
E_2	−2	2	10	1	11
E_3	−4	−10	8	−5	−11
E_4	6	7	12	4	29
Total	0	−5	35	−10	20

Correction factor:

$$= \frac{T^2}{N} = \frac{(20)^2}{16} = 25$$

$$= \frac{(0)^2}{4} + \frac{(-5)^2}{4} + \frac{(35)^2}{4} + \frac{(-10)^2}{4} - \frac{T^2}{N}$$

$$= 0 + 6.25 + 306.25 + 25 - 25 = 312.5.$$

Sum of squares between employees:

$$= \frac{(-9)^2}{4} + \frac{(11)^2}{4} + \frac{(-11)^2}{4} + \frac{(29)^2}{4} - \frac{T^2}{N}$$

$$= 20.25 + 30.25 + 30.25 + 210.25 - 25 = 266.$$

Total sum of squares:

$$= (0)^2 + (-2)^2 + (-4)^2 + (6)^2 + (-4)^2 + (2)^2 + (-10)^2 + (7)^2 + (5)^2 + (10)^2$$

$$+(8)^2 + (12)^2 + (-10)^2 + (1)^2 + (-5)^2 + (4)^2 - \frac{T^2}{N}$$

$$= 0 + 4 + 16 + 36 + 16 + 4 + 100 + 49 + 25 + 100 + 64 + 144 + 100 + 1 + 25$$

$$+16 - 25 = 675.$$

Now, drawing the ANOVA table:

Source of Variation	Sum of Square	d_f	Mean Square	F
Between column	312.5	3	104.17	$\frac{104}{10.72} = 9.72$
Between rows	266.0	3	88.67	$\frac{88.67}{10.72} = 8.27$
Residual	96.5	9	10.72	
Total	675.0	15		

For d_{f3} and d_{f9}, $F_{0.05} = 3.86$.

Since the calculated values of F are more than the table value at 5 percent level, the mean production is not the same for the four different types of printing. Also the employees differ with respect to the mean productivity. Hence, the null hypothesis is rejected.

3. A newspaper organization has purchased three new printing methods of different makes and wishes to determine whether one of them is faster than the others in producing a certain output. Five hourly production figures are observed at random from each printing machine and the results are given below:

Observation	A_1	A_2	A_3
1	25	31	24
2	30	39	30
3	36	38	28
4	38	42	25
5	31	35	28

Use ANOVA and determine whether the printing machines are significantly different in their mean speed. (Given at 5% level F=3.89 at d_f=2 and 12.)

Solution: Let us take the hypothesis that the printing machines are not significantly different in their mean speed.

Now applying ANOVA,

X_1	X_2	X_3
25	31	24
30	39	30
36	38	28
38	42	25
31	35	28
$\Sigma X_1 = 160$	$\Sigma X_2 = 185$	$\Sigma X_3 = 135$
$\overline{X}_1 = 32$	$\overline{X}_2 = 37$	$\overline{X}_3 = 27$

Grand mean or $\overline{\overline{X}} = \dfrac{32+37+27}{3} = 32.$

Variance between samples:

$(\overline{X}_1 - \overline{\overline{X}})^2$	$(\overline{X}_2 - \overline{\overline{X}})^2$	$(\overline{X}_3 - \overline{\overline{X}})^2$
0	25	25
0	25	25
0	25	25
0	25	25
0	25	25
0	125	125

Sum of squares between samples:

$$= 0 + 125 + 125 = 250.$$

Variance within samples:

X_1	$(X_1 - \bar{X}_1)^2$	X_2	$(X_2 - \bar{X}_2)^2$	X_3	$(X_3 - \bar{X}_3)^2$
25	49	31	36	24	9
30	4	39	4	30	9
36	16	38	1	28	1
38	36	42	25	25	4
31	1	35	4	28	1
	$\Sigma(X_1 - \bar{X}_1)^2 = 106$		$\Sigma(X_2 - \bar{X}_2)^2 = 70$		$\Sigma(X_3 - \bar{X}_3)^2 = 24$

Sum of squares within samples:

$$= 106 + 70 + 24 = 200.$$

Total sum of squares:

X_1	$(X_1 - \bar{\bar{X}}_1)^2$	X_2	$(X_2 - \bar{\bar{X}}_2)^2$	X_3	$(X_3 - \bar{\bar{X}}_3)^2$
25	49	31	1	24	64
30	4	39	49	30	4
36	16	38	36	28	16
38	36	42	100	25	49
31	1	35	9	28	16
	$\Sigma(X_1 - \bar{\bar{X}}_1)^2 = 106$		$\Sigma(X_2 - \bar{\bar{X}}_2)^2 = 195$		$\Sigma(X_3 - \bar{\bar{X}}_3)^2 = 149$

Total sum of squares

$$= 106 + 195 + 149 = 450.$$

Sum of squares between + Sum of squares within = Total sum of squares

That is, 250 + 200 = 450.

Hence, our calculation is correct.

ANOVA table:

Sum of Variation	Sum of Squares	d_f	Mean Square
Between samples	250	2	125
Within samples	200	12	16.667
Total	450	14	

$$F = \frac{\text{Variance between samples}}{\text{Variance within samples}} = \frac{125}{16.667} = 7.5.$$

Since the calculated value of F is more than the table value, the difference is significant. Hence, the null hypothesis is rejected. Thus, the printing machines are significantly different in their mean speed.

4. The following table gives monthly circulation of a magazine (in 1,000 rupees) in three districts by its four circulation managers:

District	I	II	III	IV
D_1	60	50	30	80
D_2	80	90	60	50
D_3	100	70	80	70

Set up the ANOVA table and test whether:

a. There is any significant difference between circulations by circulation managers.
b. There is no significant difference in circulations of three districts.

Solution: By using the coding method and dividing all the values by 10, and by taking the hypothesis that (a) there is no significant difference between circulations of circulation managers and (b) there is no significant difference in circulations between three districts:

	Circulation Managers				
District	I	II	III	IV	Total
D_1	6	5	3	8	22
D_2	8	9	6	5	28
D_3	10	7	8	7	32
Total	24	21	17	20	82
$\bar{X}$	8	7	5.67	6.67	

Correction factor:

$$= \frac{T^2}{N} = \frac{(82)^2}{12} = 560.333.$$

Total sum of square:

$$\begin{aligned}
&= (6)^2 + (8)^2 + (10)^2 + (5)^2 + (9)^2 + (7)^2 + (3)^2 + (6)^2 + (8)^2 + (5)^2 + (7)^2 - \text{CF} \\
&= 36 + 64 + 100 + 25 + 81 + 49 + 9 + 36 + 64 + 25 + 49 - 560.333 \\
&= 602 - 560.333 \\
&= 41.667.
\end{aligned}$$

Sum of squares between columns (circulation managers):

$$= \frac{1}{3}[(24)^2 + (21)^2 + (17)^2 + (20)^2] - CF$$
$$= \frac{1}{3}[576 + 441 + 289 + 400] - 560.333 = 568.7 - 560.333$$
$$= 8.337.$$

Sum of squares between rows (districts):

$$= \frac{1}{4}[(22)^2 + (28)^2 + (32)^2] - CF$$
$$= \frac{1}{4}[484 + 784 + 1024] - 560.333 = 573 - 560.333$$
$$= 12.667$$

$$\text{Residual} = 41.667 - (12.667 + 8.333)$$
$$= 41.667 - 21.004$$
$$= 20.666.$$

ANOVA table:

Source of Variation	Sum of Squares	d_f	Mean Square
Between columns	8.337	3	2.779
Between rows	12.667	2	6.334
Residual	20.666	6	3.444
Total	41.667	11	

$$F = \frac{2.779}{3.444} = 0.807.$$

For d_f=3 and d_f=5, F=4.76 at 5 percent level of significance. Since the calculated value of F is less than the table value, there is no significant difference between circulations of different circulation managers. Hence, the null hypothesis is accepted.

Now, comparing the district variance with residual variance:

$$F = \frac{6.334}{3.444} = 1.839.$$

For d_f=2 and d_f=6, F=5.14 at 5 percent level of significance. Since the calculated value of F is less than the table value, there is no significant difference in the circulations of three districts.

5. Out of three universities, that is, Cambridge, Oxford, and Sussex, a test was given to five students chosen at random from an MA (mass communication) class. Their scores are given as follows:

	Scores				
University	S_1	S_2	S_3	S_4	S_5
Cambridge	90	70	60	50	80
Oxford	70	40	50	40	50
Sussex	60	50	60	70	60

Conduct ANOVA and show if there is any significant difference between the scores of students in the three universities.

Sample I (Cambridge)		Sample II (Oxford)		Sample III (Sussex)	
X_1	X_1^2	X_2	X_2^2	X_3	X_3^2
90	8100	70	4900	60	3600
70	4900	40	1600	50	2500
60	3600	50	2500	60	3600
50	2500	40	1600	70	4900
80	6400	50	2500	60	3600
$\Sigma X_1 = 350$	$\Sigma X_1^2 = 255500$	$\Sigma X_2 = 250$	$\Sigma X_2^2 = 13100$	$\Sigma X_3 = 300$	$\Sigma X_3^2 = 18200$

The sum of all items of three samples:

$$\Sigma X_1 + \Sigma X_2 + \Sigma X_3 = 350 + 250 + 300 = 900$$

$$\therefore \text{correction factor} = \frac{T^2}{N} = \frac{(900)^2}{15} = \frac{810000}{15} = 54000$$

$$\begin{aligned} \therefore \text{Total sum of squares} &= \Sigma X_1^2 + \Sigma X_2^2 + \Sigma X_3^2 - \frac{T^2}{N} \\ &= 255500 + 13100 + 18200 - 54000 \\ &= 56800 + 54000 = 2800. \end{aligned}$$

Sum of squares between the samples:

$$\begin{aligned} &= \frac{\Sigma X_1^2}{N} + \frac{\Sigma X_2^2}{N} + \frac{\Sigma X_3^2}{N} = \frac{122500}{5} + \frac{62500}{5} + \frac{90000}{5} - 54000 \\ &= \frac{275000}{5} - 54000 = 55000 - 54000 \\ &= 1000. \end{aligned}$$

Mean sum of squares between samples $= \frac{1000}{2} = 500$ (because these are three samples and degree of freedom is $3-1=2$).

Sum of squares within samples = Total sum of squares − Sum of squares between samples $= 2800 - 1000 = 1800$.

Mean sum of squares within the samples:

$$= \frac{1800}{15-3}$$
$$= \frac{1800}{12}$$
$$= 150.$$

Now, the above information can be put in the following ANOVA table:

Sources of Variation	Sum of Squares	d_f	Mean Square
Between samples	1000	2	500
Within samples	1800	12	150
Total	2800	14	650

$$\therefore \quad F = \frac{\text{Variance between samples}}{\text{Variance within samples}}$$
$$= \frac{500}{150} = 3.33.$$

The table value of F for $d_{f1}=2$ and $d_{f2}=12$ at 5 percent level of significance is 3.89.

Since the calculated value of F is less than the table value, the difference between the mean value of the sample is not significant, that is, the samples could have come from the same universe.

6. In an advertising agency, two random samples of social media advertisements gave the following results:

Sample	Size	Sample Mean	Sum of Squares of Deviations from the Mean
1	10	15	90
2	12	14	108

Test the equality of sample variances at 5 percent level of significance.

Solution: Let us take the hypothesis that there is no significant difference in the variances of the two samples.

Now applying the *F*-test:

$$F = \frac{S_1^2}{S_2^2}$$

$$S_1^2 = \frac{\Sigma d_1^2}{N_1 - 1} = \frac{\Sigma(X_1 - \bar{X}_1)^2}{10 - 1}$$

$$= \frac{90}{9} = 10$$

$$S_2^2 = \frac{\Sigma d_2^2}{N_2 - 1} = \frac{\Sigma(X_2 - \bar{X}_2)^2}{12 - 1}$$

$$= \frac{80}{11} = 9.82$$

$$\therefore F = \frac{10}{9.82} = 1.018.$$

The table value of *F* for d_{f1}=9 and d_{f2}=11 at 5 percent level of significance is 2.9. Since the calculated value of *F* is less than the tabulated value, there is no significant difference in the variances of the two samples. Hence, the null hypothesis is accepted.

SUMMARY

The concept of ANOVA was first coined by R.A. Fisher in the 1920s. It basically provides simultaneous testing of the difference between many sample means. This type of test is very useful in communication and media research where the effects of one or two variables on a problem under study have to be determined on the basis of a number of experiments conducted simultaneously. *F*-ratio or *variance ratio* is the ratio of greater variance and smaller variance. Before applying the *F*-test, its assumptions must be followed such as (a) the universe should be normally distributed, (b) samples should be representative and should be independent of each other, and (c) there should not be significant difference between the variances of the samples. In one-way ANOVA, we take into account only one variable and we test the null hypothesis calculating the analysis one by one: (a) variance between samples, (b) variance within samples, (c) total sum of squares, (d) *F*-ratio, and (e) comparison of the calculated value of *F* with the table value of *F* for the degrees of freedom at a certain level. All these can be summarized in the following table.

ANOVA table of one-way classification:

Source of Variation	Sum of Squares	d_f	Mean Square	*F*-ratio
Between samples	SSC	$c-1$	$\text{MSC} = \frac{\text{SSC}}{c-1}$	$\frac{\text{MSC}}{\text{MSE}}$
Between rows	SSE	$N-c$	$\text{MSE} = \frac{\text{SSE}}{N-c}$	
Total	SST	$N-1$		

Further, the ANOVA table of two-way classification can be summarized as follows:

Source of Variation	Sum of Squares	d_f	Mean Square	F-ratio
Between samples	SSC	$c-1$	$MSC = \frac{SSC}{c-1}$	$\frac{MSC}{MSE}$
Between rows	SSR	$r-1$	$MSR = \frac{SSR}{r-1}$	$\frac{MSR}{MSE}$
Residual	SSE	$(c-1)(r-1)$	$MSE = \frac{SSE}{(c-1)(r-1)}$	
Total	SST	$N-1$		

After thoroughly studying the nature and behavior of multiple sample means in ANOVA (ANOVA), it will be desirably sequential, relevant, important, and useful to discuss multivariate analysis (MVA) techniques in media research in the next chapter.

IMPORTANT FORMULAE

1. Direct Method:

   a. $F = \frac{S_1^2}{S_2^2}$,

   where $S_1^2 = \frac{\Sigma d_1^2}{N_1 - 1} = \frac{\Sigma(X_1 - \bar{X}_1)^2}{N_1 - 1}$, $S_2^2 = \frac{\Sigma d_2^2}{N_2 - 1} = \frac{\Sigma(X_2 - \bar{X}_2)^2}{N_2 - 1}$.

   (Hence, S_1^2 should be greater than S_2^2 or else it will be $\frac{S_2^2}{S_1^2}$)

   b. i. $df_1 = N_1 - 1$,
   where df_1 is the degree of freedom of sample having larger variance.

   ii. $df_2 = N_2 - 1$,
   where df_2 is the degree of freedom of sample having smaller variance.

   c. i. Grand mean

$$(\bar{\bar{X}}) = \frac{\bar{X}_1 + \bar{X}_2 + \bar{X}_3 + \cdots + \bar{X}_k}{N_1 + N_2 + N_3 + \cdots + N_k}$$

   ii. If samples are of different sizes (where k is the number of samples), then

$$\bar{\bar{X}} = \frac{\bar{X}_1 N_1 + \bar{X}_2 N_2 + \bar{X}_3 N_3 + \cdots + \bar{X}_k N_k}{N_1 + N_2 + N_3 + \cdots + N_k}$$

   d. $$F = \frac{\text{Between column variance}}{\text{Between row variance}} = \frac{\text{Variance between samples}}{\text{Variance within samples}}$$

$$= \frac{MSC}{MSE},$$

where MSC = mean sum of squares between samples and
MSE = mean sum of squares within samples.

$$\text{MSC} = \frac{\text{SSC}}{c-1} \text{ and MSE} = \frac{\text{SSE}}{N-c}$$

2. Shortcut Method (One-way Classification):
   a. Correction factor (CF) $= \frac{T^2}{N} = \frac{\Sigma X_1 + \Sigma X_2 + \cdots + \Sigma X_n}{N}$
   b. $\text{SST} = \left[\Sigma X_1^2 + \Sigma X_2^2 + \cdots + \Sigma X_N^2\right] - \text{CF}$
   c. $\text{SSC} = \left[\frac{(\Sigma X_1)^2}{N_1} + \frac{(\Sigma X_2)^2}{N_2} + \cdots + \frac{(\Sigma X_N)^2}{N_N}\right] - \text{CF}$
   d. SSE = SST − SSC
   e. $F = \frac{\text{MSC}}{\text{MSE}}$,

   where $\text{MSC} = \frac{\text{SSC}}{c-1}$, $\text{MSE} = \frac{\text{SSE}}{N-c}$.
3. Shortcut Method (Two-way Classification):
   a. SSE = SST − (SSC + SSR)
   b. $\text{MSC} = \frac{\text{SSC}}{c-1}$, $\text{MSR} = \frac{\text{SSR}}{r-1}$, $MSR = \frac{\text{SSE}}{(r-1)(c-1)}$
   c. $F - \text{ratio}: F_1 = \frac{\text{MSC}}{\text{MSE}}$, $F_2 = \frac{\text{MSR}}{\text{MSE}}$

   where SSC = sum of squares between column, SSR = sum of squares between row, SSE = sum of squares due to errors, and SST = total sum of squares.

RELATED AND SUGGESTED WEBSITES

(As retrieved on December 1, 2015)

1. http://www.dartmouth.edu/~chance/teaching_aids/books_articles/probability_book/Chapter6.pdf
2. http://www.math.ubc.ca/~feldman/m302/binomial.pdf
3. http://www.csse.monash.edu.au/~smarkham/resources/anova.htm
4. http://www.cimt.plymouth.ac.uk/projects/mepres/alevel/fstats_ch7.pdf
5. http://www.sagepub.com/upm-data/26650_Chapter13.pdf
6. http://www.physics.csbsju.edu/stats/anova.html

RELATED AND RECOMMENDED READINGS

Elhance, D.N., and Veena Elhance. 1990. *Fundamentals of Statistics*, 25.1–25.30. New Delhi: Kitab Mahal.

Gupta, S.P. 2011. *Statistical Methods*, 1006–36. New Delhi: Sultan Chand & Sons.

Gupta, S.P., and Alka Gupta. 2008 *Statistical Methods in Behavioural Sciences*, 235–59. Allahabad: Sharda Pustak Bhawan.

Hussain, Shamshad. 1986. *Elementary Statistics in Psychology and Education*, 137–44. New Delhi: Motilal Banarsidass.

Kerlinger, F.N. 1973. *Foundations of Behavioural Research*, 214–239. Holt, Rinehart & Winston.

Kothari, C.R. 1990. *Research Methodology: Methods and Techniques*, 300–21. New Delhi: Wishwa Prakashan.

Mangal, S.K. 1987. *Statistics in Psychology and Education*, 192–212. New Delhi: McGraw Hill.

Wimmer, Roger D.S., and Joseph R. Dominick. 2003. *Mass Media Research: An Introduction*, 192–212. 7th ed. Belmont, CA: Thomson & Wadsworth.

QUESTIONS AND PROBLEMS

1. Describe the meaning and concept of ANOVA.
2. What is variance ratio test? Discuss the assumptions in the *F*-test and applications of the same.
3. Explain the ANOVA in one-way classification.
4. Describe the assumptions in ANOVA and techniques of this variance.
5. Describe the ANOVA in two-way classification.
6. Enlist the various formulae for *F*-test and ANOVA.
7. How is an ANOVA table written in one-way classification?
8. How is an ANOVA table constructed in two-way classification?
9. Explain the value of degrees of freedom of ANOVA in one-way and two-way classification?
10. Describe the *F*-test with regard to ANOVA. Explain the meaning and use of ANOVA. How is an ANOVA table set up and how is a test based on it performed?
11. What is ANOVA? What is the significance of its study?
12. Explain the one-way classification technique of ANOVA.
13. Describe the technique of ANOVA for two-way classification.
14. Discuss the difference between ANOVA and analysis of covariance technique for testing the significance of class difference in one-way classification.
15. Write a note on the uses of relationship between *t*, chi-square, and *F*-distributions.
16. Discuss the *F*-test for testing the equality of two sample variances.
17. What do you understand by Fisher's variance ratio test? Indicate some of its practical applications.
18. What are the basic and common assumptions made for ANOVA?
19. What is *F*-test? Mention two uses of the same.
20. What is the relevance of ANOVA in communication and media studies?
21. Distinguish between one-way and two-way ANOVA.
22. Following are the defective pieces produced by four different printing operators, in turn, on four different printing machines:

Printing Machine	Operator			
	O_1	O_2	O_3	O_4
P1	34	28	33	29
P2	31	24	35	22
P3	27	20	43	72
P4	28	28	29	26

Apply ANOVA at 0.05 level of significance to ascertain whether variability in printing production is due to variability in printing operators' performance or variability in printing machines' performance.

23. Two random samples of advertisers and journalists were drawn from two normal populations and their values are:

Advertisers	66	67	75	76	82	84	88	90	92		
Journalists	64	66	74	78	82	85	87	92	93	95	97

Test whether the two populations have the same variance at the 5 percent level of significance (F=3.11 at 5% for d_{f1}=8 and d_{f2}=10).

24. Perform a two-way ANOVA on the data given below:

Performance of Newspaper Production	Treatment			
	T1	T2	T3	T4
NP1	38	40	41	39
NP2	45	42	49	36
NP3	40	38	42	42

25. Three samples of subeditors, reporters, and graphic designers, each of size 5, were drawn from three uncorrelated normal populations with equal variances. Test the hypothesis that the population means are equal at 5 percent level.
26. To find out the effect of three different media techniques on the training of media students on a particular journalistic skill was experimented. Three groups, each consisting of seven media students, assigned randomly were trained through these three different media techniques. The scores obtained on a performance were recorded as below:

Group I	Group II	Group III
3	4	5
5	5	5
3	3	5
1	4	1
7	9	7
3	5	3
6	5	7

Test the difference between the groups by adopting the ANOVA techniques.

27. To find out the effectiveness of communication, a research study was conducted. For this purpose, three groups of advertising, print media, and public relations were considered; 10 media students each randomly selected from a media school were taken and each group was made to adopt a particular method of communication. At the end, the performance was tested. The number of irrelevant communications by the media students of these groups is presented below:

Ad group:	12,	10,	11,	11,	8,	10,	7,	9,	10,	6
Print group:	14,	8,	19,	15,	10,	11,	13,	12,	9,	12
PR group:	8,	11,	13,	9,	7,	5,	6,	8,	7,	10

Apply the ANOVA technique for testing the significance of the difference between group means.

28. There were two experimental or independent variables in a research study—a seven-member group of media students and three media teachers, who were asked to rate the media students in terms of a particular trait on a 10-point scale. The data were recorded as under:

Rating by Three Media Teachers	**Media Students**						
	1	2	3	4	5	6	7
T1	3	5	3	1	7	3	6
T2	4	5	3	4	9	5	5
T3	5	5	5	1	7	3	7

Apply the technique of ANOVA for interpreting the above data.

12

CHAPTER

Multivariate Analysis Techniques in Mass Communication

It requires a very unusual mind to undertake the multiple analysis of the obvious.

—Alfred North Whitehead

Multivariate analysis (MVA) is basically an extension of the principles of multivariate statistics. When multivariate statistics was micro-focused for the study of the specific field of communication and media studies, it emerged as a new domain called multivariate media metrics. In mass communication, MVA is a recently and newly emerging process which involves observation, examination, and analysis of more than one media metrics-related outcome variable at a time. Practically, there are often more than one or two variables in our media and society. So this type of analysis is expected to sprout, bud, and bloom more speedily in the time to come.

In the previous chapter we have broadly discussed the meaning and concept of ANOVA, variance tests ratio, ANOVA in one-way classification, ANOVA in two-way classification, precautions in the use of ANOVA, illustrations relating to ANOVA, summary, and important formulae. After systematically studying the nature and behavior of multiple sample means in ANOVA, it will be desirably sequential, relevant, important, and useful to discuss MVA techniques in media research in this chapter.

That is to say that we have discussed the inferential statistical tool of media metrics like the ANOVA in the previous chapter. Yet another inferential statistics (as shown in the flowchart of Section 2.2.1 in Chapter 2) is the MVA technique. Hence, this chapter on the MVA technique will focus on the following:

1. Meaning and concept of MVA techniques in mass communication
2. Features and uses of MVA
3. Types of multivariate techniques
4. Multiple regression analysis
5. Multiple discriminant analysis
6. Multiple analyses of variance
7. Canonical correlation analysis
8. Factor analysis
9. Cluster analysis
10. Multidimensional scaling
11. Latent structure analysis
12. Summary

In addition, the chapter will also cover the related and suggested websites, references, related and recommended readings, and questions relating to the MVA techniques in media research.

12.1 MEANING AND CONCEPT OF MVA TECHNIQUES IN MASS COMMUNICATION

MVA techniques in media research allow more than two variables of media to be analyzed simultaneously. This technique in media research takes account of the various relationships among communication and media variables, such as audience and effectiveness of communication, creativity and communication, intelligence, emotion, communication and creativity, and interrelation between growth of print media and electronic media. In recent days, this technique has come up as an effective procedure to analyze data represented in terms of many variables. The univariate or even bivariate analysis may lead to incorrect interpretation of results. This is because univariate analysis or even bivariate analysis does not take into account the correction or interdependence among several variables simultaneously. As a result, during the last 50 years, so many statisticians and mathematicians have contributed to the growth and development of so many multivariate techniques. Today these techniques are very useful and widely applicable especially in the field of communication and media studies. Applications of multivariate techniques have gone up tremendously specially after the growth of high-speed electronic devices, such as computer and internet.

12.2 FEATURES AND USES OF MVA

MVA has the potentiality to analyze complex and cumbersome data mining. In most areas and fields of communication and media studies, we generally resort to MVA techniques for realistic and practical results. It also helps us in various types of decision-making and goal-setting relating to communication and media policies. For example, when the central government chalks out media policies, then multiple issues like social, cultural, political, economic, religious spiritual, educational, and intellectual variables are considered.

This approach may sometimes turn out to be biased in favor of some variables with larger standard deviations. Under such circumstances, multivariate techniques may be properly applied for developing norms as to how should media policies be framed. If a media researcher is keen to make probability statements in light of sampled multiple measurements, then the best mechanism of data analysis is to apply some appropriate MVA technique. Multivariate techniques convert a mass of observations into a smaller number of composite scores in such a manner that they may reflect as much information as possible. Hence, the major role of these techniques is to systematically arrange a large amount of complex and cumbersome data mining into a crystal clear and easily understandable form. For even a better understanding of these techniques, one must be aware of the fundamental concepts of linear algebra, vector spaces, orthogonal and oblique projections, and univariate analysis. Before applying MVA for useful results, one must understand the nature and structure of the data and the genuine purpose of applying MVA techniques. This type of analysis involves many complex and cumbersome mathematical and statistical computations. Hence, the high-speed computers can easily facilitate the application of MVA techniques.

12.3 TYPES OF MULTIVARIATE TECHNIQUES

MVA can be broadly divided into two methods: (a) dependence methods and (b) independence methods.

Dependence methods are those that have data containing both dependent and independent variables, while *independence methods* are those that have data containing many variables without dependency relationship. Dependence methods include techniques such as: (a) multiple regression analysis, (b) multiple discriminant analysis, (c) multiple ANOVA, and (d) canonical correlation analysis. Independence methods include techniques such as: (a) factor analysis, (b) cluster analysis, (c) multidimensional scaling analysis, and (d) latent structure analysis.

J.N. Sheth in his research paper entitled "The Multivariate Revolution in Marketing Research" published in the *Journal of Marketing of American Marketing Association* has given a similar type of flowchart as drawn in Figure 12.1, which clearly explains both dependence methods and independence methods.

12.4 MULTIPLE REGRESSION ANALYSIS

There are two or more independent variables of a single dependent variable in a multiple regression analysis. Hence, in a multiple regression analysis, there are three or more variables and at least one is constant. We now take X_1 as a dependent variable and try to find out its relative movement for movements in both X_2 and X_3 which are independent variables. However, the fundamental concept of the multiple analysis is same as that of a bivariate analysis. Following are the three basic purposes of a multiple regression:

1. To find out an equation that provides estimates of the dependent variable from the values of two or more independent variables.
2. To calculate a measure of error involved in using this regression equation as a basis of estimation.
3. To compute a measure of proportion of variance in the dependent variable accounted for or "explained by" the independent variables.

The first objective is achieved by deriving an appropriate regression equation by the method of least squares. The second objective is attained by finding out a standard error of estimate. And the third objective is achieved by calculating the multiple coefficient of determination.

12.4.1 Multiple Regression Equations

1. The regression equation of X_1 on X_2 and X_3 will be as follows:

$$X_1 = a_{1.23} + b_{12.3} X_2 + b_{13.2} X_3 \quad (i)$$

In the above equation, the values of $b_{12.3}$ and $b_{13.2}$ are determined by solving simultaneously the three normal equations:

$$\Sigma X_1 = Na_{1.23} + b_{12.3} \Sigma X_2 + b_{13.2} \Sigma X_3$$

FIGURE 12.1

BROADER TYPES OF MULTIVARIATE TECHNIQUES

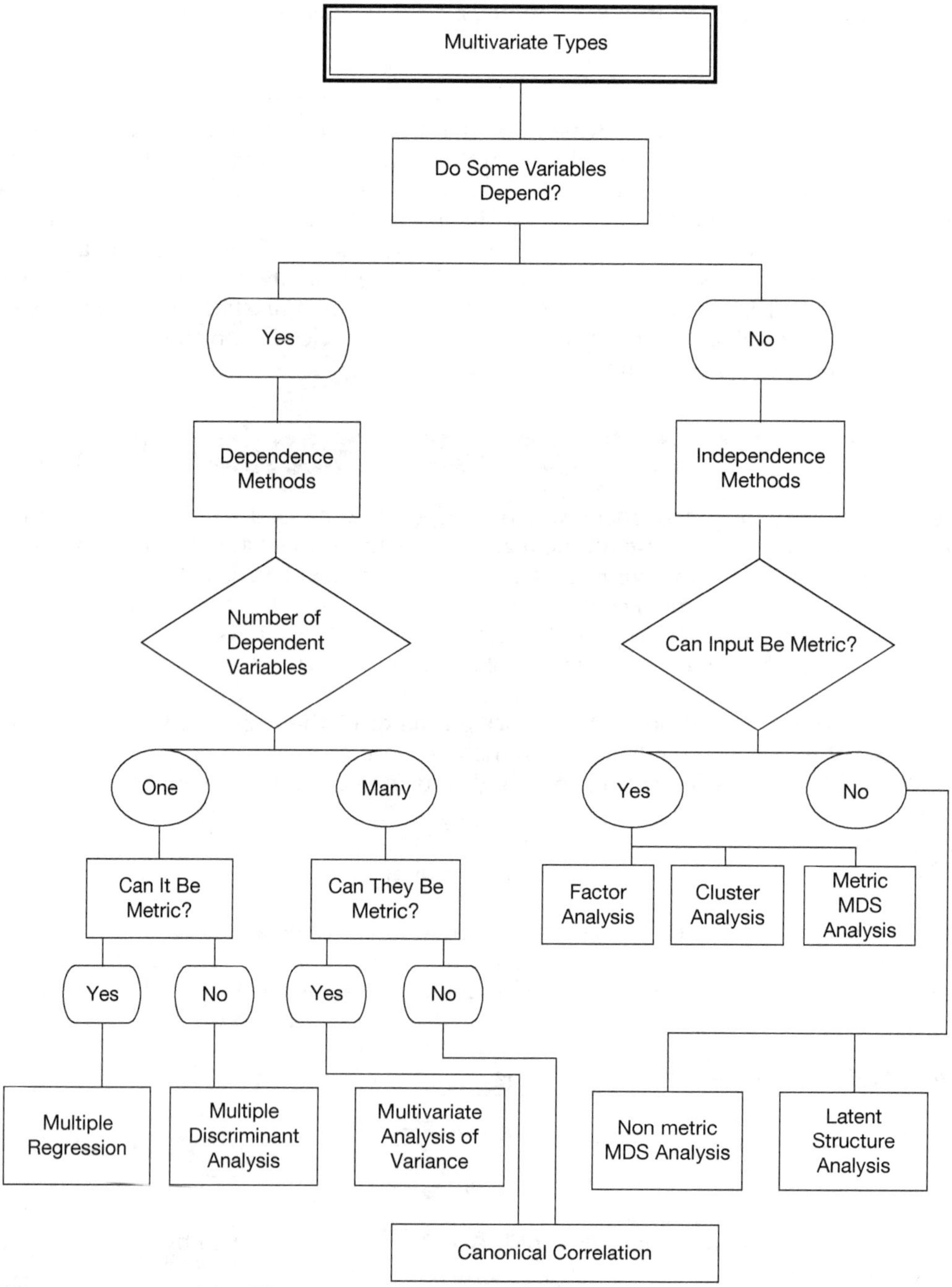

Source: Concept by Jagdish. N. Sheth, drawn by author's research scholar Bhupender Singh.

$$\Sigma X_1X_2 = a_{1.23} + b_{12.3}\,\Sigma X_2^2 + b_{13.2}\,\Sigma X_2X_3$$
$$\Sigma X_1X_3 = a_{1.23}\,\Sigma X_3 + b_{12.3}\,\Sigma X_2.X_3 + b_{13.2}\,\Sigma X_3^2$$

The last two of these three equations can be obtained if we multiply equation (*i*) by X_2 and X_3 on both sides.

2. The regression equation of X_2 on X_1 and X_3 will be as follows:

$$X_2 = a_{2.13} + b_{21.3}\,X_1 + b_{23.1}\,X_3 \qquad (ii)$$

The normal equations for fitting the above equations are:

$$\Sigma X_2 = Na_{2.13} + b_{21.3}\,\Sigma X_1 + b_{23.1}\,\Sigma X_3$$
$$\Sigma X_1X_2 = a_{2.13} + b_{21.3}\,\Sigma X_2^2 + b_{23.1}\,\Sigma X_1.X_3$$
$$\Sigma X_1X_3 = a_{2.13} + b_{21.3}\,\Sigma X_1X_3 + b_{23.1}\,\Sigma X_3^2$$

3. The regression equation of X_3 on X_1 and X_2 will be as follows:

$$X_3 = a_{3.12} + b_{31.2}\,X_1 + b_{32.1}\,X_2 \qquad (iii)$$

The normal equations for fitting the above equation are:

$$\Sigma X_3 = Na_{3.12} + b_{31.2}\,\Sigma X_1 + b_{32.1}\,\Sigma X_2$$
$$\Sigma X_1X_3 = a_{3.12} + b_{31.2}\,\Sigma X_1^2 + b_{32.1}\,\Sigma X_1X_2$$
$$\Sigma X_2X_3 = a_{3.12} + b_{31.2}\,\Sigma X_1X_2 + b_{32.1}\,\Sigma X_2^2$$

Generalization for more than three variables will be as follows:

$$X_1 = a_{1.234} + b_{12.34}\,X_2 + b_{13.24}\,X_3 + b_{14.23}\,X_4.$$

The four normal equations for determining the values of $a_{1.234}$, $b_{12.34}$, $b_{13.24}$, and $b_{14.23}$ can be obtained by multiplying the above equation on both sides by X_1, X_2, X_3, and X_4. This will give the multiple regression of X_1 on X_2, X_3, and X_4.

Example: Find the multiple regression equations of mistakes committed by advertisers, creative writers, and graphic artists from the data given below:

Advertisers	2	4	6	8
Creative writers	3	5	7	9
Graphic artists	4	6	8	10

Solution: Let us assume advertisers as X_1, creative writers as X_2, and graphic artists as X_3. Now taking the regression equation of X_1 on X_2 and X_3 is,

$$X_1 = a_{1.23} + b_{12.3}\,X_2 + b_{13.2}\,X_3.$$

The value of the constants $a_{1.23}$, $b_{12.3}$, and $b_{13.2}$ can be obtained by solving the following three normal equations:

$$\sum X_1 = Na_{1.23} + b_{12.3} \sum X_2 + b_{13.2} \sum X_3$$
$$\sum X_1X_2 = a_{1.23} + b_{12.3} \sum X_2^2 + b_{13.2} \sum X_2.X_3$$
$$\sum X_1X_3 = a_{1.23} \sum X_3 + b_{12.3} \sum X_2.X_3 + b_{13.2} \sum X_3^2$$

Calculating the required values:

X_1	2	4	6	8	$\Sigma X_1 = 20$
X_2	3	5	7	9	$\Sigma X_2 = 24$
X_3	4	6	8	10	$\Sigma X_3 = 28$
X_1X_2	6	20	42	72	$\Sigma X_1X_2 = 140$
X_1X_3	8	24	48	80	$\Sigma X_1X_3 = 160$
X_2X_3	12	30	56	90	$\Sigma X_2X_3 = 188$
X_1^2	4	16	36	64	$\sum X_1^2 = 120$
X_2^2	9	25	49	81	$\sum X_2^2 = 164$
X_3^2	16	36	64	100	$\sum X_3^2 = 216$

Substituting the values in the normal equations:

$$4a_{1.23} + 24b_{12.3} + 28b_{13.2} = 20 \quad (i)$$

$$24a_{1.23} + 164b_{12.3} + 188b_{13.2} = 140 \quad (ii)$$

$$28a_{1.23} + 188b_{12.3} + 216b_{13.2} = 160 \quad (iii)$$

Multiplying equation (*i*) by 6 and subtracting it from (*ii*),

$$24a_{1.23} + 164b_{12.3} + 188b_{13.2} = 140$$
$$\underset{-}{24a_{1.23}} + \underset{-}{134b_{12.3}} + \underset{-}{168b_{13.2}} = \underset{-}{120}$$
$$30b_{12.3} + 20b_{13.2} = 20 \quad (iv)$$

Multiplying equation (*ii*) by 7 and (*iii*) by 6 and subtracting (*vi*) from (*ii*),

$$168a_{1.23} + 1148b_{12.3} + 1316b_{13.2} = 980 \quad (v)$$

$$\underset{-}{168a_{1.23}} + \underset{-}{1128b_{12.3}} + \underset{-}{1296b_{13.2}} = \underset{-}{960} \quad (vi)$$

$$20b_{12.3} + 20b_{13.2} = 20 \quad (vii)$$

Now subtracting (*iv*) from (*vii*),

$$20b_{12.3} + 20b_{13.2} = 20$$
$$\underset{-}{30b_{12.3}} + \underset{-}{20b_{13.2}} = \underset{-}{20}$$
$$-10b_{12.3} = 0$$

$$b_{12.3}=0 \qquad (viii)$$

Now, putting the value of $b_{12.3}$ into (*vii*),

$$0+20b_{13.2}=20$$

$$b_{13.2}=1 \qquad (ix)$$

Now, substituting the value of $b_{12.3}$ and $b_{13.2}$ in equation (*i*), we get,

$$4a_{1.23}+0\times 24+28\times 1=20$$

$$4a_{1.23}=-8$$

$$a_{1.23}=-2$$

Hence, the value of $a_{1.23}=-2$, $b_{12.3}=0$, and $b_{13.2}=1$.

Thus, the required regression equation of X_1 on X_2 and X_3 is,

$$X_1=a_{1.23}+b_{12.3}\,X_2+b_{13.2}\,X_3$$

$$=-2+0+X_3$$

$$=X_3-2.$$

Assumptions of linear multiple regression analysis:

1. Dependable variables are random variables, while independent variables need not necessarily be random.
2. The relationship between independent and dependent variables is linear.

Since the calculation of multiple regression analysis is sometimes a time-consuming, tedious, complex, and cumbersome job, and even more complicated with the increase in the number of variables, the use of a high-speed computer is desirable.

12.5 MULTIPLE DISCRIMINANT ANALYSIS

It is also known as canonical variate analysis (CVA) or canonical discriminant analysis (CDA). It is a method of compressing a multivariate signal to yield a lower dimensional signal amenable to classification. This is basically an extension of linear discriminant analysis (LDA) which in its original form is applied to construct discriminant functions for the objects assigned to two groups.

When there are two groups, the discriminant function is nothing more than a multiple regression equation with the dependent variable as nominal variable (coded as 0, 1) representing group membership. With three or more groups, however, discriminant analysis goes beyond multiple regression methods. Through the discriminant analysis technique, one may classify individuals or objects into one of two or more mutually exclusive and exhaustive groups on the basis of a set of independent variables. Discriminant analysis requires interval-independent variables and a nominal dependent variable. Let us suppose that brand preference (A or B) is a dependent variable of interest and its relationship to an individual's age (X_1), education (X_2), socio-economic status (X_3), and so on is being investigated; in this case, the discriminant analysis technique is generally applied. Regression analysis in such a situation cannot be applied because the dependent variable is not intervally scaled. Under the circumstances, discriminant analysis is described to be the most suitable variable if the single dependent variable happens to be nonmetric and is to be classified into two or more groups, depending upon its relationship with many independent variables which are metric. In the above analysis, age (X_1), education (X_2), and socio-economic status (X_3) have been taken as discriminant variables. A discriminant function can be derived from discriminant analysis.

Hence, $Y = W_1X_1 + W_2X_2 + W_3X_3$,

where Y = scores of the discriminant function of an individual

X_1 = scores of the first individual on the first variable

X_2 = scores of the individual on the second variable

X_3 = scores of the individual on the third variable

W_1 = weight in the discriminant function of the first variable

W_2 = weight in the discriminant function of the second variable

W_3 = weight in the discriminant function of the third variable.

The objective in discriminant analysis is to predict an object's likelihood of belonging to a particular group based on many independent variables. When we classify the dependent variable in more than two groups, then we use the name multiple discriminant analysis. But when only two groups are to be formed, we use the term discriminant analysis.

12.6 MULTIPLE ANALYSIS OF VARIANCE

It is basically an extension of bivariate ANOVA in which the ratio of among-groups variance to within-groups variance is calculated on a set of variables instead of a single variable. This method is suitable if many metric-dependent variables are associated in a research work along with several nonmetric explanatory variables. Hence, multivariate ANOVA is particularly used if we want to test hypotheses regarding multivariate differences in group responses to experimental manipulations. For example, a media market researcher may be interested in applying one test market and one control market to study the effect of an advertising campaign on sales and awareness, knowledge, habits, aptitudes, and attitudes. Under such circumstances, MVA of variance should be applied for attaining the objectives.

12.7 CANONICAL CORRELATION ANALYSIS

It is a logical extension of multiple regression. Basically, it is a multiple regression method. It adds more than one dependent variable to the multiple regression model. It handles the relations between sets of independent variables and sets of dependent variables. Thus, the regression analysis of data with X independent variables and Y dependent variables is called canonical correction analysis. Here, both metric and nonmetric data can be applied regarding a multivariate technique. Thus, canonical correction is a generalization of multiple regression analysis and multiple regression analysis is a special case of canonical analysis. Symbolically, in canonical correction analysis, the weights of the two sets, that is, $a_1, a_2, \ldots, a_k$ and $b_1, b_2, \ldots, b_k$ are so determined that the variables $X = a_1x_1 + a_2x_2 + \cdots + a_kx_k + a$ and $Y = b_1y_1 + b_2y_2 + \cdots + b_ky_k + b$ have a maximum common variance. Hence, the canonical correction analysis gives a complete analysis of the presence or absence of a relationship between the two sets of variables and is, hence, described as a theoretically powerful method of analysis.

12.8 FACTOR ANALYSIS

As discussed earlier MVA refers to the simultaneous study or examination of more than two variables. Factor analysis is a type of multivariate statistical method that studies the independent and interactive effects of two or more independent variables on a dependent variable. It relates to the problem of analyzing the structure of the correlation or interrelationship among a large number of variables (e.g., test scores, test items, questionnaire responses, and so on) by defining a set of common underlying dimensions, called factors. In factor analysis, we first try to find out all the dependent and independent variables. Once these two types of variables are determined, the two primary uses of factor analysis—summarization and data reduction—can be achieved. In media metrics, one of the most significant and revolutionary developments is the planning and analysis of the simultaneous operation and interaction of two or more variables, for example, suppose, we have data of media person's income, education, status, and dwelling area and we want to draw a conclusion from these factors, which summarizes the commonality of all the said four variables. The method applied for this purpose is called factor analysis. This method allows us to group dependent variables and independent variables into factors which are based on correlation between variables, and the factors so derived may be considered as new variables and are described as latent variables. Their value is computed by adding the values of the original variables which have been grouped into the factor. Because the factors are linear combinations of data, the coordinates of each observation or variable are measured to get what are called factor loadings. These types of factor loadings explain the correlation between the specific variable and the factor, and are generally kept in a matrix of correlations between the variables and the factors.

Mathematical basis of factor analysis: Factor analysis is based on the study of matrix, which is an integral part of mathematical algebra. When data are presented in a few rows and columns, then it is called a "matrix" and its plural is "matrices." Matrix is a rectangular array of rows and columns in an $m \times n$ form. The following data about media students are in a 4×3 form of matrix.

	No. of Media Students of Specialized Areas			
Level	**PR**	**Print**	**Electronic**	**Advertising**
PG first yr	10	9	8	8
PG second yr	9	8	9	10
Pre-PhD	8	9	10	9

Matrix form:

$$\begin{bmatrix} 10 & 9 & 8 & 8 \\ 9 & 8 & 9 & 10 \\ 8 & 9 & 10 & 9 \end{bmatrix}$$

The Intercorrelation coefficient can be presented in the form of a matrix in the following manner:

Correlation Coefficient Table

Variable	X_1	X_2	X_3
X_1	1.00	0.45	0.38
X_2	0.45	1.00	0.27
X_3	0.38	0.27	1.00

Matrix form:

1.00	0.45	0.38
0.45	1.00	0.27
0.38	0.27	1.00

Different kinds of matrix operations such as addition, subtraction, and multiplication can be presented as follows.

A matrix which has all the numbers as zero is called a null matrix. If in a matrix, the number of rows and columns is the same, then it is called a square matrix. If in a matrix, the number of principal diagonals is 1, then it is called a unit matrix.

$$\begin{bmatrix} 0 & 0 & 0 \\ 0 & 0 & 0 \end{bmatrix} \quad \begin{bmatrix} 1 & 8 & 5 \\ 3 & 9 & 2 \\ 0 & 4 & 6 \end{bmatrix} \quad \begin{bmatrix} 1 & 0 & 0 \\ 0 & 1 & 0 \\ 0 & 0 & 1 \end{bmatrix}$$

Zero matrix　　Square matrix　　Unit matrix

If a row and a column of a matrix 'A' are exchanged, then it is called a transpose matrix, A′. And if A=A′, then it is called a symmetrical matrix.

$$A = \begin{bmatrix} 8 & 3 & 4 & 2 \\ 6 & 7 & 5 & 0 \\ 1 & 2 & 6 & 9 \end{bmatrix} \qquad \text{Transpose Matrix } (A') = \begin{bmatrix} 8 & 6 & 1 \\ 3 & 7 & 2 \\ 4 & 5 & 6 \\ 2 & 0 & 9 \end{bmatrix}$$

$$\text{Symmetrical Matrix} = \begin{bmatrix} 3 & 4 & 2 \\ 4 & 6 & 1 \\ 2 & 1 & 8 \end{bmatrix}$$

(Note: It remains unchanged even after exchanging the row and column.)

Now, let us take the examples of addition and subtraction in the following cases:

$$A = \begin{bmatrix} 4 & 5 & 2 \\ 0 & 6 & 1 \\ 2 & 7 & 8 \end{bmatrix} \quad B = \begin{bmatrix} 1 & 9 & 2 \\ 4 & 6 & 3 \\ 5 & 0 & 3 \end{bmatrix}$$

$$A + B = \begin{bmatrix} 4+1 & 5+9 & 2+2 \\ 0+4 & 6+6 & 1+3 \\ 2+5 & 7+0 & 8+3 \end{bmatrix} = \begin{bmatrix} 5 & 14 & 4 \\ 4 & 12 & 4 \\ 7 & 7 & 11 \end{bmatrix}.$$

If a matrix is multiplied by 0, then it will always be zero. Hence, A0=0 and 0A=0.

If a matrix is multiplied by a unit matrix, then the matrix remains unchanged. Hence, AI=A and IA=A.

If A and B are two such matrices that AB=I, then B is called the inverse matrix of A and is written as A^{-1}. Hence, $AA^{-1}=I=A^{-1}A$.

$$A = \begin{bmatrix} 1 & 2 & 3 \\ 2 & 5 & 7 \\ -1 & -4 & -5 \end{bmatrix}, \quad \text{then } A^{-1} = \begin{bmatrix} 3 & -2 & -1 \\ -4 & 1 & -1 \\ 2 & 0 & 1 \end{bmatrix}$$

$$A \times A^{-1} = \begin{bmatrix} 1\times3+2\times-4+3\times2 & 1\times-2+2\times1+3\times0 & 1\times-1+2\times-1+3\times1 \\ 2\times3+5\times-4+7\times2 & 2\times-2+5\times1+7\times0 & 2\times-1+5\times-1+7\times1 \\ -2\times3+-4\times-4+-5\times2 & -2\times-2+-4\times1+-5\times0 & -2\times-1+-4\times-1+-5\times1 \end{bmatrix}$$

$$= \begin{bmatrix} 1 & 0 & 0 \\ 0 & 1 & 0 \\ 0 & 0 & 1 \end{bmatrix}.$$

The inverse of any matrix is not a straight method. So it is either derived algebraically or with the help of a computer.

12.8.1 Important Methods of Factor Analysis

There are several methods of factor analysis, but the most commonly used in media metrics are as follows:

1. Centroid method
2. Principal components method
3. Maximum likelihood method

Before discussing these methods, it would be desirable here to discuss some basic key terms relating to the methods of factor analysis:

1. Factor: A factor represents the underlying dimensions that summarize the original set of observed variables. In media and communication studies, there can be one factor or more and a number of variables associated with the same.
2. Common variance: Variance shared with other variables in the factor analysis is called common variance.
3. Communality (h^2): It is denoted by h^2 and is the total amount of variance in the given item accounted for by all the factors.
4. Factor loadings: These are correlations between the original variables and the factors, and the key for understanding the nature of a particular factor. Variables with high

loadings are the distinguishing features of a factor. These are also known as factor–variable correlations.

5. Correlation matrix: Table showing correlations among all the variables.
6. Eigenvalue: If we take the sum of squared values of factor loadings relating to a factor, then such sum is called an eigenvalue, also referred to as a latent root.
7. Factor score: It is the measure of a score on a given factor. Factor scores can be helpful in explaining the meaning of the factor. With such scores, many other MVA can be carried out. Factor scores are standardized to have a mean of 0 (zero) and a standard deviation of 1.
8. Multicollinearity: The degree to which a variable can be explained by the other variables in the analysis.
9. Rotation: This is of two types, (a) orthogonal and (b) oblique. In orthogonal rotation, factors are not correlated and there exists mathematical independence of factor axes to each other (i.e., at right angles or at 90°). Each factor is independent of, or orthogonal to, all other factors. Hence, under this type, the correlation between factors is determined to be zero. And varimax is one of the most popular orthogonal rotation method. On the other hand, in oblique rotation, the factors are correlated. Thus, when the factors are independent, orthogonal rotation is performed and when the factors are correlated, an oblique rotation is carried out. Communality for all the variables will remain unaffected regardless of rotation but the eigenvalues will change due to rotation.
10. Total sum of squares: It is the final value of eigenvalues of all factors combined together. When divided by the total number of variables, the value results in an index that indicates how the specific solution accounts for what all the variables combined together represent.

Methods:

1. Centroid method of factor analysis: Before the advent of high-speed computers, this method of factor analysis, engineered by L.L. Thurstone, was applied more often till 1950. Steps of centroid method:
   a. First step is to find out a matrix of correlation *R*, with the help of a correlation coefficient.
   b. Then the first centroid factor is determined as follows:
      i. The sum of the coefficients (including the diagonal unity) in each column of the correlation matrix is worked out.
      ii. Thereafter, the sum of these column sums (*T*) is obtained.
      iii. Then the sum of each column computed as per step (i) is divided by the square root of *T* computed in step (ii), leading to what are called centroid loadings. Thus, each centroid loading is calculated. The full set of loadings so calculated constitute the first centroid factor.
   c. In order to find out the second centroid factor, one must calculate a matrix of residual coefficients. For this very reason, the loadings for the two variables on the first centroid factor are multiplied. The resulting matrix of factor cross products is named Q_1. Thereafter, Q_1 is subtracted element by element from the original correlation matrix, R, and the result is the first matrix of residual coefficients R_1. Then we must reflect some of the variables in it, meaning thereby that some of the variables are given negative signs in the sum. For any variable which is so reflected, the signs of all the coefficients in that row and column of the residual matrix are changed. When this type of change is executed, the matrix named reflected matrix, from which the

loadings are reflected, must be given negative signs. This is referred to as the second centroid factor.

d. The same process, exercised above, is adopted for the next factors. After finding out the second centroid factor, cross products are calculated after the construction of matrix Q_2. Thereafter, this is subtracted from R_1 resulting in R_2. This can be illustrated with the following example.

Example 1: Following are the data of the correlation matrix, R, relating to five variables with unities in the diagonal spaces:

Variables	1	2	3	4	5
1	0.72	0.72	0.50	0.38	0.69
2	0.72	0.81	0.81	0.54	0.47
3	0.50	0.81	0.81	0.65	0.53
4	0.38	0.54	0.65	0.65	0.41
5	0.69	0.47	0.53	0.41	0.69

Using the centroid method of factor analysis, find out the first and second centroid factors from the above information.

Solution: Let us calculate the first centroid factor as follows.
Correlation matrix and calculations of the first centroid factor:

Test	1	2	3	4	5	Σ
1	0.72	0.72	0.50	0.38	0.69	2.29
2	0.72	0.81	0.81	0.54	0.47	2.54
3	0.50	0.81	0.81	0.65	0.53	2.49
4	0.38	0.54	0.65	0.65	0.41	1.98
5	0.69	0.47	0.53	0.41	0.69	2.10
Σ	2.29	2.54	2.49	1.98	2.10	11.40
Column Sum (t_1)	15.08	3.01	3.35	3.30	2.63	2.79
1st factor centroid (A)=3.01/3.883	0.775	0.863	0.850	0.677	0.718	2.883

Sum of the column sums (T)=15.08 $\sqrt{T} = 3.883$ ΣA=3.883.

We can also state this information as follows:

Variables	Factor Loadings Concerning the First Centroid Factor (A)
1	0.775
2	0.863
3	0.850
4	0.667
5	0.718

To get the second centroid factor (B), we first develop the first matrix of factor cross product (Q_1):

	First Centroid				
Factors A	**0.775**	**0.863**	**0.850**	**0.667**	**0.718**
0.775	0.600	0.668	0.658	0.517	0.556
0.863	0.668	0.744	0.733	0.576	0.619
0.850	0.658	0.733	0.722	0.566	0.610
0.667	0.516	0.575	0.567	0.445	0.479
0.718	0.556	0.619	0.610	0.479	0.515

After this, we will now get the first matrix of residual coefficient (R_1) by subtracting Q_1 from R as follows:

Variables	1	2	3	4	5
1	0.120	–0.143	–0.158	–0.137	0.134
2	0.052	0.142	0.077	–0.036	–0.149
3	0.158	0.066	0.088	0.084	–0.08
4	–0.136	–0.193	0.083	0.205	–0.069
5	0.134	–0.149	–0.08	–0.069	0.175

Accordingly, we can derive the second centroid factor (B):

Variables	1	2	3	4	5	Σ
1	0.120	0.143	0.158	0.137	0.134	0.692
2	0.052	0.142	0.077	0.036	0.149	0.456
3	0.158	0.066	0.088	0.084	0.08	0.396
4	0.136	0.193	0.083	0.205	0.069	0.686
5	0.134	0.149	0.08	0.069	0.175	0.607
Σ	0.6	0.693	0.486	0.531	0.607	
2nd factor centroid (B) = 0.6/1.71 = 0.35	0.35	0.4	0.28	0.31	0.35	

Sum of the column sums (T) = 2.917 $\sqrt{T} = 1.71$ $\Sigma A = 3.883$.

Thus, the matrix of factor loadings can be written as follows:

	Factor Loadings	
Variables	**Centroid Factor (A)**	**Centroid Factor (B)**
1	0.775	0.35
2	0.863	0.4
3	0.850	0.28
4	0.677	0.31
5	0.718	0.35

Example 2: Find out the communality and eigenvalues from the final results obtained in Example 1.

Solution: We can find out the communality and eigenvalues for the given data as follows:

	Factor Loadings		
Variables	Centroid Factor (A)	Centroid Factor (B)	Communality (h^2)
1	0.775	0.35	$(0.775)^2+(0.35)^2=0.723$
2	0.863	0.4	$(0.863)^2+(0.4)^2=0.904$
3	0.850	0.28	$(0.850)^2+(0.28)^2=0.800$
4	0.677	0.31	$(0.677)^2+(0.31)^2=0.554$
5	0.718	0.35	$(0.718)^2+(0.35)^2=0.638$
Eigenvalue (variance accounted for, i.e., common variance)	3.026	0.593	3.619
Proportion of total variance	0.60 (60%)	0.12 (12%)	0.72 (72%)
Proportion of common variance	0.83 (83%)	0.17 (17%)	1.00 (100%)

In the above-drawn table, each communality represents the proportion of variance in all the five variables in the corresponding row and is accounted for by the two factors A and B. For example, 72.3 percent of the variance in a variable is accounted for by the centroid factors A and B and the remaining 17.7 percent of the total variance in variable 1 scores in thought of as being made up of two parts—a factor specific to the attribute represented by variable 1, and a portion due to errors of measurement associated with the assessment of variable 1. But we have not focused on these portions in the above-shown tables as our focus was generally on common variance in factor analysis.

Moreover, it has been conventionally accepted in factor analysis literature for a loading of 0.33 to be the minimum absolute value to be analyzed. The portion of a variable's variance accounted for this least loading is around 10 percent. This particular criteria, though arbitrary, is being used more or less by way of convention, and as such must be kept in view if we read and analyze the multivariate technique. In this example, factor A has loadings in excess of 0.33 on all variables. This type of factor is generally referred to as "the general factor" and is taken to represent whatever it is that all of the variables have in common. One may consider all the five variables to be the product of some unobserved variables. The name of the factor is selected in such a way that it conveys what it is that all the variables that correlate to it have in common. On the other hand, factor B has all the loadings in excess of 0.33.

Accordingly, different names can be given to the said two groups to help us in analyzing and naming factor B. The rows at the bottom of the above-mentioned table explain eigenvalue, proportion of total variance and proportion of common variance, and give us further information about the utility and application of the two factors in explaining the relations among the five variables. The total variance (V) is considered to be equal to the number of variables involved. In our present study, $V=5$ (number of rows). The row, labeled "eigenvalue" or "common variance," gives the numerical values of the portion of the variance attributed to the factor in the respective column above it.

These are calculated by adding the squared values of the corresponding factor loadings. Hence, the total value 5 is distributed into 3.026 as eigenvalue for factor A and 0.593 as eigenvalue for factor B and the total 3.619 as the sum of eigenvalues for these two factors. The corresponding distribution of the total variance 5 has been displayed in the next row where one can find that 72 percent of the total variance is related to these two factors. This means that nearly 72 percent of the total variance is common variance, while the remaining 12 percent of it is made up of portions unique to individual variables and the tools applied to measure them. The last row indicates that nearly 83 percent common variance is accounted for by factor A and the other 17 percent by factor B. Hence, we can conclude that the two factors explain the common variance simultaneously.

2. Principal components method: This method, popularly known as the PC method of factor analysis, was established by the well-known mathematician H. Hotelling. It maximizes the sum of squared loadings of each factor extracted in turn. Thus, the principal component method explains more variance than the loadings obtained from any other method of factor.

   The previous method has been explained here manually. Similarly, this method can be applied with the help of SAS, MS-Excel, or SPSS as the data are generally tedious, complex, and cumbersome keeping an eye on the fact that the aim of the PC method is the construction, out of a given set of variables and new variables referred to as principal components which are generally linear combinations.

   For example:

$$p_1 = a_{11}x_1 + a_{12}x_2 + \cdots + a_{1k}\,x_k$$

$$p_2 = a_{21}x_1 + a_{22}x_2 + \cdots + a_{2k}\,x_k$$

$$\text{\_\_\_\_\_\_\_\_\_\_\_\_\_\_\_\_\_\_\_\_\_\_\_\_}$$

$$p_k = a_{k1}x_1 + a_{k2}x_2 + \cdots + a_{kk}\,x_k$$

3. Maximum likelihood method: The maximum likelihood method provides the fundamental advantages to compute a wide range of index of the goodness of fit. Again it is quite convenient to test the statistical significance of factor loadings. Moreover, it allows researchers to find out corrections among factors and calculate confidence intervals for these parameters. This method is considered to be the best one when the data are normally distributed. This is mainly because of the fact that it permits the calculation of a wide range of indexes of goodness of fit and allows statistical significance testing of factor loadings and correlations among factors, and the calculation of confidence intervals. This method must be avoided if the data are not normally distributed. This method focuses on the population correlation matrix as estimated from the sample correlation matrix. If R_S represents sample correlation matrix, R_p represents a population correlation matrix, then this method seeks to extrapolate what is known from R_S in the best possible way to estimate R_p. Hence, this method of factor analysis is a statistical test in which one maximizes some relationship between the sample of data and the population from which the sample was taken. The statistics and mathematics of the maximum likelihood method are relatively tedious, tough, complex, and cumbersome as compared to those involved in the centroid and PC method. This can be easier when

the researcher has adequate grounding in differential calculus, integral calculus, higher algebra, and matrix algebra in particular. So for the researchers of media, communication, and other social sciences having nonmathematical backgrounds, it would again be desirable to use software such as SAS, MS-Excel, and SPSS.

12.8.2 Rotation in Factor Analysis

An extremely important feature of factor analysis is that the axes of the factor can be rotated within the multidimensional variable space. According to L.L. Thurston, a simple structure is achieved by rotating the axes until:

1. Each row of a factor matrix has at least one zero.
2. Each column of a factor matrix has p zeroes, where p is the number of factors.
3. For each pair of factors there are so many variables for which the loading on one is virtually zero and the loading on the other is substantial.
4. When there are so many factors, then for each pair of factors, there are several variables for which both loadings are zero.
5. For each pair of factors, the number of variables with non-vanishing loadings on both of them is small.

All the above-mentioned striking criteria reveal the fact that factor analysis should reduce the complexities of all the variables to a manageable level. There are generally two types of factor rotation: (a) orthogonal and (b) oblique.

In orthogonal rotation, factors are not correlated, while in oblique rotation, factors are correlated. Orthogonal rotation consists of (a) quartimax, (b) varimax, and (c) equimax.

Communality for all the variables will remain unaffected regardless of rotation. But the eigenvalue will change only due to rotation in factor.

12.8.3 R-type and Q-type Factor Analysis

On the lines of degree of correlation, factor analysis has been categorized as (a) R-type and (b) Q-type. R factor analyzes relationships among variables to identify groups of variables forming a latent dimension (factors). In R-type, high correlations occur when respondents who score high on variable 1 also score high on variable 2 and respondents who score low on variable 1 also score low on variable 2. Factors come up when there are high correlations within groups of variables. On the other hand, Q factor forms groups of respondents or cases based on their similarity on a set of characteristics. In a Q-type factor analysis, the correlations are calculated between pairs of respondents instead of pairs of variables. High correlations occur when respondent 1's pattern of responses on all the variables is much like respondent 2's pattern of responses. Factors come up when there are high correlations within groups of people.

In media metrics, factor analysis is applied to look at media readership profiles of people.

12.8.3.1 Advantages of Factor Analysis

Following are some of the advantages of factor analysis:

1. This method is very useful and highly applicable in reducing, condensing, and simplifying the huge and complex multivariate data.
2. Factor analysis is useful and instrumental in finding out relevant and important relationships among observed data that were there all the time, but were not easy to observe from the data alone.
3. This method can depict the latent factors (i.e., underlying factors not directly observable) that establish relationships among so many variables relating to a research study. For example, if readers are asked to rate different newspapers (say, *Times of India*, *Indian Express*, *Hindustan Times*, and so on) according to preference, a factor analysis may depict some striking features of newspapers that underlie the comparative choices.
4. This method may be highly applicable to empirical clustering of media, news, editorial matters, or readers/listeners/viewers/users for giving a classification scheme when data scored on various rating scales have to be grouped simultaneously.

12.8.3.2 Limitations of Factor Analysis

Factor analysis is not free from disadvantages and has definitely some glaring limitations which are as follows:

1. Like all other MVA, this method also demands complex, tedious, cumbersome, and laborious computations involving heavy cost burden. It is impossible to carry out this method without computer software packages such as SAS, MS-Excel, or SPSS. With the advancement of such software, no doubt, calculations have become easier and faster. Yet it is costly and cost-ineffective.
2. The inferences often suffer from validity, authenticity, and reliability because the data are imperfect right from the beginning in the factor analysis.
3. One can use this method properly only when he or she is well acquainted with various techniques, tools, and methods of factor analysis.

Thus, we may say that despite all such limitations, it helps a lot in reducing huge and complex data. Practically, this method is more useful as there are hardly one-variable or two-variable cases. There are often the cases of multivariable circumstances.

12.9 CLUSTER ANALYSIS

It is a very useful data reduction technique. But its application is more an art than science. If a research proceeds cautiously, it can be an invaluable tool in identifying latent patterns by suggesting useful groupings (clusters) of objects that are not discernible through other multivariate techniques.

Cluster analysis is mainly based on classifying variables in groups or clusters. It consists of clusters of different variables that correlate highly with one another and have comparatively low correlations with variables in other clusters. The main purpose of cluster analysis is to establish how many mutually and exhaustive groups or clusters, dependent on the similarities of profiles among entities, really exist in the population and then to explain the composition of this type of groups. Several groups to be determined in the cluster analysis are not pre-mentioned or pre-defined unlike in discriminate analysis.

12.10 MULTIDIMENSIONAL SCALING

It is a simultaneous examination of measuring an item in more than one dimension. There are many multidimensional scaling (MDS) methods often applied with a view of revealing patterns of one sort or another in interdependent data structures. When the data are nonmetric, MDS involves rank ordering each pair of objects in terms of analogy. The main purpose of MDS lies in the fact that it enables the researcher to find out "the perceptual structure of a set of stimuli and the cognitive processes underlying the development of this structure...MDS provides a mechanism for determining the truly salient attributes without forcing the judge to appear irrational" (Ferber, 1974) Hence, this type of scaling is very useful and applicable in revealing the most silent attributes which happen to be the primary determinants for making a specific decision in the fields of communication and media studies.

12.11 LATENT STRUCTURE ANALYSIS

Such an analysis seeks to share both of the basic objectives of factor analysis. That is to say that it extracts latent factors and expresses relationship of observed variables with these factors as their indicators and classifies a population of respondents into pure types. This analysis is highly suitable if the variables involved in the research do not hold dependency relationship and are nonmetric.

SUMMARY

MVA is simultaneous examination of more than two variables. It has the vast potentiality to analyze complex and cumbersome data mining. In most of the areas of communication and media studies, we generally depend on MVA for realistic and practical results. There are two methods of MVA: (a) dependence methods and (b) independence methods.

Dependence methods are those that have data containing both dependent and independent variables. *Independence methods* are those that have data containing many variables without dependency relationship. Dependence methods include techniques such as: (a) multiple regression analysis, (b) multiple discriminant analysis, (c) multiple ANOVA, and (d) canonical correlation analysis. Independence methods include techniques such as: (a) factor analysis, (b) cluster analysis, (c) MDS analysis, and (d) latent structure analysis.

Discriminate analysis is nothing more than a multiple regression equation with a dependent variable as a nominal variable (code as 0, 1) representing group membership. It is a technique of examining the relationship between a nominal variable and a set of interval variables. Multiple ANOVA is an extension of bivariate ANOVA in which the ratio of among-groups variance to within-groups variance is calculated on a set of variables instead of a single variable. Canonical correlation is an extension of multiple regression. Factor analysis studies the correlation among a large number of variables and then tries to explain them in terms of their common underlying dimensions called factors. Factor analysis reduces variables to a manageable number. It is described as an exploratory and confirmatory multivariate technique. It is viewed as a data reduction technique as it reduces a large number of overlapping variables to a smaller set of factors that reflect construct(s). Factor analysis is based on matrix algebra and regression analysis. That is why sometimes it is also described as a combination of correlation and regression with multiple variables. It is referred to as a specific type of multiple regression. The most commonly used methods of factor analysis in media metrics are: (a) centroid method, (b) principal components method, and (c) maximum likelihood method. Centroid method of factor analysis developed by L.L. Thurstone was applied more often till 1950 before the advent of high-speed computers. Principal component method popularly known as the PC method was engineered by H. Hotelling. This method became more popular and useful after the advent of high-speed computers. Since it is a minor extension of the centroid method, it can also be calculated manually. But since the data of multiple variables make it tedious, complex, and cumbersome, it is advisable to use software such as SAS, MS-Excel, and SPSS. Maximum likelihood method is considered to be the best when the data are normally distributed. This method allows statistical significance testing of factor loadings and correlations among factors, and the calculation of confidence intervals. Rotation in factor analysis is an extremely important feature of factor analysis. The feature is that the axes of the factor can be rotated within the multidimensional variable space. There are two types of factor rotations: (a) orthogonal and (b) oblique. In orthogonal, factors are not correlated, while in oblique, factors are correlated. Due to any rotation in factor, the communality will not change but the eigenvalue will change. On the lines of the extent of correlation, factor analysis has been categorized as R-type and Q-type. In media metrics, factor analysis is applied to look at media readership profiles of people. Factor analysis is highly applicable in reducing, condensing, and simplifying the huge and complex multivariate data. It helps in finding out relevant relationships among observed data that were there all the time, but were not easy to observe from data alone. Despite limitations like complexity of huge data, factor analysis is practically more useful as there are often the cases of multivariate circumstances. Cluster analysis is a data reduction technique which is mainly based on classifying variables in groups or clusters. MDS is a simultaneous study of measuring an item in more than one dimension. This type of scaling is very useful and applicable in revealing the most salient attributes which happen to be the primary determinants for making a specific decision in the field of communication and media studies.

Latent structure analysis seeks to share both the objectives of factor analysis. This analysis is highly suitable if the variables involved in the research do not hold dependency relationship and are nonmetric. We may conclude that in multiple regression analysis, there are many metric explanatory variables and only one metric criterion variable. In multiple discriminant analysis, there are many metric explanatory variables and one (to be classified into many groups) criterion variable. In multivariate ANOVA, there are many nonmetric explanatory variables and metric criterion variables.

In canonical correlation analysis, there are many metric explanatory variables and any one of the two, nonmetric criterion variable or metric criterion variable. In factor analysis, there are many metric explanatory variables. In cluster analysis, there are many explanatory variables. In MDS, there are many metric and many nonmetric explanatory variables and in latent square analysis, there are many nonmetric explanatory variables.

RELATED AND SUGGESTED WEBSITES

(As retrieved on December 1, 2015)

1. http://www.unt.edu/rss/class/mike/6810/IntrotoMV.pdf
2. http://www.jncasr.ac.in/chronobiology/reading%20material/multivariate%20basics%20for%20students_MewaSingh.pdf
3. http://tx.shu.edu.tw/~purplewoo/Literature/!DataAnalysis/Methods%20of%20Multivariate%20Analysis.pdf

REFERENCE

Ferber, Robert. 1974. ed., Handbook of Marketing Research, 3–52. New York, NY: McGraw-Hill.

RELATED AND RECOMMENDED READINGS

Hair, Joseph F., Rolph E. Anderson, Ronald L. Tatham, and William C. Black. 2006. *Multivariate Data Analysis*, 10–16, 87–135. 15th ed. New Jersey: Pearson Education.

Gupta, S.P and Gupta Alka. 2008. *Statistical Methods in Behavioural Sciences*. Allahabad: Sharda Pustak Bhawan.

Johnson, Richard A., and Dean W. Wichern. 2014. *Applied Multivariate Statistical Analysis*, 481–85. 6th ed. New Jersey: Pearson Education.

Kerlinger, F.N. 1978. *Foundations of Behavioural Research*, 242–70. New Delhi: Surjeet Publications.

Kothari, C.R. 2004. *Research Methodology: Methods & Techniques*, 368–401. New Delhi: New Age International Publishers.

Rencher, Alvin, and William F. Christensen. 2012. *Methods of Multivariate Analysis*, 169–548. New Jersey: Wiley.

Seth, Jagdish N. 1971. "The Multivariate Revolution in Marketing Research." *Journal of Marketing*, 35(1): 13–19.

QUESTIONS

1. What is MVA? Discuss its role in media metrics.
2. Describe the features and applications of the multivariate technique in media research.
3. Name the important multivariate techniques and explain the important characteristics of each one of such techniques.
4. Describe the various types of multivariate techniques.
5. Explain the meaning and concept of multiple regression analysis.
6. Describe the concept of multiple discriminant analysis.
7. Enumerate the steps involved in Thurstone's centroid method of factor analysis.

8. Write a brief note on rotation in factor analysis.
9. Describe the concept of multiple ANOVA.
10. What is canonical correlation analysis?
11. What is factor analysis? Discuss the role of matrix algebra in factor analysis.
12. Describe the importance of factor analysis in media metrics.
13. Explain the important methods of factor analysis.
14. What is R-type and Q-type factor analysis?
15. Describe the limitations of factor analysis.
16. Throw light on cluster analysis and its role in media research.
17. What is MDS? Discuss its application in media metrics.
18. Explain latent structure analysis.
19. Describe the different multivariate techniques in terms metric, nonmetric explanatory, and criterion variables.

13
CHAPTER

Report Writing in Quantitative Media Research

Don't show me the moon is shining; show me the glint of light on broken glass.

—Anton Chekhov

Report writing is a complete written depiction of the research design, whereas a research design is a complete plan and its profile. Research design is a structure, outline, layout, blueprint, framework, scheme, and paradigm of operation, essential for effective, efficient, systematic, and scientific research with minimum time, cost, money, energy, and resources. On the other hand, report writing is an integral part and one of the most important components of any research. Without report writing, a research is considered to be an incomplete imagination like showing the moon shining but not finding the glint of light on broken glass. In quantitative media research, an appropriate hypothesis formulation, research design, research methodology, research techniques, and findings are of no use unless converted into an effective report, communicative to others.

In the previous chapters, we have thoroughly discussed the conceptual framework of media metrics and its various tools, step by step and chapter after chapter. Hence, it will be extremely desirable to discuss report writing and computer applications in quantitative media research for more complete knowledge of media metrics and its applications.

While the next chapter will intend to focus on computer applications in quantitative media research, this chapter will throw light on the following:

1. Meaning and concept of report writing in quantitative media research
2. Structure and outline of report writing in media study
3. Importance of report writing of quantitative mass communication research
4. Precautions for writing research report
5. Qualities of a good research report

In addition, the chapter will also cover the summary, related and suggested websites, related and recommended readings, and questions of report writing in general and report writing in quantitative media research in particular.

13.1 MEANING AND CONCEPT OF REPORT WRITING IN QUANTITATIVE MEDIA RESEARCH

A research report is the full and final part of a research work. It is a description of the research work carried out by the researcher. It requires various steps to present a report in the form of a project or thesis or dissertation. The purpose of a research cannot be properly served unless the findings are made known to others including general audience and subject experts. Hence, report writing is a part and parcel of the entire research project. Report writing in quantitative media research as a whole requires a set of skills which are much different from those called for in respect of earlier stages of research activities. Thus, this final assignment should be carried out by the researcher with rapt attention and utmost care. The media researcher should not hesitate in seeking assistance and guidance of the experts, especially in quantitative media research. Report is, therefore, described as written details of the entire research. In the case of media research report writing of quantitative analysis, the researcher must be very clear about the target audience on which the given report is focused. A quantitative media research directed toward mass communication scientists will be quite different in certain respect from a report whose basic purpose is to approach the general public. Whatever may be the target audience of print media research or electronic media research or advertising research, two important points must be kept in mind by media researchers:

1. What are the expectations of this media audience from the said study?
2. How can this research work be best presented?

Thus, a report of qualitative media research is a description of research work executed in the field of media with the help of quantitative data. Mass communication scientists, toward whom the research is directed, need to be told broadly and largely about the study.

13.2 STRUCTURE AND OUTLINE OF REPORT WRITING IN MEDIA STUDY

The structure and outline of media report writing should be simple, crystal clear, and easily understandable. Its general structure and outline may be as follows:

1. Research topic
2. Introduction
3. Research problem
4. Rationale of the topic
5. Review of literature
6. Objectives
7. Hypothesis
8. Methodology
9. Data collections and analysis
10. Results/findings
11. Conclusions and suggestions
12. Limitations
13. Bibliographical references
14. Appendices

13.2.1 Research Topic

The research topic of media study, while getting it approved, should be short, simple, catchy, innovative, and highly communicative. At the time of topic selection at the personal level, supervisor level, departmental level, or organizational level, the researcher must keep an eye on the following points:

1. Is there any innovation in the topic?
2. Is the topic short, simple, and manageable?
3. Is the topic researchable?
4. Is the topic suitable to the interest of the researcher?
5. Is the topic socially relevant?
6. Is the topic objective?
7. Are the data of the said study analyzable?
8. Is the topic measurable?
9. How much time, money, energy, and resources the topic will consume?
10. Is the topic socially non-objectionable?

If any of the above is missing in the topic, then the researcher should edit and modify the topic and get it reapproved, though every effort should be made at the time of registration of the topic to make it accurate and perfect so that it may not require to be changed at the time of submission or report writing.

Hence, the report writer of the concerned topic must take pre-steps or at least post-steps that the research topic is innovative. The research must visualize whether devoting enough time, money, and energy on the topic will add and develop some new knowledge in his/her branch or area or subject. Many a time, researchers select an old and outdated topic for easy collection of data and somehow finishing the work which is rejected at the later stage. Hence, the researcher at the time of the registration or submission or report writing must be careful about the innovation of the topic and about the expected contribution in that area or branch of communication and media study.

Second, the researcher, the supervisor, and the whole team should see that the topic is short, simple, and manageable. If the topic is wide, broad, extensive, lengthy, complex, and cumbersome, then the research will neither be completed within the stipulated time nor will it give any concrete output or result. Therefore, while editing the report, it must be ensured and verified that the topic is short, simple, and manageable.

Third, the researcher, the project supervisor, and the concerned team must see either at the entry or the exit point, that is, strictly at the time of report writing whether the topic is researchable or not. If the topic is highly extensive, wide, large, and unmanageable, then it should be avoided at any point of time. For example, take a topic titled "Role of Media in Searching God." This topic is not researchable as neither the media persons nor the media audience will comfortably or reliably respond to such questions. Hence, there will be extreme lack of reliability, authenticity, validity, and so on, on such topics.

Fourth, though the suitability of the title to the interest of the researcher is a psychological issue, yet it affects the report writing and editing due to lack of negligence or casual approach by the researcher. Hence, the topic may be modified even at the 11th hour of report writing at the cost of some delay so as to satisfy effective report writing and editing.

Fifth, even at the time of report writing, it may be noticed and realized that the topic is not socially relevant, and then it may be rectified to make it relevant and useful at the cost of a tolerable delay. Such step will add to an effective report editing and writing.

Sixth, it must be ensured at least at the time of report writing that the topic is neither subjective nor biased. It must be ensured that the topic is not editorialized or full of personal comments breaking the objectivity of the research. Hence, for proper editing and effective report writing, the subjective title must be modified and converted to an objective title for appropriate report writing.

Seventh, the data of the said study must be worth analyzing or else it cannot be properly written or edited in the report. If the data are irrelevant and do not meet the requirements of the work and its objectives, then it adversely affects the report writing.

Eighth, in case of quantitative media research, the topic must be measurable. There are a few words in media and communication research which are not measurable or measuring them is a cumbersome process. Hence, words such as "applicability," "communicability," "flexibility," "credibility," and "effectiveness" are very complex to measure. Similarly, a few abstract words such as "pleasure," "nature," and "character" are immeasurable. Thus, immeasurable words in the title should be avoided and more so in quantitative study of media research.

Ninth, if the topic is time-consuming, money-consuming, energy-consuming, and resource-consuming and if due to one reason or the other, the proper time, required money, desired energy, and applicable resources cannot been arranged, then ultimately it affects the work, the research writing, and editing of the report.

Last, the topic must not be socially objectionable. If it is socially objectionable, the whole data, facts, and information become socially objectionable which adversely affect the editing of research work and effective report writing.

Thus, the research topic must be selected carefully at the entry point or it will require to be improved or modified at the submission level or report writing stage.

13.2.2 Introduction

In this chapter, the topic is introduced. It mainly contains the origin and growth of the terms used in the topic. That is to say it states the historical background. It also states the nature, merits, demerits, characteristics, qualities, relevance, and importance of the topic very briefly. Though it is an essay-type writing, yet personal opinion or editorialization should be avoided as far as it is possible. That is to say that subjectivity should be minimized and objectivity should be maximized. Further, it is important to briefly quote at least the expert's or another researcher's surname who has added some new knowledge, year of the work in bracket just after his comment, and his opinion or statement. For example, if Marshall McLuhan opines in the year 1997, "It is not the economic deprivation, but lack of corruption is a serious concern for media." Then it will be written as follows: It is not the economic deprivation, but lack of communication is a serious concern for media (McLuhan, 1975).

Further, all the terms used in the topic should be defined properly and systematically. While defining the terms, first of all its general meaning should be explained and then its specific or technical meaning should be elaborated. For that, we may use prominent popular dictionaries such as Oxford Advanced Learner's Dictionary, Oxford Dictionaries, Cambridge Dictionary, and Webster's Dictionary. Then the same term may be defined with the help of technical or scientific or media dictionaries in our case. And lastly, the researcher should present the exact final meaning of the word in the said study so that the word will be taken and considered the same throughout the study as it was defined in the opening chapter called "Introduction."

Thus, stating "Introduction" in a research report is a highly skillful and experienced task and it definitely follows the principle, "Well begun is half done."

13.2.3 Research Problem

Practically, it is the research problem that comes first in the mind of the researcher, even before finalizing the topic. But, theoretically the topic is written first whether it is the cover page or inside page, even though the topic emerges from the problem. Research problems are generally research questions, which gradually become the base of the research objectives and the research hypothesis. Research problem is presented in its detailed form in a major project or thesis. But it is kept to a minimum in published research reports in any research journal. It should preferably be written in a question form.

Thus, the research problem writing is the second stage or step of the structure and outline of the quantitative media research.

13.2.4 Rationale of the Topic

Here, the researcher has to reason out as to why this topic was selected. Any topic is generally selected when it has some social significance and the researcher is keenly interested in the topic with his heart and soul. The researcher is the first unit of the society. Hence, deep interest or background or future prospect of the topic for the researcher cannot be avoided. That is why "Rationale of the Topic" is also sometimes replaced by another chapter called "Social Significance of the Topic."

Hence, it is important in this chapter as to why the researcher thinks that a particular topic has social significance. And he starts with his personal significance and then relates it to the social significance.

Thus, stating the rationale of the topic in report writing is very important and relevant and it should be related to the social significance of the study.

13.2.5 Review of Literature

Then comes literature review which is based on the research topic and research problem. When the literature is reviewed from the previous research work in the concerned area or field or topic or problem, then it should be preferably written chronologically either in ascending order or in descending order while editing and writing the report. Sometimes, it is written alphabetically (author's name) in report writing depending upon the significance, relevance, and usefulness.

In a review literature, it can be the previous related work of international refereed research journals of high impact factor, national refereed research journals of high impact factor, websites, books, periodicals, journals, websites, CDs of audios as well as audiovisuals, and articles in standard magazines and standard newspapers including editorials and features. But the preference and chronology should start from international refereed research journals of high repute and high impact factor.

Sometimes, a review of literature is explored even before the selection of the topic and research problem. It is executed only on the basis of a research area or tentative topic.

Therefore, literature review helps even in the finalization or modification of the topic and the research problem. The literature also helps in creating and deleting objectives. Sometimes the objectives are framed by the researcher and it is reviewed objective-wise. Hence, it is like a chicken-egg situation. We may describe literature review as pre-topic and post-topic phenomena, pre-problem and post-problem phenomena, pre-objective and post-objective phenomena, and also as pre-hypothesis and post-hypothesis phenomena. In fact, all these areas, titles, problems, review literatures, objectives, and hypotheses are so interlinked and interwoven that each one is pre- and post-operations of one another.

Thus, writing a review of literature is an art and craft. It is a highly skilled task depending on the researcher's maturity and experience.

13.2.6 Objectives

Objectives are basically the core and needle of the research. At the end in results and conclusions it is minutely and meticulously verified whether all the objectives have been systematically achieved or not. Objectives also give birth to a few general hypotheses which are gradually converted into statistical hypotheses.

Objectives are of two types: (a) broad objectives and (b) specific objectives.

In broad objectives, generally, topic or its different main parts are written. Or it may be the main research problem and its different parts. For example, "Content Analysis of Economic News and Its Impact." Then the broad objectives will be: (a) to analyze the contents of economic news in the concerned media of the research study, and (b) to study the impact of economic news of the concerned media of the research study.

As far as specific objectives are concerned, these are the further break-up of the broad objectives, for example, (a) to study the coverage of economic news of three English dailies, (b) to compare the coverage of economic news of three English dailies, (c) to know the level of economic news in three English dailies, and so on and so forth.

Earlier, more and more research problems and more and more objectives were considered suitable for any media research. But in the present time, only one or two research problems and very few objectives from these one or two problems are considered to be suitable for more effective media research. Thus, the trend is that the area of the operation of media research should be minimized and variables should be maximized for more intensive, deep, and consolidated research, findings, and results.

13.2.7 Hypothesis

A hypothesis is a pre-statement of any thought or theory. It is a prior assumption of the expected results. It is also the general statement about the population. It is of general nature as well as of statistical nature. When we convert the general hypothesis into statistical hypothesis, the latter is further broken into two types, that is, null hypothesis and alternative hypothesis. When the null hypothesis, also called a no relation hypothesis, is proved, the alternative hypothesis is disproved. Thus, the null hypothesis and alternative hypothesis are described as mathematical opposites.

Formulating an appropriate hypothesis means completing half of our research work. Not only that, hypothesis automatically deletes and minimizes the unwanted data and, like a supervisor, directs us toward the specific data. Thus hypothesis not only gives us direction but also reduces our research work to a great extent.

In perception study of communication and media studies, a hypothesis is a must. In any other media research where responses of so many have been taken, a hypothesis is a must. However, in a few exceptionally experimental researches, hypothesis may be avoided as things are self-explanatory and self-directed, and facts are automatically minimized.

The shortest and the most distinctive definition of research is that it is and must be a scientific study. But communication and media research often lacks scientific approach. It is the proper statistical hypothesis testing which makes a media research or any other social science research scientific. Thus, a hypothesis is an integral part of media research. Sometimes, it is directly generated from the topic, sometimes from the problem, sometimes from the objectives, and sometimes it is the general observation of the population. In all these cases, statistical hypothesis testing is a must in quantitative media research.

Thus, hypothesis formulation and then writing it in a report requires a specific research skill. It is an art and craft and must be properly placed and suitably written in a media research report.

13.2.8 Methodology

A methodology is a science of methods or a systematic study of method. A research methodology, which is a subset and an integral part of research design, includes research methods, research techniques/tools/apparatus, and statistical testing. Thus, the methods, tools, and statistical testing are all scientifically approved devices. There are so many types of qualitative research methods, quantitative research methods, and a triangulation (combination of both). Therefore, a researcher must be aware of merits and demerits of all the research methods. Then only he can decide which method/methods is/are most suitable for his research problem. Similarly, the researcher should also be fully aware of all the research tools and statistical testing. Then only he/she can best judge which one/ones is/are most appropriate for his particular research problem.

Thus, the main function of the methodology of the research report is to inform the intended general public/audience and the experts what was done to solve the problem. Therefore, research methodology should not only be selected scientifically, systematically, and properly, but it should also be written effectively in a research report.

13.2.9 Data Collection and Analysis

All the concerned primary data, secondary data, and tertiary data are collected as per the research methods with the help of research tools. Then the data are analyzed in light of research problems, objectives, and hypothesis to get results/findings.

The first part of the primary data collection should tell what sample or samples were used, how they were selected, and then the reason for selecting them including the sample size and sample design. If the samples were stratified random sampling, then it should also be stated in the follow-up action of the methodology. The sample size and the whole sample design should be justified and should be scientifically logical. In the data collection process and analysis, the details of graphs, tables, charts, diagrams, and the likes are used and that must be properly stated in the research report.

Thus, stating data collection and analysis in the research report is a highly artistic job. It must pay attention to all the proper arrangements and sequences of graphs, tables, charts, diagrams, and the likes, with suitable and symbolic headlines.

13.2.10 Results/Findings

The results or findings are stated in the research report in terms of data. These are objective-oriented results or findings in the form of available data. Hence, these are data within data. That is to say that these are the most relevant and useful data according to the requirements of the research problems, objectives, and hypothesis.

Thus, writing results or findings with the help of available data, charts, tables, diagrams, and the likes is a highly skillful job as far as the research report is concerned, more so as the results or findings are extremely relevant and significant in the process of formation of conclusions and finally giving effective suggestions or recommendations.

13.2.11 Conclusions and Suggestions

This is another important and challenging part of writing a research report, more so in the case of quantitative communication and media research. Conclusion is a generalization of results or findings. It further edits the unwanted data to its minimum level.

Though in a research journal, results and conclusions are clubbed together, yet in a thesis or major project, these are preferably separated.

The results or findings are written for both general readers and subject experts. But the conclusions are written for general readers. So it should be written in a readers-friendly manner. The language should be very simple and easily understandable.

Thus, the real skill of a research report lies in simplifying the results or findings to their simplest form to make them useful and socially relevant conclusions.

Then comes the role of suggestions. It is based on the existing and emerging problems relating to the topic and then suggestions by the researcher on the basis of his/her skills and experiences that he/she has gained before, during, and after the research.

Thus, stating conclusions and suggestions in a research report is a matter of extreme maturity and ability of the researcher. The researcher must be minute and meticulous while executing this art and craft in the report.

13.2.12 Limitations

Some of the researchers often get confused with the research problems and limitations. Limitations are basically related to the problems and crisis of time, money, energy, and resources. In every research there is generally either lack of time or lack of money or lack of energy or lack of resources. The researcher in the report must highlight this to defend his research work's deficiencies and shortcomings. If he has studied only a small village and it should have been compared with an outer small village, then the researcher should highlight his limitations indicating that it may be executed by some other researchers in the next study, since research is a continuous ongoing process and one researcher directly or indirectly hands over his remaining tasks to the next, next to next, and so on. Hence, the limitations must be stated in the research report so that, in a series, another unit and then yet another unit may covered by the new and prosperous researchers. In a way, it gives a way to a new researcher to study the topic from yet another point of view.

Thus, stating limitations in a research report is yet another skillful challenge and requires experiences and maturity to pin-point the most vital limitations, opening vistas and scope for the remaining researchers.

13.2.13 Bibliographical References

This is another very important part of research report writing. It provides the complete details of the sources of information and papers cited in a standardized format. This not only helps the readers about the various other sources, but it is also a legal requirement to cite an author, the publisher, the title, and so on. If the researcher has directly or indirectly taken some reference material from somewhere and if he does not give proper biographical reference, then it is also a violation of the Copyright Act.

Broadly speaking, there are so many types of referencing styles which are as follows:

1. Harvard style
2. Vancouver style
3. American Psychological Association (APA) style
4. Modern Language Association (MLA) style
5. OSCOLA style
6. Chicago style
7. Turabian style

First, we have the *Harvard style* which mainly covers names, date, month, and year; most importantly, the name(s) of the author(s) are written with the first letter of each author's last name and each initial capitalized. It will become crystal clear with the following examples of different types.

1. Journal article:
   Denzin, N. K., et al. (2016). *Internet and Mass Media*, 10(1), pp. 210–220.
2. Book:
   Saunders, M. (2016). *Research methods for media students*. 3rd ed. Open University Press study skills. Maidenhead: Open University Press.
3. Newspaper:
   Woodward, B. (2016, 15 February). Growing Plagiarism Among Media Researchers. *Independent Education.*

Second, we have the *Vancouver style* which mainly relates to numeric and running notes. Here, the name(s) of the author(s) are written with the first letter of each author's last name and each initial capitalized like in the Harvard style. And the year is written at the end. The following examples of different types will make it easily understandable.

1. Journal article:
   Denzin NK, et al. Internet and mass media. 2016, 10 (1): 210–20.

2. Book:
   Saunders M. Research methods for media students. 3rd ed. Open University Press study skills. Maidenhead: Open University Press; 2016.
3. Newspaper:
   Woodward B. Growing plagiarism among media researchers. Independent Education; 2016 Feb 15.

Third we have the *American Psychological Association (APA) style*, which is most commonly and frequently used in media research, especially in quantitative analysis. In this style, the first letter of the first word of the title and subtitles, as well as the first letter of any proper noun, is capitalized. Moreover, the full title of the book including any subtitles should be written clearly and italicized or underlined. The following examples of different nature will make it easily understandable:

1. Journal article:
   Denzin, N.K. et al. (2016). Web 3.0 authorship: issues of referencing and citation for academic integrity. *Internet and mass media, 10*(1), 210–220.
2. Book:
   Saunders, M. (2016). *Research methods for media students* (3rd ed.). Open University Press study skills. Maidenhead: Open University Press.
3. Newspaper:
   Woodward, Bob. (2016, February 15). Growing plagiarism among media researchers. *Independent Education.*

Fourth, we have the *Modern Language Association (MLA)* which is often used in writing research papers and citing sources in liberal arts and humanities. But it is used in media research also and of course in quantitative analysis when qualitative data are quantified. It is just like APA style. But the year is written at the end. The following examples of different nature will make it extremely clear and easily understandable:

1. Journal article:
   Denzin, N.K. et al. *Internet and mass media*, vol. 10, no. 1, 2016, pp. 210–20.
2. Book:
   Saunders, M. *Research methods for media students*. 3rd ed., Open University Press study skills. Open University Press, Maidenhead, 2016.
3. Newspaper:
   Woodward, Bob. "Growing plagiarism among media researchers." *Independent Education*, 15 February 2016.

Fifth, we have the *OSCOLA* style which is appropriately known as Oxford Standard for Citation for Legal Authorities. It is mostly used for any report of different periodicity while referencing manually or electronically. It can be made quite clear with the following example.

OXFORD STANDARD FOR CITATION OF LEGAL AUTHORITIES, [2016].

Sixth, we have the *Chicago style* which is mainly of two types: (a) notes and bibliography, and (b) author–date. The first one is mostly used in humanities including history, literature, and fine arts. As far as media research is concerned, it is primarily used in qualitative research of mass communication. But it is also used in qualitative media analysis when the qualitative data are quantified. On the other hand, the author–date style is mainly used in physical, natural, and social sciences including media studies of both qualitative and quantitative nature.

Seventh, the *Turabian style* is a citing and referencing system which is almost similar to the Chicago style. It is named after Kate Turabian from the University of Chicago who has written a manual to guide the aspiring students in referencing and citing when writing research papers. One difference from Chicago style is that of font size and point size. It is generally different from that of the Chicago style. Both Chicago style and Turabian style are not very comprehensive but allow using footnotes and endnotes unlike APA and MLA.

Further, with tremendous growth in computer technology, the Microsoft Office Window 2007 onwards can automatically generate a bibliographical reference based on the information sources provided in the document. Moreover, yet another method of citation is in the form of footnotes.

Thus, stating a bibliography reference in the research report not only requires the knowledge of media research and its references but also the knowledge and skills of computer technology.

13.2.14 Appendices

In appendices, generally the different questionnaires, schedules, related pictures, maps, interviews, and the likes are provided. This is also called a space for miscellany, where any charts, diagrams, or tables which are indirectly related to the research work may also be presented.

It is important to mention here that all the filled questionnaires/schedules should never be attached to this chapter. Only one copy of the related questionnaires/schedules should be provided here so that the general public or experts may be able to assess the research work from inside.

Thus, even appendices writing as a part of a research report is not so easy. It requires a lot of proper care and rapt attention to properly place each and everything in this chapter. Anything that could not be projected earlier due to one reason or the other may also be projected in this chapter. Hence, stating appendices in a research report is really an art and craft with minute and meticulous observation.

13.3 IMPORTANCE OF REPORT WRITING OF QUANTITATIVE MASS COMMUNICATION RESEARCH

First of all report writing of qualitative media research can help in heaping up a vast reservoir of knowledge in this field. Hence, it adds to the knowledge of this section, branch, area, and finally subject. By virtue of a vast reservoir of such knowledge, so many theories, models, paradigms of communication, and media can be developed.

Second, this helps in the expansion and development of branch and subject of mass communication in general and qualitative media research in particular.

Third, the results and conclusions of the properly written research report can be published in newspapers due to its social significance. Hence, the research which remains confined to the microscope minority of experts and researchers can be popularized and brought to the level of common men and general public.

Fourth, a well-written research report can also be published in research journals in pieces to reach more researchers for further addition and exploration in the field.

Fifth, a systematically written research report can become the basis for formulation of new hypothesis. This can activate and continue the process of research in this section, branch, area, and finally subject.

Sixth, a suitably written research report relates the past work and present work of the said research which develops a scope for further useful comparisons and new studies.

Seventh, the research design, research methods, research techniques, and statistics used are largely and broadly reflected in a research report. This helps the new researchers to a great extent in understanding all these and applying new methods, techniques, and statistical applications.

Eighth, a properly documented research report is very much helpful to the researchers in devising new ways of exploring the research problems.

Thus, preparing a research report is not only the final stage of the research process, but it is also a functional art and craft. It is basically an outcome of researcher's labor, skill, maturity, ability, experience, and knowledge. Moreover, it is important and helps in creating a vast reservoir of knowledge, expansion and development of qualitative media research, popularizing such research to general public, publication in research journals in pieces, formulation of new hypothesis, relating past work and present work, developing new methods, techniques and statistical applications, and in devising new ways of exploring research problems.

13.4 PRECAUTIONS FOR WRITING RESEARCH REPORT

Research report is a medium of providing results and conclusions to the many readers of the report. Hence, there are some precautionary measures for writing a research report:

1. A research report must have conceptual, linguistic, and thematic clarity. It must be simple and easily understandable.
2. It should not be so lengthy that it becomes dull and dismal and should not be so short that it loses the gist and essence of the research.
3. A research report must have proper sequencing and interlinking between chapters and within chapters. This is extremely important to sustain reader's interest.
4. The report must have conceptual, thematic, and linguistic correctness. It should be free from grammatical and linguistic errors. It must appropriately contain the use of quotations, footnotes, documentation, and proper use of abbreviations in footnotes.
5. A research report must be an original work of the researcher and the researcher is legally required to sign a declaration of the originality and exclusiveness of the work.
6. It must highlight the policy implications with reference to the research questions and research problems. It is extremely desirable that the report makes the forecast of the probable future of the subject concerned. It must also hint at the type of research that still needs to be carried out in that section, branch, area, or subject.
7. Appendices must be endorsed to give details of questionnaires, schedules, and technical data in the report.
8. Bibliographical references are important not only from the knowledge point of view, but also from the legal point of view. It often protects the researcher from infringement of the Copyright Act.
9. Indexing is an integral part of a good research. So it must be minutely, meticulously, and carefully prepared by the researcher in the report.

13.5 QUALITIES OF A GOOD RESEARCH REPORT

A good and well-written research report must have the following qualities:

1. The most important quality of a report is that it should have a nice appearance. It must look attractive and appealing. Its cover page must have a fascination. Its paper must be of high quality and standard and typing or printing must be neat and clean with proper line spacing and four-sided margins.
2. A good report must have conceptual, thematic, visual, and pictorial clarity.
3. Intensive, extensive, large, wide, and logical clarification of the research problem is one of the most important angles of a good research report.
4. A good report avoids frequent repetition of facts and its chapters are very well interlinked and interwoven within and between. Thus, continuity and logical sequencing are important aspects.
5. In a good research report, the results and conclusions are full of factuality, objectivity, authenticity, validity, and reliability.
6. In a good report, small sentences and small paragraphs are used so that it should be simple and easily understandable.
7. In a well-documented report, scientific and technical words are minimized. And if at all they are used, these are well supported by simple words or such words are explained in brackets with easily understandable expressions.
8. A good report is one which has a vast readership. And that is possible only when it is highly communicative. It should be full of 7Cs of communication, that is, clarity, conciseness, continuity, correctness, credibility, and completeness.
9. In a good report, there should be proper reference of title, author, page number, publisher, place, time, and so on.
10. A well-written report contains tables, charts, diagrams, and the likes, in proper sequencing with telegraphic headlines containing only nouns.

Thus, a good research report is factual, clear, easily understandable, free from errors and duplication, result-focused and result-oriented, well-analyzed, organized, synthesized, structured, reader-friendly, purposefully communicative, timely prepared, straight-forward, law-abiding, and ethical. It is not a child's play. It is a herculean task. But constant and continuous practice brings perfection to it.

SUMMARY

Report of a qualitative media research is a description of research work carried out by the media researcher with the help of quantitative data. It requires various steps and innumerable skills to present a report in the form of a project or thesis or dissertation. Its structure should be simple, reader-friendly, easily understandable, timely prepared, and result-oriented. Its general outline includes: (a) research topic, (b) introduction, (c) research problem, (d) rationale of the topic, (e) review of literature, (f) objectives, (g) hypothesis, (h) methodology, (i) data collection and analysis, (j) results/findings, (k) conclusions, (l) limitations, (m) bibliography, and (n) appendices. The importance of research report writing is that it tremendously helps in creating a vast reservoir of knowledge, expansion and development of quantitative media research popularizing such research to general public, publication in research journals in pieces, formulation of new hypothesis, relating past research work and present work, developing new methods, techniques and statistical applications, and in devising new ways of exploring research problems. The precautions for writing a good research report demands that it should be factual, clear, easily understandable, free from errors and duplication, result-oriented, well-analyzed, organized, synthesized, reader-friendly, purposefully communicative, timely prepared, straightforward, law-abiding, and ethical. After thoroughly studying the report writing in quantitative media research, it will be desirably relevant, important, and useful to discuss computer applications in quantitative media research (especially electronic data collection techniques, internet, and referencing techniques, and a brief overview of use of various software packages for media metrics and mass communication research activities) in the next chapter so as to make the textbook complete and more useful for the students.

RELATED AND SUGGESTED WEBSITES

(As retrieved on June 30, 2016)

1. https://www.dlsweb.rmit.edu.au/lsu/content/pdfs/2_assessmenttasks/super_report.pdf
2. http://www.monash.edu.au/lls/llonline/quickrefs/06-essay-or-report.pdf
3. http://www.isentia.com.my/assets/whitepapers/isentia_whitepaper_malaysia_v2.pdf
4. http://www.cisco.com/c/dam/en_us/solutions/industries/docs/education/Multimodal-Learning-Through-Media.pdf
5. https://www.google.co.in/search?q=spss+23.0.0&biw=1242&bih=566&source=lnms&tbm=isch&sa=X&sqi=2&ved=0ahUKEwjsuc26s_7NAhWKro8KHWTwDTwQ_AUICCgD#tbm=isch&q=computer+typing&imgrc=3LS1yl_Ikb-mCM%3A

RELATED AND RECOMMENDED READINGS

Chawla, Deepak, and Neena Sondhi. 2011. *Research Methodology Concepts and Cases*, 607–18. 1st ed. New Delhi: Vikas Publishing House Pvt. Ltd.

Kerlinger, F.N. 1983. *Foundations of Behavioural Research*, 694–700. New Delhi: Surjeet Publications.

Kothari, C.R. 2000. *Research Methodologies: Methods and Techniques*, 344–60. New Delhi: Wishwa Prakashan.

Sarangi, Prasant. 2010. *Research Methodology*. Delhi: Taxman Publication.

Wilkinson, T.S., and P.L. Bhandarkar. 1996. *Methodologies and Techniques of Social Research*, 388–95. Mumbai: Himalaya Publishing House.

Wimmer, Roger D., and Joseph R. Dominick. 2003. *Mass Media Research: An Introduction*. 7th ed. Belmont: Wadsworth Publishing Company.

Zina, O. Leary. 2010. *The Essential Guide to Doing Your Research Project*. 3rd ed. London: SAGE Publications.

QUESTIONS

1. What do you mean by report writing of a quantitative media research? Describe its outline.

2. Differentiate between a research topic and research problem.
3. Explain the importance of report writing of mass communication research.
4. Throw light on different steps in report writing of a media project.
5. Differentiate between a research problem and limitations of a report. Describe the precautionary measures for report writing of a quantitative media study.
6. What should a media research keep in mind while writing "Introduction" of a quantitative research topic?
7. Differentiate between a general hypothesis and a statistical hypothesis. Convert five general hypothesis of your choice into statistical hypothesis.
8. Describe the importance of review of literature in a quantitative media research.
9. Differentiate between broad objectives and specific objectives.
10. Write short notes on the following: (a) rationale of the topic, (b) data analysis, and (c) bibliographical references.
11. Differentiate between research report, research design, research methodology, research method, and research tool.
12. Why is it desirable to insert a copy of questionnaires/schedules into "Appendices"? Explain.

14

CHAPTER

Computer Applications in Quantitative Media Studies

Computers are magnificent tools for the realization of our dreams, but no machine can replace the human spark of spirit, compassion, love and understanding.

—L.V. Gerstner

Computer, which is basically a data processing electronic devise, is highly applicable in all those fields where quantitative data are largely and widely used. Such quantitative data often create lot of complexities. But all these complexities are easily overcome with the help of computers having high speed and perfect accuracy. In media research also where quantitative data are used in bulk, the use of computer to analyze the difficult, problematic, and complex data has made complicated media research designs easy and practical. It has now become an integral and indispensable part in quantitative research of communication and media. Hence, media researchers are required to be exposed to the various applications of computer including the internet.

In the last chapter, we have extensively and intensively discussed the meaning and concept of report writing in quantitative media research report, outline and structure of quantitative media research report, precautions in quantitative media research writing, and qualities of a good research report of quantitative media research. All our knowledge of media metrics and even research report writing will remain incomplete if we do not enlighten ourselves about the fundamentals of *computer applications in quantitative media research.*

Hence, this chapter on computer applications in quantitative media research will briefly but desirably discuss the following:

1. Meaning and concept of computer applications in quantitative media research
2. Computer and quantitative media research
3. Internet and media research of quantitative data
4. Electronic data collection techniques in quantitative media research
5. Internet and referencing techniques in qualitative media study
6. Applications of software packages in quantitative media research

In addition, the chapter will also cover the summary, related and suggested website, references, related and recommended readings, and questions.

14.1 MEANING AND CONCEPT OF COMPUTER APPLICATIONS IN QUANTITATIVE MEDIA RESEARCH

In the present scenario, computer application has become omnipotent and omnipresent. It is applicable in every walk of life as a major tool of providing a large data bank of information. It helps in time tabling, calculations of lengthy and complex data, model processing, data analysis and collection of secondary and tertiary data, scheduling of projects, learning processes, provides profiles, security and efficiency, and also helps in production of text material such as books, reports, theses and research papers. Hence, it has become one of the most useful tools of research in modern times. In quantitative media research, it is ideally suitable in data collection and analysis concerning large research projects. Media researchers generally face a lot of difficulties with huge storage of data, their quicker retrieval as and when required, and processing of the same with the help of different methods and techniques. In all such activities, computer is helpful to a great extent. Apart from speeding up the media research operations with high accuracy, it has tremendously reduced human drudgery and added to the quality of communication and media research work. Computer can easily and quickly execute the complex and cumbersome statistical computations such as, measurers of central tendencies, measure of dispersions, measure of symmetry, measure of relationship, chi-square test, *t*-test, ANOVA, *Z*-test, *F*-test, multivariate analysis, and several nonparametric hypotheses tests such as *U* test and *H* test.

At present, a variety of software packages are easily and readily available for most of the simple and complicated analytical and quantitative data of which media researchers often make use. While analyzing the quantitative data of communication and media, the only work a researcher is supposed to do is to feed the data he has collected after loading the operating system and specific software packages on the computer. The results/findings will be easily and readily available within a fraction of minutes depending on the extent and load of the research work.

14.2 COMPUTER AND QUANTITATIVE MEDIA RESEARCH

The methods, techniques, and statistical applications involving the trial and error process are often used in quantitative media research methodology. These types of activities involve a lot of computer work of repetitive nature. A computer is ideally suitable for such methods, techniques, and statistical applications. In this way, a computer tremendously reduces the drudgery of such media researchers on the one hand and produces the final results quickly on the other. Thus, a variety of opportunities are easily available to a media researcher by computers within a very short span of time which otherwise may have taken an abnormally longer time. Moreover, the storage capacity and facility which the computer provides is of utmost help to a quantitative media researcher. This is simply because such media researcher can make the fullest use of stored up data whenever he so desires. Hence, computers facilitate the communication and media research to a great extent. A large chunk of data can be processed, interpreted, and analyzed comfortably with an accelerated pace. A media researcher, specially carrying out quantitative research, must develop an appropriate skill in computer data analysis and he must be acquainted with the following steps:

1. Data organization and coding
2. Storing the required data in a computer

3. Applying suitable statistical applications
4. Selecting an appropriate software package
5. Computer program execution.

First of all, a quantitative media researcher must focus his attention toward data organization and coding before the input stage of data analysis. The researcher will come across many problems and complexities if the available data are not properly organized. In order to overcome such difficulties, the data must be appropriately coded. There may be numerical coding, zero coding, alphabetic coding, and abbreviative coding. For "Very much," "Much," "Normal," "Little," and "Not at all," we may code as 5, 4, 3, 2, and 1, respectively. A "0" code refers to no response. The alphabetic coding is assigned when the data is just to be presented in tabulation and frequency count or geographical representation. An abbreviate coding is assigned to organizational categories, for example, Pb for "Public," Pvt for "Private," and G for "Government." Similarly, interval or ratio data are also coded. For example, income data classified in class intervals such as ₹3 lakhs and above, ₹2 lakhs and above, and ₹1 lakh and above may respectively be coded as 1, 2, and 3. The moment the data is coded, it is ready and fit to be stored in a computer. For this purpose, the input devices may be used. Thereafter, the researcher is supposed to decide as to which statistical tools will be suitable for the scientific analysis of the available data. For that he will be required to select the proper program to be used. Consequently, the computer is used to carry out the instructions. Hence, media researchers operating computers for quantitative analysis may execute their task with high speed and accuracy. The changing and newly emerging technology will give further impetus to the use of computers by media researchers.

14.3 INTERNET AND MEDIA RESEARCH OF QUANTITATIVE DATA

Internet has emerged as a vehicle for quantitative media research, especially in inexpensive data collection. It has tremendously reduced the time, money, and energy for quantitative data collection in the field of media and communication. In some cases, the quantitative data can be collected effortlessly without any cost. Several media researchers, who want quantitative data of this field, have placed reduced costs ahead of validity and reliability of media research in terms of what is relevant and significant. Moreover, web technology and data collected with the help of this technology has opened several avenues for all types of media researchers. Collecting such quantitative media data does not need much time, money, energy, and resources these days. It is not so costly any longer. Now researchers can carry out a research study with the help of web technology. Such an astronomical reduction in the cost of quantitative media research will open the doors for the general public of both private and public sectors. Media researchers, professional, and academicians, who were earlier quite unable to carry out any research, can now pursue almost every type of research project.

Quantitative media research executed with the help of web technology or internet has so many plus points. First of all, it is very easy to collect data and conduct surveys with the help of internet. The moment a media researcher becomes aware of the process, a thesis or dissertation or project can be easily designed within a very short span of time for the respondents on the internet anywhere in the world.

Second, there is ample scope of changing, modifying, and correcting a questionnaire if the quantitative media researcher is working on the internet. This is not only done easily and smoothly, but it also saves a lot of time, money, and energy.

Third, a quantitative media researcher with the help of the internet not only reduces the cost of data collection and analysis, but in this case each respondent is comfortable enough to read questions several times as per his requirement and understanding. Moreover, a respondent can fill the questionnaire in several sessions just by saving the previous data. When the respondent restarts, all his previous data are already available on the screen. He may again change, modify, and correct it and then proceed on for the next questions. Hence, it is very easy for the respondent to fill the questionnaire in several sessions according to the availability of his time, mood, and interest.

Fourth, in many countries including the United States, there are no laws relating to conducting internet surveys unlike laws regulating telephone surveys.

Fifth, the researcher can ask questions not only textually, but he may ask questions in the form of audio or visual or audiovisual. Respondents may listen to the talk or deliberation or song many times till he fully understands and satisfies himself with the content. Similarly, he can watch visual or audiovisual of a news, events, or television advertisements.

Sixth, both the researcher and the respondent can interact while filling the questionnaire to sort out any queries or doubts. A respondent may ask the researcher to come to a specific section of the questionnaire and may clear his doubts easily.

Seventh, unlike telephone surveys, internet survey does not disturb either the researcher or respondent. A respondent can start it as per his suitability and convenience.

Eighth, due to extreme flexibility of time adjustment, a researcher can track respondents' answers over time.

Ninth, in the case of data mining of quantitative media research, large samples are extremely easy to achieve, especially when the research project is useful, interesting, significant, and relevant to several respondents.

Last but not the least, the use and acceptability of the internet is not confined to specific types of audience any longer. Respondents are now fast becoming internet users and representatives of the whole universe. Governments even in developing countries are now extremely keen to enhance the penetration rate of the internet, opening the door to a variety of respondents throughout the world.

On the other hand, quantitative media research executed with the help of the internet also has some limitations. Though it is time-saving, money-saving, energy-saving, and resource-saving, yet the research methodology used with the help of the internet may not have an inherent authenticity, reliability, and validity. Again, the method used by the internet is not universally accepted as a valid methodology. So many top-notch companies of the world are still executing the statistical analysis manually. This is mainly because when software packages such as SPSS, SAS, Statistica, StatView, Stata, SISA, General Inquirer, Textpack, TACT, TextSTAT, MS-Excel, Corpus, Tableau, and webometrics are used directly, the researchers are not able to visualize all the variables properly. And some of the researchers, even if they know how to use these software packages, are not in a position to feed the data properly because of the very poor understandings of the variables used. That is why most of the researchers who use these software packages without proper understanding of the variables are not able to address the queries raised by the examiners during their viva. Due to the lack of manual knowledge, they are not able to understand which statistics to be applied to which data.

A few researchers apply chi-square test, *t*-test, ANOVA, MANOVA, and so on, without any understanding. These statistical tools are used to test hypotheses. But some researchers apply these statistical tools even without mentioning the basics of their hypothesis.

Although internet research has become extremely popular in no time in quantitative media research, there is lack of true and proper media research of reputation comparing internet research to other universally accepted data collection procedures, methods, techniques, and statistical applications.

Hence, some of the major problems relating to internet research in the field of communication and media are sequentially highlighted below:

First of all there is an extreme problem of control over the research situation in the case of collection of quantitative media research data with the help of an internet. Hence, the researcher is quite unaware as to who answers an internet questionnaire. This type of complexity also prevails with mail surveys. But seldom or never is this type of survey conducted in quantitative media research.

Second, at present there is no way to determine whether the internet sample is representative of the universe from which the sample was chosen. This again relates to the first problem of control over the research situation as to who completed the survey.

Third, a large number of internet users turn down the option of taking part in any type of internet research projects of quantitative media research as they are highly concerned with security problems.

Fourth, there is another complex problem of having no way to identify the respondents of quantitative media research with the help of an internet that is operated for the completion of a data collection. Despite the fact that the responses from the same internet unit can be controlled with the help of the computer IP address, yet this problem persists in quantitative data of media analysis.

Fifth, there is yet another serious problem in quantitative media study due to internet. That is to say that people who have absolutely no background of research and have virtually no experience and knowledge of research have merged as well-known internet researchers. This is like "a little learning is a dangerous thing." For example, in the broadcasting world of radio and television industry, so many former program directors who have hardly executed any proper research throughout their career have developed websites to conduct broadcasting research. More dangerous is that such nonprofessional researchers have publicized and marketed themselves in such a cleverly camouflaged manner that they have somehow won the confidence of the people.

14.4 ELECTRONIC DATA COLLECTION TECHNIQUES IN QUANTITATIVE MEDIA RESEARCH

Any quantitative media research will always be considered to be efficient and effective provided it attains its goal with minimum time, money, energy, and resources. To best achieve this goal, the traditional methods need to be avoided as these are cost ineffective and more time-consuming, energy-consuming, and resource-consuming. And new methods need to be adopted for an effective outcome. Successful media researchers are continually changing with technology and its adaptive nature.

There are umpteen number of methods currently used in electronic data collections in quantitative media research from internet users. The current electronic data collection procedures include the following.

14.4.1 Email

A tool of exchanging digital messages between computer users, emails are the most commonly used tool in media and communication research. A researcher can send his questionnaires to several respondents simultaneously by email. The questionnaires can be attached as a file with a persuasive covering letter including all ethical aspects. The email by the researcher can also direct the respondents to a website. The respondents fill all the questions of a questionnaire electronically and send the data back to the researcher by clicking on a "submit" button or via fax, WhatsApp, Facebook, hike, Evernote, Dropbox, and the likes after printing the complete questionnaire with the help of a camScanner. Email addresses can be gathered from the internet or may be purchased from companies which regularly and economically sell such data.

14.4.2 Pop-up

In this electronic data collection technique of quantitative media research, an invitation to take part in a research project pops up in a small box on the internet user's monitor as and when he visits a website. In order to participate in such research activities, the user is just supposed to click on a button contained in the pop-up, which easily directs him/her to the questionnaire.

14.4.3 Database Email

It includes sending heavy email messages from the SQL Server Database Engine which may contain heavy tables, heavy files, heavy findings, and the likes. Those respondents who are keenly interested and voluntarily ready to have their names included on a company's database get an email along with an invitation by the company's website to take part in a research project. This type of technique is largely and widely used by broadcasting stations.

14.4.4 Randomly Selected Pop-up

This is yet another technique of electronic data collection which is frequently used in quantitative media analysis. The technique is almost the same as in the pop-up technique. But in this case, respondents are selected randomly, generally every *N*th visitor to a website. For example, the offer to take part in quantitative media study can be presented to every 10th visitor to the website. Since it is randomly selected, the possibility of its being biased is automatically minimized.

14.4.5 Pre-recruit

In this type of electronic data collection of quantitative media research, respondents are usually contacted by telephone, internet, mail, or regular mail and are invited to take part in the quantitative media analysis. In case the respondents accept the invitation and agree to take part, then he/she is given an internet address to visit with a view to participate in such media study.

14.4.6 Instant Messaging

This is yet another type of apparatus of electronic data collection for quantitative media research. In this type of technique, the respondents take part in focus groups and other kinds of discussions and debate by simultaneously logging onto the same instant message service or the like proprietary site. This type of messaging is of immense help to media researchers as far as quantitative data are concerned.

14.4.7 Stationary Display

In this type of electronic data collection for the in-depth study of quantitative media analysis, a well-known company website includes a permanent display, generally a very small box at the corner of the monitor, that invite users to take part in such quantitative media research. Here, in this case, the respondents are supposed to click on a button by which they are automatically directed to a questionnaire.

Though the simple email technique is the most friendly and easiest to operate, yet comparatively it requires more and frequent work in the data entry phase of the research project. This is simply because the data must be coded and entered. Anyway, the media researchers of quantitative analysis should not fight shy of pursuing any of the previously discussed techniques. The most significant benefit of operating the internet for collecting such media data is that there are umpteen number of software packages easily and cheaply available these days. Some of these packages are readily available without any cost to help such media researchers.

Moreover, the skills and abilities to operate internet websites and computer programming differ significantly in accordance with the type of electronic data collection techniques used. A quantitative media study can be simple as well as complex. It solely depends on the approach of such media researchers. One can make it as simple as he desires and as complicated as he dares. On the other hand, the simple email technique does not require any skillful computer and internet expertise. However, the fully automated techniques applied in pop-up questionnaires and other "turn key" techniques require the highest degree of expertise, knowledge, and skill.

14.5 INTERNET AND REFERENCING TECHNIQUES IN QUANTITATIVE MEDIA STUDIES

As we have discussed earlier in the previous chapter that bibliographical references are an extremely important and integral part of any research as they acknowledge the source and help the readers in tracking the source. Like manual referencing, internet referencing is also a standard method of formatting the information sources the researcher has used in his dissertation or project or thesis or assignments or any other written work. It is an ethical issue also, failing which, partially or totally, is described as an academic misconduct. So it is considered to be an important aspect for any scholarly communication. It has now become a standard for any communication in most of the professional organizations. There are so many academic institutions, universities, colleges, libraries, and even departments which provide the style guidelines, online tutorials, or reference management software tools such as EndNote™ or Reference Manager™. Moreover, there are so many word processing tools easily available these days which include referencing features like the option to insert citations and references from different templates for various systems. In case we use a referencing software tool such as EndNote™ or Reference Manager™, then the process is direct and straightforward and most of the functions are easily executed by these software tools.

Broadly speaking, there are many types of referencing styles, some of which are as follows:

1. Harvard style
2. Vancouver style
3. American Psychological Association (APA) style
4. Modern Language Association (MLA) style
5. OSCOLA style
6. Chicago style
7. Turabian style

First, we have the *Harvard style* which mainly covers names, date, month, and year; most importantly, the name(s) of the author(s) are written with the first letter of each author's last name and each initial capitalized. Electronic and other references of the Harvard style will become crystal clear with the following examples of different types.

1. Electronic journal article:
   Denzin, N.K. et al. (2016). Web 3.0 authorship: issues of referencing and citation for academic integrity. *Internet and Mass Media*. [Online]. 10(1), pp. 210–220. Available at http://www.sciencedirect.com [Accessed 25 Feb. 2016].
2. Electronic book:
   Saunders, M. (2016). *Research methods for media students*. 3rd ed. [Online]. Open University Press study skills. Maidenhead: Open University Press. Available from http://lib.myilibrary.com [Accessed 20 Feb. 2016].
3. Electronic newspaper:
   Woodward, B. (2016, 15 February). Growing Plagiarism Among Media Researchers. *Independent Education*. Available from: http://www.lexisnexis.com [Accessed 28 Feb. 2016].
4. Website:
   Bernstein, Carl. (Ed.) (2016). *Quantitative Media Research: Learn Higher Avoiding Plagiarism*. Brandfold: Learn Higher at Branford University. Available at http://www.learnhigher.ac.uk/site/index.php [Accessed 25 Feb. 2016].
5. Online tutorial:
   Cronkite, Walter. et al. (2016). [Online Tutorial Version 5]. *Plagiarism learning in media research and teaching online*: PLATO. Derby: Innovation 10 Learning at the University of Derby. Available online at: http: //www.ilolearn.co.uk/education [Accessed on 15 Feb. 2016].

Second, we have the *Vancouver style* which mainly relates to numeric and running notes. Here, the name(s) of the author(s) is written with the first letter of each author's last name and each initial capitalized like in the Harvard style. And the year is written before the retrieving description. As far as the electronic and other references of Vancouver style are concerned, the following examples of different types will make it easily understandable.

1. Electronic journal article:
   Denzin, NK, et al. Web 3.0 authorship: issues of referencing and citation for academic integrity. *Internet and mass media*. [Online]. 2016, 10 (1): 210–20. Available at http://www.sciencedirect.com [Accessed 25 Feb. 2016].

2. Electronic book:
   Saunders, M. *Research methods for media students*. 3rd ed. [Online]. Open University Press study skills. Maidenhead: Open University Press. 2016. Available from http://lib.myilibrary.com [Accessed 20 Feb. 2016].
3. Electronic newspaper:
   Woodward, B. Growing plagiarism among media researchers. *Independent Education*; 2016 Feb 15. Available from: http://www.lexisnexis.com [Accessed on 28 Feb. 2016].
4. Website:
   Bernstein, Carl. (Ed.). *Quantitative media research: Learn higher avoiding plagiarism*. Brandfold: Learn Higher at Branford University, 2016. Available at http://www.learnhigher.ac.uk/site/index.php [Accessed 25 Feb. 2016].
5. Online tutorial:
   Cronkite, Walter. et al. [Online Tutorial Version 5]. *Plagiarism learning in media research and teaching online*: PLATO. Derby: Innovation 10 Learning at the University of Derby. 2016. Available online at: http: //www.ilolearn.co.uk/education [Accessed on 15 Feb. 2016].

Third we have the *American Psychological Association (APA) style*, which is most commonly and frequently used in media research, especially in quantitative analysis. In this style, the first letter of the first word of the title and subtitles, as well as the first letter of any proper noun, is capitalized. Moreover, the full title of the book including any subtitles should be written clearly and italicized or underlined. The following examples of different types will make it easily understandable.

1. Electronic journal article:
   Denzin, N.K. et al. (2016). Web 3.0 authorship: issues of referencing and citation for academic integrity. *Internet and mass media*. [Online]. *10*(1), 210–220. Available at http://www.sciencedirect.com [Accessed 25 Feb. 2016].
2. Electronic book:
   Saunders, M. (2016). *Research methods for media students*. 3rd ed. [Online]. Open University Press study skills. Maidenhead: Open University Press. Available from http://lib.myilibrary.com [Accessed 20 Feb. 2016].
3. Electronic newspaper:
   Woodward, Bob. (2016, February 15). Growing plagiarism among media researchers. *Independent Education*. Available from: http://www.lexisnexis.com [Accessed 28 Feb. 2016].
4. Website:
   Bernstein, Carl. (Ed.) (2016). *Quantitative media research: Learn higher avoiding plagiarism*. Brandfold: Learn Higher at Branford University. Available at http://www.learnhigher.ac.uk/site/index.php [Accessed 25 Feb. 2016].
5. Online tutorial:
   Cronkite, Walter. et al. (2016). [Online Tutorial Version 5]. *Plagiarism learning in media research and teaching online*: PLATO. Derby: Innovation 10 Learning at the University of Derby. Available online at: http: //www.ilolearn.co.uk/education [Accessed on 15 Feb. 2016].

Fourth, we have the *Modern Language Association (MLA) style* which is often used in writing research papers and citing sources in liberal arts and humanities. But it is used in media research also and, of course, in quantitative analysis when qualitative data are quantified. It is just like the APA style. But the year is written before the retrieving description. As far as the internet and referencing with the *MLA style* are concerned, the following examples of different types will make it extremely clear and easily understandable:

1. Electronic journal article:
   Denzin, N.K. et al. Web 3.0 authorship: issues of referencing and citation for academic integrity. *Internet and mass media*. [Online]. 2016, Vol. 10, no. 1. pp 210–220. Available at http://www.sciencedirect.com [Accessed 25 Feb. 2016].
2. Electronic book:
   Saunders, M. *Research methods for media students*. 3rd ed. [Online]. Open University Press study skills. Maidenhead: Open University Press. 2016. Available from http://lib.myilibrary.com [Accessed 20 Feb. 2016].
3. Electronic newspaper:
   Woodward, Bob. (2016). Growing plagiarism among media researchers. *Independent Education*. 15 February 2016. Available from: http://www.lexisnexis.com [Accessed 28 Feb. 2016].
4. Website:
   Bernstein, Carl. (Ed.). *Quantitative media research: Learn higher avoiding plagiarism*. Brandfold: Learn Higher at Branford University, 2016. Available at http://www.learnhigher.ac.uk/site/index.php [Accessed 25 Feb. 2016].
5. Online tutorial:
   Cronkite, Walter. et al. [Online Tutorial Version 5]. *Plagiarism learning in media research and teaching online*: PLATO. Derby: Innovation 10 Learning at the University of Derby. 2016. Available online at: http: / /www.ilolearn.co.uk/education [Accessed on 15 Feb. 2016].

Fifth, we have the *OSCOLA* style which is appropriately known as Oxford Standard for Citation for Legal Authorities. It is mostly used for any report of different periodicity while referencing manually or electronically. It can be made quite clear with the following example:

OXFORD STANDARD FOR CITATION OF LEGAL AUTHORITIES. [2016]. Available at: http://denning.law.ax.uk/published/oscola.shtml [Accessed 17 Feb. 2016].

Sixth, we have the *Chicago style* which is mainly of two types: (a) notes and bibliography, and (b) author–date. The first one is mostly used in humanities including history, literature, and fine arts. As far as media research is concerned, it is primarily used in qualitative research of mass communication. But it is also used in qualitative media analysis when the qualitative data are quantified. On the other hand, the author–date style is mainly used in physical, natural, and social sciences including media studies of both qualitative and quantitative nature.

Seventh, the *Turabian style* is a citing and referencing system which is almost similar to the Chicago style. It is named after Kate Turabian from the University of Chicago who has written a manual to guide the aspiring students in referencing and citing while writing research papers. One difference from the Chicago style is that of font size and point size. It is generally different from the Chicago style. Both Chicago style and Turabian style are not very comprehensive but allow using footnotes and endnotes unlike APA and MLA.

Moreover, while checking various referencing systems for specific items such as journals, books, magazines, or newspapers, the worldcat online catalogue[1] can be easily used to search for items of quantitative media research and then cite the reference information from their catalogue, choosing the reference system that the researcher is required to use.

Further, it is important to mention here that social media sites such as Facebook, WhatsApp, YouTube, hike, and LinkedIn are also used as data collecting techniques. Googledoc links are these days most frequently and commonly used for this purpose. This googledoc link can be easily and comfortably shared amongst social networks and a group can be requested to fill an online questionnaire.

14.6 APPLICATIONS OF SOFTWARE PACKAGES IN QUANTITATIVE MEDIA RESEARCH

There are broadly two types of software packages which are used in quantitative media research:

1. Statistical software
2. Content analysis software

And the most commonly used statistical software packages are as follows:

1. SPSS: The most frequently used statistical software in quantitative media research is SPSS, that is, Statistical Package for Social Sciences. SPSS version 2015 is officially called IBM SPSS statistics. SPSS 23 is the most current version of this software. This statistical package is largely and widely used in social sciences including media research of its quantitative data. Its manuals are wide, clear, comprehensive, and well-indexed. Other than SPSS, there are several other useful software packages for application in quantitative media research, such as Statistica, SAS, StatView, Data Desk and JMP, MS-Excel, and many other generalized and specialized statistical programs.
2. Statistica: This is similar to SPSS, but slightly easier to operate. Its unique feature is its graphical potentiality. Its cheapest version is called Quick Statistica which is faster also. It basically provides the most comprehensive array of data analysis, data management, data visualization, and data mining.
3. SAS: It is meant for advanced analytics, multivariate analysis, data management, and predictive analytics. It is basically a database system which can also be used as a statistical tool. The special characteristics of SAS are that it can handle large samples. Millions and billions of cases can be handled in a fraction of seconds and data mining can be executed within a very short span of time.

[1] www.worldcat.org/

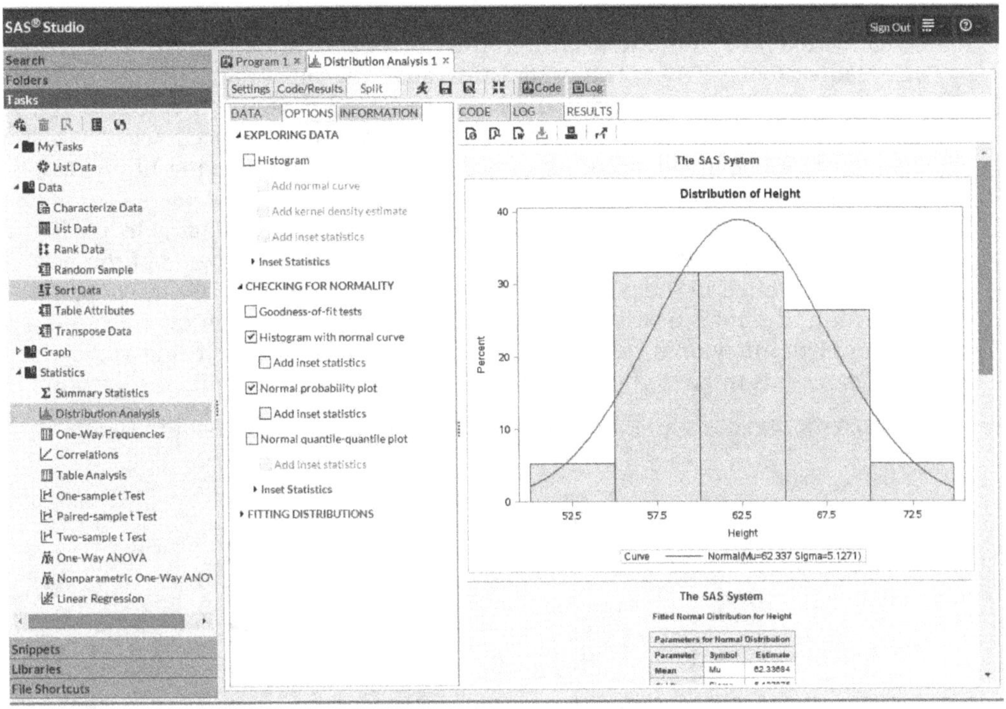

Source: http://www.sas.com/en_us/software/university-edition.html#for-students-learners

4. StatView: Being the first statistical application to have a graphical user interface, it was earlier a Macintosh program. But now it has a windows version also. It is quite different from other statistical software packages in the sense that it creates quite a lot of confusion in the beginning. But once the researcher gets used to it, the advantages are astronomical. Moreover, it works with an accelerated pace and it can easily produce a wide variety of graphs in no time.[2]
5. Data Desk and JMP: These two programs add tremendously in exploratory statistics and are displayed in a graphic format. Both these software packages are instrumental in understanding a bunch of data quickly with accuracy and perfection. Sometimes heavy-duty programs are not performed by SPSS so efficiently. But this tool is very helpful in easily executing heavy-duty programs.
6. Generalized statistical programs: In general parlance, most of the data are measured at a primitive level where these are mostly nominal, occasionally ordinal, and seldom ratio. But most of the statistical programs are devised for ratio data or interval data and not

[2] Source: https://www.google.co.in/search?q=sas+software&biw=1242&bih=566&source=lnms&tbm=isch&sa=X&ved=0ahUKEwjE7Zf8s_7NAhXEPY8KHcSACZ8Q_AUICCgD#tbm=isch&q=statview+software&imgrc=4z3miE960G2boM%3A (accessed November 15, 2016).

nominal data. Even SPSS demands its input to be in a numerical form. No response can be converted into its numeric form in the case of a question like "which newspaper did you read yesterday?" But for any statistical analysis, each newspaper has to be allocated an arbitrary number. Statistical programs which are known for their reliability, validity, and authenticity will report the mean of the newspaper to an accuracy of at least 8 decimal points. For extreme accuracy of even decimals, the following heavy-duty number crunchers may be used:

a. Stata: Created in 1985 by StataCorp., this is intercooled. That is to say like a newsprint van, complete with a plain DOS-style interface; the owner of the newspaper is only interested in the power of the van and not its beauty. In this context, the latest version of Stata can easily produce publication quality graphics. Thus, it is a perfect, complete, integrated package which provides almost everything which the media researcher is interested in for data analysis, data management, and graphics.

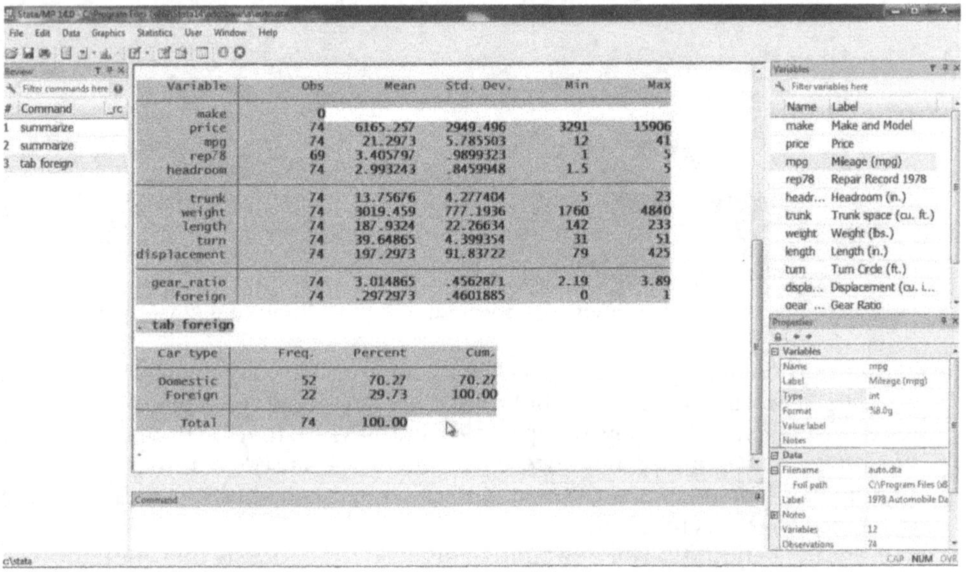

Source: http://www.stata.com/disciplines/behavioral-sciences/ (accessed November 15, 2016).

b. S-Plus: Founded by R. Douglas Martin, it is another very effective statistical programming language which has a powerful graphics capacity. But file handling in this case is not a child's play. It is rather a herculean task in the sense that it requires some kind of a trick. Like Stata, it was devised for expert and professional statisticians who apply it most frequently.

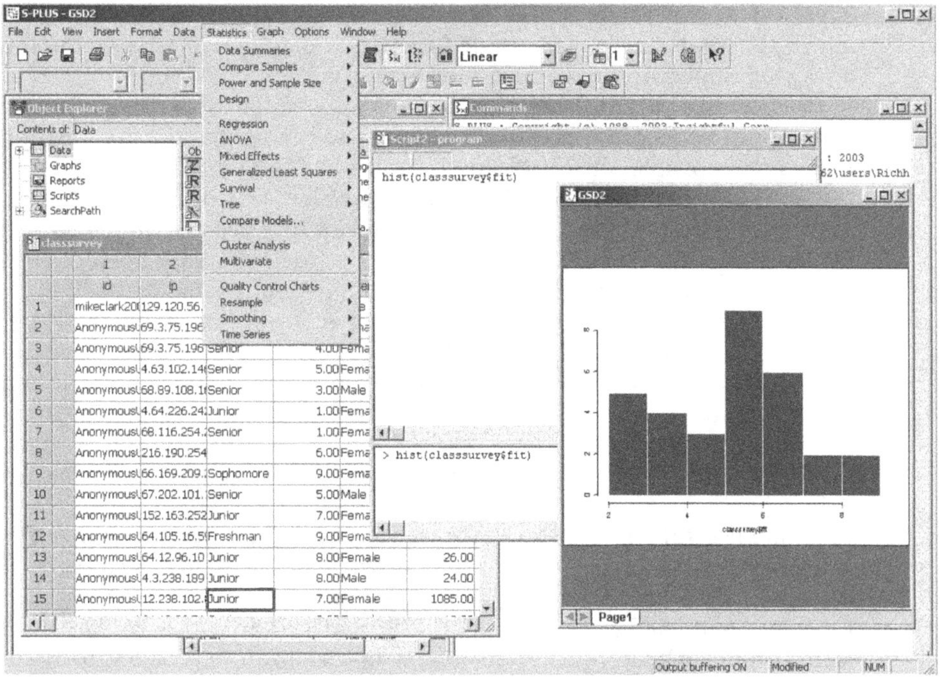

Source: http://www.msmiami.com/S_PLUS_s/39.htm (accessed November 15, 2016).

c. R like S-Plus: Designed by John Chambers to blur the distinction between users and programmers, it is primarily based on the statistical programming language S. But its freeware and its Windows and Macintosh versions are easily and readily available.

7. Specialized statistical programs: The most important and relevant statistical software packages for quantitative media research are as follows:

a. Instat Plus: Designed to support statistics teaching, it is basically an interactive statistical package. Such packages are exceptional and rare. It is quite easy and simple and has the power to be instrumental in media research that requires analysis of data. Moreover, it has the capability to help explain many of the key concepts, such as confidence intervals that users in media research often find confusing.
b. WinIDAMS: It is a free statistical software which was produced for UNESCO. At present, it has more than 9,000 registered users in 180 countries the world over.
c. SISA: Its full form is Simple Interactive Statistical Analysis. In this case, the researcher does not need a statistical software. Here, the media researcher is just supposed to feed data and the results will be easily calculated online by this statistical package. But data feeding is not so easy in any of the statistical software packages. The researcher needs complete knowledge of the dependent and the independent variables and all other sorts of variables. But when there is very little data to feed which the researcher is quite in a position to comprehend, then this package will do wonders within a very short span of time. Hence, it allows the researcher to do statistical interpretation directly on the internet.
d. Bayesware Discoverer: This is the only statistical package which has the capacity to handle incomplete and unstructured data. The most commonly used and popular version of this software among media researchers is 1.0. It is also called bwd10.exe.

e. Amelia: This is a unique type of statistical software. It is called "Imputation Software" which substitutes a plausible value for missing data. Amelia II executes multiple and advanced imputation to data with missing value.
f. MANET: This is yet another interactive software which takes care of the missing data. Media researchers often ask this question as to how to handle the missing data. And here is the possible answer of application of MANET in this case. However, when the researcher handles the missing data, he/she is definitely going to make some assumptions despite the fact that he/she is not in a position to realize it. Therefore, for academic data analysis and interpretation, the researcher must be fully aware of the various assumptions he/she is postulating.
g. Clarify: This statistical software is mainly used for interpreting and presenting statistical results. It makes all the data fed crystal clear and then data processing is started within the software. In a fraction of time, the whole data is interpreted and then presented in the form of statistical findings. Moreover, it is a computer-aided software which applies Monte Carlo simulation to transform the raw output of statistical analysis into findings which are of great help to media researchers of quantitative data.
h. TURNER: It is primarily a Mac software which is highly instrumental in exploratory data analysis. It is a computer-based statistical devise which is relevant and important for exploratory and semi-exploratory media research of quantitative analysis.
i. Tableau: Founded by Pat Hanrahan and Chris Stolte, it is an American software which produces a family of interactive data visualization products focused on advertising and media marketing research. It is a visualization tool for exploring and interpreting the relational database and data cubes led research in the use of table-oriented presentation to browse multidimensional relational databases.

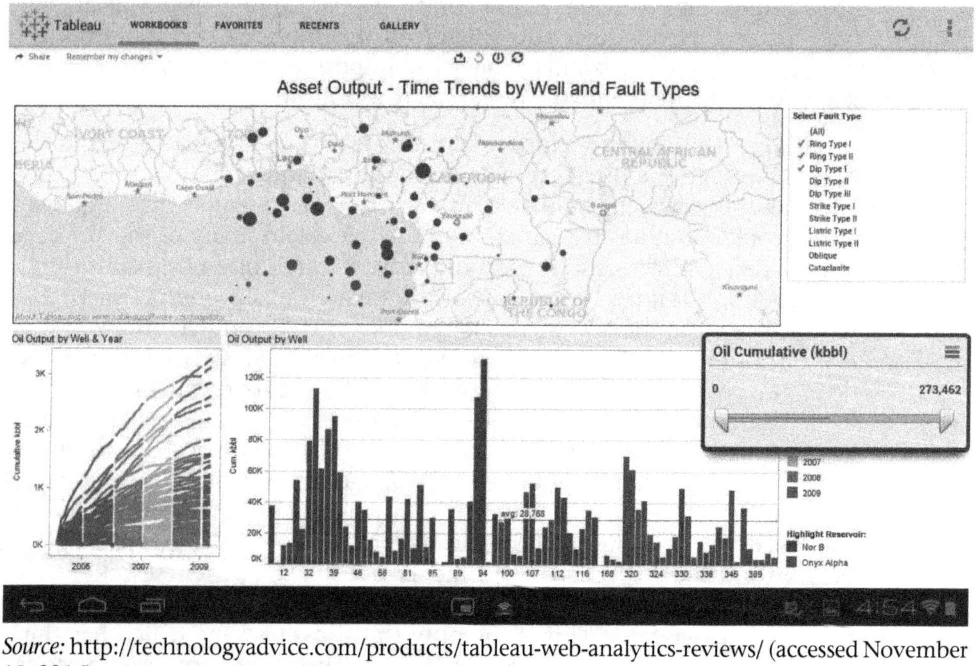

Source: http://technologyadvice.com/products/tableau-web-analytics-reviews/ (accessed November 15, 2016).

j. Webometrics: The word webometrics was first coined by Almind and Ingwersen of the USA in 1997. Also called cybermetrics, it is used to measure methodically the World Wide Web to attain basic information about the number and types of hyperlinks, structure of the World Wide Web, and usage patterns.

Yet another concept of webometrics has also been designed which describes it as "the study of web-based content with mainly quantitative techniques for social science research goals applying tools that are not particular to one field of research" (Thelwall 2009).

It gives importance and emphasis to the development of applied techniques for its appropriate application in wider social sciences. It helps in developing the proper techniques away from the IT world so as to apply it to social sciences including quantitative media research.

All the above packages are easily available on John Pezzullo's Statpages website. This website is highly instrumental in computing statistical data. Therefore, when a media researcher is using MS-Excel, he may do some statistical tests, and if he does not want to do it using the lengthy process of MS-Excel, then he can find a suitable and proper calculator here in which he can paste his data and get the results. In addition to the above mentioned statistical packages, we have some survey tabulation and web survey tabulation software packages too. The survey tabulation software packages are Statpac, The Survey System, and Quantrix, while web survey tabulation software packages are Powertab for Macintosh and Perseus Survey Solutions for Windows. But at present, Powertab has become outdated and Perseus is used on a much larger and wider scale.

On the other hand, the most frequently used content analysis software packages are: Corpus, General Inquirer, VBPro, Wordsmith, Textpack, TACT, and TextSTAT. Corpus is a statistical process and software technique for linguistic analysis, whereas General Inquirer is used for a dictionary-based content analysis program. VBPro is a baseline text analysis software for quantitative content analysis of communication and media studies, whereas Wordsmith's main objective is quantitative analysis of textual data which mainly functions with concordance, wordlist, and keywords. Textpack is very expensive as compared to VBPro and is applied for text analysis and automatic coding, whereas TACT (Text Analysis Computing Tool) helps with a text retrieval and analysis program which is designed to allow users to ask questions about words and patterns in a given text. It uses digital radiographic images and this computer-based research device correlates the individual images of a subject with a layering of images that can be minutely and meticulously observed in slices. On the other hand, TextSTAT is mainly used for the analysis of word frequencies in the texts and has the function to choose a specific word and display all the sentences.

Now a very pertinent question arises as to which software is the best for survey data in the present scenario. Although we also have another age-old software called MS-Excel which has now come up with its latest version in 2016 and is soon coming as "Excel on steroids," yet SPSS version 23.0 has many more advantages over MS-Excel. Though MS-Excel, which was well-known for its elegant looking charts, crystal-clear graphs, fascinating diagrams, and preliminary statistics, yet at present SPSS has all the advantages. SPSS is much quicker in its approach. It can handle even incomplete, missing, and unstructured data and is quite superior and more appropriate even for advanced statistical tools whether it is descriptive statistics or inferential statistics and whether it is parametric testing or nonparametric testing.

Thus, computer applications in quantitative media research have several advantages. Despite some limitations, complexities, and problems, computer applications including internet media research have many gainful aspects. When the problem of ignorance as to who is responding to a questionnaire and sample representativeness will be addressed in the time to come, online tools will most probably become the primary data collection technique used by researchers including media analysts. Till then, computer and online research may be applied as an adjunct approach to try to assist or refute data collected with other methods. Hence, computers and internets are excellent tools of quantitative media research. But it is an undisputed fact that ultimately no tool can replace the human spirit and compassion.

SUMMARY

Computer application has become omnipotent and omnipresent. Its unique software packages can easily execute complex statistical calculations such as measurers of central tendencies, measure of dispersions, measure of symmetry, measure of relationship, chi-square test, *t*-test, ANOVA, *Z*-test, *F*-test, multivariate analysis, and several nonparametric hypotheses tests such as *U* test and *H* test.

A media researcher while carrying out quantitative analysis must be aware of the following steps: (a) data organization and coding, (b) storing the required data in computer, (c) applying suitable statistical applications, (d) selecting an appropriate software package, and (e) computer program execution. Though quantitative media research with the help of offline and online computer software packages is time-saving, money-saving, energy-saving, and resource-saving, yet the research methodology used with the help of internet may not have an inherent authenticity, reliability, and validity. Again, the method used by the internet is not universally accepted as a valid methodology. So many top-notch companies of the world are still executing the statistical analysis manually. This is mainly because when software packages such as SPSS, SAS, Statistica, StatView, Stata, SISA, General Inquirer, Textpack, TACT, TextSTAT, MS-Excel, Corpus, Tableau, and webometrics are used directly, the researchers are not able to visualize all the variables properly.

There are umpteen methods currently used in electronic data collections in quantitative media research from internet users. The current electronic data collection procedures include: email, database email, Pop-up, randomly selected pop-up, prerecruit, instant messaging, and stationary display.

Broadly speaking, there are many types of referencing styles which include: Harvard style, Vancouver style, American Psychological Association (APA) style, Modern Language Association (MLA) style, OSCOLA style, Chicago style, and Turabian style.

Moreover, while checking various referencing systems for specific items such as journals, books, magazines, or newspapers, the worldcat online catalogue[3] can be easily used to search for items of quantitative media research and then to cite the reference information from their catalogue, choosing the reference system that the researcher is required to use.

Further, it is important to mention here that social media sites such as Facebook, WhatsApp, YouTube, hike, and LinkedIn are also used as data collecting techniques. Googledoc links are these days most frequently and commonly used for this purpose. This googledoc link can be easily and comfortably shared amongst social networks and a group can be requested to fill an online questionnaire.

There are broadly two types of software packages which are used in quantitative media research. The first one is statistical software (SPSS, Statistica, SAS, StatView, Data Desk and JMP, Stata, S-Plus, R like S-Plus, WinIDAMS, SISA, Bayesware Discoverer, Amelia, Clarify, Turner, MANET, Tableau, webometrics, and the likes). The second one is content analysis software (Corpus, General Inquirer, VBPro, Wordsmith, Textpack, TACT, TextSTAT, and the likes).

In addition to the above-mentioned statistical packages, we have some survey tabulation and web survey tabulation software packages. The survey tabulation software packages are Statpac, The Survey System, and Quantrix and the web survey tabulation software packages are Powertab for Macintosh and Perseus Survey Solutions for Windows. But at present, Powertab has become outdated and Perseus is used on a much larger and wider scale. Here, a very relevant question arises as to which software is the best for survey data in the present scenario. Although we also have another age-old software called MS-Excel which has now come up with its latest version in 2016 and is soon coming as "Excel on steroids," yet SPSS version 23.0 has many more advantages over MS-Excel. Though MS-Excel was well-known for its elegant-looking charts, crystal-clear graphs, fascinating diagrams, and preliminary statistics, yet at present SPSS has all the advantages. SPSS is much quicker in its approach. It can handle even incomplete, missing, and unstructured data and is quite superior and more appropriate even for advanced statistical tools whether it is descriptive statistics or inferential statistics and whether it is parametric testing or nonparametric testing. Hence, computer applications in quantitative media research have several advantages.

Despite some limitations, computer applications including internet media research has many gainful aspects. Thus, computers are excellent tools of quantitative media research. But no tool can replace the human spirit and understanding.

RELATED AND SUGGESTED WEBSITES

(As retrieved on July 18, 2016)

1. http://www.audiencedialogue.net/software.html
2. http://www.statsoft.com/Products/STATISTICA/Product-Index
3. https://www.google.co.in/?gfe_rd=cr&ei=mUCMV9OEJqj98weVoJXYBQ#q=sas+statistics
4. http://www.stata.com/why-use-stata/
5. http://faculty.washington.edu/tlumley/b514/R-fundamentals.pdf
6. http://instat.software.informer.com/3.3/
7. http://unesdoc.unesco.org/images/0021/002112/211276eo.pdf
8. http://www.quantitativeskills.com/sisa/
9. https://www.google.co.in/webhp?sourceid=chrome-instant&ion=1&espv=2&ie=UTF-8#q=Bayesware+Discoverer

REFERENCE

Thelwall, M. 2009. *Introduction to Webometrics: Quantitative Web Research for the Social Sciences*. Chapel Hill: Morgan & Claypool Publishers.

RELATED AND RECOMMENDED READINGS

Chawla, Deepak, and Neena Sondhi. 2011. *Research Methodology Concepts and Cases*, 607–18. 1st ed. New Delhi: Vikas Publishing House Pvt. Ltd.

Jesson Jill K., Lydia Matheson, and Fiona M. Lacey. 2011. *Doing Your Literature Review Traditional and Systematic Techniques*, 146–51. London: SAGE Publications Ltd.

Kothari, C.R. 2000. *Research Methodologies: Methods and Techniques*, 370–73. 2nd rev. ed. New Delhi: New Age International Publishers.
Wimmer, Roger D., and Joseph R. Dominick. 2003. *Mass Media Research: An Introduction*, 431–41. 7th ed. Wadsworth Publishing Company.
Zina, O. Leary. 2010. *The Essential Guide to Doing Your Research Project*. 3rd ed. London: SAGE Publications.

QUESTIONS

1. Describe the role of computer applications in quantitative media research.
2. What skills in computer data analysis of quantitative media research should a researcher be acquainted with?
3. Discuss the advantages of web technology in quantitative media research.
4. Throw light on the limitations of online research in quantitative media research.
5. Explain the major problems relating to internet research in the field of communication and media.
6. Describe the various electronic data collection techniques in quantitative media research.
7. Explain the referencing techniques in quantitative media research.
8. Throw light on various styles of referencing. How is it written in the case of online referencing in quantitative media research?
9. Describe the various applications of statistical software packages in quantitative media research.
10. List the content analysis software packages in media research of quantitative data.
11. Throw light on generalized statistical programs in quantitative media research.
12. Explain specialized statistical programs in quantitative media research.
13. List the survey tabulation and web survey tabulation software packages used in quantitative media research.
14. Compare between MS-Excel and SPSS. Which software do you consider the best for quantitative media research? Justify.

GLOSSARY

Amelia: This is a unique type of software that is also called "Imputation software." It substitutes plausible values for missing data. Its latest version, Amelia II, executes multiple and advanced imputation for data with missing values.

Analysis of Variance (ANOVA): It provides a statistical analysis for testing simultaneously the difference between so many sample means.

ANOCOVA: A kind of linear model which is basically a mixture of ANOVA and regression. Under this, simple regression replaces the influence of uncontrolled variable and the residual sums of squares are used to provide variance estimates which, in turn, are used to make tests of significance.

ANOVA table of one-way classification: In one-way classification, only one variable is taken into account. That means the data are classified according to only one criterion. One-way classification is fast cropping up in media and communication research, especially after the realization of application of statistical testing of a hypothesis for more scientific study.

ANOVA table of two-way classification: Two-way classification is used when the data are classified on the basis of two factors. For example, a newspaper may be classified on the basis of periodicity and theme.

APA style: American Psychological Association style is the most commonly and the most frequently used style in media research. In this style, the first letter of the first word of the titles and subtitles, as well as the first letter of any proper noun, is capitalized. Moreover, the full title of books, including any subtitles, should be written clearly and italicized or underlined.

Appendices: It is plural of appendix which means a section of table of subsidiary matter at the end of a thesis or project or dissertation or book, or the like. In appendices, generally the different questionnaires, schedules, related pictures, maps, interviews, and the likes are provided. This is also called a space for miscellany or a space for additional matter.

Applied research: It solves a specific problem rather than developing a theory.

Average deviation: It is measure of dispersion also known as mean deviation and is denoted by AD or MD or δ(del). It is computed by taking the arithmetic mean of the absolute values of deviations of the functional values from any measure of central tendency like mean, median, or mode. Average deviation is considered to be the least from the median and is also called the first moment dispersion.

Asymmetry: Symmetry means a balance between two halves and asymmetry is just the reverse. The dictionary meaning of asymmetry is "lack of symmetry," "skewness," "uneven," "odd," "unequal," "not straight," "dichotomy," or "uneven position" on each side of a central point or line.

Averages of the second order: Same as measures of dispersion.

Bar chart: It illustrates frequencies and scores.

Bayesware Discoverer: This is the only statistical package which has the capacity to handle the incomplete and unstructured data. The most commonly used and popular version of this software among media researchers is 1.0. It is also called bwd10.exe.

Bibliographical references: It provides the complete details of the sources of information and papers cited in a standardized format. This not only helps the readers about the various other sources, but it is also a legal requirement to cite author, publisher, title, and so on. If the researcher has directly or indirectly taken some reference material from somewhere and if he does not give proper biographical reference, then it is also a violation of the Copyright Act.

Blog: It is a short form of a weblog. It is a regularly updated website or web page which is run by an individual or a group and is written in an informal or conversational style.

Bowley's coefficient of skewness: This formula was propounded by the well-known statistician Professor Bowley. He does not take into account the values of mean and mode. It depends on the values of quartiles and median. This measure of skewness is also known as the second measure of skewness.

Call our research: A kind of technique used in radio research to determine the popularity of different recorded programs.

Canonical correlation: It simultaneously predicts a set of criteria variables from their joint covariance to a set of explanatory variables. In this, there are many metric explanatory variables and any one (out of two) nonmetric criteria variable.

Cardinal no. of finite set: The number of elements in a finite set A is known as cardinal number and is denoted by $n(A)$. For example, if $A=\{1,2,3,4,5\}$, then $n(A)=5$ and if $B=\{a,b,e,f,g\}$, then $n(B)=5$.

Census: When every unit or element of a population is considered for the study, it is called census.

Central limit theorem: A large sample leads to normalcy in the distribution of the data.

Central tendency: A single value that represents the large and widely scattered data, either in the form of a mathematical average or positional average or concentration of the highest frequency, mean, median, and mode.

Chicago style: It is mainly of two types: (a) notes and bibliography, (b) author–date. The first one is mostly used in humanities including history, literature, and fine arts. As far as media research is concerned, it is primarily used in qualitative research of mass communication. But it is also used in qualitative media analysis when the qualitative data are quantified. On the other hand, the author–date style is mainly used in physical, natural, and social sciences including media studies of both qualitative and quantitative nature.

Chi-square (χ^2): It is a specific type of cross-tabulation between observed frequencies and expected frequencies which is followed by a certain formula.

Circulation: It is the total number of copies sold in context with print media such as newspapers, magazines, journals, and so on.

Classification of sets: Sets may be classified in a variety of forms which are as follows: finite set, Infinite set, singleton set, null or empty or void set, universal set, subset, proper subset, power set, equal sets, equivalent sets, multiple sets, and so on.

Closed-ended question: It is a type of multiple choice question, where the respondent is supposed to mark an answer making a selection from a prepared set of options.

Cluster sample: When a sample is taken as a group or category, forming several groups or categories.

Codebook: Categorizing the unit of analysis.

Coding: Coding, a process of assigning a code to something for classification or identification, is a proper placement of the unit of analysis into a particular category. It is a method of assigning numerals or symbols to replies from respondents so that the answers can be put into a limited number of categories or classes. It is essential for effective and efficient analysis which will reduce the data to a small number of classes. In the case of manual coding, the standard method is to code in the "margin" with a colored pencil. Whether the coding is executed electronically or manually, the researcher must see that coding errors are eliminated or minimized. It is better to keep a record sheet of codes, that is, a code sheet. Coding should be executed while preparing the data instrument. This helps in directly entering the code of each variable to the recording sheet. The codes can be numeric, alphabetic, or zero.

Coefficient of correlation: when the numeric value of correlation is presented, it is called the coefficient of correlation.

Coefficient of determination: This relates to correlational study, in which the amount of variation in the criterion variable is accounted for by the antecedent variable.

Coefficient of nondetermination: This relates to correlational analysis in which the amount of variation in the criterion variable is left unexplained.

Cohort analysis: A study of specific population over different period of time.

Common variance: Variance started with other variables in the factor analysis is called common variance.

Communality: It is denoted by h^2 and is the total amount of variance in the given item accounted for by all the factors.

Comparable set: Two sets A and B are said to be comparable if one of them is a subset of the other. For example, the sets {4,5,6,7} and {4,5,6,7,8,10} are comparable sets.

Complimentary of a set: The compliment of a given set is a set which contains all those members of the universal set that do not belong to the given set. For example (a) If the universe set U={4,5,6,7,8,9,10}, and A={4,5,6,7,8}, then $A'=A^C=\{9,10\}$ (where A' or A^C denotes compliment of a set)

Concurrence deviation method of correlation: It is described as the simplest and quickest method of calculating the coefficient of correlation. This method mainly focuses on the direction of change of two variables (say X and Y) independently.

Correlation: Interrelationship between two or more variables.

Correlation matrix: It is a table showing correlations among all the communalities which are denoted by h2 and are the total amount of variance in the given item accounted for by all the factors.

Communication audit: It generally relates to public relations in which a study of internal and external means of communication is conducted by an organization.

Confidence interval: The range within which a parameter value is estimated is called the "confidence interval." This range will vary on the basis of the extent of precision which is the target to be attained. This is a specific area in which there is a marked probability that the parameter will fall. The bigger the extent of precision required, the larger will be the range between the lower limit and the upper limit of the range.

Confidence level: This is also called the alpha level in which the probability of 0.05 or 0.01 of rejecting a null hypothesis is true.

Confidence level of μ: If the sample is a random sample from a normal population of unknown mean, the 95 percent confidence or fiducial limits of the population mean (μ) are: $\mu = \bar{X} \pm \frac{S}{\sqrt{N}} t_{0.01}$ (where $\bar{X}$ is the mean of the sample, N is the sample size, and S is the standard deviation of the sample).

Confidence limits: Same as confidence level or fiducial limits.

Construct: A number of concepts that are made to describe a specific situation.

Continuous variable: Variables that can take any value in a certain range. For example, height, time, distance, and the likes are continuous variables.

Control group: A group in a scientific research, which does not receive any experimental treatment and, thus, serves as a basis for a comparison in an experiment.

Control variable: A variable that is constant and unchanged in order to assess the relationship between two other variables.

Convenience sample: It is a non-probability sample in which respondents or subjects are selected because of their convenient accessibility, availability, and proximity to the researcher.

Criterion variable: In general, the criterion variable is the dependent variable. In regression analysis, criterion variable is the variable which is predicted. So it is also called the predictor (independent) variable.

Curvilinear correlation: If the change of two variables is not in the same proportion, then the curve will not be straight, but it will be skewed. Hence, it is called curvilinear correlation. It is also called nonlinear correlation.

Data: Facts or statistics or information in raw or unorganized or unstructured form are called data.

Database email: It sends heavy email messages from SQL Server Database Engine which may contain heavy tables, heavy files, heavy findings, and so on. Those respondents who are keenly interested and voluntarily ready to have their names included on a company's database get an email along with an invitation by company's website to take part in a research project. This type of technique is largely and widely used by broadcasting stations.

Data editing: It is a process of converting the raw data into useful information by detecting errors and omissions. It includes perusal and careful examination of filled questionnaires and/or schedules. Editing is an art and craft which is executed to assure that the data are accurate, consistent with other facts gathered, uniformly entered as complete as possible, and have been systematically arranged to facilitate coding and tabulation. Editing techniques relates to a range of procedures used for handling and detecting mistakes and omissions in data.

Data coding: Same as coding.

Data classification: It is basically a data management process of sorting, classifying, and categorizing data into various forms, groups, types, and so on. The data collected generally becomes a large volume of raw data which must be reduced to homogeneous groups to make meaningful relationships. This is executed by creating classes through classification of data, through the process of arranging data in groups or classes on the basis of common characteristics.

Data processing: It is basically a type of data operation especially with the help of a computer in the present era. It generally implies editing, coding, classification, tabulation, and general explanation of the table.

Data analysis: It means to consider the data in light of hypothesis or research questions, research objectives, and the ever evolving as well as prevailing theories and drawing conclusions that are as amenable as theory formation.

Data interpretation: It means drawing inference as per data behavior. This is a very significant and ending step in the process of research as it is the phase where the findings as per objectives and set hypotheses are highlighted. Through processing, the information gathered is given a valid form to be analyzed. Through applying statistical techniques, certain measures are computed which are selected as per data's nature and measures' applicability. After this, the outputs are interpreted and inferences are drawn.

Database journalism: A journalism which is dependent on computer-assisted analysis is called database journalism.

Data Desk and JMP: These two programs add tremendously in exploratory statistics and are displayed in graphic format. Both these software packages are instrumental in understanding a bunch of data quickly with accuracy and perfection. Sometimes when heavy-duty programs are not performed by SPSS so efficiently, then these software packages work most effectively. Thus, these tools are very helpful in easily executing heavy-duty programs.

Degree of freedom: It is denoted by d_f or v. During the comparison between the calculated value and the table value, we are supposed to find out the degree of freedom which is calculated by the formula $d_f=(c-1)\ (r-1)$, where c is the number of columns and r is the number of rows. For example, if the $d_f=2$, then we will see the table value from the second row according to our freedom at any value of confidence level (i.e., at 0.995 or at 0.990 or at 0.975 or at 0.950 or at 0.900 or at 0.100 or at 0.050 or at 0.025 or at 0.010 or at 0.005).

During the comparison between the calculated value and the table value of χ^2, we are supposed to find out the degrees of freedom. Here, the degrees of freedom (d_f or v) is calculated by the following formula: $d_f=(c-1)\ (r-1)$, where c is the number of columns and r is the number of rows.

De Moivre Curve: De Moivre used the normal curve mathematically in practice, so it is also called the De Moivre curve.

De Morgan's law: It is a law which states that the compliment of union of two sets is equal to the intersection of their complements, and the complements and the intersection of two sets is equal to the union of their compliments, for example, $(A \cup B)^c = A^c \cap B^c$.

Dependent methods of MVA: These are multiple regression analysis, multiple discriminant analysis, multiple analysis for variance, and canonical correlation.

Dependent variable: This variable is a consequence of some cause. For example, if we increase the size of the audience, the effectiveness of communication will decrease. Here, the effectiveness of communication is a dependent variable. That is why it is also called uncontrolled variable, result variable, outcome variable, effects variable, consequence variable, criterion variable, or attribute variable. In a scientific experiment, we cannot have a dependent variable without an independent variable. Thus, its value is presumed to depend on the independent variable (which is also called controlled variable or cause variable or active variable or predictor or antecedent variable).

Descriptive media metrics: It has got its birth from descriptive statistics. It is used to quantitatively describe the basic features of the media data. It reduces the data-sets of media problems and media issues for easier interpretation and provides the simple summaries about the measures. Technically speaking, it includes measures of central tendency (mean, median, mode), measures of dispersion (mean deviation, standard deviation, range, quartile deviation), measures of asymmetry (skewness, kurtosis), and measures of relationship (correlation, regression).

Descriptive statistics: When descriptive media metrics is broadened and is used in general parlance rather than media problems and issues, it is called descriptive statistics.

Differentiation: It is an operation which allows media researchers to find out a function which gives the rate of change of one variable with respect to another variable. It is frequently used in engineering research, but often used in advanced media research to differentiate the media variables and subvariables.

Discrete variable: Those which can take only finite number of invisible values are called discrete variables, for example, the number of students in a class.

Disjoint set: If A and B are two sets such that $A \cap B = \emptyset$, that is, there are no common elements in A and B, then these are called disjoint sets. For example, $A=\{1,2,3,4\}$, $B=\{8,9,10,11\}$, then A and B are disjoint sets because there are no common elements between the two sets.

Dispersion: It is the degree of variability in a set of scores.

Disproportionate stratified sampling: When the proportion of different strata is not equal, even though their size is equal, then it is called disproportionate stratified sampling (e.g., in a population of 200 media persons, if there are 100 journalists, 60 public relation officers, and 40 advertisers and we take 25 each from the three strata for study which are equal in number, but disproportionate according to the population).

Dummy variable: When a variable at the nominal level is converted into a form more suitable for higher order statistics.

Eigenvalue: If we take sum of squared values of factor loadings related to a factor, then such sum is called eigenvalue also referred to as a latent root.

Editing: Same as data editing.

Effects variable: Same as dependent variable.

Email: A method of exchanging digital messages between computer users and is the most frequently used tool in media and communication research. Here, a researcher can send his questionnaires to several respondents simultaneously by email. The questionnaires can be attached as a file with a persuasive covering letter including all ethical aspects. The email by the researcher can also direct the respondents to a website. The respondents electronically fill all the questions of a questionnaire and send the data back to the researcher by clicking on a "submit" button or via fax WhatsApp, Facebook, hike, Evernote, Dropbox, and the likes after printing the complete questionnaire with the help of CamScanner. Email addresses can be gathered from the Internet or may be purchased from companies which regularly and economically sell such data.

Empty set: It is also called null set or empty set or void set. It does not have any member or element or component and is denoted by O| or by { }, for example, set of all those integers whose square is 7.

Equal set: Two sets A and B are said to be equal, if every element of A is an element of B and every element of B is an element of A, for example, {5,9,11}={9,11,5}. Another example is: {3,5,9}={3,5,5,9,9,3} (the repetition of elements of a set is immaterial).

Equivalent set: Two finite sets A and B are said to be equivalent sets if the number of elements in A are equal to those in B, that is, $n(A)=n(B)$. Equivalence of two sets is denoted by the symbol ≃. Thus, if A and B are equivalent sets, we write A≃B and it is read as "A is equivalent to B," for example, if A={1,2,3} and B={x,y,z}, then $n(A)=n(B)=3$ and, therefore, A and B are equivalent sets and we write A=B.

Note: Each pair of equal sets are equivalent sets, but equivalent sets need not be equal sets.

Errors in hypothesis testing: There are two types of errors in hypothesis testing: (a) type I error (b) type II error. Type I error is that when the hypothesis is true, but our tests reject it. Type II error is that in which the hypothesis is false, but our tests accept it.

Estimation: It generally refers to the technique and methods by which population parameters are studied from sample studies.

Estimating lines: They study the average relationship between two series and highlight their covariance.

Estimator of parameters: It is a particular single numeric value of the sample which is used to estimate the parameter value. It is used as an estimate of the unknown population parameter.

Evaluation research: It is a specific type of media and communication research in which an evaluation culture is developed to measure an organization's social, communication, or media performance.

Experimental design: A planning for laboratory research.

External validity: The extent to which the results of a research project can be generalized to other situations.

Factor: It represents the underlying dimensions that summarizes the original set of observed variables. In media and communication studies, there can be one or more factors and the number of variables associated with the same.

Factor analysis: Originated in psychometrics, but now widely used in media metrics and other social sciences, factor analysis is a multivariate statistical technique. It is used for data reduction to a manageable level, constructing development, and examination of interrelationships between variables.

Factor loadings: These are correlations between the original variables and the factors and the key for understanding the nature of a particular factor. Variables with high loadings are distinguishing features of the factor. These are also known as factor variable correlations.

Factor score: Summary of the score obtained after factor analysis.

Factor design: A simultaneous study of two or more factors or independent variables.

Fiducial limits: Same as confidence level or confidence limits.

Finite set: When the element of a set are countable, the set is called a finite set. For example, (a) set of all registered newspapers in a particular city or set of all private TV channels in a particular city; (b) The set of all countries on the earth is a finite set, (c) The set of all states in India is a finite set; (d) The set of months in a year is a finite set.

First degree dispersion: Average deviation or mean deviation is called first-degree dispersion.

First moment about origin: Mean is called the first moment about origin.

First moment about mean: It is always zero.

Flesch reading ease formula: It is known as an early readability formula which is dependent on the number of words per sentence and the number of syllables per word.

Focus group: It is type of qualitative research in which a group of 6–12 persons are interviewed simultaneously by a moderator to know about their perceptions, opinions, and attitudes about specific issue or product.

Fog index: It is a kind of readability scale which is dependent on sentence length and the number of syllables per word.

Fourth moment about mean: Kurtosis is called the fourth moment about mean.

Frequency curve: It is a graphical representation of frequency distribution.

Frequency distribution: It is a visual display of various collection of scores ordered according to magnitude.

Frequency polygon: It is a graphical depiction of the frequencies of scores.

Friedman's test: It is a nonparametric test and an alternative to one-way ANOVA with measures. It is applied to test for differences between groups when the dependent variable is ordinal.

Gaussian curve: Because the normal curve was discovered by Laplace and Gauss, the curve is also known as the Gaussian curve in the honor of Gauss.

Goodness of fit: It is also known as a test of concordance which enables us to understand how well the assured theoretical distribution fits to the observed data.

Graph: It is a diagrammatical representation of a set of data in which the data is represented by symbols.

Graphic method of correlation: This method finds out correlation between two distributions and also the direction whether it is positively correlated or negatively correlated. When in a graph the two curves representing the two variables show similar tendency, it is an indication of positive correlation, on the other hand, when the two curves move in different directions, correlation is negative.

Graphical representation: A graph or chart is a diagrammatical representation of a set of data in which the data is represented by symbols. A diagrammatical representation is also called a graphic representation which is also described as a geometrical image of a set of data. It is basically a mathematical visualization. It helps us in visual thinking about a statistical problem. Hence, the graphic representation of data is a highly effective and more communicative method of processing, presenting, understanding, analyzing, and interpreting the collected data.

Gross rating points: It is the total of all rating points, representing the size of the gross of an advertising or radio or television program.

Guttman's scale: Also known as cumulative scaling or scalogram analysis, it is quite different from the Likert scale or Thurstone scale. It applies to a series of items in other kinds of tests, such as achievement tests that have binary outcomes.

Histogram: A type of bar chart which represents frequencies or scores.

Homogeneity: In research, it means equality of experimental groups before conducting an experiment.

Homogeneity test: It tries to understand whether two or more independent random samples are drawn from the same universe or from different universe.

Hook: It is a small representative sample of radio recordings applied in a call-out research.

Hypertext: A text which is displayed on computer or electronic devices to link electronic documents.

Hypothesis: It is an assumed proposition and a tentative generalization of significance of relationship between two or more variables.

***H* test:** It was propounded by Kruskal and Wallis. So it is also known as the *Kruskal–Wallis H test* which is an extension of the Mann–Whitney test and the best nonparametric substitute of ANOVA if there is no assumption. That is why it is also called ANOVA by ranks.

Index no.: It is used to measure changes over time in magnitudes, which are not capable of direct measurement.

Independence test: It is related to the problem whether one attribute is independent of the other or not. It involves a single sample taken from one universe.

Independent methods of MVA: These are factor analysis, cluster analysis, multidimensional scaling analysis, and latent structure analysis.

Independent variable: This variable is a cause which gives some consequence. For example, if we increase the size of the audience, the effectiveness of communication will decrease. Here, the size of the audience is an independent variable. It is such a variable which is varied, controlled, guided, governed, and manipulated by the researcher. That is why it is also called a controlled variable or cause variable or active variable or predictor, or antecedent variable. In a scientific experiment, we cannot have an independent variable without a dependent variable.

Inferential media metrics: It has got its birth from inferential statistics. It tries to infer what the population might think from sample data of the media issues and problems. Technically speaking, it includes parametric statistics or nonparametric hypothesis testing (*F*-test, *t*-test, *Z*-test, ANOVA, ANOCOVA, and so on) and nonparametric statistics or nonparametric hypothesis testing (chi-square, *U* test, *H* test, and so on).

Inferential statistics: When inferential media metrics is broadened and is used in general parlance rather than media problems and issues, it is called inferential statistics.

Infinite set: When the elements of a set are uncountable, the set is called an infinite set. For example, set of hairs in our head or set of stars in the sky, or set of natural numbers, real numbers, whole numbers, complex numbers, rational numbers, and so on, are instances of infinite sets.

Instant plus: Designed to support statistics teaching, it is basically an interactive statistical package. Such packages are exceptional and rare. It is quite easy and simple and has the power to be instrumental in media research that requires analysis of data. Moreover, it has the capability to help explain many of the key concepts, such as confidence intervals that users in media research often find confusing.

Instant messaging: This is yet another type of apparatus of electronic data collection for quantitative media research. In this type of technique, the respondents take part in focus groups and other kinds of discussions and debates by simultaneously logging onto the same instant message service or the like proprietary site. This type of messaging is of immense help to media researchers as far as quantitative data are concerned.

Interval data: It is like ordinal data with equal split such as time and temperature. For example, the interval between 8.00 am and 8.05 am, 9.00 am and 9.05 am, and that between 10.00 am and 10.05 am is same unlike the difference between I, II, III of a race or an examination (ordinal data).

Interval level: Like interval data, It is a level of measurement in which the interval between adjacent points on a scale are equal.

Interval estimates: Unlike point estimate, an interval estimate is a statement of two values between which it is estimated that the parameter lies. Hence, it is a range instead of a particular point.

Instrumental replication: It is duplication of dependent variables of the earlier researches.

Integration: It is a process of finding a function when its derivatives are given. It is also called anti-differentiation. It is frequently applied in engineering research, but is applied in advanced media research only when variables and subvariables are integrated to find their function from the established derivatives. If $F'(X)=f(X)$, then we say $F(X)$ is anti-derivative of $f(X)$.

Intensive interview: It is a one-to-one personal interview by probing deeply on a certain issue.

Internal consistency: It is based on correlations between different variables and is usually the level of consistency of performance among variables within a scale.

Internal validity: In this the results are dependent on expected conditions rather than on extraneous variables.

Karl Pearson's coefficient of skewness: It is based on the difference between mean and mode divided by standard deviation to give a relative measure. This method of measuring skewness has been propounded by the well-known British biometrician and statistician Karl Pearson.

Karl Pearson's coefficient of correlation: It is a formula given by the well-known Biometrician and Mathematician Karl Pearson for the measurement of coefficient of correlation of many mathematical methods of calculating correlation.

Kelly's coefficient of skewness: A well-known statistician Kelly has suggested that instead of quartiles, deciles and percentiles may be used in computation of skewness. According to him, the 10th and 90th percentiles or the 1st and 9th deciles may be used for measuring skewness.

Kruskal–Wallis *H* test: Same as *H* test.

Kurtosis: It refers to the degree of flatness or peakedness about the mode of a frequency curve pertaining to media problems and issues. It tells us the extent to which a distribution is more peaked or flat-topped than the normal curve. It enlightens us whether the distribution, if plotted on a graph, will give us a normal curve more flat than the normal curve or a curve more peaked than the normal curve.

Latent structure analysis: Such an analysis seeks to share both of the basic objectives of factor analysis. That is to say that it extracts latent factors and expresses relationship of observed variables with these factors as their indicators, and classifies a population of respondents into pure types.

Leptokurtic curve: This curve is higher than the normal curve having bigger kurtosis.

Life stream: Coined by two Americans Eric Freeman and David Gelernter in the mid-1990s, it functions as a diary of researcher's electronic life in which every document the researcher creates and every document the respondents and other people send to the researcher is stored.

Linear correlation: When there is change in two variables in the same proportion, the graph plotted thereby is a straight line and such correlation is described as linear correlation.

Likert scale: It is a scale of measurement in which the respondents are strongly positive, positive, neutral, negative, and strongly negative with the statements.

Limitations: These are basically related to the problems and crisis of time, money, energy, and resources. In every research there is generally either lack of time or lack of money or lack of energy or lack of resources. The researcher in the report must highlight this to defend his research work's deficiencies and shortcomings.

Literature review: It is based on the research topic and research problem. When the literature is reviewed from the previous research work in the concerned area or field or topic or problem, then it should be preferably written chronologically either in ascending order or in descending order while editing and writing the report. It can be taken from many other sources such as books, journals, periodicals, magazines, newspapers, electronic devices, websites, and CDs.

Longitudinal study: It is a research based on the data at different periods of time.

MANET: This is an interactive software which takes care of the missing data. Media researchers often ask this question as to how to handle the missing data. And here is the possible answer of application of MANET in this case.

MANOVA: It is an ANOVA with multiple dependent variables and is an integral part of multivariate analysis. While ANOVA tests for difference in means between two or more groups, MANOVA tests for the difference in two or more vectors of means.

Mann–Whitney *U* test: It is an alternative of *t*-test in a nonparametric form when the data is ordinal. It is used to (a) compare two population means that come from the same population, (b) test whether two population means are equal or not, (c) test equal sample sizes, and (d) to test the median of two populations.

Marker variable: A variable that highlights the different constructs under the research.

Mathematical notation: It is a well-known written symbol or symbolic expression of mathematical concepts. It gives a precise semantic meaning.

Matrix: It is an integral part of mathematical algebra, highly instrumental in factor analysis, which can be conducive to search media issues, problems, variables, and subvariables.

Matrix algebra: Same as matrix.

Mean: It is the mathematical average of the given set of scores.

Mean deviation: Same as average deviation.

Measures of asymmetry: It enlightens us in the direction and extent of asymmetry or skewness in a series and permits us to compare two or more series.

Measures of central tendency: Same as central tendency.

Measures of dispersion: They give an average of the differences of various items from one average. They are also called averages of the second order. Measures of dispersion include average deviation (mean deviation), standard deviation, variance, range, quartile, quartile deviation, and so on.

Measures of relationship: When there is directional relationship or cause and effect relationship between two or more variables, then it can be measured numerically which is called measures of relationship.

Measures of skewness: Same as measures of asymmetry.

Measurement: It is the technique of assignment of numbers to objects or events in accordance with certain prescribed guidelines.

Measurement error: It is an error created by any sort of inconsistency by the instruments applied in the study.

Median: It is a positional average, that is, mid-point of a given set of scores.

Median test: Alexander M. Mood propounded this nonparametric median test which is used to test the equality of medians from two or more populations. Hence, it gives a nonparametric alternative to the one-way ANOVA and sometimes also Pearson's chi-square test. This test works when Y variable is continuous, discrete-ordinal, or discrete-nominal and X variable is discrete with two or more attributes.

Media metrics: Metrics is a method of measuring something scientifically. Hence, media metrics is a scientific method of measuring the variables and subvariables of media and communication. Broadly speaking, it is a use of statistics and mathematics in media and communication research.

Mesokurtic curve: It is higher than normal curve having bigger kurtosis.

Meta-analysis: A quantitative summation of various research scores and findings.

Methodology: It is a science of methods or a systematic study of methods.

Methods of dispersion: It includes average deviation or mean deviation, standard deviation, variance range, range deviation, quartile deviation, and the likes.

Micro blog: It is a type of blog in which very short, mini, and tiny messages of texts, pictures, video, or audio are sent which can be further sent to a website to show either to a small group or to the public.

MMO: It is a massively multiplier online game in which a very large number of participants interact with one another within a game world of endless size.

Mode: it is the score having the highest frequency.

Moments: Used to explain the different features of a frequency distribution such as central tendency, variation and skewness.

Moments of arbitrary origin: If the mean is in fraction, it is difficult to calculate moments. In such a situation, we calculate moments about an arbitrary origin and then convert these moments about the mean. Moments about the arbitrary origin also called "raw moments" are denoted by the symbol δ.

Mood's median test: Same as median test.

Multicollinearity: The degree to which a variable can be explained by the other variable in the analysis.

Multiple analysis of variance: Same as MANOVA.

Multiple correlation: In multiple correlation, there are three or more variables and all are changing or variating simultaneously, and the change is also studied simultaneously.

Multidimensional scaling analysis: It is a simultaneous test of measuring an item in more than one dimension.

Multiple discriminant analysis: Also known as canonical variate analysis (CVA) or canonical discriminant analysis (CDA), multiple discriminant analysis is a method of compressing a multivariate signal to yield a lower dimensional signal amenable to classification. This is basically an extension of linear discriminant analysis (LDA) which in its original form is applied to construct discriminant functions for the objects assigned to two groups.

Multiple regression: It is a simultaneous examination of two or more independent variables and their interrelation to a single dependent variable.

Multiple correlation analysis: In a multiple correlation analysis, there are three or more variables and at least one will be constant.

Multiple regression analysis: In a multiple regression analysis, there are three or more variables and at least one will be constant.

Multistage sampling: It is a complex type of cluster sampling at different stages in which units, not groups, are chosen.

Multiple set: It is an unordered collection of elements in which an element may occur as a member more than once. The multiplicity of an element is the number of times the element occurs in the set. For example, the set A={b,c,c,d,d,e,e,e} is a multiple set. Multiplicity of element b in set A=1. Multiplicity of element c in set A=2. Multiplicity of element d in set A=2. Multiplicity of element e in set A=3.

Multivariate analysis: It is basically an extension of the principles of multivariate statistics. In media research, it allows more than two variables of media to be analyzed simultaneously.

This technique in media research takes account of the various relationships among communication and media variables, such as audience and effectiveness of communication, creativity and communication, intelligence, emotion, communication and creativity, and interrelation between growth of print media and electronic media.

Mutually exclusive: It is a unit of analysis which can be placed in one and only one category.

Nominal data: Nominal relates to name and both nominal and name have the same Latin root. Hence, it refers to categorically discrete data such as name of your university, name of media book, and category of gender. That is why it is also called categorical data.

Nominal level: Like nominal data, it is a form of level of measurement in which arbitrary numbers are leveled to classify names, persons, or objects.

Nonparametric testing of hypothesis: It does not depend on the random sampling or normal distribution. It can be applicable on any data. This type of hypothesis testing does not require any assumptions or conditions or parameters. Hence, it is simple to understand and easy to apply.

Non-probability sample: When a sample is selected without following the law of probability, it is called a non-probability sample.

Nonparametric statistics: It is also known as distribution free statistics or assumption free statistics or order statistics. It is a statistical process which is used with variables measured at the nominal or ordinal level.

Normal curve: It is a bell-shaped symmetrical curve showing a particular distribution of probability over the values of a random variable.

Normal distribution: It has a graph of continuous, symmetrical, and bell-shaped curve.

Null hypothesis: It refers to a general statement that there is no significant relationship between two variables, or the two variables are independent of each other.

Null set: Same as empty set.

Numbers: Mathematical objects or statistical data used to count, measure, and label.

Objectives: Basically, the core and needle of the research. At the end, in results and conclusions it is minutely and meticulously verified whether all the objectives have been systematically achieved or not

One-tailed test of hypothesis: It relates to only one side of the normal curve.

One-sample Wilcoxon test: It assumes the data to be a symmetric distribution, such as the uniform or Cauchy distribution. If the researcher cannot verify this assumption of symmetry, he should use the nonparametric one-sample sign test. That is why this is not very popular as it is neither properly parametric nor nonparametric. Hence, a better option is always preferred.

Open-ended question: It is a form of unstructured question in which possible answers are not given as a choice.

Ordinal data: The word ordinal sounds like order. Hence, order of a race or order of a rank in an examination I, II, III are glaring examples of ordinal data. Similar examples are high–low, minimum–maximum, more than/less than, short–average–tall, primary–secondary–higher education, lower–lower middle–middle–higher middle–higher–smallest to largest, etc.

Ordinal level: It is a type of level of measurement in which ranking of items are done on the lines of ordinal data.

OSCOLA style: It is known as Oxford Standard for Citation for Legal Authorities. It is mostly used for any report of different periodicity while referencing manually or electronically.

Outcome variable: Same as a dependent variable.

Panel study: It is a research procedure in which the same sample of respondents is measured at a different period of time.

Parameter: It is a specific characteristic of a universe.

Parametric statistics: A form of statistical technique suitable for variables measured at the interval or ratio level. It is related to certain parameters or assumptions or conditions when applied.

Parametric testing of hypothesis: This type of hypothesis testing requires certain assumptions or conditions or parameters.

Partial correlation: When there are more than two variables in an event, but the interrelation of only two is measured keeping other variables as constant.

People meter: It is a television audience data collection tool capable of measuring individual viewing behavior.

Periodicity: Any type of bias occurring due to nonrandom selection of a sample.

Platykurtic curve: It is lower than normal curve having lesser kurtosis.

Point estimates: Same as estimator of parameter.

Population variance test: This type of test is applied to find out whether the variance in the population could be a specified numeric value. This has a vital role in scientific accuracy of media analysis.

Pop-up: In this procedure of electronic data collection technique of quantitative media research, an invitation to take part in a research project pops up in a small box on internet user's monitor as and when he visits a website. In order to participate in such research activities, the user is just supposed to click on a button contained in the pop-up and, thus, he is easily directed to the questionnaire.

Positive correlation: When two variables change in the same direction and with a change in one variable, the other also changes, it is called positive correlation.

Power of hypothesis test: The measure of how effectively the test is working is called the power of the test. For hypothesis to be powerful, β (probability of accepting H_0 when H_0 is not true) should to be as small as possible. Reversely $1-\beta$ (probability of rejecting H_0 when H_0 is not true) should be as big as possible. If $(1-\beta)$ is near to unity, we can say that the test is working effectively, leading to the fact that the test is rejecting H_0 when H_0 is not true. Thus, $(1-\beta)$ value is the measure of how effectively the test is working or what is called the "power of a hypothesis test."

Power set: It is a collection of subsets.

Precision journalism: A procedure of investigation in which media research methods are applied to collect the news.

Pre-recruit: In this type of electronic data collection of quantitative media research, respondents are usually contacted by telephone, internet, mail, or regular mail and are invited to take part in the quantitative media analysis. In case the respondents accept the invitation and agree to take part, then he is given an internet address to visit with a view of participating in such media study.

Primary source: It is a first-hand direct source which provides the original data.

Primary data: The collection of first-hand data is called primary data.

Probability sample: When a sample is chosen according to the law of probability, then it is called probability sample.

Proper set: A set B is said to be a proper subset of set A if every element of set B is an element of A, whereas every element of A is not an element of B.

Proportionate stratified sample: When the proportion of different strata is equal, then it is called proportionate stratified sample.

Prosocial: Behavior which is positive or beneficial to other people or society as a whole.

Psychographics: Mindset or attitudinal profile of respondents in a research.

Public relations audit: An elaborate and comprehensive study of the public relations status of an organization.

Purposive sample: When a sample is deliberately selected, to be representative of universe.

Qualitative research method: It relates to qualitative aspects of a research (which are usually immeasurable) which uses flexible questioning.

Quantitative research method: It is related to the quantitative aspects of research which uses standardized questioning.

Quasi-experiment: It is a form of research design which does not associate with random assignment of subjects to an experimental group.

Quota sample: It is a procedure of collecting representative data from subgroup of certain characteristics of interest. It is basically strata within strata.

Random error: Such an error is always there in the measurement during a research study and it cannot be controlled by the researcher under any circumstance.

Random sample: It is a subset or subgroups of individuals (a sample) of a universe chosen from the universe in such a way that each unit in a universe has equal chance of being selected.

Range: It is a measure of dispersion which can be obtained by subtracting the smallest score from the largest score in a set of distribution.

Ratio data: This data is the same as interval data with a natural or true zero such as height and weight.

Ratio level: Like ratio data, It is a level of measurement in which the interval between adjacent points on a scale are equal with a true zero.

Randomly selected pop-up: This is a technique of electronic data collection which is frequently used in quantitative media analysis. The technique is almost the same as in the pop-up. But in this case, respondents are selected randomly, generally every *N*th visitor to a website. For example, the offer to take part in a quantitative media study can be presented to every 10th visitor to the website. Since it is randomly selected, hence the possibility of its being biased is automatically minimized.

Rank correlation test: Developed by Spearman, it is described as a measure of association based on the ordinal feature of data. This test is one of the simplest statistical methods to use and the easiest to apply. It is even superior to Karl Pearson's product moment correlation coefficient in the sense that unlike the Pearson approach, it does not require normal distribution of data and random sampling.

Rank sum test: Propounded by Mann and Whitney, it is a nonparametric test of hypothesis testing that two samples come from the same population against an alternative hypothesis. It is a highly adjustable test in the sense that it does not have any assumption. Unlike *t*-test, there is no normal distribution of data in the application of this test. This test was sporadically presented by Frank Wilcoxon. But it was properly picked up and suitably developed by H.B. Mann and D.R. Whitney. So it is popularly known as the Mann–Whitney test. But a few statisticians are of the view that it should be called the Wilcoxon–Mann–Whitney test. So it is occasionally referred to as the Wilcoxon–Mann–Whitney test.

Rationale of the topic: Here, the researcher has to reason out as to why this topic was selected. Any topic is generally selected when it has some social significance and the researcher is keenly interested in the topic by heart and soul. The researcher is the first unit of the society. Hence, his deep interest or background or future prospect of the topic cannot be avoided. That is why "rationale of the topic" is also sometimes replaced by another phrase called "social significance of the topic."

R like S-plus: Designed by John Chambers to blur the distinction between users and programmers, it is primarily based on the statistical programming language S. Its freeware and its windows and Macintosh versions are easily and readily available.

Readability: When a text is so presented that it becomes worth reading, then it is called readability.

Regression: It basically implies going back or returning towards the mean and it is the measure of the average relationship between two or more variables in terms of the original units.

Regression analysis: It is carried out for estimating or predicting the unknown value of one variable from the unknown value of the other variable.

Regression lines: Same as estimating lines.

Replication: It is an independent checking, cross-checking and multi-checking.

Report writing: A research report is the full and final part of a research work. It is a description of the research work carried out by the researcher. It requires various steps to present a report in the form of a project or thesis or dissertation. The purpose of a research cannot be properly served unless the findings are made known to others including general audience and subject experts. Hence, report writing is a part and parcel of the entire research project.

Research problem: Practically, the research problem comes first in the mind of the researcher even before finalizing the topic. But, theoretically, the topic is written first whether it is the cover page or inside page, even though the topic emerges from the problem. Research problems are generally research questions, which gradually become the base of the research objectives and the research hypothesis. Research problem is presented in its detailed form in major project or thesis.

Research question: When some very basic question is generated from the research problem, we may call it a research question.

Research design: It is structure, outline, layout, blueprint, framework, scheme, and paradigm of operation essential for effective, efficient, systematic, and scientific research with minimum time, cost, money, energy, and resources.

Result variable: Same as dependent variable.

Review of literature: Same as literature review.

Roaster form: In this form, all the members of a set are separated by commas, and are enclosed in curly or middle brackets. For example, the set N of natural numbers may be written as N={1,2,3,4,...}.

Here. the dots denote that the set contains all the natural numbers.

Rule method: Here, the set is written by some special properties satisfied by all its members like N={x|x is a natural number}. The symbol | stands for "such that" x is a natural number. Yet another example of all real numbers greater than 5, but less than 9 can be expressed symbolically as follows: N={x|5<x<9}. In this case, the rule lays down that "N" is a set of all elements x such that x is an integer and 5<x<9.

Sample: It is a part or subset or subgroup of population.

Sample distribution: It is the frequency distribution of all the variables in a sample from a given set of data.

Sample size: It is selecting the number of observations or replicates in the sample from the universe. For example, if the sample size is 350, it means that 350 units from the universe have been chosen for the study.

Sampling distribution: It is a probability distribution of a given databased on a random sample.

Sampling error: The extent to which measurements of a sample differ from measurements that would be obtained from the universe.

Sampling interval: It is a form of frequency of data collection and is a random interval applied for choosing the units in the systematic sampling method.

SAS: It is meant for advanced analytics, multivariate analysis, data management, and predictive analytics. It is basically a database system which can also be used as a statistical tool. The special characteristics of SAS are that it can handle large samples. Millions and billions of cases can be handled in a fraction of seconds and data mining can be executed within a very short span of time.

Scale: It is a type of measurement such as Likert scale, Guttman scale, semantic differential scale, three-point scale, five-point scale, or seven-point scale.

Scatter diagram: It is the graphic representation of the correlation between two variables.

Scientific method: It is a systematic, evaluative, comparative, controlled, empirical, and critical investigation of hypothesis about presumed relationship.

Semantic differential: It is a seven-point scale between two bipolar adjectives like outstanding, excellent, very good, good, average, bad, very bad.

Second degree dispersion: Standard deviation is called second-degree dispersion.

Second moment about mean: Variance is called second moment about mean.

Set: It is defined as a collection of well-defined object.

Set builder form: Same as the rule method.

Set theory: It is a branch of mathematics which studies, set description, set classification and set operation. It is applied mostly to the objects which are relevant to mathematics.

Singleton: A set which has only one element.

Sigma: The Greek capital letter Σ which means summation or sum of all.

Sign test: It is one of the simplest nonparametric tests which is based on (+) or (–) sign of observations. It is not based on any numeric value and can be categorized as (a) one-sample sign test, (b) two-sample sign test

SISA: Its full form is simple interactive statistical analysis. In this case, the researcher does not need statistical software. Here, the media researcher is just supposed to feed his data, and the results will be easily calculated online by this statistical package. But data feeding is not so easy in any of the statistical software. The researcher needs complete knowledge of the dependent and the independent variables and all other sorts of variables. But when there is very little data to feed which the researcher is quite in a position to comprehend, and then this package will do wonders within a very short span of time. Hence, it allows the researcher to do statistical interpretations directly on the internet.

Skewness: It is a measure of asymmetry which calculates the extent of departure of a curve from the normal distribution either positively or negatively.

Social audit: It generally relates to public relations research in which an analysis of social performance of an organization is observed.

Social marketing: Coined by two Americans Philip Kotler and Gerald Zaltman, it is a kind of marketing for social welfare and benefit.

Social networking service: Also called social networking site, SNS or social media is a forum to establish social associations, social relations, and social interface among online users who share personal activities, ideas, information, interests, or thoughts.

SPSS: The most frequently used statistical software in quantitative media research is SPSS, that is, statistical package for social sciences. SPSS version 2015 is officially called IBM SPSS statistics. But the most current version of SPSS is 2016 which is called SPSS 23.

S-plus: Founded by R. Douglas Martin, it is another very effective statistical programming language which has a powerful graphics capacity. But file handling in this case is not a child's play. It is, rather, a herculean task in the sense that it requires some kind of a trick. Like Stata, it was devised for expert and professional statisticians who apply it most frequently.

Standard deviation: It is the square root of the variance which measures the amount of variation or dispersion from the average.

Standard error: It is the estimate of the degree of error in a measurement.

Stationary display: In this type of data collection electronically for the in-depth study of quantitative media analysis, a well-known company website included a permanent display, generally a very small box at the corner of the monitor, that invites users to take part in such quantitative media research. Here, in this case, the respondents are supposed to click on a button by which they are automatically directed to a questionnaire.

Statistica: Created in 1985 by StataCorp, this is intercooled. That is to say like a newsprint van, complete with a plain DOS-style interface, the owner of the newspaper is only interested in the power of the van and not its beauty. In this context, the latest version of Stata can easily produce publication quality graphics. Thus, it a perfect, complete, and integrated package which provides almost everything which the media researcher is interested in for data analysis, data management, and graphics.

Statistics: It is a science which applies mathematical procedure to collect, organize, summarizes, and analyze the available data.

StatView: Being the first statistical application to have a graphical user interface, it was earlier a Macintosh program. But now it is a Windows version also. It is quite different from other statistical software packages in the sense that it is quite confusion-creating in the beginning. But once the researcher gets used to it, then the advantages are astronomical. Moreover, it works with an accelerated pace and it can easily produce a wide variety of graphs in no time.

Stratified sample: When a sample is selected after the universe has been divided into homogenous subgroups or categories, then it is called a stratified sample.

Structured interview: It is also called a standardized interview or researcher-administered survey in which standard questions are asked in a predetermined order.

Subset: A subset is an integral part of a set.

Superset: The set, having a subset as an integral part, is described as a superset.

Systematic random sampling: It is a form of probability sampling technique in which there is an equal chance of choosing each unit from within the universe during sample formulation.

Systematic variance: It is a systematic rise or fall in a set of data by a known factor.

Tableau: Meticulously engineered by Pat Hanrahan and Chris Stolte, it is an American software which produces a family of highly interactive data visualization products focused on advertising, corporate communication, and media marketing research. It is basically a visualization apparatus for searching, exploring, and interpreting the relational database and data cubes led research in the use of table-oriented presentation to browse multidimensional relational databases.

Tabular form of set: Same as roaster form.

Telephone survey: It is a type of research method in which relevant data are collected over the telephone by experienced interviewers who ask questions and record the answers.

Test of significance for attributes: In this type of a test, we can only find out the presence or absence of attributes (that is, quality, property, characteristics, or traits).

Test for the number of successes: In this type of test for the number of successes, the sampling distribution follows a binomial probability distribution.

Test for the proportion of significance: In this type of test for the proportion of successes, instead of recording the number of successes in each sample, we may record the proportion of successes, that is, 1/*N*th of the number of successes in each sample.

Test for difference between proportions: In this type of test, primarily the difference of proportions is studied. Suppose that we draw two samples from universe. We may be interested in calculating whether the difference between the proportion of successes is significant or not. Under such circumstances, we take the hypothesis that the difference between p_1, that is, the proportion of successes in one sample, and p_2, that is, the proportion of successes in another sample is because of the variation in the random sampling.

Test of goodness of fit: Same as goodness of fit.

Test of homogeneity: Same as homogeneity test.

Theory: It is a scientific and systematic generalization of facts or phenomena.

Theory of runs: same as one-sample test.

Third moment about mean: Skewness is called third moment about mean.

Test of population variance: Same as population variance test.

Tools of media metrics: The mathematical and statistical tools of media metrics are: different numbers, set theory, matrix, differentiation, integration, data processing, measures of central tendency, measures of dispersion, measures of relationship, multivariate analysis, parametric testing, nonparametric testing, and so on.

Trends study: It is the simplest form of longitudinal study of the data which examines the overall change over a period of time.

Triangulation: It is a combination of qualitative and quantitative method of research to solve a research problem.

Turabian style: It is a citing and referencing system which is almost similar to the Chicago style. It is named after Kate Turabian from the University of Chicago who has written a manual to guide the aspiring students in referencing and citing while writing research papers. One more difference with that of Chicago style is that of font size and point size. It is generally different from Chicago style. Both Chicago style and Turabian style are not very comprehensive but allow using footnotes and endnotes unlike APA and MLA.

Turner: It is primarily a Mac software which is highly instrumental in exploratory data analysis. It is a computer-based statistical devise which is useful, relevant, and important for exploratory and semi-exploratory media research of quantitative analysis.

Two-tailed test of hypothesis: It relates to both sides of the normal curve.

Types of correlation: It is broadly of the following types: positive, negative, zero, simple, partial, multiple, linear, nonlinear, scatter diagram, graphic, and so on.

Types of correlation coefficient: Broadly speaking, these are of four types: Karl Pearson's product moment, Spearman's rank, concurrent deviation, and least squares.

Types of nonparametric test: In a broader parlance, it has the following types: chi-square, Mann–Whitney *U* test, Kruskal–Wallis *H* test, sign test, Wilcoxon test, Mood's median test, Friedman's test, and so on.

Types of parametric test: In broader sense, it has the following types: *F*-test, *Z*-test, one-sample *t*-test, two-sample *t*-test, one way ANOVA, and so on.

Types of number: There are whole, natural, integer, rational, and irrational numbers.

Type I error: It is a type of error in hypothesis testing in which the null hypothesis is rejected while it should have been usually accepted.

Type II error: It is another form of error in hypothesis testing in which the null hypothesis is accepted while it should have been usually rejected.

***t*-test:** It is a parametric test applied to determine the significance between group means.

Uncontrolled variable: Same as dependent variable.

Universal set: It is a set of all components or elements that come in a particular situation and serves as a frame of reference. For example, in circumstances where reference is made to students of journalism and mass communication, all students of journalism and mass communication will constitute a universal set. It is generally denoted by U.

Unstructured interview: In this type of interview, questions are not pre-planned or pre-arranged or pre-determined, which allows questions to develop during the course of interview.

***U* test:** Same as the rank sum test.

Validity: It is the degree to which a concept, conclusion, or measurement is well-founded and reacts exactly to the real-world situation.

Variable: It is an event or phenomenon which can be measured or manipulated and it may change from group to group, person to person, or within one person over a period of time.

Variance: It is the square of standard deviation and is a mathematical index of the degree to which scores deviate from the mean.

Venn diagram: It represents sets logically, mathematically, and pictorially as circles or closed curves within an enclosing rectangles called the universal set, and common members of the sets being represented by interactions of the circle.

Void set: Same as empty set or null set.

Web browser: It is a program which systematically searches the World Wide Web.

Webometrics: Coined by two Americans Almind and Ingwersen in 1997, it is used to methodically measure the World Wide Web in order to attain basic information about the number and types of hyperlinks and the structure of the World Wide Web. It is also called cybermetrics and is also described as the study of web-based content with mainly quantitative techniques for social science research goals applying tools that are not particular to one field of research.

Wilcoxon signed-rank test: It assumes the data to be a symmetric distribution, such as the uniform or Cauchy distribution. If the researcher cannot verify this assumption of symmetry, he should use the nonparametric one-sample sign test.

WinIDAMS: It is a free statistical software which is produced for UNESCO. At present, it has more than 9000 registered users in 180 countries the world over.

World Wide Web: It is a system of interlinked computers and electronic information sites which are accessed via internet.

***Z*-test:** Same as *t*-test. But in this case, the sample size is more than 30, while in *t*-test it is equal to or less than 30.

STATISTICAL VALUE TABLES

TABLE 1

NORMAL DISTRIBUTION

Entry is area A under the standard normal curve from $-\infty$ to $z(A)$

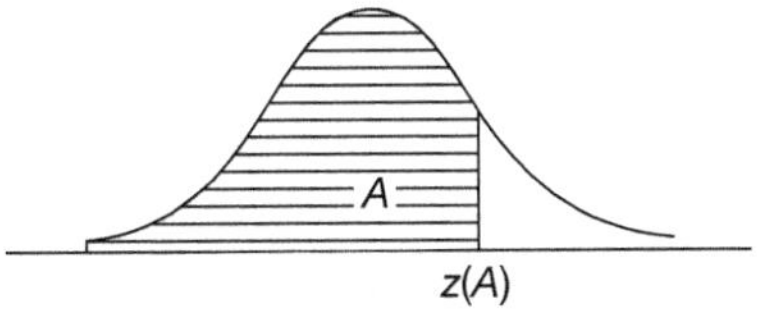

z	.00	.01	.02	.03	.04	.05	.06	.07	.08	.09
.0	.5000	.5040	.5080	.5120	.5160	.5199	.5239	.5279	.5319	.5359
.1	.5398	.5438	.5478	.5517	.5557	.5596	.5636	.5675	.5714	.5753
.2	.5793	.5832	.5871	.5910	.5948	.5987	.6026	.6064	.6103	.6141
.3	.6179	.6217	.6255	.6293	.6331	.6368	.6406	.6443	.6480	.6517
.4	.6554	.6591	.6628	.6664	.6700	.6736	.6772	.6808	.6844	.6879
.5	.6915	.6950	.6985	.7019	.7054	.7088	.7123	.7157	.7190	.7224
.6	.7257	.7291	.7324	.7357	.7389	.7422	.7454	.7486	.7517	.7549
.7	.7580	.7611	.7642	.7673	.7704	.7734	.7764	.7794	.7823	.7852
.8	.7881	.7910	.7939	.7967	.7995	.8023	.8051	.8078	.8106	.8133
.9	.8159	.8186	.8212	.8238	.8264	.8289	.8315	.8340	.8365	.8389
1.0	.8413	.8438	.8461	.8485	.8508	.8531	.8554	.8577	.8599	.8621
1.1	.8643	.8665	.8686	.8708	.8729	.8749	.8770	.8790	.8810	.8830
1.2	.8849	.8869	.8888	.8907	.8925	.8944	.8962	.8980	.8997	.9015
1.3	.9032	.9049	.9066	.9082	.9099	.9115	.9131	.9147	.9162	.9177
1.4	.9192	.9207	.9222	.9236	.9251	.9265	.9279	.9292	.9306	.9319
1.5	.9332	.9345	.9357	.9370	.9382	.9394	.9406	.9418	.9429	.9441
1.6	.9452	.9463	.9474	.9484	.9495	.9505	.9515	.9525	.9535	.9545
1.7	.9554	.9564	.9573	.9582	.9591	.9599	.9608	.9616	.9625	.9633
1.8	.9641	.9649	.9656	.9664	.9671	.9678	.9686	.9693	.9699	.9706
1.9	.9713	.9719	.9726	.9732	.9738	.9744	.9750	.9756	.9761	.9767
2.0	.9772	.9778	.9783	.9788	.9793	.9798	.9803	.9808	.9812	.9817
2.1	.9821	.9826	.9830	.9834	.9838	.9842	.9846	.9850	.9854	.9857
2.2	.9861	.9864	.9868	.9871	.9875	.9878	.9881	.9884	.9887	.9890
2.3	.9893	.9896	.9898	.9901	.9904	.9906	.9909	.9911	.9913	.9916
2.4	.9918	.9920	.9922	.9925	.9927	.9929	.9931	.9932	.9934	.9936
2.5	.9938	.9940	.9941	.9943	.9945	.9946	.9948	.9949	.9951	.9952
2.6	.9953	.9955	.9956	.9957	.9959	.9960	.9961	.9962	.9963	.9964
2.7	.9965	.9966	.9967	.9968	.9969	.9970	.9971	.9972	.9973	.9974
2.8	.9974	.9975	.9976	.9977	.9977	.9978	.9979	.9979	.9980	.9981
2.9	.9981	.9982	.9982	.9983	.9984	.9984	.9985	.9985	.9986	.9986
3.0	.9987	.9987	.9987	.9988	.9988	.9989	.9989	.9989	.9990	.9990
3.1	.9990	.9991	.9991	.9991	.9992	.9992	.9992	.9992	.9993	.9993
3.2	.9993	.9993	.9994	.9994	.9994	.9994	.9994	.9995	.9995	.9995
3.3	.9995	.9995	.9995	.9996	.9996	.9996	.9996	.9996	.9996	.9997
3.4	.9997	.9997	.9997	.9997	.9997	.9997	.9997	.9997	.9997	.9998

TABLE 2

CHI-SQUARE DISTRIBUTION

Entry is $\chi^2(A;\, v)$ where $P\{\chi^2(v) \le \chi^2(A;\, v)\} = A$

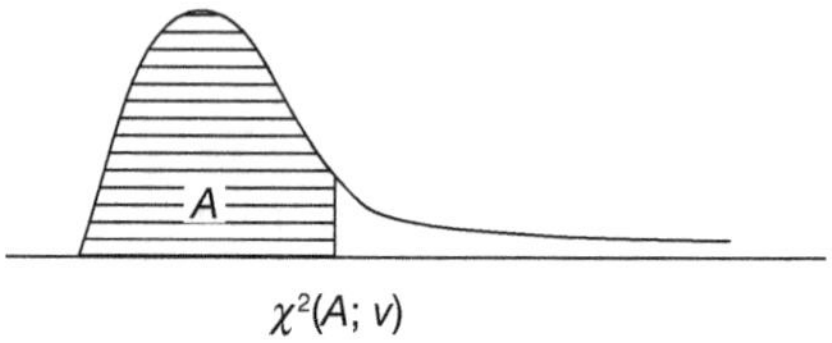

	A									
v	.005	.010	.025	.050	.100	.900	.950	.975	.990	.995
1	$0.0^{4}393$	$0.0^{3}157$	$0.0^{3}982$	$0.0^{2}393$	0.0158	2.71	3.84	5.02	6.63	7.88
2	0.0100	0.0201	0.0506	0.103	0.211	4.61	5.99	7.38	9.21	10.60
3	0.072	0.115	0.216	0.352	0.584	6.25	7.81	9.35	11.34	12.84
4	0.207	0.297	0.484	0.711	1.064	7.78	9.49	11.14	13.28	14.86
5	0.412	0.554	0.831	1.145	1.61	9.24	11.07	12.83	15.09	16.75
6	0.676	0.872	1.24	1.64	2.20	10.64	12.59	14.45	16.81	18.55
7	0.989	1.24	1.69	2.17	2.83	12.02	14.07	16.01	18.48	20.28
8	1.34	1.65	2.18	2.73	3.49	13.36	15.51	17.53	20.09	21.96
9	1.73	2.09	2.70	3.33	4.17	14.68	16.92	19.02	21.67	23.59
10	2.16	2.56	3.25	3.94	4.87	15.99	18.31	20.48	23.21	25.19
11	2.60	3.05	3.82	4.57	5.58	17.28	19.68	21.92	24.73	26.76
12	3.07	3.57	4.40	5.23	6.30	18.55	21.03	23.34	26.22	28.30
13	3.57	4.11	5.01	5.89	7.04	19.81	22.36	24.74	27.69	29.82
14	4.07	4.66	5.63	6.57	7.79	21.06	23.68	26.12	29.14	31.32
15	4.60	5.23	6.26	7.26	8.55	22.31	25.00	27.49	30.58	32.80
16	5.14	5.81	6.91	7.96	9.31	23.54	26.30	28.85	32.00	34.27
17	5.70	6.41	7.56	8.67	10.09	24.77	27.59	30.19	33.41	35.72
18	6.26	7.01	8.23	9.39	10.86	25.99	28.87	31.53	34.81	37.16
19	6.84	7.63	8.91	10.12	11.65	27.20	30.14	32.85	36.19	38.58
20	7.43	8.26	9.59	10.85	12.44	28.41	31.41	34.17	37.57	40.00
21	8.03	8.90	10.28	11.59	13.24	29.62	32.67	35.48	38.93	41.40
22	8.64	9.54	10.98	12.34	14.04	30.81	33.92	36.78	40.29	42.80
23	9.26	10.20	11.69	13.09	14.85	32.01	35.17	38.08	41.64	44.18
24	9.89	10.86	12.40	13.85	15.66	33.20	36.42	39.36	42.98	45.56
25	10.52	11.52	13.12	14.61	16.47	34.38	37.65	40.65	44.31	46.93
26	11.16	12.20	13.84	15.38	17.29	35.56	38.89	41.92	45.64	48.29
27	11.81	12.88	14.57	16.15	18.11	36.74	40.11	43.19	46.96	49.64
28	12.46	13.56	15.31	16.93	18.94	37.92	41.34	44.46	48.28	50.99
29	13.12	14.26	16.05	17.71	19.77	39.09	42.56	45.72	49.59	52.34
30	13.79	14.95	16.79	18.49	20.60	40.26	43.77	46.98	50.89	53.67
40	20.71	22.16	24.43	26.51	29.05	51.81	55.76	59.34	63.69	66.77
50	27.99	29.71	32.36	34.76	37.69	63.17	67.50	71.42	76.15	79.49
60	35.53	37.48	40.48	43.19	46.46	74.40	79.08	83.30	88.38	91.95
70	43.28	45.44	48.76	51.74	55.33	85.53	90.53	95.02	100.4	104.2
80	51.17	53.54	57.15	60.39	64.28	96 58	101.9	106.6	112.3	116.3
90	59.20	61.75	65.65	69.13	73.29	107.6	113.1	118.1	124.1	128.3
100	67.33	70.06	74.22	77.93	82.36	118.5	124.3	129.6	135.8	140.2

TABLE 3

PERCENTILES OF THE *T* DISTRIBUTION

Entry is $t(A;\, v)$ where $P\{t(v) \le \chi^2(A;\, v)\} = A$

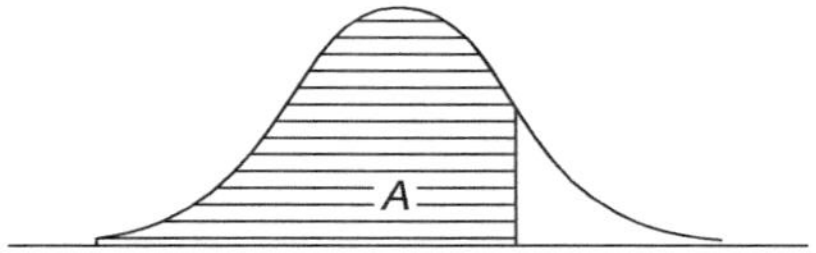

$t\,(A;\, v)$

	A													
v	.60	.70	.80	.85	.90	.95	.975	.98	.985	.99	.9925	.995	.9975	.9995
1	0.325	0.727	1.376	1.963	3.078	6.314	12.706	15.895	21.205	31.821	42.434	63.657	127.322	636.590
2	0.289	0.617	1.061	1.386	1.886	2.920	4.303	4.849	5.643	6.965	8.073	9.925	14.089	31.598
3	0.277	0.584	0.978	1.250	1.638	2.353	3.182	3.482	3.896	4.541	5.047	5.841	7.453	12.924
4	0.271	0.569	0.941	1.190	1.533	2.132	2.776	2.999	3.298	3.747	4.088	4.604	5.598	8.610
5	0.267	0.559	0.920	1.156	1.476	2.015	2.571	2.757	3.003	3.365	3.634	4.032	4.773	6.869
6	0.265	0.553	0.906	1.134	1.440	1.943	2.447	2.612	2.829	3.143	3.372	3.707	4.317	5.959
7	0.263	0.549	0.896	1.119	1.415	1.895	2.365	2.517	2.715	2.998	3.203	3.499	4.029	5.408
8	0.262	0.546	0.889	1.108	1.397	1.860	2.306	2.449	2.634	2.896	3.085	3.355	3.833	5.041
9	0.261	0.543	0.583	1.100	1.383	1.833	2.262	2.398	2.574	2.821	2.998	3.250	3.690	4.781
10	0.260	0.542	0.879	1.093	1.372	1.812	2.228	2.359	2.527	2.764	2.932	3.169	3.581	4.587
11	0.260	0.540	0.876	1.088	1.363	1.796	2.201	2.328	2.491	2.718	2.879	3.106	3.497	4.437
12	0.259	0.539	0.873	1.083	1.356	1.782	2.179	2.303	2.461	2.681	2.836	3.055	3.428	4.318
13	0.259	0.537	0.870	1.079	1.350	1.771	2.160	2.282	2.436	2.650	2.801	3.012	3.372	4.221
14	0.258	0.537	0.868	1.076	1.345	1.761	2.145	2.264	2.415	2.624	2.771	2.977	3.326	4.140
15	0.258	0.536	0.866	1.074	1.341	1.753	2.131	2.249	2.397	2.602	2.746	2.947	3.286	4.073
16	0.258	0.535	0.865	1.071	1.337	1.746	2.120	2.235	2.382	2.583	2.724	2.921	3.252	4.015
17	0.257	0.534	0.863	1.069	1.333	1.740	2.110	2.224	2.368	2.567	2.706	2.898	3.222	3.965
18	0.257	0.534	0.862	1.067	1.330	1.734	2.101	2.214	2.356	2.552	2.689	2.878	3.197	3.922
19	0.257	0.533	0.861	1.066	1.328	1.729	2.093	2.205	2.346	2.539	2.674	2.861	3.174	3.883

(Continued)

(*Continued*)

	A													
v	.60	.70	.80	.85	.90	.95	.975	.98	.985	.99	.9925	.995	.9975	.9995
20	0.257	0.533	0.860	1.064	1.325	1.725	2.086	2.197	2.336	2.528	2.661	2.845	3.153	3.849
21	0.257	0.532	0.859	1.063	1.323	1.721	2.080	2.189	2.328	2.518	2.649	2.831	3.135	3.819
22	0.256	0.532	0.858	1.061	1.321	1.717	2.074	2.183	2.320	2.508	2.639	2.819	3.119	3.792
23	0.256	0.532	0.858	1.060	1.319	1.714	2.069	2.177	2.313	2.500	2.629	2.807	3.104	3.768
24	0.256	0.531	0.857	1.059	1.318	1.711	2.064	2.172	2.307	2.492	2.620	2.797	3.091	3.745
25	0.256	0.531	0.856	1.058	1.316	1.708	2.060	2.167	2.301	2.485	2.612	2.787	3.078	3.725
26	0.256	0.531	0.856	1.058	1.315	1.706	2.056	2.162	2.2%	2.479	2.605	2.779	3.067	3.707
27	0.256	0.531	0.855	1.057	1.314	1.703	2.052	2.158	2.291	2.473	2.598	2.771	3.057	3.690
28	0.256	0.530	0.855	1.056	1.313	1.701	2.048	2.154	2.286	2.467	2.592	2.763	3.047	3.674
29	0.256	0.530	0.854	1.055	1.311	1.699	2.045	2.150	2.282	2.462	2.586	2.756	3.038	3.659
30	0.256	0.530	0.854	1.055	1.310	1.697	2.042	2.147	2.278	2.457	2.581	2.750	3.030	3.646
40	0.255	0.529	0.851	1.050	1.303	1.684	2.021	2.123	2.250	2.423	2.542	2.704	2.971	3.551
60	0.254	0.527	0.848	1.045	1.296	1.671	2.000	2.099	2.223	2.390	2.504	2.660	2.915	3.460
120	0.254	0.526	0.845	1.041	1.289	1.658	1.980	2.076	2.196	2.358	2.468	2.617	2.860	3.373
∞	0.253	0.524	0.842	1.036	1.282	1.645	1.960	2.054	2.170	2.326	2.432	2.576	2.807	3.291

TABLE 4
PERCENTILES OF THE *F* DISTRIBUTION

Den. df	*A*	Numerator df 1	2	3	4	5	6	7	8	9
1	.50	1.00	1.50	1.71	S.82	1.89	1.94	1.98	2.00	2.03
	.90	39.9	49.5	53.6	55.8	57.2	58.2	58.9	59.4	59.9
	.95	161	200	216	225	230	234	237	239	241
	.975	648	800	864	900	922	937	948	957	963
	.99	4,052	5,000	5,403	5,625	5,764	5,859	5,928	5,981	6,022
	.995	16,211	20.000	21,615	22,500	23,056	23,437	23,715	23,925	24,091
	.999	405,280	500,000	540,380	562,500	576,400	585,940	592,870	598,140	602,280
2	.50	0.667	1.00	1.13	1.21	1.25	1.28	1.30	1.32	1.33
	.90	8.53	9.00	9.16	9.24	9.29	9.33	9	9.37	9.38
	.95	18.5	19.0	19.2	19.2	19.3	19.3	19.4	19.4	19.4
	.975	38.5	39.0	39.2	39.2	39.3	39.3	39.4	39.4	39.4
	.99	98.5	99.0	99.2	99.2	99.3	99.3	99.4	99.4	99.4
	.995	199	199	199	199	199	199	199	199	199
	.999	998.5	999.0	999.2	999.2	999.3	999.3	999.4	999.4	999.4
3	.50	0.585	0.881	1.00	1.06	1.10	1.13	1.15	1.16	1.17
	.90	5.54	5.46	5.39	5.34	5.31	5.28	5.27	5.25	5.24
	.95	10.1	9.55	9.28	9.12	9.01	8.94	8.89	8.85	8.81
	.975	17.4	16.0	15.4	15.1	14.9	14.7	14.6	14.5	14.5
	.99	34.1	30.8	29.5	28.7	28.2	27.9	27.7	27.5	27.3
	.995	55.6	49.8	47.5	46.2	45.4	44.8	44.4	44.1	43.9
	.999	167.0	148.5	141.1	137.1	134.6	132.8	131.6	130.6	129.9
4	.50	0.549	0.828	0.941	1.00	1.04	1.06	1.08	1.09	1.10
	.90	4.54	4.32	4.19	4.11	4.05	4.01	3.98	3.95	3 94
	.95	7.71	6.94	6.59	6.39	6.26	6.16	6.09	6.04	600
	.975	12.2	10.6	9.98	9.60	9.36	9.20	9.07	8.98	8.90
	.99	21.2	18.0	16.7	16.0	15.5	15.2	15.0	14.8	14.7
	.995	31.3	26.3	24.3	23.2	22.5	22.0	21.6	21.4	21.1
	.999	74.1	61.2	56.2	53.4	51.7	50.5	49.7	49.0	48.5
5	.50	0.528	0.799	0.907	0.965	1.00	1.02	1.04	1.05	1.06
	.90	4.06	3.78	3.62	3.52	3.45	3.40	3.37	3.34	3.32
	.95	6.61	5.79	5.41	5.19	5.05	4.95	4.88	4.82	4.77
	.975	10.0	8.43	7.76	7.39	7.15	6.98	6.85	6.76	6.68
	.99	16.3	13.3	12.1	11.4	11.0	10.7	10.5	10.3	10.2
	.995	22.8	18.3	16.5	15.6	14.9	14.5	14.2	14.0	13.8
	.999	47.2	37.1	33.2	31.1	29.8	28.8	28.2	27.6	27.2

(Continued)

(*Continued*)

Den. df	A	Numerator df 1	2	3	4	5	6	7	8	9
6	.50	0.515	0.780	0.886	0.942	0.977	1 00	1.02	1.03	1.04
	.90	3.78	3.46	3.29	3.18	3.11	3.05	3.01	2.98	2.96
	.95	5.99	5.14	4.76	4.53	4.39	4.28	4 21	4.15	4.10
	.975	8.81	7.26	6.60	6.23	5.99	5.82	5.70	5.60	5.52
	.99	13.7	10.9	9.78	9.15	8.75	8.47	8.26	8.10	7.98
	.995	18.6	14.5	12.9	12.0	11.5	11.1	10.8	10.6	10.4
	.999	35.5	27.0	23.7	21.9	20.8	20.0	19.5	19.0	18.7
7	.50	0.506	0.767	0.871	0.926	0.960	0.983	1.00	1.01	1.02
	.90	3.59	3.26	3.07	2.96	2.88	2.83	2.78	2.75	2.72
	.95	5.59	4.74	4.35	4.12	3.97	3.87	3.79	3.73	3.68
	.975	8.07	6.54	5.89	5.52	5.29	5.12	4.99	4.90	4.82
	.99	12.2	9.55	8.45	7.85	7.46	7.19	6.99	6.84	6.72
	.995	16.2	12.4	10.9	10.1	9.52	9.16	8.89	8.68	8.51
	.999	29.2	21.7	18.8	17.2	16.2	15.5	15.0	14.6	14.3

Den. df	A	Numerator df 10	12	15	20	24	30	60	120	∞
1	.50	2.04	2.07	2.09	2.12	2 13	2.15	2.17	2.18	2.20
	.90	60.2	60.7	61.2	61.7	62.0	62.3	62.8	63.1	63.3
	.95	242	244	246	248	249	250	252	253	254
	.975	969	977	985	993	997	1,001	1,010	1,014	1,018
	.99	6,056	6,106	6,1 57	6,209	6,235	6,261	6,313	6,339	6,366
	.995	24,224	24,426	24,630	24.836	24,940	25,044	25.253	25,359	25.464
	.999	605,620	610,670	615,760	620,910	623,500	626J 00	631,340	633,970	636,620
2	.50	1.34	1.36	1.38	1 .39	1.40	1.41	1.43	1.43	1.44
	.90	9.39	9.41	9.42	9.44	9.45	9.46	9.47	9.48	9.49
	.95	19.4	19.4	19.4	19.4	19.5	19.5	19.5	19.5	19.5
	.975	394	39.4	39.4	39.4	39.5	39.5	39.5	39.5	39.5
	.99	99.4	99.4	99.4	99.4	99.5	99.5	99.5	99.5	99.5
	.995	199	199	199	199	199	199	199	199	200
	.999	999.4	999.4	999.4	999.4	999.5	999.5	999.5	999.5	999.5
3	.50	1.18	1.20	1.21	1.23	1.23	1.24	1.25	1.26	1.27

(*Continued*)

(*Continued*)

Den. df	*A*	Numerator df 10	12	15	20	24	30	60	120	∞
	.90	5.23	5.22	5.20	5.18	5.18	5.17	5.15	5.14	5.13
	.95	8.79	8.74	8.70	8.66	8.64	8.62	8.57	8.55	8.53
	.975	14.4	14.3	14.3	14.2	14.1	14.1	14.0	13.9	13.9
	.99	27.2	27. i	26.9	26.7	26.6	26.5	26.3	26.2	26.1
	.995	43.7	43.4	43.1	42.8	42.6	42.5	42.1	42.0	41.8
	.999	129.2	128.3	127.4	126.4	125.9	125.4	124.5	124.0	123.5
4	.50	1.11	1.13	1.14	1.15	1.16	1.16	1.18	1.18	1.19
	.90	3.92	3.90	3.87	3.84	3.83	3.82	3.79	3.78	3.76
	.95	5.96	5.91	5.86	5.80	5.77	5.75	5.69	5.66	5.63
	.975	8.84	8.75	8.66	8.56	8.51	8.46	8.36	8.31	8.26
	.99	14.5	14.4	14.2	14.0	13.9	13.8	13.7	13.6	13.5
	.995	21.0	20.7	20.4	20.2	20.0	19.9	19.6	19.5	19.3
	.999	48.1	47.4	46.8	46.1	45.8	45.4	44.7	44.4	44.1
5	.50	1.07	1.09	1.10	1.11	1.12	1.12	1.14	1.14	1.15
	.90	3.30	3.27	3.24	3.21	3.19	3.17	3.14	3.12	3.11
	.95	4.74	4.68	4.62	4.56	4.53	4.50	4.43	4.40	4.37
	.975	6.62	6.52	6.43	6.33	6.28	6.23	6.12	6.07	6.02
	.99	10.1	9.89	9.72	9.55	9.47	9.38	9.20	9.11	9.02
	.995	13.6	13.4	13.1	12.9	12.8	12.7	12.4	12.3	12.1
	.999	26.9	26.4	25.9	25.4	25.1	24.9	24.3	24.1	23.8
6	.50	1.05	1.06	1.07	1.08	1 09	1.10	1.11	1.12	1.12
	.90	2.94	2.90	2.87	2.84	2.82	2.80	2.76	2.74	2.72
	.95	4.06	4.00	3.94	3.87	3.84	3.81	3.74	3.70	3.67
	.975	5.46	5.37	5.27	5.17	5.12	5.07	4.96	4.90	4.85
	.99	7.87	7.72	7.56	7.40	7.31	7.23	7.06	6.97	6.SS
	.995	10.2	10.0	9.81	9.59	9.47	9.36	9.12	9.00	8.88
	.999	18.4	18.0	17.6	17.1	16.9	16.7	16.2	16.0	15.7
7	.50	1.03	1.04	1.05	1.07	1.07	1.08	1.09	1.10	1.10
	.90	2.70	2.67	2.63	2.59	2.58	2.56	2.51	2.49	2.47
	.95	3.64	3.57	3.51	3.44	3.41	3.38	3.30	3.27	3.23
	.975	4.76	4.67	4.57	4.47	4.42	4.36	4.25	4 20	4.14
	.99	6.62	6.47	6.31	6.16	6.07	5.99	5.82	5.74	5.65
	.995	8.38	8.18	7.97	7.75	7.65	7.53	7.31	7.19	7.08
	.999	14.1	13.7	13.3	12.9	12.7	12.5	12.1	11.9	11.7

(*Continued*)

(Continued)

Den. df	*A*	**Numerator df**								
		1	2	3	4	5	6	7	8	9
8	.50	0.499	0.757	0.860	0.915	0.948	0.971	0.988	1.00	1.01
	.90	3.46	3.11	2.92	2.81	2.73	2.67	2.62	2.59	2.56
	.95	5.32	4.46	4.07	3.84	3.69	3.58	3.50	3.44	3.39
	975	7.57	6.06	5.42	5.05	4.82	4.65	4.53	4.43	4.36
	.99	11.3	8.65	7.59	7.01	6.63	6.37	6.18	6.03	5.91
	.995	14.7	11.0	9.60	8.81	8.30	7.95	7.69	7.50	7.34
	.999	25.4	18.5	15.8	14.4	13.5	12.9	12.4	12.0	11.8
9	.50	0.494	0.749	0.852	0.906	0.939	0.962	0.978	0.990	1.00
	.90	3.36	3.01	2.81	2.69	2.61	2.55	2.51	2.47	2.44
	.95	5.12	4.26	3.86	3.63	3.48	3.37	3.29	3.23	3.18
	.975	7.21	5.71	5.08	4.72	4.4S	4.32	4.20	4.10	4.03
	.99	10.6	8.02	6.99	6.42	6.06	5.80	5.61	5.47	5.35
	.995	13.6	10.1	8.72	7.96	7.47	7.13	6.88	6.69	6.54
	.999	22.9	16.4	13.9	12.6	11.7	11.1	10.7	10.4	10.1
10	.50	0.490	0.743	0.845	0.899	0.932	0.954	0.971	0.983	0.992
	.90	3.29	2.92	2.73	2.61	2.52	2.46	2.41	2.38	2.35
	.95	4.96	4.10	3.71	3.48	3.33	3.22	3.14	3.07	3.02
	.975	6.94	5.46	4.83	4.47	4.24	4.07	3.95	3.85	3.78
	.99	10.0	7.56	6.55	5.99	5.64	5.39	5.20	5.06	4.94
	.995	12.8	9.43	8.08	7.34	6.87	6.54	6.30	6.12	5.97
	.999	21.0	14.9	12.6	11.3	10.5	9.93	9.52	9.20	8.96
12	.50	0.484	0.735	0.835	0.888	0.921	0.943	0.959	0.972	0.981
	.90	3.18	2.81	2.61	2.48	2.39	2.33	2.28	2.24	2.21
	.95	4.75	3.89	3.49	3.26	3.11	3.00	2.91	2.85	2.80
	.975	6.55	5.10	4.47	4.12	3.89	3.73	3.61	3.51	3.44
	.99	9.33	6.93	5.95	5.41	5.06	4.82	4.64	4.50	4.39
	.995	11.8	8.51	7.23	6.52	6.07	5.76	5.52	5.35	5.20
	.999	18.6	13.0	10.8	9.63	8.89	8.38	8.00	7.71	7.48
15	.50	0.478	0.726	0.826	0.878	0.911	0.933	0.949	0.960	0.970
	.90	3.07	2.70	2.49	2.36	2.27	2.21	2.16	2.12	2.09
	.95	4.54	3.68	3.29	3.06	2.90	2.79	2.71	2.64	2.59
	.975	6.20	4.77	4.15	3.80	3.58	3.41	3.29	3.20	3.12
	.99	8.68	6.36	5.42	4.89	4.56	4.32	4.14	4.00	3.89
	.995	10.8	7.70	6.48	5.80	5.37	5.07	4.85	4.67	4.54
	999	16.6	11.3	9.34	8.25	7.57	7.09	6.74	6.47	6.26

Den. df	A	Numerator df 1	2	3	4	5	6	7	8	9
20	.50	0.472	0.718	0.816	0.868	0.900	0.922	0.938	0.950	0.959
	.90	2.97	2.59	2.38	2.25	2.16	2.09	2.04	2.00	1.96
	.95	4.35	3.49	3.10	2.87	2.71	2.60	2.51	2.45	2.39
	.975	5.87	4.46	3.86	3.51	3.29	3.13	3.01	2.91	2.84
	.99	8.10	5.85	4.94	4.43	4.10	3.87	3.70	3.56	3.46
	.995	9.94	6.99	5.82	5.17	4.76	4.47	4.26	4.09	3.96
	.999	14.8	9.95	8.10	7.10	6.46	6.02	5.69	5.44	5.24
24	.50	0.469	0.714	0.812	0.863	0.895	0.917	0.932	0.944	0.953
	.90	2.93	2.54	2.33	2.19	2.10	2.04	1.98	1.94	1.91
	.95	4.26	3.40	3.01	2.78	2.62	2.51	2.42	2.36	2.30
	.975	5.72	4.32	3.72	3.38	3.15	2.99	2.87	2.78	2.70
	.99	7.82	5.61	4.72	4.22	3.90	3.67	3.50	3.36	3.26
	.995	9.55	6.66	5.52	4.89	4.49	4.20	3.99	3.83	3.69
	999	14.0	9.34	7.55	6.59	5.98	5.55	5.23	4.99	4.80

Den. df	A	Numerator df 10	12	15	20	24	30	60	120	∞
8	.50	1.02	1.03	1.04	1.05	1.06	1.07	1.08	1.08	1.09
	.90	2.54	2.50	2.46	2.42	2.40	2.38	2.34	2.32	2.29
	.95	3.35	3.28	3.22	3.15	3.12	3.08	3.01	2.97	2.93
	.975	4.30	4.20	4.10	4.00	3.95	3.89	3.78	3.73	3.67
	.99	5.81	5.67	5.52	5.36	5.28	5.20	5.03	4.95	4.86
	.995	7.21	7.01	6.81	6.61	6.50	6.40	6.18	6.06	5.95
	.999	11.5	11.2	10.8	10.5	10.3	10.1	9.73	9.53	9.33
9	.50	1.01	1.02	1.03	1.04	1.05	1.05	1.07	1.07	1.08
	.90	2.42	2.38	2.34	2.30	2.28	2.25	2.21	2.18	2.16
	.95	3.14	3.07	3.01	2.94	2.90	2.86	2.79	2.75	2.71
	.975	3.96	3.87	3.77	3.67	3.61	3.56	3.45	3.39	3.33
	.99	5.26	5.11	4.96	4.81	4.73	4.65	4.48	4.40	4.31
	.995	6.42	6.23	6.03	5.83	5.73	5.62	5.41	5.30	5.19
	.999	9.89	9.57	9.24	8.90	8.72	8.55	8.19	8.00	7.81
10	.50	1.00	1.01	1.02	1.03	1.04	1.05	1.06	1.06	1.07
	.90	2.32	2.28	2.24	2.20	2.18	2.16	2.11	2.08	2.06
	.95	2.98	2.91	2.84	2.77	2.74	2.70	2.62	2.58	2.54
	.975	3.72	3.62	3.52	3.42	3.37	3.31	3.20	3.14	3.08
	.99	4.85	4.71	4.56	4 41	4.33	4.25	4.08	4.00	3.91

(Continued)

(*Continued*)

Den. df	A	Numerator df 10	12	15	20	24	30	60	120	∞
	.995	5.85	5.66	5.47	5.27	5.17	5.07	4.86	4.75	4.64
	.999	8.75	8.45	8.13	7.80	7.64	7.47	7.12	6.94	6.76
12	.50	0.989	1.00	1.01	1.02	1.03	1.03	1.05	1.05	1.06
	.90	2.19	2.15	2.10	2.06	2.04	2.01	1.96	1.93	1.90
	.95	2.75	2.69	2.62	2.54	2.51	2.47	2.38	2.34	2.30
	.975	3.37	3.28	3.18	3.07	3.02	2.96	2.85	2.79	2.72
	.99	4.30	4.16	4.01	3.86	3.78	3.70	3.54	3.45	3.36
	.995	5.09	4.91	4.72	4.53	4.43	4.33	4.12	4 01	3.90
	.999	7.29	7.00	6.71	6.40	6.25	6.09	5.76	5.59	5.42
15	.50	0.977	0.989	1.00	1.01	1.02	1.02	1.03	1.04	1.05
	.90	2.06	2.02	1.97	1.92	1.90	1.87	1.82	1.79	1.76
	.95	2.54	2.48	2.40	2.33	2.29	2.25	2.16	2.11	2.07
	.975	3.06	2.96	2.86	2.76	2.70	2.64	2.52	2.46	2.40
	.99	3.80	3.67	3.52	3.37	3.29	3.21	3.05	2.96	2.87
	.995	4.42	4.25	4.07	3.88	3.79	3.69	3.48	3.37	3.26
	.999	6.08	5.81	5.54	5.25	5.10	4.95	4.64	4.48	4.31
20	.50	0.966	0.977	0.989	1.00	1.01	1.01	1.02	1.03	1.03
	.90	1.94	1.89	1.84	1.79	1.77	1.74	1.68	1.64	1.61
	.95	2.35	2.28	2.20	2.12	2.08	2.04	1.95	1.90	1.84
	.975	2.77	2.68	2.57	2.46	2.41	2.35	2.22	2.16	2.09
	.99	3.37	3.23	3.09	2.94	2.86	2.78	2.61	2.52	2.42
	.995	3.85	3.68	3.50	3.32	3.22	3.12	2.92	2.81	2.69
	.999	5.08	4.82	4.56	4.29	4.15	4.00	3.70	3.54	3.38
24	.50	0.961	0.972	0.983	0.994	1.00	1.01	1.02	1.02	1.03
	.90	1.88	1.83	1.78	1.73	1.70	1.67	1.61	1.57	1.53
	.95	2.25	2.18	2.10	2.03	1.9 8	1.94	1.84	1.79	1.73
	.975	2.64	2.54	2.44	2.33	2.27	2.21	2.08	2.01	1.94
	99	3.17	3.03	2.89	2.74	2.66	2.58	2.40	2.31	2.21
	.995	3.59	3.42	3.25	3.06	2.97	2.87	2.66	2.55	2.43
	.999	4.64	4.39	4 14	3.87	3.74	3.59	3.29	3.14	2.97

Den. df	A	Numerator df 1	2	3	4	5	6	7	8	9
30	.50	0.466	0.709	0.807	0.858	0.890	0.912	0.927	0.939	0.948
	.90	2.88	2.49	2.28	2.14	2.05	1.98	1.93	1.88	1.85
	.95	4.17	3.32	2.92	2.69	2.53	2.42	2.33	2.27	2.21
	.975	5.57	4.18	3.59	3.25	3.03	2.87	2.75	2.65	2.57
	.99	7.56	5.39	4.51	4.02	3.70	3.47	3.30	3.17	3.07
	.995	9.18	6.35	5.24	4.62	4.23	3.95	3.74	3.58	3.45
	.999	13.3	8.77	7.05	6.12	5.53	5.12	4.82	4.58	4.39
60	.50	0.461	0.701	0.798	0.849	0.880	0.901	0.917	0.928	0.937
	.90	2.79	2.39	2.18	2.04	1.95	1.87	1.82	1.77	1.74
	.95	4.00	3.15	2.76	2.53	2.37	2.25	2.17	2.10	2.04
	.975	5.29	3.93	3.34	3.01	2.79	2.63	2.51	2.41	2.33
	.99	7.08	4.98	4.13	3.65	3.34	3.12	2.95	2.82	2.72
	.995	8.49	5.80	4.73	4.14	3.76	3.49	3.29	3.13	3.01
	.999	12.0	7.77	6.17	5.31	4.76	4.37	4.09	3.86	3.69
120	.50	0.458	0.697	0.793	0.844	0.875	0.896	0.912	0.923	0.932
	.90	2.75	2.35	2.13	1.99	1.90	1.82	1.77	1.72	1.68
	.95	3.92	3.07	2.68	2.45	2.29	2.18	2.09	2.02	1.96
	.975	5.15	3.80	3.23	2.89	2.67	2.52	2.39	2.30	2.22
	.99	6.85	4.79	3.95	3.48	3.17	2.96	2.79	2.66	2.56
	.995	8.18	5.54	4.50	3.92	3.55	3.28	3.09	2.93	2.81
	.999	11.4	7.32	5.78	4.95	4.42	4.04	3.77	3.55	3.38
∞	.50	0.455	0.693	0.789	0.839	0.870	0.891	0.907	0.918	0.927
	.90	2.71	2.30	2.08	1.94	1.85	1.77	1.72	1.67	1.63
	.95	3.84	3.00	2.60	2.37	2.21	2.10	2.01	1.94	1.88
	.975	5.02	369	3.12	2.79	2.57	2.41	2.29	2.19	2.11
	.99	6.63	4.61	3.78	3.32	3.02	2.80	2.64	2.51	2.41
	.995	7.88	5.30	4.28	3.72	3.35	3.09	2.90	2.74	2.62
	.999	10.8	6.91	5.42	4.62	4.10	3.74	3.47	3.27	3.10

(Continued)

(*Continued*)

Den. df	A	Numerator df 10	12	15	20	24	30	60	120	∞
30	.50	0.955	0.966	0.978	0.989	0.994	1.00	1.01	1.02	1.02
	.90	1.82	1.77	1.72	1.67	1.64	1.61	1.54	1.50	1.46
	.95	2.16	2.09	2.01	1.93	1.89	1.84	1.74	1.68	1.62
	.975	2.51	2.41	2.31	2.20	2.14	2.07	1.94	1.87	1.79
	.99	2.98	2.84	2.70	2.55	2.47	2.39	2.21	2.11	2.01
	.995	3.34	3.18	3.01	2.82	2.73	2.63	2.42	2.30	2.18
	.999	4.24	4.00	3.75	3.49	3.36	3.22	2.92	2.76	2.59
60	.50	0.945	0.956	0.967	0.978	0.983	0.989	1.00	1.01	1.01
	.90	1.71	1.66	1.60	1.54	1.51	1.48	1.40	1.35	1.29
	.95	1.99	1.92	1.84	1.75	1.70	1.65	1.53	1.47	1.39
	.975	2.27	2.17	2.06	1.94	1.88	1.82	1.67	1.58	1.48
	.99	2.63	2.50	2.35	2.20	2.12	2.03	1.84	1.73	1.60
	.995	2.90	2.74	2.57	2.39	2.29	2.19	1.96	1.83	1.69
	.999	3.54	3.32	3.08	2.83	2.69	2.55	2.25	2.08	1.89
120	.50	0.939	0.950	0.961	0.972	0.978	0.983	0.994	1.00	1.01
	.90	1.65	1.60	1.55	1.48	1.45	1.41	1.32	1.26	1.19
	.95	1.91	1.83	1.75	1.66	1.61	1.55	1.43	1.35	1.25
	.975	2.16	2.05	1.95	1.82	1.76	1.69	1.53	1.43	1.31
	.99	2.47	2.34	2.19	2.03	1.95	1.86	1.66	1.53	1.38
	.995	2.71	2.54	2.37	2.19	2.09	1.98	1.75	1.61	1.43
	.999	3.24	3.02	2.78	2.53	2.40	2.26	1.95	1.77	1.54
∞	.50	0.934	0.945	0.956	0.967	0.972	0.978	0.989	0.994	1.00
	.90	1.60	1.55	1.49	1.42	1.38	1.34	1.24	1.17	1.00
	.95	1.83	1.75	1.67	1.57	1.52	1.46	1.32	1.22	1.00
	.975	2.05	1.94	1.83	1.71	1.64	1.57	1.39	1.27	1.00
	.99	2.32	2.18	2.04	1.88	1.79	1.70	1.47	1.32	1.00
	.995	2.52	2.36	2.19	2.00	1.90	1.79	1.53	1.36	1.00
	.999	2.96	2.74	2.51	2.27	2.13	1.99	1.66	1.45	1.00

TABLE 5

QUANTILES OF THE MANN–WHITNEY TEST STATISTIC

n	p	m=2	3	4	5	6	7	8	9	10	11	12	13	14	15	16	17	18	19	20
2	.001	3	3	3	3	3	-	3	3	3	3	3	3	3	3	3	3	3	3	3
	.005	3	3	3	3	3	3	3	3	3	3	3	3	3	3	3	3	3	4	4
	.01	3	3	3	3	3	3	3	3	3	3	3	4	4	4	4	4	4	5	5
	.025	3	3	3	3	3	3	4	4	4	5	5	5	5	5	5	6	6	6	6
	.05	3	3	3	4	4	4	5	5	5	5	6	6	7	7	7	7	8	8	8
	.10	3	4	4	5	5	5	6	6	7	7	8	8	8	9	9	10	10	11	11
3	.001	6	6	6	6	6	6	6	6	6	6	6	6	6	6	6	7	7	7	7
	.005	6	6	6	6	6	6	6	7	7	7	8	8	8	9	9	9	9	10	10
	.01	6	6	6	6	6	7	7	8	8	8	9	9	9	10	10	11	11	11	12
	.025	6	6	6	7	8	8	9	9	10	10	11	11	12	12	13	13	14	14	15
	.05	6	7	7	8	9	9	10	11	11	12	12	13	14	14	15	16	16	17	18
	.10	7	8	8	9	10	11	12	12	13	14	15	16	17	17	18	19	20	21	22
4	.001	10	10	10	10	10	10	10	10	11	11	11	12	12	12	13	13	14	14	14
	.005	10	10	10	10	11	11	12	12	13	13	14	14	15	16	16	17	17	18	19
	.01	10	10	10	11	12	12	13	14	14	15	16	16	17	18	18	19	20	20	21
	.025	10	10	11	12	13	14	15	15	16	17	18	19	20	21	22	22	23	24	25
	.05	10	11	12	13	14	15	16	17	18	19	20	21	22	23	25	26	27	28	29
	.10	11	12	14	15	16	17	18	20	21	22	23	24	26	27	28	29	31	32	33
5	001	15	15	15	15	15	15	16	17	17	18	18	19	19	20	21	21	22	23	23
	.005	15	15	15	16	17	17	18	19	20	21	22	23	23	24	25	26	27	28	29
	.01	15	15	16	17	18	19	20	21	22	23	24	25	26	27	28	29	30	31	32
	.025	15	16	17	18	19	21	22	23	24	25	27	28	29	30	31	33	34	35	36
	.05	16	17	18	20	21	22	24	25	27	28	29	31	32	34	35	36	38	39	41
	.10	17	18	20	21	23	24	26	28	29	31	33	34	36	38	39	41	43	44	46
6	.001	21	21	21	21	21	21	23	24	25	26	26	27	28	29	30	31	32	33	34
	.005	21	21	22	23	24	25	26	27	28	29	31	32	33	34	35	37	38	39	40

(*Continued*)

(*Continued*)

n	*p*	*m*=2	3	4	5	6	7	8	9	10	11	12	13	14	15	16	17	18	19	20
	.01	21	21	23	24	25	26	28	29	30	31	33	34	35	37	38	40	41	42	44
	.025	21	23	24	25	27	28	30	32	33	35	36	38	39	41	43	44	46	47	49
	.05	22	24	25	27	29	30	32	34	36	38	39	41	43	45	47	48	50	52	54
	.10	23	25	27	29	31	33	35	37	39	41	43	45	47	49	51	53	56	58	60
7	.001	28	28	28	28	29	30	31	32	34	35	36	37	38	39	40	42	43	44	45
	.005	28	28	29	30	32	33	35	36	38	39	41	42	44	45	47	48	50	51	53
	.01	28	29	30	32	33	35	36	38	40	41	43	45	46	48	50	52	53	55	57
	.025	28	30	32	34	35	37	39	41	43	45	47	49	51	53	55	57	59	61	63
	.05	29	31	33	35	37	40	42	44	46	48	50	53	55	57	59	62	64	66	68
	.10	30	33	35	37	40	42	45	47	50	52	55	57	60	62	65	67	70	72	75
8	.001	36	36	36	37	38	39	41	42	43	45	46	48	49	51	52	54	55	57	58
	.005	36	36	38	39	41	43	44	46	48	50	52	54	55	57	59	61	63	65	67
	.01	36	37	39	41	43	44	46	48	50	52	54	56	59	61	63	65	67	69	71
	.025	37	39	41	43	45	47	50	52	54	56	59	61	63	66	68	71	73	75	78
	.05	38	40	42	45	47	50	52	55	57	60	63	65	68	70	73	76	78	81	84
	.10	39	42	44	47	50	53	56	59	61	64	67	70	73	76	79	82	85	88	91
9	.001	45	45	45	47	48	49	51	53	54	56	58	60	61	63	65	67	69	71	72
	.005	45	46	47	49	51	53	55	57	59	62	64	66	68	70	73	75	77	79	82
	01	45	47	49	51	53	55	57	60	62	64	67	69	72	74	77	79	82	84	86
	.025	46	48	50	53	56	58	61	63	66	69	72	74	77	80	83	85	88	91	94
	.05	47	50	52	55	58	61	64	67	70	73	76	79	82	85	88	91	94	97	100
	.10	48	51	55	58	61	64	68	71	74	77	81	84	87	91	94	98	101	104	108
10	.001	55	55	56	57	59	61	62	64	66	68	70	73	75	77	79	81	83	85	88
	.005	55	56	58	60	62	65	67	69	72	74	77	80	82	85	87	90	93	95	98
	.01	55	57	59	62	64	67	69	72	75	78	80	83	86	89	92	94	97	100	103
	.025	56	59	61	64	67	70	73	76	79	82	85	89	92	95	98	101	104	108	111
	.05	57	60	63	67	70	73	76	80	83	87	90	93	97	100	104	107	111	114	118
	.10	59	62	66	69	73	77	80	84	88	92	95	99	103	107	110	114	118	122	126

n	p	$m=2$	3	4	5	6	7	8	9	10	11	12	13	14	15	16	17	18	19	20
11	.001	66	66	67	69	71	73	75	77	79	82	84	87	89	91	94	96	99	101	104
	.005	66	67	69	72	74	77	80	83	85	88	91	94	97	100	103	106	109	112	115
	.01	66	68	71	74	76	79	82	85	89	92	95	98	101	104	108	111	114	117	120
	.025	67	70	73	76	80	83	86	90	93	97	100	104	107	111	114	118	122	125	129
	.05	68	72	75	79	83	86	90	94	98	101	105	109	113	117	121	124	128	132	136
	.10	70	74	78	82	86	90	94	98	103	107	111	115	119	124	128	132	136	140	145
12	.001	78	78	79	81	83	86	88	91	93	96	98	102	104	106	110	113	116	118	121
	.005	78	80	82	85	88	91	94	97	100	103	106	110	113	116	120	123	126	130	133
	.01	78	81	84	87	90	93	96	100	103	107	110	114	117	121	125	128	132	135	139
	.025	80	83	86	90	93	97	101	105	108	112	116	120	124	128	132	136	140	144	148
	.05	81	84	88	92	96	100	105	109	111	117	121	126	130	134	139	143	147	151	156
	.10	83	87	91	96	100	105	109	114	118	123	128	132	137	142	146	151	156	160	165
13	.001	91	91	93	95	97	100	103	106	109	112	115	118	121	124	127	131	134	137	140
	.005	91	93	95	99	102	105	109	112	116	119	123	126	130	134	137	141	145	149	152
	.01	92	94	97	101	104	108	112	115	119	123	127	131	135	139	143	147	151	155	159
	.025	93	96	100	104	108	112	116	120	125	129	133	137	142	146	151	155	159	164	168
	.05	94	98	102	107	111	116	120	125	129	134	139	143	148	153	157	162	167	172	176
	.10	96	101	105	108	115	120	125	130	135	140	145	150	155	160	166	171	176	181	186
14	001	105	105	107	109	112	115	118	121	125	128	131	135	138	142	145	149	152	156	160
	.005	105	107	110	113	117	121	124	128	132	136	140	144	148	152	156	160	164	169	173
	.01	106	108	112	116	119	123	128	132	136	140	144	149	153	157	162	166	171	175	179
	.025	107	111	115	119	123	128	132	137	142	146	151	156	161	165	170	175	180	184	189
	.05	109	113	117	122	127	132	137	142	147	152	157	162	167	172	177	183	188	193	198
	.10	110	116	121	126	131	137	142	147	153	158	164	169	175	180	186	191	197	203	208
15	.001	120	120	122	125	128	133	135	138	142	145	149	153	157	161	164	168	172	176	180
	.005	120	123	126	129	133	137	141	145	150	154	158	163	167	172	176	1S1	185	190	194
	.01	121	124	128	132	136	140	145	149	154	158	163	168	172	177	182	187	191	196	201
	.025	122	126	131	135	140	145	150	155	160	165	170	175	180	185	191	196	201	206	211
	.05	124	128	133	139	144	149	154	160	165	171	176	182	187	193	198	204	209	215	221
	.10	126	131	137	143	148	154	160	166	172	178	184	189	195	201	207	213	219	225	231

(Continued)

(*Continued*)

n	*p*	*m*=2	3	4	5	6	7	8	9	10	11	12	13	14	15	16	17	18	19	20
16	.001	136	136	139	142	145	148	152	156	100	164	168	172	176	180	185	189	193	197	202
	.005	136	139	142	146	150	155	159	164	160	173	178	182	187	192	197	202	207	211	216
	.01	137	140	144	149	153	158	163	168	173	178	183	188	193	198	203	208	213	219	224
	.025	138	143	148	152	158	163	168	174	179	184	190	196	201	207	212	218	223	229	235
	.05	140	145	151	156	162	167	173	179	185	191	197	202	208	214	220	226	232	238	244
	.10	142	148	154	160	166	173	179	185	191	198	204	211	217	223	230	236	243	249	256
17	.001	153	154	156	159	163	167	171	175	179	183	188	192	197	201	206	211	215	220	224
	.005	153	156	160	164	169	173	178	183	188	193	198	203	208	214	219	224	229	235	240
	01	154	157	162	167	172	177	182	187	192	198	203	209	214	220	225	231	236	242	247
	.025	156	160	165	171	176	182	188	193	199	205	211	217	223	229	235	241	247	253	259
	.05	157	163	169	174	180	187	193	199	205	211	218	224	231	237	243	250	256	263	269
	.10	160	166	172	179	185	192	199	206	212	219	226	233	239	246	253	260	267	274	281
18	.001	171	172	175	178	182	186	190	195	199	204	209	214	218	223	228	233	238	243	248
	.005	171	174	178	183	188	193	198	203	209	214	219	225	230	236	242	247	253	259	264
	.01	172	176	181	186	191	196	202	208	213	219	225	231	237	242	248	254	260	266	272
	.025	174	179	184	190	196	202	200	214	220	227	233	239	246	252	258	265	271	278	284
	.05	176	181	188	194	200	207	213	220	227	233	240	247	254	260	267	274	281	288	295
	.10	178	185	192	199	206	213	220	227	234	241	249	256	263	270	278	285	292	300	307
19	.001	190	191	194	198	202	206	211	216	220	225	231	236	241	246	251	257	262	268	273
	.005	191	194	198	203	208	213	219	224	230	236	242	248	254	260	265	272	278	284	290
	.01	192	195	200	206	211	217	223	229	735	241	247	254	260	266	273	279	285	292	298
	.025	193	198	204	210	216	223	229	236	243	249	256	263	269	276	283	290	297	304	310
	.05	195	201	208	214	221	228	235	242	249	256	263	271	278	285	292	300	307	314	321
	.10	198	205	212	219	227	234	242	249	257	264	272	280	288	295	303	311	319	326	334
20	.001	210	211	214	218	223	227	232	237	243	248	253	259	265	270	276	281	287	293	299
	.005	211	214	219	224	229	235	241	247	253	259	265	271	278	284	291	297	303	310	316
	.01	212	216	221	227	233	239	245	251	258	264	271	278	284	291	298	304	311	318	325
	025	213	219	225	231	238	245	251	259	266	273	280	287	294	301	309	316	323	330	338
	.05	215	222	229	236	243	250	258	265	273	280	288	295	303	311	318	326	334	341	349
	.10	218	226	233	241	249	257	265	273	281	289	297	305	311	321	330	338	346	354	362

TABLE 6

QUANTILES OF THE KRUSKAL-WALLIS TEST STATISTIC FOR SMALL SAMPLE SIZES

Sample Sizes	$w_{0.90}$	$w_{0.95}$	$w_{0.99}$
2, 2, 2	3.7143	4.5714	4.5714
3, 2, 1	3.8571	4.2857	4.2857
3, 2, 2	4.4643	4.5000	5.3571
3, 3, 1	4.0000	4.5714	5.1429
3, 3, 2	4.2500	5.1389	6.2500
3, 3, 3	4.6000	5.0667	6.4889
4, 2, 1	4.0179	4.8214	4.8214
4, 2, 2	4.1667	5.1250	6.0000
4, 3, 1	3.8889	5.0000	5.8333
4, 3, 2	4.4444	5.4000	6.3000
4, 3, 3	4.7000	5.7273	6.7091
4, 4, 1	4.0667	4.8667	6.1667
4, 4, 2	4.4455	5.2364	6.8727
4, 4, 3	4.773	5.5758	7.1364
4, 4, 4	4.5000	5.6538	7.5385
5, 2, 1	4.0500	4.4500	5.2500
5, 2, 2	4.2933	5.0400	6.1333
5, 3, 1	3.8400	4.8711	6.4000
5, 3, 2	4.4946	5.1055	6.8218
5, 3, 3	4.4121	5.5152	6.9818
5, 4, 1	3.9600	4.8600	6.8400
5, 4, 2	4.5182	5.2682	7.1182
5, 4, 3	4.5231	5.6308	7.3949
5, 4, 4	4.6187	5.6176	7.7440
5, 5, 1	4.0364	4.9091	6.8364
5, 5, 2	4.5077	5.2462	7.2692
5, 5, 3	4.5363	5.6264	7.5429
5, 5, 4	4.5200	5.6429	7.7914
5, 5, 5	4.5000	5.6600	7.9800

TABLE 7

QUANTILES OF THE WILCOXON SIGNED RANKS TEST STATISTIC

	$w_{0.005}$	$w_{0.01}$	$w_{0.025}$	$w_{0.05}$	$w_{0.10}$	$w_{0.20}$	$w_{0.30}$	$w_{0.40}$	$w_{0.50}$	$\frac{n(n+1)}{2}$
5	0	0	0	1	3	4	5	6	7.5	15
6	0	0	1	3	4	6	8	9	10.5	21
7	0	1	3	4	6	9	11	12	14	28
8	1	2	4	6	9	12	14	16	18	36
9	2	4	6	9	11	15	18	20	22.5	45
10	4	6	9	11	15	19	22	25	27.5	55
11	6	8	11	14	18	23	27	30	33	66
12	8	10	14	18	22	28	32	36	39	78
13	10	13	18	22	27	33	38	42	45.5	91
14	13	16	22	26	32	39	44	48	52.5	105
15	16	20	26	31	37	45	51	55	60	120
16	20	24	30	36	43	51	58	63	68	136
17	24	28	35	42	49	58	65	71	76.5	153
18	28	33	41	48	56	66	73	80	85.5	171
19	33	38	47	54	63	74	82	89	95	190
20	38	44	53	61	70	83	91	98	105	210
21	44	50	59	68	78	91	100	108	115.5	131
22	49	56	67	76	87	100	110	119	126.5	153
23	55	63	74	84	95	110	120	130	138	176
24	62	70	82	92	105	120	131	141	150	300
25	69	77	90	101	114	131	143	153	162.5	325
26	76	85	99	111	125	142	155	168	175.5	351
27	84	94	108	120	135	154	167	178	189	378
28	92	102	117	131	146	166	180	192	203	406
29	101	111	127	141	158	178	193	206	217.5	435
30	110	121	138	152	170	191	207	220	232.5	465
31	119	131	148	164	182	205	221	235	248	496
32	129	111	160	176	195	219	236	250	264	528
33	139	152	171	188	208	233	251	266	280.5	561
34	149	163	183	201	222	248	266	282	297.5	595
35	160	175	196	214	236	263	283	299	315	630
36	172	187	209	228	251	279	299	317	333	666
37	184	199	222	242	266	295	316	335	351.5	703

	$w_{0.05}$	$w_{0.01}$	$w_{0.025}$	$w_{0.05}$	$w_{0.10}$	$w_{0.20}$	$w_{0.30}$	$w_{0.40}$	$w_{0.50}$	$\frac{n(n+1)}{2}$
38	196	212	236	257	282	312	334	353	370.5	741
39	208	225	250	272	298	329	352	372	390	780
40	221	239	265	287	314	347	371	391	410	820
41	235	253	280	303	331	365	390	41 1	430.5	861
42	248	267	295	320	349	384	409	431	451.5	903
43	263	282	311	337	366	403	429	452	473	946
44	277	297	328	354	385	422	450	473	495	990
45	292	313	344	372	403	442	471	495	517.5	1035
46	308	329	362	390	423	463	492	517	540.5	1081
47	324	346	379	408	442	484	514	540	564	1 128
48	340	363	397	428	463	505	536	563	588	1176
49	357	381	416	447	483	527	559	587	612.5	1225
50	374	398	435	467	504	550	583	611	637.5	1275

For n larger than 50, the pth quantile wp of the Wilcoxon signed ranked test statistic may be applied.

INDEX

absolute measures of asymmetry, 137
alphabetic coding, 55
alternate hypothesis, 256
Amelia, 454
ANOVA, variance, 387
applied media metrics, 2
asymmetrical distribution, 136
asymmetry, 135
  absolute measures, 137
  kurtosis, 151
  moment, 146
    arbitrary origin, 147
    measures, 148
  normal curve and normal distribution, 153
    applications of, 158
    characteristics and properties, 154
    illustration, applications, 159
  relative measures, 138
  tests of, 137
average, 73

bar graph, 61
Bayesware Discoverer, 453
bi-modal values
  classified frequency distribution, 89
  unclassified frequency distribution, 87
Bowley's coefficient of skewness, 142

cardinal number, 37
Carli, 226
Cartesian product, 34
central editing, 54
central tendency, 72
  meaning and concept of, 73
    median, 79
    mode, 85
Chi-square, 332
  additive property, 343
  alternative method, 341
  applications, 342
  homogeneity, 343
  illustration of various applications, 345
  independence, test of, 342
  misuse and precaution, 344
chi-square, 340
  constant, 341
  freedom, degrees of, 340
circle graph, 63
Clarify, 454
class intervals, 56
classified frequency distribution method 188
cluster analysis, 421
coefficient
  mean deviation, 104
  standard deviation and variation, 112
coding 55
coefficient
  correlation, 179
  determination, 191
  skewness, 154
combined standard deviation, 113
common variance, 414
comparable sets, 34
complex numbers, 31
complex tabulation, 59
compliment of a set, 37
computer applications, 440
  computer and quantitative media research, 441
  electronic data collection techniques, 444
  Internet
    and media research, 442
    and referencing techniques, 446
  meaning and concept, 441
  softwares applications, 450
concurrent deviation method, 197
continuous variable, 4
corporate communication, 13
correlation index, 179
correlation matrix, 414
correlation
  calculation, 203
  coefficient, 179
  lag and lead, 205
  linear and nonlinear, 179
  meaning and concept, 176
  method
    concurrent deviation method, 197
    graphic method, 182
    Karl Pearson's coefficient, 183
    least squares, 200
    scatter diagram, 181
    Spearman's correlation coefficient method, 192
  positive and negative, 178
  properties, 180
  regression analysis vs., 208
  significance, 177
  simple, partial and multiple, 178
cross-partitions, 39
cumulative frequency graph, 66

data analysis, 67
  interpretation, 68
  types of, 67
Data Desk and JMP, 451
data processing, 53
  analysis, meaning and concept of, 52
  classification
    attributes, 56
    tabulation, 58
  coding, 55
  data, 52

editing, 54
graphical representation, 61
grouped data, 64
ungrouped data, 61
media metrics, 69
prominent studies of, 68
data, 52
database email, 445
database journalism, 2011
De Morgan's law, 38
dependent variable, 5
descriptive media metrics, 2
descriptive statistics, 69
development communication, 16
difference of sets, 38
differentiation
first principle, 42
power function, 43
direct correlation, 178
direct/nondeviation method, 185
discrete variable, 4
disjoint sets 34
dispersion
meaning and concept, 100
mean deviation, 101
coefficient of mean deviation, 104
frequency distribution, 102
merits and demerits, 103
simple distribution, 101
range, 119
interquartile range and quartile deviation, 120
standard deviation, 104
coefficient, 112
combined standard deviation, 113
frequency distribution 105
mean deviation vs., 112
merits and demerits, 111
non-deviation method, 110
shortcut method, 107
simple distribution, 105
step deviation method, 109
variance, 117

econometrics, 2
eigenvalue, 414
electronic data collection techniques, 444
electronic media, 12
email, 445
empty set, 33
estimation theory, 262

factor, 413
factor analysis, 411
advantages, 420
centroid method, 414
limitations, 420
R-type and Q-type, 419
factor loadings, 414
field editing, 54
finite set, 32, 37
frequency distribution
mean deviation, 102
mean, 76
median, 81
mode, 85
standard deviation, 105
frequency polygon, 65
Friedman's test, 332

generalized statistical programs, 451
good estimator, qualities of, 263
goodness of fit test, 342
graphic method, 182
grouped data, graphical representation, 64

homogeneity, 343
hypothesis
attributes, significance, 264
estimation theory, 262
good estimator, qualities of, 263
larger samples, 271
correlated samples, 285
sample with pooled mean, comparing mean, 287
small *vs.*, 271
standard error, 283
two-tailed test, 274
meaning and concept, 255
parametric testing, 254
proportions, 267
report writing, 430
small sample, significance, 293
standard error and sampling distribution, 260
steps, 255
errors in, 257
judging, power of, 259
two-tailed and one-tailed test, 258
successes, number of, 265
successes, proportion, 266

imaginary numbers, 31
independence, test of, 342
independent variable, 5
Index Numbers
characteristics, 227
meaning and concept, 226
methods, 228
unweighted index numbers, 229
weighted index numbers, 231
uses of, 228
inferential media metrics, 2
inferential statistics, 69
infinite set, 32
instant messaging, 445
Instat Plus, 453
integers, 30
integration, 46
Internet, 442, 446
interquartile range, 120
interval estimates, 263
interval level of measurement, 7
inverse correlation, 178
irrational numbers, 31

Journalism Quarterly, 10

Karl Pearson's coefficient, 183

simple deviation method, 185
assumptions, 190
classified frequency distribution method, 188
coefficient of correlation and probable error, 190
determination, 191
direct/non deviation method, 185
merits and demerits, 190
shortcut method, 186
skewness, 139

Kelly's coefficient of skewness, 143
Kruskal–Wallis test, 327
kurtosis, 151

latent structure analysis, 421
least squares method, 200
line graph, 63
linear correlation, 179

Mac software, 454
Mann–Whitney test, 320
mathematics, 24
differentiation, power function, 43
differentiation, 42
integration, 46
matrix, 47
meaning and concept, 25
notation, procedures, 28
numbers, types of, 30
partitions and cross-partitions, 39
sets
classification, 32
descriptions, 31
operations, 35
use of, 26
matrix, 47
maximum likelihood method, 418
mean, 73
mean deviation, 101
coefficient of mean deviation, 104
frequency distribution, 102
merits and demerits, 103
simple distribution\ unclassified\ ungrouped distribution, 102
vs. standard deviation, 112
mean
deviations from, 212
difference, 298
frequency distribution
classified data with, 76
unclassified data with, 75
shortcut method, 76
simple distribution, 74
step deviation method, 78
media metrics, 1
application, 7
advertising 13
development communication, 16
electronic media, 12
print media, 9
social marketing, 17
social media, 18
web media, 17
data processing, 69
meaning and concept of, 1
nature of, 3
measurement levels, 5
variables, 4
tools of, 27
types of, 2
median, 79
frequency distribution, 81
simple distribution, 80
mode, 85
bi-modal values, 87
simple distribution, 85
moment, 146
arbitrary origin, 147
measures, 148
Mood's median test, 332
MS-Excel, 455
multicollinearity, 414
multidimensional scaling, 421
multiple analysis of variance, 410
multiple correlation, 178
multiple discriminant analysis, 409
multiple regression analysis, 405
multiple sets, 33
multivariate analysis (MVA), 403
canonical correlation analysis, 410
cluster analysis, 421
factor analysis, 411
advantages, 420
centroid method, 414
limitations, 420
maximum likelihood method, 418
R-type and Q-type 419
features and uses, 404
latent structure analysis, 421
meaning and concept, 404
multidimensional scaling, 421
multiple analysis of variance, 410
multiple discriminant analysis, 409
multiple regression analysis, 405

natural numbers, 30
negative correlation, 178
negatively skewed distribution, 136
nominal level of measurement, 6
nonparametric inferential media metrics, 3
non-deviation method, 110
nonparametric hypothesis testing, 317
one sample runs test, 325
advantages, 332
Kruskal–Wallis test, 327
limitations of, 333
Mood's median test, 332
one sample Wilcoxon rank test, 327
one-sample sign test, 318

rank correlation test, 330
rank sum test, 320
two-sample sign test, 318
nonlinear correlation, 179
normal curve, 153
applications of, 158
characteristics and properties 154
illustration, applications 159
null hypothesis, 255
null set, 33
numeric coding, 55

oblique rotation, 414
ogive 66
one sample runs test, 325
one sample Wilcoxon rank test, 327
one-tailed test, 258
one-way classification, 377
ordinal level of measurement, 6
orthogonal rotation, 414

parametric inferential media metrics, 2
partitions, 39
pictogram, 64
pie-chart, 63
point estimate, 263
pop-up, 445
positive correlation, 178
positively skewed distribution, 136
power set, 33
Powertab, 455
precision journalism, 10, 20
prerecruit, 445
primary data sources, 52
principal component methods, 418
print media, 9
database journalism, 11
precision journalism, 10
Product Moment correlation coefficient, 184
product rule, 45
proper subset, 33
psychometrics, 2
Q-type factor analysis, 419
qualitative variable, 5
quartile deviation, 120
quotient rule, 45

R-type Factor Analysis, 419
R like S-Plus, 453
randomly selected pop-up, 445
range, 119
interquartile range and quartile deviation, 120
rank difference correlation coefficient *See* Spearman's correlation coefficient method, 192
rank sum test, 320
ratio level of measurement, 7
rational numbers, 31
referencing techniques, 446
regression analysis, 207
assumed mean, deviation, 215
coefficients, properties, 213
computation, 224
correlation vs., 208
least squares, 209
means, deviations from, 212
regression equations, 209
significance, 208
standard error of estimate, 224
regression equations, 209
relationship, 176
relative measures of asymmetry, 138
report writing, 425
appendices, 435
bibliographical references, 433
conclusions and suggestions, 432
data collection and analysis, 431
hypothesis, 430
importance of, 435
literature review, 429
meaning and concept, 426
methodology, 431
objectives, 430
origin and growth, 428
precautions, 436
qualities of, 437
research problem, 429
research topic, 427
results/findings, 432
structure and outline, 426
topic, rationale, 429
rotation, 419

S-Plus, 452
SAS, 450
scatter diagram method, 181
secondary data sources, 52
sets
classification, 32
descriptions, 31
operations, 35
shortcut method
standard deviation, 107
shortcut method, 76
Karl Pearson's coefficient, 186
sign test, 317
signed numbers, 31
significance test
correction coefficient, 304
limitations of, 307
simple aggregative method, 229
simple average of relatives method, 230
simple correlation, 178
simple deviation method, 185
simple distribution
mean, 76
mean deviation, 102
median, 80
mode, 85
standard deviation, 104
Simple Interactive Statistical Analysis (SISA), 453
simple tabulation, 59
singleton set, 33
skewness *See* asymmetry, 135
social marketing, 17
social media, 18
sociometrics, 2
softwares applications, 450

Spearman's correlation coefficient method, 192, 330
characteristics, 193
equal ranks, 195
merits and demerits, 197
specialized statistical programs, 453
spiritual feature, 352
SPSS, 450
standard deviation, 104
coefficient, 112
combined standard deviation, 113
frequency distribution, 105
mean deviation vs., 112
merits and demerits, 111
non-deviation method, 110
shortcut method, 107
simple distribution, 105
step deviation method, 109
standard error, 260
larger samples, 283
Stata, 452
stationary display, 446
Statistica, 450
Statistical Inference, 262
StatView, 451
step deviation method
mean, 79
standard deviation, 109
Stevens, S.S., 5
subset, 33
sum rule, 44
symmetrical distribution, 135, 153

t-distribution, 293
confidence, 295
correction coefficient, significance, 304
means, difference, 298
properties of, 294
two dependent samples, 302
Tableau, 454
tabulation, 58
Text Analysis Computing Tool (TACT), 455
theoretical media metrics, 2
transcriptions, 58
TURNER, 454
two-sample sign test, 318
two-tailed test, 258
two-way classification, 384

ungrouped data, graphical representation, 61
universal set, 33, 34
unweighted index numbers, 229

variables, 4
variance, 373117
ANOVA, precautions, 387
illustrations, 388
meaning and concept, 374
one-way classification, 377
two-way classification, 384
variance tests ratio, 374
applications, 375
assumptions, 374
variation, coefficient, 112
VBPro, 455
void set, 33

web media, 17
webometrics, 455
weighted aggregative method, 231
weighted average of relatives method, 232
weighted index numbers, 231
whole numbers, 30
WinlDAMS, 453

zero coding, 55

ANSWERS TO QUESTIONS AND PROBLEMS

CHAPTER 4

(5) AM=39.8,
(6) AM=₹22,265,
(7) $\bar{X}=53$, $M=52$, $M_0=50$,
(8) AM=₹16,516.66,
(9) AM=45.4,
(10) AM=18,
(11) AM=49.9,
(12) Unknown frequency=126,
(13) AM=63.83,
(14) AM=26.34,
(15) AM=34.56,
(16) AM=237,
(17) AM=39.5,
(18) AM=166.35,
(19) AM=3,
(20) AM=35.37,
(21) Missing Frequency=1,
(22) Unknown frequency=2 and 5, respectively,
(23) AM=12.12,
(24) $\bar{X}=40.34$, $M=40.9$, $M_0=42.02$,
(25) (a) $\bar{X}=22.71$, $M=18$, (b) $\bar{X}=12.22$, $M=12$, (c) $\bar{X}=17.8$, $M=16.5$, (d) $\bar{X}=18.71$, $M=17$, (e) $\bar{X}=3.3$, $M=3.1$, (*f*) $\bar{X}=6.11$, $M=7.7$
(26) $M=54.5$, $M_0=47.83$,
(27) (a) $\bar{X}=91.3$, $M=91.1$, $M_0=90.7$, (b) $\bar{X}=64.43$, $M=64$, $M_0=65$
(28) $\bar{X}=75.16$, $M=72.5$, $M_0=67.18$
(29) (a) $\bar{X}=14.43$, $M=10$, (b) $\bar{X}=3.61$, $M=3.9$, (c) $\bar{X}=7.06$, $M=6.8$, (d) $\bar{X}=12$, $M=12$, (e) $\bar{X}=119.37$, $M=118$, (f) $\bar{X}=8.12$, $M=7$,
(30) $\bar{X}=116.79$, $M=116.87$, $M_0=117.04$,
(31) Crude mode=42, True mode=43.25,
(32) $\bar{X}=53.32$, $M=53$, $M_0=52.35$; crude mode is not possible as highest frequency of the adjacent class intervals is equal.
(33) $\bar{X}=104$,
(34) $\bar{X}=49.36$, $M=49.05$, $M_0=48.44$,
(35) $\bar{X}=46.26$, $M=44.5$, $M_0=40.98$
(36) $\bar{X}=68.13$, $M=67.65$, $M_0=66.69$
(37) $\bar{X}=59.88$, $M=59.14$, $M_0=57.66$
(38) $\bar{X}=61$, $M=61.37$, $M_0=62.11$
(39) $\bar{X}=47.75$, $M=47.31$, $M_0=46.43$
(40) $\bar{X}=37.16$, $M=36.33$, $M_0=34.68$
(41) (a)=Mean, (b)=Mode, (c)=Median
(42) $M_0=35$

CHAPTER 5

(14) $\delta=6.425$,
(15) $\sigma=7.63$,
(16) $\sigma=9.98$,
(17) $\delta=7.937$, $\sigma=8.783$, variance=77.185,
(18) $\delta=18.08$, $\sigma=21.35$, variance=456
(19) $\sigma=10.58$,
(20) $\sigma=12.92$, coefficient of SD=0.38,
(21) $\sigma=10.58$,
(22) $\delta=2.4$
(23) $\delta=1.16$
(24) $\delta_M=10.40$,
(25) $\delta_{\bar{X}}=4.1$, $\delta_{M_0}=6.9$, $\delta_M=4.1$,
(26) $\delta=2.4$
(27) $\delta_{\bar{X}}=1.1$, $\delta_{M_0}=1$, $\delta_M=1$
(28) $\delta_M=1.79$,
(29) $\delta_M=4.1$
(30) $\delta_M=12.89$
(31) $\delta_{\bar{X}}=10.36$,
(32) $\sigma=785.6$,
(33) $\sigma=3.39$,
(34) $\sigma=2.15$,
(35) $\sigma=9.54$,

(36) $\sigma=2.77$,
(37) $\sigma=5.86$,
(38) $\sigma=19.76$ years,
(39) $\bar{X}=34.25$, $\sigma=12.92$, coefficient of SD=0.38,
(40) CV of $R_1=123.6\%$, CV of $R_2=109\%$ but 123.6>109, reporter R_2 more consistent in performance,
(41) $\delta_{\bar{X}}=22.816$, $\sigma=27.49$,
(42) sum of all scores=5000, sum of squares of items=251,600,
(43) $\sigma=2.9$, variance=8.25,
(44) $\bar{X}=19.72$, $\sigma=7.57$,
(45) $\sigma=90.25$,
(46) $\bar{X}=36.9$, $\sigma=11.92$,
(47) $\sigma=14.04$, CV=49.7,
(48) $\sigma=$₹128.70,
(49) Editor X is more consistent (Hint: for X, CV=67.08 and for Y, CV=69.52),
(50) A (Hint: Because CV is lesser),
(51) $\delta_{\bar{X}}=10.47$, $\sigma=12.69$,
(52) $\delta_M=16.94$, $\sigma=21.67$,
(53) $\sigma=4$,
(54) $\bar{X}=4$ $\sigma=6.67$,
(55) $N_2=60$, $\bar{X}_2=120$, $\sigma=8$,
(56) A is more equitable because its CV is lesser,
(57) $\bar{X}$ =₹72.63, $\sigma_{12}=6.65$,
(58) Coefficient of quartile deviation=0.273, coefficient of variation=42.65%,
(59) Interquartile range=45.623, coefficient of quartile deviation=0.55,
(60) $\sigma_X=11.08$, $\sigma_Y=7.68$,
(61) Sum of all items=9600, sum of squares of all items=4,62,600,
(62) Correct $\bar{X}=10.2$, correct $\sigma=1.989$,
(63) Correct $\bar{X}=19.15$, correct $\sigma=4.6615$.

CHAPTER 6

(17) $\bar{X}=147.2$, $\sigma=7.21$, $S_{k_p}=0.07$,
(18) $\bar{X}=18.07$, $M_0=18.4$, $S_{k_p}=-0.186$,
(19) $S_{k_p}=-0.75$,
(20) $S_{k_p}=-0.228$,
(21) The first statement is false (Hint: CV of the broadcast journalists is more); the second statement is true (Hint: The coefficient of skewness is the same in both cases)
(22) $S_{k_p}=-0.266$,
(23) CV=49.84,
(24) $S_{k_p}=-0.031$,
(25) CV=42.01,
(26) $S_{k_p}=0.008$,
(27) $M=28.93$, $M_0=26.8$,
(28) $S_{k_B}=0.025$,
(29) $S_{k_B}=-0.035$,
(30) Since the value of β_2 is less than 3, the curve is platykurtic,
(31) $\mu_1=0$, $\mu_2=2$, $\mu_3=0$, $\mu_4=11$, curve is symmetrical, but not normal,
(32) Moments about mean $\mu_1=0$, $\mu_2=14.75$, $\mu_3=39.75$, $\mu_4=142.312$
(33) $\mu_1=0$, $\mu_2=236.76$, $\mu_3=264.336$, $\mu_4=14190.11$, $\beta_1=0.005$, $\beta_2=2.521$,
(34) $\beta_2=2$, since β_2 is less than 3, so the curve is platykurtic.
(35) $S_{k_p}=0.08$,
(36) $\mu_1=0$, $\mu_2=1.5$, $\mu_3=0$, $\mu_4=6$, $Z_1=3$, $Z_2=10.5$, $Z_3=40.5$, $Z_4=168$,
(37) $M_0=80$, CV=38.46,
(38) $\beta_1=0.504$, $\beta_2=3.782$,
(39) $M_0=27.5$,
(40) CV=31.25, $S_{k_K}=0.06$, $M=159$
(41) $\beta_1=0.006$, $\beta_2=2.306$,
(42) $\sigma=20$, $M_0=58$, $M=52.67$,
(43) $Q_1=61.56$, $Q_2=66.9$, $Q_3=75.58$, Dispersion: QD=7.01,
(44) CV (A)=20%, CV (B)=22% Skew (A)=–1, Skew (B)=–0.5,
(45) $M_0=195.2$, $M=198.4$,
(46) $S_{k_p}=0.202$,
(47) $S_{k_p}=0.202$,
(48) $S_{k_p}=-0.754$,
(49) coeff. of skew.=0.5,
(50) 0.1106,
(51) CV=49.84%,
(52) $S_{k_p}=0.046$,
(53) $S_{k_p}=0.8$,
(54) $\bar{X}=18.07$, $\sigma=1.776$, $M_0=18.4$, $S_{k_p}=-0.187$,

(55) $\overline{X}=28.54$, $\sigma=7.89$, $M_0=26.875$, $S_{k_P}=0.211$,
(56) $S_{k_B}=0$,
(57) $S_{k_B}=-0.032$,
(58) $Q_1=22.625$, $Q_2=32.07$, $M=26.73$, coeff. of skew.$=0.131$,
(59) $S_{k_B}=0.064$,
(60) $S_{k_B}=-0.191$,
(61) $\mu_1=0$, $\mu_2=159.24$, $\mu_3=80.352$, $\mu_4=83659.87$, $\beta_1=0.0016$, $\beta_2=3.3$, since β_1 is close to zero, so the distribution is almost symmetrical. Since $\beta_2>3$, so the distribution is platykurtic,
(62) $\sigma=22.5$,
(63) 0.020,
(64) 70,
(65) $S_{k_B}=0.023$,
(66) $\beta_1=0$, so the distribution is symmetrical. $\beta_2=2.89$. Since $\beta_2<3$, the distribution is platykurtic.
(67) $\overline{X}=7$, $\sigma^2=16$,
(68) $S_K=0.714$,
(69) $\mu_1=0$, $\mu_2=1.5$, $\mu_3=0$, $\mu_4=6$. Moment about zero 3, 40.5, 10.5, 168,
(70) $S_{k_P}=0.65$,
(71) $\overline{X}=7.2$, $\sigma=4.4$,
(72) $\sigma=22.5$,
(73) $\mu_1=0$, $\mu_2=3$, $\mu_3=0$, $\mu_4=27$, $\beta_1=0$, $\beta_2=3$. Since $\beta_1=0$, so the curve is symmetrical, and $\beta_2=3$, so the curve is normal,
(74) $S_{k_P}=0.159$, $\beta_1=0.0114$, $\beta_2=2.048$,
(75) $Z_1=10$, $Z_2=116$, $Z_3=1545$, $Z_4=23184$,
(76) $S_K=0.07$,
(77) $\beta_1=0.031$, $\beta_2=2$. The curve is almost symmetrical and platykurtic,
(78) $S_{k_P}=0.355$,
(79) $\mu_1=0$, $\mu_2=2.5$, $\mu_3=166$, $\mu_4=1132$,
(80) $\mu_1=0$, $\mu_2=8$, $\mu_3=36$, $\mu_4=180$, $\beta_2=2.8125$; since $\beta_1<3$, so the curve is platykurtic,
(81) $\overline{X}=100$, $M=96$,
(82) $\overline{X}=50$, $M_0=40.4$,
(83) $Z=2.13$,
(84) $x=53$,
(85) Reporting ($\therefore$ $3.78\sigma>1.25\sigma$),
(86) a. 50.65 and 57.35, b. 50.65 and 57.35, c. 435,
(87) a. 10.466, b. 4.68 and 32.4,
(88) a. 11.9, b. 96, c. 75%, d. 107, e. 85 to 115,
(89) 1.036σ, 0, -0.253σ, -0.675σ

CHAPTER 7

(31) $r=0.786$,
(32) $r=-0.92$,
(33) $r=+0.92$,
(34) $r=-0.97$
(35) $r=+0.603$,
(36) $r=+0.774$,
(37) $r=+0.7804$,
(38) $r=+0.603$,
(39) $r=-0.989$,
(40) $\sigma_y=+9.048$,
(41) $r=+0.7803$,
(42) $r=-0.6742$,
(43) $r=-0.95$,
(44) $r=-0.96$,
(45) $r=+0.95$,
(46) $r=+0.955$, $PE_r=0.021$
(47) $r=+0.375$,
(48) $r=-0.919$,
(49) $r=+0.956$,
(50) $r=-0.7744$,
(51) $r=+0.5329$,
(52) $r=-0.9$,
(53) $r=+0.415$,
(54) $r=+0.833$,
(55) $r=+0.885$,
(56) $r=+0.795$,
(57) $r=+0.907$,
(58) $r=r_c=0$,
(59) $X=-4.4+1.3Y$, $Y=4.1+0.65X$
(60) $X=16.4-1.3Y$, $Y=11.9-0.65X$,
(61) $X=16.4-1.3Y$, $Y=11.9-0.65X$,
(62) $Y=0.96X-2$, $X=0.54Y+37.2$,
(63) -2.473,
(64) A_2 would have awarded $33.5=34$ marks,
(65) $P_{01}=125.33$,
(66) ρ (Rho)$=0.51$,
(67) ρ (Rho)$=0.786$,

(68) SD_1 and SD_3, since their rank correlation coefficients were maximum,
(69) ρ (Rho)=0.539,
(70) ρ (Rho)=−0.071,
(71) ρ (Rho)=+0.80,
(72) ρ (Rho)=− 0.8176,
(73) ρ (Rho)=+ 0.394,
(74) ρ (Rho)=+ 0.734,
(75) r_c=+ 0.774,
(76) r=+ 0.415,
(77) r=+ 0.578,
(78) r=+ 0.578,
(79) PE_r=0.054, Limits: 0.054–0.654
(80) r=+ 0.005,
(81) r=+0.36,
(82) r=+ 0.833,
(83) σ_y=8.333,
(84) N=9.94=10,
(85) Since r is less than 6 times the probable error, it cannot be regarded as significant,
(86) r=+ 0.915
(87) N=10,
(88) r=+ 0.894,
(89) r=− 0.951 (there is a high degree of negative correlation between level of unemployment and crime rate),
(90) $X=26.72+0.5714Y$, $Y=1.12X-5.8$,
(91) Mean marks in editing is 62.4 and r=+0.8
(92) $X=-\ 41.1375+0.9075Y$, $Y=67.72+0.48X$, value of X=26.925,
(93) b_{xy}=0.041, b_{yx}=0.152; Regression equation of X on $Y=55.88+0.041Y$ and Y on $X=99.93+0.152X$
(94) X on $Y=0.064Y+7.2$, Y on $X=5.667X-86.66$,
(95) Y on $X=0.942X+6.08$; Estimate of Y, when X=55, Y=57.89,
(96) r=0.87, σ_y=6.14,
(97) $X=-\ 13.3+0.333Y$, $Y=61.6+1.92X$, when X=25, Y will be 109.6, when Y=130, X=29.99,
(98) $X=40.892-0.234Y$, $Y=59.248-0.664X$, r=−0.394, most likely marks in PR=39.
(99) b_{xy}=1.25, b_{yx}=0.556,
(100) Y on $X=12+0.8X$, X on $Y=1+0.45Y$,
(101) (a) 29.968, (b) 31.75 lakh,
(102) (a) ₹41.65 crore, (b) ₹102.325,
(103) $X=0.8+0.16Y$, $Y=40+4X$, (b) 140 crore, (c) 24.8 crore
(104) $X=0.596Y+26.26$, $Y=1.168X-10.92$, Y_{92}=96.536,
(105) X_{25}=87.646, Y_{90}=25.22 crore
(106) (a) 2007=125, 2008=150, 2009=175, 2010=200, 2011=250, 2012=225, 2013=250, 2014=275, (b) 2006=40, 2007=50, 2008=60, 2009=70, 2010=80, 2011=100, 2012=90, 2013=100, 2014=110, (c) 2007 will be taken as 100,
(107) P_{01}=134.9

CHAPTER 8

(33) limit=6.1–13.9.
(34) Z=2.43; significant and null hypothesis rejected,
(35) t=1.44; insignificant and null hypothesis accepted,
(36) Z=6.42; Significant and null hypothesis rejected,
(37) Z=1.36; insignificant and null hypothesis accepted,
(38) Z=4.12; significant and null hypothesis rejected,
(39) Z=1.51; insignificant and null hypothesis accepted,
(40) t=3.70; significant and null hypothesis rejected,
(41) t=3.04; significant and null hypothesis rejected,
(42) t=2.43; significant and hypothesis rejected,
(43) t=3.75; significant at both 5 percent and 1 percent level

(44) $Z=59.78$; highly significant and null hypothesis rejected,
(45) $Z=4.61$; significant and null hypothesis rejected,
(46) $Z=2.18$; significant and hypothesis rejected,
(47) $Z=2.58$; significant and hypothesis rejected,
(48) $Z=4.19$; significant and hypothesis rejected,
(49) $t=0.607$; insignificant and null hypothesis accepted,
(50) $Z=2.67$; significant and hypothesis rejected. Hence, "yes,"
(51) $t=2$, $t_{0.05}=1.72$, $t_{0.01}=2.50$, (a) significant at 5 percent and insignificant at 1 percent (b) population mean at the final test is significantly lower at 5 percent, but not at 1 percent (c) at 5 percent level "yes," introduction of anxiety adversely affects the ability but at 1 percent "no," it doesn't affect the ability.
(52) $Z=4.22$; significant and hypothesis rejected. Answer: No,
(53) $Z=10.87$; significant and hypothesis rejected.
(54) $Z=1.265$; insignificant and null hypothesis accepted. Answer: Both equally exist.
(55) $Z=1.67$; insignificant and null hypothesis accepted. Answer: No.

CHAPTER 9

(23) $r=14$; not significant; yes, the arrangement of applicants can be accepted as "random."
(24) $Z=0.091$; not significant.
(25) (a) $Z=5$; not significant, (b) $Z=0.61$; not significant.
(26) $H=7.88$ significant at 0.05 level.

CHAPTER 10

(15) $\chi^2=10$, yes
(16) $\chi^2=5.37$, significant,
(17) $\chi^2=2$, equal distribution,
(18) $\chi^2=5.86$, significant
(19) $\chi^2=2.434$, not significant,
(20) $\chi^2=70.162$, significant
(21) Not independent of age group,
(22) $\chi^2=8.166$, significant,
(23) $\chi^2=0.01$,
(24) $\chi^2=65.27$, yes
(25) $\chi^2=4.3$, yes
(26) $\chi^2=1.685$, fit is good
(27) $\chi^2=2.098$, not significant,
(28) $\chi^2=22.5$, not independent,
(29) $\chi^2=8.888$, significant,
(30) $\chi^2=8.166$,
(31) $\chi^2=3.10$, not significant,
(32) $\chi^2=12.8$, yes
(33) $\chi^2=7.94$, yes (normal distribution),
(34) $\chi^2=14.24$, significant
(35) $\chi^2=16.498$, yes (significant),
(36) $\chi^2=2.09$, not significant,
(37) $\chi^2=3$, not significant,
(38) $\chi^2=1.24$, not significant.

CHAPTER 11

(22) $F_1=0.812$, $F_2=0.928$.
(23) $F=1.415$.
(24) No significant difference between treatment and performance of newspaper production,
(25) $F=4$; F is more than the table value, indicating that the population means of three samples do not seem to be equal. Null hypothesis is rejected.

(26) $F=0.444$; difference between groups not significant at both levels. Null hypothesis is accepted.
(27) $F=6.27$; F is more than the table value at both levels. There is a significant difference between group means.
(28) $F_r=8.56$, $F_{css}=1.56$; $F_r>$, null hypothesis is rejected. Media teachers did discriminate between students; $F_c<$, null hypothesis is accepted. It means teachers did not differ significantly. Thus, teachers' rating was trustworthy and reliable.

CPSIA information can be obtained
at www.ICGtesting.com
Printed in the USA
LVHW101717220419
615086LV00008B/323/P

9 789386 062161